The Economics of Contracting : Foundations, Applications and Empirical Investigations

7
Bibliothèque Scientifique Francqui
Francqui Scientific Library
Wissenschaftliche Bibliothek Francqui
Wetenschappelijke Bibliotheek Francqui

The Economics of Contracting : Foundations, Applications and Empirical Investigations

Proceedings of
the Eigth Francqui Colloquium,
Brussels, 19 - 21 November 1999

Mathias Dewatripont (Ed.)

de boeck

La Bibliothèque Scientifique Francqui est publiée avec le concours de la Fondation Francqui.

Editions De Boeck Université
Rue des Minimes 39, B-1000 Bruxelles

1re édition

Imprimé en Belgique

Dépôt légal :
Bibliothèque nationale, Paris : décembre 2006
Bibliothèque royale de Belgique : 2006/0074/037

ISSN 1374-0911
ISBN 2-8041-4905-6
ISBN13 : 978-2-8041-4905-5

Alphabetical list of authors, with main current affiliation

Philippe Aghion, Harvard University, USA.

Abhijit Banerjee, Massachusetts Institute of Technology, USA.

Roland Bénabou, Princeton University, USA.

Erik Berglof, European Bank for Reconstruction and Development, London, UK.

Patrick Bolton, Columbia University, USA.

Pierre-André Chiappori, Columbia University, USA.

Jenny Corbett, Oxford University, UK.

Mathias Dewatripont, ECARES, Université Libre de Bruxelles, Belgium.

Esther Duflo, Massachusetts Institute of Technology, USA.

Antoine Faure-Grimaud, London School of Economics, UK.

Ernst Fehr, Universitat Zurich, Switzerland.

Oliver Hart, Harvard University, USA.

Ian Jewitt, Oxford University, UK.

Steven N. Kaplan, University of Chicago, USA.

Jean-Jacques Laffont, IDEI, Université des Sciences Sociales, Toulouse, France.[1]

Patrick Legros, ECARES, Université Libre de Bruxelles, Belgium.

David Martimort, IDEI, Université des Sciences Sociales, Toulouse, France.

Eric Maskin, Institute for Advanced Study, Princeton, USA.

1. Jean-Jacques Laffont founded IDEI and was his Director until his untimely death in 2004.

Janet Mitchell, National Bank of Belgium.

John Moore, University of Edinburgh, UK.

Andrew Newman, Boston University, USA.

Patrick Rey, IDEI, Université des Sciences Sociales, Toulouse, France.

Jean-Charles Rochet, IDEI, Université des Sciences Sociales, Toulouse, France.

Bettina Rockenbach, Universitat Erfurt, Germany.

Gérard Roland, University of California-Berkeley, USA.

Bernard Salanié, Columbia University, USA.

Ilya Segal, Stanford University, USA.

Lars Stole, University of Chicago, USA.

Per Stromberg, Swedish Institute for Financial Research.

Jean Tirole, IDEI, Université des Sciences Sociales, Toulouse, France.

Ernst-Ludwig von Thadden, Universitat Mannheim, Germany.

Etienne Wasmer, Université du Québec à Montréal, Canada.

Philippe Weil, ECARES, Université Libre de Bruxelles, Belgium.

1

Introduction

Mathias Dewatripont

Contract theory is by now a central pillar of microeconomic theory. Several of its contributors have been rewarded with the Nobel Prize for their contributions in this general area, including Ronald Coase, Herbert Simon, William Vickrey, James Mirrlees, George Akerlof, Joseph Stiglitz and Michael Spence. Textbooks have also started to appear on the subject, *e.g.* those of Salanié (1997), Laffont and Martimort (2002) or Bolton and Dewatripont (2005).

These textbooks discuss in details the achievements of contract theory, beginning with its maintained hypothesis, that is, its emphasis on optimal contracting. Classical contract theory is a search for constrained Pareto optima. Constraints include hidden actions, or moral hazard, and hidden information, or adverse selection (in its screening and signaling modes). One can analyze settings with only two parties (one principal and one agent) or with multiple parties (moral hazard in teams, auctions, ...). One can also extend the analysis to multiple periods. This paradigm has proved extremely fruitful for the analysis of many economic applications, in fields as diverse as labor economics, corporate finance, industrial organization, public economics, macroeconomics, development economics or international trade for example.

Optimal contracts can at times be quite sophisticated and complex, so much so that their realism has been contested. This has prompted the emergence of an alternative paradigm, dubbed "incomplete contracting" following the seminal contribution by Grossman and Hart (1986).[1] This paradigm introduces "non-contractability" assumptions and restricts the contract set to simple contract provisions like asset ownership and its associated "residual rights of control". By introducing these concepts in the analysis, it allows for a discussion of dimensions like the boundaries of the firm, which traditional contract theory had not really been able to address. But the paradigm has been criticized for its exogenous restrictions of the contract set, leading to a vigorous intellectual debate on the subject.

1. See also Hart and Moore (1990) as well as the book by Hart (1995).

It is fair to say that contract theory, in both its complete and incomplete contract versions, has been extremely insightful and influential in economics in the last decades. Researchers have moreover started to confront theories with data, taking advantage as in other fields of economics of fast-improving databases and computers, and much progress — and impetus for new theoretical developments — is to be expected on that front.[2] The same can be said of attempts to analyze contracting problems in an experimental setting, which should also deliver very interesting insights.[3]

*

* *

The set of papers included in this volume are a very good illustration of what the methods of contract theory can deliver. Written by a set of first-rate researchers, they tackle foundational problems of contract theory, applications of models to areas like macroeconomics, regulation, development or finance and insurance, as well as some empirical and experimental investigations. They are thus an excellent illustration of the diversity of issues and research strategies that can be pursued in contract economics.

The first six papers in this volume are all related to questions of incomplete contracting, albeit from quite a variety of perspectives. The first three, by Maskin and Tirole, Segal and Hart and Moore, have been quite influential in the debate on the foundations of incomplete contracts.[4] The paper by Maskin and Tirole is the one that has indicated the logical limitations of the incomplete contract paradigm: It has identified conditions under which the lack of contractability of actions *ex ante*, at the time of contracting (but not *ex post*, at the time of trade) can be circumvented through (very) sophisticated contracting. To be specific, Maskin and Tirole show that, in a world where the payoff consequences of these actions can be foreseen — even if actions cannot be written down in a contract — sophisticated contracts can very often "get around the noncontractability". This result is interesting because the Grossman-Hart approach does assume full rationality of the players and therefore predictability of the payoff consequences of future actions. It means that some insights derived under incomplete contracting come from exogenous restrictions on the contract set. While such restrictions — like "only property rights can be contracted upon" — sound realistic in various contexts, it would be better to be able to endogenize them rather than assuming them from the start. In this respect, the paper by Segal is very interesting: It takes a complete contract perspective, allowing for sophisticated contracts, including contract contingencies based on parties' announcements of what they observe as the realization of the uncertainty in the environment. But it shows that, if this uncertainty becomes very "rich", *i.e.* if the environment becomes very "complex",

2. See for example the surveys by Chiappori and Salanié (2003), Gibbons and Waldman (1999), Laffont (1997) and Prendergast (1999).
3. See for example Fehr and Schmidt (2003).
4. See also Tirole (1999) for a general discussion of this topic.

the value of sophisticated contracting tends to zero, so that the parties might as well not write any contract at all! As stressed very nicely by Hart and Moore, in their discussion of the foundations of incomplete contracting, the environment analyzed by Segal embodies two key assumptions, namely, (i) that the parties cannot precommit not to renegotiate the initial contract, and (ii) that they are risk neutral. They explain how these two assumptions lead the Maskin-Tirole irrelevance result to fail, so that noncontractability assumptions do make a difference in Segal's environment. Beyond obtaining this result, the Segal approach also offers a very promising notion of contractual complexity which delivers a correlation between complexity and the emergence of (extremely) simple contracts.

The paper by Legros and Newman offers an interesting additional perspective on this debate. It points out that traditional complete contract theory often relies on sophisticated mechanisms in which parties make announcements to third parties — think of them as courts — about the information they have observed, announcements which are then taken into account to determine the contractual outcome. Legros and Newman argue that, in reality, it may be possible at times for some parties to "interfere" with these announcements, *e.g.* by effectively casting doubt on them. They show that this possibility may significantly influence the outcomes that optimal contracting can achieve. And they argue that situations where one party manages to invest enough in interference so as to be able to "silence" the other party in court can be usefully interpreted as managing to acquire "authority". Theirs is a promising avenue in the attempt to introduce real-world limitations on the power of contracting, but also to make more precise the important concept of authority.

Much of the debate on the foundations of incomplete contracting has focused on the case where actions (*e.g.* trade) are noncontractable *ex ante* but contractable *ex post*. This debate can however be avoided when actions are contractable neither *ex ante* not *ex post*. While this may sound like assuming a fair amount of contractual incompleteness, this is an assumption not unfamiliar to complete contract theorists: In moral hazard models, "effort" is an action which is never contractable! Classical moral hazard models have however focused on the issue of the optimal design of incentive schemes, rather than control issues. Once we allow however to contract on "who has the right to take the effort/action", one can derive interesting insights on the optimal allocation of authority. The paper by Aghion, Dewatripont and Rey takes this route and shows that the nature of optimal contracts can depend very significantly on the extent to which the parties can contractually commit to allocate control rights. They consider a world where a principal is interested to learn about the extent to which an agent is "cooperative" and therefore a good long-run partner. One way to get the agent to reveal her "type" is to put her in control of the relationship for some amount of time, during which good agents "behave" and are rewarded by a long-run contract, while bad agents find it too tempting to "take the money and run". In fact, such *ex ante* allocation of control to the agent is the optimal contract if the principal can only put the agent in control of the relationship if he finds it profitable to do so, a setting which Aghion *et al.* call "transferable control", as opposed to "contractable control". Indeed, under contractable control, they show that the principal is better off eliciting information on the agent's type by offering her control in the short run with a positive probability only if she admits that she is a "bad type". This contract improves upon unconditionally granting short-run control to the agent because the principal is in control more often in the short run while nevertheless still managing to learn the agent's type. But such a contract clearly requires the principal to be able to commit to granting control to the agent even after having learnt that the agent is not trustworthy.

The above result is in a sense consistent with empirical evidence presented by Banerjee and Duflo, who detail the contractual dynamics between small Indian software producers and typically larger buyers, some of which are Fortune 500 firms in the U.S. The dynamics they uncover concerns the extent of risk sharing: While relative sizes suggest that the small — and therefore more risk averse — producer should be to some extent insulated from the risk in the environment, this is not the case at the start of the relationships in their sample. This is consistent with the idea that at the beginning these small producers are "unknown entities", so that the first contract they are awarded serves as a way for the buyer to learn about them. Having them bear a substantial share of the risk is then a way to maximize learning, because good types will have strong incentives to perform. Once learning has taken place, more efficient risk-sharing can then be put in place. This paper is a very good example of what empirical analyses of contracting can deliver: Interesting insights — in this case on the importance of reputation effects for contract form — applied to rich market environments.

The above papers share a desire to understand the role of contract incompleteness. They all start from the idea of limits to observability of some dimensions that translate into noncontractability of some sort. An alternative idea, coming from psychology and sociology, is that contractual incentives may backfire because they crowd out "intrinsic motivation". The paper by Bénabou and Tirole discusses this issue by looking at the effect the provision of incentives can have on an agent when she takes such provision as a signal about what the principal believes about her ability. Specifically, incentives may undermine the agent's self-confidence, and therefore potentially her effort, if she concludes that their presence reflects the principal's concern about her productivity. In a similar vein, the paper by Fehr and Rockenbach provides experimental evidence showing how economic incentives, in the form of sanctions, end up undermining altruistic cooperation, *if and only if they are perceived as unfair*. The paper therefore makes the important point that one needs to integrate into the analysis of explicit incentives their impact on human altruism.

These two papers are very interesting examples of the recent attempts at bridging the gap between the "homo-economicus paradigm" and the insights of other social sciences in order to enrich our understanding of human behavior. While this research agenda naturally starts with the analysis of single-person decision-making, it has important implications too for contracting environments. And the Fehr-Rockenbach paper clearly shows the value of bringing experimental evidence in the picture.

The remaining papers in this volume are all concerned with applications of contract theory. The next two, by Dewatripont, Jewitt and Tirole and by Faure-Grimaud and Martimort, concern incentives in the public sector. The first one extends a career concerns model à la Holmstrom (1999) — where agents exert effort to "impress" outsiders and generate attractive subsequent job offers — to a multi-task environment. This fits reasonably well the environment faced by civil servants, with limited financial incentives and at times ill-defined public "missions". In such a setting, where effort increases when outsiders form a more precise judgment about agents' productivity by looking at their performance, one is able to rationalize the idea that "better focused" missions enhance the performance or "accountability" of public agencies, a stylized fact that has been documented in political science (see for example Wilson (1989)).

The paper by Faure-Grimaud and Martimort is concerned with the incentives of regulatory agencies in a world with a risk of collusion[5] between regulators and interest groups. It argues that, while for a current Government, granting independence to a regulatory agency raises that risk, it can also serve to constrain future Governments whose policy preferences may differ from those of the current one. Moreover, independence creates a higher degree of stability of policy over time. Since it also derives results on the optimal design of regulatory statutes by Governments, this paper is a very good example of the potential of contract-theoretic analyses for political economy questions.

The next seven papers are all concerned with financial contracting, an area which has proved a very fertile ground for contract-theoretic applications. Just like the Faure-Grimaud and Martimort paper, the first finance application, by Laffont, considers the role of collusion in contracting. It looks at "group lending", a technique used

5. A topic first analyzed by Tirole (1986).

by the Grameen Bank and similar institutions to successfully lend to poor people in developing countries. The paper analyzes a setting where borrowers have limited liability and also private information on the returns of their projects. Such returns are assumed to be correlated across borrowers. The paper shows how collusion between borrowers makes it attractive to design group lending contracts, where borrower repayments depend on other borrowers' performance. By doing so, it illustrates the power of the contract-theoretic methodology to derive insights on "microfinance" questions, which have attracted a lot of attention among development experts in recent years.

The next paper, by Kaplan and Stromberg, provides a very welcome empirical look at real-world contracts. This allows the authors to discuss in detail the relevance of the vast literature on financial contracting. Looking at a sample of venture-capital contracts, they show how these contracts allocate income rights and various control rights, in a way that evolves over the life of the project. They conclude that the evidence is quite consistent with the insights from both the classical moral-hazard literature[6] as well as the more recent control-rights approach to the capital structure of the firm.[7]

The remaining finance applications explicitly consider contracts in a market context. Chiappori and Salanié's is an empirical paper, which has a methodological as well as a more applied objective. It first derives a simple and general test of the presence of asymmetric information in a competitive market for contracts. It then performs this test on the French automobile insurance market. Interestingly, it finds no evidence of asymmetric information in this market. This means that insurers are able to effectively price insurance according to effective risk thanks to the observable variables at their disposal. Just like the Kaplan-Stromberg paper, this empirical exercise is more than welcome, in a field where theory has traditionally been much "ahead" of empirical analyses.

While the previous paper argued against the importance of asymmetric information in the market it analyzed, the paper by Wasmer and Weil does the opposite. It considers a macroeconomic perspective, continuing a line of research that emphasizes asymmetric information and the associated contracting imperfections that can lead to aggregate losses. The originality of the paper is to allow for the simultaneous presence of labor and credit market imperfections. It introduces endogenous search frictions in both markets. It shows how these frictions reinforce one another, thereby pointing to the need to simultaneously think about reducing credit as well as labor market imperfections in order to fight unemployment.

One sector where imperfections in contracting can have significant aggregate consequences is banking. Two papers, by Corbett and Mitchell and by Berglof and Roland, consider this sector. Con-

6. *E.g.* Holmstrom (1979).

7. See for example Aghion and Bolton (1992), Dewatripont and Tirole (1994a) and Hart (1995).

tracting here is relevant at various levels: Between banks and their borrowers, between banks and their funders — be they depositors or shareholders — and also between banks and regulators, especially when banks risk insolvency and regulators step in order to avoid having to cover losses through deposit insurance.[8] Corbett and Mitchell consider such a case where regulators have decided to offer banks rescue packages in order to reduce their risk of insolvency. They show however that reputation concerns can very well induce reluctance on the part of banks to accept recapitalization offers. Berglof and Roland take a look at the banking sector in transition economies. Their focus is on the relation between banks and their borrowers. It has been well-known since Kornai (1980) that a key concern facing economies at the beginning of their transition was the "soft budget constraint", or the refinancing of loss-making entreprises. Dewatripont and Maskin (1995) have argued that the soft budget constraint can arise as a result of the inability of lenders to commit not to bail out firms with initially negative net-present-value projects, because refinancing happens at a time where significant costs have already been sunk, so that refinancing is *ex post* optimal. Berglof and Roland analyze a variety of transmission channels for soft budget constraints. They show that they all share the property of *ex post* attractive refinancing. This points to the need to find ways to restore the credibility of *ex post* liquidation when one wants to introduce *ex ante* borrower discipline in the transition phase.

The last finance application in this volume is by Bolton and von Thadden. Theirs is a model of corporate ownership structure analyzing the tradeoff between liquidity and control when choosing the degree of ownership concentration. The analysis considers two alternative ways to discipline management: Through monitoring by *existing* shareholders or through the threat of takeovers. The first mechanism requires ownership concentration. In comparison with the second one, it reduces the liquidity of the market for the stock, but it does not suffer from the "free-rider problem" which plagues takeovers. Building upon these ideas, the paper offers an interesting analysis of the link between simple contractual features — in this case, the endogenous concentration of control rights among shareholders — and the features of the market environment — namely the intensity of trading on stock markets and the nature of takeover regulations.

After these seven contracting papers devoted to banking and financial markets, the volume ends with a paper, by Rochet and Stole, which considers an Industrial Organization context. The paper has an ambitious objective: To analyze a nonlinear pricing model which simultaneously includes two-dimensional adverse selection and type-dependent outside opportunities for consumers. The authors are in fact

8. See Dewatripont and Tirole (1994b) for an analysis of the extent to which, in their relation with banks, bank regulators "mimic" the role debtholders play with their nonfinancial borrowers.

able to provide a characterization of this setting, and they moreover discuss two applications: monopoly and duopoly pricing. Among other results, the paper identifies conditions for the duopoly case where a very simple outcome emerges: simple cost-plus-fee pricing and efficient quality allocations. As argued by the authors, the theoretical results of the paper are useful for recent econometric analyses, which in this case have been "ahead" of theory, by typically allowing for a significant amount of consumer heterogeneity.

The set of papers published in this book are very impressive in their breadth. They demonstrate the usefulness of the contract-theoretic methodology. On the other hand, it is clear that many more economic issues are left to analyze. This is particularly true for empirical and experimental investigations, but it also applies to further theoretical inquiries.

Thanks to the generous support of the Francqui Foundation, many of these papers were presented in a conference held in Brussels in November 1999.[9] I would like to thank Prof. Dr. Luc Eyckmans for his help in its organization. I am also grateful to the scientific publishers who have accepted to see the papers they had published to be included in this volume.

9. The authors of the papers presented in this volume all participated in the Francqui conference held in November 1999. Given the long publications lags which are unfortunately very common in economics, some of these papers are yet unpublished, which is why some of the papers of this volume are reprints of alternative, already published papers.

REFERENCES

[1] Aghion, P., and P. Bolton. (1992). "An Incomplete Contracts Approach to Financial Contracting." *Review of Economic Studies*, 77, 338-401.

[2] Bolton, P., and M. Dewatripont. (2005). *Contract Theory*. Cambridge, MA: MIT Press.

[3] Chiappori, P.A., and B. Salanié. (2003). "Testing Contract Theory: A Survey of Recent Work." In M. Dewatripont, L. Hansen and S.J. Turnovsky (eds), *Advances in Economics and Econometrics, Theory and Applications, Eighth World Congress of the Econometric Society, Volume I*. Cambridge, UK: Cambridge University Press.

[4] Dewatripont, M., and E. Maskin. (1995). "Credit and efficiency in Centralized and Decentralized Economies." *Review of Economic Studies*, 62, 541-55.

[5] Dewatripont, M., and J. Tirole. (1994a). "A Theory of Debt and Equity: Diversity of Securities and Manager-Shareholder Congruence." *Quarterly Journal of Economics*, 109, 1027-54.

[6] Dewatripont, M., and J. Tirole. (1994b). *The Prudential Regulation of Banks*. Cambridge, MA: MIT Press.

[7] Fehr, E., and K. Schmidt. (2003). "Theories of Fairness and Reciprocity: Evidence and Economic Applications." In M. Dewatripont, L. Hansen and S.J. Turnovsky (eds), *Advances in Economics and Econometrics, Theory and Applications, Eighth World Congress of the Econometric Society, Volume I*. Cambridge, UK: Cambridge University Press.

[8] Gibbons, R., and M. Waldman. (1999). "Careers in Organizations: Theory and Evidence." In O. Ashenfelter and D. Card (eds), *Handbook of Labor Economics, Volume 3*. Amsterdam: North-Holland.

[9] Grossman, S., and O. Hart. (1986). "The Costs and Benefits of Ownership: A Theory of Vertical and Lateral Integration." *Journal of Political Economy*, 94, 691-719.

[10] Hart, O. (1995). *Firms, Contracts and Financial Structure*. Oxford: Oxford University Press.

[11] Hart, O., and J. Moore. (1990). "Property Rights and the Nature of the Firm." *Journal of Political Economy*, 98, 1119-58.

[12] Holmstrom, B. (1979). "Moral Hazard and Observability." *Bell Journal of Economics*, 10, 74-91.

[13] Holmstrom, B. (1999). "Managerial Incentive Problems: A Dynamic Perspective." *Review of Economic Studies*, 66, 169-82.

[14] Kornai, J. (1980). *Economics of Shortage*. Amsterdam: North-Holland.

[15] Laffont, J.J. (1997). "Game Theory and Empirical Economics: The Case of Auction Data." *European Economic Review*, 41, 1-35.

[16] Laffont, J.J., and D. Martimort. (2002). *The Theory of Incentives: The Principal-Agent Model*. Princeton, NJ: Princeton University Press.

[17] Prendergast, C. (1999). "The Provision of Incentives in Firms." *Journal of Economic Literature*, 37, 7-63.

[18] Salanié, B. (1997). *The Economics of Contracts: A Primer*. Cambridge, MA: MIT Press.

[19] Tirole, J. (1986). "Hierarchies and Bureaucracies: On the Role of Collusion in Organizations." *Journal of Law, Economics and Organization*, 2, 181-214.

[20] Tirole, J. (1999). "Incomplete Contracts: Where Do We Stand?" *Econometrica*, 67, 741-81.

[21] Wilson, J.Q. (1989). *Bureaucracy: What Government Agencies Do and Why They Do It*. New York: Basic Books.

2

Unforeseen Contingencies and Incomplete Contracts

Eric Maskin
Jean Tirole

Abstract

We scrutinize the conceptual framework commonly used in the incomplete contract literature. This literature usually assumes that contractual incompleteness is due to the transaction costs of describing — or of even foreseeing — the possible states of nature in advance. We argue, however, that such transaction costs need not interfere with optimal contracting (*i.e.* transaction costs need not be *relevant*), provided that agents can probabilistically forecast their possible future *payoffs* (even if other aspects of the state of the nature cannot be forecast). In other words, all that is required for optimality is that agents be able to perform dynamic programming, an assumption always invoked by the incomplete contract literature. The foregoing optimality result holds very generally provided that parties can commit themselves not to renegotiate. Moreover, we point out that renegotiation may be hard to reconcile with a framework that otherwise presumes perfect rationality. However, even if renegotiation is allowed, the result still remains valid provided that parties are risk averse.

1 • Introduction

Most real contracts are vague or silent on a number of significant matters. For example, in government, the mandates of agencies, courts, or legislators make almost no mention of the many contingencies that may affect the set of feasible options, nor of how the choice among options should reflect those contingencies. Moreover, this "contractual incompleteness" appears to be important to understanding why the structure of government matters. Similarly, incompleteness is often thought to be crucial to explaining the boundaries of the firm, corporate control, and the patent system.

While there has been a flurry of contributions to the economics of property and control rights since the early work of Grossman and Hart (1986) and Hart and Moore (1990), there is no well-accepted incomplete contracting paradigm, unlike for the phenomena of moral hazard and adverse selection. A few papers study very structured environments in a complete-contracting framework to show that in specific instances in which there are many constraints the optimal complete contract reduces to something that looks quite "incomplete": *e.g.* no contract at all (Che-Hausch (1998), Hart-Moore (1999), Segal (1995, 1999)), an authority relationship (Aghion-Tirole (1997)), an option to buy (Nöldeke-Schmidt (1998)), a property right (Maskin-Tirole (1999)), or some other simple decision process (see Tirole (1999) for a discussion). But the bulk of the papers on incomplete contracting (for epistemological reasons or else for simplicity) do not attempt to derive complete contract foundations for the restricted class of contracts they study. Rather, following Williamson (1975, 1985), they invoke *transaction* costs (difficulty of foreseeing contingencies, cost of writing numerous contingencies, cost of enforcement by a court) to motivate the restriction to a simple class of contracts such as property rights or authority.

This paper is a methodological discussion of the incomplete contract literature. We question existing modelling by pointing out a tension between two important features of the literature: the postulation of significant transaction costs and the use of dynamic programming. Roughly, we argue that the rationality needed to perform dynamic programming is in standard models strong enough to ensure that transaction costs are *irrelevant*. More specifically, we show that even if such costs prevent agents from describing physical contingencies *ex ante*, and in the class of models on which the incomplete contracting literature usually focuses, they do not constrain the set of payoffs that can be reached through contracting in the absence of contract renegotiation. Thus, although we certainly acknowledge that transaction costs matter in reality, we believe that more attention needs to be devoted to the conceptual underpinnings of incomplete contract models.

The basic idea behind the *irrelevance theorem* is very simple. If parties have trouble foreseeing the possible *physical* contingencies, they can write contracts that *ex ante* specify only the possible *payoff* contingencies. (After all, it is only payoffs that ultimately matter.) Then, later on, when the state of the world is realized, they can fill in the physical details. The only serious complication is incentive-compatibility: Will it be in each agent's interest to specify these details truthfully? But the techniques of the implementation literature can be used to ensure that truthful specification occurs in equilibrium.[1]

A rough analogy can be made with the use of securities in competitive markets. As Arrow (1953) showed, the competitive equilibrium of an economy with complete contingent markets can be replicated by having agents first trade in (a properly chosen set of)

1. Just as we do, Wernerfelt (1989) argues that contracts can be written in terms of payoffs even when future physical contingencies are unknown. The main focus of his analysis, however, is the implementation of implicit contracts through infinitely repeated games.

securities and then, after the state of nature is realized, conducting spot markets. The securities — which can be denominated in money rather than physical goods — are analogous to our payoff-denominated contracts. The spot markets correspond to "filling in the physical details."

The paper is organized as follows. Section 2 lays out the classic framework of complete contracting with describable states of nature. Section 3 defines the agents' (minimal) representation of their environment in the polar case in which states of nature are indescribable, under the maintained assumption that the agents can perform dynamic programming and so are able to envision the payoff consequences of their contract and investments. Section 4 illustrates through an example the possibility that indescribability does not constrain the payoffs that can be obtained by rational parties. Then for general environments, Section 5 establishes the irrelevance theorem (Theorem 1). It shows that in the absence of contract renegotiation the indescribability of states of nature does not interfere with optimal contracting if the optimal contract when states are describable is "welfare-neutral". A contract is welfare-neutral if, whenever two states are payoff-equivalent (*i.e.* they are distinguishable only by features not affecting the von Neumann-Morgenstern utilities), it gives rise to the same utilities in both states; welfare-neutrality is then shown to be unrestrictive under two more primitive assumptions (Section 6): a generalization of the requirement that the ratio of the agent's marginal utilities of money be independent of the state of nature (a condition which holds for instance if preferences are quasi-linear), and the condition that the relative likelihood of two payoff-equivalent states not convey information about prior unverifiable actions, if any (Theorem 2). These two assumptions are satisfied in most incomplete contract models in the literature that we are aware of. Hence, the irrelevance theorem applies to these models. However, we also provide examples in which the assumptions do not hold and indescribability matters. We then show that the optimal contract can be implemented in a parsimonious way, namely through the announcement of a single action on the equilibrium path, even when states of nature are indescribable (Section 7).

Section 8 examines the issue of contract renegotiation. Starting with the work of Dewatripont (1989), the economics literature has examined optimal complete contracts under the constraint that parties cannot commit not to renegotiate to their mutual advantage (see *e.g.* Fudenberg-Tirole (1990), Hart-Tirole (1988) and Maskin-Moore (1999). In this respect, it should be noted that this literature on complete contracts with renegotiation (CCR) adheres to the standard complete contracting methodology, and does not, directly at least, invoke indescribable contingencies. By contrast, the incomplete contracting approach, although usually allowing for renegotiation, seems at least motivationally distinct from this CCR literature. Indeed, the papers just mentioned are usually not associated with the incomplete contracting literature). First, we point out that renegotiation may be hard to reconcile with a framework that otherwise presumes perfect rationality. We suggest how rational parties could, in principle, commit themselves not to renegotiate. While, like transaction costs, renegotiation is pervasive in practice, we should devote more research toward reconciling its existence with current modelling practices. Nevertheless, we feel that exploring the implications of renegotiation for those models is worthwhile. Hence, we attempt to delineate when the indescribability of states of nature is costly given the possibility of renegotiation. In particular, we show that it is *not* costly in the sort of models typically considered in the literature provided that agents are at least slightly risk averse (Theorem 3).

Short of a theory of bounded rationality, one can either focus on simple institutions on *a priori* grounds or study the implications of complete contract theory in structured environments. Section 9 discusses the implications of the irrelevance results and outlines some avenues for further research.

2 • The Complete Contracting Benchmark

There are two agents ($i = 1, 2$) and three dates. [Our analysis generalizes immediately to n agents.] Date 0 is the contracting date. Date 1 is the investment date; each agent i makes an *ex post* unverifiable investment $e_i \in E_i$. Finally, at date 2, an *ex post* verifiable action a is chosen. Each pair $e = (e_1, e_2) \in E_1 \times E_2$ gives rise, stochastically, to a *verifiable* state of nature θ characterized by:

(i) a finite[2] action set A^θ,

and

(ii) payoff functions $u^\theta = (u_1^\theta, u_2^\theta)$, where $u_i^\theta : A^\theta \to \mathbb{R}$.

The assumption that payoff functions themselves are verifiable *ex post* is obviously strong. But our goal is to show that indescribability of states by itself does not reduce welfare, and this conclusion is strengthened the more we stack the deck in favour of complete contracts. Our conclusions would continue to hold *a fortiori* were we to suppose that only some *partial* signal z^θ of θ is verifiable.

Of course, given the stochastic nature of action sets and payoff functions, parties will not in general know the state in advance, even if they know the investment levels. We assume, however, that they have prior probabilistic beliefs about states and that they share a common prior expressed by the conditional probabilities $p(\theta \mid e)$.[3]

2. The assumption of a finite action space for each state of nature is made for expositional and notational simplicity.
3. The common prior assumption is certainly strong, but is usually invoked in both the complete and incomplete contract literatures. Relaxing it by allowing agents to "agree to disagree" on their priors would affect the optimal complete contract but we conjecture that it would not affect the irrelevance theorem.

Let Θ denote the set of states, and let $A \equiv \bigcup_{\theta \in \Theta} A^{\theta}$. A complete contract is a function

$$f : \Theta \to A \quad \text{such that } f(\theta) \in A^{\theta} \quad \text{for all } \theta.$$

The contract f induces an investment "game" between the players in which, given $e = (e_1, e_2)$, player i's payoff is

$$\sum_{\theta \in \Theta} p(\theta \mid e) u_i^{\theta}(f(\theta)) - c_i(e_i),$$

where $c_i(e_i)$ is agent i's cost of investment.[4]

We say that the pair (e^*, f) is *feasible* if, given f, the unique equilibrium of the investment "game" consists of each agent i selecting $e_i = e_i^*$:

(i) e^* constitutes a Nash equilibrium:

$$\sum_{\theta \in \Theta} p(\theta \mid e^*) u_i^{\theta}(f(\theta)) - c_i(e_i^*) \geqq \sum_{\theta \in \Theta} p(\theta \mid e_i, e_j^*) u_i^{\theta}(f(\theta)) - c_i(e_i) \quad (1)$$

for $i = 1, 2$ and all $e_i \in E_i$, and

(ii) there is no other equilibrium: if we replace e^* with $e^{**} \neq e^*$, (i) no longer holds.

The complete contracting literature usually focuses on allocations that are Pareto optimal in the set of feasible allocations. When the state is verifiable, as it is here, the revelation of the state is no concern and the search for (in general second best) Pareto optimal allocations is a standard multi-person moral hazard problem.

Dividing the Action Space into State-Dependent and State-Independent Components

In practice, the feasibility of some aspects of an action may be state-dependent (*e.g.* which goods are to be produced) while others (*e.g.* monetary transfers) are state-independent. Let

$$A^{\theta} = X^{\theta} \times Y$$

where X^{θ} is state-dependent and Y is state-independent. For concreteness, we shall assume that the choice of $y \in Y$ specifies the distribution of some private good, such as money. That is, $y = (y_1, y_2)$, where y_i is agent i's allotment of private good. Suppose that the set of feasible allocations Y of this private good is

$$Y = \{(y_1, y_2) \mid \underline{y}_i \leqq y_i \leqq \bar{y}_i, i = 1, 2 \quad \text{and} \quad y_1 + y_2 \leq \bar{y}\}.$$

4. We adopt the common but strong assumption that the cost of effort is additively separable from terms involving θ because, as already noted, we are invoking the implausibly strong but expositionally useful supposition that θ is verifiable *ex post*. Thus if there were terms in the utility function involving both θ and e, it might be possible to infer e from θ, which would dispose of the moral hazard problem entailed in e not being verifiable.

Without loss of generality take $\bar{y} = 0$. We shall suppose that u_i^θ depends on x and y_i only, and that for all $\theta \in \Theta$ and all $x \in X^\theta$, $u_i^\theta(x, y_i)$ is strictly increasing and continuous in y_i in the feasible set, labelled Y_i.

Welfare-Neutral Complete Contracts

In what follows, we will be particularly concerned with complete contracts that are *welfare-neutral.* To define this concept, let us call two states θ and θ' *equivalent* ($\theta \sim \theta'$) if $|X^\theta| = |X^{\theta'}|$ and there exists a bijection $\pi : X^\theta \to X^{\theta'}$ and scalars $a_i > 0$ and β_i, such that

$$u_i^\theta(x, y_i) = a_i u_i^{\theta'}(\pi(x), y_i) + \beta_i \quad \text{for all } x \in X^\theta,\ y_i \in Y_i \text{ and } i = 1, 2. \qquad (2)$$

That is, two states are equivalent if, up to a renaming of the state-dependent actions, the von Neumann-Morgenstern preferences are the same. A complete contract $f : \Theta \to A$ is *welfare-neutral* if, whenever θ and θ' are equivalent, we have

$$u_i^\theta(f(\theta)) = a_i u_i^{\theta'}(f(\theta')) + \beta_i \quad \text{for all } i.$$

In other words, if the von Neumann-Morgenstern utility functions are the same (modulo a positive affine transformation) in states θ and θ', then $f(\theta)$ and $f(\theta')$ give rise to the same utilities (modulo that transformation).

Section 6 will provide a detailed study of the welfare neutrality assumption. At this stage, let us content ourselves with two illustrations. First, welfare neutrality is violated in the standard *principal-agent model.* In this model, only the agent exerts effort at date 1. The state of nature θ realized at date 2 is the principal's profit or benefit from the agent's activity, and there is no decision to be taken at date 2 (X^θ is a singleton for all θ). If the principal either is risk neutral or has exponential (CARA) utility function, the principal's profit does not affect her von Neumann-Morgenstern preferences over income, and so all states are payoff equivalent. Yet, if θ is verifiable, as is assumed in the principal-agent literature, the optimal contract in general specifies a state-contingent transfer. And so welfare neutrality is not satisfied in this standard model.

In contrast, welfare neutrality is trivially satisfied in the two-sided-investment *buyer-seller model,* which has been one of the main applications of the incomplete contracting literature. In the complete contract counterpart to this model, the buyer's and the seller's date-1 investments in human capital, say, are denoted e_B and e_S, respectively. The buyer and the seller trade one unit of a single good at date 2 (by convention, "no trade" corresponds to a trade of a useless and costless good). There are n goods $k = 1, \ldots, n$, generating value $v_B^k(\theta)$ for the buyer and cost $c_S^k(\theta)$ for the seller. So, the decision set is $X = \{1, \ldots, n\}$. The utilities if good k is traded are

$$u_B[v_B^k(\theta) + y_B] - e_B \quad \text{and} \quad u_S[-c_S^k(\theta) + y_S] - e_S,$$

respectively. [Applications of this model to property rights usually also assume that the parties have outside opportunities, in that the seller can sell to alternative buyers instead, and the buyer similarly can buy from alternative sellers instead. These outside opportunities do not affect the fact that the optimal complete contract is welfare neutral.] The incomplete contracting literature usually further assumes that e_B induces a probability distribution over ordered valuation vector $\{v_B(1), v_B(2), \ldots, v_B(n)\}$ where $v_B(k)$ is the kth statistic, and that the ordered valuation vector is a sufficient statistic for θ to learn e_B; and similarly for the seller. In these circumstances, the optimal complete contract (can be chosen so as to) yield the same valuation, cost and transfers in two states θ and θ' that have the same ordered valuation and cost vectors. So welfare neutrality holds.

3 • Indescribable States

As we have laid out the model of Section 2, the complete contract f is chosen to solve a pure moral hazard problem as formulated in (1). If we drop the assumption that u^θ is verifiable *ex post* but keep the assumption that X^θ is describable and verifiable, the model is in the spirit of the contributions of Hart and Moore (1988), Aghion *et al.* (1994) and Nöldeke and Schmidt (1995), among others.[5] In this case, however, $f(\theta)$ can no longer be directly implemented because the action it specifies depends on unverifiable information. The agents have to play a *mechanism* (see below) in order to determine the appropriate action a. More generally, we want to know what can be achieved not only when u^θ is unverifiable, but also when the states of nature are indescribable.

Since the goal of this paper is to assess inefficiencies resulting from the indescribability of actions and contingencies *ex ante*, we must compare two payoff-equivalent representations of the world: one in which the agents can perfectly describe the actions and contingencies *ex ante*, and another in which they cannot. Either way we follow the incomplete contract literature by assuming that both agents learn θ *ex post*,[6] and that whether or not a given action x is feasible can be verified *ex post*.

If parties are able to perform dynamic programming (which incomplete contract models always assume), then at the very least

5. One interpretation of this modified model (where u^θ is unverifiable) is that, for each θ, agents can describe the possible actions X^θ well enough in advance so that these can be specified in the contract (in the articles mentioned above, agents know *ex ante* which good they should trade), but that they are uncertain *ex ante* about how much utility the actions bring.

6. This rules out *ex post* asymmetric information. We conjecture, however, that the irrelevance theorem extends the case of *ex post* asymmetric information in the sense that the *ex ante* describability or indescribability of states continues not to matter under our assumptions.

they can formulate a probability distribution over the possible payoffs. To represent possible payoffs, let

$$v_i : \{1, \ldots, m\} \times Y_i \to \mathbb{R},$$

be a "dummy" or "number-based" payoff function for agent *i*, where $\{1, \ldots, m\}$ is a set of positive integers. The only difference between v_i and an ordinary (*action-based*) payoff funtion u_i is that, in the former, the domain of physical actions has been replaced by this set of integers. The integers are a dummy index reflecting the fact that agents cannot forecast physical actions.[7]

Viewed this way, a state $\theta = (X^\theta, u^\theta) \in \Theta$ can alternatively be expressed as $(X^\theta, v^\theta, \sigma^\theta)$, where:

(i) X^θ is the (physical) action space in state θ, where $|X^\theta| = m^\theta$;

(ii) $v^\theta = (v_1^\theta, v_2^\theta)$, where $v_i^\theta : M^\theta \times Y_i \to \mathbb{R}$ constitutes agent *i*'s number-based payoff function and $M^\theta = \{1, \ldots, m^\theta\}$; and

(iii) $\sigma^\theta : M^\theta \to X^\theta$ is a state-θ mapping from numbers into actions in X^θ. That is, $\sigma^\theta(k)$ is a physical action that implements the payoff pair $v^\theta(k, y) = (v_1^\theta(k, y_1), v_2^\theta(k, y_2))$ in state θ: $u_i^\theta(\sigma^\theta(k), y_i) = v_i^\theta(k, y_i)$ for $i = 1, 2$. The function σ^θ can be interpreted as a *deciphering key*.

We let *V* denote the set of *ex ante* possible number-based payoff functions pairs $v = (v_1, v_2)$.

When we say that agents can perform dynamic programming in the case of indescribable states, we mean that they can formulate prior beliefs $\hat{p}(v \mid e)$ about how investments affect payoffs. Beliefs $\hat{p}(\cdot \mid \cdot)$ are consistent with beliefs in the describable states model if, for all $v \in V$ and all $e \in E$,

$$\hat{p}(v \mid e) = \sum_{\theta \in \Theta_v} p(\theta \mid e), \tag{3}$$

where

$$\Theta_v = \{\theta \in \Theta \mid v^\theta = v\}.$$

Number-Based Contracts

When actions are no longer describable in advance, parties cannot pre-specify the action they would like to implement in each state. However, they can in principle pre-specify the *utilities* they would like to implement. Call

$$\hat{f} : V \to Z_+ \times Y,$$

7. Jean-Charles Rochet has suggested that there is a rough analogy between this construction and Kolmogorov's approach to probabilities (in probability theory, we need not know the physical properties of states of nature, since we care only about the probability distribution over consequences.)

a *number-based contract*, where for any number-based payoff functions $v = (v_1, v_2)$, $\hat{f}(v)$ specifies an integer k and a describable action $y \in Y$ such that $(v_1(k, y_1), v_2(k, y_2))$ are the corresponding utilities to be implemented.

By analogy with the definition for action-based contracts, a number-based contract $\hat{f}$ is *welfare-neutral* if, whenever $\theta \sim \theta'$ (so that there exist a one-to-one mapping $\pi : M^{\theta} \to M^{\theta'} = M^{\theta}$ and scalars $a_i > 0$ and β_i for $i = 1, 2$ such that $v_i^{\theta}(k, y_i) = a_i v_i^{\theta'}(\pi(k), y_i) + \beta_i$ for $i = 1, 2$ and all (k, y_i)), then

$$v_i^{\theta}(k^{\theta}, y_i^{\theta}) = a_i v_i^{\theta'}(k^{\theta'}, y_i^{\theta'}) + \beta_i \quad \text{for} \quad i = 1, 2,$$

where $\hat{f}(v_1^{\theta}, v_2^{\theta}) = (k^{\theta}, y^{\theta})$ and $\hat{f}(v_1^{\theta'}, v_2^{\theta'}) = (k^{\theta'}, y^{\theta'})$.

The number-based contract $\hat{f}$ *corresponds* to the complete contract $f: \Theta \to A$, if for all $v \in V$ and for all $\theta \in \Theta$ such that $v^{\theta} = v$,

$$v_i(\hat{f}(v)) = u_i^{\theta}(f(\theta)) \quad \text{for } i = 1, 2.$$

It is not hard to see that a complete contract f is welfare-neutral if, and only if, there exists a welfare-neutral number-based contract corresponding to f.

Mechanisms

There are two difficulties with ensuring that the utilities prescribed by number-based contract $\hat{f}$ actually get implemented: (i) the true number-based payoff functions $(v_1^{\theta}, v_2^{\theta})$ are not verifiable and (ii) the true deciphering key σ^{θ}, mapping integers to physical actions, is not verifiable. Accordingly, $\hat{f}$ must be implemented indirectly; the agents' contract must specify a mechanism for them to play. A *mechanism* (or game form) g is a procedure in which, once θ is realized, one or both agents propose a feasible action or actions as part of their strategies (strategies may involve more than just proposing actions, *e.g.* making claims about the true utility functions). On the basis of the agents' strategies, g determines a physical action. In view of the *ex ante* indescribability of the action space, however, the rule mapping strategies to actions cannot depend on any physical property of these actions. (Thus, the rule "implement the action that agent 1 has proposed" is permissible, but the rule "implement the action involving production of the higher quality good" is not.) In any state $\theta \in \Theta$, g induces a game between the two agents — each agent i chooses a strategy to maximize the expected value of u_i^{θ}.

We shall say that g with joint strategy space $S_1 \times S_2$ *implements* the number-based contract $\hat{f}$ if, for all $\theta \in \Theta$ and all (subgame-perfect) equilibria $(s_1^{\theta}, s_2^{\theta})(\in S_1 \times S_2)$ in state θ,

$$u_i^{\theta}(g(s_1^{\theta}, s_2^{\theta})) = v_i^{\theta}(\hat{f}(v_1^{\theta}, v_2^{\theta})) \quad \text{for } i = 1, 2.$$

That is, the equilibrium utilities[8] in state θ are the same as those prescribed by $\hat{f}$ for agents' number-based payoff functions in state θ.

Our "irrelevance theorem" provides conditions under which a number-based contract $\hat{f}$ is implementable. A necessary requirement is that $\hat{f}$ be welfare-neutral. To see this, note that if $\theta \sim \theta'$ then the game induced by an implementing mechanism after θ is strategically equivalent to that induced after θ'. Hence, if (μ_1, μ_2) is an equilibrium payoff for the latter game, $(a_1\mu_1 + \beta_1, a_2\mu_2 + \beta_2)$ is an equilibrium payoff for the former, *i.e.* $\hat{f}$ is welfare-neutral.

Before turning to this result, we first examine the simpler special case in which unlimited monetary transfers can be made and payoff functions are quasi-linear.[9]

4 An Example of Implementation with Large Penalties

Assume that:

(a) for all $\theta \in \Theta$, utility functions are quasi-linear[10] between actions in X^θ and Y

$$u_i^\theta(x, y_i) = w_i^\theta(x) + y_i, \qquad i = 1, 2;$$

(b) there is no bound on the magnitude of individual agents' transfers

$$Y = \{(y_1, y_2) \mid y_1 + y_2 \leqq 0\};$$

(c) there exists a describable action x^0 (which can be interpreted as the "no-trade" point) such that, for all $\theta \in \Theta$, $x^0 \in X^\theta$. We shall normalize the payoff from x^0 to zero

$$w_i^\theta(x^0) = 0 \quad \text{for all } \theta \in \Theta, \qquad i = 1, 2;$$

(d) $\hat{f}$ is a Pareto-optimal number-based contract.

Consider the following mechanism:

Stage 1: Agent 1 announces:

- an action set X;
- number-based payoff functions $v_i : M \to \mathbb{R}$, $i = 1, 2$, where $|M| = |X|$ and $(v_1, v_2) \in V$; and
- a deciphering key $\sigma : M \to X$.

(If agent 1 fails to do this, the outcome is $(x^0, (-P, P))$, where P is a large monetary payment; *i.e.* action x^0 is implemented and agent 1

8. In the implementation literature, a contract — or, more generally, a *social choice rule* — is said to be implemented by a mechanism if, for each state $\theta \in \Theta$, the equilibrium *physical outcome* of the mechanism is the same as that prescribed by the contract. When physical outcomes cannot be described in advance, however, the best we can do is to ensure that equilibrium *utilities* are the same as those prescribed by the contract.

9. A well-known but highly special illustration of the idea that details of a contract may be filled in *ex post* is the following. A seller is to sell one unit of a good to a buyer. The unit has value v if the good is the "relevant good" and 0 otherwise. What constitutes the relevant good is *ex ante* unknown, and perhaps even the possibilities are "indescribable". Yet there exists an efficient contract as follows: (i) the seller describes a good *ex post*, (ii) the buyer accepts or rejects the good. If she accepts, she must pay v; if she rejects, she pays 0. In the absence of renegotiation (an issue to be discussed later), this contract achieves the efficient outcome, and gains from trade can be divided *ex ante* through an arbitrary transfer between the two parties.

10. The assumption that $u_i^\theta(x, y_i)$ is *linear* in y_i simplifies but is not crucial to the following construction. A nonlinear function $q_i(y_i)$ would do as well. The key property of assumption *(a)* used in the construction below is that u_i^θ is separable in x and y_i.

pays agent 2 a penalty P). Note that, because utility is separable, we can ignore the utility from money and view $v_i(k)$ as an announcement of the *gross* surplus $w_i^{\theta}(\sigma(k))$.

Stage 2: Agent 2 decides to challenge or not to challenge agent 1's announcement.

- If he does not challenge, the outcome is (x^*, y^*), where $x^* = \sigma(k^*)$ and $(k^*, y^*) = \hat{f}(v_1, v_2)$.
- If he does challenge, then agent 1 must pay a large penalty P to agent 2.

Agent 2 can challenge in one of three ways:

(i) Agent 2 can challenge the action space X either by exhibiting a feasible action $x \notin X$ or by exhibiting an infeasible $x \in X$. In either case, the implemented action is x^0. That is, the outcome is

$$(x^0, (-P, P));$$

(ii) Agent 2 can challenge agent 1's implicit claim that $v_1(\sigma^{-1}(\cdot))$ is agent 1's actual surplus function. Namely, he chooses integer k and a number $\varepsilon \neq 0$, and gives agent 1 the choice between options (a) and (b), where (a) consists of action $\sigma(k)$ and agent 1 receiving no monetary transfer (except for the transfer $-P$ corresponding to the penalty he paid) and (b) consists of the action x^0 and a transfer of $v_1(k) + \varepsilon$ (beyond the penalty $-P$). Agent 1 then chooses between (a) and (b). The challenge is successful if either $\{\varepsilon > 0$ and agent 1 picks option (a)$\}$ or $\{\varepsilon < 0$ and agent 1 picks option (b)$\}$. Otherwise, it is unsuccessful. In the case of an unsuccessful challenge, agent 2 must himself pay a penalty $2P$, and this goes to a third party. To summarize, if agent 1 selects (a), the outcome is

$(\sigma(k), (-P, P))$ if the challenge is successful $(\varepsilon > 0)$,

$(\sigma(k), (-P, -P))$ if the challenge is unsuccessful $(\varepsilon < 0)$.

If agent 1 selects (b), the outcome is

$(x^0, (v_1(k) + \varepsilon - P, P - v_1(k) - \varepsilon))$ if the challenge is successful $(\varepsilon < 0)$, and

$(x^0, (v_1(k) + \varepsilon - P, -P))$ if the challenge is unsuccessful $(\varepsilon > 0)$;

(iii) Agent 2 can challenge agent 1's claim that $v_2(\sigma^{-1}(\cdot)) = w_2(\cdot)$ is agent 2's actual utility function. Specifically, agent 2 can announce a number-based payoff function v_2'. In this case agent 2 pays P (the penalty received from agent 1) to a third party. Agent 1 then has the opportunity to counter-challenge. If he refrains from doing so, the alternative (x^{**}, y^{**}) is implemented, where $x^{**} = \sigma(k^{**})$, $(k^{**}, y^{**}) = \hat{f}(v_1, v_2')$. If agent 1 does counter challenge, then agent 2 must pay a second penalty P to agent 1 (implying that agent 2's overall net payment is P) and challenge (ii) is carried out with the roles reversed.

We claim that the mechanism implements $\hat{f}$ if P is big enough. Challenge (i) exploits the fact that a court can verify whether a specific action is feasible or not. This challenge thus guarantees that agent 1 will not misstate the true action space. Challenge (ii) guarantees that agent 1 (and the counter-challenge in (iii) guarantees that agent 2) will not lie about his own payoff function. Finally, challenge (iii) ensures that agent 1 will not lie about agent 2's payoff function in a way that reduces the latter's payoff beyond that prescribed by $\hat{f}$. Given that $\hat{f}$ is Pareto optimal, agent 1 therefore cannot obtain more than the payoff that $\hat{f}$ specifies.

5 • The Irrelevance Theorem

Let us drop the assumptions of Section 4 that payoff functions are separable and that unbounded monetary transfers are possible. Instead let us assume that, given the number-based contract $\hat{f}$, the following two technical assumptions are satisfied:

Assumption 1. There exist a describable alternative x^0 and transfers $y^0 \in Y$ ((x^0, y^0) could be a "no-trade" point) such that, for all $\theta \in \Theta$,

(i) $x^0 \in X^\theta$,

(ii) $v_i^\theta(\hat{f}(v^\theta)) > u_i^\theta(x^0, y_i^0)$, and

(iii) $\underline{y}_i < y_i^0 < \bar{y}_i$, for $i = 1, 2$

and

Assumption 2. For all $\theta \in \Theta$, if $\hat{f}(v^\theta) = (k^\theta, y^\theta)$ then $\underline{y}_i < y_i^\theta < \bar{y}_i$ for $i = 1, 2$.

Remark. Assumptions 1 and 2 are usually satisfied in economic models. In some models they may hold with only weak inequalities, as is the case when an agent i is protected by limited liability but, because of the moral hazard problem, it is desirable to "punish" him by assigning the lowest possible transfer $\underline{y}_i$. In such a case, Theorem 1 below says that one can approximate the outcome with describable actions arbitrarily closely even if actions are indescribable. Hence, Assumptions 1 and 2 are not very restrictive.

Theorem 1. *If the number-based contract $\hat{f}$ corresponds to a complete contract f that is welfare-neutral, Pareto-optimal, and satisfies Assumptions* 1 *and* 2,[11] *then $\hat{f}$ can be implemented in subgame-perfect equilibrium when states are indescribable.*

Remark. The proof of Theorem 1 builds on standard implementation theory. In the implementation literature (see Moore (1992) and Palfrey (1998) for recent surveys), the objective is to construct mechanisms that elicit agents' payoffs when the action space is known in advance but payoffs are neither known *ex ante* nor verifiable *ex post*. We show that such mechanisms can be extended to the case in which the action space cannot be forecast. Specifically, after the state θ is realized, we have agent 1 announce what he claims are (i) the realized action space X and (ii) a mechanism g^X that, given X, implements the number-based contract $\hat{f}$ (the existence of an implementing mechanism is assured by the implementation literature). We then allow agent 2 to challenge either announcement. Because we assume (as does the incomplete contract literature) that courts can verify *ex post* whether or not any given action is feasible, it is easy for agent 2 to challenge successfully agent 1 if he has omitted a feasible action from X or included an infeasible one. (In the contract we construct here, agent 1 must announce the entire feasible action space. In Section 7, however we will show that the parties can make do with much more parsimonious announcements). Moreover, assuming that X is the true feasible set, agent 2 can mechanically prove when a mechanism g^X fails to implement $\hat{f}$ by simply exhibiting a nonoptimal equilibrium (which also constitutes a successful challenge). The incentive for agent 2 to challenge successfully is that she is then rewarded with the opportunity to pick her favourite action (this deters agent 1 from announcing a false action space or non-implementing mechanism). If agent 2 does not challenge — which will occur only if agent 1's claim is true — the mechanism g^X is then played.

Proof. Note first that, from part (iii) of Assumption 1, there exists $y^{00} \in Y$ such that $y_i^{00} < y_i^0$, $i = 1, 2$. Hence,

$$u_i^\theta(x^0, y_i^{00}) < u_i^\theta(x^0, y_i^0) \quad \text{for all } \theta \in \Theta, \qquad i = 1, 2.$$

Given action space X, we shall call a mechanism g^X, with joint strategy space $S_1^X \times S_2^X$, *successful* provided that, for all possible pairs of number-based payoff functions $v \in V$ (where $v_i : M \times Y_i \to \mathbb{R}$, $i = 1, 2$) for which $|X| = |M|$ and all possible deciphering keys $\sigma : M \to X$, the unique subgame-perfect equilibrium payoffs of the game g^X when agents have utility functions $(v_1(\sigma^{-1}(\cdot), \cdot), v_2(\sigma^{-1}(\cdot), \cdot))$ are $v(\hat{f}(v))$.

11. We could drop the stipulation that $\underline{y}_i < y_i^\theta$ in Assumption 2 and also the hypothesis that f is Pareto optimal if instead we assumed:
Assumption 3. For all $\theta \in \Theta$ and all $i = 1, 2$, if $(\hat{x}, \hat{y})$ satisfies $u_i^\theta(\hat{x}, \hat{y}) \geqq u_i^\theta(x, y)$ for all (x, y) such that $u_j^\theta(x, y) \geqq u_j^\theta(x^0, y^0)$, where $j \neq i$, then $v_j^\theta(\hat{f}(v^\theta)) > u_j^\theta(\hat{x}, \hat{y})$. In words, if agent i chooses his favorite alternative subject to agent j getting at least the utility of (x^0, y^0), then agent j's utility is strictly less than that from the number-based contract $\hat{f}$. In fact, Assumption 3 is implied by Assumption 2 and Pareto optimality of $\hat{f}$.

For the time being, suppose that, for all action spaces that could arise — *i.e.* for all X for which there exists $\theta \in \Theta$ with $X^{\theta} = X$ — there exists a successful mechanism. (We will show this is so below. This is where we make use of implementation theory.) Then the parties can sign a contract that stipulates that, once the state of nature is realized:

(i) agent 1 proposes a feasible set of actions X and a corresponding mechanism g^X;

(ii) agent 2 can accept the proposal or challenge it;

(iii) if agent 2 challenges, then he can (a) exhibit a feasible action $x \notin X$, or (b) exhibit an infeasible action $x \in X$, or (c) demonstrate that, given X, the proposed mechanism g^X is not successful;

(iv) if agent 2 succeeds with any of (a)-(c) then he can name an action (x, y), which is implemented; if he fails with the challenge the outcome is (x^0, y^{00}); in either case, the execution of the contract ends at this point;

(v) if agent 2 accepts agent 1's proposal, then the mechanism g^X is played and the action that this leads to is implemented, provided it is feasible (if not, the outcome is (x^0, y^{00})).

We claim that, for all $\theta \in \Theta$, the unique equilibrium payoffs of this contract are $v^{\theta}(\hat{f}(v^{\theta}))$. To see this, note that if agent 1 proposes the true feasible set X^{θ} and a corresponding successful mechanism $g^{X^{\theta}}$ and if agent 2 accepts, then, by definition of "successful mechanism," the resulting continuation equilibrium payoffs are indeed $v^{\theta}(\hat{f}(v^{\theta}))$. Moreover, it is (uniquely) optimal for agent 2 to accept this proposal, since any challenge would fail and therefore result in outcome (x^0, y^{00}), which from Assumption 1 (ii) is worse than $v_2^{\theta}(\hat{f}(v^{\theta}))$. It remains only to show that in equilibrium agent 1 must make such a proposal. Observe that if he did not make such a proposal, then agent 2 could challenge successfully (either by showing that X is not the true feasible set or by exhibiting number-based payoff functions $(v_1, v_2) \in V$, a deciphering key σ, and an equilibrium of g^X when agents have utility functions $(v_1(\sigma^{-1}(\cdot), \cdot), v_2(\sigma^{-1}(\cdot), \cdot))$ such that agents' equilibrium payoffs are not $v(\hat{f}(v))$. Moreover, since $\underline{y}_1 < y_1^{\theta}$ and $y_2^{\theta} < \bar{y}_2$, by doing so, agent 2 could get a strictly higher payoff than $v_2^{\theta}(\hat{f}(v^{\theta}))$. But because f is Pareto optimal, this would imply a payoff strictly less than $v_1^{\theta}(\hat{f}(v^{\theta}))$ for agent 1, a suboptimal outcome.

To complete the proof, we must show that, for all $\theta \in \Theta$, there exists a successful mechanism $g^{X^{\theta}}$. To do this, it is enough to show that the sufficient conditions in Moore and Repullo (1988) are satisfied. We relegate this portion of the proof to Appendix 1. ■

6 How Restrictive is Welfare-Neutrality?

The crucial hypothesis in Theorem 1 is the welfare-neutrality of the contract f. We next show (Theorem 2) that this hypothesis is unrestrictive provided that two more fundamental conditions hold: (i) state-independence of the ratios of the marginal utilities of money and (ii) unidentified effort.

Definition. Preferences satisfy the property of state-independence of the ratios of the marginal utilities of money if, for θ, $\theta' \in \Theta$, whenever θ and θ' are equivalent — *i.e.* there exist one-to-one mapping $\pi : X^\theta \to X^{\theta'}$ and scalars $a_i > 0$, β_i such that (2) holds — then

$$a_1 = a_2 .$$

Observe that a sufficient condition for state-independence is that payoff functions take a separable form:

$$u_i^\theta(x, y_i) = w_i^\theta(x) + a(\theta) q_i(y_i) . \tag{4}$$

Definition. Effort is unidentified if whenever θ and θ' are equivalent

$$p(\theta \mid e, \{\theta, \theta'\}) = p(\theta \mid e', \{\theta, \theta'\}) \quad \text{for all } e \text{ and } e' .$$

That is, effort is unidentified when the only information conveyed by the realized state about the effort levels chosen is that inherent in the von Neumann-Morgenstern preferences.

Theorem 2. *Suppose that the preferences satisfy the property of state-independence of the ratios of the marginal utilities of money and effort is unidentified. Then for any complete contract f, there exists a welfare-neutral complete contract f′ such that*

$$\sum_{\theta \in \Theta} p(\theta \mid e) u^\theta(f(\theta)) = \sum_{\theta \in \Theta} p(\theta \mid e) u^\theta(f'(\theta)) \text{ for all } e.$$

Proof. Consider two equivalent states θ and θ'. From state-independence there exist $\pi : X^\theta \to X^{\theta'}$ and scalars $a > 0$, β_i such that

$$u_i^\theta(x, y_i) = a u_i^{\theta'}(\pi(x), y_i) + \beta_i \quad \text{for all } (x, y_i) \in X^\theta \times Y_i \text{ and } i = 1, 2 . \tag{5}$$

Now, conditional on e and $\{\theta, \theta'\}$, agent i's expected utility from the complete contract is

$$p u_i^\theta(x^\theta, y_i^\theta) + (1 - p) u_i^{\theta'}(x^{\theta'}, y_i^{\theta'}) , \tag{6}$$

where $f(\theta) = (x^\theta, y^\theta)$ and $f(\theta') = (x^{\theta'}, y^{\theta'})$ and

$$p = p(\theta \mid e, \{\theta, \theta'\}) . \tag{7}$$

Thanks to (5) we can rewrite (6) as:

$$pau_i^{\theta'}(\pi(x^{\theta}), y_i^{\theta}) + (1-p)u_i^{\theta'}(x^{\theta'}, y_i^{\theta'}) + p\beta_i. \tag{8}$$

Now consider a contract f' in which, when θ occurs, there is a $[t, 1-t]$ randomization between (x^{θ}, y^{θ}) and $(\pi^{-1}(x^{\theta'}), y^{\theta'})$. And when θ' occurs, there is a $[t, 1-t]$ randomization between $(\pi(x^{\theta}), y^{\theta})$ and $(x^{\theta'}, y^{\theta'})$. Notice that this is welfare-neutral. Moreover, it results in conditional expected utility

$$p(tu_i^{\theta}(x^{\theta}, y_i^{\theta}) + (1-t)u_i^{\theta}(\pi^{-1}(x^{\theta'}), y_i^{\theta'}))$$
$$+ (1-p)(tu_i^{\theta'}(\pi(x^{\theta}), y_i^{\theta}) + (1-t)u_i^{\theta'}(x^{\theta'}, y_i^{\theta'})),$$

which, from (5) can be rewritten as:

$$(apt + (1-p)t)u_i^{\theta'}(\pi(x^{\theta}), y_i^{\theta})$$
$$+ (ap(1-t) + (1-p)(1-t))u_i^{\theta'}(x^{\theta'}, y_i^{\theta'}) + p\beta_i. \tag{9}$$

Take

$$t = \frac{ap}{ap + 1 - p}.$$

This is well-defined since, from unidentified effort, p does not depend on e. With this substitution (9) reduces to (8). That is, we can replicate the expected utility from f — conditional on e, θ and θ' — using the welfare-neutral contract f'. Continuing in the same way, we can establish the same thing for all equivalent pairs θ and θ'. ■

To understand the role of state-independence of the ratios of the marginal utilities of money in Theorem 2, it may be helpful to consider an example in which it is violated and Theorem 1 does not hold. There are two actions a_1 and a_2 and two equally likely states of nature θ and θ'. The utility functions are

$$u_1^{\theta}(a) = \begin{cases} -e^{2\delta}, & a = a_1, \\ -1, & a = a_2, \end{cases} \qquad u_2^{\theta}(a) = \begin{cases} -e^{-2\delta}, & a = a_1, \\ -1, & a = a_2, \end{cases}$$

and

$$u_1^{\theta'}(a) = \begin{cases} -e^{-2\delta}, & a = a_1, \\ -1, & a = a_2, \end{cases} \qquad u_2^{\theta'}(a) = \begin{cases} -e^{2\delta}, & a = a_1, \\ -1, & a = a_2. \end{cases}$$

[The interpretation is that the two agents have exponential utility functions $-e^{-c_i}$, and face endowment shocks $(-\delta, \delta)$ in state θ, and $(\delta, -\delta)$ in state θ'. Action a_1 is a "gambling action," which doubles the individual shocks, and a_2 is a "hedging action."] Note that, if π

denotes the permutation in which $\pi(a_1) = a_2$ and $\pi(a_2) = a_1$, then, for all a,

$$u_1^{\theta}(a) = e^{2\delta} u_1^{\theta'}(\pi(a))$$

and

$$u_2^{\theta}(a) = e^{-2\delta} u_2^{\theta'}(\pi(a)).$$

Hence states θ and θ' are equivalent, but state-independence is violated.

Consider the complete contract f for which $f(\theta) = f(\theta') = a_2$. This is an efficient contract since a_2 provides perfect insurance, *i.e.* it results in expected payoffs $(-1, -1)$. Note, however, that it is not welfare-neutral and therefore cannot be implemented in the indescribable actions case. Indeed, the only expected payoff pairs that are possible in that case are

$$\Big\{\lambda[-\tfrac{1}{2}(1+e^{-2\delta})] + (1-\lambda)[-\tfrac{1}{2}(1+e^{2\delta})],$$
$$(1-\lambda)[-\tfrac{1}{2}(1+e^{-2\delta})] + \lambda[-\tfrac{1}{2}(1+e^{2\delta})]\Big\},$$

where $\lambda \in [0, 1]$. This follows because the endowment shocks are payoff-irrelevant at the implementation stage and therefore cannot be elicited, implying that for $i = 1, 2$, the probability that the action preferred by player i is chosen by the complete contract is the same in both states of nature.

Next, let us turn to an example illustrating the role of unidentified effort. There are two states of nature, θ and θ', and a pair of actions, $\{a_1, a_2\}$ and $\{a'_1, a'_2\}$, in each state respectively. The payoff functions are

$$u_1^{\theta}(a) = \begin{cases} 3, & a = a_1, \\ 5, & a = a_2, \end{cases} \qquad u_2^{\theta}(a) = \begin{cases} 1, & a = a_1, \\ 4, & a = a_2, \end{cases}$$

and

$$u_1^{\theta'}(a) = \begin{cases} 2, & a = a'_1, \\ 0, & a = a'_2, \end{cases} \qquad u_2^{\theta'}(a) = \begin{cases} 5, & a = a'_1, \\ 2, & a = a'_2. \end{cases}$$

Note that if π is the mapping $a'_2 = \pi(a_1)$ and $a'_1 = \pi(a_2)$

$$u_1^{\theta}(a) = u_1^{\theta'}(\pi(a)) + 3,$$

and

$$u_2^{\theta}(a) = u_2^{\theta'}(\pi(a)) - 1,$$

for $a = a_1, a_2$. Hence θ and θ' are equivalent and state-independence of the ratios of the marginal utilities of money holds. At date 1, agent 2 "works" or "shirks." Working (which costs agent 2 one util) results in state θ and shirking (which has no cost) in state θ'. So the unidentified effort condition is violated. With a complete contract it is straightforward to obtain the overall payoffs $(5, 4)$: It suffices to specify that actions a_2 and a_2' will be chosen in states θ and θ' respectively. This induces agent 2 to work, as $4 > 2$. However, in the case of indescribable states, if a_2 is implemented in state θ then $\pi(a_2) = a_1'$ must be implemented in state θ'. Hence, agent 2 cannot be induced to work, and the only possible *ex ante* utilities are $(2, 5)$ or $(0, 2)$ or mixtures thereof. This is because effort is payoff-irrelevant at date 2 and the probability of action a $(a = a_1, a_2)$ in state θ must therefore be equal to the probability of action $\pi(a)$ in state θ'. Hence, if π is the probability of action a_1 in state θ, agent 2 obtains net utility

$$\lambda + 4(1-\lambda)\,, \quad \text{if he works,}$$

and

$$2\lambda + 5(1-\lambda)\,, \text{ if he shirks.}$$

The agent therefore always shirks when the actions are indescribable.

We defined "complete contracting" in Section 2 as the case in which all aspects of a state — including payoffs — are verifiable *ex post*. Our work/shirk example illustrates one situation in which payoffs are verifiable indirectly. Specifically, note that the action sets are different in the two states and that there is a one-to-one correspondence between action sets and utility functions. Thus it need not literally be true that utility functions can be inspected for them to be verifiable; it may suffice that action spaces be verifiable.

Finally, let us consider a slightly different example of unidentified effort. Suppose that at date 1 agent 2 can either work or shirk to produce a widget, which is consumed by agent 1. The widget can turn out to be of either high or low quality, but agent 2 working raises the probability of a high-quality widget. Let us suppose that if agent 2 works, the widget, whatever its quality, has a blue colour, whereas if he shirks it is red. Color is entirely payoff-irrelevant. Nevertheless it ensures that in a complete contract setting, agent 2 can be perfectly insured (let us suppose that he is risk averse): The contract can stipulate that agent 1 pay agent 2 if, and only if, the widget is blue. In the case where colors cannot be foreseen, however, agent 2 must bear some risk: for proper incentives, the payment he receives must be strictly monotonic in the quality of the widget. Moreover, this is true whether or not quality itself is verifiable. (If quality is not verifiable, then there must be some probability of no trade in the lower quality state to implement such a monotonic schedule.)

We have provided three illustrations of how Theorems 1 and 2 can break down. The assumption of welfare neutrality is by no means innocuous. Indeed, complete contract theory often focuses on situations in which welfare neutrality is violated; for example, and as we already observed, in moral hazard models, the agent's reward depends on signals of performance, such as the principal's profit, that once realized, have no impact on the parties' von Neumann-Morgenstern preferences. Such measures of performance could not be elicited from the parties *ex post*, and so they have to be describable *ex ante*.

We must point out, however, that the features driving these examples in which describability matters have not been invoked by the incomplete contract literature. Indeed, virtually all the models from that literature of which we are aware satisfy the hypotheses of Theorem 2, so that the irrelevance theorem applies.

7 Parsimony

The mechanisms described in Sections 4 and 5 are demanding in the sense that agents are required to fully specify the realized state of nature *ex post*. Although this is presumably a less arduous task than describing the entire space Θ *ex ante*, it may still be formidable.

Fortunately, there is a simple modification of these mechanisms that, in equilibrium, requires agents to do nothing more than describe a single action. Specifically, suppose (for expositional simplicity only) that preferences are quasi-linear. Let us add two preliminary stages to the mechanism described in Section 4. In the first stage, agent 1 proposes an action (x, y). In stage 2, agent 2 accepts or rejects the proposal. If he accepts, the outcome is (x, y), provided that this is feasible. (If it is infeasible, the "fall-back" option (x^0, y^0) is implemented.) If he rejects, then agent 2 pays an (arbitrarily small) fee ε to a third party and the mechanism constructed in Section 4 is played. Thus, we have introduced a preliminary round in which agent 1 can avoid the (possibly costly) enumeration of the action space by offering to settle on a particular action. The fee ε paid by agent 2 is invoked only to prevent frivolous challenges by that agent.

This mechanism implements the complete contract outcome arbitrarily closely (as ε goes to 0), and yet elicits only a single action on the equilibrium path: If $\hat{f}$, the number-based contract to be implemented, is Pareto-optimal, then, in any state θ, it is an equilibrium of this modified mechanism for agent 1 to propose an alternative a^θ that is ε-optimal and for agent 2 to accept. To see this, note that agent 1 cannot get away with proposing an alternative a that yields him a payoff more than $v_1^\theta(\hat{f}(v^\theta)) + \varepsilon$, since, given $\hat{f}$'s Pareto-optimality, player 2 would necessarily get less than $v_2^\theta(\hat{f}(v^\theta)) - \varepsilon$. That is, agent 2 would be better off rejecting a, since, by the Section 4 construction, the equilibrium of the continuation game gives him utility $v_2^{\theta}(\hat{f}(v^{\theta}))$. Any other equilibrium of the modified mechanism must yield the same payoffs.

We have observed that the mechanism can be chosen such that, in equilibrium, agents describe a single action. To show this, we assumed that describing the entire realized action space X^{θ} is feasible, although possibly very costly. We now show that a parsimony result obtains in the case in which describing the realized action space is infeasible. Assume that utilities are quasi-linear and that, as in Section 4, punishments can be large (our first parsimony result does not rely on this assumption and so, strictly speaking the second result is not a generalization of the first; however, we believe that quasi-linearity can be dropped in the second case as well.) Let us remind the reader of our convention that, in the quasi-linear case, $v_i(k)$ is a *gross* surplus.

Consider the following mechanism: At stage 1, agent 1 announces (i) number-based payoff function (v_1, v_2), (ii) an action x, and (iii) the deciphering key $x = \sigma(k)$ for this action only. [So, player 1 announces only a single physical action.] The implicit claim in this announcement is that (v_1, v_2) are the true payoff functions and that $x = \sigma(k)$, where $(k, y) = \hat{f}(v_1, v_2)$ and σ is the true deciphering key. At stage 2, agent 2 can (i) accept agent 1's announcement, in which case (x, y) is implemented; (ii) challenge agent 1, in which case, as in the mechanism of Section 4, agent 1 must pay 2 a large fine P; or (iii) query agent 1. If agent 2 challenges, he is, in effect, denying at least one of agent 1's claims that (a) x is feasible, (b) $(v_1(\sigma^{-1}(\cdot)), v_2(\sigma^{-1}(\cdot)))$ are the true gross surplus functions and (c) $x = \sigma(k)$. How the challenge (and possible counter-challenge) is conducted and the consequences thereof are exactly as in Section 4. If agent 2 queries, then he must pay a small fee ε and can either (a) name an integer l and ask agent 1 to specify an action $\sigma(l) \in X$ such that the gross surpluses from $\sigma(l)$ are $(v_1(l), v_2(l))$, or else (b) specify an action $x' \in X$ and ask agent 1 to specify an integer l' such that $\sigma(l') = x'$. After agent 1 responds, agent 2 can either challenge or not. If not, the outcome is (x, y). If he challenges, he is in effect denying in case (a) that the action $\sigma(l)$ actually generates gross surpluses $(v_1(l), v_2(l))$, and in case (b) that the action l' generates gross surpluses $(v_1(l'), v_2(l'))$. In either case, the challenges are exactly as in Section 4.

Let us assume that the contract to be implemented is *strongly welfare-neutral*, in the sense that it picks the same utilities in states θ and θ' whenever the utility possibility sets are the same in those two states (in which case we will say that θ and θ' are weakly equivalent). Strong welfare-neutrality ensures that our parsimonious mechanism implements the contract.

Note that strong welfare-neutrality is indeed stronger than welfare-neutrality because two states can be weakly equivalent without being equivalent.[12] Still, Theorem 2 can be extended to strong welfare-neutrality if we replace equivalence by weak equivalence. Moreover strong welfare-neutrality is satisfied by the economic models in the literature.

8 Renegotiation

One possible objection to the mechanisms constructed in Sections 4 and 5 is that they are vulnerable to renegotiation. That is, even though in equilibrium the outcomes of these mechanisms are efficient, this is not so off the equilibrium path. Moreover, the out-of-equilibrium inefficiencies are important because they deter agents from deviating from their equilibrium strategies. If agents anticipated that all inefficient outcomes would be renegotiated, the mechanisms' equilibria might collapse.

Although we agree that in practice most private contracts do not prohibit renegotiation, (and both of us have invoked the possibility of renegotiation from time to time in our own work), we should point out that the assumption that renegotiation cannot be prevented is motivated in the literature by considerations that lie outside the existing models.

It is not obvious why rational agents must allow renegotiation to constrain them, *i.e.* why they cannot simply write an irrevocability clause into their contracts (indeed, we see such clauses in practice in the case of irrevocable trusts). One answer sometimes offered is that under our legal system, the contract enforcer (*i.e.* the court) is not brought into the picture unless one of the contracting parties sues the other. Thus, there is no one to stop the parties if they choose to tear up their old contract and write a new one. (This point of view is formally embodied in the renegotiation models of Hart and Moore (1988, 1999), Maskin and Moore (1999), and Segal (1995)). However, parties could in principle register their contract publicly and play out the mechanism before an arbitrator.[13] Indeed, the current legal system already accommodates similar arrangements in the realm of labour negotiations.

An alternative argument offered for renegotiation is that, even if parties can successfully prevent themselves from invalidating their original contract, they may be able to write a second separate contract that "undoes" some of the provisions of the first. Of course, for such a scenario to be problematic, there would have to be more than

12. Here is an example in which the optimal contract is not strongly welfare-neutral. There is an infinite number of indescribable actions. Agent 1 is the "agent" and agent 2 the "principal." The agent can work or shirk at date 1. If he works, half the actions yield $(1, 5)$ and the other half $(0, 4)$. If he shirks, a third of the actions yield $(2, 3)$ and the other two thirds yield $(1, 2)$. So, working costs 1 to the agent and increases the principal's utility by 2. The two states, which are identified with the two efforts, are not equivalent, and so a contract that induces effort is vacuously welfare-neutral. On the other hand, the two states of nature are weakly equivalent and any strongly welfare-neutral contract induces shirking. Indeed, distinguishing between the two states requires the specification of an infinite number of actions.

13. One might object to such an arrangement by pointing out that the cost of hiring an arbitrator could make contracting prohibitively expensive. However, the need for arbitrators can be dispensed with as long as (i) the actions that parties take in the implementing mechanism can be verified after the fact and (ii) the original contract is registered and contains a "penalty" clause, as in the text below, ensuring that if either party produces evidence of an attempt to recontract he can collect a large fine from the other. Such a contract need not involve the courts or arbitrators unless one of the parties appeals to them after the terms of the contract have already been violated.

one enforcement authority (a unique authority could simply invalidate any second contract between the parties)[14], which raises the question of why enforcement is not centralized. But even putting that issue aside, there seems a straightforward way that parties can commit themselves not to write subsequent contracts. Namely, they can write a clause into the original contract stating that if either party produces evidence of a second contract (or an equivalent set of contracts with third parties,[15] see footnote 14), he is entitled to collect a large penalty from the other party, and that in this circumstance the second contract is not enforceable (where precedence is defined by the registration date). In this way, the parties can ensure that, were they to write a second contract, they would find themselves in a "prisoner's dilemma" situation, in which each had the incentive to inform on the other.

As with our discussion of transactions costs, we do not mean to suggest that renegotiation is irrelevant in practice. Indeed, we acknowledge that it is both important and pervasive. Although we wish only to point out that a rational theory underlying renegotiation is still lacking, we remain hopeful that one (perhaps based on bounded rationality) may yet be constructed. In this respect we agree with Hart-Moore (1999), which contains an interesting discussion of the renegotiation assumption. Moreover, despite the fact that allowing for renegotiation may be at odds with full rationality, we remain interested in analyzing the effect of renegotiation on the irrelevance theorem.

To model renegotiation, let us adhere to Hart and Moore (1988, 1998), Maskin and Moore (1999) and Segal (1995, 1999) by assuming that:

(i) the contract is not registered publicly,

(ii) if the mechanism prescribed by the contract generates an *ex post* inefficient outcome, the parties renegotiate this outcome and move to a Pareto dominating point on the Pareto frontier,

(iii) renegotiation is "payoff-relevant." That is, the point that is reached on the Pareto frontier is entirely determined by the payoffs at the inefficient outcome and by the von Neumann-Morgenstern equivalence class of the number-based payoff functions. [As we will see, this implies that if two states are equivalent before renegotiation, they are still equivalent after renegotiation.]

There are *two types of irrelevance theorems* that can be looked for: One can search for conditions under which neither renegotiation nor indescribability constrains the set of implementable payoffs. Alternatively, one can consider cases in which renegotiation possibly

14. Actually, this is not necessarily true, as Oliver Hart pointed out to us; in some circumstances the parties might be able to undo the first contract through a set of contracts with third parties rather than through direct transactions. For example, suppose that *ex post* the buyer and seller of some good want to exchange more of that good than the original contract specified. Instead of the seller directly selling the buyer an additional amount, they could go through a middleman. And since the arrangements with the middleman would be *first* contracts, they would not be invalid under a "no second contract" rule.

15. Alternatively, the contract could ban *all* subsequent transactions with third parties. This would, in general, be inefficient, since some trades with third parties might be legitimate and have nothing to do with the initial contract. However, the contract could take care to ban such transactions only *off* the equilibrium path, so that the ban would serve simply as a punishment for deviation.

restricts the set of implementable allocations, but in which indescribability does not further delimit feasible payoffs.[16]

We first obtain a result of the first type. We show that, under risk aversion and unbounded transfers, renegotiation quite generally does not constrain the set of implementable allocations even if states are indescribable. The key assumption is renegotiation welfare-neutrality, which is somewhat stronger than the ordinary welfare-neutrality invoked in Theorem 1, and, like its predecessor, guarantees that the payoffs to be implemented do not depend on information that cannot be elicited when actions are indescribable. As in Sections 4 and 5, we make further assumptions that guarantee that an agent's utility can be decreased (the agent can be punished) when he misrepresents the state of nature and is challenged. In Sections 4 and 5, this punishment could take the form of an inefficient allocation, or, relatedly, of a transfer to a third party. However, such punishments are vulnerable to renegotiation (in the case of an inefficient allocation) or to collusion between the two agents (in the case of transfers to third parties). To devise punishments that are immune to renegotiation and/or collusion, we assume agents are (at least slightly) risk averse and, as in Section 4, that penalties can be large. Thus, we make the following assumptions:

(a) for all $\theta \in \Theta$, utility functions take the form

$$u_i^\theta(x, y_i) = U_i(w_i^\theta(x) + y_i) \quad \text{for } i = 1, 2,$$

where $U_i : \mathbb{R} \to \mathbb{R}$ is increasing and strictly concave;

(b) there is no bound on the magnitude of individual agents' transfers

$$Y = \{(y_1, y_2) \mid (y_1 + y_2) = 0\}.$$

Suppose, to simplify matters, that for each state θ, there is a unique efficient action x^θ and that the action profile (x, y_1, y_2) is renegotiated to the point $(x^\theta, y_1 + \Delta y_1^\theta(x), y_2 + \Delta y_2^\theta(x))$ where $\Delta y_1^\theta(x)$ and $\Delta y_2^\theta(x)$ $(\Delta y_1^\theta(x) + \Delta y_2^\theta(x) = 0)$ depend on x and θ, but not on (y_1, y_2). (The assumption that the renegotiation is independent of (y_1, y_2) is strong but is invoked only for expositional convenience).

Renegotiation ensures that each agent i ends up with the same surplus $w_i^\theta(x^\theta)$ in state θ, regardless of the action x and the transfers (y_1, y_2) that result as the outcome of a mechanism. In keeping with requirement (ii) that renegotiation lead to Pareto improvements, we assume that

$$w_i^\theta(x^\theta) + \Delta y_i^\theta(x) \geqq w_i^\theta(x) \quad \text{for } i = 1, 2. \tag{10}$$

16. The latter sort of irrelevance theorem asserts that a second form of contract incompleteness, namely that due to renegotiation, does not interfere with incompleteness due to indescribability. Similar irrelevance theorems may hold when other reasons for contract incompleteness such as uncoordinated contracts (multiprincipal situations) are introduced, but we have not investigated the matter.

As for requirement (iii) that renegotiation be payoff-relevant, consider two equivalent states θ and θ'. By definition, for $i = 1, 2$, there exist $a_i > 0$, β_i, and a bijection $\pi : X^{\theta} \to X^{\theta'}$ with $\pi(x^{\theta}) = x^{\theta'}$ such that

$$U_i(w_i^{\theta}(x) + y_i) = a_i U_i(w_i^{\theta'}(\pi(x)) + y_i) + \beta_i, \tag{11}$$

for all $x \in X^{\theta}$ and all y_i. Now, for any (y_1, y_2) the outcome (x, y_1, y_2) in state θ is equivalent to the outcome $(\pi(x), y_1, y_2)$ in state θ'. The requirement of payoff-relevant renegotiation demands that these two outcomes still be equivalent after renegotiation; *i.e.*,

$$\begin{aligned} &U_i(w_i^{\theta}(x^{\theta}) + y_i + \Delta y_i^{\theta}(x)) \\ &\qquad = a_i U_i(w_i^{\theta'}(x^{\theta'}) + y_i + \Delta y_i^{\theta'}(\pi(x))) + \beta_i. \end{aligned} \tag{12}$$

But (11) and (12) imply that

$$\Delta y_i^{\theta}(x) = \Delta y_i^{\theta'}(\pi(x)), \tag{13}$$

for all $x \in X^{\theta}$.

In the no-renegotiation case (Theorem 1) the crucial hypothesis ensuring that a complete context be implementable was welfare-neutrality. When renegotiation is possible, *renegotiation welfare-neutrality* becomes the pertinent condition. To define this, we shall call two states θ and θ' *renegotiation equivalent* if there exists a bijection $\pi : X^{\theta} \to X^{\theta'}$ with $\pi(x^{\theta}) = x^{\theta'}$ such that

$$\Delta y_i^{\theta}(x) = \Delta y_i^{\theta'}(\pi(x)) \quad \text{for } i = 1, 2, \quad \text{for all } x \in X^{\theta}.$$

Notice, from (13), that two states are renegotiation equivalent if they are equivalent in the ordinary sense. The converse, however, is not true (see below for a discussion of this).

We now define a contract f to be *renegotiation welfare-neutral* if, whenever θ is renegotiation equivalent to θ', $f(\theta) = (x^{\theta}, y^{\theta})$ and $f(\theta') = (x^{\theta'}, y^{\theta'})$ where x^{θ} and $x^{\theta'}$ are the efficient actions in states θ and θ', and

$$y^{\theta} = y^{\theta'}.$$

Because renegotiation equivalence is weaker than ordinary equivalence, renegotiation welfare-neutrality is stronger than ordinary welfare-neutrality. Nevertheless, it is not a very restrictive assumption in typical incomplete contract models. Consider, for example, a buyer-seller framework in which in each state θ, there is one "relevant" good and a number of "irrelevant" goods that could be produced by the seller. Suppose that it is uniquely optimal for the buyer to consume one unit of the relevant good. The buyer's valuation is then $V(e_B, \kappa)$ and the seller's *ex post* production cost

$C(e_S, \kappa)$ where e_B and e_S are the investments by the buyer and seller and κ is a random variable that is realized before trade. Let $\theta = (e_B, e_S, \kappa)$ be the "state of nature." Denote "no trade" by x^0 and suppose that it yields zero surplus: $w_i^{\theta}(x^0) = 0$ for all i and θ. Assume further that renegotiation follows a generalized Nash bargaining process: The buyer and the seller receive fractions τ_B and τ_S of the gain from renegotiating $(\tau_B + \tau_S = 1)$. In particular, at the no trade outcome total surplus is zero. Hence the total gain from renegotiating is

$$w_B^{\theta}(x^{\theta}) + w_S^{\theta}(x^{\theta}) = V(e_B, \kappa) - C(e_S, \kappa),$$

and so the buyer's and seller's payoffs after renegotiating from the no-trade point are, respectively,

$$V(e_B, \kappa) + \Delta y_B^{\theta}(x^0) = \tau_B[V(e_B, \kappa) - C(e_S, \kappa)] \tag{14}$$

and

$$-C(e_S, \kappa) + \Delta y_S^{\theta}(x^0) = \tau_S[V(e_B, \kappa) - C(e_S, \kappa)]. \tag{15}$$

Hence, (13)-(15) imply that a necessary condition for two states $\theta = (e_B, e_S, \kappa)$ and $\theta' = (e'_B, e'_S, \kappa')$ to be renegotiation equivalent is thus that

$$\tau_B C(\theta) + \tau_S V(\theta) = \tau_B C(\theta') + \tau_S V(\theta'). \tag{16}$$

Suppose that the set $Z = \{(c, v) \mid \text{there exists } \theta \text{ such that } (C(\theta), V(\theta)) = (c, v)\}$ contains m elements. Then for generic choices of these m elements, (16) holds only if

$$(C(\theta), V(\theta)) = (C(\theta'), V(\theta')). \tag{17}$$

But if, as in Segal (1995) and Hart-Moore (1999), the irrelevant goods' values and costs are independent of the state, then two states satisfying (17) are equivalent in the usual sense. Hence, the fact that (16) implies (17) means that renegotiation welfare-neutrality is no stronger than ordinary welfare-neutrality. In other words, there exist first-best efficient contracts in Segal's model satisfying renegotiation welfare-neutrality. We can now state:

Theorem 3. *Assume that utility functions take the form $u_i^{\theta}(x, y_i) = U_i(w_i^{\theta}(x) + y_i)$ for $i = 1, 2$ with U_i increasing and strictly concave, that there is no bound on feasible transfers: $Y = \{(y_1, y_2) \mid y_1 + y_2 = 0\}$, that there exists a describable action x^0 such that $x^0 \in X^{\theta}$ for all θ, and that the contract f is Pareto-optimal and renegotiation welfare neutral. Then the number-based contract $\hat{f}$ associated with f can be implemented in subgame perfect equilibrium subject to renegotiation when states are indescribable.*

Proof. See Appendix 2. ■

There are two senses in which implementing a contract is potentially harder when renegotiation is possible than when it is not. The first is that renegotiation welfare-neutrality is, in principle, stronger than ordinary welfare-neutrality. Even so, we argued above that, in typical incomplete-contract models, renegotiation welfare-neutrality is not very restrictive. We also already alluded to the second difficulty; namely, that of punishing parties for deviating from equilibrium. This unlike the first problem, is a serious constraint in many models of the literature. However these models invariably assume that parties are risk-neutral, and it turns out that when this assumption is relaxed the problem entailed in devising punishments vanishes. To see how renegotiation can make punishment problematic, recall the mechanism of Section 4. There, agent 1 pays a fine P to agent 2 if challenged by agent 2. And agent 2 pays a fine $2P$ to a third party, if his challenge turns out to be unsuccessful. If renegotiation is possible, however, then the agents will write a new contract rather than turn over any money to the third party. In this new contract, agent 1 will presumably get part of the $2P$ that would otherwise have gone to the third party. Thus he may well be better off inducing the challenge to fail even if the challenge was valid. Hence renegotiation interferes with our mechanism in a fundamental way.

Suppose, however, that we modify the mechanism so that, if his challenge fails, agent 2 pays his fine to agent 1 rather than to a third party. Moreover, assume that the magnitude of the fine is a random variable, whose realization is determined only after the challenge fails. If the agents are both risk neutral, then the randomness of the fine is irrelevant; only its expectation matters. Moreover, the fact that agent 1 receives the fine means that he has the incentive to cause a valid challenge to fail. Suppose, however, that at least agent 2 is risk averse. Then we can find a lottery such that, for agent 1, the certainty equivalent of the payment he receives is zero, but, for agent 2, the certainty equivalent of the payment he makes is negative. Indeed, by adjusting the lottery, we can make the latter certainty equivalent as negative as we like. Hence, by penalizing agent 2 for failed challenges in this way, we can ensure that he does not have the incentive to challenge falsely, while at the same time avoiding giving agent 1 the incentive to make a valid challenge fail.

Now, one might ask, shouldn't the randomness in agent 2's penalty cause the parties to renegotiate it beforehand?[17] Notice, however, that if agent 2 has indeed made a valid challenge, then in the continuation equilibrium, the penalty will not be invoked, and so renegotiation is not an issue. Indeed, agent 2 would resist renegotiating since otherwise he might give agent 1 the incentive to cause the valid challenge to fail. On the other hand, if agent 2 has challenged falsely, then the parties *should* anticipate the penalty will be invoked.

17. Another possibility (raised by Oliver Hart) is that one party or the other might attempt to obtain insurance against the lottery from a risk-neutral third party. But such an insurance arrangement could be forestalled if the parties kept the details of the randomizing device (*e.g.* a computer program) to themselves.

Hence, in this case, they will want to renegotiate before the challenge succeeds or fails. Nevertheless, if the penalty is severe enough, then, even after renegotiation, agent 2 will still be worse off than had he refrained from challenging falsely. So he will be deterred from doing so. Details are provided in Appendix 2.

Even though the proof of Theorem 3 makes use of large penalties (as in the example of Section 4), we conjecture that, as in the proof of Theorem 1, these are not needed, *i.e.*, that arbitrarily small penalties (combined with an arbitrarily small degree of risk aversion) will do.

More generally, though, once the possibility of renegotiation is admitted, the set of implementable payoffs when states are describable may be reduced. The pertinent issue for us, however, is whether or not this set is further reduced by indescribability. Hence we simply *assume* that a contract is implementable (under renegotiation) when the states are describable and ask whether the contract remains implementable (under renegotiation) when the states are indescribable.

We provide conditions under which indescribability makes no difference at all. Let us say that the set of states Θ is *maximal* if for all $\theta, \theta' \in \Theta$ such that $|X^\theta| = |X^{\theta'}|$ and all bijections $\pi : X^\theta \to X^{\theta'}$, there exists $\theta'' \in \Theta$ such that $X^{\theta''} = X^\theta$ and $u^{\theta''}(x, y) = u^{\theta'}(\pi(x), y)$, for all $(x, y) \in X^\theta \times Y$. Note that maximality *per se* is a weak assumption since the state θ'' need not have high probability (as we will see, however, the assumptions of maximality and welfare neutrality are together quite restrictive).

Now, when renegotiation *à la* Assumptions (i)-(iii) is possible, we can introduce a "renegotiation function" $h(\cdot, \cdot)$, where $h^\theta(x, y) \in X^\theta \times Y$ is the Pareto-optimal alternative to which (x, y) is renegotiated in state θ. For all θ, let $\tilde{u}_i^\theta(x, y) = u_i^\theta(h^\theta(x, y))$. Then $h^\theta(x, y)$ must satisfy

$$\tilde{u}_i^\theta(x, y_i) \geqq u_i^\theta(x, y_i), \qquad i = 1, 2.$$

Moreover, the payoff-relevance requirement (iii) dictates that if $\theta \sim \theta'$ — so that for some bijection $\pi : X^\theta \to X^{\theta'}$ and scalars $a_i > 0$, β_i, condition (2) holds — and

$$u_i^\theta(x, y_i) = a_i u_i^{\theta'}(\pi(x), y_i) + \beta_i, \qquad i = 1, 2,$$

then

$$\tilde{u}_i^\theta(x, y_i) = a_i \tilde{u}_i^{\theta'}(\pi(x), y_i) + \beta_i, \qquad i = 1, 2.$$

Theorem 4. *Suppose that the set of describable states is maximal. Assume that the number-based contract $\hat{f}$ corresponds to a complete contract f that is renegotiation welfare-neutral, is Pareto optimal* *but not one of the extreme points on the Pareto frontier, and is implementable in subgame-perfect equilibrium when states are describable and renegotiation is allowed (according to Assumptions (i)-(iii)). Then* $\hat{f}$ *can also be implemented in subgame-perfect equilibrium subject to renegotiation when states are indescribable.*

Theorem 4, which is proved in Appendix 3, indicates that the key to the indescribability being irrelevant is, once again, a form of welfare-neutrality. We now show however, that renegotiation welfare-neutrality is a more demanding condition than ordinary welfare-neutrality. Recall from Theorem 2 that state-independence of the ratios of the marginal utilities of money and the unidentifiability of effort imply welfare-neutrality. We show that in general the requirement that these two assumptions be satisfied for renegotiated utilities $\tilde{u}^{\theta}(\cdot)$ is strictly stronger than they hold for $u^{\theta}(\cdot)$

Theorem 5. (i) *Suppose that state-independence of the ratios of the marginal utilities of money and unidentifiability of effort conditions hold under renegotiation, that is for payoffs* $\tilde{u}^{\theta}(\cdot)$. *Then, these two conditions also hold in the absence of renegotiation, that is for payoffs* $u^{\theta}(\cdot)$.

(ii) *However, the converse is not true: either (or both) of the two conditions may hold in the absence of renegotiation, yet be violated under renegotiation.*

Proof. (i) First recall that, from payoff-relevant renegotiation, if $\theta \sim \theta'$, then $\theta \overset{r}{\sim} \theta'$, where $\theta \overset{r}{\sim} \theta'$ means that the two states are equivalent for the payoffs functions $\tilde{u}(\cdot)$ that obtain under renegotiation.

Suppose that the state-independence condition holds under renegotiation. Then, if $\theta \overset{r}{\sim} \theta'$, there exist scalars $\tilde{a} > 0$, $\tilde{\beta}_1$, $\tilde{\beta}_2$, and a bijection $\pi : X^{\theta} \to X^{\theta'}$ such that

$$\tilde{u}_i^{\theta}(x, y_i) = \tilde{\alpha}\tilde{u}_i^{\theta'}(\pi(x), y_i) + \tilde{\beta}_i$$

$$\text{for all } x \in X^{\theta},\ y_i \in Y_i \text{ and } i = 1, 2.$$

Suppose, furthermore, that $\theta \sim \theta'$. Then, for $i = 1, 2$, there exist scalars $a_i > 0$ and β_i, and a bijection $\pi : X^{\theta} \to X^{\theta'}$ such that

$$u_i^{\theta}(x, y_i) = a_i u_i^{\theta'}(\pi(x), y_i) + \beta_i$$

$$\text{for all } x \in X^{\theta},\ y_i \in Y_i \text{ and } i = 1, 2.$$

But, $u^{\theta}(\cdot)$ and $\tilde{u}^{\theta}(\cdot)$ coincide on the Pareto frontier as do $u^{\theta'}(\cdot)$ and $\tilde{u}^{\theta'}(\cdot)$. And because there are at least two points on that frontier by assumption, we conclude that $a_1 = a_2$ and so the state-independence condition also holds in the absence of renegotiation.

That the unidentifiability of effort under renegotiation implies that effort is also unidentified in the absence of renegotiation results directly from the definition of unidentifiability and from the fact that two states that are equivalent in the absence of renegotiation are also equivalent under renegotiation.

(ii) That the converse does not hold is established through an example; see below. ■

Example showing that the state-independence and the unidentified-effort assumptions are stronger under renegotiation:

There are two states of nature, θ and θ', and four actions, a_1, a_2, a_3, a_4. Let $X^{\theta} = \{a_1, a_2, a_3\}$ and $X^{\theta'} = \{a_1, a_2, a_4\}$. The action-based payoff matrices (with columns corresponding to actions and rows to agents) are

$$\begin{matrix} a_1 & a_2 & a_3 \end{matrix} \qquad\qquad \begin{matrix} a_1 & a_2 & a_4 \end{matrix}$$
$$\begin{bmatrix} 1 & 0 & -1 \\ 0 & 1 & -2 \end{bmatrix} \text{ in state } \theta \text{, and } \begin{bmatrix} 0 & 1 & -1 \\ 2 & 0 & -3 \end{bmatrix} \text{ in state } \theta'.$$

Note that $\theta \not\sim \theta'$: the only bijection from X^{θ} to $X^{\theta'}$ that preserves the ordering of preferences is π: $\pi(a_1) = a_2$, $\pi(a_2) = a_1$, $\pi(a_3) = a_4$, but condition (2) is violated for any $\{a_2, \beta_2\}$. Because the two states are not equivalent, state-independence holds vacuously in the absence of renegotiation. Now consider renegotiation and assume that the inefficient action a_3 is renegotiated to a_1 in state θ and similarly a_4 is renegotiated to a_2 in state θ'. So, the action-based payoff matrices under renegotiation are

$$\begin{matrix} a_1 & a_2 & a_3 \end{matrix} \qquad\qquad \begin{matrix} a_1 & a_2 & a_4 \end{matrix}$$
$$\begin{bmatrix} 1 & 0 & 1 \\ 0 & 1 & 0 \end{bmatrix} \text{ in state } \theta \text{, and } \begin{bmatrix} 0 & 1 & 1 \\ 2 & 0 & 0 \end{bmatrix} \text{ in state } \theta'.$$

Hence for the permutation π defined above.

$$\tilde{u}_1^{\theta}(a) = \tilde{u}_1^{\theta'}(\pi(a)) \quad \text{and} \quad \tilde{u}_2^{\theta}(a) = \frac{1}{2}\,\tilde{u}_2^{\theta'}(\pi(a)).$$

So, $\theta \overset{r}{\sim} \theta'$, and state-independence fails to hold under renegotiation ($a_1 = 1 \neq a_2 = \frac{1}{2}$). It is also easy to see (indeed, the hypotheses of Theorem 1 are satisfied) that one can implement the contract that prescribes action a_1 in both states θ and θ' (an efficient "risk-sharing" arrangement) in the absence of renegotiation, whether or not actions are describable. This contract can also be implemented under renegotiation if actions are describable (the mechanism can simply specify the constant action a_1), but cannot be implemented under renegotiation in the case of indescribable actions (from welfare neutrality, agent 2 must have payoff 1 in state θ if he has payoff 2 in state θ').

This example also illustrates the point that the unidentified-effort assumption is more easily satisfied in the absence of renegotiation. Suppose that agent 1, say, chooses between efforts e and e' and that the two states θ and θ' result from e and e', respectively. Because $\theta \not\sim \theta'$, the unidentified-effort assumption is vacuously satisfied in the absence of renegotiation. On the other hand, $\theta \overset{r}{\sim} \theta'$ and

$$p(\theta \mid e, \{\theta, \theta'\}) = 1 \neq p(\theta \mid e', \{\theta, \theta'\}) = 0,$$

and so the unidentified-effort assumption is not satisfied under renegotiation.

Thus Theorem 5 suggests that indescribability of actions is more likely to matter when renegotiation is allowed. Intuitively, under dynamic programming, indescribability is analogous to a "Blackwell garbling" of the information structure. This garbling is more costly when contract designers cannot use the threat of Pareto-suboptimal actions in order to elicit the state of nature.

Although Theorem 3 and 4 provide sufficient conditions under which indescribability does not matter, future research ought to delineate more carefully when it *does* matter. We must emphasize, however, that the fact that indescribability may interfere with contract efficiency does not, by itself, justify a focus on specific classes of contracts. More work remains to be done in order to unveil the exact implications of indescribability for contract design.

9 • Discussion

What morals should we draw from the irrelevance theorem? One possible reaction is to dismiss the mechanisms constructed in the proof of Theorems 1 and 3 as hopelessly "unrealistic." Indeed, the lack-of-realism charge is sometimes leveled at the implementation literature more generally. In our view, however, this criticism is misguided. The implementation literature makes no pretense that anything resembling its general mechanisms are or should be used in practice. [One reason for the complexity of the mechanisms in this literature is that they are constructed to handle very general environments.] Rather it is an effort to determine which allocations are consistent with contracting by rational agents and which are not. Specifically, Theorems 1 and 3 demonstrate that in a large class of cases, the transaction costs of foreseeing contingencies have no bearing on implementable contracts. Hence, in our view, a more justifiable reaction to Theorems 1 and 3 would be to call for a weaker form of rationality. Unfortunately, our profession has, for the most part, made little progress toward modelling bounded rationality in a satisfactory way.[18]

If we are to explain "simple institutions" such as property rights, authority (or more generally, decision processes), short-term contracts, and so forth, a theory of bounded rationality is certainly an important, perhaps ultimately essential, ingredient. But for now, it is not the only reasonable approach as we argue below. In the short run there are really two options: to focus on simple institutions by assumption, or to reject the conventional wisdom that complete contract theory is incapable of explaining simple institutions.

Focus on Simple Institutions

One way to proceed is to decide at the outset to consider nothing but "simple contracts" or "simple institutions." Our view is that there is nothing wrong with this approach as long as we are aware of its shortcomings (insiders are quite aware of its limitations, but outsiders or new entrants in the field need not be).

The first difficulty relates to the definition of "simplicity." Is an *ex post* auction of an asset, a contract indexed on the value of publicly traded financial assets, or an option-to-sell contract complex? Are message games such as those observed in tenure reviews or regulatory hearings complex? It does not seem so; yet such apparently simple contracting clauses are rarely allowed in the literature. To be sure, the spirit of the literature is to incorporate such clauses if they seem relevant to the context, but there is no algorithm that enables us to know when we have exhausted the range of "simple contracting opportunities."

Second, and relatedly, there is the question of the value of the short-cut. All economic models are caricatures of reality. They provide a metaphor that can be used to better understand the world, to suggest reforms, and to derive testable implications. The insights we have so far gleaned from incomplete contract models (restricting attention to ownership contracts, authority relationships, short-term contracts, *etc.*) are quite encouraging. But, as usual, taking a short-cut (here restricting the set of feasible contracts on *a priori* grounds rather than from first principles) requires faith that what actually justifies the short-cut does not interact with the rest of the reasoning. In the history of economic thought, examples abound in which taking a short-cut turned out to be a rewarding exercise (*e.g.* developing general equilibrium theory before having a model of large-number-of-traders price formation, or building the paradigms of moral hazard and adverse selection before formally introducing costs of information

18. For a recent attempt in the context of contracts, see MacLeod (1996).

acquisition to explain the asymmetry of information); sometimes, however, conclusions do not seem robust to an endogenization of the short-cut (*e.g.* some of the pre-rational-expectations macroeconomics). At this stage, the literature on simple institutions seems to fall within the former category, but we must await more fundamentalist modeling in order to confirm this intuition.

How Far Can Complete Contract Theory Take Us?

A number of recent papers have argued that in certain *very structured environments*, the optimal complete contract outcome could be implemented through an apparently incomplete contract or simple institution. Before we briefly discuss these, we should point out that the purpose of these exercises is not to show that "simple contracts" are in fact optimal; indeed the papers must invoke extreme assumptions in order to obtain such results. Rather, this literature attempts to derive circumstances in which, *under full rationality*, the loss from using simple contracts rather than optimal complex ones is small. In such circumstances, one would expect bounded rationality considerations to dominate such losses and weigh in favor of simple contracts over slightly more efficient, but also more complex contracts. So, the approach consists of identifying factors that reduce the power of complex contracts relative to simple ones, with the hope that, with the advent of a theory of bounded rationality, small amounts of bounded rationality will indeed induce contracts to be simple.

Several papers fall within this "complete contracting approach to simple institutions." We already mentioned in the introduction papers showing that in specific environments, the optimal complete contract is equivalent to a complete absence of contract or to a simple looking contract such as a property right or an authority relationship. A second branch has looked for complete contract foundations for short-term contracts. Aghion-Bolton (1987), Hermalin (1988), Diamond (1993) and others have argued in various contexts that parties who contract with private information may want to signal that they are "not afraid of returning to the market in the future" in order to obtain better terms of trade today, and that signing a short-term contract is the practical way of doing so.[19] Third, authority relationships (or more generally decision processes) may find a natural habitat in complete contracting models in which at least one party responds little to monetary incentives. Private benefits attached to decisions are then the primary determinants of the parties' incentives to participate and to behave. Put simply, the parties then care primarily about who will have his say in picking decisions, and it is therefore not surprising that authority-like contracts emerge from the analysis.[20] In contrast, strong responsiveness to monetary incentives

19. Laffont and Tirole (1993, Ch. 16) analyze an overlapping-regulators environment and show that, in some circumstances, the optimal regulatory contract with a firm is a short-term contract despite the fact that such a contract creates ratcheting. The idea is that the corresponding inefficiency is dominated by the possibility for the new regulator to "undo" an improper contract signed by a captured former regulator.

20. See Aghion-Tirole (1997) and Tirole (1999) on this point.

creates scope for more efficient schemes in which messages and monetary transfers are used to take total-surplus-maximizing decisions and to compensate parties for foregone private benefits. One would then expect contracts to differ substantially from simple authority relationships. As a last illustration, one can, following Aghion-Bolton (1992), view the financial structure of firms as packages of return streams and decision rights. One can then consider that the return stream attached to a claim is but an incentive scheme designed to induce holders of this claim to interfere in the "right way" (that is, in a way that properly disciplines the insiders), an idea well in line with standard complete contract theory.[21]

To sum up, we do not argue that complete contract theory *per se* explains the observed simplicity of contracts, but rather that it provides clues as to when bounded rationality considerations (yet to be investigated) are likely to dominate inefficiencies linked with the simplicity restriction.

Appendix

1. Verification of the Moore and Repullo (1988) Sufficient Conditions

Claim. *If Assumptions* 1 *and* 2 *are satisfied, then, for any action space X, there exists a successful mechanism* g^X, *i.e., a mechanism such that, for all pairs of number-based payoff functions* $v \in V$ (*where* $v_i : M \times Y_i \to \mathbb{R}$, $i = 1, 2$) *for which* $|M| = |X|$, *and for all deciphering keys* $\sigma : M \to X$, *the unique subgame-perfect equilibrium payoffs of the game* g^X *when agents have utility functions* $(v_1(\sigma^{-1}(\cdot), \cdot), v_2(\sigma^{-1}(\cdot), \cdot))$ *are* $v(\hat{f}(v))$.

Proof. We are dealing with a specified action set X and so standard implementation theory applies. We will show that the sufficient conditions for subgame-perfect implementation in Moore and Repullo (1988) are satisfied.

Let us assume that for any $v \in V$ with $v : M \times Y_i \to \mathbb{R}^2$, for any X for which $|M| = |X|$, and for any deciphering key $\sigma : M \to X$, there exists $\theta \in \Theta$ such that

$$u^{\theta}(\cdot, \cdot) = v(\sigma^{-1}(\cdot), \cdot).$$

This condition was not hypothesized. However, if it is violated, then there are fewer payoff functions to deal with, and so implementation is all the easier. That is, the claim holds *a fortiori*. For any X, let $\Theta_X = \{\theta \in \Theta \mid X^{\theta} = X\}$.

21. For instance, the debt-equity financial structure obtained in Dewatripont-Tirole (1994) can alternatively be interpreted as an incomplete or complete contract outcome.

The first condition that we must verify is:

(a) Existence of actions for which there is "preference reversal."

We must show that, for all states θ, $\varphi \in \Theta_X$, where u^θ is not von Neumann-Morgenstern equivalent (VNM-equivalent) to u^φ, there exist actions $a(\theta, \varphi)$, $b(\theta, \varphi) \in X \times Y$ and agents $i_1(\theta, \varphi)$ and $i_2(\theta, \varphi)$ such that

$$u^\theta_{i_1(\theta, \varphi)}(\hat{f}(v^\theta)) \geqq u^\theta_{i_1(\theta, \varphi)}(a(\theta, \varphi)), \tag{A.1}$$

$$u^\theta_{i_2(\theta, \varphi)}(a(\theta, \varphi)) \geqq u^\theta_{i_2(\theta, \varphi)}(b(\theta, \varphi)), \tag{A.2}$$

and

$$u^\varphi_{i_2(\theta, \varphi)}(a(\theta, \varphi)) < u^\varphi_{i_2(\theta, \varphi)}(b(\theta, \varphi)). \tag{A3}$$

That is, we must show that there exist actions for which there is preference reversal between states θ and φ. In particular, we want agent i_2 to weakly prefer $a(\theta, \varphi)$ to $b(\theta, \varphi)$ in state θ (A.2), but to strictly prefer $b(\theta, \varphi)$ to $a(\theta, \varphi)$ in state φ (A.3). Such a preference reversal allows Moore and Repullo to build a mechanism in which each agent first announces the state of the world θ^i, and can challenge these announcements (θ^1, θ^2) by announcing φ if $\theta^1 = \theta^2$. There are four crucial properties to the construction. The first is (i) if $\theta^1 \neq \theta^2$, the outcome is a "bad" action for both agents. Next, if $\theta^1 = \theta^2 = \theta$, then (ii) provided that these announcements are true, the outcome is $\hat{f}(\theta)$ if there is no challenge and a choice between $a(\theta, \varphi)$ and $b(\theta, \varphi)$ by agent $i_2(\theta, \varphi)$ if there is a challenge by agent $i_1(\theta, \varphi)$. From (A.2) agent $i_2(\theta, \varphi)$ will choose $a(\theta, \varphi)$ and so from (A.1), agent $i_1(\theta, \varphi)$ does not gain by the challenge in state θ. But (iii) if the announcements $\theta^1 = \theta^2 = \theta$ are false, then either player can challenge with the true state φ. Moreover, from (A.3), agent $i_2(\theta, \varphi)$ now would choose $b(\theta, \varphi)$ over $a(\theta, \varphi)$, and the threat of this choice destroys the continuation equilibrium in which either $a(\theta, \varphi)$ or $b(\theta, \varphi)$ are the outcomes. In fact, the mechanism can be constructed so that the only possible continuation equilibrium is one in which $i_1(\theta, \varphi)$ chooses his favorite alternative subject to the other agent getting at least the utility he would from a "bad" outcome. Finally, (iv) the mechanism has these properties so that if the other agent anticipates that $i_1(\theta, \varphi)$ will challenge then he can "pre-challenge" and therefore choose his own favourite action, but if agent $i_1(\theta, \varphi)$ anticipates this, he can pre-pre-challenge etc.

Conditions (i) and (iii) ensure that we cannot have an equilibrium in which $\theta^1 \neq \theta^2$: The outcome is "bad" when the announcements differ but if, say, θ^2 is false then agent 1 can change his announcement to θ^2 and simultaneously challenge so as to get his favourite alternative. Condition (iv), however, guarantees that there cannot be an equilibrium in which both agents announce the same false state: each agent would try to pre-challenge the other. Finally, condition (ii) ensures that truthful relevation by both agents *is* an equilibrium (and, given the foregoing argument, the *only* equilibrium).

In view of conditions (i)-(iv) it remains to show that there exist (a) $a(\theta, \varphi)$ and $b(\theta, \varphi)$ satisfying (A.1)-(A.3), (b) a "favourite alternative" for each agent (actually, each agent may have multiple favourite alternatives, *i.e.* a *maximal set*) and (c) a "bad" action.

To demonstrate (A.1)-(A.3), we note that if u^θ is not VNM-equivalent to u^φ, there exists agent $i_2(\theta, \varphi)$, actions (x, y), (x', y'), (x'', y'') and scalar $\alpha \in [0, 1]$ such that

$$\alpha u^\theta_{i_2(\theta,\varphi)}(x, y) + (1-\alpha)u^\theta_{i_2(\theta,\varphi)}(x'', y'') = u^\theta_{i_2(\theta,\varphi)}(x', y'), \quad \text{(A.4)}$$

and

$$\alpha u^\varphi_{i_2(\theta,\varphi)}(x, y) + (1-\alpha)u^\varphi_{i_2(\theta,\varphi)}(x'', y'') < u^\varphi_{i_2(\theta,\varphi)}(x', y'). \quad \text{(A.5)}$$

Let $\hat{a}(\theta, \varphi)$ be a randomization between (x, y) and (x'', y'') with probabilities α and $1-\alpha$ respectively. Let $\hat{b}(\theta, \varphi) = (x', y')$. Then (A.4) and (A.5) can be rewritten as

$$u^\theta_{i_2(\theta,\varphi)}(\hat{a}(\theta, \varphi)) = u^\theta_{i_2(\theta,\varphi)}(\hat{b}(\theta, \varphi)) \quad \text{(A.6)}$$

and

$$u^\varphi_{i_2(\theta,\varphi)}(\hat{a}(\theta, \varphi)) < u^\varphi_{i_2(\theta,\varphi)}(\hat{b}(\theta, \varphi)). \quad \text{(A.7)}$$

Now, for $\beta \in (0, 1)$, let $a(\theta, \varphi)$ be a randomization between (x^0, y^0) (with probability β) and $\hat{a}(\theta, \varphi)$ (with probability $1-\beta$). Let $b(\theta, \varphi)$ be a randomization between (x^0, y^0) (with probability β) and $\hat{b}(\theta, \varphi)$ (with probability $1-\beta$). Notice that as long as $\beta < 1$, (A.6) and (A.7) continue to hold when $\hat{a}(\theta, \varphi)$ and $\hat{b}(\theta, \varphi)$ are replaced by $a(\theta, \varphi)$ and $b(\theta, \varphi)$. Hence (A.2) and (A.3) hold. Moreover for β near enough 1, (A.5) implies that

$$u_i^{\theta'}(a(\theta, \varphi)) > \frac{1}{2}\, u_i^{\theta'}(x^0, y^{00}) + \frac{1}{2}\, u_i^{\theta'}(x^0, y^0) \quad \text{for all } \theta', i, \quad \text{(A.8)}$$

and

$$u_i^{\theta'}(b(\theta, \varphi)) > \frac{1}{2}\, u_i^{\theta'}(x^0, y^{00}) + \frac{1}{2}\, u_i^{\theta'}(x^0, y^0) \quad \text{for all } \theta', i. \quad \text{(A.9)}$$

Now, for β sufficiently close to 1, there exists $i = i_1(\theta, \varphi)$ such that

$$u^{\theta}_{i_1(\theta,\varphi)}(f(\theta)) \geqq u^{\theta}_{i_1(\theta,\varphi)}(a(\theta, \varphi)), \tag{A.10}$$

as (A.1) claimed.

(b) Existence of maximal set.

Let

$$Q = \bigcup_{\theta, \varphi \in \Theta_X} \{f(\theta), a(\theta, \varphi), b(\theta, \varphi)\},$$

with the provision that if a mechanism ever specifies an outcome in Q, either agent has the alternative option of implementing a 50-50 randomization between (x^0, y^0) and (x^0, y^{00}) instead. That is, in any state $\theta \in \Theta_X$, an alternative $a \in Q$ is really a contingent alternative $\hat{a}$ in which

$$\hat{a} = \begin{cases} a, \text{ if } u^{\theta}_i(a) \geqq \frac{1}{2}\, u^{\theta}_i(x^0, y^0) \\ \qquad\qquad + \frac{1}{2}\, u^{\theta}_i(x^0, y^{00}), & \text{for } i = 1, 2, \\ \frac{1}{2}\,(x^0, y^0) + \frac{1}{2}\,(x^0, y^{00}), & \text{otherwise.} \end{cases} \tag{A.11}$$

The next condition to verify is that there exists a subset $B \subseteq X \times Y$ containing Q such that, for $i = 1, 2$ and all $\theta \in \Theta_X$, if

$$M_i(\theta) = \{a \in B \mid u^{\theta}_i(a) \geqq u^{\theta}_i(b) \quad \text{for all } b \in B\},$$

then

$$M_i(\theta) \text{ is non-empty,} \tag{A.12}$$

$$M_i(\theta) \cap M_j(\theta) \text{ is empty,} \tag{A.13}$$

and

$$M_i(\theta) \cap Q \text{ is empty.} \tag{A.14}$$

For state θ, the sets $M_1(\theta)$ and $M_2(\theta)$ are, respectively, 1's and 2's favourite alternatives in the set B, which includes the optimal alternative $f(\theta)$ as well as the preference reversal alternatives. $a(\theta, \varphi)$ and $b(\theta, \varphi)$ for each φ.

To demonstrate (A.12)-(A.14), let $R = X \times Y - Q$ with the provision that if a mechanism ever specifies an alternative in R, each agent has the option of implementing a 25-75 randomization between

(x^0, y^0) and (x^0, y^{00}) instead. That is, in any state $\theta \in \Theta_X$, an alternative $a \in R$ is really a contingent alternative $\hat{a}$ in which

$$\hat{a} = \begin{cases} a, \text{ if } u_i^\theta(a) \geqq \frac{1}{4} u_i^\theta(x^0, y^0) \\ \qquad\qquad + \frac{3}{4} u_i^\theta(x^0, y^{00}), \quad i = 1, 2 \\ \frac{1}{4}(x^0, y^0) + \frac{3}{4}(x^0, y^{00}), \quad \text{otherwise.} \end{cases} \tag{A.15}$$

Take

$$B = Q \cup R.$$

As long as X and Θ_X are finite, the continuity of $u_i^\theta(x, y)$ ensures that (A.12) holds for all $\theta \in \Theta_X$ and $i = 1, 2$. Now, if $a \in M_1(\theta)$, then, from Assumption 1 (ii) and Assumption 2,

$$u_1^\theta(a) > v_1^\theta(\hat{f}(v^\theta)),$$

and so, from the Pareto-optimality of $\hat{f}$, $v_2^\theta(\hat{f}(v^\theta)) > u_2^\theta(a)$. Hence, $a \notin M_2(\theta)$, and we conclude that (A.13) holds.

Finally, to establish (A.14), consider $a \in Q$. Then, for some $\theta', \varphi' \in \Theta$,

$$a = \begin{matrix} f(\theta') \\ \text{or} \\ a(\theta', \varphi') \\ \text{or} \\ b(\theta', \varphi'). \end{matrix} \tag{A.16}$$

If θ is the true state of the world, then as we have noted, a mechanism designating the outcome a is really prescribing outcome $\hat{a}$ satisfying (A.11). From (A.11) and (A.16) we see that there are four cases:

(i) $\hat{a} = f(\theta')$;

(ii) $\hat{a} = a(\theta', \varphi')$;

(iii) $\hat{a} = b(\theta', \varphi')$;

and

(iv) $\hat{a} = \frac{1}{2}(x^0, y^0) + \frac{1}{2}(x^0, y^{00})$.

Consider case (i) first: $\hat{a} = f(\theta')$. Then, from (A.11),

$$u_j^\theta(f(\theta')) \geqq \frac{1}{2} u_j^\theta(x^0, y^0) + \frac{1}{2} u_j^\theta(x^0, y^{00}), \quad j = 1, 2. \tag{A.17}$$

From Assumption 2, the definition of R, and (A.17), there exists for each $i = 1, 2$, $a^i \in R$ such that

$$u_i^\theta(a^i) > u_i^\theta(f(\theta')) \tag{A.18}$$

and

$$u_j^\theta(a^i) > \frac{1}{4}\, u_j^\theta(x^0, y^0) + \frac{3}{4}\, u_j^\theta(x^0, y^{00}), \quad j \neq i, \tag{A.19}$$

and $f(\theta') \notin M_i(\theta)$. Next consider case (ii): $\hat{a} = a(\theta', \varphi')$. Then, (A.11) implies that

$$u_j^\theta(a(\theta', \varphi')) \geqq \frac{1}{2}\, u_j^\theta(x^0, y^0) + \frac{1}{2}\, u_j^\theta(x^0, y^{00}), \quad j = 1, 2. \tag{A.20}$$

From Assumption 1 (iii) and (A.20) there exists, for each $i = 1, 2$, $a^i \in R$ satisfying $u_i^\theta(a^i) > u_i^\theta(a(\theta', \varphi'))$ and (A.19). Hence $a(\theta', \varphi') \notin M_i(\theta)$. Similarly, in case (iii), $b(\theta', \varphi') \notin M_i(\theta)$.

Finally, consider case (iv): $\hat{a} = \frac{1}{2}(x^0, y^0) + \frac{1}{2}(x^0, y^{00})$. In that case $v_i^\theta(\hat{f}(\theta)) > u_i^\theta(\hat{a})$ for $i = 1, 2$, and so, once again, $\hat{a} \notin M_i(\theta)$ for $i = 1, 2$. We conclude that (A.14) holds, as claimed.

(c) Existence of "bad" actions.

To conclude the verification of the Moore-Repullo conditions, we must show that there exists an action a^* such that for all $\theta \in \Theta_x$ and $i = 1, 2$,

$$u_i^\theta(a) > u_i^\theta(a^*) \quad \text{for all } a \in M_1(\theta) \cup M_2(\theta) \cup Q. \tag{A.21}$$

But from the above choices of $M_i(\theta)$ and Q, it is easy to see that (A.21) is satisfied when $a^* = (x^0, y^{00})$. ■

2. Proof of Theorem 3

Consider the following mechanism:

(i) agent 1 announces

- an action set X
- payoff functions $w_i : X \to \mathbb{R}$, $i = 1, 2$,
- an outcome $(x^{\hat{\theta}}, y^{\hat{\theta}})$ where $(x^{\hat{\theta}}, y^{\hat{\theta}}) = f(\hat{\theta})$ and $\hat{\theta} = (X, w_1, w_2)$.

[Note that the assumption that f is welfare neutral and renegotiation ensure that it is possible to determine what $f(\hat{\theta})$ is without $\hat{\theta}$ having been described in advance.]

Choose P big enough so that

$$\Delta y_1^{\theta}(x) - P < y_1^{\theta}$$

and

$$\Delta y_2^{\theta}(x) + P > y_2^{\theta}$$

for all θ and $x \in X^{\theta}$. [Note that here we are again invoking the assumption that f is welfare neutral.]

If agent 1 fails to do the above, the outcome is $(x^0, -P, P)$.

(ii) agent 2 can challenge or not

- if not, the outcome is $(x^{\hat{\theta}}, y^{\hat{\theta}})$
- if he does challenge, agent 1 must pay him P
- he can either challenge X (in which case we proceed as usual) or (w_1, w_2)
- if he challenges w_1, then he must choose x, $x' \in X$ and $y \in \mathbb{R}$ such that

$$\Delta y_1^{\hat{\theta}}(x) < y_1^{\hat{\theta}}(x') + \gamma.$$

Agent 1 can choose between x and x'. If he chooses x, the challenge succeeds (agent 2 proves that agent 1's claim that the state is $\hat{\theta}$ is false) and the outcome is $(x, 0, 0)$ (before renegotiation). If he chooses x', the challenge fails; and agent 1 should end up with utility (assuming $\hat{\theta}$ is the true state)

$$w_1^{\hat{\theta}}(x^{\hat{\theta}}) + \Delta y_1^{\hat{\theta}}(x') + \gamma - P.$$

We want to punish agent 2 for having challenged falsely. Accordingly choose $K > 0 > L$ so that

$$\frac{1}{2} U_1(w_1^{\hat{\theta}}(x^{\hat{\theta}}) + \Delta y_1^{\hat{\theta}}(x') + K - P) + \frac{1}{2} U_1(w_1^{\hat{\theta}}(x^{\hat{\theta}}) + \Delta y_1^{\hat{\theta}}(x') + L - P)$$
$$= U_1(w_1^{\hat{\theta}}(x^{\hat{\theta}}) + \Delta y_1^{\hat{\theta}}(x') + \gamma - P).$$

For $|L|$ very big, K will also have to be very big. Indeed note that given our assumption about strict risk aversion, for a sequence satisfying the previous equation

$$\lim_{|L| \to \infty} \left\{ \frac{1}{2} U_2(w_2^{\hat{\theta}}(x^{\hat{\theta}}) + \Delta y_2^{\hat{\theta}}(x') - K + P) + \frac{1}{2} U_2(w_2^{\hat{\theta}}(x^{\hat{\theta}}) + \Delta y_2^{\hat{\theta}}(x') - L + P) \right\} = -\infty.$$

Accordingly, at the same time that agent 2 challenges, have him choose K and L (satisfying the equality above) so big that

$$\frac{1}{2}\,U_2(w_2^{\hat\theta}(x^{\hat\theta})+\Delta y_2^{\hat\theta}(x')-K+P) + \frac{1}{2}\,U_2(w_2^{\hat\theta}(x^{\hat\theta})+\Delta y_2^{\hat\theta}(x')-L+P) < U_2(w_2^{\hat\theta}(x^{\hat\theta})+y_2^{\hat\theta}).$$

Then if agent 2's challenge fails, the outcome is $(x^{\hat\theta}, K-P+\Delta y_1^{\hat\theta}(x'), -K+P+\Delta y_2^{\hat\theta}(x'))$ with probability 1/2 and $(x^{\hat\theta}, L-P+\Delta y_1^{\hat\theta}(x'), -L+P+\Delta y_2^{\hat\theta}(x'))$ with probability 1/2. Hence agent 2 is deterred from challenging falsely. If agent 1 chooses x', the outcome of the lottery is known immediately, so there is no renegotiation once agent 1 has chosen x'. Thus agent 1 cannot choose x' in order to "blackmail" agent 2 and force renegotiation to something he prefers to the x choice. [Because the (K, L) lottery entails risk, it is inefficient and, therefore, one might expect it to be possibly renegotiated before agent 1's choice between x and x'. Note, however, that if agent 2 has challenged validly, the (K, L) lottery won't be invoked, and so there is no need to renegotiate it. Indeed, agent 2 will refuse to renegotiate it to eliminate any incentive agent 1 might have to falsely demonstrate that agent 2's challenge is invalid. If agent 2's challenge is invalid, then the (K, L) lottery will be renegotiated, but as long as $|K|$ and $|L|$ are big enough, agent 2 will still be worse off than if he had not challenged.]

A symmetric argument applies if agent 2 challenges w_2. ■

3. Indescribability and Renegotiation

Notice that, for a Pareto-optimal complete contract f as defined in Section 2, renegotiation is not an issue: $f(\theta)$ is Pareto for each state θ, and so there is nothing to renegotiate. Let us therefore drop the assumption that utilities are verifiable in the describable states case (*i.e.* let us now suppose that states are describable but not verifiable). Hence, as in Section 4, agents have to resort to a mechanism in order to implement a complete contract. However, since agents can describe the possible action sets, the mechanism can be made contingent on the realized action space. Specifically, we shall denote a contingent mechanism by $\{g^X\}_X$ where, for each possible X,

$$g^X : S_1^X \times S_2^X \to X \times Y,$$

and S_i^X is agent i's strategy space when $X^\theta = X$. We shall say that $\{g^X\}_X$ *implements* the complete contract f in the describable states case if, for all $\theta \in \Theta$ and all subgame-perfect equilibria (s_1^θ, s_2^θ) in state θ,

$$u_i^\theta(g^{X^\theta}(s_1^\theta, s_2^\theta)) = u_i^\theta(f(\theta)), \quad i = 1, 2.$$

We first establish a general lemma and then apply it to the case of renegotiation.

Lemma 1. *Suppose that the set of states Θ is maximal. If the number-based contract $\hat{f}$ corresponds to a complete contract f that is welfare-neutral, implementable in subgame-perfect equilibrium in the describable states case, is Pareto optimal and not one of the two extreme points on the Pareto frontier, then $\hat{f}$ can be implemented in subgame-perfect equilibrium when states are indescribable.*

Proof. Suppose that f is welfare-neutral and is implemented by $\{g^X\}_X$ in the case where actions are describable in advance. When states are not describable, agents can no longer describe the elements of the set X in advance. However, they can regard these as *dummy* sets (in the same way that actions are dummy variables in number-based contracts).

Accordingly, consider the following three-stage mechanism. In the first stage agent 1 announces (i) a set of actions $\hat{X}$, (ii) a set of dummy actions X with $|X| = |\hat{X}|$, and (iii) a bijection $\gamma : X \to \hat{X}$. In stage 2, agent 2 can accept or challenge. If he accepts, the mechanism moves to stage 3. If he challenges, then he must either exhibit a feasible $x \notin \hat{X}$ or an infeasible $x \in \hat{X}$, in which case he has the right to implement any feasible action of his choosing and the game ends. If the game goes to stage 3, the agents play the mechanism g^X "transformed by γ" (the γ-transformed g^X): If they play strategies (s_1, s_2) such that

$$g^X(s_1, s_2) = (x, y), \tag{A.22}$$

then the outcome is

$$(\gamma(x), y). \tag{A.23}$$

If at any point some agent i fails to follow these rules, then the other agent gets the opportunity to choose any feasible alternative he wishes.

We claim that this mechanism implements $\hat{f}$. To see this, suppose first that agent 1 has announced the true action space $\hat{X}$ as well as dummy action space X and bijection $\gamma : X \to \hat{X}$, and that agent 2 has accepted. Let $\hat{\theta} \in \Theta$ be the true state of nature.

Now perform the thought-experiment in which, instead of a dummy set, agent 1 announces a real set X. Then, from maximality, there exists $\theta \in \Theta$ such that $X^\theta = X$ and

$$u^\theta(x, y) = u^{\hat{\theta}}(\gamma(x), y). \tag{A.24}$$

Now, because, by hypothesis, g^X implements f when the action space is X,

$$u^\theta(g^X(s^*)) = v^\theta(\hat{f}(\theta)), \tag{A.25}$$

for any equilibrium s^* in state θ. But from (A.24), s^* is an equilibrium for g^X in state θ if and only if it is a continuation equilibrium for the γ-transformed g^X in state $\hat{\theta}$. Hence, from (A.24) and (A.25) the equilibrium payoffs of the γ-transformed g^X in state $\hat{\theta}$ are $v^\theta(\hat{f}(\theta))$. But from welfare-neutrality and (A.24)

$$v^{\hat{\theta}}(\hat{f}(\hat{\theta})) = v^\theta(f(\theta)). \tag{A.26}$$

Hence, regardless of the γ announced, the continuation equilibrium payoffs of our mechanism are $v^{\hat{\theta}}(\hat{f}(\theta))$, and so agent 1 can announce any such bijection. We have been arguing as though X were a real action set. But note that everything continues to go through if X consists only of numbers.

It remains only to note that if agent 1 fails to announce the true action space $\hat{X}$, then agent 2 can successfully challenge him, and the assumption that $f(\theta)$ is on the Pareto frontier, but not one of the extreme points, implies that he does worse than (A.26). Hence (A.26) constitutes the overall equilibrium payoffs, that is, the mechanism implements $\hat{f}$.

Turning to the case of renegotiation, and given renegotiation function $h(\cdot, \cdot)$ described in the text, mechanism g and state $\theta \in \Theta$, let

$$g^\theta(s_1, s_2) = h^\theta(g(s_1, s_2))$$

for all feasible strategies (s_1, s_2). It is straightforward to verify that each step of the proof of Lemma 1 continues to hold when we replace each mechanism g with g^θ, and replace welfare-neutrality with renegotiation welfare-neutrality. In particular, note that payoff-relevant renegotiation implies that maximality holds for the utility functions $\tilde{u}_i^\theta$ provided that it does for the utility functions u_i^θ.

Acknowledgements. The authors are grateful to Oliver Hart, Jean-Jacques Laffont, John Moore, Jean-Charles Rochet and a referee for helpful discussions and comments.

REFERENCES

[1] Aghion, P. and Bolton, P. (1992). "An Incomplete Contracts Approach to Financial Contracting", *Review of Economic Studies*, **59**, 473-493.

[2] Aghion, P. and Tirole, J. (1997), "Formal and Real Authority in Organizations", *Journal of Political Economy*, **105**, 1-29.

[3] Aghion, P., Dewatripont, M. and Rey, P. (1994), "Renegotiation Design with Unverifiable Information", *Econometrica*, **62**, 257-282.

[4] Arrow, K. (1953), "Le Rôle des Valeurs Boursières pour la Répartition la Meilleure des Risques", *Économétrie* (Paris: Centre National de la Recherche Scientifique) [Translated as: Arrow, K. (1964), "The role of Securities in the Optimal Allocation of Risk Bearing", *Review of Economic Studies*, **31**, 91-96].

[5] Che, Y.K. and Hausch, D. (1998), "Cooperative Investments and the Value of Contracting: Coase vs Williamson", *American Economic Review* (forthcoming).

[6] Dewatripont, M. (1989), "Renegotiation and Information Relevation over Time: The Case of Optimal Labor Contracts", *Quarterly Journal of Economics*, **104**, 589-620.

[7] Dewatripont, M. and Tirole, J. (1994), "A Theory of Debt and Equity: Diversity of Securities and Manager-Shareholder Congruence", *Quarterly Journal of Economics*, **109**, 1027-1054.

[8] Diamond, D. (1993), "Seniority and Maturity of Debt Contracts", *Journal of Financial Economics*, **33**, 341-368.

[9] Fudenberg, D. and Tirole, J. (1990), "Moral Hazard and Renegotiation in Agency Contracts", *Econometrica*, **58**, 1279-1320.

[10] Grossman, S. and Hart, O. (1986), "The Costs and Benefits of Ownership: A Theory of Lateral and Vertical Integration", *Journal of Political Economy*, **94**, 691-719.

[11] Hart, O. (1995) *Firms, Contracts, and Financial Structure*, (Oxford: Oxford University Press).

[12] Hart, O. and Moore, J. (1990), "Property Rights and the Nature of the Firm", *Journal of Political Economy*, **98**, 1119-1158.

[13] Hart, O. and Moore, J. (1999), "Foundations of Incomplete Contracts", *Review of Economic Studies*, **66**, 115-138.

[14] Hart, O. and Tirole, J. (1988), "Contract Renegotiation and Coasian Dynamics", *Review of Economic Studies*, **55**, 509-540.

[15] Hermalin, B., (1988), "Adverse Selection, Contract Length, and the Provision of On-the-Job Training," in *Three Essays on the Theory of Contracts*, PhD thesis, Massachusetts Institute of Technology.

[16] Holmström, B. and Tirole, J. (1991), "Transfer Pricing and Organizational Form", *Journal of Law, Economics and Organization*, **7**, 201-228.

[17] Laffont, J.-J. and Tirole, J. (1993) *A Theory of Incentives in Procurement and Regulation* (Cambridge: MIT Press).

[18] MacLeod, B. (1996) "Complexity, Contracts, and the Employment Relationship" (Mimeo).

[19] Maskin, E. and Moore, J. (1999), "Implementation and Renegotiation", *Review of Economic Studies*, **66**, 39-56.

[20] Maskin, E. and Tirole, J. (1999), "Two Remarks on the Property Rights Literature", *Review of Economic Studies*, **66**, 139-149.

[21] Moore, J. (1992), "Implementation in Environments with Complete Information", in *Advances in Economic Theory*, J. J. Laffont, (ed.), (Cambridge: Cambridge University Press) p. 182-282.

[22] Moore, J., and Repullo, R. (1988), "Subgame Perfect Implementation", *Econometrica*, **56**, 1191-1220.

[23] Nöldeke, G. and Schmidt, K. (1995), "Option Contracts and Renegotiation: A Solution to the Hold-Up Problem", *Rand Journal of Economics*, **26**, 163-179.

[24] Nöldeke, G. and Schmidt, K. (1998), "Sequential Investments and Options to Own", (Mimeo, University of Bonn and Munich).

[25] Palfrey, T. (1998), "Implementation Theory", in R. Aumann and S. Hart (eds.) *Handbook of Game Theory*, vol. 3 (Amsterdam: North Holland).

[26] Segal, I. (1995) *Essays on Commitment, Renegotiation, and Incompleteness of Contracts*, PhD thesis, Harvard University.

[27] Segal, I. (1999), "Complexity and Renegotiation: A Foundation for Incomplete Contracts", *Review of Economic Studies*, **66**, 57-82.

[28] Tirole, J. (1999), "Incomplete Contracts: Where Do We Stand?" *Econometrica* (forthcoming).

[29] Wernerfelt, B. (1989), "Unforeseen Contingencies and Market Failure", (Mimeo, MIT).

[30] Williamson, O. (1975) *Markets and Hierarchies: Analysis of Antitrust Implications* (New York: Free Press).

[31] Williamson, O. (1985) *The Economic Institutions of Capitalism* (New York: Free Press).

3

Complexity and Renegotiation: A Foundation for Incomplete Contracts

Ilya Segal

Abstract

The paper considers a hold-up model where only one of n future trading opportunities will prove to be efficient, and where *ex post* renegotiation of the *ex ante* contract cannot be prevented. As the environment becomes more complex $(n \to \infty)$, the outcome under any message-contingent long-term contract converges to that of the "incomplete contracting" model where trade is contractible *ex post*, but not *ex ante*. When trades are costly to describe, both *ex ante* and *ex post*, the incomplete contracting result is extended to a broader class of environments.

1 Introduction

According to the modern paradigm of complete contracting which has grown out of implementation theory and incentive theory, optimal contracts should precisely specify an outcome conditional on all relevant information that is observable by a court (*i.e. verifiable*). Moreover, if some relevant information is observed by some of the contracting parties but not by a court, the optimal contract will be contingent on the parties' announcements of this information (see *e.g.* Laffont and Maskin (1982), Moore (1992)). This implies, in particular, that the parties would never prefer to leave some variables open to future negotiation.

While some contracts do seem to conform to these predictions,[1] most real-life contracts are far less sophisticated. This observation has recently provoked significant interest in so-called *incomplete contracting* models, which assume that certain "transaction costs" prevent some aspects of the future trade from being contracted *ex ante* (while still allowing the parties to contract on these aspects *ex post*). Thus, the parties have to leave future outcomes open to

1. For example, coal and natural gas contracts often precisely specify quantities and prices for up to fifty years ahead, possibly conditional on such relevant information as the international price of a similar product and verifiable measures of the seller's cost (Joskow (1988), Crocker and Masten (1988)). Some contractual clauses, such as unilateral options, make the outcome indirectly contingent on the parties' non-verifiable valuations for the trade by giving them choices ("messages") within the contractual framework. For example, a party may be given the right to opt out of the contract by paying some contractually specified damages (as under the widely used "take or pay" clause — see Schwartz (1992)), and/or to choose

future renegotiation, which compromises their incentives to undertake *ex ante* relationship-specific investments (Williamson (1975)).[2] An important application of this approach has been to study asset ownership as an incomplete contract which affects *ex ante* investment incentives by determining the parties' bargaining positions in *ex post* renegotiation (Hart, (1995)). Since its emergence, however, the incomplete contracts literature has been under attack for its failure to provide a rigorous foundation for "transaction costs" (see *e.g.* Maskin and Tirole (1999)).[3]

This paper takes a step towards explaining the prevalence of simple contracts. It considers a variation of the hold-up model, which is a staple of the incomplete contracting literature (for early treatments, see Williamson (1975, 1985), Grout (1984), Hart and Moore (1988)). It departs from existing hold-up models by introducing a new variable, complexity of the contracting environment, which is defined as the number of potentially relevant future trade opportunities. As the environment's complexity grows without a bound, the outcome in our hold-up model converges to that of the "incomplete contracting" model where trade is contractible *ex post*, but not *ex ante*. This happens through two channels: by reducing the benefit of writing the optimal complete contract, and/or by raising the cost of writing such a contract.

The vanishing of contracting gains in a complex hold-up environment is due to the fact that inefficient future trades, while not affecting the total surplus available, introduce additional incentive constraints. Each inefficient future trade is a potential hold-up opportunity: each party may claim that it is the efficient trade, in the hope of extracting a greater share of *ex post* surplus. The greater is the number of inefficient trades, the more incentive constraints need to be satisfied to prevent the parties from misrepresenting the efficient trade, and the lower is the value of contracting. This effect is illustrated in a particular environment in which incentive constraints asymptotically rule out any improvement over the no-contract outcome.

In more general environments, incentive constraints by themselves do not necessarily preclude implementation of the first-best. However, improving investment incentives in a complex environment may require a contract in which the parties describe an unbounded number of trades to the court. This highlights the second effect of environmental complexity: the cost of certain complex contracts in such an environment may be prohibitive. To capture this effect formally, it is assumed that (i) trades cannot be described in advance, in the sense of Maskin and Tirole (1999), and (ii) at most a finite number of trades can be described in the *ex post* message game. These assumptions are reasonable as long as describing a

the quantity to trade at a contractually specified price (within contractually specified limits).

2. Fudenberg *et al.* (1990) and Rey and Salanie (1990) offer sets of assumptions which ensure that the outcome of an optimal long-term contract can be replicated with short-term contracts and subsequent renegotiation. These assumptions, in particular, require that at every renegotiation stage a *verifiable* sufficient statistic for the past actions given all the potentially observable information be produced. This requirement is not satisfied in hold-up models, where investments, even though observable at the renegotiation stage, are not verifiable.

3. See Section 5 for a critique of existing justifications for incomplete contracting.

trade involves a positive cost or delay. Under these assumptions, asymptotic improvement upon the no-contract outcome is impossible as the environment's complexity grows without a bound.

The rest of the paper is organized as follows. Section 2 presents a model of a complex hold-up environment and its preliminary analysis. Section 3 considers a particular case of the model where incentive constraints asymptotically result in incomplete contracting. Section 4 considers the general case, incorporating a restriction on contractual complexity. Section 5 relates the paper's results to existing justifications of contractual incompleteness and suggests some directions for future research.

2 The Model

Consider a model where a buyer and a seller can trade one (but no more than one) of n widgets, indexed 1 to n. Trade is represented by a number $w \in \{0, 1, \ldots, n\}$, where $w = 0$ stands for "no trade". Let $\boldsymbol{v} = (v_0, v_1, \ldots, v_n)$ denote the vector of the buyer's valuations for the trades, and $\boldsymbol{c} = (c_0, c_1, \ldots, c_n)$ denote the vector of the seller's costs, with the convention that $v_0 = c_0 = 0$ (throughout the paper, boldface letters will be used to denote vectors). Assume that $\boldsymbol{v} \in V^{n+1}$, $\boldsymbol{c} \in C^{n+1}$, where V and C are compact subsets of $\Re$.

Both vectors depend stochastically on the parties' *ex ante* relationship-specific investments. Let $\sigma \in \Sigma$ denote the cost of the seller's investment, and $\lambda \in \Lambda$ denote the cost of the buyer's investment, where Λ and Σ are compact subsets of $\Re$. Let $\boldsymbol{v}(\lambda, \zeta)$, $\boldsymbol{c}(\sigma, \zeta)$ denote the parties' valuations as functions of their investments and the realization of uncertainty $\zeta \in Z$, where Z is a measurable set in a Euclidean space. Assume that these valuations are observed by the parties *ex post*.

If the parties' *ex post* valuations are $\boldsymbol{v}$, $\boldsymbol{c}$, the total *ex post* surplus available to the parties is

$$S(\boldsymbol{v}, \boldsymbol{c}) = \max_{w \in \{0, 1, \ldots, n\}} [v_w - c_w].$$

Assume that $E_\zeta[S(\boldsymbol{v}(\lambda, \zeta), \boldsymbol{c}(\sigma, \zeta))]$ is a continuous function of λ, σ.

Assuming that the maximum *ex post* surplus is always realized, a socially efficient investment pair (λ^*, σ^*) must maximize the expected *ex ante* surplus, *i.e.*

$$(\lambda^*, \sigma^*) \in \arg\max_{(\lambda, \sigma) \in \Lambda \times \Sigma} E_\zeta S(\boldsymbol{v}(\lambda, \zeta), \boldsymbol{c}(\sigma, \zeta)) - \lambda - \sigma. \quad (1)$$

Let $\mathscr{E}_n^*$ denote the set of such "first-best" investment pairs (λ^*, σ^*).

The parties' individual investment incentives, on the other hand, will be affected by the *ex ante* contract they write. The contract can specify future trade as a function of verifiable information, and, possibly, the parties' messages about non-verifiable information. It is assumed, however, that the parties cannot commit not to renegotiate contractual inefficiencies:

Assumption 1. Whenever the contractual outcome is not *ex post* efficient, the parties renegotiate to an efficient outcome, splitting the renegotiation surplus equally.[4]

If the contract specifies trading a widget w at a price t, the renegotiation surplus is $S(\boldsymbol{v}, \boldsymbol{c}) - (v_w - c_w)$, and the parties' post-renegotiation utilities U_B, U_S can be calculated as

$$\begin{aligned} U_B &= -t + \frac{v_w + c_w}{2} + \frac{1}{2} S(\boldsymbol{v}, \boldsymbol{c}), \\ U_S &= t - \frac{v_w + c_w}{2} + \frac{1}{2} S(\boldsymbol{v}, \boldsymbol{c}). \end{aligned} \tag{2}$$

For example, suppose that the parties abstain from writing an *ex ante* contract (equivalently, they write a contract specifying $w = 0$). In this case, each party's *ex post* payoff will be $\frac{1}{2} S(\boldsymbol{v}, \boldsymbol{c})$. Therefore, an investment pair (λ^0, σ^0) constitutes a Nash equilibrium of the *ex ante* investment game without a contract if, and only if,

$$\begin{aligned} \lambda^0 &\in \arg\max_{\lambda \in \Lambda} \frac{1}{2} E_\zeta S(\boldsymbol{v}(\lambda, \zeta), \boldsymbol{c}(\sigma^0, \zeta)) - \lambda, \\ \sigma^0 &\in \arg\max_{\sigma \in \Sigma} \frac{1}{2} E_\zeta S(\boldsymbol{v}(\lambda^0, \zeta), \boldsymbol{c}(\sigma, \zeta)) - \sigma. \end{aligned} \tag{3}$$

Let $\mathcal{E}_n^0$ denote the set of such "no-contract" investment pairs (λ^0, σ^0).

In general, without a contract one should expect underinvestment relative to the first-best, since each party internalizes only 50% of its investment's contribution to *ex post* surplus. The following result formalizes this intuition using the techniques of monotone comparative statics (Milgrom and Shannon (1994), Edlin and Shannon (1998)).[5]

Proposition 1. *Choose any* $(\lambda^0, \sigma^0) \in \mathcal{E}_n^0$ *and any* $(\lambda^*, \sigma^*) \in \mathcal{E}_n^*$. *Suppose that* $E_\zeta[S(\boldsymbol{v}(\lambda, \zeta), \boldsymbol{c}(\sigma, \zeta))]$ *has positive partial derivatives on* $\Lambda \times \Sigma$. *Then*

(i) *If* $\Lambda = \{\bar{\lambda}\}$ *(the buyer has no investment choice) and* $\sigma^* \in \operatorname{int} \Sigma$, *then* $\sigma^0 < \sigma^*$.

(ii) *If* $\Sigma = \{\bar{\sigma}\}$ *(the seller has no investment choice) and* $\lambda^* \in \operatorname{int} \Lambda$, *then* $\lambda^0 < \lambda^*$.

4. Equal split of renegotiation surplus is assumed only to simplify exposition. It is straightforward to verify that all of the paper's results hold if renegotiation splits the surplus in any fixed proportion.

5. All proofs are in the Appendix.

(iii) *If there exists an ex post efficient trade* $w^*(\zeta) \in \arg\max_w [\boldsymbol{v}_w(\lambda, \zeta) - \boldsymbol{c}_w(\sigma, \zeta)]$ *which is independent of* (λ, σ), *and* $\lambda^* \in \text{int}\ \Lambda$, $\sigma^* \in \text{int}\ \Sigma$, *then* $(\lambda^0, \sigma^0) < (\lambda^*, \sigma^*)$.

According to parts (i) and (ii) of the proposition, in the absence of a contract, each party underinvests *given the other party's investment.*[6] Therefore, in the absence of a contract, a socially optimal investment pair cannot be sustained. As it turns out, however, first-best investments can be implemented with a contract which prevents renegotiation in equilibrium by specifying a widget that is *ex post* efficient given these investments, at a price that is independent of the parties' investments:

Proposition 2. *If* $(\lambda^*, \sigma^*) \in \mathscr{E}_n^*$, *then* (λ^*, σ^*) *is an equilibrium investment pair in a contract in which a widget* $w^*(\zeta) \in \arg\max_w [v_w(\lambda^*, \zeta) - c_w(\sigma^*, \zeta)]$ *is traded at a price* $t(\zeta)$.

The proof is based on the following simple argument. Observe that each party's investment does not affect the other party's utility at the contractual outcome, which serves as the disagreement point for renegotiation. Therefore, if (for example) the buyer had all the bargaining power, he would be the residual claimant for *ex post* surplus, so he would find any deviation from a first-best investment level unprofitable. When the buyer has only partial bargaining power, his *ex post* payoff after any deviation is even lower (while his equilibrium payoff is not affected, since in equilibrium there is no renegotiation). Therefore, any deviation would remain unprofitable.[7]

According to Proposition 2, if the *ex post* efficient trade is either known *ex ante* or verifiable *ex post*, the hold-up problem can be easily resolved. To eliminate this possibility, two assumptions are made:

Assumption 2. The parties' investments λ and σ, their valuation vectors $\boldsymbol{v}$ and $\boldsymbol{c}$, and the realization of uncertainty ζ are not verifiable.

Assumption 3. For any pair of vectors $\boldsymbol{v}$ and $\boldsymbol{c}$, and a permutation π of the set $\{1, \ldots, n\}$ of widgets, define new valuation vectors $\boldsymbol{v}\pi$ and $\boldsymbol{c}\pi$ such that for all $w \in \{1, \ldots, n\}$,

$$(\boldsymbol{v}\pi)_w = v_{\pi(w)},$$
$$(\boldsymbol{c}\pi)_w = c_{\pi(w)}.$$

Then for any $\lambda \in \Lambda$ and $\sigma \in \Sigma$, the distributions of $\boldsymbol{v}(\lambda, \zeta)\pi$ and $\boldsymbol{c}(\sigma, \zeta)\pi$ do not depend on the permutation π.

Assumption 2 implies, in particular, that the efficient trade is not verifiable *ex post*. Assumption 3 postulates that any permutation of widgets does not affect the parties' priors. Intuitively, this means that any *ex ante* structure on the set of possible trades is lacking, *i.e.*

6. If investments are substitutes in expected total surplus, one party's underinvestment encourages the other party to invest more. If this indirect effect outweighs the direct effect, one party (but not both) may invest more without a contract than in the first best.

7. The argument fails when a party's investment directly affects the other party's valuation (for example, the seller's investment improves non-verifiable quality of the good). Che and Hausch (1997) show that in this case the parties cannot improve upon the no-contract outcome even when the efficient *quantity* of trade is known *ex ante*. Their model is similar to ours in that contractual incompleteness is due to a court's inability to distinguish between "widgets" of different qualities. (If quality could be contracted in advance, investment would have no direct external effect, and Proposition 2 would apply.)

widgets are indistinguishable *ex ante*. In particular, all trades are *ex ante* equally likely to be efficient.[8]

The next assumption will rule out asymptotic improvement by a contract that specifies a noncontingent trade $w \in \{1, \ldots, n\}$ at a fixed price t_0. By Assumption 3, for all $w > 0$ we have $E_\zeta v_w(\lambda, \zeta) = 1/n \sum_{n=1}^{n} E_\zeta v_i(\lambda, \zeta)$ and $E_\zeta c_w(\sigma, \zeta) = 1/n \sum_{i=1}^{n} E_\zeta c_i(\sigma, \zeta)$, which implies that specifying a noncontingent trade gives each party the same expected utility as a randomization that picks every widget with probability $1/n$. This expected utility is assumed to be insensitive to investments as $n \to \infty$:

Assumption 4. The average trade is asymptotically non-responsive to investments: for every $\zeta \in Z$, $\lambda, \lambda' \in \Lambda$, and $\sigma, \sigma' \in \Sigma$, as $n \to \infty$,

$$\frac{1}{n}\left|\sum_{w=1}^{n} [v_w(\lambda', \zeta) - v_w(\lambda, \zeta)]\right| \to 0,$$

$$\frac{1}{n}\left|\sum_{w=1}^{n} [c_w(\sigma', \zeta) - c_w(\sigma, \zeta)]\right| \to 0.$$

Using expressions (2), this assumption implies that in any noncontingent contract, each party asymptotically receives 50% of its investment's contribution to total surplus, just as it would without a contract.

So far we have not ruled out the possibility that the parties would reveal the efficient trade (or another trade that is responsive to investments) in a message-contingent contract. However, expressions (2) imply that given a fixed price, each party will have an incentive to "hold up" the other party by suggesting a trade that improves its bargaining position: the buyer will suggest a widget w that maximizes $(v_w + c_w)/2$, and the seller will suggest a widget that minimizes $(v_w + c_w)/2$. Assume that there are many such "hold-up" widgets, which are not responsive to investments:

Definition 1. *Widget w is non-responsive to investments in contingency ζ if $v_w(\lambda, \zeta)$ and $c_w(\sigma, \zeta)$ do not depend on λ and σ respectively (and otherwise it is said to be responsive to investments in contingency ζ).*

Definition 2. *Widget w is good (G) [bad (B)] in contingency ζ if*

(a) *it is non-responsive to investments in contingency ζ, and*

(b) $[v_w(\lambda, \zeta) + c_w(\sigma, \zeta)]/2 > [<] [v_i(\lambda, \zeta) + c_i(\sigma, \zeta)]/2$ *for all responsive widgets i and contingency ζ, and for all* $(\lambda, \sigma) \in \Lambda \times \Sigma$.

8. Observe that the uncertainty postulated in Assumption 3 is different in nature from the uncertainty about the *ex post* optimal *quantity* of trade, considered *e.g.* in Edlin and Reichelstein (1996). In their model, *ex ante* uncertainty about the optimal trade does not necessarily prevent implementation of first-best investments. For example, under a certain separability assumption, both parties can be made to invest efficiently using a contract that specifies the expected efficient trade given optimal investments. In our model, different trades cannot be ranked *ex ante* as representing higher or lower quantities.

An example of a good (G) widget would be a "goldplated" widget, which is worth a lot to the buyer, but is very costly to produce. A bad (B) widget, on the other hand, could be a "cheap imitation" widget, which costs little to the seller, and is worth little to the buyer. Expression (2) implies that given a fixed price t, the buyer would prefer suggesting a G widget rather than a responsive widget, while the seller would prefer suggesting a B widget rather than a responsive widget.[9] In order to make revelation of responsive widgets difficult, assume that the numbers of G and B widgets are large:

Assumption 5. The numbers of G and B widgets go to infinity in probability[10] as $n \to \infty$.

3 Incentive Constraints and Contracting Benefits

This section analyzes a particular model satisfying Assumptions 1–5, in which incentive constraints asymptotically reduce contracting benefits to zero. In this model, in every contingency there is exactly one responsive widget, which will be called widget R (for "regular"). This responsive widget is assumed to always represent the *ex post* efficient trade. All remaining widgets will represent hold-up opportunities (either G or B). The *ex ante* probability of each widget being the R widget is $1/n$, and the types of the remaining widgets are distributed i.i.d., with the probability that a given non-responsive widget is G rather than B being equal to $1/2$. Call the vector $\boldsymbol{N} \in \{R, G, B\}^n$ of the realized types of all widgets the *configuration*.

Let $v \in \overline{V}$ denote the buyer's valuation for the R widget, and $c \in \overline{C}$ denote the seller's cost for this widget, where $\overline{V}$, $\overline{C}$ are assumed to be compact subsets of $\Re$. Assume that for all B widgets b, for all G widgets g, and for any $v \in \overline{V}$, $c \in \overline{C}$, we have

$$\begin{aligned} v - c &> \max\{0, v_b - c_b, v_g - c_g\}, \\ \underline{a} = \frac{v_b + c_b}{2} &< \frac{v + c}{2} < \frac{v_g + c_g}{2} = \overline{a}. \end{aligned} \tag{4}$$

The first inequality says that the R widget is always the efficient widget to trade. To understand the second line, recall that, according to (2), specifying the trade of widget w in a contract provides the transfer $(v_w + c_w)/2$ from the seller to the buyer. The second line of (4), therefore, says that all B widgets provide the same transfer $\underline{a}$, all G widgets provide the same transfer $\overline{a}$, and that the R widget provides an intermediate transfer (which is consistent with Definition 2).

9. Truthful revelation of the efficient widget would be easier to achieve if renegotiation could be prevented, or if the split of bargaining power in renegotiation could be affected by the *ex ante* contract. For example, if the contract gave the seller the right to make an *ex post* take-it-or-leave-it offer to the buyer, the seller would become the residual claimant for total surplus. This would give the seller an incentive to suggest the efficient widget *ex post*, and to invest efficiently *ex ante*. More generally, Proposition 5 of Rogerson (1992) establishes that in the absence of renegotiation, first-best investments can be implemented using multi-stage *ex post* message games. In a related vein, Aghion *et al.* (1994) show that if the renegotiation game uses the original contract as an outside option, rather than as the disagreement point, the contract can make the responder accept an offer leaving it no surplus over the contractual outcome (*e.g.*, by imposing per diem penalties or using a financial hostage), which would again induce the proposer to choose a first-best investment level.

10. Convergence in probability means that for any fixed number m, the probability that the numbers of G and B widgets exceed m goes to one as $n \to \infty$.

Since the efficient trade in this model does not depend on investments, Proposition 1(iii) establishes that in the absence of a contract, both parties underinvest. For convenience, assume that the distribution of the parties' valuations for the efficient trade, v and c, does not depend on n. This assumption ensures that neither the set $\mathscr{E}^*$ of first-best investments nor the set $\mathscr{E}^0$ of no-contract investments depend on n. At the same time, the efficiency improvement achieved by writing an *ex ante* contract will depend on n.

As discussed earlier, Assumptions 3 and 4 imply that a contract specifying a noncontingent trade will provide no asymptotic improvement over the no-contract outcome as $n \to \infty$. An improvement may be achieved with message-contingent contracts which provide the parties with the incentives to reveal the efficient trade. When n is small, message-contingent contracts in which the equilibrium price depends on the realized configuration may substantially improve upon noncontingent contracts:

Example 1. Let $n = 2$. Suppose that $\underline{a} = 0 < v + c < \bar{a}$ for all $v \in \bar{V}$, $c \in \bar{C}$ (observe that this requires $\bar{a}$ to be at least twice as large as stipulated in (4)). Then the following message-contingent contract implements the first-best:

1. The buyer proposes a widget to trade.
2. The seller agrees or challenges.
3. If the seller agrees, the widget proposed by the buyer is traded at t_0. If the seller challenges, he chooses which widget to trade, and the price is $t_0 - \bar{a}/2$.
4. The contractual outcome can be renegotiated.

If the configuration is *BR* or *RB*, the seller will never challenge: according to (2), challenging the *R* widget and offering the *B* widget instead saves him $(v + c)/2$, which is less than the penalty $\bar{a}/2$ he pays for challenging. Therefore, using (2) again, we see that the buyer will propose the *R* widget.

If the configuration is *GR* or *RG*, the seller will always challenge the *G* widget and offer the *R* widget instead, since according to (2) this saves him $\bar{a} - (v + c)/2$, which exceeds the penalty $\bar{a}/2$ he pays for challenging. The buyer will nevertheless propose the *G* widget, since this allows him to extract the penalty from the seller.[11]

Therefore, in both cases, the *R* widget is traded in equilibrium, and the trading price does not depend on v, c. Thus, by Proposition 2 the first-best is achieved.

To characterize the set of incentive-compatible contracts, the model can be cast in the framework of implementation with renegotiation developed by Maskin and Moore (1999). An *ex post* state of the

11. Formally speaking, this argument derives the subgame-perfect equilibrium of the message game. However, since this is a zero-sum game (renegotiation always restores efficiency), all the Nash equilibrium outcomes are also subgame-perfect equilibrium outcomes. This point also applies to Examples 2 and 3 in Section 4 below.

world can be described by a triple $(\boldsymbol{N}, v, c)$, where v is the buyer's valuation for the R widget, c is the seller's cost for this widget, and $\boldsymbol{N}$ is the configuration. Let Θ denote the set of all such states, *i.e.*

$$\Theta = \{\boldsymbol{N} \in \{R, G, B\}^n\text{: for some } i, N_i = R \text{ and } \boldsymbol{N}_j \neq R \text{ for all } j \neq i\} \times \overline{V} \times \overline{C}.$$

An *ex post* outcome can be described as $(\boldsymbol{x}, t)$, where $\boldsymbol{x} \in \{(x_0, x_1, \ldots, x_n) \in \Re^{n+1}_+ \text{: } \sum_{w=0}^{n} x_w = 1\}$ is the randomized trade (x_w is the probability that widget w is traded), and $t \in \Re$ is the monetary transfer from the buyer to the seller.[12,13] Let Y denote the set of all such outcomes. Denote the buyer's and seller's utilities from outcome $y \in Y$ in the state $\theta \in \Theta$ by $u_B(y, \theta)$ and $u_S(y, \theta)$ respectively.

The contractual outcome will be renegotiated whenever it is Pareto inefficient. Maskin and Moore consider an arbitrary exogenously given renegotiation function $h\colon \Theta \times Y \to Y$, so that $h(y \mid \theta)$ specifies the final outcome in state θ when the contractually stipulated outcome in that state is y. Maskin and Moore postulate three properties of the renegotiation function:

(R1) The function $h(\cdot)$ is single-valued (*i.e.* the outcome of renegotiation is uniquely defined).

(R2) The outcome $h(y \mid \theta)$ is strongly Pareto efficient in state θ for all $\theta \in \Theta$ and all $y \in Y$.

(R3) Renegotiation is individually rational, *i.e.* $u_j(h(y \mid \theta), \theta) \geqq u_j(y, \theta)$ for $j \in \{B, S\}$, all $\theta \in \Theta$, and all $y \in Y$.

In our model, the renegotiation function $h(\cdot)$ is given by the Nash bargaining solution, which always implements the *ex post* efficient trade, splitting the renegotiation surplus equally between the parties. This renegotiation function clearly satisfies properties (R1)–(R3).

The objective of an *ex ante* contract is to implement a given *choice rule* $f\colon \Theta \to Y$ as the post-renegotiation outcome. In general, this can be achieved via a message game. A general message game can be described as $M = \langle M_B, M_S, g \rangle$, where M_B, M_S are the parties' message spaces, and $g\colon M_B \times M_S \to Y$ is the outcome function. The message game M is said to implement a choice rule f with renegotiation h if in any state $\theta \in \Theta$ the unique Nash equilibrium outcome of $h \circ g$ is $f(\theta)$. A choice rule is implementable if there exists a message game implementing it. Observe that any social choice rule that is implementable with renegotiation has to be strongly Pareto efficient (any Pareto inefficient outcome would be renegotiated

12. Randomization will play no role in the analysis of this section, but it will play a role in the next section. Allowing for randomized monetary transfers would not change anything because the risk-neutral parties care only about expected transfers.

13. The contract could also specify destruction of wealth when the parties disagree. However, since this inefficiency would be renegotiated in the same way in any state of the world, it would not affect the parties' incentives in any way.

away). The following theorem characterizes social choice rules that are implementable with renegotiation in a two-party environment:

Theorem 0. (Maskin and Moore (1999)) *A strongly Pareto efficient choice rule f is implementable with renegotiation h satisfying assumptions* (R1)–(R3) *if, and only if, for any ordered pair of states* θ, $\phi \in \Theta$ *there exists an outcome* $y \in Y$ *such that*

$$u_B(f(\theta), \theta) \geqq u_B(h(y \mid \theta), \theta) \text{ and } u_S(f(\phi), \phi) \geqq u_S(h(y \mid \phi), \phi).$$

The intuition behind the theorem runs as follows. Since the post-renegotiation outcome is always *ex post* efficient, "contract plus renegotiation" is a game with opposing interests, hence the equilibrium payoffs (and the equilibrium outcome) are unique by a version of the Minimax theorem.[14] Therefore, one should not worry about multiplicity of equilibria, and the Revelation Principle can be used to restrict attention to so-called direct revelation mechanisms. In such mechanisms the parties' messages to the court are complete reports of what they know about the state of the world (*i.e.* $M_B = M_S = \Theta$) and the parties do not lie in equilibrium.

Note that we can restrict attention to contracts that prescribe the choice rule directly when both parties agree on the state of the world. When the parties disagree, on the other hand, we know that one party is lying, but we do not know which one. Therefore, in the case of a disagreement, the mechanism must specify an outcome y that punishes the lying party, whoever it is. Informally, we will say that such an outcome "resolves" the disagreement. The requirement that all potential disagreements be resolved yields the incentive-compatibility constraints described in Theorem 0.

Application of Theorem 0 to our model is not straightforward because of the daunting number of possible disagreements. Fortunately, we will be able to obtain an upper bound on what can be achieved in an incentive-compatible contract using only a small subset of all possible disagreements. Intuitively, we can do this because some disagreements are much easier to resolve than others.

Suppose, for example, that a certain widget is described as bad by the seller and as good by the buyer. Stipulating the trade of this widget would then "call the bluff" by punishing the liar, whoever it is. Indeed, if the seller is lying and the buyer is telling the truth, the seller will have to provide a good widget, which will punish him severely; if instead the buyer is lying and the seller is telling the truth, the buyer will receive a bad widget, which will punish him as well. More generally, if there is a widget that is described as more valuable by the buyer than by the seller, stipulating the trade of this widget would easily resolve the disagreement.

14. Moreover, in our context of transferable utility "contract plus renegotiation" is a zero-sum game, therefore the equilibrium outcome is unique even when mixed strategies are allowed.

The disagreements that are hard to resolve are those in which no widget is described as more valuable by the buyer than by the seller. We will focus on a set of such disagreements, which will be called *critical disagreements*. An ordered pair of configurations $(\boldsymbol{M}, \boldsymbol{N})$ is related by critical disagreement if there exist widgets i, j such that

$$\begin{aligned} \boldsymbol{M}_i &= R, \boldsymbol{N}_i = B, \\ \boldsymbol{M}_j &= G, \boldsymbol{N}_j = R, \\ \boldsymbol{M}_w &= \boldsymbol{N}_w \text{ for } w \notin \{i, j\}. \end{aligned} \tag{5}$$

In words, $\boldsymbol{M}$ is in critical disagreement with $\boldsymbol{N}$ when the widget described as regular in $\boldsymbol{N}$ is described as good in $\boldsymbol{M}$, the widget described as regular in $\boldsymbol{M}$ is described as bad in $\boldsymbol{N}$, and the two configurations agree on the types of all the other widgets.

Let $\mathfrak{D}$ denote the set of ordered configuration pairs related by critical disagreement. The relation of critical disagreement can be represented with a directed graph, whose vertices are configurations, and whose edges are pairs from $\mathfrak{D}$. To draw this graph, let $|\boldsymbol{N}|$ denote the number of B widgets in configuration $\boldsymbol{N}$, and note that $(\boldsymbol{M}, \boldsymbol{N})$ can be related by critical disagreement only if $|\boldsymbol{N}| = |\boldsymbol{M}| + 1$. Therefore, it is convenient to draw the graph of critical disagreements by levels, configurations with $|\boldsymbol{N}| = l$ being located at the lth level, and the edges connecting vertices from neighbouring levels. An example for $n = 3$ is drawn in Figure 1.

The proof of this section's result can now be sketched as follows (a complete proof is in the Appendix). Suppose we want to implement a choice rule $(\boldsymbol{x}(\boldsymbol{N}, v, c), t(\boldsymbol{N}, v, c))$, where $t(\boldsymbol{N}, v, c)$ is the monetary transfer and $\boldsymbol{x}(\boldsymbol{N}, v, c)$ is the randomized trade prescribed for the state of the world $(\boldsymbol{N}, v, c)$. Pareto efficiency of the choice rule dictates that $x_w(\boldsymbol{N}, \boldsymbol{v}, \boldsymbol{c})$ for $\boldsymbol{N}_w = \boldsymbol{R}$, but leaves us the freedom to design the transfer function $t(\boldsymbol{N}, v, c)$. Consider the

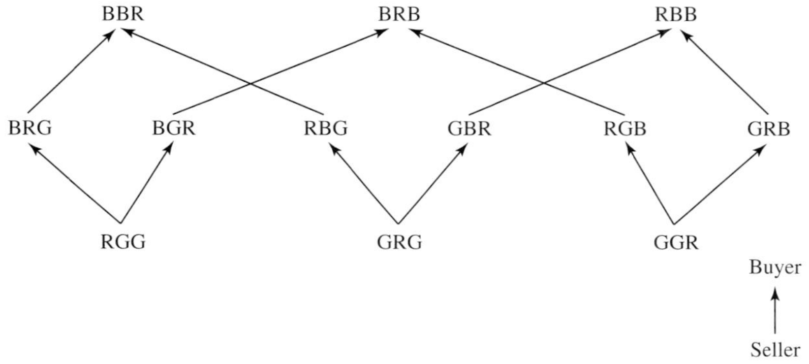

FIGURE 1

The graph of critical disagreements for $n = 3$.

restrictions on the transfer function that are imposed by Maskin-Moore incentive constraints associated with critical disagreements. Namely, suppose that the buyer's announcement is $\theta_B = (\boldsymbol{N}, v_B, c_B)$, while the seller's announcement is $\theta_S = (\boldsymbol{M}, v_S, c_S)$, where $(\boldsymbol{M}, \boldsymbol{N}) \in \mathfrak{D}$, and look for an outcome $(\boldsymbol{x}, t)$ that resolves the disagreement.

Intuitively, trading the widget that is described as $\boldsymbol{R}$ by the seller or the widget that is described as $\boldsymbol{R}$ by the buyer would not be very useful for resolving the critical disagreement, since each widget is ascribed a higher value by the seller than by the buyer. Trading another widget, on whose characteristics the parties agree, can be shown to be equivalent to specifying "no trade" (*i.e.* $x_0 = 1$). In either case, using (2), the incentive constraints of Theorem 0 can be written as

$$-t + \frac{v_S - c_S}{2} \leqq v_S - t(\boldsymbol{M}, v_S, c_S),$$

$$t + \frac{v_B - c_B}{2} \leqq t(\boldsymbol{N}, v_B, c_B) - c_B.$$

Adding the two inequalities, we obtain

$$t(\boldsymbol{N}, v_B, c_B) - t(\boldsymbol{M}, v_S, c_S) \geqq \frac{v_B + c_B}{2} - \frac{v_S + c_S}{2}. \tag{6}$$

Suppose first that the transfer function $t(\boldsymbol{N}, v, c)$ does not depend on the configuration $\boldsymbol{N}$, *i.e.* $t(\boldsymbol{N}, v, c) = t(v, c)$. In that case, by switching (v_B, c_B) and (v_S, c_S) in inequality (6), we can also write

$$t(v_B, c_B) - t(v_S, c_S) \leqq \frac{v_B + c_B}{2} - \frac{v_S + c_S}{2}.$$

Together with (6), this implies that

$$t(v_B, c_B) - t(v_S, c_S) = \frac{v_B + c_B}{2} - \frac{v_S + c_S}{2}.$$

This means that $t(v, c) \equiv (v + c)/2 + \text{const}$; that is, up to a constant, the transfer equals that obtained without an *ex ante* contract. Such a transfer rule, of course, would not improve investment incentives upon the no-contract outcome.

This argument shows that the only hope to improve incentives upon the no-contract outcome lies in having the transfer rule depend on the configuration. Substituting $(v_B, c_B) = (v_S, c_S)$ in inequality (6), we see that in an incentive-compatible contract, the transfer has to be non-decreasing along a critical disagreement.

Having the transfer increase along critical disagreements may help improve incentives, as can already be seen from Example 1. In that example, the buyer is able to extract a fine $\bar{a}/2$ from the seller when the configuration contains no B widgets, but not when the configuration contains a B widgets. The fact that the transfer is increasing in the number of B widgets helps create the incentives for the parties to reveal the R widget. To understand this, observe that when the transfer is increasing along critical disagreements, the buyer is less willing to enter into a critical disagreement with the seller: when he is believed, he pays a higher transfer than that implied by the seller's report. Symmetrically, the seller in that case is less willing to enter into a critical disagreement with the buyer: when he is believed, he receives a lower transfer than that implied by the buyer's report.

At the same time, it can be shown that the transfer difference between *any* two configurations $\boldsymbol{N}'$, $\boldsymbol{N}''$ is bounded by $A = \bar{a} - \underline{a}$. Indeed, if we had $t(\boldsymbol{N}', v, c) - t(\boldsymbol{N}'', v, c) > A$, the disagreement in which the seller reports $(\boldsymbol{N}', v, c)$ and the buyer reports $(\boldsymbol{N}'', v, c)$ could not be resolved by specifying any trade. Intuitively, since the stakes involved in trading different widgets are bounded by A, transfers in different states of the world cannot differ by more than that amount.

Finally, observe from Figure 1 that as n goes to infinity, so does the number of critical disagreements squeezed between the top and the bottom of the graph. Since the transfer difference between the top and the bottom of the graph is bounded by A for any n, this implies that the (properly defined) "average" transfer difference between two configurations related by critical disagreement, $t(\boldsymbol{N}, v, c) - t(\boldsymbol{M}, v, c)$, goes to zero as $n \to \infty$. In the limit, the transfer does not change along the "average" critical disagreement, in which case our earlier discussion suggests that investment incentives converge to those without a contract. Formally, we obtain the following result:

Theorem 1. *In an environment with n widgets, choose an incentive-compatible message contingent contract, and let* $U_j^n(\boldsymbol{N}, v, c)$ *denote the* ex post *payoff of party* $j \in \{B, S\}$ *in the contract in the state of the world* $(\boldsymbol{N}, v, c)$. *Then for all* $v, v' \in \overline{V}$, $c, c' \in \overline{C}$,

$$\left| E_N U_j^n(\boldsymbol{N}, v', c') - E_N U_j^n(\boldsymbol{N}, v, c) - \left(\frac{v' - c'}{2} - \frac{v - c}{2}\right) \right|$$

$$\leq \frac{A}{2^{n-1}} \left[1 + \binom{n-1}{\left\lceil \frac{n-1}{2} \right\rceil} \right],$$

where $A = \bar{a} - \underline{a}$.

Using Stirling's formula $(n! \sim n^n e^{-n}\sqrt{2\pi n})$, we can see that the right-hand side of the above inequality goes to zero as $n \to \infty$. Therefore, asymptotically for each party j we have

$$E_N U_j^n(\boldsymbol{N}, v, c) \simeq \frac{v-c}{2} + \text{const},$$

i.e. each party shares 50% of the total *ex post* surplus with the other party, just as it would without a contract.

This result can be translated into convergence of investments to the no-contract investments. Since the set of Nash equilibrium investment pairs (λ, σ) (with or without a contract) may not be single-valued, we need to define convergence of sets. We do this using the notion of Hausdorff distance $\rho(X, Y)$ between two sets X, Y in a metric space, defined as

$$\rho(X, Y) = \max\left\{\sup_{x \in X} \text{dist}\,(x, Y), \sup_{y \in Y} \text{dist}\,(y, X)\right\},$$

$$\text{where dist}\,(x, Y) = \inf_{y \in Y} |x - y|,$$

(Hausdorff (1962)).

Let $\mathscr{E}_n \subset \Lambda \times \Sigma$ denote the set of all investment pairs attainable in a Nash equilibrium of a contract with n widgets. Since a "no trade" contract is always feasible, we have $\mathscr{E}^0 \subset \mathscr{E}_n$ for all n. Also, let $W(\lambda, \sigma)$ denote the total expected surplus given the parties' investments (λ, σ), *i.e.*

$$W(\lambda, \sigma) = E_\zeta[S(\boldsymbol{v}(\lambda, \zeta), \boldsymbol{c}(\sigma, \zeta))] - \lambda - \sigma.$$

By assumption, $W(\cdot)$ is a continuous function.

Now we can use Theorem 1 to establish convergence of investments and welfare to the incomplete contracting outcomes:

Corollary 1. As $n \to \infty$,

(i) $\rho(\mathscr{E}_n, \mathscr{E}^0) \to 0$,

(ii) $\rho(W(\mathscr{E}_n), W(\mathscr{E}^0)) \to 0$.

Part (ii) implies, in particular, that $\sup W(\mathscr{E}_n) \to \sup W(\mathscr{E}^0)$, *i.e.* the maximum total surplus achievable in an incentive-compatible contract with n widgets converges to the maximum total surplus achieved without a contract as $n \to \infty$.

4 • The Role of Contracting Costs

Consider two perturbations of the last section's model, in which an incentive-compatible message-contingent contract can approach the first-best for a large n:

Example 2. Consider a model whose only difference from that described in Section 3 is that the number of G widgets is known *ex ante* to be $g(n)$. Then the first-best outcome can be implemented for any n using a game in which the seller can veto $g(n)$ widgets, and the buyer chooses one of the remaining widgets to be traded at a fixed price t_0. The seller will veto the widgets that provide him with the lowest post-renegotiation payoff. According to expressions (2), the seller will veto all the G widgets. Out of the remaining widgets, the buyer will choose the one maximizing his post-renegotiation transfer, which according to (2) will be the R widget. Therefore, in equilibrium the R widget is traded at a fixed price, which according to Proposition 2 gives the parties first-best investment incentives.

Example 3. Consider a model whose only difference from that described in Section 3 is that instead of one there are $[\rho n]$ responsive (R) widgets $(0 < \rho < 1)$, *i.e.* the asymptotic proportion of R widgets is ρ. Then the first-best outcome can be approached asymptotically as $n \to \infty$. Indeed, consider a mechanism in which the seller can veto $[n/2]$ widgets, and the buyer chooses one of the remaining widgets to be traded at a fixed price t_0. This game will result in selecting a widget yielding the median post-renegotiation transfer from the seller to the buyer. The median transfer will be provided by an R widget when the numbers of G and B widgets in the configuration do not differ by more than $[\rho n]$, the number of R widgets. By the Law of Large Numbers, the probability of this event goes to one as $n \to \infty$, and therefore the parties' incentives approach the first-best.

Intuitively, the previous section's result does not apply in Example 2 because no critical disagreements exist when the number of G widgets is known. Whenever the parties disagree on which is the R widget, there exists a widget which is ascribed a higher value by the buyer than by the seller. Trading this widget resolves the disagreement. In Example 3, critical disagreements exist, but their number is much smaller than in the previous section. This allows asymptotic implementation of the first-best.

One feature shared by the two examples is that the message game achieving the first-best involves describing a large number of widgets. In Example 2, under Assumption 5 we have $g(n) \to \infty$ as $n \to \infty$, thus the message game requires the seller to describe an unbounded number of widgets. The message game in Example 3 also involves the seller describing an unbounded number of widgets, $[n/2]$. When n is very large, such contracts would be impractical.

To formalize this idea, we will measure the complexity of a message-contingent contract by the number of widgets that are described in the contract. If the parties write no *ex ante* contract, *ex post* they only need to describe one widget to a court — the one they have renegotiated to trade. A natural question to ask is what can be asymptotically achieved by an *ex ante* contract in which the parties only describe a finite number of widgets to a court. In this section we show that under the assumptions presented in Section 2, asymptotically such contracts cannot improve upon the no-contract outcome.

As in the previous section, we apply the Maskin-Moore concept of implementation with renegotiation to characterize incentive-compatibility constraints, the only modification being that an *ex post* state of the world is now described by a pair $(\boldsymbol{v}, \boldsymbol{c}) \in \Re^{2(n+1)}$. In addition to the incentive constraints, however, we now introduce constraints on the content and size of the messages the parties send. For example, direct revelation mechanisms, in which each party describes all of the widgets, will be ruled out due to their complexity. Therefore we need to consider more general mechanisms of the form $M = \langle M_B, M_S, g \rangle$, where M_B, M_S are the parties' message spaces, and g: $M_B \times M_S \rightarrow Y$ is the outcome function. For the sake of generality, we allow extensive-form message games, in which case the parties' messages $(m_B, m_S) \in M_B \times M_S$ should be understood as contingent strategies. Write the outcome function as $g(m_B, m_S) = (\boldsymbol{x}(m_B, m_S), t(m_B, m_S))$, where $\boldsymbol{x}(m_B, m_S)$ is the randomized trade prescribed for the message pair $(m_B, m_S) \in M_B \times M_S$, and t is the transfer prescribed for this message pair.

In this setup, we introduce two contracting restrictions. The first restriction, first introduced by Maskin and Tirole (1999), is that widgets cannot be described *ex ante*, because at this point the parties cannot foresee them, and cannot give them names. *Ex post*, once widgets' names are known, the parties can communicate by describing widgets to the court, and by reporting their valuations for the widgets that have been described. Therefore, the likelihood of a given widget being chosen in the message game cannot depend on its name. The message games described in Examples 2 and 3 are two examples of such communication. The parties would be able to specify these games in the *ex ante* contract without using widgets' names.

To formalize this restriction on contractual communication, consider two different numberings of widgets: "old" and "new". Suppose that the old numbering could be obtained from the new numbering by means of a permutation π, *i.e.* the old number of a widget whose new number is $w \in \{1, \ldots, n\}$ is $\pi(w) \in \{1, \ldots, n\}$. Suppose that in the old numbering, the parties' messages are $(m_B, m_S) \in M_B \times M_S$, and the contract prescribes the outcome $(\boldsymbol{x}(m_B, m_S), t(m_B, m_S))$. In the new numbering, the same messages will be represented differently. Denote the parties' messages in the new numbering by $(m_B\pi, m_S\pi) \in M_B \times M_S$. For these messages, the mechanism $g(\cdot)$ will prescribe the outcome $(\boldsymbol{x}(m_B\pi, m_S\pi), t(m_B\pi, m_S\pi))$.

If the parties cannot describe widgets in advance, the contractual outcome cannot depend on the numbering of widgets. Therefore, we require that the physical outcome under the new numbering is exactly the same as the physical outcome under the old numbering. This requirement consists of two parts: (i) the new monetary transfer is the same as the old monetary transfer, and (ii) the new randomization over physical trades is the same as the old randomization over physical trades, which in the new numbering can be written as $(\boldsymbol{x}(m_B, m_S))\pi$. Therefore the parties' inability to describe widgets *ex ante* can be formalized with the following contracting restriction:[15]

(C1) For any message pair $(m_B, m_S) \in M_B \times M_S$, and any permutation π of $\{1, \ldots, n\}$,

$$t(m_B\pi, m_S\pi) = t(m_B, m_S),$$

$$\boldsymbol{x}(m_B\pi, m_S\pi) = (\boldsymbol{x}(m_B, m_S))\pi.$$

Theorem 4 of Maskin and Tirole (1999) implies that in our setup, impossibility to describe widgets *ex ante by itself* places no constraint on what can be achieved in a message-contingent contract. Intuitively, even though widgets cannot be described *ex ante*, the parties can always write a message game describing all the widgets *ex post*. In our Examples 2 and 3, widgets need not be described *ex ante*, but a large number of them is described in the *ex post* message game, and the first-best outcome is achieved.

In our view, however, if widgets are hard to describe *ex ante*, it may also be hard to describe a large number of them *ex post*. Therefore, we impose a second contracting restriction, which says that at most a finite number of widgets can be described *ex post*. Formally, say that a set of widgets $\Omega \subset \{1, \ldots, n\}$ is *undescribed* by a message pair (m_B, m_S) if for any permutation π of widgets that only affects Ω,

$$(m_B\pi, m_S\pi) = (m_B, m_S).$$

This means that the parties' messages do not distinguish between the "undescribed" widgets that constitute Ω.

Observe that when the parties communicate sequentially, the sets of undescribed widgets may depend on the parties' messages. For example, which widgets the buyer chooses to describe may, in

15. Any mechanism satisfying (C1) implements a choice rule that is *welfare-neutral* as defined in Maskin and Tirole (1999), and *neutral* as defined in Segal (1996). See the two papers for further discussion.

general, depend on what the seller has previously reported. Let $\Omega(m_B, m_S)$ denote the (largest) set of undescribed widgets given the message pair (m_B, m_S). Our second contracting restriction can now be formalized as follows:

(C2) For any message pair $(m_B, m_S) \in M_B \times M_S$, at most k widgets are described, *i.e.* $|\Omega(m_B, m_S)| \geqq n - k$.[16]

To get some intuition for how restrictions (C1) and (C2) affect the set of implementable choice rules, consider the environment of Example 2. Consider a game in which widgets are sequentially described by one or the other party, and the parties announce the types of the described widgets. If the buyer decides to lie, one strategy for him would be to veto every widget described by the seller, by claiming that it is a "bad" widget. Similarly, if the seller decides to lie, one strategy for him would be to veto every widget described by the buyer, by claiming that it is a "good" widget. Of course, since the numbers of bad and good widgets in the configuration are known in advance, there are only so many widgets each party can veto. Thus, after sufficiently many widgets have been described, eventually there will be named a widget for which the buyer will have to concede that it is not "bad", and the seller will have to concede that it is not "good". Trading this widget would "resolve" the disagreement. However, if the configuration contains large numbers of bad and good widgets, a large number of widgets will have to be described before the bluff is called. If attention is restricted to message games in which a bounded number of widgets is described, for a large n the bluff may never be called. Thus, a disagreement which would not be "critical" in the definition of the previous section (it can in principle be resolved by finding a widget ascribed a higher value by the buyer than by the seller), becomes critical when at most a finite number of widgets can be described. Formalization of this argument yields the following result:

Theorem 2. *In an environment with n widgets satisfying Assumptions* 1–3, *choose any incentive-compatible message contingent contract which satisfies* (C1) *and* (C2). *Let* $U_j^n(\boldsymbol{v}, \boldsymbol{c})$ *denote the* ex post *payoff of party* $j \in \{B, S\}$ *in the contract in the state of the world* $(\boldsymbol{v}, \boldsymbol{c})$. *Then for all* $\boldsymbol{v}, \boldsymbol{v}' \in V^{n+1}$, $\boldsymbol{c}, \boldsymbol{c}' \in C^{n+1}$,

$$\left| U_j^n(\boldsymbol{v}', \boldsymbol{c}') - U_j^n(\boldsymbol{v}, \boldsymbol{c}) - \frac{S(\boldsymbol{v}', \boldsymbol{c}') - S(\boldsymbol{v}, \boldsymbol{c})}{2} \right|$$
$$\leqq \max_{l \leqq k} \left\{ \begin{array}{c} \left| \dfrac{(\boldsymbol{v}' + \boldsymbol{c}')^{(l)} - (\boldsymbol{v} + \boldsymbol{c})^{(l)}}{2} \right| \\ \left| \dfrac{(\boldsymbol{v}' + \boldsymbol{c}')^{(n-l+1)} - (\boldsymbol{v} + \boldsymbol{c})^{(n-l+1)}}{2} \right| \\ \dfrac{1}{n-k} \left(\left| \sum_{i=1}^{n} \dfrac{(\boldsymbol{v}' + \boldsymbol{c}')_i - (\boldsymbol{v} + \boldsymbol{c})_i}{2} \right| + kA \right) \end{array} \right\},$$

16. In Segal (1996), this restriction is obtained by applying the computer science concept of communication complexity to the contractual message game. For example, the concept of "tree complexity" defines complexity of an extensive-form message game by the number of its terminal nodes (Karchmer (1989)). Intuitively, if a message game involves describing k widgets, this can be done in $\binom{n}{k}$ possible ways, which gives a lower bound on the number of terminal nodes in the game. If k is bounded regardless of n, as stipulated by (C2), the tree complexity of the message game is polynomial in n, and otherwise it is exponential.

where $\boldsymbol{v}^{(l)}$ *denotes the lth lowest component (rank order statistic) of a vector* $(\boldsymbol{v}_1, \ldots, \boldsymbol{v}_N)$, *and* $A = (\max V + \max C)/2 - (\min V + \min C)/2$.

The left-hand side of the inequality is the absolute value of the difference between the change in party j's *ex post* payoff and 50% of the change in total surplus (compare with Theorem 1). The right-hand side is a maximum of several expressions. The first two expressions represent the changes in the valuations of the k best and k worst widgets. The last expression contains the change in the valuations for the average widget. To understand the result intuitively, observe that the buyer will always suggest the best widgets, and the seller will always suggest the worst widgets out of those which have not yet been described. Therefore, in a contract in which at most k widgets are described, only the best k and the worst k widgets have a chance of being described. The contract can either specify trading one of those widgets, or randomize with equal probabilities over the undescribed widgets.

Under Assumption 5, the k best and the k worst widgets are very likely to be non-responsive to investments for a large n. Under Assumption 4, the average widget is also asymptotically non-responsive to investments. Therefore, the expectation of the right-hand side of the above inequality goes to zero, which implies that equilibrium investments with and without a contract converge:

Corollary 2. *In a sequence of environments where Assumptions* 1–5 *are satisfied and A is bounded regardless of n, as* $n \to \infty$,

(i) $\rho(\mathscr{E}_n, \mathscr{E}_n^0) \to 0$,

(ii) $\rho(W(\mathscr{E}_n), W(\mathscr{E}_n^0)) \to 0$.

Part (ii) implies, in particular, that the maximum contracting gain converges to zero as $n \to \infty$.

5 Discussion

This section relates the paper's results to existing justifications for incomplete contracting, which can be classified along the four types of "transaction costs" identified by Tirole (1994) — unforeseen contingencies, writing costs, enforcement costs, and renegotiation.

Enforcement Costs: When it is difficult to verify parties' *ex post* valuations for different trades, the complete long-term contract specifying the efficient *ex post* trade in all states of the world may be infeasible. It has been argued that whenever the parties' valuations are mutually observable *ex post* but not verifiable, it may be optimal to negotiate the trade after these valuations are observed, rather than rigidly contract the trade *ex ante*.

This argument does not provide a rigorous foundation for incomplete contracting because whenever parties' valuations are mutually observable *ex post*, a long-term contract can be made indirectly contingent on these valuations by allowing the parties to send messages and conditioning the trade on these messages (see Moore (1992) for a survey of the relevant implementation literature). In the context of the holdup problem, Rogerson (1992) shows that using multi-stage message games and the concept of subgame-perfect implementation suggested by Moore and Repullo (1988), first-best investments can be implemented. Therefore, the cost of verifying publicly observable information *by itself* does not impose a serious constraint on contracting.

Unforeseen Contingencies: Some aspects of future trades may not be foreseeable at the contracting date, and therefore have to be left to future negotiation.

However, incomplete contracting theories assume that the contracting parties can foresee their payoffs in each future contingency. Maskin and Tirole (1999) observe that using this minimum foresight consistent with rationality, the parties can design a message game that effectively describes *ex post* all the trades that have not been described *ex ante*. They show that when the parties can use such a game, inability to foresee future contingencies *by itself* does not constrain contracting.[17]

Writing Costs: If specifying contractual contingencies is costly, the optimal contract should trade off the loss from contractual incompleteness against the cost of adding contractual clauses.

A model of contractual incompleteness based on this idea has been offered by Dye (1985). Taken on its face value, this view predicts that when stakes are very large relative to writing costs, contracts should be very close to being complete, and the relative effects of contractual incompleteness should be negligible. Unfortunately, we do not have a good idea of the magnitude and composition of writing costs, and we are not convinced of their significance relative to stakes in important economic situations. Therefore, existence of writing costs *by itself* does not explain why incompleteness of contracts should be an important economic phenomenon.

Renegotiation: The prevailing legal system does not allow contracting parties to prevent consensual renegotiation of their original contract. Since optimal message-contingent contracts often punish lying parties with inefficient outcomes, the possibility of renegotiation constrains the set of feasible contracts.

While a complete survey of the literature on contracting in hold-up models in the presence of renegotiation would be beyond

17. In the absence of renegotiation, this generally implies that first-best investments can be implemented, in accordance with Rogerson's result. Maskin and Tirole also show that when the parties are risk-averse and unbounded transfers can be used, renegotiation does not constrain the set of implementable outcomes when lotteries can be used to punish both parties for a disagreement. When the parties are risk-neutral (as they are in our model), Maskin and Tirole only establish (in Theorem 4) that undescribability places no *additional* constraint on contracting, but do not rule out renegotiation-proofness constraints.

the scope of this paper, it should be pointed out that different papers have adopted different views of the renegotiation procedure. In the models of Hart and Moore (1988), Aghion *et al.* (1994), MacLeod and Malcomson (1993), and Noldeke and Schmidt (1995), renegotiation outcome is given by some version of the Outside Option Principle, as described *e.g.* in Sutton (1986).[18] By setting a high penalty for breach, a contract can make one party's outside option bind, so that the other party receives the entire renegotiation surplus. This allows to implement the first-best in one-sided investment models (see footnote 9), and to achieve a substantial improvement over the no-contract outcome in two-sided models.

In contrast to these papers, Edlin and Reichelstein (1996) assume that the split of renegotiation surplus over the contractual outcome is exogenously given. In particular, they consider the renegotiation function that splits the surplus in fixed proportions, which is the model of renegotiation adopted in this paper. In this case, they find that a noncontingent ("specific performance") contract can achieve or approximate the first-best. In summary, in all the mentioned hold-up models with renegotiation, a substantial improvement upon the no-contract outcome is possible.[19]

In contrast to previous explanations of incomplete contracts, this paper emphasizes the role of environmental complexity. It shows that *in a complex environment*, all four aforementioned sources of "transaction costs" may be important ingredients in explaining contractual incompleteness. Theorem 1 demonstrates that in a complex environment, the parties' inability to verify publicly observable information and their inability to prevent renegotiation place severe constraints on contracting and may explain contractual incompleteness. Theorem 2 shows that in a complex environment, the parties' inability to foresee all possible trades *ex ante* and the cost of describing them *ex post* impose additional constraints on contracting and extend the applicability of the incomplete contracting result.

While much has been said about the role of bounded rationality in explaining contractual incompleteness, existing models of bounded rationality have not been able to explain how people could be irrational enough not to be able to describe all the possible contingencies *ex ante*, yet rational enough to foresee their payoffs *ex ante* and to describe any given contingency *ex post* (see *e.g.* Maskin and Tirole 1999). In our view, any attempt to model bounded rationality in a simple environment is doomed to fall into the trap of describing decision makers as either "completely dumb" or "perfectly rational". Neither is an attractive alternative for modeling "transaction costs". It is only in environments reflecting the real world's complexities that an intermediate region of "bounded rationality" emerges. For example,

18. This is not to overlook the substantial differences among the papers. Thus, Hart and Moore and MacLeod and Malcomson assume that the court cannot verify which party has refused to trade, while Aghion *et al.* and Noldeke and Schmidt make the opposite assumption. Also, Aghion *et al.* and MacLeod and Malcomson allow trading to occur at different points in time, while Hart and Moore and Noldeke and Schmidt only allow trading at a single fixed date. In addition, MacLeod and Malcomson, unlike the other three papers, allow the parties to have external trading options, as well as consider external investments (those that directly benefit the other party).

19. A recent paper by Che and Hausch (1997) obtains incomplete contracting in a hold-up model with "external" investments. See footnote 7 for a comparison of their model to our setup.

in a complex environment, it may be easy to describe any given potential trade, but prohibitively costly to describe all of them, or any positive fraction of them. Theorem 2 suggests that this difference may be important for understanding incomplete contracts.[20]

An important challenge for a theory of bounded rationality in complex environments is to explain the role of renegotiation in the real world. This paper has followed the traditional view of renegotiation as a constraint on contracting. The parties' inability to legally bind themselves not to renegotiate is an important element of our explanation of incompleteness of contracts. However, theorists have suggested various ways of eliminating renegotiation or tilting its outcome, such as contracting with an outsider (Holmstrom (1982)), using financial hostages (Aghion *et al.* (1994)), and setting up a public registry of contracts (Maskin and Tirole (1999)). In practice, non-renegotiable contracts have sometimes been successfully enforced in the past (*e.g.*, non-renegotiable marriage contracts in some countries). Therefore, the absence of legal provisions allowing contracting parties to prevent out-of-contract renegotiation calls for an explanation.

The explanation may come from bounded rationality. In a complex environment in which contracting parties possess private information about trade opportunities, the renegotiation game may be more complex than mere haggling over surplus. Given the considerable cost of administering complicated contractual message games ("formal communication"), the parties may prefer not to write the renegotiation game directly in the *ex ante* contract, instead leaving the option of renegotiation ("informal communication") open. Thus, the "transaction costs" of formal communication may help explain why contracting parties would *strictly* prefer to write an incomplete renegotiable contract, rather than a complete non-renegotiable one.

Appendix

Proof of Proposition 1. Observe that both (λ^0, σ^0) and (λ^*, σ^*) solve a maximization program of the form

$$\max_{(\lambda, \sigma) \in \Lambda \times \Sigma} \quad \alpha E_\zeta S(\boldsymbol{v}(\lambda, \zeta), \boldsymbol{c}(\sigma, \zeta)) - \lambda - \sigma,$$

where $z = 1/2$ for no-contract investments (λ^0, σ^0) and $z = 1$ for first-best investments (λ^*, σ^*). The assumptions imply that the objective function has increasing marginal returns both in $(\sigma; z)$ and in $(\lambda; z)$, as defined in Edlin and Shannon (1998), and parts (i) and (ii) follows by their Strict Monotonicity Theorem.

20. Anderlini and Felli (1994) and MacLeod (1996) also model complex environments in which bounded rationality can result in contractual incompleteness. In the model of MacLeod, the optimal contract is exponentially complex. Anderlini and Felli describe contracting problems in which the process of arriving at the optimal contract is not computable at all.

In case (iii), the above maximization program can be separated into two:

$$\max_{\lambda \in \Lambda} [zE_\zeta v_{w^*(\zeta)}(\lambda, \zeta) - \lambda],$$

$$\max_{\sigma \in \Sigma} [-zE_\zeta c_{w^*(\zeta)}(\sigma, \zeta) - \sigma].$$

The first objective function has increasing marginal returns in $(\lambda; z)$, and the second objective function has increasing marginal returns in $(\sigma; z)$. The Strict Monotonicity Theorem of Edlin and Shannon (1998) implies that $\lambda^0 < \lambda^*$ and $\sigma^0 < \sigma^*$. ■

Proof of Proposition 2. Suppose the buyer considers deviating to $\lambda' \in \Lambda$. Using (2), the buyer's *ex post* utility in contingency ζ will then be

$$\begin{aligned}
&-t(\zeta) + \frac{v_{w^*}(\lambda', \zeta) + c_{w^*}(\sigma^*, \zeta)}{2} + \frac{1}{2} S(\boldsymbol{v}(\lambda', \zeta), \boldsymbol{c}(\sigma^*, \zeta)) \\
&\quad = -t(\zeta) + c_{w^*}(\sigma^*, \zeta) + \frac{1}{2} [v_{w^*}(\lambda', \zeta) - c_{w^*}(\sigma^*, \zeta)] \\
&\qquad + \frac{1}{2} S(\boldsymbol{v}(\lambda', \zeta), \boldsymbol{c}(\sigma^*, \zeta)) \\
&\quad \leqq -t(\zeta) + c_{w^*}(\sigma^*, \zeta) + S(\boldsymbol{v}(\lambda', \zeta), \boldsymbol{c}(\sigma^*, \zeta)),
\end{aligned}$$

where the last inequality follows from the definition of $S(\boldsymbol{v}(\lambda', \zeta), \boldsymbol{c}(\sigma^*, \zeta))$. Using in addition the fact that (λ^*, σ^*) solves (1), the buyer's expected *ex ante* utility after a deviation can be bounded as follows

$$\begin{aligned}
&E_\zeta[-t(\zeta) + c_{w^*}(\sigma^*, \zeta) + S(\boldsymbol{v}(\lambda', \zeta), \boldsymbol{c}(\sigma^*, \zeta))] - \lambda' \\
&\quad \leqq E_\zeta[-t(\zeta) + c_{w^*}(\sigma^*, \zeta) + S(\boldsymbol{v}(\lambda^*, \zeta), \boldsymbol{c}(\sigma^*, \zeta))] - \lambda^* \\
&\quad = E_\zeta[-t(\zeta) - v_{w^*}(\lambda^*, \zeta)] - \lambda^*,
\end{aligned}$$

which is the buyer's equilibrium payoff. Therefore, the deviation does not make the buyer better off. Similarly for the seller. ■

Proof of Theorem 1. Let $\boldsymbol{v}(\theta)$ and $\boldsymbol{c}(\theta)$ denote the two parties' valuation vectors in the state of the world θ, *i.e.*

$$v_w(\boldsymbol{N}, v, c) = \begin{cases} v \text{ if } \boldsymbol{N}_w = R, \\ v_g \text{ if } \boldsymbol{N}_w = G, \\ v_b \text{ if } \boldsymbol{N}_w = B, \\ 0 \text{ if } w = 0, \end{cases} \qquad c_w(\boldsymbol{N}, v, c) = \begin{cases} c \text{ if } \boldsymbol{N}_w = R, \\ c_g \text{ if } \boldsymbol{N}_w = G, \\ c_b \text{ if } \boldsymbol{N}_w = B, \\ 0 \text{ if } w = 0. \end{cases}$$

Consider the disagreement in which the buyer announces that the state of the world is θ_B and the seller announces that the state of the world is θ_S. Using Theorem 0 and expressions (2), this disagreement can be resolved if, and only if, there exists an outcome $(\boldsymbol{x}, t)$ such that

$$-t+\sum_{w=0}^{n} x_w \frac{v_w(\theta_S)+c_w(\theta_S)}{2}+\frac{1}{2}S(\boldsymbol{v}(\theta_S),\boldsymbol{c}(\theta_S)) \geqq U_B(\theta_S),$$

$$t-\sum_{w=0}^{n} x_w \frac{v_w(\theta_B)+c_w(\theta_B)}{2}+\frac{1}{2}S(\boldsymbol{v}(\theta_B),\boldsymbol{c}(\theta_B)) \geqq U_S(\theta_B).$$

Adding up, and taking into account that $U_B(\theta_S) = S(\boldsymbol{v}(\theta_S), \boldsymbol{c}(\theta_S)) - U_S(\theta_S)$, yields

$$U_S(\theta_B)-U_S(\theta_S) \geqq \frac{S(\boldsymbol{v}(\theta_B),\boldsymbol{c}(\theta_B))-S(\boldsymbol{v}(\theta_S),\boldsymbol{c}(\theta_S))}{2} + \sum_{w=0}^{n} x_w\left[\frac{v_w(\theta_S)+c_w(\theta_S)}{2}-\frac{v_w(\theta_B)+c_w(\theta_B)}{2}\right]. \qquad (7)$$

It is possible to find $\boldsymbol{x} \in \{(x_0, x_1, \ldots, x_n) \in \Re_+^{n+1}: \sum_{w \in \{0, 1, \ldots, n\}} x_w = 1\}$ satisfying this inequality if, and only if,

$$U_S(\theta_B)-U_S(\theta_S) \geqq \frac{S(\boldsymbol{v}(\theta_B),\boldsymbol{c}(\theta_B))-S(\boldsymbol{v}(\theta_S),\boldsymbol{c}(\theta_S))}{2} + \min_{w \in \{0,1,\ldots,n\}}\left[\frac{v_w(\theta_S)+c_w(\theta_S)}{2}-\frac{v_w(\theta_B)+c_w(\theta_B)}{2}\right]. \qquad (8)$$

The following three lemmas will apply this incentive constraint to three types of disagreements. Lemma A.1 considers critical disagreements, Lemma A.2 considers disagreements where parties agree on the valuations for the efficient trade and disagree on the configuration, and Lemma A.3 considers disagreements where parties agree on a configuration and disagree on the valuations for the efficient trade.

Lemma A.1. *In an incentive-compatible contract, for all* $(\boldsymbol{M}, \boldsymbol{N}) \in \mathfrak{D}$ *and all* $v_B, v_S \in \overline{V}$, $c_B, c_S \in \overline{C}$ *we must have*

$$U_S(\boldsymbol{N}, v_B, c_B) - U_S(\boldsymbol{M}, v_S, c_S) \geqq \frac{v_B - c_B}{2} - \frac{v_S - c_S}{2}.$$

Proof of Lemma A.1. Let $\theta_B = (\boldsymbol{N}, v_B, c_B)$ and $\theta_S = (\boldsymbol{M}, v_S, c_S)$, where $(\boldsymbol{M}, \boldsymbol{N}) \in \mathfrak{D}$, with $\boldsymbol{M}_i = \boldsymbol{N}_j = R$. Using (4), we can write

$$\frac{v_w(\theta_S)+c_w(\theta_S)}{2}-\frac{v_w(\theta_B)+c_w(\theta_B)}{2} = \begin{cases} (v_S+c_S)/2-\underline{a}>0 \text{ when } w=i, \\ \overline{a}-(v_B+c_B)/2>0 \text{ when } w=j, \\ 0 \text{ when } \boldsymbol{M}_w=\boldsymbol{N}_w \in \{B,G\} \text{ or } w=0. \end{cases}$$

Substituting in the incentive constraint (8), we obtain the lemma's statement. ■

Lemma A.2. *In an incentive-compatible contract, for any two configurations* $\boldsymbol{N}$, $\boldsymbol{M}$, *and for all* $v \in \overline{V}$, $c \in \overline{C}$ *we must have*

$$U_S(\boldsymbol{M}, v, c) - U_S(\boldsymbol{N}, v, c) \leqq A .$$

Proof of Lemma A.2. Let $\theta_B = (\boldsymbol{N}, v, c)$ and $\theta_S = (\boldsymbol{M}, v, c)$. Using (4), we can write

$$\min_{w \in \{0, 1, \ldots, n\}} \left[\frac{v_w(\theta_S) + c_w(\theta_S)}{2} - \frac{v_w(\theta_B) + c_w(\theta_B)}{2}\right]$$

$$\geqq \min_w \frac{v_w(\theta_S) + c_w(\theta_S)}{2} - \max_w \frac{v_w(\theta_B) + c_w(\theta_B)}{2} \geqq \underline{a} - \bar{a} = -A .$$

Substituting in the incentive constraint (8), we obtain the lemma's statement. ■

Lemma A.3. *In an incentive-compatible contract, for all* $\boldsymbol{N}$ *and all* v_B, $v_S \in \overline{V}$, c_B, $c_S \in \overline{C}$ *we must have*[21]

$$U_S(\boldsymbol{N}, v_B, c_B) - U_S(\boldsymbol{N}, v_S, c_S) \geqq \frac{v_B - c_B}{2} - \frac{v_S - c_S}{2} + \min\left\{0, \frac{v_S + c_S}{2} - \frac{v_B + c_B}{2}\right\}.$$

Proof of Lemma A.3. Let $\theta_B = (\boldsymbol{N}, v_B, c_B)$, and $\theta_S = (\boldsymbol{N}, v_S, c_S)$, where $\boldsymbol{N}_i = R$. Using (4), we can write

$$\frac{v_w(\theta_S) + c_w(\theta_S)}{2} - \frac{v_w(\theta_B) + c_w(\theta_B)}{2} = \begin{cases} \dfrac{v_S + c_S}{2} - \dfrac{v_B + c_B}{2} & \text{when } w = i, \\ 0 \text{ when } \boldsymbol{N}_w \in \{B, G\} \text{ or } w = 0. \end{cases}$$

Substituting in the incentive constraint (8), we obtain the lemma's statement. ■

Now we introduce some useful notation. Define the *length* of an edge $(\boldsymbol{M}, \boldsymbol{N}) \in \mathfrak{D}$ as $\tau(\boldsymbol{M}, \boldsymbol{N}, v, c) \equiv U_S(\boldsymbol{N}, v, c) - U_S(\boldsymbol{M}, v, c)$. Substituting $v_B = v_S = v$, $c_B = c_S = c$ in the statement of Lemma A.1, we obtain

$$\tau(\boldsymbol{M}, \boldsymbol{N}, v, c) \geqq 0 \text{ for all } (\boldsymbol{M}, \boldsymbol{N}) \in \mathfrak{D}, \tag{9}$$

i.e. the length of an edge is non-negative, which vindicates the term. Using this notation, we can rewrite the statement of Lemma A.1 as follows

$$U_S(\boldsymbol{N}, v_B, c_B) - U_S(\boldsymbol{N}, v_S, c_S) \geqq \frac{v_B - c_B}{2} - \frac{v_S - c_S}{2} - \tau(\boldsymbol{M}, \boldsymbol{N}, v_S, c_S).$$

21. An interesting corollary of this lemma can be obtained by substituting $v_B = v_S = v$, $c_B = c' < c_S = c$. Then the statement can be rewritten as $U_S(\boldsymbol{N}, v, c') - U_S(\boldsymbol{N}, v, c) \geqq (c - c')/2$. This implies that in any incentive compatible contract, the seller receives at least 50% of his contribution to total surplus. Therefore, for any n, the seller's investment incentive cannot be lower than that without a contract. (The same conclusion can be obtained for the buyer).

The inequality holds for every configuration $\boldsymbol{M}$ adjacent to $\boldsymbol{N}$ from below, *i.e.* satisfying $(\boldsymbol{M}, \boldsymbol{N}) \in \mathfrak{D}$. Observe that there are $|\boldsymbol{N}|$ such configurations. To see this, let $\boldsymbol{N}_j = R$ and observe that for each widget i such that $\boldsymbol{N}_i = B$, there is one critical disagreement terminating in $\boldsymbol{N}$, namely the disagreement $(\boldsymbol{M}, \boldsymbol{N})$ satisfying (5). Thus, the number of edges adjacent to $\boldsymbol{N}$ from below equals the number of type B widgets in $\boldsymbol{N}$, *i.e.* $|\boldsymbol{N}|$. (Similarly, it can be shown that the number of edges adjacent to $\boldsymbol{N}$ from above equals the number of type G widgets in $\boldsymbol{N}$, *i.e.* $n - |\boldsymbol{N}| - 1$.)

After averaging the right-hand side of the above inequality over all the edges adjacent to $\boldsymbol{N}$ from below, we obtain the following bound for $|\boldsymbol{N}| \geqq 1$

$$U_S(\boldsymbol{N}, v_B, c_B) - U_S(\boldsymbol{N}, v_S, c_S)$$

$$\geqq \frac{v_B - v_B}{2} - \frac{v_S - c_S}{2} - \frac{1}{|\boldsymbol{N}|} \sum\nolimits_{(\boldsymbol{M}, \boldsymbol{N}) \in \mathfrak{D}} \tau(\boldsymbol{M}, \boldsymbol{N}, v_S, c_S). \quad (10)$$

To see how the seller's expected utility can depend on the parties' valuations, we use (10) for $|\boldsymbol{N}| \geqq 1$, and the statement of Lemma A.3 for $|\boldsymbol{N}| = 0$, taking into account that

$$\min\left\{0, \frac{v_S + c_S}{2} - \frac{v_B + c_B}{2}\right\} \geqq \underline{a} - \bar{a} = -A:$$

$$E_N U_S(\boldsymbol{N}, v_B, c_B) - E_N U_S(\boldsymbol{N}, v_S, c_S)$$

$$= \sum\nolimits_N p[U_S(\boldsymbol{N}, v_B, c_B) - U_S(\boldsymbol{N}, v_S, c_S)]$$

$$\geqq \frac{v_B - c_B}{2} - \frac{v_S - c_S}{2} - pnA$$

$$- p \sum\nolimits_{|\boldsymbol{N}| \geqq 1} \frac{1}{|\boldsymbol{N}|} \sum\nolimits_{(\boldsymbol{M}, \boldsymbol{N}) \in \mathfrak{D}} \tau(\boldsymbol{M}, \boldsymbol{N}, v_S, c_S), \quad (11)$$

where $p = 1/(n2^{n-1})$ is the probability of any given configuration. This expression can be bounded from below by maximizing the following sum

$$p \sum\nolimits_{|\boldsymbol{N}| \geqq 1} \frac{1}{|\boldsymbol{N}|} \sum\nolimits_{(\boldsymbol{M}, \boldsymbol{N}) \in \mathfrak{D}} \tau(\boldsymbol{M}, \boldsymbol{N}, v, c) \quad (12)$$

We are going to bound the sum using Lemma A.2. For this purpose, define a *path* P as a set of $n - 1$ pairwise adjacent edges leading from the bottom to the top of the graph of critical disagreements: $P = \{(\boldsymbol{N}^0, \boldsymbol{N}^1), (\boldsymbol{N}^1, \boldsymbol{N}^2), \ldots, (\boldsymbol{N}^{n-2}, \boldsymbol{N}^{n-1})\} \subset \mathfrak{D}$. Denote the set of all paths by Π. Using this notation, we can use Lemma A.2 to write

$$\sum_{(\boldsymbol{M},\boldsymbol{N}) \in P} \tau(\boldsymbol{M}, \boldsymbol{N}, v, c) = U_S(\boldsymbol{N}^{n-1}, v, c) - U_S(\boldsymbol{N}^0, v, c) \leqq A$$

for all $P \in \Pi$.

We will use a weaker inequality obtained by adding up the inequality above for all paths. To do this, first observe that Π contains $n!$ elements. Indeed, there are n ways to choose a configuration from the top, and each configuration at a level $l \in \{1, \ldots, n-1\}$ is connected via a critical disagreement to l configurations at level $l-1$. Thus, a path can be chosen in $n \cdot (n-1) \cdot \ldots \cdot 1 = n!$ different ways. Second, using a similar counting argument, we can see that an edge $(\boldsymbol{M}, \boldsymbol{N}) \in \mathfrak{D}$ belongs to $(n-1-|\boldsymbol{N}|)!(|\boldsymbol{N}|-1)!$ different paths. Therefore, by adding up the above inequalities for all paths, we obtain

$$\sum_{(\boldsymbol{M},\boldsymbol{N}) \in \mathfrak{D}} (n-1-|\boldsymbol{N}|)!(|\boldsymbol{N}|-1)!\tau(\boldsymbol{M}, \boldsymbol{N}, v, c) \leqq n! \cdot A. \quad (13)$$

Now, consider the linear programming problem of maximizing (12) subject to (13) and (9). The solution to this program is achieved at a vertex, where the length of all edges but one is set to zero. When we put all the weight on an edge $(\boldsymbol{M}, \boldsymbol{N}) \in \mathfrak{D}$, we obtain $\tau(\boldsymbol{M}, \boldsymbol{N}, v, c) = n!/((n-1-|\boldsymbol{N}|)!(|\boldsymbol{N}|-1)!)A$, and the value of the objective function is

$$p\frac{n!}{(n-1-|\boldsymbol{N}|)!(|\boldsymbol{N}|-1)!|\boldsymbol{N}|}A = pn\binom{n-1}{|\boldsymbol{N}|}A = \frac{1}{2^{n-1}}\binom{n-1}{|\boldsymbol{N}|}A.$$

The maximum value is achieved at $|\boldsymbol{N}| = [(n-1)/2]$, which gives us the following lower bound on the left-hand side of (11)

$$E_N U_S(\boldsymbol{N}, v_B, c_B) - E_N U_S(\boldsymbol{N}, v_S, c_S) - \left(\frac{v_B - v_B}{2} - \frac{v_S - c_S}{2}\right)$$
$$\geqq -\frac{A}{2^{n-1}} - \frac{1}{2^{n-1}}\binom{n-1}{[(n-1)/2]}A.$$

Substituting $(v_B, c_B) = (v', c')$, $(v_S, c_S) = (v, c)$, we obtain a lower bound on $E_N U_S(\boldsymbol{N}, v', c') - E_N U_S(\boldsymbol{N}, v, c) - ((v'-c')/2 - (v-c)/2)$. Substituting instead $(v_B, c_B) = (v, c)$, $(v_S, c_S) = (v', c')$, we obtain an upper bound on the same expression. Combining the two bounds, we obtain the theorem's statement for $j = S$. Expressing the buyer's utility as $U_B(\boldsymbol{N}, v, c) = v - c - U_S(\boldsymbol{N}, v, c)$, we obtain the theorem's statement for $j = B$. ■

Proof of Corollary 1. Let $u_j^n(\lambda, \sigma)$ denote party j's expected *ex post* utility in the contract with n widgets as a function of investments (λ, σ). Using the fact that $\boldsymbol{N}$ is distributed independently of (v, c), we can write

$$u_j^n(\lambda, \sigma) = E_\zeta U_j^n(\boldsymbol{N}(\zeta), v(\lambda, \zeta), c(\sigma, \zeta))$$
$$= E_\zeta[E_N U_j^n(\boldsymbol{N}, v(\lambda, \zeta), c(\sigma, \zeta))]$$

where $v(\lambda, \zeta)$, $c(\sigma, \zeta)$ are the parties' valuations for the R widget in contingency ζ given investments λ, σ, and $\boldsymbol{N}(\zeta)$ is the configuration in contingency ζ.

Stirling's formula implies that

$$\frac{1}{2^{n-1}}\binom{n-1}{[(n-1)/2]}A \sim \sqrt{\frac{2}{\pi(n-1)}}\,A \to 0 \text{ as } n \to \infty.$$

Therefore, Theorem 1 implies that as $n \to \infty$, for $j \in \{B, S\}$ we have

$$E_N U_j^n(\boldsymbol{N}, v', c') - E_N U_j^n(\boldsymbol{N}, v, c) \to \frac{v' - c'}{2} - \frac{v - c}{2},$$

where convergence is uniform on $v, v' \in \overline{V}$, $c, c' \in \overline{C}$. Substituting $v = v(\lambda, \zeta)$, $v' = v(\lambda', \zeta)$, $c = c(\sigma, \zeta)$, $c' = c(\sigma', \zeta)$, and taking the expectation over ζ, we obtain that for all $\lambda, \lambda' \in \Lambda$, $\sigma, \sigma' \in \Sigma$, as $n \to \infty$,

$$u_j^n(\lambda', \sigma') - u_j^n(\lambda, \sigma) \to \frac{1}{2}\,[E_\zeta v(\lambda', \zeta) - E_\zeta v(\lambda, \zeta)]$$
$$- \frac{1}{2}\,[E_\zeta c(\sigma', \zeta) - E_\zeta c(\sigma, \zeta)]. \quad (14)$$

Now, suppose in negation that part (i) of the Corollary's statement is not true. Since $\mathscr{E}^0 \subset \mathscr{E}_n$ for all n, the supposition implies that $\sup_{(\lambda_n, \sigma_n) \in \mathscr{E}_n} \text{dist}\,((\lambda_n, \sigma_n), \mathscr{E}^0)$ does not go to zero as $n \to \infty$. Therefore, there exists a sequence $\{(\lambda_n, \sigma_n)\}_{n=1}^{\infty}$ such that $(\lambda_n, \sigma_n) \in \mathscr{E}_n$ for all n and $\text{dist}\,((\lambda_n, \sigma_n), \mathscr{E}^0)$ does not converge to zero. Since the sequence lies in a compact set $\Lambda \times \Sigma$, we can pick a subsequence $\{(\lambda_k, \sigma_k)\}_{k=1}^{\infty} \subset \mathscr{E}_k$ that converges to a point $(\hat{\lambda}, \hat{\sigma}) \notin \mathscr{E}^0$.

Since (λ_k, σ_k) is a Nash equilibrium investment pair given the contract, for all $\lambda \in \Lambda$ we must have

$$u_B^k(\lambda, \sigma_k) - u_B^k(\lambda_k, \sigma_k) \leqq \lambda - \lambda_k. \quad (15)$$

The left-hand side of this inequality can be rewritten as

$$\left(u_B^k(\lambda, \sigma_k) - u_B^k(\lambda_k, \sigma_k) - \frac{1}{2}\,[E_\zeta v(\lambda, \zeta) - E_\zeta v(\lambda_k, \zeta)]\right)$$
$$+ \frac{1}{2}\,[E_\zeta v(\lambda, \zeta) - E_\zeta v(\lambda_k, \zeta)].$$

As $k \to \infty$, the first term converges to zero by the uniform convergence in (14), while the second term converges to $\frac{1}{2}[E_\zeta v(\lambda, \zeta) - E_\zeta v(\hat{\lambda}, \zeta)]$ by the assumption that $E_\zeta v(\lambda, \zeta) = E_\zeta S(\boldsymbol{v}(\lambda, \zeta), \boldsymbol{c}(\sigma, \zeta)) - E_\zeta c(\sigma, \zeta)$ is continuous in λ. Thus, taking the limit $k \to \infty$ in inequality (15), we obtain

$$\frac{1}{2} E_\zeta v(\lambda, \zeta) - \frac{1}{2} E_\zeta v(\hat{\lambda}, \zeta) \leqq \lambda - \hat{\lambda}.$$

Since this should be true for any $\lambda \in \Lambda$, $\hat{\lambda}$ must satisfy the first condition in (3), *i.e.* it must be the buyer's equilibrium investment without a contract. In the same way it can be shown that $\hat{\sigma}$ is the seller's equilibrium investment without a contract. Therefore, $(\hat{\lambda}, \hat{\sigma}) \in \mathscr{E}^0$, which contradicts an earlier statement. This establishes part (i) of the Corollary. Part (ii) follows by the continuity of $W(\cdot)$. ■

Proof of Theorem 2. First we prove two lemmas which establish certain useful consequences of contracting restriction (C1).

Lemma B.1. *For any* $i, j \in \Omega(m_B, m_S)$, *we must have* $x_i(m_B, m_S) = x_j(m_B, m_S)$.

Proof of Lemma B.1. Take $\pi = (ij)$, *i.e.* the permutation that transposes widgets *i* and *j*, holding other widgets fixed. This permutation only affects $\Omega(m_B, m_S)$. Using the fact that $\Omega(m_B, m_S)$ is undescribed by (m_B, m_S) and condition (C1), we can write

$$x_i(m_B, m_S) = x_i(m_B\pi, m_S\pi) = x_{\pi(i)}(m_B, m_S) = x_j(m_B, m_S). \quad ■$$

Lemma B.2. *For each party* $j \in \{B, S\}$, *all states of the world* $(\boldsymbol{v}, \boldsymbol{c})$, *and all permutations* π *of widgets, we must have* $U_j^n(\boldsymbol{v}\pi, \boldsymbol{c}\pi) = U_j^n(\boldsymbol{v}, \boldsymbol{c})$.

Proof of Lemma B.2. Follows immediately from (C1). ■

Let $\hat{m}_B(\cdot)$, $\hat{m}_S(\cdot)$ be the parties' equilibrium strategies. Consider disagreements in which the buyer and seller send messages of the form $\hat{m}_B(\boldsymbol{v}_B\pi_B, \boldsymbol{c}_B\pi_B)$ and $\hat{m}_S(\boldsymbol{v}_S\pi_S, \boldsymbol{c}_S\pi_S)$ respectively. Fixing $(\boldsymbol{v}_B, \boldsymbol{c}_B)$ and $(\boldsymbol{v}_S, \boldsymbol{c}_S)$, there exists a pair of permutations (π_B, π_S) such that:

(i) For every widget *i* described by the seller, there exists $l \leqq k$ such that

$$(\boldsymbol{v}_B\pi_B + \boldsymbol{c}_B\pi_B)_i = (\boldsymbol{v}_B + \boldsymbol{c}_B)^{(l)},$$
$$(\boldsymbol{v}_S\pi_S + \boldsymbol{c}_S\pi_S)_i \geqq (\boldsymbol{v}_S + \boldsymbol{c}_S)^{(l)}. \qquad (16)$$

In words, the buyer reports that it is one of the k lowest-ranked widgets, and that its rank l is not higher than what it is according to the seller's report.

(ii) For every widget i described by the buyer, there exists $l \leqq k$ such that

$$\begin{aligned}(\boldsymbol{v}_S\pi_S + \boldsymbol{c}_S\pi_S)_i &= (\boldsymbol{v}_S + \boldsymbol{c}_S)^{(n-l+1)},\\ (\boldsymbol{v}_B\pi_B + \boldsymbol{c}_B\pi_B)_i &\leqq (\boldsymbol{v}_B + \boldsymbol{c}_B)^{(n-l+1)}.\end{aligned} \tag{17}$$

In words, the seller reports that it is one of the k highest-ranked widgets, and that its rank $n-l+1$ is not lower than what it is according to the buyer's report.

The outcome $(\boldsymbol{x}, t)$ for this message pair should satisfy the Maskin-Moore incentive constraint (7) derived in the proof of Theorem 1, which here can be written as

$$\begin{aligned}&U_S(\boldsymbol{v}_B\pi_B, \boldsymbol{c}_B\pi_B) - U_S(\boldsymbol{v}_S\pi_S, \boldsymbol{c}_S\pi_S)\\ &\quad \geqq \frac{S(\boldsymbol{v}_B, \boldsymbol{c}_B) - S(\boldsymbol{v}_S, \boldsymbol{c}_S)}{2}\\ &\quad + \sum_{i=0}^{n} x_i\left[\frac{(\boldsymbol{v}_S\pi_S + \boldsymbol{c}_S\pi_S)_i}{2} - \frac{(\boldsymbol{v}_B\pi_B + \boldsymbol{c}_B\pi_B)_i}{2}\right].\end{aligned}$$

Using Lemmas B.1 and B.2, the constraint can be rewritten as

$$\begin{aligned}&U_S(\boldsymbol{v}_B, \boldsymbol{c}_B) - U_S(\boldsymbol{v}_S, \boldsymbol{c}_S) - \frac{S(\boldsymbol{v}_B, \boldsymbol{c}_B) - S(\boldsymbol{v}_S, \boldsymbol{c}_S)}{2}\\ &\geqq \frac{1 - \sum_{i \notin \Omega} x_i}{|\Omega|} \sum_{i \in \Omega}\left[\frac{(\boldsymbol{v}_S\pi_S + \boldsymbol{c}_S\pi_S)_i}{2} - \frac{(\boldsymbol{v}_B\pi_B + \boldsymbol{c}_B\pi_B)_i}{2}\right]\\ &\quad + \sum_{i \in \Omega} x_i\left[\frac{(\boldsymbol{v}_S\pi_S + \boldsymbol{c}_S\pi_S)_i}{2} - \frac{(\boldsymbol{v}_B\pi_B + \boldsymbol{c}_B\pi_B)_i}{2}\right]\\ &\geqq \min_{w \notin \Omega}\left\{\begin{array}{c}\left\{\dfrac{(\boldsymbol{v}_S\pi_S + \boldsymbol{c}_S\pi_S)_w}{2} - \dfrac{(\boldsymbol{v}_B\pi_B + \boldsymbol{c}_B\pi_B)_w}{2}\right\}\\ \dfrac{1}{|\Omega|}\sum_{i \in \Omega}\left[\dfrac{(\boldsymbol{v}_S\pi_S + \boldsymbol{c}_S\pi_S)_i}{2} - \dfrac{(\boldsymbol{v}_B\pi_B + \boldsymbol{c}_B\pi_B)_i}{2}\right]\end{array}\right\},\end{aligned} \tag{18}$$

where Ω is the largest set of undescribed widgets for this message pair. To bound the first term in the min in (18), consider the following two cases:

(i) If widget w has been described by the seller, then by (16) we know that for some $l \leqq k$,

$$\frac{((\boldsymbol{v}_S + \boldsymbol{c}_S)\pi_S)_w}{2} - \frac{((\boldsymbol{v}_B + \boldsymbol{c}_B)\pi_B)_w}{2} \geqq \frac{(\boldsymbol{v}_S + \boldsymbol{c}_S)^{(l)}}{2} - \frac{(\boldsymbol{v}_B + \boldsymbol{c}_B)^{(l)}}{2}$$
$$\geqq -\left|\frac{(\boldsymbol{v}_B + \boldsymbol{c}_B)^{(l)}}{2} - \frac{(\boldsymbol{v}_S + \boldsymbol{c}_S)^{(l)}}{2}\right|$$

(ii) If widget w has been described by the buyer, then by (17) we know that for some $l \leqq k$,

$$\frac{((\boldsymbol{v}_S + \boldsymbol{c}_S)\pi_S)_w}{2} - \frac{((\boldsymbol{v}_B + \boldsymbol{c}_B)\pi_B)_w}{2} \geqq \frac{(\boldsymbol{v}_S + \boldsymbol{c}_S)^{(n-l+1)}}{2} - \frac{(\boldsymbol{v}_B + \boldsymbol{c}_B)^{(n-l+1)}}{2}$$
$$\geqq -\left|\frac{(\boldsymbol{v}_B + \boldsymbol{c}_B)^{(n-l+1)}}{2} - \frac{(\boldsymbol{v}_S + \boldsymbol{c}_S)^{(n-l+1)}}{2}\right|.$$

To bound the second term in the min in (18), we use the fact that $|\Omega| \geqq n - k$ and the definition of A

$$\frac{1}{|\Omega|}\sum_{i \in \Omega} \frac{((\boldsymbol{v}_S + \boldsymbol{c}_S)\pi_S)_i - ((\boldsymbol{v}_B + \boldsymbol{c}_B)\pi_B)_i}{2}$$
$$\geqq -\frac{1}{|\Omega|}\left|\sum_{i=1}^{n} \frac{(\boldsymbol{v}_S + \boldsymbol{c}_S)_i - (\boldsymbol{v}_B + \boldsymbol{c}_B)_i}{2} - \sum_{i \notin \Omega} \frac{((\boldsymbol{v}_S + \boldsymbol{c}_S)\pi_S)_i - ((\boldsymbol{v}_B + \boldsymbol{c}_B)\pi_B)_i}{2}\right|$$
$$\geqq -\frac{1}{n-k}\left(\left|\sum_{i=1}^{n} \frac{(\boldsymbol{v}_S + \boldsymbol{c}_S)_i - (\boldsymbol{v}_B + \boldsymbol{c}_B)_i}{2}\right| + kA\right).$$

Putting all this together, we can use (18) to write

$$U_S(\boldsymbol{v}_B + \boldsymbol{c}_B) - U_S(\boldsymbol{v}_S + \boldsymbol{c}_S) - \frac{S(\boldsymbol{v}_B, \boldsymbol{c}_B) - S(\boldsymbol{v}_S, \boldsymbol{c}_S)}{2}$$
$$\geqq -\max_{l \leqq k} \left\{ \begin{array}{c} \left|\frac{(\boldsymbol{v}_B + \boldsymbol{c}_B)^{(l)}}{2} - \frac{(\boldsymbol{v}_S + \boldsymbol{c}_S)^{(l)}}{2}\right| \\ \left|\frac{(\boldsymbol{v}_B + \boldsymbol{c}_B)^{(m-l+1)}}{2} - \frac{(\boldsymbol{v}_S + \boldsymbol{c}_S)^{(m-l+1)}}{2}\right| \\ \frac{1}{n-k}\left(\left|\sum_{i=1}^{n} \frac{(\boldsymbol{v}_B + \boldsymbol{c}_B)_i - (\boldsymbol{v}_S + \boldsymbol{c}_S)_i}{2}\right| + kA\right) \end{array} \right\}.$$

Substituting $(\boldsymbol{v}_B, \boldsymbol{c}_B) = (\boldsymbol{v}', \boldsymbol{c}')$, $(\boldsymbol{v}_S, \boldsymbol{c}_S) = (\boldsymbol{v}, \boldsymbol{c})$, we obtain a lower bound on $U_S(\boldsymbol{v}', \boldsymbol{c}') - U_S(\boldsymbol{v}, \boldsymbol{c}) - (S(\boldsymbol{v}', \boldsymbol{c}') - S(\boldsymbol{v}, \boldsymbol{c}))/2$. Substituting instead $(\boldsymbol{v}_B, \boldsymbol{c}_B) = (\boldsymbol{v}, \boldsymbol{c})$, $(\boldsymbol{v}_S, \boldsymbol{c}_S) = (\boldsymbol{v}', \boldsymbol{c}')$, we obtain an upper bound on the same expression. Combining the two bounds, we obtain the theorem's statement for $j = S$. Expressing the buyer's utility as $U_B(\boldsymbol{v}, \boldsymbol{c}) \equiv S(\boldsymbol{v}, \boldsymbol{c}) - U_S(\boldsymbol{v}, \boldsymbol{c})$, we obtain the theorem's statement for $j = B$. ■

Proof of Corollary 2. Let $u_j^n(\lambda, \sigma)$ denote party j's expected *ex post* utility in the contract with n widgets as a function of investments (λ, σ), *i.e.*

$$u_j^n(\lambda, \sigma) = \int U_j^n(\boldsymbol{v}(\lambda, \zeta), \boldsymbol{c}(\sigma, \zeta))\, dF(\zeta).$$

Using Theorem 2 and the fact that $|E(R)| \leqq E(R)$ for any random variable R, we can write

$$\left| u_j^n(\lambda', \sigma') - u_j^n(\lambda, \sigma) - \frac{E_\zeta S(\boldsymbol{v}(\lambda', \zeta), \boldsymbol{c}(\sigma', \zeta')) - E_\zeta S(\boldsymbol{v}(\lambda, \zeta), \boldsymbol{c}(\sigma, \zeta))}{2} \right|$$

$$\leqq E_\zeta \left| U_j^n(\boldsymbol{v}(\lambda', \zeta), \boldsymbol{c}(\sigma', \zeta)) - U_j^n(\boldsymbol{v}(\lambda, \zeta), \boldsymbol{c}(\sigma, \zeta)) - \frac{S(\boldsymbol{v}(\lambda', \zeta), \boldsymbol{c}(\sigma', \zeta)) - S(\boldsymbol{v}(\lambda, \zeta), \boldsymbol{c}(\sigma, \zeta))}{2} \right|$$

$$\leqq E_\zeta \max_{l \leqq k} \left\{ \begin{array}{l} \left| \dfrac{(\boldsymbol{v}(\lambda', \zeta) + \boldsymbol{c}(\sigma', \zeta))^{(l)} - (\boldsymbol{v}(\lambda, \zeta), \boldsymbol{c}(\sigma, \zeta))^{(l)}}{2} \right| \\ \left| \dfrac{(\boldsymbol{v}(\lambda', \zeta) + \boldsymbol{c}(\sigma', \zeta))^{(n+l+1)} - (\boldsymbol{v}(\lambda, \zeta) + \boldsymbol{c}(\sigma, \zeta))^{(m-l+1)}}{2} \right| \\ \dfrac{1}{n-k} \left| \sum_{i=1}^{n} \dfrac{(\boldsymbol{v}(\lambda', \zeta) + \boldsymbol{c}(\sigma', \zeta))_i - (\boldsymbol{v}(\lambda, \zeta) + \boldsymbol{c}(\sigma, \zeta))_i}{2} \right| + kA \end{array} \right\}$$

$$\leqq \rho_n \frac{1}{n-k} E_\zeta \left(\left| \sum_{i=1}^{n} \frac{(\boldsymbol{v}(\lambda', \zeta) + \boldsymbol{c}(\sigma', \zeta))_i - (\boldsymbol{v}(\lambda, \zeta) + \boldsymbol{c}(\sigma, \zeta))_i}{2} \right| + kA \right) + (1 - \rho_n)A,$$

where ρ_n is the probability that there are at least k of G and B widgets. By Assumption 5, $\rho_n \to 1$ as $n \to \infty$. Using in addition Assumption 4, we see that for all $\lambda, \lambda' \in \Lambda$, $\sigma, \sigma' \in \Sigma$, the right-hand side of the above inequality goes to zero as $n \to \infty$. Therefore,

$$u_j^n(\lambda', \sigma') - u_j^n(\lambda, \sigma) - \frac{E_\zeta S(\boldsymbol{v}(\lambda', \zeta), \boldsymbol{c}(\sigma', \zeta')) - E_\zeta S(\boldsymbol{v}(\lambda, \zeta), \boldsymbol{c}(\sigma, \zeta))}{2} \to 0 \text{ as } n \to \infty.$$

The remainder of the proof is analogous to that of Corollary 1. ■

Acknowledgement. This paper is a revised and extended version of Chapter 3 of my 1995 Ph.D. thesis at Harvard University. I gratefully acknowledge the financial support of the Alfred P. Sloan Foundation during my dissertation work. I am greatly indebted to Oliver Hart and Eric Maskin, my dissertation advisors, for many invaluable discussions and continuous encouragement. I am also grateful to Bengt Holmstrom, Boaz Moselle, Andrei Shleifer, Steve Tadelis, Jean Tirole, Michael Whinston, and participants of seminars at

Berkeley, Boston University, CalTech, Chicago, Harvard, IDEI, LSE, MIT, Northwestern, Penn, Stanford, UCSD, ULB, and Yale for valuable comments. I thank Patrick Bolton (an editor) and two anonymous referees for their thorough reading of the manuscript and suggestions for improvement. I am grateful to Federico Echenique for valuable research assistance. Any errors that still remain are my own.

REFERENCES

[1] Aghion, P., Dewatripont, M., and Rey, P. (1994), "Renegotiation Design with Unverifiable Information", *Econometrica*, **62**, 257-282.

[2] Anderlini, L. and Felli, L. (1994), "Incomplete Written Contracts: Undescribable States of Nature", *Quarterly Journal of Economics*, **109**, 1085-1124.

[3] Che, Y.-K. and Hausch, D. (1997), "Cooperative Investments and the Value of Contracting (Social Systems Research Institute Working Paper No. 9714, University of Wisconsin-Madison).

[4] Crocker, K. J. and Masten, S. E. (1988), "Mitigating Contractual Hazards: Unilateral Options and Contract Length", *Rand Journal of Economics*, **19**, 327-43.

[5] Dye, R. (1985), "Costly Contract Contingencies", *International Economic Review*, **26**, 233-250.

[6] Edlin, A. and Reichelstein, S. (1996), "Holdups, Standard Breach Remedies, and Optimal Investment", *American Economic Review*, **86**, 478-501.

[7] Edlin, A. and Shannon, C. (1998), "Strict Monotonicity in Comparative Statics", *Journal of Economic Theory*, **18**, 201-219.

[8] Fudenberg, D., Holmstrom, B. and Milgrom, P. (1990), "Short-term Contracts and Long-term Agency Relationships", *Journal of Economic Theory*, **51**, 1-31.

[9] Grout, P. (1984), "Investment and Wages in the Absence of Binding Contracts: A Nash Bargaining Approach", *Econometrica*, **52**, 449-460.

[10] Hart, O. (1995) *Firms, Contracts, and Financial Structure*, (Oxford: Oxford University Press).

[11] Hart, O. and Moore, J. (1988), "Incomplete Contracts and Renegotiation", *Econometrica*, **56**, 755-785.

[12] Hausdorff, F. (1962) *Set Theory* (New York: Chelsea).

[13] Holmstrom, B. (1982), "Moral Hazard in Teams", *Bell Journal of Economics*, **13**, 324-340.

[14] Joskow, P. L. (1988), "Price Adjustment in Long-Term Contracts: The Case of Coal", *Journal of Law and Economics*, **31**, 47-83.

[15] Karchmer, M. (1989) *Communication Complexity: A New Approach to Circuit Depth* (Cambridge: MIT Press).

[16] Laffont, J. J. and Maskin, E. (1982), "The Theory of Incentives: An Overview", in W. Hildenbrand (ed.) *Advances in Economic Theory*, (Cambridge: Cambridge University Press).

[17] MacLeod, B. (1996), "Complexity, Contract, and the Employment Relationship" (Mimeo, Université de Montreal).

[18] MacLeod, B. and Malcomson, J. (1993), "Investments, Holdup, and the Form of Market Contracts", *American Economic Review*, **83**, 811-837.

[19] Maskin, E. and Moore, J. (1999), "Implementation and Renegotiation", *Review of Economic Studies*, **66**, 39-56.

[20] Maskin, E. and Tirole, J. (1999), "Unforeseen Contingencies, and Incomplete Contracts", *Review of Economic Studies*, **66**, 83-114.

[21] Milgrom, P. and Shannon, C. (1994), "Monotone Comparative Statics", *Econometrica*, **62**, 157-180.

[22] Moore, J. (1992), "Implementation in Environments with Complete Information", in J. J. Laffont (ed.) *Advances in*

Economic Theory, (Cambridge: Cambridge University Press).

[23] Moore, J. and Repullo, R. (1988), "Subgame Perfect Implementation", *Econometrica*, **56**, 1191–1220.

[24] Noldeke, G. and Schmidt, K. M. (1995), "Option Contracts and Renegotiation: A Solution to the Hold-Up Problem", *Rand Journal of Economics*, **26**, 163–179.

[25] Rey, P. and Salanie, B. (1990), "Long-Term, Short-Term, and Renegotiation: On the Value of Commitment in Contracting", *Econometrica*, **58**, 597–619.

[26] Rogerson, W. (1992), "Contractual Solutions to the Hold-Up Problem", *Review of Economic Studies*, **59**, 777-793.

[27] Segal, I. (1996), "Communication Complexity and Coordination by Authority" (Mimeo, UC Berkeley).

[28] Schwartz, A. (1992), "Legal Theories and Incomplete Contracts", in L. Werin and H. Wijkander (eds.), *Contract Economics*, (Oxford: Blackwell).

[29] Sutton, J. (1986), "Non-Cooperative Bargaining Theory: An Introduction", *Review of Economic Studies*, **53**, 709-724.

[30] Tirole, J. (1994), "Incomplete Contracts: Where do we Stand?" (Walras–Bowley lecture at the North American Summer Meetings of the Econometric Society in Quebec City).

[31] Williamson, O. (1975) *Markets and Hierarchies: Analysis and Antitrust Implications* (New York: Free Press).

[32] Williamson, O. (1985) *The Economic Institutions of Capitalism* (New York: Free Press).

4

Foundations of Incomplete Contracts

Oliver Hart
John Moore

Abstract

In the last few years, a new area has emerged in economic theory, which goes under the heading of "incomplete contracting". However, almost since its inception, the theory has been under attack for its lack of rigorous foundations. In this paper, we evaluate some of the criticisms that have been made of the theory, in particular, those in Maskin and Tirole (1999*a*). In doing so, we develop a model that provides a rigorous foundation for the idea that contracts are incomplete.

1 Introduction

In the last ten to fifteen years, a new area has emerged in economic theory, which goes under the heading of "incomplete contracting".[1] This approach has been useful for understanding topics such as the meaning of ownership and the nature and financial structure of the firm. Yet almost since its inception, the theory has been under attack for its lack of rigorous foundations. In this paper, we evaluate some of the criticisms that have been made of incomplete contracting theory, in particular, those in Maskin and Tirole (1999*a*) (henceforth MT). In doing so we develop a model that provides a rigorous foundation for the idea that contracts are incomplete.

Many papers in the incomplete contracts literature motivate the idea of contractual incompleteness as follows. Imagine a buyer, B, who requires a good (or service) from a seller, S. Suppose that the exact nature of the good is uncertain; more precisely, it depends on a state of nature which is yet to be realized. In an ideal world, the parties would write a contingent contract specifying exactly which good is to be delivered in each state. However, if the number of states is very large, such a contract would be prohibitively expensive. So instead the parties will write an incomplete contract. Then, when the

1. The incomplete contracts literature can be seen as a development of the earlier transactions cost literature. See *e.g.* Williamson (1975).

state of nature is realized, they will renegotiate the contract, since at this stage they know what kind of good should be traded.

MT have criticized this informal story on the following grounds. They argue that there is a tension between the (standard) assumption made in the incomplete contracts literature that the parties are unboundedly rational, and the appeal to the transaction cost of describing the *ex ante* nature of trade. MT develop a number of irrelevance theorems showing that the parties can design clever contracts, involving the exchange of commonly held information via messages, that overcome the inability to describe trade in advance. They conclude that the informal justification of contractual incompleteness based on the *ex ante* indescribability of actions or trades is unconvincing.

In this paper we evaluate the MT critique. We argue that MT's irrelevance theorems are less damaging to the theory than might appear at first sight. Our argument has two parts. First, we develop a model, inspired by Segal (1995, 1999), in which it is *costless* to delineate the set of possible trades in advance ("trades are describable"), and yet where the "null contract" — the quintessentially incomplete contract — is optimal. Applied to our model, the MT irrelevance theorems say that the optimal contract without describability of trades cannot be *worse* than the optimal contract with describability, *i.e.* it must be the null contract too. However, this result in no way undermines the conclusion that the optimal contract is incomplete.

Second, moving beyond our model, one finds that what we consider to be MT's potentially most important result, their Theorem 4, requires quite restrictive assumptions. If these assumptions are relaxed, describability *does* matter. In fact, we provide an extension of our basic model in which the optimal contract with describability yields the first-best, whereas the optimal contract without describability is the null contract.

An important feature of our model, found also in Segal's work, is that there is no natural metric or ordering on the good to be traded; that is, it is not the case that a good can be represented by its quantity or quality (with higher quantity or quality being more valuable for the buyer). Instead, in each state of nature a particular type of good is uniquely appropriate.[2] Although our model is closely related to that of Segal (1995, 1999), our formulation is somewhat different, and this greatly simplifies the analysis and proofs of the theorems.

We should emphasize that we are not wedded to the idea that contracts are totally incomplete. We also provide a simple extension of the basic model in which the optimal contract is partially incomplete. Moreover, we find in this extension that describability again matters: the degree of partial incompleteness depends on the parties' ability to describe the nature of trade.

2. In this respect our model differs from much of the literature on the foundations of incomplete contracts, where it is supposed that agents contract over the quantity of a homogeneous good to be traded. A paper that obtains similar results to ours, although using a different approach, is Che and Hausch (1998). In Che and Hausch's model, a good can be represented by its quality (with higher quality being better for the buyer), but there are externalities: the seller's investment affects the value of the good to the buyer, and the buyer's investment affects the seller's cost.

Our conclusions rely heavily on the assumption that parties to a contract are unable to commit not to renegotiate their contract (and also to some extent on the assumption that they cannot commit not to collude with a third party). In contrast, MT take the point of view that, at least in an ideal world, commitment should be possible. Indeed, much of their analysis pertains to this case (see their Theorems 1 and 2). We examine their reasoning in some detail but do not find their arguments entirely convincing. Ultimately, however, our view is that the degree of commitment is something about which reasonable people can disagree: both cases — where there is and where there is not commitment — are worthy of study.

The paper is organized as follows. In Section 2 we discuss MT's notion of describability and their irrelevance theorems, using as a vehicle a simple buyer-seller model in which the buyer and seller cannot specify in advance the efficient good to trade. Section 3 is devoted to an examination of the commitment issue. In Section 4 we present a preliminary discussion of the role of property rights (asset ownership) when contracts are incomplete. Finally, Section 5 asks to what extent the optimal contracts we derive should be interpreted as incomplete, given that we employ the mechanism-design machinery of maximizing subject to incentive constraints, and do not impose exogenous restrictions on contracting.

2 • A Model of Incomplete Contracts

Consider a buyer B and a seller S, who are involved in a two-date relationship, as illustrated in Figure 1. The parties meet and contract at date 0, and trade at date 1. In between, at date $1/2$, say, one or both of the parties may invest. For expositional purposes, in the text we assume that only S invests, but we deal with the more general case in the Appendix. Both parties are risk neutral (and are not wealth-constrained) and the rate of interest is zero. Also, both parties are sufficiently rational that they can compute and maximize expected payoffs.

We assume that the parties trade one unit of a good, which we call a widget. To capture the idea that it is hard to contract on this good in advance, we assume that there are N different widgets. In any

FIGURE 1

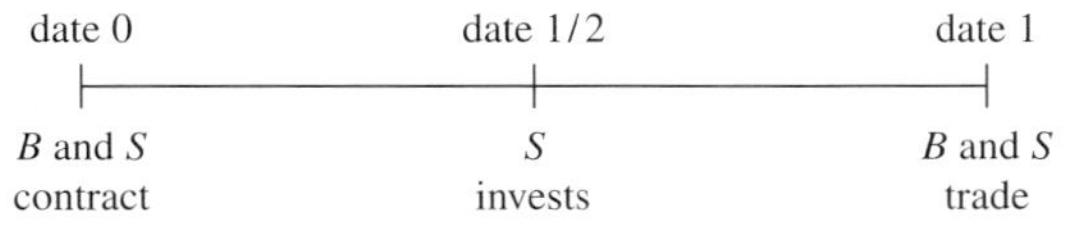

state of nature, exactly one of these widgets should be traded.[3] We call this the "special" (or specific) widget. It yields a (monetary) value v to B and costs S a (monetary) amount $\tilde{c}$ to produce (this cost is incurred if and only if trade takes place). Here $\tilde{c}$ is stochastic as of date 0. For simplicity, in the text we suppose that $\tilde{c}$ takes on two values: $\tilde{c} = c_1$ with probability $\pi(\sigma)$ and $\tilde{c} = c_2$ with probability $1 - \pi(\sigma)$, where σ represents the cost of S's date $1/2$ investment. We assume that $0 \leqq c_1 < c_2 < v$; that $0 < \pi(\sigma) < 1$, $\pi'(\sigma) > 0$, $\pi''(\sigma) < 0$ for all $\sigma \geqq 0$; and that $\pi'(0) = \infty$. Note that, among other things, there are always gains from trade at date 1.

The other $N-1$ widgets are "generic" (or general purpose) widgets. These generic widgets have cost g_n for S, where $g_n = c_1 + (n/N)(c_2 - c_1)$, $n = 1, \ldots, N-1$. In other words, the costs of the generic widgets lie evenly between c_1 and c_2. It will become clear that the exact specification of these costs is not important. What matters is that as the number of widgets, N, increases, no large "gaps" remain between c_1 and c_2. Also, it makes no difference if there are other generic widgets whose costs lie outside this range; see the analysis of the general case in the Appendix.

As will be seen, the value of a generic widget to B is unimportant, provided that such a widget generates strictly less surplus than the special widget (*i.e.* strictly less than $v - c_2$); we assume this in what follows.

We suppose that there is complete symmetry among the widgets at date 0, in the sense that each widget is equally likely to be the special widget or to be one of the $N-1$ generic widgets. That is, there are $2N!$ possible states of nature at date 1: for each of the two possible realizations of S's cost of producing the special widget (c_1 with probability $\pi(\sigma)$; c_2 with probability $1 - \pi(\sigma)$), there are $N!$ equally likely possible permutations of how costs are allocated across widgets.[4]

We assume that both parties observe the state of nature at date 1 (including the realization of $\tilde{c}$). However the state is not verifiable, and nor are the parties' final payoffs: that is, these things cannot be observed by outsiders, such as the courts. In the parlance of incomplete contract theory, the state and parties' payoffs are "observable, but not verifiable".[5]

We follow MT in distinguishing between two cases. One is where the widgets can be described in advance, and the other is where they cannot.

Case D. The N widgets can be costlessly described at date 0.

Case ND. It is prohibitively costly to describe the N widgets at date 0, but it is costless to describe them at date 1.

3. We assume that it is technologically infeasible to trade more than one widget.

4. The assumption that S's investment affects only the cost of the special widget, and yet S does not know which widget this is when she invests, requires some justification. We have in mind a situation where S's investment is *relationship*-specific rather than *widget*-specific. For example, S's investment might be in learning how to do business with B more efficiently. Such an investment will pay off whatever widget B needs at date 1, *i.e.* whichever widget is special, but will not pay off with respect to the widgets B does not need (the generic ones).
Note that, if we had assumed that B invests rather than S, then it would be quite standard to suppose that B's investment pays off only if B receives the special widget from S (in spite of the fact that B does not know in advance which the special widget is).

5. The assumption that the state of nature is unverifiable is important. If the state were verifiable, then the parties could achieve the first-best by writing a contract that specifies that S must supply the widget that is "special" in whatever state occurs, at a fixed price. The assumption that the state of nature is observable is probably less important. We make this assumption for two reasons. First, it greatly simplifies the analysis. Second, the informal motivation of contractual incompleteness given in the introduction does not rely on an asymmetry of information between the parties.

In Case D, for example, it is possible to write a specific performance contract at date 0 to the effect that S must supply a particular widget at date 1 — although, by assumption, this widget will turn out to be the special widget only with probability $1/N$. In Case ND, such a contract is infeasible.

The focus of MT's paper is on what differences, if any, there are between these polar cases, in terms of what contracts can achieve.

We begin our analysis of optimal contracting by considering the first-best. In the first-best, the special widget is always traded and the investment σ is chosen to maximize total expected surplus:

$$\underset{\sigma}{\text{maximize}} \ \pi(\sigma)[v - c_1] + (1 - \pi(\sigma))[v - c_2] - \sigma. \qquad (2.1)$$

One simple way to achieve the first-best is for the parties to write a contract that specifies the optimal value of σ; and then rely on bargaining at date 1 to ensure that the special widget is traded. Following the literature (including MT), however, we assume that this is impossible: either σ is too complicated to describe in an enforceable way, or it is observed only by S.

2.1 Commitment

When the parties can commit not to renegotiate their contract, there is another way to achieve first-best: give S the right to make a take-it-or-leave-it offer to B at date 1. This way S captures all the date 1 surplus, and, anticipating this, makes the efficient investment decision at date $1/2$. Moreover, such a contract does not require that the widgets are described at date 0, and so works in Case ND (even in Case ND, the parties can describe, and hence contract on, the special widget at date 1).

Proposition 1. *Suppose Case ND holds. If the parties can commit not to renegotiate, then the first-best can be achieved.*

Proof. Under a take-it-or-leave-it contract, at date 1, S will ask B to pay v for the special widget, and B will agree. S's private incentive to invest is aligned with the social objective, (2.1), and the first-best is achieved. ■

If the first-best can be achieved when widgets cannot be described at date 0 (Case ND), then *a fortiori* it can also be achieved when widgets can be described (Case D).

Corollary. *The conclusion of Proposition 1 also holds in Case D.*

This corollary serves to illustrate MT's Theorem 1, albeit in a very particular setting. Their theorem states that, if the parties can commit not to renegotiate, then the ability to describe the nature of trade in advance does not matter. This is clearly true in Proposition 1, since there is an optimal contract that does not require *S* to describe the widget at date 0, but only at date 1 when she makes a take-it-or-leave-it offer.

The strength of MT's Theorem 1 lies in its *general* applicability to implementation problems. They have shown that in environments with complete information, where agents can commit not to renegotiate, implementation does not require the *ex ante* specification of a mechanism that maps messages into actions (widgets). Instead, the mechanism can be specified *ex ante* in terms of a mapping from messages into utilities (which are numbers). The description of actions (over which utilities are defined) can be postponed until *ex post*, as part of the message game. In other words, MT have shown that, with commitment, it does not matter if actions are impossible to describe *ex ante*, provided they can be described *ex post* — as in Case *ND*. Unquestionably, this is a major contribution to implementation theory. However, as will become clear shortly, much depends on the assumption that agents are committed not to renegotiate the mechanism *ex post*.

2.2 No Commitment

Proposition 1 relies heavily on the commitment assumption. The reason why *B* accepts *S*'s take-it-or-leave-it offer is that if he rejects then the contract specifies "no trade", and, even though there are gains from trade still outstanding, the two parties are committed to abide by the contract.[6]

Suppose instead that the parties cannot commit not to renegotiate.[7] We will see that the positive conclusion of Proposition 1 is dramatically reversed.

For concreteness, let us assume that if the outcome of the contract at date 1 is inefficient and the parties renegotiate, then *B has all the bargaining power.* (The Appendix deals with the case of a general division of bargaining power.) Under this assumption, the take-it-or-leave-it contract of Proposition 1 works very badly, because *B* can reject *S*'s offer and rely instead on bargaining to extract all the surplus, which gives *S* absolutely no incentive to invest at date $1/2$ to reduce her expected costs. In fact, this take-it-or-leave-it contract works no better than no contract at all: under the "null contract", too, *B* extracts all the surplus in the date 1 bargain.

The question arises: can contracts achieve anything in these circumstances? For the moment we will assume that we are in Case *D*: the *N* widgets can be described at date 0. This puts us squarely in the

6. The same applies were *S* to offer the wrong widget (one of the generic ones) and *B* were to accept: they precommit not to switch to the special widget.

7. We assume that there is a (short) period of time after the formal provisions of the contract are carried out and before trade actually occurs; it is during this period that the parties have an incentive to renegotiate *ex post* (even though they would like to prevent such renegotiation *ex ante*). See Section 3 for a detailed discussion of commitment.

world of mechanism design and classical implementation theory. That is, the parties can write into the date 0 contract a mechanism which is to be played at date 1, once they have learned the state; and, by design, the equilibrium of the mechanism will differ across states, so the contractual outcome is thereby *indirectly* conditioned on the state.[8] The important difference here from most of the literature on implementation is that we are supposing that the parties are free to renegotiate the outcome once the mechanism has been played. For this class of problem, where there is renegotiation, Maskin and Moore (1999) provides a general characterization of the set of implementable choice rules. In what follows, although we implicitly rely on their characterization theorem, we will try to argue from first principles, so as to clarify the logic of the argument.

By "state" we mean actually two things: first, the realization of S's cost of producing the special widget; and, second, the realization of the permutation of the N widgets (*i.e.* the identity of the special widget, and the cost permutation of the generic widgets). Now, in terms of providing S with an incentive to reduce her expected costs, the only aspect of the state that matters is the realization of the cost of the special widget. That is, S is only concerned with the (expected) price p_1 she receives if her cost of producing the special widget is c_1, as opposed to the (expected) price p_2 she receives if the cost is c_2. The symmetry of the model — the fact that all permutations are equally likely — suggests that there can be no gain from having p_1 or p_2 depend on the realization of the permutation.[9]

S's choice of investment σ at date $1/2$ is given by the solution to

$$\underset{\sigma}{\text{maximize}}\ \pi(\sigma)[p_1 - c_1] + (1 - \pi(\sigma))[p_2 - c_2] - \sigma . \qquad (2.2)$$

Notice that her private incentive to invest will be aligned with the first-best if p_1 and p_2 are equal: in that case, she enjoys the full benefit from any cost reduction. However, as the gap between the prices, $p_2 - p_1$, grows, she shares any cost reduction with B, and her incentive to invest is diluted. Hence the parties' aim is to find a contractual mechanism that implements prices p_1 and p_2 for which the gap $p_2 - p_1$ is as small as possible.

As we have argued, the take-it-or-leave-it contract of Proposition 1 is useless, no better than having no contract at all. The point is that, because B has all the bargaining power at date 1, the difference between the prices, $p_2 - p_1$, ends up being equal to the difference between S's costs, $c_2 - c_1$; and from (2.2) this implies that S has no incentive to invest.

The surprising fact is that, for large N, no other contract can do significantly better!

8. See Moore (1992) for an introduction to the theory of mechanism design and implementation in environments with complete information. (Here, B and S both observe the state at date 1, and so have complete information.)

9. This assertion is justified within the formal proof of Proposition 2 below. Note that it would not be true if some permutations were more likely to occur than others. For example, suppose a particular widget were much more likely to be the special widget than any of the others. Then a specific performance contract — the parties agree to trade that particular widget at a fixed price — would work well. (Under the specific performance contract, p_1 would equal p_2 whenever the widget was the special widget, but not otherwise; and so the realization of the permutation would matter.)

Proposition 2. *Suppose Case D holds. If the parties cannot commit not to renegotiate, then irrespective of the contract, as the number of widgets N tends to infinity, S's investment* σ *approaches zero. That is, in the limit, contracts cannot make any difference to expected total surplus, and the parties may as well use the null contract.*

In fact, we will show that the most that can be gained from writing any contract is to reduce the price gap $p_2 - p_1$ from $c_2 - c_1$ to $((N-1)/N)(c_2 - c_1)$: a reduction of the order of $O(1/N)$.

Given a sufficient range of costs for the generic widgets, Proposition 2 generalizes to any *ex post* division of bargaining power, and to a model in which both parties make investments, which may be multi-dimensional. See the Appendix.

Proposition 2 is closely related to Theorem 1 of Segal (1999), except that we dispense with his extreme widgets — what he terms "gold-plated" and "cheap imitation" widgets. Segal's construction relies on there being uncertainty over the number (and identity) of extreme widgets, and hence uncertainty over the ranking (in terms of cost) of the special widget. In our model, the generic widgets have costs similar to the special widget, and, crucially, the ranking of the special widget depends *only* on S's investment: there is no "aggregate uncertainty". This greatly simplifies the analysis and the proofs of the theorems.

The intuition behind Proposition 2 is as follows. Consider the problem the parties face in designing a contractual mechanism whose equilibrium depends on the realization of S's cost of producing the special widget. When this cost is c_i, $i = 1, 2$, let us say that "state i" has occurred.[10] The parties are in effect playing a composite game: the contractual mechanism followed by renegotiation. *Whichever* widget, W say, is specified by the mechanism, even if it is one of the $N-1$ generic ones, renegotiation ensures that at the end of the day the special widget will be traded. Moreover, since B has all the bargaining power, S's payoff is minus the cost of producing W, $C(W)$ say. (This is gross of any transfer that the mechanism might specify. Note that such transfers can depend on the outcome of the mechanism, but not on c_i directly.) Now, given renegotiation, B's payoff and S's payoff sum to the gains from trade $v - c_i$. Hence B's payoff equals $C(W) + v - c_i$. Also, we must not forget that the mechanism might specify "no trade" as the outcome; this costs S nothing, and, following renegotiation, yields B a payoff $v - c_i$. Ignoring permutations, then, in either state there are $N+1$ possible (nonstochastic) outcomes to the composite game, each corresponding to a different point along the Pareto frontier. In Figure 2 we list them in descending order of S's payoff (continuing to ignore transfers specified by the mechanism).

10. This terminology is loose. Strictly speaking, both of these "states" comprise a subset of $N!$ states, each corresponding to a different permutation of the widgets.

FIGURE 2

Final payoffs following renegotiation
(gross of transfer specified by mechanism)

		Seller S	*Buyer B*
State 1			
	no trade	0	$v - c_1$
	special widget	$-c_1$	v
		$-c_1 - \frac{1}{N}(c_2 - c_1)$	$v + \frac{1}{N}(c_2 - c_1)$
	generic widgets	$\vdots$	
		$-c_1 - \frac{N-1}{N}(c_2 - c_1)$	$v + \frac{N-1}{N}(c_2 - c_1)$
State 2			
	no trade	0	$v - c_2$
		$-c_1 - \frac{1}{N}(c_2 - c_1)$	$v - c_2 + c_1 + \frac{1}{N}(c_2 - c_1)$
	generic widgets	$\vdots$	
		$-c_1 - \frac{N-1}{N}(c_2 - c_1)$	$v - c_2 + c_1 + \frac{N-1}{N}(c_2 - c_1)$
	special widget	$-c_2$	v

Note that in state 1, the cheapest of the N widgets is the special one. And in state 2, the special widget is the most expensive. However this is only a matter of labelling: following renegotiation, *all* contractually specified outcomes, even "no trade", lead to the special widget being traded. In effect, we can ignore the labels ("no trade", "special widget", "generic widgets") that appear in the lists in Figure 2.

Unfortunately, this leaves very little to screen on. To see why, consider the limit $N \to \infty$, where the only difference between the lists is that a constant, $c_2 - c_1$, is added to B's payoff in state 1 relative to state 2. (This amount is the additional surplus from S having a lower cost of producing the special widget.) Clearly, for the purpose of mechanism design, adding a constant to one of the parties' payoffs does not help screen the states.

For finite N, we claim that S's payoff cannot differ by more than $(1/N)(c_2 - c_1)$ across states 1 and 2. To check this, consider a simple mechanism in which S is allowed to choose one of the N widgets. Then she will always select the cheapest widget — *viz.* the special one (cost c_1) in state 1, and the cheapest generic one (cost $c_1 + (1/N)(c_2 - c_1)$) in state 2. Correspondingly, if B is allowed to choose, he will always select the most expensive widget — *viz.* the most expensive generic one (cost $c_1 + ((N-1)/N)(c_2 - c_1)$) in state 1, and the special one (cost c_2) in state 2. Under either mechanism, S's payoff differs by only $(1/N)(c_2 - c_1)$ across states 1 and 2, as claimed.

Other, more sophisticated mechanisms might be considered. For example, one party might be entitled to veto a certain number of widgets prior to the other party choosing. It is easy to see that this does not succeed in widening the gap in S's payoff between states.

A specific performance contract does no better either. Consider the contract specifying that a certain widget should be traded at a fixed price. The payoffs associated with this widget are equally likely to be any one of those listed above (excepting "no trade"). Again, S's (expected) payoff differs by only $(1/N)(c_2 - c_1)$ across states 1 and 2.

An equivalent way of saying this is that the price difference $p_2 - p_1$ equals $((N-1)/N)(c_2 - c_1)$. In terms of S's incentive to invest, this is only $O(1/N)$ better than the null contract.

Now for the formal proof of the proposition.

Proof of Proposition 2. Take any abstract mechanism M. Consider a state, $(1, \tau)$ say, in which the special widget costs S c_1 to produce, and the N widgets are arranged according to some permutation τ.[11] Without loss of generality, suppose that τ is such that widget 1 is the special widget, and that widgets 2, …, N are generic widgets costing $c_1 + (1/N)(c_2 - c_1), \ldots, c_1 + ((N-1)/N)(c_2 - c_1)$ respectively.

In state $(1, \tau)$, let the equilibrium strategies of M for B and S be $\mu^b(1, \tau)$ and $\mu^s(1, \tau)$. And, following any renegotiation, let $p(1, \tau)$ denote the overall price that B pays S for delivery of the special widget: $p(1, \tau)$ equals any transfer specified in the mechanism *plus* any amount agreed by the parties during renegotiation. In other words, B's and S's final equilibrium payoffs are respectively $v - p(1, \tau)$ and $p(1, \tau) - c_1$.

Now consider another state, $(2, \tau^*)$ say, in which the special widget costs S c_2 to produce, and the N widgets are arranged according to some new permutation τ^* in which widgets 1, …, $N-1$ are generic widgets costing $c_1 + (1/N)(c_2 - c_1), \ldots, c_1 + ((N-1)/N)(c_2 - c_1)$ respectively, and widget N is the special widget. Note that τ^* is a simple rotation of τ: widget $n = 1, \ldots, N-1$ now has the characteristics that widget $n+1$ formerly had; and now widget N is the special widget rather than widget 1.

11. State $(1, \tau)$ is thus one of the $N!$ constituent states of what in the text we loosely called "state 1".

In state $(2, \tau^*)$, let the equilibrium strategies of M for B and S be $\mu^b(2, \tau^*)$ and $\mu^s(2, \tau^*)$. After renegotiation, let their respective payoffs be $v - p(2, \tau^*)$ and $p(2, \tau^*) - c_2$.

The question arises: What outcome does M specify if the strategy pair $(\mu^b(2, \tau^*), \mu^s(1, \tau))$, is played? Suppose some general stochastic outcome is specified: B pays S an amount q; widget $n = 1, \ldots, N$ is traded with probability $\alpha_n \geqq 0$; and there is no trade with probability $1 - (\alpha_1 + \cdots + \alpha_N) \geqq 0$.[12]

There are two incentive constraints that $q, \alpha_1, \ldots, \alpha_N$ must satisfy. First, in state $(2, \tau^*)$, S must not have an incentive to deviate to $\mu^s(1, \tau)$. Second, in state $(1, \tau)$, B must not have an incentive to deviate to $\mu^b(2, \tau^*)$.

Suppose strategy pair $\mu^b(2, \tau^*)$, $\mu^s(1, \tau)$ *is* played. The contractually-specified outcome is typically inefficient, and will be renegotiated: when the outcome of the lottery $(\alpha_1, \ldots, \alpha_N)$ specifies either that a generic widget is traded, or that there is no trade, the parties must bargain in order to exploit the gains from trading the special widget (and, by assumption, B has all the bargaining power). The final payoffs depend on the state, as indicated in Figure 2. In state $(2, \tau^*)$, following the play of $\mu^b(2, \tau^*)$, $\mu^s(1, \tau)$, S's final payoff is

$$q - \alpha_1\left(c_1 + \frac{1}{N}(c_2 - c_1)\right) - \cdots - \alpha_{N-1}\left(c_1 + \frac{N-1}{N}(c_2 - c_1)\right) - \alpha_N c_2,$$

which, according to the first incentive constraint, cannot be *more* than what she gets in equilibrium, $p(2, \tau^*) - c_2$. And in state $(1, \tau)$, following the play of $\mu^b(2, \tau^*)$, $\mu^s(1, \tau)$, S's final payoff is

$$q - \alpha_1 c_1 - \alpha_2\left(c_1 + \frac{1}{N}(c_2 - c_1)\right) - \cdots - \alpha_N\left(c_1 + \frac{N-1}{N}(c_2 - c_1)\right),$$

which, according to the second incentive constraint, cannot be *less* than what she gets in equilibrium, $p(1, \tau) - c_1$, since if S were worse off B would be better off (all final payoffs lie along the Pareto frontier).

Combining these two constraints, we have

$$p(2, \tau^*) - p(1, \tau) \geqq c_2 - c_1 - (\alpha_1 + \cdots + \alpha_N)\frac{1}{N}(c_2 - c_1)$$
$$\geqq \frac{N-1}{N}(c_2 - c_1).$$

Since this lower bound applies for any permutation τ (and associated rotation τ^*), we can take expectations across permutations, which are equally probable, to deduce that the difference

12. As both parties are risk neutral, there is no gain from making the transfer q depend on which widget (if any) the mechanism specifies is traded.

between the expected price S receives if it costs her c_2 to produce the special widget and the expected price she receives if it costs her c_1 is at least $((N-1)/N)(c_2-c_1)$.

In other words, as the realization of S's cost falls from c_2 to c_1, her payoff rises by at most $(1/N)(c_2-c_1)$. But this gives her only $O(1/N)$ more incentive to reduce her expected costs than does the null contract (under which her payoff would be independent of the cost realization). ■

Given that, when there is no commitment, almost nothing can be achieved in Case D, it follows *a fortiori* that the same must be true in Case ND.

Corollary. *The conclusion of Proposition* 2 *also holds in Case ND.*

This corollary serves to illustrate MT's Theorem 4, albeit again in a very particular setting. Their theorem states that, subject to certain additional conditions, if the parties cannot commit not to renegotiate, then the inability to describe the nature of trade in advance does not matter. This is clearly true in Proposition 2, since even when the parties can describe widgets in advance, they achieve little more than under the null contract.

Before we move on, it is worth reviewing the role of our assumption that the costs of the generic widgets fill the whole interval from c_1 to c_2. Suppose this were not true; *e.g.* suppose instead that the costs of the generic widgets were spread evenly between $\frac{1}{2}(c_1+c_2)$ and c_2. Then the following contract would be useful: S is allowed to choose which widget to supply at date 1 and receives a fixed price. S will always choose the cheapest widget, which is the special widget if $\tilde{c} = c_1$ and the cheapest generic widget if $\tilde{c} = c_2$. Thus S's payoff differs by $\frac{1}{2}(c_1+c_2)-c_1$ across the high cost and low cost states of nature, which gives S an incentive to invest in cost reduction.

2.3 Does Describability Matter?

The main message to emerge from the analysis of Sections 2.1 and 2.2 is that the inability to commit not to renegotiate makes a crucial difference. In contrast, the issue of whether or not actions (widgets) can be described *ex ante* — whether Case D or ND prevails — appears not to matter; this is consistent with MT's thesis.

These findings shed light on the informal story with which the paper began. It turns out that the usual "observable but not verifiable" assumption is enough to justify a high degree of contractual incompleteness (taking the null contract to be the quintessentially incomplete contract), provided (i) the parties cannot commit not to renegotiate, and (ii) the environment is rich enough (here, there are enough generic widgets). That is, the incentive constraints that emerge from dealing with Case *D*, and treating the problem as one of classical mechanism design (constrained by renegotiation), are enough to reduce massively the contractual possibilities. At a formal level, there is no need to invoke additional — and less traditional — assumptions like nondescribability in order to give the informal story solid theoretical foundations. This raises the question: should contracts that are optimal subject to well-defined incentive constraints be thought of as "incomplete" at all? We address this question in Section 5.

The matter of describability should not be ignored altogether. It is clearly ridiculous to assume that all actions can be costlessly described in advance, and for this reason, MT's Theorem 4 is a potentially important result, because, stripped of its auxiliary conditions, the theorem appears to conclude that nondescribability is irrelevant even when there is no commitment. We believe that such a broad-brush conclusion would be misleading, however. The inability to describe the widgets *ex ante* can make a big difference.

For example, consider a model where there is *no* uncertainty. Without loss of generality, suppose widget 1 is always the special widget, and that widgets 2, ..., N are always generic widgets costing $c_1 + (1/N)(c_2 - c_1), \ldots, c_1 + ((N-1)/N)(c_2 - c_1)$ respectively. In this deterministic model, the first-best can obviously be achieved if widgets can be described at date 0 (Case *D*): the parties simply write a specific performance contract under which the parties agree to trade widget 1 at a fixed price, say v. Since this outcome is efficient, there is nothing to renegotiate, and S enjoys all of any cost saving: $p_1 = p_2 = v$. S has first-best incentives.

Things look very different, however, if the N widgets cannot be described at date 0 (Case *ND*). Now a specific performance contract is no longer feasible (widget 1 cannot be specified). The parties have to rely instead on a mechanism which reveals the identity of the special widget at date 1, while at the same time keeping $p_1 = p_2$. We assert that this implementation problem is essentially the same as that of Proposition 2, and that the conclusion is therefore the same: *in approximate terms, no contract can do any better than the null contract.*

A simple way to prove this assertion is to suppose that there are N "names" at date 0, each of which will describe a widget at date 1. However, it is not known which name will attach to which widget: the meaning of the vocabulary (the list of N names) only becomes established at date 1. And there is no other way of describing widgets at date 0. In particular, even though B and S know at date 0 which widget is the special one, they have no words to describe it, other than the N names, any one of which may turn out to be appropriate at date 1. It is clear that this implementation problem is isomorphic to the problem in Section 2.2, where it was not known at date 0 which widget would have which costs/values. The conclusions of Proposition 2 thus carry over to the present setting, where widgets have fixed costs/values but cannot be described at date 0.

We introduce names here only as a device to simplify the argument. *A fortiori*, our assertion holds when there are no names, or any other vocabulary for describing the widgets at date 0.

This example is *not* covered by MT's Theorem 4. Their result requires two conditions: first, that the set of states is "maximal"; and, second, that the final outcome is "renegotiation welfare neutral". Roughly, maximality means that every permutation of the N widgets has to be possible (which rules out our deterministic example); and renegotiation welfare neutrality means that final payoffs have to be the same across permutations. The first condition is not restrictive, but the second one is. To see this, notice that the example can be modified to include a small measure of fringe states so as to meet MT's maximality condition. Moreover, such a modification does not rob the example of its force: it is still the case that the specific performance contract is approximately first-best in Case D, whereas in Case ND the null contract is almost optimal. However, although this modified example satisfies maximality, it does not satisfy MT's renegotiation welfare neutrality condition, and so is not covered by their Theorem 4.

We may conclude this section as follows: nondescribability *is* generally an important constraint in the absence of a commitment not to renegotiate.

2.4 Partially Incomplete Contracts

Proposition 2 can be criticized for going too far: there is no point in writing any contract at all. What is needed is a theory of partial incompleteness.

The model can also be criticized on the grounds that the effects of S's investment σ are too jagged: only the *special* widget's cost is affected by σ; the costs/values of the other (generic) widgets are fixed. In principle, investment may reduce the cost of any widget.

Here we make a start in responding to these criticisms. Consider a variant of our model. There are N widgets, each of which can be described at date 0: we are in Case D. Of these N widgets, M are "defined". Defined widgets are simply a category of widget distinct from the others: *e.g.* they may all have a common shape, which is not shared by the other $N-M$ widgets. And each defined widget is distinct from the other defined widgets: *e.g.* each may have its own colour. We take M to be large, and N large relative to M: $N \gg M \gg 1$.

There is one "special" widget, which is the widget that yields the greatest surplus at date 1. This is the widget that will be traded at date 1 (possibly following renegotiation). Let its value to B be v. Crucially, *the special widget is always one of the M defined widgets*: previously, we assumed that the special widget could be any of the N widgets.

The second important change we make to our model is to suppose that the cost of producing *all* of the M defined widgets is affected by σ. With probability $\pi(\sigma)$, the cost of producing a given defined widget, other than the special widget, is reduced by $\Delta > 0$.[13] And with probability $\pi(\sigma)$, the cost of producing the special widget is reduced by $k\Delta$. We assume $k > 1$: in other words, we assume that σ has a greater impact on the expected cost of producing the special widget than on the other $M-1$ defined widgets. These cost reductions are perfectly correlated.[14] That is, with probability $1-\pi(\sigma)$, there are no cost reductions. Without cost reductions, we suppose that costs are evenly spread from $\underline{c}$ to $\bar{c}$, with the cost of the special widget lying somewhere in the middle, say at c. Assume Δ is small enough that $\underline{c} < c - k\Delta$ and $c < \bar{c} - \Delta$; *i.e.* the special widget always has cost lying within the range of costs of the other defined widgets. All permutations of the M defined widgets (*viz.* the identity of the special widget, and the permutation of the costs of the other $M-1$ widgets) are equally probable at date 1.

The costs of the remaining $N-M$ widgets are unaffected by σ.[15] We suppose that these costs are evenly spread from $\underline{g}$ to $\bar{g}$, a range which encompasses the costs of the defined widgets: $\underline{g} < \underline{c} - \Delta$ and $\bar{c} < \bar{g}$. All cost permutations of these $N-M$ widgets are equally probable at date 1.

The expected total surplus is

$$\pi(\sigma)[v - c + k\Delta] + (1-\pi(\sigma))[v - c] - \sigma. \tag{2.3}$$

And hence the first-best investment level σ^* satisfies

$$\pi'(\sigma^*) = 1/(k\Delta). \tag{2.4}$$

Just as in our earlier model, the first-best cannot be attained, since the identity of the special widget is not known in advance. Moreover, as in Proposition 2, the incentive constraints impose severe restrictions on what can be achieved through contracting. However, unlike in Proposition 2, the parties can do appreciably better than under the null contract. With the null contract, S would have

13. $\pi(\sigma)$ is assumed to satisfy our earlier assumptions: $0 < \pi(\sigma) < 1$, $\pi'(\sigma) > 0$ and $\pi''(\sigma) < 0$ for all $\sigma \geqq 0$; and $\pi'(0) = \infty$.

14. This is not an important assumption.

15. As in Section 2, we do not need to specify the values to B of the $N-1$ non-special widgets, other than to assume that their surplus (value minus cost) is always strictly less than the surplus of the special widget.

no incentive to invest since she gets no surplus from the date 1 bargain (the price B pays is perfectly correlated with the realized cost of producing the special widget). That is, σ would equal zero. The same would be true in a contract where, for example, either B or S were free to choose any of the N widgets (*i.e.* without limiting the choice to the defined widgets): S would always choose the cheapest widget (costing $\underline{g}$), B would always choose the most expensive (costing $\overline{g}$), and, either way, S's payoff would not depend on σ, which would give her no incentive to invest.

Instead, the parties can write a contract specifying that S supplies one of the defined widgets for a fixed price p. The choice of which defined widget may be left to S, in which case she will supply the cheapest, costing her either $\underline{c}-\Delta$ (with probability $\pi(\sigma)$) or $\underline{c}$ (with probability $1-\pi(\sigma)$). This is not the special widget, and so the parties will renegotiate at date 1. But since S gets none of the surplus, her expected payoff, net of investment costs, equals

$$\pi(\sigma)[p-\underline{c}+\Delta]+(1-\pi(\sigma))[p-\underline{c}]-\sigma. \tag{2.5}$$

And hence her choice of investment $\hat{\sigma}$ satisfies

$$\pi'(\hat{\sigma}) = 1/\Delta. \tag{2.6}$$

Comparing (2.6) with (2.4), we see that there is underinvestment: $\hat{\sigma}<\sigma^*$. However, there is more investment than under the null contract: $\hat{\sigma}>0$. That is, a "partially incomplete" contract — a contract defining the set of widgets from which S must supply one, and fixing the price — is better than no contract; but it does not implement first-best.

Notice that if the contract allowed B to select from the set of defined widgets, then he would choose the most expensive, costing either $\bar{c}-\Delta$ (with probability $\pi(\sigma)$) or $\bar{c}$ (with probability $1-\pi(\sigma)$). And S's investment would again be given by $\hat{\sigma}$. In other words, aside from a transfer difference $\bar{c}-\underline{c}$, it does not matter if B or S has the right to select one of the defined widgets.

For large M, these partially incomplete contracts are almost as good as any contract can be. Consider a specific performance contract: at date 0 the parties agree that one specified defined widget should be supplied at date 1 for a fixed price. Since there is a small probability, $1/M$, that this widget will turn out to be the special one, S's incentives are slightly improved; but as $M\to\infty$ her investment drops to $\hat{\sigma}$.

We can appeal to the same logic of Proposition 2 to prove that this is as far as contracts can take us.

Proposition 3. *Suppose Case D holds. If the parties cannot commit not to renegotiate, then as M, the number of defined widgets, tends to infinity, the optimal level of S's investment converges to* $\hat{\sigma}$, *the solution to* (2.6). *In the limit, it is optimal to contract for the delivery of one of the defined widgets at a fixed price; the particular widget may be chosen by B or S at date* 1, *or may be specified in advance at date* 0.

Proposition 3 goes some way towards meeting the criticism that we lack a theory of partial incompleteness. It should be recognized that this is not really a framework in which agents *choose* the degree of contractual incompleteness, because there are no "margins": in Proposition 3, the set of defined widgets is exogenously given.

Before leaving this model, we should point out that Proposition 3 does *not* hold in Case *ND*, where the widgets cannot be described at date 0. In fact, in this case, one can adapt the argument of Section 2.3 to show that as the total number of widgets N tends to infinity (and the ratio N/M also approaches infinity), S's investment approaches zero, irrespective of the contract. Thus, here we have another example (like that in Section 2.3) where nondescribability matters.

3 Commitment

In Section 2 we saw that, although nondescribability matters in incomplete contracting models, the crucial assumption is the lack of commitment. If the parties can commit not to renegotiate their contract, then they can achieve the first-best (Proposition 1).

In this section we consider how reasonable it is to assume that the parties cannot commit not to renegotiate.[16] We will also discuss the role of third parties to a contract. It will be convenient from an expositional point of view to gear our discussion fairly closely to that of MT.

One obvious way for B and S to commit not to renegotiate is for them to write in their contract an irrevocability clause; or, equivalently, a clause that says that B must pay S a huge sum of money if renegotiation occurs. The problem with this is that, under the current legal system, there is nothing to stop B and S from writing a *new* contract that cancels the irrevocability clause or waives the penalty. The point is that the courts will enforce the new contract rather than the original one. Anticipating that the irrevocability clause will not stand, B will decline S's take-it-or-leave-it offer in the model of Section 2, and renegotiate.

MT argue that this justification for lack of commitment is unsatisfactory because in an ideal world B and S could register their first contract with the court, and could instruct the court to enforce

16. For an interesting discussion of this question, see Tirole (1998).

the first contract and ignore any revised contract. However, a registration system like this does not exist anywhere in the world as far as we know, and would require a system-wide institutional change.[17]

Even if such a registration system were put in place, it might not prevent renegotiation. B and S might be able to renegotiate indirectly by writing side-contracts with third parties. For example, B and S could agree *ex post* to operate through a middleman: S will supply the widget to the middleman, who will supply it to B; in return B pays the middleman, who pays S. These side-contracts do not violate the first contract (which states that no renegotiation will occur) because they do not involve B and S directly.

Of course, the original contract could state that not only can it not be renegotiated, but also no equivalent set of contracts with third parties should be enforced. The question, though, is: What is an "equivalent set of contracts with third parties"? There may be quite legitimate sequences of trade linking S to B through various middlemen, and it may be hard for a judge to distinguish between the legitimate ones and the ones that are designed to circumvent a "no renegotiation" provision.

Note that side-contracting also interferes with the use of third parties as a commitment device. Suppose that B and S sign a contract with a third party T stating that B and S will each pay T a huge sum of money if renegotiation occurs. Then *ex post* B and S can avoid the penalty by contracting indirectly through a middleman. Moreover, if B and S try to prevent this *ex ante* by promising to pay a penalty in the event that a middleman is used, then the same problem arises as above: it might be hard to distinguish between cases where the middleman is used for legitimate business purposes and cases where he is used to circumvent renegotiation.

Now that we have raised the issue of third parties, it is worth asking whether they can be used in other ways than just to prevent renegotiation. The answer is yes. Third parties can drive a wedge between B's and S's payoffs: B can be penalized without rewarding S, and *vice versa*. This may improve incentives even if the parties cannot commit not to renegotiate their contract.

To see how a third party can improve matters, consider the following contract in the model of Section 2.2:

At date 1, B chooses between the following possibilities: (1) B pays $c_2 - c_1$ to S and no trade occurs; or (2) B pays nothing to S. If B chooses (2), S has a choice of "accepting" B's offer or "rejecting" B's offer. If S "accepts" B's offer, no trade occurs. If S "rejects" B's offer, then S supplies a widget of her choice to B, and B pays $c_1 + (1/2N)(c_2 - c_1)$ to S and a fine $F \geqq c_2 - c_1$ to a third party T.

17. Such a change might be quite costly and the benefits may not be all that great: the majority of contracting parties may choose not to register their contracts, since they recognize that they will think of new things to include as time passes (they are "boundedly rational"). Thus, to the extent that a registration system has a fixed cost, it might not be worth introducing for the minority of people like B and S, who are unboundedly rational and for whom contract renegotiation is an impediment.

An important part of this contract is that it does not prohibit renegotiation. Thus, if a "no trade" outcome occurs, or if S "rejects" B's offer and supplies an inefficient widget, then this is not the end of the matter: since there are gains from trade the parties will always renegotiate and trade the efficient widget (the special widget). As in Section 2, we assume that B has all the bargaining power in the renegotiation process.

Consider first the case where S's cost of producing the special widget at date 1 equals c_1: state 1 occurs. If B chooses (1), then S's payoff is $c_2 - c_1$, and B's payoff is $(v - c_1) - (c_2 - c_1) = v - c_2$, since B gets all the gains from renegotiation. On the other hand, if B chooses (2), then it is easy to see that S will prefer to "reject" (she supplies the special widget, costing c_1, and her payoff is $-c_1 + c_1 + (1/2N)(c_2 - c_1) = (1/2N)(c_2 - c_1) > 0$) than to "accept" (her payoff is zero). Hence B has to pay the fine, which reduces his payoff below $v - c_2$. The conclusion is that in state 1, B chooses (1), and S's payoff is $c_2 - c_1$.

Consider next the case where S's cost of producing the special widget at date 1 equals c_2: state 2 occurs. If B chooses (1), then S's payoff is $c_2 - c_1$, and B's is $(v - c_2) - (c_2 - c_1) = v + c_1 - 2c_2$. If B chooses (2), then it is easy to see that S prefers to "accept" (her payoff is zero) than to "reject" (she supplies the cheapest generic widget, costing $c_1 + (1/N)(c_2 - c_1)$, and her payoff is $-c_1 - (1/N)(c_2 - c_1) + c_1 + (1/2N)(c_2 - c_1) = -(1/2N)(c_2 - c_1) < 0$). Hence, under (2) B avoids the fine and his payoff is $v - c_2 > v + c_1 - 2c_2$ (he gets all the gains from renegotiation). The conclusion is that in state 2, B chooses (2), and S's payoff is zero.

We see that S's payoff decreases from $c_2 - c_1$ in state 1 to zero in state 2. In other words, her payoff falls by the exact amount that her costs rise. But this means that S has first-best investment incentives: at date $1/2$, S will solve

$$\underset{\sigma}{\text{maximize}}\ \pi(\sigma)[c_2 - c_1] - \sigma,$$

which is equivalent to (2.1). Since renegotiation ensures that the efficient widget is supplied, the three-party contract yields the first-best outcome.

Let us now discuss some potential problems with the above contract. First, the mechanism is very fragile. It relies on the fact that there are discrete differences between the costs of the various widgets; the mechanism is designed so that when state 1 is the true state "rejection" by S gives her a small positive payoff, whereas when state 2 is the true state "rejection" by S gives her a small negative payoff. There is reason to think that if there is a continuum of widgets, it may be difficult to screen state 1 from state 2, even if third parties are allowed. Certainly, contracts like that above will not work. And general implementation theorems that employ devices such as getting one agent to announce the state of nature (which can then be challenged by the other agent) are unlikely to be operational because the description of a state is so rich: the entire (infinite) vector of costs has to be announced.[18] We conjecture that in some properly articulated model with a continuum of widgets, the conclusions of Proposition 2 will hold, even allowing for third parties; but this awaits further research.

Even if we stick to the case of a finite number of generic widgets, the above contract is vulnerable to collusion. In particular, either B and T or S and T can gain by writing a (secret) side-contract in which it is agreed that any fine received by T is handed over to the other party.

Consider a side-deal between B and T. Suppose state 1 occurs. Then if B chooses (2) in the above game, S will "reject" as before, but B's payoff will be $v - c_1 - (1/2N)(c_2 - c_1) > v - c_2$, since B pays the fine to himself. Thus B will choose (2), and S's payoff is $(1/2N)(c_2 - c_1)$.

On the other hand, if state 2 occurs, collusion makes no difference: B chooses (2), S "accepts" and S's payoff is zero.

We see that collusion has a devastating effect on S's investment incentives. Recognizing that B and T will collude after she has made her investment decision, S will choose σ to solve

$$\underset{\sigma}{\text{maximize}}\ \pi(\sigma)\left[\frac{1}{2N}\,(c_2 - c_1)\right] - \sigma,$$

which leads to a very low value of σ. In fact, as $N \to \infty$, $\sigma \to 0$, which is the same outcome as when there is no contract at all (see Proposition 2).[19]

Can collusion be avoided? An obvious approach is to prohibit collusion in the original three-party contract, *i.e.* to instruct the courts not to enforce any side-deals between a subset of the parties. The difficulty with this, however, is that B and T (or S and T) can disguise their side-deal by using a middleman.

Another approach to avoiding collusion, suggested by MT, is to replace the single third party T by a collection of third parties. For example, MT propose that the contract between B and S could state that any fines should be paid to the "community of citizens", *i.e.* to the general public. The idea is that it is hard — if not impossible — for B or S to collude with a whole community.

18. Note that these mechanisms are designed to rule out unwanted equilibria. If uniqueness is not required, then the mechanisms can be much simpler.

19. It is not difficult to show that S and T also have an incentive to collude (assuming B and T do not). Collusion between S and T makes no difference in state 1, when B chooses (1). However, in state 2, S will "reject" if B chooses (2), since S now receives the fine. Thus, if B understands the collusion between S and T, B will choose (1) in order to avoid paying the fine. Hence S's, payoff is the same in state 2 as in state 1. The conclusion is that S will choose $\sigma = 0$, which is the same outcome as when there is no contract.

However, such an arrangement raises new problems. First, as a matter of contract law, there appears to be nothing to stop B and S from cancelling the fine, *after* S has "rejected" an offer from B, but *before* the fine has been paid, *i.e.* they could simply change their mind. The point is that the community is not a true party to the contract — the citizens never signed anything — and so they would have no grounds to complain or sue. Of course, B and S could pick a representative of the community to be a signatory, but this would raise the possibility of collusion between B (or S) and the representative.

Second, even if we put this issue aside, it is unclear who would collect the fine on behalf of the community. For example, suppose the contract states that S must reject B's offer by placing an advertisement in a designated newspaper, and this advertisement must include an offer from B to pay F to the first person who responds to it, *e.g.* by sending an e-mail to a particular address. Then S could always tip off a friend, thereby ensuring that the friend is the first to respond, *i.e.* in effect S receives the fine herself.

The use of lotteries

MT have proposed an even more ingenious way to solve the problem of third-party collusion: eliminate third parties altogether and use lotteries to introduce a wedge between what S receives and what B pays. Specifically, suppose that B is (at least slightly) risk averse, rather than risk neutral.[20] Then it is possible to find a random variable $\tilde{p}$ whose mean, $E\tilde{p}$, equals $c_1 + (1/2N)(c_2 - c_1)$, but the certainty equivalent of $-\tilde{p}$ is very low to B. (Simply raise the variance of $\tilde{p}$.) Now replace the previous three-party contract with a two-party one, where there are no fines, but if S "rejects" B's offer, B pays the random amount $\tilde{p}$ to S. This is equivalent to the previous contract since the lottery has the effect of a penalty on B.[21]

This approach has its own difficulties, however. The simplest way to introduce randomness in $\tilde{p}$ is to make $\tilde{p}$ contingent on an objective, nonmanipulable event, *e.g.* the change in a stock market index over a short interval following S's announcement.[22] However, the problem is that, if the event is objective, B can insure against it in advance, *i.e.* B could go to a (competitive) insurance company and agree, conditional on S's announcement and a particular realization of the stock market index, to exchange the actual value of $\tilde{p}$ for its expected value, $E\tilde{p}$. If S "rejects", this makes B's combined payment to S and the insurance company equal to $E\tilde{p} = c_1 + (1/2N)(c_2 - c_1)$, and the effect of the penalty is removed.

In a private communication, Eric Maskin has suggested that B and S could avoid the possibility of insurance by making $\tilde{p}$ depend

20. We continue to suppose that S is risk neutral. The argument can easily be modified if S is also risk averse.

21. We are assuming that B is not wealth-constrained. Wealth constraints may limit the maximum penalty that can be imposed through a lottery.

22. The reason the interval must be short is that, if it were not, then this would give time for B and S to renegotiate the contract after S's announcement, to avoid the unwanted randomness.

on the realization of a subjective event, or an event whose probability distribution is private information to B and S. For example, B and S could construct a randomization device, *e.g.* a machine, whose structure is known only to B and S. However, this would seem to open the door to manipulation of the device by B or S. That is, there appears to be a trade-off: the more objective a lottery is, the less it can be manipulated, but the more it can be insured against; the less objective a lottery is, the less it can be insured against, but the more it can be manipulated.[23]

At this point, perhaps we ought to bring to a halt this rather protracted tennis match between the believers in commitment and the believers in no commitment. Let the match be declared an honourable draw. To repeat what we said in the Introduction: the degree of commitment is something about which reasonable people can disagree.

4 • Property Rights

We saw in Section 2 that the inability to specify trade in advance and/or the inability to commit not to renegotiate can lead to an inefficient outcome, in which S underinvests. In this section we consider whether some form of vertical integration can alleviate the situation. In particular, following the property rights literature (see Grossman and Hart (1986), Hart and Moore (1990) and Hart (1995)), we ask whether S would invest more if she owned B's (nonhuman) assets.

We will assume that, as owner, S has residual rights of control over B's assets, in the sense that S has access to B's downstream technology. What this means is that S can turn the special widget into final output that can be sold on the downstream market at price $\hat{v} < v$. Here $v - \hat{v}$ represents the contribution of B's (specialized) human capital; even though S owns B's nonhuman assets, S cannot capture this amount.

To see how downstream integration changes S's incentives, let us stick to the setup of Section 2.2 where B has all the bargaining power in renegotiation and where, in the limit $N = \infty$, it is optimal to have no contract at date 0. Consider first the case where $\hat{v} \geqq c_2 > c_1$. Then, at date 1, S can always threaten to produce without B and obtain $\hat{v} - c_1$ in state 1 or $\hat{v} - c_2$ in state 2. Of course, renegotiation will occur, since there is an extra $v - \hat{v}$ to be gained if B participates, but since B has all the bargaining power this does not affect S's payoff. Thus S chooses σ to maximize $\pi(\sigma)[\hat{v} - c_1] + (1 - \pi(\sigma))[\hat{v} - c_2] - \sigma$, which yields the same solution as (2.1), *i.e.* the first-best.

23. Yet another possibility, suggested to us by Andy Postlewaite, is that, instead of constructing a machine, the parties can induce endogenous (*i.e.* subjective) randomness by agreeing to play a game, with a publicly observed outcome, that has a mixed strategy equilibrium. The idea is that, although the players' strategies are not observable to outsiders, they are self-enforcing. See Barany (1992) for an analysis of this kind of idea. The advantage of a game over a machine is that a game is not manipulable by one party. However, the disadvantage of a game is that it may be difficult to arrange that the parties play the game simultaneously with S's "rejection" of B's offer. If there is even a short interval of time between S's "rejection" and the playing of the game, then the parties can (and will) renegotiate the contract during this interval, to avoid the randomness induced by the mixed strategies (see also footnote 22).

On the other hand, suppose $c_2 > \hat{v} > c_1$.[24] Then, S will obtain $\hat{v} - c_1$ in state 1 but nothing in state 2 (it is not worth her while producing without B's participation in this state). Hence S solves:

$$\underset{\sigma}{\text{maximize}}\ \pi(\sigma)[\hat{v} - c_1] - \sigma, \tag{4.1}$$

which yields the first order condition $\pi'(\sigma) = 1/(\hat{v} - c_1)$. Comparing this with the first order condition for (2.1), $\pi'(\sigma) = 1/(c_2 - c_1)$, we see that S will underinvest relative to the first-best, but will generally set $\sigma > 0$, *i.e.* downstream integration has a positive effect.

The conclusion so far is that a reallocation of property rights can help when contracts are incomplete. In fact, this is also the conclusion obtained in Maskin and Tirole (1999*b*). However, MT make two further observations. First, they point out that the parties can obtain an even better outcome by including a third party in their contract. Second, they note that there may be several property rights allocations which yield the same outcome, *i.e.* the theory lacks predictive power.

Although we have given arguments against the use of third parties in Section 3, it is worthwhile to consider MT's first point. Since the first-best can be achieved without a third party if $\hat{v} \geqq c_2$, the interesting case to study is where $c_1 < \hat{v} < c_2$. The contract MT propose is the following. B and S agree at date 0 that they will *jointly* own B's assets, *i.e.* that neither party has the right to use the assets without the other's permission. However, B has the option to sell his share in the joint venture to S at date 1 at price $0 < P < \hat{v} - c_1$; moreover, if B exercises his option, S must not only pay P to B but also a fine F to a third party.

To see how this works, suppose first that S's cost of producing the special widget at date 1 equals c_1: state 1 occurs. Then, if B does not exercise his option to sell, S obtains a zero payoff in the absence of renegotiation since S cannot use B's assets without B's permission. Since B gets all the gains from renegotiation, B's post-renegotiation payoff is $v - c_1$, and S's is zero. On the other hand, if B exercises his option to sell, S's payoff equals $\hat{v} - c_1 - P - F$, and B's payoff equals $v - \hat{v} + P$, since B obtains the full amount $v - \hat{v}$ in renegotiation. It follows that, since $P < \hat{v} - c_1$, B will choose not to exercise his option, and so S's payoff in state 1 is zero.

Consider next the case where S's cost of producing the special widget at date 1 equals c_2: state 2 occurs. Then, whether or not B exercises his option to sell, S will not use the assets without B's participation since $\hat{v} < c_2$. Hence B will obtain the full surplus $v - c_2$ in renegotiation and his payoff will equal $v - c_2$ if he does not exercise his option and $v - c_2 + P$ if he does. Since $P > 0$, B prefers to exercise his option, and so S's payoff in state 2 equals $-(P + F)$.

24. If $\hat{v} \leqq c_1$, downstream integration obviously has no effect, since S will not produce in either state without B's participation.

Notice that as S's cost of producing the special widget at date 1 rises from c_1 to c_2, the fall in her payoff can be made equal to $c_2 - c_1$ if the parties choose $F = c_2 - c_1 - P$. In other words, the appropriate choice of F induces S to make the first-best level of investment.

Given the discussion of Section 3, it is not altogether surprising that third parties can be used to enhance a simple property rights outcome (or for that matter to achieve the first-best).[25] However, we argued in Section 3 that third parties may be problematic because they are vulnerable to collusion. These considerations apply with equal force to the property rights model presented here. Thus, in practice B and S may find it difficult to use a third party in the way that MT suggest.

Even in the absence of third parties, MT's joint ownership scheme has interesting properties. In particular, set $F = 0$ (*i.e.* eliminate the third party). Then the difference between S's gross payoffs in states 1 and 2 equals P, which can be set as high as $\hat{v} - c_1$. Thus, the same outcome can be achieved with joint ownership, plus an option to sell, as by letting S have 100% ownership of the asset: in both cases, S will solve (4.1).

This is in fact MT's second point: there may be more than one allocation of property rights that sustains the second-best optimum.[26] However, this observation does not seem terribly damaging to the property rights approach. First, the theory is still capable of ruling out *most* allocations of property rights (for example, in the case where only S invests, ownership structures in which S (resp. B) owns B's assets with probability ρ (resp. $(1-\rho)$) are suboptimal for all $0 \leqq \rho < 1$). Second, MT's joint ownership contract seems very fragile. P must be chosen so that B has an incentive to exercise his option in state 2 but not in state 1. However, if, say, $\hat{v}$ is stochastic with support (c_1, c_2), then B will exercise his option to sell with positive probability in state 1, which will reduce S's incentives to invest. In contrast, the contract where S owns B's assets with probability 1 is robust to the introduction of uncertainty in $\hat{v}$. In fact, we conjecture that the indeterminacy in optimal ownership structure will be much reduced, and may disappear, in a world of uncertainty.

In concluding this section, we should point out that the above analysis falls some way short of providing a fully satisfactory foundation for a theory of ownership. The property rights approach takes the view that an owner has *residual* control rights. However, the above model does not distinguish between specific and residual rights, and in fact equates residual rights with complete control rights (in particular, the right to have access to B's downstream technology). A more satisfactory model would proceed by assuming that certain decisions need to be taken with respect to assets, some of which can be

25. MT show that their scheme generalizes to the case where B invests as well as S.

26. The reader may wonder whether the solution to (4.1) does indeed represent the second-best optimum in the two-party case where only S invests; or whether the parties could do better by having ownership of S's assets be a function of verifiable messages sent by the parties at date 1. The answer is that they cannot do any better (under the assumption that S's gross payoff in the absence of renegotiation with B, $\hat{v}$, is non-verifiable). This can be demonstrated using the results of Maskin and Moore (1999).

described in advance (the specific control rights), but others of which cannot. (These nonspecifiable decisions are similar to the characteristics of the widget that cannot be described in advance in Section 2, Case *ND*.) Suppose that there is a large number of hard-to-describe uses of the assets, only one of which, say, will be relevant in a particular state of nature; and the states of nature are equally likely. Then it seems probable that an analysis along the lines of Section 2 will lead to the conclusion that the best the parties can do is to allocate residual control rights over assets, *i.e.* ownership rights. However, a formal demonstration of this must await further work.

5 Interpreting Contractual Incompleteness

A question that is sometimes asked about incomplete contracting models is: are the optimal contracts really incomplete? To put it another way, what *is* an incomplete contract?[27]

Some contracts are manifestly incomplete in the sense that they leave something out or are ambiguous.[28] For example, consider a contract that says that S must supply B with a widget on February 29, 1998, even though no such date exists. Or, to give a deeper example, consider a specific performance contract which says that S must supply B with a particular widget, but which does not indicate the damages if performance turns out to be impossible. Incompleteness like this is very common in reality, but unfortunately it is very hard to model. It would seem necessary to assume that the parties are boundedly rational in the sense that they do not foresee even relatively obvious events. In contrast, in this paper, we have assumed that the parties are constrained in contracting only by the fact that complicated states of nature cannot be verified.[29]

The contracts that we have derived in this paper are therefore not incomplete in the above sense. In particular, the parties' obligations are fully specified in all circumstances. This is true even of the null contract that was (approximately) optimal in Proposition 2. The null contract is complete in that it is absolutely clear what everybody's obligations are: nobody has any!

However, there is another sense in which one can say that a contract is incomplete: it is incomplete if the parties would like to add contingent clauses, but are prevented from doing so by the fact that the state of nature cannot be verified (or because states are too expensive to describe *ex ante*).[30] For example, a contract that says that S must supply X widgets to B at a fixed price (and pay huge damages if

27. For illuminating discussions of this question, see Ayres and Gertner (1992) and Tirole (1998).

28. Ayres and Gertner (1992) call such contracts "obligationally incomplete".

29. Actually, it is not entirely clear that parties who write obligationally incomplete contracts are boundedly rational. Douglas Baird has suggested that it may be rational for parties to write contracts with missing provisions or ambiguities, to the extent that they anticipate that the courts will fill in the gaps or remove the ambiguities. Viewed this way, obligationally incomplete contracts and the "insufficiently state contingent" contracts described below are not fundamentally different.

30. Ayres and Gertner (1992) refer to such contracts as "insufficiently state contingent".

she does not supply) is incomplete if the parties would really have liked to make the number of widgets contingent on the state.

Viewed in this way, the optimal contract in Proposition 2 (under the noncommitment assumption) — that is, no contract — is incomplete. It is true that the parties' obligations are fully specified and that renegotiation at date 1 always "completes" the contract (*i.e.* makes it contingent). However, the way the contract is completed is not optimal from an *ex ante* perspective. The parties would like to ensure that the price of the special widget is independent of S's cost, but, as we have seen, this may not be compatible with their *ex post* incentive constraints.

Of course, at some level this is all a matter of semantics — one could just as well call the contracts in Section 2 "optimal complete contracts subject to commitment and incentive constraints (and possibly also describability constraints)". However, we believe that there is a qualitative difference between the contracts of Section 2 and the complete or comprehensive contracts studied in the traditional mechanism design literature (including that based on asymmetric information or moral hazard) — not least because the contracts of this paper provide the beginnings of a foundation for a theory of ownership or property rights — and thus it is reasonable to have a different term for them.

Appendix

In this Appendix we generalize Proposition 2 to the case where both parties make investments at date $1/2$: B invests β, costing $C^b(\beta)$; and S invests σ, costing $C^s(\sigma)$. Now β and σ may be multidimensional. Also, we allow for any division of surplus in the date 1 bargaining. Specifically, we suppose that, if the outcome of the contractually-specified mechanism is inefficient, then with probability λ, S makes a take-it-or-leave-it offer to B, and with probability $1-\lambda$, B makes a take-it-or-leave-it offer to S.

As in the text, there are N widgets, numbered $1, \ldots, N$, which can be described at date 0 (we are in Case D).[31] In each state of nature at date 1, one of these widgets is special, yielding value v to B and costing S c to produce. The stochastic mapping from (β, σ) to (v, c) is arbitrary, except that we suppose v and c are always ranked and bounded: there exist $\bar{v} < \infty$ and $\underline{c} \geqq 0$ such that $\bar{v} \geqq v \geqq c \geqq \underline{c}$ with probability 1.[32] The fact that the mapping from (β, σ) to (v, c) is arbitrary means that we can allow for any degree of correlation between v and c, and also for externalities where B's investment β affects S's cost c, or where S's investment σ affects B's value v.

31. As in the corollary to Proposition 2, our result holds *a fortiori* if the N widgets cannot be described in advance (Case ND).

32. The restriction $v \geqq c$ is made so that, at worst, the special widget is like a generic widget for which value equals cost (see below). Our results still hold if the value of a widget (special or generic) to B is strictly less than the cost to S. In such a case, the parties will typically renegotiate in order to avoid inefficient trade.

The remaining $N-1$ widgets are generic, and, for $n = 1, \ldots, N-1$, have cost $g_n = \underline{c} + (n/N)(\bar{v} - \underline{c})$. To simplify matters, we now assume that the value of each of these special widgets equals its cost.[33]

We assume that there is complete symmetry among the widgets at date 0, in the sense that each widget is equally likely to be the special widget or to be one of the $N-1$ generic widgets. (This uniform distribution over permutations is unaffected by β and σ.)

At date 1, both B and S observe the state: the realized permutation of the N widgets, and the cost c to S and the value v to B of the special widget. However, no-one else observes the state. In other words, the state is observable (to the two parties) but not verifiable (to outsiders, such as the courts).

As a preliminary exercise, suppose a contractual mechanism specifies that some widget W is traded. If the state of nature is such that, first, W is a generic widget with cost/value g_n, and, second, the special widget has cost c to S and value v to B, then, following renegotiation, S's final payoff will be $-g_n + \lambda(v-c)$, and B's final payoff will be $g_n + (1-\lambda)(v-c)$. (These payoffs are gross of any transfer that the mechanism might specify.) Equally, if the mechanism specifies that there is no trade, then, following renegotiation, S's final payoff will be $\lambda(v-c)$, and B's final payoff will be $(1-\lambda)(v-c)$.

To provide a benchmark for Proposition 2*, let β^0 and σ^0 denote the equilibrium investment levels at date $1/2$ if no contract were written at date 0 and the terms of trade were bargained from scratch at date 1 — in other words, if the "null contract" were in place. Under the null contract, for a given realization of c and v, the trade price equals $(1-\lambda)c + \lambda v$, S's payoff equals $\lambda(v-c)$, and B's payoff equals $(1-\lambda)(v-c)$. So β^0 and σ^0 jointly solve

$$\begin{aligned} \beta^0 &= \arg\max_{\beta} E[(1-\lambda)(v-c) - C^b(\beta) \mid \beta, \sigma^0], \\ \sigma^0 &= \arg\max_{\sigma} E[\lambda(v-c) - C^s(\sigma) \mid \beta^0, \sigma], \end{aligned} \qquad \text{(A.1)}$$

where $E[\cdot \mid \beta, \sigma]$ denotes the expectation operator with respect to the date 1 joint distribution of c and v conditional on investments β and σ having been made at date $1/2$. We assume that the solution (β^0, σ^0) to (A.1) is unique.

Proposition 2*. *Suppose Case D holds. If the parties cannot commit not to renegotiate, then, irrespective of the contract, as $N \to \infty$ their investments β and σ approach the values β^0 and σ^0 given by* (A.1). *That is, in the limit, contracts cannot make any difference to expected total surplus, and the parties may as well use the null contract.*

33. As in Section 2, the exact specification of these costs/values is not important. What matters is that as the number of widgets, N, increases, no large "gaps" in cost or value remain between $\underline{c}$ and $\bar{v}$. (In fact, if one knows the value of λ, this range can be reduced; but, by "covering" the full range from $\underline{c}$ to $\bar{v}$, we ensure that Proposition 2* below holds for all λ.) Also, it makes no difference if there are other generic widgets whose costs/values lie outside this range.

Proof. Take any abstract mechanism M. A state is defined by the permutation τ, say, of the widgets, and the cost c to S and value v to B of the special widget. In state (c, v, τ), let the equilibrium strategies of M for B and S be $\mu^b(c, v, \tau)$ and $\mu^s(c, v, \tau)$. And, following any renegotiation, let $p(c, v, \tau)$ denote the overall price that B pays S for delivery of the special widget: $p(c, v, \tau)$ equals any transfer specified in the mechanism *plus* any amount agreed by the parties during renegotiation. In other words, B's and S's final equilibrium payoffs are respectively $v - p(c, v, \tau)$ and $p(c, v, \tau) - c$.

Let $P(c, v)$ denote the expected value of $p(c, v, \tau)$ taken over all permutations τ (which are equally probable).

Without loss of generality, we may suppose that τ is such that widget 1 is the special widget, and that widgets $2, \ldots, N$ are generic widgets costing $\underline{c} + (1/N)(\bar{v} - \underline{c}), \ldots, \underline{c} + ((N-1)/N)(\bar{v} - \underline{c})$ respectively.

Now consider another state (c^*, v^*, τ^*), where τ^* is a rotation of τ: widgets $1, \ldots, N-1$ are generic widgets costing $\underline{c} + (1/N)(\bar{v} - \underline{c}), \ldots, \underline{c} + ((N-1)/N)(\bar{v} - \underline{c})$ respectively, and widget N is the special widget. Without loss of generality, we suppose that

$$(1 - \lambda)(c^* - c) + \lambda(v^* - v) \geqq 0. \qquad \text{(A.2)}$$

The proof of Proposition 2* proceeds via two lemmas, which together pin down the size of the gap between the expected prices, $P(c^*, v^*) - P(c, v)$. The first lemma provides a lower bound.

Lemma 1. $P(c^*, v^*) - P(c, v) \geqq (1 - \lambda)(c^* - c) + \lambda(v^* - v) - (1/N)(\bar{v} - \underline{c})$.

Proof of Lemma 1. Consider the outcome of the mechanism M if B plays strategy $\mu^b(c^*, v^*, \tau^*)$ and S plays strategy $\mu^s(c, v, \tau)$. Suppose M specifies: B pays S an amount q: widget $n = 1, \ldots, N$ is traded with probability $\alpha_n \geqq 0$: and there is no trade with probability $1 - (\alpha_1 + \cdots + \alpha_N) \geqq 0$. (As both parties are risk neutral, there is no loss of generality in not having the transfer q depend on which widget — if any — the mechanism specifies is traded.)

There are two incentive constraints that $q, \alpha_1, \ldots, \alpha_N$ must satisfy. First, in state (c^*, v^*, τ^*), S must not have an incentive to deviate to $\mu^s(c, v, \tau)$. Second, in state (c, v, τ), B must not have an incentive to deviate to $\mu^b(c^*, v^*, \tau^*)$.

Suppose strategy pair $\mu^b(c^*, v^*, \tau^*)$, $\mu^s(c, v, \tau)$ is played. The contractually-specified outcome is typically inefficient, and will be renegotiated: when the outcome of the lottery $(\alpha_1, \ldots, \alpha_N)$ specifies either that a generic widget is traded, or that there is no trade, the parties must bargain in order to exploit the gains from trading the special widget. The final payoffs depend on the state. In state

(c^*, v^*, τ^*), following the play of strategy pair $\mu^b(c^*, v^*, \tau^*)$, $\mu^s(c, v, \tau)$, S's final payoff is

$$q + \alpha_1\left(-\underline{c} - \frac{1}{N}(\bar{v} - \underline{c}) + \lambda(v^* - c^*)\right) + \cdots$$
$$+ \alpha_{N-1}\left(-\underline{c} - \frac{N-1}{N}(\bar{v} - \underline{c}) + \lambda(v^* - c^*)\right)$$
$$+ \alpha_N(-c^*) + (1 - \alpha_1 - \ldots - \alpha_N)(\lambda(v^* - c^*)),$$

which, according to the first incentive constraint, cannot be *more* than what she gets in equilibrium, $p(c^*, v^*, \tau^*) - c^*$. And in state (c, v, τ), following the play of strategy pair $\mu^b(c^*, v^*, \tau^*)$, $\mu^s(c, v, \tau)$, S's final payoff is

$$q + \alpha_1(-c) + \alpha_2\left(-\underline{c} - \frac{1}{N}(\bar{v} - \underline{c}) + \lambda(v - c)\right) + \cdots$$
$$+ \alpha_N\left(-\underline{c} - \frac{N-1}{N}(\bar{v} - \underline{c}) + \lambda(v - c)\right)$$
$$+ (1 - \alpha_1 - \cdots - \alpha_N)(\lambda(v - c)),$$

which, according to the second incentive constraint, cannot be *less* than what she gets in equilibrium, $p(c, v, \tau) - c$, since if S were worse off B would be better off (all final payoffs lie along the Pareto frontier).

Combining these two constraints, we have

$$p(c^*, v^*, \tau^*) - p(c, v, \tau)$$
$$- (1 - \lambda)(c^* - c) - \lambda(v^* - v) + \frac{1}{N}(\bar{v} - \underline{c})$$
$$\geqq \alpha_1(c - \underline{c} + \lambda(v - c)) + \alpha_N(\bar{v} - v^* + (1 - \lambda)(v^* - c^*))$$
$$+ (1 - \alpha_1 - \cdots - \alpha_N)\left(\frac{1}{N}(\bar{v} - \underline{c})\right),$$

which is nonnegative, given that $\bar{v} \geqq v^* \geqq c^* \geqq \underline{c}$ and $\bar{v} \geqq v \geqq c \geqq \underline{c}$.

Since this lower bound applies for any permutation τ (and associated rotation τ^*), we can take expectations across permutations to deduce that

$$P(c^*, v^*) - P(c, v) \geqq (1 - \lambda)(c^* - c) + \lambda(v^* - v) - \frac{1}{N}(\bar{v} - \underline{c}).$$

This proves Lemma 1. ■

The second lemma provides an upper bound for the gap between the expected prices $P(c^*, v^*) - P(c, v)$.

Lemma 2. $P(c^*, v^*) - P(c, v) \geqq (1 - \lambda)(c^* - c) + \lambda(v^* - v)$.

Proof of Lemma 2. Consider the outcome of the mechanism M if B plays strategy $\mu^b(c, v, \tau)$ and S plays strategy $\mu^s(c^*, v^*, \tau)$. (Note that, in contrast to the proof of Lemma 1, the selected states here differ only in the costs and values of the special widget; in both states, the permutation of the widgets is τ. And recall that the choice of τ is without loss of generality.) Suppose M specifies: B pays S an amount $\hat{q}$; widget $n = 1, \ldots, N$ is traded with probability $\hat{\alpha}_n \geqq 0$; and there is no trade with probability $1 - (\hat{\alpha}_1 + \cdots + \hat{\alpha}_N) \geqq 0$.

There are two incentive constraints that $\hat{q}, \hat{\alpha}_1, \ldots, \hat{\alpha}_N$ must satisfy. First, in state (c, v, τ), S must not have an incentive to deviate to $\mu^s(c^*, v^*, \tau)$. Second, in state (c^*, v^*, τ), B must not have an incentive to deviate to $\mu^b(c, v, \tau)$.

Suppose strategy pair $\mu^b(c, v, \tau)$, $\mu^s(c^*, v^*, \tau)$ *is* played. The contractually-specified outcome is typically inefficient, and will be renegotiated: when the outcome of the lottery $(\hat{\alpha}_1, \ldots, \hat{\alpha}_N)$ specifies either that a generic widget is traded, or that there is no trade, the parties must bargain in order to exploit the gains from trading the special widget. The final payoffs depend on the state. In state (c, v, τ), following the play of the strategy pair $\mu^b(c, v, \tau)$, $\mu^s(c^*, v^*, \tau)$, S's final payoff is

$$\hat{q} + \hat{\alpha}_1(-c) + \hat{\alpha}_2\Big(-\underline{c} - \frac{1}{N}(\bar{v} - \underline{c}) + \lambda(v - c)\Big) + \cdots$$
$$+ \hat{\alpha}_N\Big(-\underline{c} - \frac{N-1}{N}(\bar{v} - \underline{c}) + \lambda(v - c)\Big)$$
$$+ (1 - \hat{\alpha}_1 - \cdots - \hat{\alpha}_N)(\lambda(v - c)),$$

which, according to the first incentive constraint, cannot be *more* than what she gets in equilibrium, $p(c, v, \tau) - c$. And in state (c^*, v^*, τ), following the play of strategy pair $\mu^b(c, v, \tau)$, $\mu^s(c^*, v^*, \tau)$, S's final payoff is

$$\hat{q} + \hat{\alpha}_1(-c^*) + \hat{\alpha}_2\Big(-\underline{c} - \frac{1}{N}(\bar{v} - \underline{c}) + \lambda(v^* - c^*)\Big) + \cdots$$
$$+ \hat{\alpha}_N\Big(-\underline{c} - \frac{N-1}{N}(\bar{v} - \underline{c}) + \lambda(v^* - c^*)\Big)$$
$$+ (1 - \hat{\alpha}_1 - \cdots - \hat{\alpha}_N)(\lambda(v^* - c^*)),$$

which, according to the second incentive constraint, cannot be *less* than what she gets in equilibrium, $p(c^*, v^*, \tau) - c^*$, since if S were worse off B would be better off.

Combining these two constraints, we have

$$p(c^*, v^*, \tau) - p(c, v, \tau) - (1-\lambda)(c^* - c) - \lambda(v^* - v)$$
$$\leqq -\hat{\alpha}_1((1-\lambda)(c^* - c) + \lambda(v^* - v)),$$

which is nonpositive by (A.2).

Since this upper bound applies for any permutation τ, we can take expectations across permutations to deduce that

$$P(c^*, v^*) - P(c, v) \leqq (1-\lambda)(c^* - c) + \lambda(v^* - v).$$

This proves Lemma 2. ■

Together, Lemma 1 and Lemma 2 show that as $N \to \infty$, the gap between $P(c^*, v^*)$ and $P(c, v)$ approaches $(1-\lambda)(c^* - c) + \lambda(v^* - v)$, whatever the contractually-specified mechanism. But this means that, up to an additive constant, the expected price paid by B to S is the same as if the parties bargained from scratch at date 1 — as if the null contract were in place. This in turn means that B and S will make equilibrium investments β^0 and σ^0 at date $1/2$. Proposition 2* is proved. ■

Acknowledgements. We are grateful to Douglas Baird, Martin Hellwig, Eric Maskin, Andy Postlewaite, Ilya Segal, and Jean Tirole for helpful discussions on this topic. We also thank Philippe Aghion, Patrick Bolton, Malcolm Baker, V. Bhaskar, Mathias Dewatripont, Bentley MacLeod, Leeat Yariv, and an anonymous referee for comments on an earlier draft. We acknowledge financial support from the U.S. National Science Foundation, the Leverhulme Trust, the LSE Financial Markets Group, and the Suntory Toyota International Centre for Economics and Related Disciplines at the LSE.

REFERENCES

[1] Ayres, I. and Gertner, R. (1992), "Strategic Contractual Inefficiency and the Optimal Choice of Legal Rules", *The Yale Law Journal*, **101**, 729-773.

[2] Barany, I. (1992), "Fair Distribution Protocols or How the Players Replace Fortune", *Mathematics of Operations Research*, **17**, 327-340.

[3] Che, Y.-K. and Hausch, D. (1998), "Cooperative Investments and the Value of Contracting", *American Economic Review* (forthcoming).

[4] Grossman, S. and Hart, O. (1986), "The Costs and Benefits of Ownership: A Theory of Vertical and Lateral Integration", *Journal of Political Economy*, **94**, 691-719.

[5] Hart, O. (1995) *Firms, Contracts, and Financial Structure* (Oxford: Oxford University Press).

[6] Hart, O. and Moore, J. (1990), "Property Rights and the Nature of the Firm", *Journal of Political Economy*, **98**, 1119-1158.

[7] Maskin, E. and Moore, J. (1999), "Implementation and Renegotiation", *Review of Economic Studies*, **66**, 39-56.

[8] Maskin, E. and Tirole, J. (1999*a*), "Unforeseen Contingencies and Incomplete Contracts", *Review of Economic Studies*, **66**, 83-114.

[9] Maskin, E. and Tirole, J. (1999*b*), "Two Remarks on the Property-Rights Literature", *Review of Economic Studies*, **66**, 139-149.

[10] Moore, J. (1992), "Implementation in Environments with Complete Information", in J. J. Laffont (ed.), *Advances in Economic Theory* (Cambridge: Cambridge University Press).

[11] Segal, I. (1995), "Essays on Commitment, Renegotiation, and Incompleteness of Contracts" (Ph.D. dissertation, Harvard University).

[12] Segal, I. (1999), "Complexity and Renegotiation: A Foundation for Incomplete Contracts", *Review of Economic Studies*, **66**, 57-82.

[13] Tirole, J. (1998), "Incomplete Contracts: Where Do We Stand?" (Mimeo, Institut d'Economie Industrielle, Toulouse).

[14] Williamson, O. (1975) *Markets and Hierarchies: Analysis and Antitrust Implications* (New York: Free Press).

5

Courts, Contracts, and Interference

Patrick Legros
Andrew F. Newman

Abstract

This paper shows that the possibility of interference in court proceedings, or more generally jamming other agents' messages, has significant consequences for the form of optimal contracts and the flexibility of decisions that can be made inside firms. Our approach offers a new view of authority, basing it on the ability of parties to have their say in court. Interference gives authority a role in worlds where it is traditionally absent in contract theory, like simple employment relationships without specific investments.

1 Introduction

A recurrent question raised in response to the incomplete contracting literature is why mechanisms like authority and ownership should be used in place of "message games". In many economic environments, particularly those in which contracting parties have symmetric information, message games would be more efficient. At the same time, many researchers acknowledge the empirical dubiousness of such message games.

Avoiding the unpleasant territory between theoretical unfoundedness and empirical irrelevance calls for an account of what limits the set of feasible mechanisms. Recently, some authors have begun to focus on the role of the court as enforcer of contracts and to ask how limitations on this form of enforcement might in turn generate limits to contracting.

Court enforcement has several possible sources of imperfection. First, it is voluntary: if both parties to a contract decide not to call on the court, or if they decide afterward to ignore the court's decision

(Anderlini *et al.*, 2001), the contract is not enforced. In other words, commitment to the contract is limited by renegotiation.

Second, the court itself may have a commitment problem: judges and juries may be corruptible, subject to bribes or threats by the parties in dispute (Bond, 2001). While doubtless an important issue, especially in developing countries, it strains credulity that, for instance, corruptible judges are at bottom the source of the widespread use of such "incomplete contracts" as the employment relation.

Third, there may be limits to the amount of information the court can extract. This is certainly plausible when the contracting parties have asymmetric information. But as we suggested, in the symmetric information environments that are the favorite haunt of incomplete contracting models, it is often "easy" to extract the common information with message games (*e.g.* Maskin, 2002).

In Legros and Newman (1999), we develop a theory of *interference* in mechanism design based on a kind of imperfection in the technology of communication. We depart from standard mechanism design theory by admitting the possibility that an agent might jam messages sent by other agents and for agents to attempt to secure (at a cost) their communication channels from such jamming.

It is natural to think of a court proceeding as a mechanism: an exchange of messages takes place in the form of testimony by experts and witnesses along with various pieces of "hard" evidence; these are aggregated into a decision by the judge (or jury) and an allocation is implemented. We think of this aggregation process as subject to manipulation: rhetorical ploys, outright forgery, ambiguous evidence and cognitive limitations all contribute to the possibility of interference.[1] The quality of one's lawyer, as well as the resources spent on record keeping, are likely to have considerable influence on what the judge "hears".

In this paper, we illustrate this theory in a very simple contracting environment. The parties to a contract can influence the court proceeding not only by what they announce (as in standard mechanism design) but by influencing the message the judge receives from their opponent. We think of this as dependent on the quality of one's lawyer, which is determined by an endogenous investment: if he is good, and your opponent's is bad, then your message will be heard, and your opponent's message will be unheard.

This simple model yields a number of insights. When good lawyers are expensive or when the conflicts of interest are small, first-best contracting will be achieved. Otherwise, optimal contracts assume forms that fall short of the first-best. They may be "flat", with

1. For a discussion of some aspects of the "technology" of debate, see Glazer and Rubinstein (2001).

less variation in production decisions than the first-best would require. In addition, the model gives a new interpretation to the idea of *authority*: one party may invest in good lawyers, so that only his voice is heard, and decisions then follow his interests. In our example, the one who invests is the one whose interests are more consonant with total welfare, and the decision made is the same as the first-best. This view of authority is distinct, though complementary to the standard ones which identify it with the right to decide (Grossman and Hart, 1986) or being better informed (Aghion and Tirole, 1997).

A feature of this approach is that we introduce an imperfection in the technology of communication, but otherwise maintain the usual commitment assumptions of static mechanism design. Moreover, authority arises even in environments that are simpler than the usual ones in which it is studied. In particular, authority may play a role in organizations even if there are no hold up problems, relationship specific investments, sequential decisions, or renegotiation.

2 • A Model

Consider the following simple problem of decision-making in a firm. The value of the firm is a function of the worker's (observable) action and of a state of the world that is known to the worker and to the employer but not to outside parties. The initial "contract" specifies a wage w paid to the worker and a list of actions that might be required from the worker; this list should be interpreted as the set of state contingent decisions.[2] If decision $a \in \mathbb{R}_+$ is chosen in state θ, payoffs are

$$V(a, \theta) = y - w - \frac{a^2}{2} + \alpha\theta a \quad \text{for the employer,}$$

$$U(a) = w - \beta a \quad \text{for the worker.}$$

Assuming no wealth effects, the problem for the employer and the worker is to find state contingent decisions that maximize the total expected surplus. To simplify again, assume that the state can take one of two values, $\theta \in \{0, 1\}$, with $Pr(\theta = 0) = 1 - \pi$. The first-best decision in state θ maximizes $V(a, \theta) + U(a)$ for each θ; simple computations lead to

$$a^{FB}(0) = 0, \quad a^{FB}(1) = \alpha - \beta,$$

$$W^{FB} = y + \pi \frac{(\alpha - \beta)^2}{2}. \tag{1}$$

2. For simplicity, we assume that it is not possible to write monetary contracts as a function of the action. Allowing such contracts would not eliminate the fundamental conflict of interest between the two parties, and the issues we discuss here would remain.

Two different approaches to this problem lead to the conclusion that the first-best allocation can be implemented. In the *mechanism design* approach each player is asked to reveal the state of the world. If their messages agree, the first-best decision corresponding to the state they announce is imposed by the center or court. If they disagree, then a severe punishment is imposed. Under this scheme, it is a Nash equilibrium to truthfully reveal the state, and the first-best allocation results (we ignore the problem of multiplicity of equilibria in this paper).

In the *incomplete contract* approach, one focuses on instruments such as authority. Note that the employer prefers $a^{FB}(0)$ to $a^{FB}(1)$ in state $\theta = 0$, and prefers $a^{FB}(1)$ to $a^{FB}(0)$ in state $\theta = 1$.[3] Hence a contract which limits action choices to $\{a^{FB}(0), a^{FB}(1)\}$ and gives the employer "authority" to choose between them will replicate the first-best decision rule. The worker, on the other hand, has the same preferences over these actions as the employer in state $\theta = 0$ but has the reverse preference in state $\theta = 1$. Hence, the worker would like to disobey the employer in state $\theta = 1$ and do $a^{FB}(0)$ instead of $a^{FB}(1)$.

How does authority avoid such disobedience? One possibility is to write in the contract that "if the employer tells the worker to do d but the worker decides to do $d' \neq d$, then the worker has to pay a penalty". Such a clause requires that the order given by the employer to the worker is verifiable in court, *e.g.*, that the employer keeps track of his orders. Generally, whether or not the employer has collected evidence (hard or soft), his authority relies on his ability to convince the court to compel the worker to obey his orders.[4] If he can always do this, the worker will obey because he does not expect a better outcome by going to court.

Indeed, one could simply let the judge ask the employer what he told the worker to do and enforce this order. As long as the employer can communicate perfectly with the judge, such a decision rule can enforce any outcome the employer desires. The employer has authority, not because this authority is "given" by the contract but because the employer has "voice" in court *and* that the judge will go along with what he says in court.

But in fact court proceedings are not perfect. Communication between the judge (and/or the jury) and the parties is subject to noise, misinterpretation, and interference. The quality of each side's lawyer may affect the outcome as much as the facts of the case. Moreover, the law itself can make it difficult for some parties to have effective voice in courts (*e.g.*, by putting the burden of proof on one party). In short, justice does not just happen, it is manufactured, and the technology with which it is done is an imperfect one.

3. $V(a, 1)$ is maximized at $a = \alpha$, below which (in particular, at $a^{FB}(1)$) it is increasing.

4. We assume that there is no direct cost of going to court.

This point applies with equal force whatever the approach one takes to thinking about contracting. It will impose limits to what can be accomplished via the design of mechanisms. But it also increases the cost of enforcing authority, and it may provide natural restrictions on its scope.

2.1 Interference

We introduce an imperfection in court proceedings by allowing each party's lawyer to "jam" the message that is sent by the other party's lawyer to the judge.[5] Lawyers come in two varieties: good and bad. A bad lawyer can always be interfered with, either by a bad lawyer or by a good lawyer. A good lawyer cannot be interfered with. "Good" refers to the ability to give an argument that cannot be nullified by a counter-argument. Bad lawyers come for free in this world; good lawyers cost $c \geq 0$. This model resembles the form of court proceedings in "common law" countries wherein advocates compete for the judge's (or jury's) attention.[6]

Formally, each lawyer can send an argument and a counter-argument. Let m_P be the argument and n_P be the counter-argument sent by the lawyer of the employer; let m_A be the counter-argument and n_A the argument of the lawyer of the worker. If both lawyers are good, the judge will hear their arguments, i.e., will hear (m_P, n_A); if the employer's lawyer is good while the worker's lawyer is bad, the judge will hear (m_P, n_P). Hence, the benefit of having a good lawyer when the other lawyer is bad is that one can effectively be the only one to communicate with the judge. Note that if both lawyers are bad, the judge will hear the counter-arguments only, i.e., (m_A, n_P); this case is similar to the case where both lawyers are good: each lawyer has effectively a way to transmit a message to the judge.

This is similar to the standard mechanism design approach: each lawyer can send arguments to the judge, m for the employer's lawyer and n for the worker's lawyer. With a perfect communication technology, the judge would hear (m, n) and, knowing that the two parties have common information, mechanism design tells us that it is simple for a judge to extract this common information.[7] In our case, each lawyer can try to interfere, to replace the message of the other lawyer by his own; whether or not this interference succeeds is a function of the quality of the other lawyer.

This interference technology could be interpreted literally: legal procedures often allow the judge to "strike" from the record some arguments if the other party has valid objections; evidence might be tampered with by the other party, either physically (forgery)

5. See Legros and Newman (1999) for a general analysis of such interference.
6. For the benefits of an advocacy regime see Dewatripont and Tirole (1999).
7. Typically, the judge can threaten to enforce a "bad" outcome for both parties if they do not agree on the state of the world. However, there may be other equilibria which do not implement this outcome; we ignore this issue here.

or by having outside experts re-interpreting the meaning of the evidence. More broadly, though, the interference technology also captures the "bounded rationality" of the judge: hearing the rhetorical arguments of both parties' lawyers, the judge makes up his mind about the meaning of the message of each lawyer, perhaps forgetting in the process the sequence of messages sent by each party.

While neither the entrepreneur nor the worker wants to be interfered with in court, this comes at a cost, and unless the stakes built into the contract and the anticipation of the court outcome are important enough, they may decide not to invest in good quality lawyers. Since there is an interplay between contract stakes and incentives to invest, we make this an integral part of the model.

The natural model that should be considered is one where the decision to go to court is endogenous; doing so weakens the commitment to play the court mechanism. However, with private investments in lawyers, a number of issues involving signalling one's investment arise that distract from the issue of interference per se.

Thus to remain as close to the standard framework as possible, and to focus on what interference alone implies for limitations on mechanisms, we assume here that the worker and the entrepreneur go to court automatically.[8]

2.2 A Revelation Principle

The timing of the model is as follows:

1. Each party decides — privately — to invest at cost c in good quality lawyers (the *ex ante* nature of the investment means these lawyers are on retainer) or in organizational structures that will facilitate the presentation of persuasive evidence once in court.
2. The state θ is realized.
3. Parties go to court and play the mechanism $(M, N, g : M \times N \to \mathbb{R}_+ \cup \{bad\})$, where "*bad*" is a decision that the court can impose on the parties and that bring each of them a payoff of zero, M is the set of messages of the entrepreneur's lawyer and N is the set of messages of the worker's lawyer.

An equilibrium in pure strategies is then *an investment strategy* $I_i \in \{0, c\}$ at the first stage and a *message sending strategy* $\sigma_i(\theta, I_i) = (m_i, n_i)$ in court, where (θ, I_i) is the information set of agent i. As explained before, each lawyer will send two messages: an

8. If there were no possibility of interference and court itself is costless, then the outcome is the same whether or not the parties are committed to go to court.

argument (m_p for the entrepreneur, n_A for the worker) and will try to interfere with the other lawyer's argument by sending a counter-argument (n_P for the entrepreneur, m_A for the worker). The messages eventually received by the judge depend on the initial investments. Precisely, if the entrepreneur sends (m_P, n_P) and the worker sends (m_A, n_A), the judge receives

$$\begin{array}{ll} (m_P, n_P) & \text{if } I_P = c\,,\ I_A = 0\,, \\ (m_P, n_A) & \text{if } I_P = c\,,\ I_A = c\,, \\ (m_A, n_A) & \text{if } I_P = 0\,,\ I_A = c\,, \\ (m_A, n_P) & \text{if } I_P = 0\,,\ I_A = 0\,. \end{array}$$

We show in Legros and Newman (1999) that it is possible to appeal to a revelation principle in order to characterize the set of equilibrium allocations. Since with interference, the judge may confound the sources of the messages m and n, the direct revelation mechanism asks each lawyer to send a message (θ, i), where θ is the state and $i \in \{P, A\}$ is the identity of the party's lawyer and specifies an outcome $h((0, i), (\phi, j)) \in \mathbb{R}_+ \cup \{bad\}$. The revelation principle is then: consider a mechanism $(M, N, g : M \times N \rightarrow \mathbb{R}_+ \cup \{bad\})$ together with equilibrium investments (I_P, I_A) and equilibrium message sending strategies $(\sigma_P(\theta, I_P), \sigma_A(\theta, I_A))$; there is a direct revelation game

$$(\{0, 1\} \times \{P, A\}, \{0, 1\} \times \{P, A\}, h : (\{0, 1\} \times \{P, A\})^2 \rightarrow \mathbb{R}_+ \cup \{bad\})$$

such that (I_P, I_A) are equilibrium investment levels and both P and A use equilibrium message sending strategies that reveal the state and their identity, i.e., $\sigma_i(\theta, I_i) = ((\theta, i), (\theta, i))$ for $i = P, A$, that generates the same equilibrium allocations as in the initial mechanism.

3 The First-Best

In the first-best, no party should invest in good quality lawyer. Our revelation principle implies that in state θ, P will make argument (θ, P) and a counter-argument (θ, P), A will make argument (θ, A) and a counter-argument (θ, A) and moreover neither P nor A wants to invest in a good quality lawyer and then send other messages.

Assume first that neither P nor A invests and that each lawyer is truthful (in our sense). The judge will hear the counter-argument (θ, P) of P and the counter-argument (θ, A) of A. The outcome will then be $h((\theta, A), (\theta, P))$. Since we must have the first-best decisions we need

$$h((0, A), (0, P)) = 0,$$
$$h((1, A), (1, P)) = \alpha - \beta. \quad (2)$$

The easiest way to insure incentive compatibility is to have

$$h((\theta, i), (\phi, j)) = bad \text{ whenever } \theta \neq \phi, \text{ or } ij \neq AP. \quad (3)$$

For then, as long as w and $y - w$ are large enough (which we will assume from now on), deviating from equilibrium messages generates a payoff of zero. Because P's preferences are consonant with the first-best, he has no reason to invest in a good lawyer. This is not the case for A however. Assume that A spends c for a good lawyer. The judge will hear the argument and counter-arguments of A, and A can select the decision $a = 0$ in any state of the world by using the argument $(0, P)$ and the counter-argument $(0, A)$ (note that he lies twice: in his argument since $(0, P) \neq (\theta, A)$ and in his counter-argument since $(0, A) \neq (1, A)$ in the high state). By doing so, he saves on effort and his *ex ante* utility is

$$w - c.$$

If A does not invest in a good lawyer, his *ex ante* utility is

$$w - \pi\beta(\alpha - \beta).$$

Therefore,

Proposition 1. *The first-best is implementable if and only if* $c \geq \pi\beta(\alpha - \beta)$.

This is quite sensible; interfering is not worth the expense when the stakes in the contract are smaller than the cost of investment, that is

- when high-quality lawyers are expensive;
- when the expected marginal cost of effort $\pi\beta$ is small;
- when the conflict of interests (as measured by $(\alpha - \beta)$) is small.

4 Second-Best and Authority

4.1 Which Allocations are Consistent with $q = (0, 0)$ when $c < \pi\beta(\alpha - \beta)$?

From the previous result, it is necessary to distort the allocation from the first-best. We show that it is, in fact, sometimes optimal to distort both decisions: A will exert higher effort than in the first-best in the low state and a lower effort than in the first-best in the high state. As before, consider the judge decision given by (3) and by

$$h((0, P), (0, A)) = a,$$
$$h((1, P), (1, A)) = b. \qquad (4)$$

Without loss of generality, let $a \leq b$. As long as $a \leq b$ and $b \leq \alpha$, P does not want to invest in high-quality lawyers (since his preferences are consonant with $a \leq b$): A, however, would prefer to have a in the high state. He can do so by investing in a high-quality lawyer and give an argument $(0, P)$ and a counter-argument $(0, A)$. His expected utility is then

$$w - \beta a - c$$

while by having a bad lawyer his expected utility is

$$w - (1 - \pi)\beta a - \pi\beta b.$$

Incentive compatibility therefore requires

$$b - a \leq \frac{c}{\pi\beta}. \qquad (5)$$

Note that since by assumption $c < \pi\beta(\alpha - \beta)$, $b - a < \alpha - \beta$. The variation in actions in between the two states is strictly bounded above by the first-best variation. Total welfare is

$$W(a, b) = y - (1 - \pi)\left[\frac{a^2}{2} + \beta a\right] - \pi\left[\frac{b^2}{2} - (\alpha - \beta)b\right]. \qquad (6)$$

Note that W_b is negative for $b > \alpha - \beta$ and that $W_a < 0$. It follows that $b \leq \alpha - \beta$ and that a should be as small as possible. It follows that the constraint (5) binds and that $a = b - c/\pi\beta$. Substituting this value in W and maximizing with respect to b (ignoring the constraints $b \leq \alpha - \beta$, $a \geq 0$) yields

$$b^* = \pi\alpha - \beta + \frac{1 - \pi}{\pi}\frac{c}{\beta}. \qquad (7)$$

The right-hand side is indeed less than $\alpha - \beta$, therefore this is the solution to the constrained problem if

$$a^* = \pi\alpha - \beta - \frac{c}{\beta} \qquad (8)$$

is non-negative. Hence, if $c \geq \beta(\pi\alpha - \beta)$, the optimal solution is $a^* = 0$, $b^* = c/\pi\beta$ and only the high-state decision is distorted, but if $c < \beta(\pi\alpha - \beta)$, the solution is given by (8) and (7) and both the low-state and the high-state decisions are distorted. Thus, when good lawyers are cheap, they may, nevertheless, be avoided by making the contract sufficiently "flat". Whether this is optimal remains to be addressed.

5 • One Sided-Investment by the Employer may be Optimal

Assume now that P invests in a high-quality lawyer while A does not. We show that the first-best decision is achieved, but at cost c. If there is truth telling, in state θ the judge should hear the argument of P, (θ, P) and his counter-argument (θ, P) and choose

$$h((0, P), (0, P)) = 0,$$

$$h((1, P), (1, P)) = \alpha - \beta.$$

Assume as before that

$$h((\theta, i), (\phi, j)) = bad \quad \text{whenever } \theta \neq \phi, \text{ or } ij \neq PP. \qquad (9)$$

If A deviates to investing in a good lawyer, his argument will be heard by the judge (his counter-argument will not however since P has a good lawyer). Since P is truthful, the judge will hear $((\theta, P), (\phi, i))$ in state θ, where (ϕ, i) is the argument of A. By interfering A can have his argument (ϕ, i) heard, but by (9), the best argument that A can make is $(0, P)$ in order to avoid *bad* and getting 0. Hence, A cannot improve on the previous outcome by investing. The total *ex ante* welfare is $W^* - c$. For certain values of the parameters (*e.g.* c small, π moderately large), this will exceed the welfare achieved by the second-best contract described above.

Suppose that the worker is the only one to invest. Since the worker now controls the messages that the judge receives, he will send messages that induce the lowest decision in the range of h. Hence, the equilibrium decision is a constant; but this is not optimal, since by simply writing a contract with a constant decision, the employer and the employee can save c.

We identify this arrangement in which the employer invests and the worker does not with giving the employer authority: not only are his preferred decisions implemented, but it is he who is "believed" in court: he has the good lawyer and the employee dare

FIGURE 1

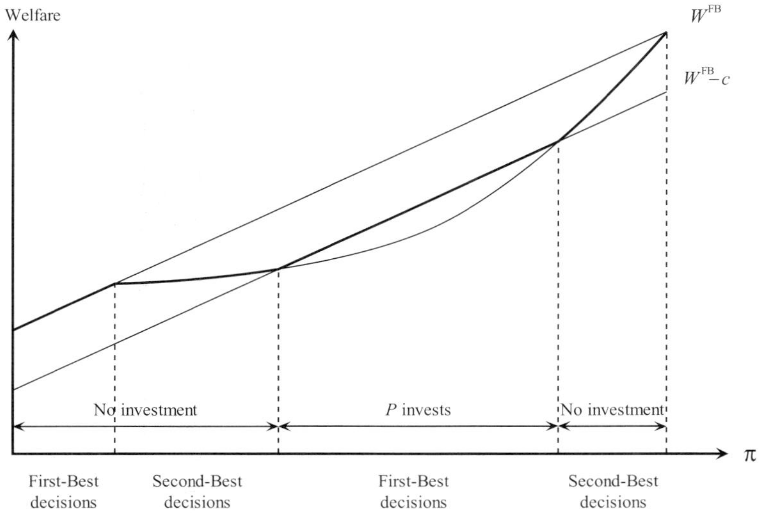

not gainsay him. A summary of what contracts are optimal over the parameter space is provided in Fig. 1.

What about mixed strategies in investment? It is possible to show that having the worker invest with some probability is never optimal.[9] However, there could be welfare gains when P invests with a probability < 1. A full analysis of this possibility is somewhat intricate, and we defer it to future work.

6 Conclusion

This example shows that the possibility of interference in court proceedings, or more generally jamming other agents' messages, has significant consequences for the form of optimal contracts and the flexibility of decisions that can be made inside firms. We believe that our approach brings a fresh look to the question of authority. Authority is here based on the ability of parties to have their say in court. It is therefore of a different nature than previous approaches to authority that were based on ownership of assets (Grossman and Hart, 1986), or on the ability to take informed decisions (Aghion and Tirole, 1997). Interference gives authority a role in worlds where it is traditionally absent in contract theory, like simple employment relationships where parties tend to have symmetric information and where there are no significant relationship specific investments.

Often, these views of authority are complementary. For instance, ownership of assets might confer authority if the courts are

9. Conditional on P investing with probability q, incentive compatibility for A implies a condition similar to (??). Having A invest does not weaken the incentive problem for P but introduces additional constraints. In more general situations of conflicts — for instance when P has (and A has not) consonant preferences with the first-best in some states and when A has (and P has not) consonant preferences with the first-best in other states — it can be welfare enhancing to have both parties make the investment. See Legros and Newman (1999) for an example.

biased in favor of property owners, if owners can afford better lawyers, etc. Particularly in environments with wealth effects and/or credit constraints, the latter possibility suggests there should be a positive correlation between wealth and authority. Similarly, better informed agents might be better at giving convincing arguments or evidence in court proceedings.

The legal system itself will also affect the allocation of authority. For example, shifting the burden of proof can be modelled by changes in the efficacy of a given investment in lawyers; this will typically result in changes to the firms's contractual structure.

Acknowledgements. We would like to thank Mathias Dewatripont, Eric Maskin and Jean Tirole for helpful discussions. Patrick Legros benefited from the financial support of the Communauté française de Belgique (projects ARC 98/03-221 and ARC00/05-252) and EU TMR Network contract no FMRX-CT98-0203.

REFERENCES

[1] Aghion, P., Tirole, J., 1997. Formal and real authority in organizations. *Journal of Political Economy* 105, 1-29.

[2] Anderlini, L., Felli, L., Postlewaite, A., 2001. Courts of law and unforeseen contingencies. Discussion Paper No. 2835, CEPR, London.

[3] Bond, P., 2001. A theory of contractual incompleteness based on judicial agency. Mimeo., Northwestern University.

[4] Dewatripont, M., Tirole, J., 1999. Advocates. *Journal of Political Economy* 107, 1-39.

[5] Glazer, J., Rubinstein, A., 2001. Debates and decisions: On a rationale of argumentation rules. *Games and Economic Behavior* 36, 158-173.

[6] Grossman, S., Hart, O., 1986. The costs and benefits of ownership: A theory of vertical and lateral integration. *Journal of Political Economy* 94, 691-719.

[7] Legros, P., Newman, A., 1999. Interference: Contracts and authority under insecure communication. Mimeo., ULB and UCL.

[8] Maskin, E., 2002. On indescribable contingencies and incomplete contracts. *European Economic Review* 46, 4/5.

6

Transferable Control

Philippe Aghion
Patrick Rey
Mathias Dewatripont

Abstract

In this paper, we introduce the notion of transferable control, defined as a situation where one party (the principal, say) can transfer control to another party (the agent) but cannot commit herself to do so. One theoretical foundation for this notion builds on the distinction between formal and real authority introduced by Aghion and Tirole, in which the actual exercise of authority may require noncontractible information, absent which formal control rights are vacuous. We use this notion to study the extent to which control transfers may allow an agent to reveal information regarding his ability or willingness to cooperate with the principal in the future. We show that the distinction between contractible and transferable control can drastically influence how learning takes place: with contractible control, information about the agent can often be acquired through revelation mechanisms that involve communication and message-contingent control allocations; in contrast, when control is transferable but not contractible, it can be optimal to transfer control unconditionally and learn instead from the way in which the agent exercises control.

1 Introduction

Much progress has been accomplished in the last fifteen years in modelling control allocation and in using this notion to analyze vertical and lateral integration,[1] financing decisions,[2] and the allocation of authority within firms.[3]

In all these models, although actions may not be contractible (either *ex ante*, or both *ex ante* and *ex post*), the allocation of control is. However, this assumption is not always warranted. For example:

- The president of France cannot contractually commit not to change (that is, withdraw control from) his/her prime minister:

1. See for example Grossman and Hart (1986), Hart and Moore (1990), and more generally Hart (1995).
2. See for example Aghion and Bolton (1992). Hart and Moore (1994), and Dewatripont and Tirole (1994).
3. See for example Aghion and Tirole (1997), Dessein (2000, 2002), Hart and Moore (1999b), and Hart and Holmström (2002).

Even if reputation considerations make it credible that he/she will not fire the new prime minister right after having appointed him/her, this obviously changes subsequently depending on the prime minister's performance on the job.

- More generally, the promotion/demotion of a subordinate in an organization (that is, the withdrawing/granting of control for a given set of tasks) rarely involves prior contractual commitment, but instead relies on (often soft) information about job performance.
- As for the provision of new credit lines by banks or credit card companies, there is typically no contractual commitment for these lines to be maintained, as banks want to protect themselves against possible abuses by customers; at the same time, credit lines will not be withdrawn right after having been granted, and control over the future course of action lies with the customer until the credit line is removed.

All these examples have the following two features in common: (i) control is clearly not fully contractible *ex ante*, but can be transferred somewhat irreversibly, at least in the short run when the party doing so finds it in his or her interest; (ii) putting a party "in control" allows the other party to test and learn more about the agent's ability or loyalty to the organization. In this paper, we therefore explore the implications of *transferable control*, defined as a situation where one party (the principal, say) can transfer control to another party (the agent) but cannot commit herself to do so. One theoretical foundation for this notion of transferable control builds on the distinction between formal and real authority introduced by Aghion and Tirole (1997), in which the actual exercise of authority may require certain critical information, absent which formal control rights are vacuous[4]; and while formal control rights could be contracted upon, information transfers may not (if for instance the informed party claims that she has no useful information, or provides useless information, when she does not consider the information transfer to be in her interest).

In this paper, we use this notion to study the extent to which control transfers may allow an agent to reveal information regarding his willingness to cooperate with the principal. We show that the distinction between contractible and transferable control can drastically influence how learning takes place: with contractible control, information about the agent can often be acquired through revelation mechanisms that involve communication and message-contingent control allocations; in contrast, when control is transferable but not contractible, it can be optimal to transfer control unconditionally and learn instead from the way in which the agent exercises this control.

4. Alternatively, undertaking an action may require the acquisition of unverifiable skills and knowledge. The party initially in charge may decide to transfer the required skills (or provide the adequate training) without being in a position to contractually commit to do so.

To position the notion of transferable control within the contract theory literature, it is convenient to refer to the degree of contractibility of actions. More specifically, consider the following polar cases:

(i) At one extreme, a world with fully contractible actions: contracts can then fully determine the entire interaction between the parties; this case encompasses the implementation literature à la Maskin (1999) or Moore and Repullo (1988), where one can contract on entire game forms. In such a world, who "chooses" the action is irrelevant: the contracting parties can limit themselves to sending (possibly sequential) messages to a "planner," who then takes or dictates all relevant actions.[5]

(ii) At the other extreme, a world with only noncontractible, preassigned actions: here, contracts hardly affect the structure of the game played by the parties; this case encompasses both game-theoretic models (such as Kreps *et al.* (1982), Sobel (1985), and Watson (1999)), which assume away any contracting, and moral hazard models (à la Mirrlees 1999, Holmström 1979, 1982, Legros and Matthews 1993), where noncontractible actions are preassigned to one or the other party and can only be influenced indirectly, by contracting over related variables (*e.g.*, output).

In between, there is *partial contracting* (see Aghion *et al.* 2002), where formal contracts do not determine the entire relation between the contracting parties but can influence the underlying game between them.[6] These are situations in which some actions are *ex post* nonverifiable and therefore not contractible *ex ante*, so that they cannot be delegated to (or dictated by) a social planner. Yet, control over such actions can influence the dynamic interaction between the parties. Much of the existing literature on control rights and authority has concentrated on situations where such control is fully contractible.[7]

Our paper is first related to the prior literature on control rights and authority, to which we add the possibility of credible control transfers. We thus focus on a case intermediate between contractible control and preassigned actions (or "moral hazard"), where control over particular actions is not contractible but still credibly transferable. Second, our model relates to the game-theoretic literature on reputation; allowing for contracting before the actual game takes place, however, allows us to study under which conditions — *e.g.*, contractible versus transferable control — information is transmitted by action choices rather than through revelation mechanisms. Third, since we focus on control allocation as a way to induce cooperation,

5. The implementation results of this literature have been generalized by Maskin and Tirole (1999) to the case where actions are noncontractible *ex ante*, before the revelation of the state of nature, but become contractible *ex post*, after the revelation of the state of nature.

6. Aghion *et al.* (2002) discuss the connection between partial contracting and the debate on the foundations of incomplete contracts (*e.g.*, in Segal 1999, Hart and Moore 1999a, Maskin and Moore 1999, Maskin and Tirole 1999, and Tirole 1999).

7. See *e.g.* Aghion and Bolton 1992, Dewatripont and Tirole 1994, Aghion and Tirole 1997, Legros and Newman 1999, and Hart and Moore 1999b. See also Dewatripont 2001.

our analysis also relates to the literature on formal versus informal contracting, and in particular to Baker *et al.* (2002) and Halonen (1997). In a repeated model of ownership allocation à la Grossman and Hart (1986), where all parties have complete information, Baker *et al.* (2002) show that vertical integration may help the parties to hold on to their promises of taking costly actions or making costly monetary transfers. Based also on a repeated ownership allocation model, but with imperfect information about the parties' disutility from cheating on effort or investment commitments, Halonen (1997) argues that joint ownership may emerge as a desirable contractual outcome *ex ante*, because both parties will then find it particularly costly for their reputation to renege on their promises. This rationale for control allocation is reminiscent of the argument of Boot *et al.* (1993), who stress that "loan commitment contracts" that allow banks to unilaterally renege on their commitments imply that the bank's reputation for "fairness" is enhanced when they do not actually renege. These papers, however, do not distinguish between contractible control and transferable control, and they restrict attention to simple contracts, even though revelation mechanisms would be more effective (for example, in Halonen's framework, where trade is supposed to be *ex post* verifiable, relatively simple contracts could be quite powerful).

The paper is organized as follows. Section 2 describes the framework. Section 3 focuses on contractible control and shows that in a broad range of situations the optimal contract is a revelation mechanism promising control to the agent when he announces a noncooperative type. This kind of mechanism ceases to be credible when control is not contractible but only transferable. In this case, as shown in Section 4, the power of revelation mechanism is greatly reduced and unconditional control transfers emerge as an optimal learning device. While Sections 3 and 4 went for simplicity in not allowing for monetary responsiveness, Section 5 shows that our results are robust to its introduction. Finally, Section 6 connects our analysis to the Aghion and Tirole (1997) concepts of formal and real authority, briefly discusses its implications for the study of delegation, and suggests some obvious extensions for future research.

2 • Framework

This Section outlines an incomplete information framework where control allocation serves as a natural instrument to enhance trust and cooperation. Specifically, we consider a relationship between a principal (she) and an agent (he), hereafter P and A, meant to carry out a project: P has overall control over the project but needs A for implementing it. More precisely, the project involves two stages, design and implementation. In the design stage, the party in charge chooses between two actions, C and N; action C is the "cooperative" action that is best for the project, whereas action N is a "non-cooperative" action that A may favor — for example, it may enhance A's human capital or, more generally, A's market value. In the implementation stage, P decides whether to implement the project (I), or to stop it (S). A can be "good" or "bad," and the project is worth implementing only if A is good. Initially, P does not know A's type; we denote by μ her prior probability that A is bad.

Specifically:

- In Stage 1, the design decision has to be made; P can either take the decision or let A take it; we shall distinguish between the case where P and A can contract over who is in charge of design and the case where P can simply *transfer* control to A, without contractually committing herself to do so. The design decision itself (C or N) is observed by both parties but not contractible. We normalize to zero the parties' payoffs from C; adopting instead the noncooperative action N does not affect a good A but entails a loss $(-l)$ for P and a benefit B for a bad A. P's and A's payoffs from N are thus respectively:[8]

$$(-l, 0) \text{ when } A \text{ is good,}$$

$$(-l, B) \text{ when } A \text{ is bad.}$$

- In Stage 2, P freely decides whether to implement or stop the project (actions I and S respectively): this decision is not contractible and cannot be delegated to A. Stopping the project yields zero payoffs for both parties. Implementing the project brings instead an additional gain G to P and g to A when A is good, while it brings a loss $-L$ to P and a gain b to A if A is bad. P's and A's payoffs from I are thus respectively:

$$(G, g) \text{ when } A \text{ is good,}$$

$$(-L, b) \text{ when } A \text{ is bad.}$$

We assume away discounting between the two stages; P's and A's overall payoffs are thus simply the sum of the first- and second-stage payoffs and can be summarized as follows:

- When A has a good type:

Action	I	S
C	G, g	$0, 0$
N	$G-l, g$	$-l, 0$

8. At the end of Section 3 and in Section 5, we discuss the robustness of our results with respect to changes in the payoff matrix.

- when A has a bad type:

Action	I	S
C	$-L, b$	$0, 0$
N	$-L-l, B+b$	$-l, B$

We shall restrict attention to the case where:

$$B > b > 0,$$

$$L > l > 0.$$

Thus a good A is willing to cooperate in Stage 1 and gains g from P's implementing the project; in contrast, a bad A gains B from the noncooperative design action N; he also gains b from the implementation of the project, but prefers the noncooperative design action N even if this induces P to stop the project $(B > b)$. P incurs a loss l from the noncooperative action at the design stage and an even bigger loss L from implementing the project when the agent has a bad type; P is thus willing to let a bad A choose the noncooperative action at the design stage to learn his type (and stop the project).

This payoff structure is that of a typical signalling game, where preference heterogeneity between the two types of A can allow for separation. It is however particular in one important respect: there is congruence in both periods between the preferences of P and the good type of A (in particular, both prefer C followed by implementation to N followed by stopping the project).[9] At the end of Section 3, we discuss the role of this congruence.

If P is uninformed about A's type when deciding whether to implement or stop the project in Stage 2, she will stop the project (whatever action has been chosen in Stage 1 since utilities are all separable over time) whenever:

$$(1-\mu)G + \mu(-L) < 0;$$

(the left-hand side is the expected Stage-2 payoff of the principal if she implements the project, the right-hand side is her Stage-2 payoff if she stops the project); this can be reexpressed as:

$$\mu > \mu^* \equiv \frac{G}{G+L}.$$

Incomplete information thus generates two types of problems: first, when μ is too large, P prefers to stop the project since she cannot obtain a positive payoff in Stage 2. Second, when μ is small enough, P cooperates (does not stop the project) but loses L when A

9. Fixing the implementation decision, a good A is here indifferent between cooperating or not on design. The analysis applies unchanged when a good A gains ε from adopting N, where ε is small but either negative (a good A strictly prefers to cooperate) or positive (a good A is slightly reluctant to cooperate). What matters is that a good type is willing to cooperate if this induces P to implement the project (i.e., $g > \varepsilon$).

is a bad type. We now explore alternative means by which these two problems can be solved.

We start our analysis by assuming that payoffs are private benefits and that the parties are not responsive to monetary incentives. Therefore, contracts consist of revelation mechanisms to be played at the beginning of each stage; as a function of messages sent at the beginning of Stage 1, control over project design is allocated to the agent or kept by the principal, and given the messages exchanged between the two parties up to Stage 2, the principal decides whether to implement the project. When parties are instead responsive to monetary incentives (in Section 5), optimal contracts also include message-contingent transfer payments.

3 • Contractible Control: The Power of Revelation Mechanisms

In this Section we assume that control over Stage 1 can be specified by an enforceable contract between *P* and *A*. The set of feasible strategies and contracts and the timing of moves can then be described as follows (in the absence of monetary responsiveness).

In the contracting phase, *P* offers a contract to *A*; this contract dictates an allocation of control over the Stage 1 action, possibly contingent upon messages sent by *A* at that stage. The agent then decides whether or not to accept this contract; if he refuses, the game ends and both parties get zero; if he accepts, the game proceeds as follows:

- In Stage 1, *A* sends messages and control is then (possibly randomly) allocated to *P* or *A* according to the contract; whoever ends up in charge of Stage 1 chooses between *C* and *N*.
- In Stage 2, *A* may again send messages; *P* then decides whether or not to implement the project.

Note however that, without loss of generality, one can restrict attention to contracts in which the agent sends no message in Stage 2. This follows from the cheap-talk nature of the Stage 2 message game: a bad *A* only sees advantages and no cost in mimicking a good type at Stage 2, since doing so can only encourage *P* to implement the project, which is good for him. And since *P*'s decision to implement the project or not is not contractible, she will do it if and only if it is in her interest to do so.

For simplicity, we concentrate next on contracts where pure strategies are played (and we explain in footnotes how the results are robust to the possibility of mixed strategies). Two types of contracts are therefore possible:

- Contracts where the agent does not send any message (equivalently, both types send the same message, which is then useless). P can for example simply choose to keep control over the Stage 1 action, and implement the project in Stage 2 if and only if $\mu < \mu^*$. P's payoff is then $\max\{(1-\mu)G - \mu L, 0\}$. Alternatively, P could give control to A and infer A's type from his choice of action; we further explore this latter possibility in the following section.
- Revelation mechanisms, where P learns A's type through the messages sent in Stage 1 and then implements the project only if A reports a good type.

Intuitively, in such a revelation mechanism a bad A could gain b in Stage 2 by misreporting a good type. To prevent this, P must reward a bad A for revealing himself, and can do so by giving a bad A control over Stage 1. Since a bad A can obtain B by choosing N, to induce truth-telling P must grant control to a bad A with at least probability b/B; in addition, in order to minimize a bad A's incentive to misreport his type, P should not give control to a good A. The following proposition confirms this intuition:

Proposition 1. *P's optimal revelation mechanism, M_C, is such that:* (i) *P keeps control in Stage* 1 *when A announces a good type, and* (ii) *P allocates control to A with probability b/B when A announces a bad type. In the associated equilibrium, action N is chosen if and only if a bad A gets control and the project is implemented if and only if A announces a good type.*[10]

Proof. In any revealing equilibrium, P implements the project if the agent reports a good type and stops it otherwise. Thus, a good A is always willing to report his type, since he gets g by doing so and 0 by behaving as a bad type.

Let x and y denote the probabilities that A obtains control when announcing a good and a bad type. P will clearly choose action C when she has control over Stage 1. When a good A gets control, he is indifferent between actions C and N while P benefits from action C. In contrast, a bad A always chooses action N when in control. Therefore, the best for P is that a good A chooses C whenever in control: this improves P's payoff, and also helps P deterring a bad A from misreporting a good type. P's expected payoff is then given by

$$(1-\mu)G - \mu y l,$$

while the bad A's incentive compatibility condition for truth-telling is:

$$yB \geq (1-x)b + xB.$$

10. This result remains valid when equilibrium mixed strategies are considered, which can be seen as follows: (i) first, if A obtains control in Stage 1, he will play a pure strategy for sure, and so will P in Stage 2; (ii) if P is in control in Stage 1, she will not mix in Stage 2 (between I and S) if her posterior probability assessment that A is bad is not equal to μ^*. But if P does not mix in Stage 2, she prefers the bad A also not to mix (between saying he is bad or good), since the loss from $I(L)$ outweighs the loss from Stage 1 control (as for the good A, he never wants to mix, since he is indifferent between C and N, and only cares about the Stage 2 action); (iii) finally, an outcome where P is in control in Stage 1 and mixes in Stage 2 is also unattractive for P, because it means she obtains a zero payoff upon having Stage 1 control (and a negative one upon not having Stage 1 control).

Since $B > b$, the optimal probabilities of control are thus $x = 0$ and $y = b/B$. ■

The mechanism M_c gives P an expected payoff equal to

$$(1-\mu)G - \mu \frac{b}{B} l,$$

and is thus positive whenever

$$\mu < \mu_c \equiv \frac{G}{G + \frac{b}{B} l}.$$

The mechanism M_c addresses the two problems mentioned before: the revelation of A's type allows P to implement the project when — and only when — it is desirable to do so. However, this revelation has a cost: P must "reward" a bad type A for telling the truth, namely by granting control to that bad type in Stage 1 with probability b/B, in which case action N is implemented instead of action C.

Note that P prefers M_c over "keeping control with probability 1 and implementing the project": $L > l$ and $B > b$ imply

$$(1-\mu)G - \mu \frac{b}{B} l > (1-\mu)G - \mu L.$$

Note moreover that $\mu_c < \mu^*$, so there are cases ($\mu_c < \mu < \mu^*$) where M_c is profitable even when, if uninformed, P would have chosen to stop the project in Stage 2.

Remark. We stressed above that the payoff structure was particular in having P's preferences congruent with that of a good A. Indeed, the above revelation mechanism no longer works when the principal's preferences become sufficiently noncongruent with those of both types of agents. Suppose for example[11] that, at Stage 1, there are three possible actions to be taken: C, N, and N'. The payoffs from C and N are the same as before, and N' brings zero to P and a bad A; but a good A now gains $B_g > 0$ from N'. Therefore, P prefers C to N and N', and a bad A prefers N to C and N', but a good A now prefers N' to C and N.

Let as before x and y denote the probabilities that A obtains control when announcing a good and a bad type. To induce A to tell the truth, we must have

$$xB_g + g \geq yB_g + yg \tag{1}$$

for the good type, and

$$yB \geq xB + (1-x)b \tag{2}$$

for the bad type.

11. We thank a referee for suggesting this example.

Indeed, if a good A report his type truthfully, in Stage 1 he obtains control with probability x and can then choose his preferred action N', while in Stage 2 P implements the project; if he reports instead a bad type, with probability y he gets control and reveals his true type by choosing N', inducing P to implement the project,[12] otherwise P chooses C and then stops the project. Similarly, if a bad A reports his type truthfully he obtains control and chooses N with probability y, while P stops the project to avoid losses in Stage 2; if he pretends instead to be a good type, with probability x he acquires control and then reveals his type by choosing N, otherwise the principal keeps control and implements the project.

The two incentive conditions can be rewritten as

$$(1+\alpha)(1-y) \geq 1-x \geq \frac{1}{1-\beta}(1-y),$$

where $\alpha = g/B_g$ and $\beta = b/B$. Therefore, if

$$(1+\alpha) < \frac{1}{1-\beta},$$

both conditions can be simultaneously satisfied only if $x = y = 1$, which amounts to simply transferring control to A and learning from his choice of action.

4 • Transferable Control and Learning by Delegation

While M_c illustrates how control allocation can be used to induce truth-telling through a standard revelation mechanism, this contract suffers from obvious credibility problems: P has no incentives to transfer control to a bad A once his type has been revealed. Hence our interest in exploring the case where control is transferable but noncontractible: in that case, P can choose to transfer control (given A's messages) at the beginning of Stage 1, but cannot commit to do so at the contracting stage. The set of strategies and the timing of events are then modified as follows. In the contracting phase, P offers a contract to A, which again allows for messages to be sent by A at the beginning of each stage, but can no longer dictate the allocation of control over the first stage. As before, A then decides whether or not to accept the contract; if he refuses, the game ends and both parties get zero; if he accepts, the game proceeds as follows.

12. Alternatively, P could stick to the belief that A has a bad type; however, such a belief would contradict, for example, the Cho-Kreps intuitive criterion, since only a good A gains from choosing N', even if doing so is the only way to induce P to implement the project.

- In Stage 1, A sends messages; then P decides with full discretion whether or not to transfer control to A; whoever ends up in charge of Stage 1 chooses between C and N.
- Stage 2 is unchanged: A may again send messages before P decides whether or not to implement the project.

We can immediately establish the following lemma:

Lemma 1. *When control over Stage 1 is transferable but not contractible, there is no loss of generality in not asking the agent to send messages.*

Proof. When control over Stage 1 is not contractible, message games involve cheap talk not only in Stage 2 but also in Stage 1: in both stages, a bad A sees only advantages and no cost in reporting a good type. Therefore the principal may as well ignore any message A might send at any stage. ■

Given this lemma, at the contracting stage P must simply choose between keeping control, in which case she remains uninformed about A's type by the end of Stage 1, or transferring Stage-1 control to A. The cost of such a control transfer is that the bad A will choose action N, which is his dominant strategy. The good A instead is happy to choose action C, especially since this signals his good type and ensures that P implements the project.[13] In comparison with the case where P keeps control in Stage 1, transferring control to A clearly improves A's expected payoff. It also increases P's expected payoff whenever the (short-term) loss from losing control in Stage 1 is more than compensated by the (long-term) benefit of learning A's type prior to Stage 2.

The Stage-1 loss comes from the fact that a bad A chooses action N. The expected loss for P, who then stops the project in Stage 2, is therefore equal to μl. The Stage-2 informational gain now depends upon the equilibrium that would prevail if A did not signal his type:

- If the probability of a bad type agent is sufficiently small $(\mu \leq \mu^*)$, an uninformed principal P would always implement the project; learning A's type then allows P to stop the project and avoid the loss L when A turns out to be a bad type. Thus, for $\mu \leq \mu^*$ learning A's type allows P to save μL in expected terms; P will thus prefer to grant control to A in Stage 1 since $L > l$ implies

$$\mu L \geq \mu l.$$

- If the probability of a bad type agent is sufficiently high $(\mu > \mu^*)$, an uninformed principal P would instead stop the project; learning A's type then allows P to implement the project and gain G if A turns out to be a good type. Thus,

13. There may also exist pooling equilibria where both types of agents choose action N. These equilibria are however dominated by those in which P keeps control over the Stage-1 action.

learning A's type when $\mu > \mu^*$ generates an additional expected gain equal to $(1-\mu)G$ to the principal; for such values of μ, P will thus prefer to grant control to A in Stage 1 if:

$$(1-\mu)G > \mu l,$$

or equivalently:

$$\mu < \mu_t \equiv \frac{G}{G+l}.$$

This establishes our main result:

Proposition 2. *P's optimal transferable-control contract,* M_t, *is such that:* (i) *no messages are sent before Stage* 1 *(and a fortiori after that stage);* (ii) *P transfers control over the Stage* 1 *action to A if* $\mu < \mu_t$ *and keeps control (and stops the project in Stage* 2*) otherwise;* (iii) *if A obtains control in Stage* 1, *he chooses action C if his type is good and action N otherwise, and P implements the project if and only if action C has been chosen.*[14]

It is therefore in P's interest to transfer control to A for small values of μ: if μ is too high, the hope that a good A will act cooperatively in Stage 1 in order to keep the project going in Stage 2 is too small compared with the short-term loss from a bad A's noncooperating in the first stage.

To summarize, when A's willingness to cooperate is initially unknown by P, two problems may potentially arise: either cooperation is impossible in Stage 2 (P stops the project), or "excessive" cooperation imposes losses on P. Then, "testing" A by giving him control over Stage 1 creates an opportunity for A to reveal his willingness to cooperate, which in turn helps overcome each of the preceding two problems. By transferring control of Stage 1 to A, P may not lose that much since a good A will want to choose action C to induce the implementation of the project; furthermore, any early loss induces P to take "appropriate measures" (that is, to stop the project) to prevent subsequent losses.[15]

A final remark to conclude this section: by transferring control to A, which is optimal when $\mu < \mu_t$, P achieves an expected payoff equal to:

$$(1-\mu)G - \mu l.$$

This payoff achieved through M_t is lower than what she gets with the contractible-control revelation mechanism M_c described in the previous section, namely:

$$(1-\mu)G - \frac{b}{B}\mu l.$$

14. Once again, mixed strategies will not alter the result: whatever the equilibrium messages sent by A, the probability that P transfers control cannot be increasing in her probability assessment that A is bad. On the other hand, it is also impossible that it be strictly decreasing in equilibrium, because this would violate the bad A's incentive constraint. Therefore, messages can be ignored and we are left with unconditional control transfers.

15. On the other hand, P must be able to commit to let A exert control over a number of actions and/or for some time, so as to allow a bad A to gain sufficiently from the exercise of this control. If for example P had the right to "withdraw" control from A at any moment, then P would indeed be tempted to overrule A's choice of N. Anticipating this, a bad A would then "choose" C to preserve his benefit from implementation and the principal would thus never learn the agent's "exercise" of control. More generally, P must be in a position to transfer control irreversibly for at least some time, for such control to be useful as a learning device.

Therefore:

- When control is contractible, it is optimal for P to have A's type revealed through a direct revelation mechanism rather than through trust-building; specifically, the relationship is profitable when $\mu < \mu_c$ and M_c is then the optimal contract for P, since it induces truth-telling with a smaller probability (b/B instead of 1) of control allocated to a bad A.
- When control is transferable but not contractible, the relationship is profitable only when

$$\mu < \mu_t = \frac{G}{G+l},$$

and M_t is then the optimal contract for P; control is then transferred with higher probability (1 instead of b/B) but only for a smaller interval of μ's (since $\mu_t < \mu_c$).

5 Monetary Responsiveness

We have thus far restricted attention to the case where the contracting parties do not respond to monetary incentives. But now suppose that P's and A's utilities are given by:

$$U_P = \pi_P + p \text{ and } U_A = \pi_A - p$$

where π_P and π_A denote the private benefits of the two parties (defined as in the previous section), and p is a monetary transfer from A to P. Since we now have transferable utilities, what matters for efficiency is the sum of the parties' payoffs; in keeping with the analysis of the previous sections, we assume in this section

$$L > l > B > b,$$

so that it is efficient to stop the project when the agent is bad.

Allowing for monetary responsiveness means that contracts can require transfers contingent on messages, which in turn can provide additional ways to acquire the information over A's type. In particular, if $b < g$, P can simply keep control and obtain full revelation at Stage 2 by having the good A pay g against project implementation.[16] The possibility of monetary transfers thus eliminates the role for allocating or transferring control to A in that case. When $b > g$, however, the previous insights remain valid, as we show next.

16. If $b < g$, in the absence of any messages, there exists a separating equilibrium in which: (i) P keeps control and chooses C in Stage 1 and implements the project in Stage 2 only if A pays $p = g$; (ii) only a good A makes the payment. In this equilibrium, P implements the project only when A is good and both types of agent get zero rent.

5.1 Contractible Control

Introducing monetary transfers allows P to extract rents from A and also to "sell" Stage 1 control. The following proposition extends the previous analysis:

Proposition 3. *Assume that $b > g$. Then, the optimal separating contract for P consists in selling control at price g with probability $(b-g)/(B-g)$ when A reports a bad type, while keeping control and requiring a payment of g when A reports a good type.*[17] *In this mechanism, a good A obtains no rents while a bad A obtains $b-g$ and P obtains a positive expected payoff as long as*

$$\mu < \mu_c^m \equiv \frac{1}{1+[(b-g)/(B-g)][(l-g)(G+g)]}.$$

Proof. See Appendix.

In other words, when $b > g$ the introduction of monetary transfers does not eliminate the role for (contractible) control allocation; in particular, it can be checked that, whenever the relationship is profitable $(\mu < \mu_c^m)$, P prefers this separating contract to staying uninformed and keeping control over Stage 1. However, the optimal separating contract still allocates control with positive probability to a bad A and never to a good A; thus, while monetary transfers allow for a reduction in the probability of control given to a bad A, the optimal contract still suffers from the same credibility problem as in Section 3.

Remark. As shown in Aghion *et al.* (2003), allowing for monetary transfers tends to increase the power of revelation mechanisms: Charging for control allocation reduces a good A's net gain from acquiring control, and therefore reduces the degree of noncongruence between a good A and P. Yet, we show that these revelation mechanisms only work if the lack of congruence between the good A's preferences and P's preferences is not too severe.

5.2 Transferable Control

When $b > g$, a bad type is more eager than a good one to get control over Stage 1 and/or convince P to implement a project; however, P would never transfer control or implement the project if she learned that A was bad. It is therefore impossible to have A's type revealed through type-contingent messages or payments. In fact we can show:

Lemma 2. *Assume $b > g$. When control over Stage 1 is transferable but not contractible, then payments and control allocation*

17. Once again, this result is robust to the consideration of mixed strategies. Essentially the same arguments apply as in footnote 10, since the mechanism is very similar — although with a different probability of giving control to A — except that there is a price g to be paid by A whenever he actually receives Stage 1 control: (i) first, if A obtains control in Stage 1, he will play a pure strategy for sure, and so will P in Stage 2; (ii) if P is in control in Stage 1, she will not mix in Stage 2 (between I and S) if her posterior probability assessment that A is bad is not equal to μ^*. But if P does not mix in Stage 2, she prefers the bad (resp. good) A also not to mix (between saying he is bad or good), because I (resp. S) is inefficient; (iii) finally, an outcome where P is in control in Stage 1 and mixes in Stage 2 is also unattractive for P, because, on the one hand, it means she does not benefit from the gain of implementation of the project and, on the other hand, by lowering the probability of implementation, she will moreover obtain a lower expected payment from the good A (whose participation constraint is binding) and in turn from the bad A (whose incentive constraint is binding) at the initial message stage.

cannot depend on the agent's type; there is thus no loss of generality in not asking the agent to send messages.

Proof. See Appendix.

Given this lemma, at the contracting stage P must simply stipulate a price (which must be the same for both types) and choose between: (i) keeping control, in which case she remains uninformed about A's type by the end of Stage 1; (ii) transferring Stage-1 control to A. The same analysis as in Section 4 then leads to:

Proposition 4. *Assume $b > g$. When control over Stage 1 is transferable but not contractible, the relationship is profitable as long as $\mu < \mu_t = G/(G+l)$, in which case P's optimal contract is such that: (i) no messages are sent before Stage 1 (and a fortiori after that stage); (ii) A pays g and P transfers control over Stage 1 to A; (iii) in Stage 1, a good A chooses C whereas a bad A chooses N, and in Stage 2 P implements the project if and only if C has been chosen in Stage 1. In comparison with the contractible control optimum, the good A still gets no rents, the bad A gets higher rents and P gets lower rents. Finally, if $\mu \geq \mu_t$, it is optimal for P to keep control and stop the project.*[18]

Proof. See Appendix.

Introducing monetary transfers thus allows P to extract some of the agent's rents (when the relationship is profitable) but does not otherwise affect the optimal contract. Transferring control remains the only way for P to learn A's type in Stage 1.[19]

6 • Discussion and Conclusions

This paper provides contract theoretic foundations for games in which a principal needs to transfer control rights to her agent in order to "test" her ability or propensity to cooperate in the future. Specifically, we have shown that when control is transferable, as opposed to being contractible, simple control transfers emerge as optimal learning devices. Thus, moving from contractible to transferable control can significantly reduce the power of revelation mechanisms: the principal may no longer rely on communication and message-based control transfers, but simply put the agent in charge and learn from the agent's exercise of control.

Taking a contractual perspective moreover generates additional insights for the theory of organizations. In this section, we discuss two applications of our framework to, respectively, the transfer of "real" authority and the scope of delegation.

18. Just as without monetary responsiveness, mixed strategies will not alter the result: whatever the equilibrium messages sent by A, the probability that P transfers control cannot be increasing in her probability assessment that A is bad. On the other hand, it is also impossible that it be strictly decreasing in equilibrium, because this would violate the bad A's, incentive constraint. Moreover, the condition $b > g$ also rules out any separation between types, even a probabilistic one, using monetary payments. Therefore, we are left with unconditional control transfers and monetary payments.

19. However, when control is contractible, P does better using the revelation mechanism described in Subsection 5.1, which minimizes the probability of giving control to a bad A.

6.1 Transferring Real Authority

Aghion and Tirole (1997) (hereafter AT) stress that the exercise of authority requires more than the formal right to make decisions: it also requires relevant information in order to take appropriate decisions. AT investigate this issue in the context of an investment problem where one project has to be chosen among n *ex ante* indistinguishable projects. Contracting first takes place over formal authority, then effort is exerted by the parties in order to acquire information about the payoffs of the various investment projects, and finally the investment project can be chosen. Since the parties have partially congruent payoffs, it may be in the interest of the party endowed with formal authority, when she is uninformed, to grant real authority to the other party, by following his recommendation.

In order to connect AT's basic setup to our analysis, let us reinterpret Stage 1 of our model in the light of the AT framework: label party P's favorite project as "action C," while A's favorite project is "action N." Knowing which actions are C and N is however not obvious, because they are among n possible actions that are *ex ante* indistinguishable. A's type in our model can be interpreted as the degree of congruence of A's payoff function with P's payoff function: a "good type" is congruent with P, while a "bad type" is not. The difference in information structure between the AT model and our model is that AT assume that both parties are initially uninformed about project returns but know the degree of congruence of their payoffs. Here instead, P knows the various project returns, but does not know the degree of congruence between A's interest and her own. This matters because P has to rely on A in Stage 2 if she does not stop the project. The question then is whether P can learn about A's payoff structure by giving him (real) authority in Stage 1.

Let us first assume that the formal Stage-1 decision rights necessarily belong to A (suppose for example, as in the classical moral hazard literature, that P is either too busy or unable to actually take the action in that stage). In this case, the relevant notion of control is, who has the information needed to take decision, that is, who has real authority. And to the extent that the relevant information is not "verifiable," this control is not contractible but it is transferable: since A has formal authority, providing him with the relevant information indeed amounts to an irreversible transfer of real authority.

To be specific, assume as in AT that, except for C and N, all the other projects are so bad that choosing at random is worse than doing nothing at all. Since A is initially uninformed about project returns, he then needs information from P to make any Stage-1 decision. It is natural to assume that, in many instances, P cannot commit *ex ante* to transmit the appropriate information.[20] On the other hand, if P informs A about the identity of both "action C" and "action N," control is irreversibly transferred to A: once A knows about action N, there is nothing to prevent him from choosing it, given that he has received formal Stage-1 control rights initially.

With this reinterpretation of the Stage-1 actions along the lines of the AT setup, we can now apply straightforwardly the results of the previous Section: provided that the probability μ that A is not congruent enough with P is not too large, it can become optimal for P to give away (or sell, under monetary responsiveness) formal authority over the Stage-1 action to A, and also to transmit information to A about which among the n actions are actions C and N. Through this transfer of control, P has the opportunity to learn about A's type, and to stop the project in Stage 2 if and only if A has chosen action N in Stage 1.

Let us now assume that formal Stage-1 decision rights can be contractually allocated to either P or A. Two cases might then be considered:

- if P can provide A with the relevant information about C and N before allocating formal Stage-1 decision rights, we are back to the case of contractible control: indeed, by informing A beforehand, P can credibly grant real authority through the (possibly message-contingent) allocation of formal Stage-1 decision rights. As in Section 3, P may then find it optimal to first provide A with the relevant information and, second, offer formal control to A with positive probability when reporting a bad type.
- if instead the relevant information about C and N cannot be understood by A until after he has already been allocated formal authority over Stage 1, then the logic of transferable control applies again. Contractually allocating formal authority to A is indeed no longer a credible way to grant him real authority. However, once formal authority has been allocated to A, P can also grant him real authority by providing the relevant information. The analysis is then essentially the same as in the beginning of this section, where A was always endowed with formal Stage-1 control.

6.2 The Scope of Delegation

In the previous subsection, we identified circumstances under which P informs A about both actions C and N, in order to let him reveal his willingness to cooperate. In contrast, in AT, no such dynamic consideration exists and implementing one's favorite project is the only thing that matters. As a result, transfers of real

20. In particular, if contractually instructed to identify x actions for A, P could decide to only tell A about action C and "bad" actions (possibly identifying several times the same action), but not action N.

authority never occur: when the party endowed with formal authority turns to the other party for advice, it receives information about at most one project, and therefore has no choice but to follow the recommendation. In our setup, P finds it instead optimal to transfer real authority to A in Stage 1 in order to learn about his type, which is helpful for Stage 2. We therefore have true delegation here, motivated by the concern for future cooperation.

We can build on this insight to analyze the optimal scope or size of delegation. To this end, we extend the action set to include convex combinations of actions C and N. Specifically, for any a $\alpha \in [0, 1]$, action N_α generates payoffs $-\alpha l$ for the principal, 0 for a good agent and αB for a bad agent. P can now grant partial control to A over any subset of actions N_α. In the AT interpretation, this amounts to giving A the relevant information about these actions. An alternative interpretation is that Stage 1 consists of several projects, each of which involves two actions N and C, with payoffs as described before. P then decides which fraction of projects to delegate to A.

This convexification of the action set allows P to replicate the contractible control optimum with only transferable control. Namely, it is optimal for P to transfer control over the actions N_α for $\alpha \in [0, \bar{\alpha}]$, where $\bar{\alpha} = b/B$ represents the minimal amount of delegation required for a bad A to reveal his type. The extent of delegation thus increases with B and decreases with b: since the goal is to induce a bad A to signal his type by choosing action N, it is easier, the higher the short-term gain B of doing so, and the smaller the long-term loss b of doing so.

This extension leads for example to intuitive comparative statics results:

- Suppose for example that, with exogenous probability ρ, the principal-agent relationship disappears after Stage 1, for example, due to the technological obsolescence of the firm or of the agent's firm-specific skills. Then b must be replaced with $(1-\rho)b$ and the optimal amount of delegation becomes $\bar{\alpha}(\rho) = (1-\rho)b/B$. Thus, delegation decreases with the rate of obsolescence.
- Alternatively, one could assume that the benefit αB that the bad agent obtains from action N_α now only arises if the agent receives an outside job offer. This would for example be the case if action N corresponds to an investment in the agent's general human capital or, more generally, in his market value, at the expense of the firm. Call this probability ρ'. Now, the optimal amount of delegation is defined by $\alpha = b/(\rho' B)$. Thus, delegation decreases with labor market mobility as measured by ρ'.

6.3 Further Possible Extensions

We have focused on a simple model with two periods, two types of agents, and two actions. Yet, we have allowed for a full-blown mechanism design approach, in which the contracting set becomes particularly rich in the case with monetary responsiveness. The main insights should generalize to the case of multiple types and actions, but investigating optimal learning through control allocation in a dynamic setting is an interesting avenue for further research.

The previous discussion illustrates the potential for the notion of transferable control to enrich the analysis of delegation in organizations in a dynamic context. In particular, we have been able to rationalize transfers of real authority as a learning device. This could be a useful building block for further investigating the interaction between information flows, the design of hierarchies and trust-building in organizations.

Appendix

1. Proof of Proposition 3

As in Section 3, we can restrict attention to direct mechanisms where, at each stage, A sends one of two messages — "good" and "bad." We proceed again by backward induction.

We first check that there is no scope for revelation of A's type in Stage 2. Consider a candidate equilibrium where A reveals his type at Stage 2, in which case P implements the project only if A is good. In order for a bad A not to pretend to be good, announcing a good type must involve an additional transfer p in P's favor. Whatever the Stage 1 action (C or N), a good A would find it profitable to pay p (and have the project implemented) only if

$$g - p > 0,$$

and a bad A will not find it profitable to mimic a good type if

$$b - p < 0.$$

But these two conditions cannot be simultaneously satisfied when $b > g$.

Moving back one step, consider the control allocation stage. A can in principle reveal his type by "acquiring control" at some specified price. More precisely, consider a separating equilibrium and let (x_g, p_g) and (x_b, p_b) denote the agent's probabilities of obtaining control and the payments in P's favor respectively attached to reporting a good type and a bad type. In any such separating equilibrium, when P keeps control of Stage 1 she chooses C and then implements the project only if A reported a good type. A bad A chooses N whenever in control, and P then stops the project. Without loss of generality, a good A can be assumed to choose C when in control,[21] and P then implements the project.

The two participation constraints are thus:

$$g - p_g \geq 0$$

and:

$$x_b B - p_p \geq 0 .$$

If a bad A falsely reports a good type, he reveals his type when in control (by choosing N), in which case P then stops the project, and induces P to implement the project when P keeps control. A bad A is thus willing to report the truth if:

$$x_b B - p_b \geq (1 - x_g)b + x_g B - p_g .$$

If a good A falsely announces a bad type, P chooses C when in control and then stops the project. When A gets control, choosing N would again lead P to stop the project; however, at this point A may try to "signal" his good type by choosing C instead. Indeed, following the Cho-Kreps intuitive criterion, a choice of action C can only be attributed to a good A, and must therefore be followed by project implementation, irrespective of previous announcements. The good A's incentive constraint is then[22]:

$$g - p_g \geq x_b g - p_b .$$

The optimal contract leading to a separating equilibrium maximizes P's expected payoff:

$$(1 - \mu)(p_g + G) + \mu[p_b + (1 - x_b) \times 0 - x_b l] ,$$

subject to the above constraints. Two things can be noted at this point. First, giving control less often to a good type (reducing x_g) relaxes the bad A's incentive constraint (since $B > b$) without affecting P's payoff, so that it is optimal for P to set $x_g = 0$. Second, since $B \geq b > g$, the participation constraint of the bad A is satisfied whenever his incentive constraint and the participation constraint of the good A are. These two observations allow us to rewrite the relevant constraints as:

$$g - p_g \geq 0 ,$$

$$g - p_g \geq x_b g - p_b ,$$

21. As before, requiring a good A to choose N is inefficient and gives a bad A additional incentives to falsely report a good type.

22. Absent the Cho-Kreps criterion, P may refuse A's signal and stick to the reported type, which would reduce A's benefit from falsely reporting a bad type. The analysis would be similar, although P could then reduce the probability of control given to a bad type (from $(b-g)/(B-g)$ to $(b-g)/B$).

and:

$$x_b B - p_b \geq b - p_g .$$

The last condition must be binding, otherwise P could increase p_b. Using this condition to determine p_b, P's expected payoff can be expressed as

$$p_g + (1-\mu)G - \mu[x_b(l-B) + b],$$

while the first two conditions become

$$p_g \leq g,$$

$$b - g \leq x_b(B-g).$$

The optimal contract thus satisfies

$$p_g = g,\ x_b = \frac{b-g}{B-g},$$

and the corresponding expected transfer p_b is

$$p_b = x_b B - b + p_g = \frac{b-g}{B-g} g = x_b g,$$

which can be implemented by asking for a price g whenever control is allocated to A.

This separating equilibrium yields 0 to a good A and $x_b(B-g) = b-g$ to a bad A, while P obtains a payoff of:

$$(1-\mu)(G+g) - \mu \frac{b-g}{B-g}(l-g),$$

which is positive provided:

$$\mu \leq \mu_c^m = \frac{1}{1 + \frac{b-g}{B-g}\frac{l-g}{G+g}}.$$

This establishes the Proposition.

2. Proof of Lemma 2

It suffices to show that A's payments and P's decisions cannot be message or type-contingent. We first show that there is no scope for revelation of A's type at Stage 2. If separation were to occur at that stage, a bad A would not pay anything since an informed P would then stop the project. A good A could try to credibly report his type by making a specific payment p, in order to induce P to implement the project. However, a good A would be willing to pay only $p \leq g$, and a bad A would then also report a good type since $p < b$.

We now show that there is no scope for messages at Stage 1 either. In any separating equilibrium, P would keep control and stop the project when a bad A reveals his type. A bad A would thus not pay anything. A good A could try to reveal his type by making a specific payment p in order to influence P's decision over the allocation of Stage 1 control. But again a good A would be willing to pay p only if $p \leq g$, in which case a bad A would pay p to obtain control and choose action N, even if this leads P to stop the project. The lemma is proved.

3. Proof of Proposition 4

The previous lemma establishes that P cannot learn A's type simply through message-contingent payments and the reasoning is then similar to that of Section 4. If $\mu < \mu_t$, P prefers learning A's type by transferring control over Stage 1. A good A then obtains g (by choosing C and inducing P to implement the project) and a bad A obtains $B > g$ (it is a dominant strategy to choose N, even though it then leads P to stop the project). The maximal price P can ask is thus $p = \min(g, B) = g$; a good A then gets no rent while a bad A gets $B - g$, and P's expected payoff is

$$g + (1-\mu)G - \mu l = (1-\mu)(G+g) - \mu(l-g),$$

which is lower than when control is contractible.

If P opted instead for keeping control with probability 1, she would remain uninformed about A's type and implement the project only if $\mu < \mu^*$; in that case, she could still require at most a price $p = g$, which is the maximal price a good A is willing to pay. She would thus get $(1-\mu)(G+g) - \mu(L-g)$, which is lower than what she can get with the above revelation mechanism. And if $\mu > \mu^*$, P would stop the project and thus earn zero (since she could not ask for any positive payment in that case). Therefore, P prefers the previous mechanism to keeping control with probability 1.

If $\mu > \mu_t$, P prefers keeping control and stopping the project; anticipating this, A does not pay anything.

This completes the proof.

Acknowledgments. We thank Oliver Hart, Jean Tirole, participants in the International Francqui Conference (Brussels, November 1999) on the Economics of Contracting, various seminar audiences, and especially three referees for very useful comments and suggestions.

REFERENCES

[1] Aghion, Philippe and Patrick Bolton (1992). "An Incomplete Contracts Approach to Financial Contracting." *Review of Economic Studies*, 59, 473-494.

[2] Aghion, Philippe, Mathias Dewatripont, and Patrick Rey (2002). "On Partial Contracting." *European Economic Review*, 46(4-5), 745-753.

[3] Aghion, Philippe, Mathias Dewatripont, and Patrick Rey (2003). "Transferable Control," Working paper, Cambridge, Massachusetts: Harvard University, ECARES and IDEI.

[4] Aghion, Philippe and Jean Tirole (1997). "Formal and Real Authority in Organizations." *Journal of Political Economy*, 105, 1-29.

[5] Baker, George, Robert Gibbons, and Kevin J. Murphy (2002). "Relational Contracts and the Theory of the Firm." *Quarterly Journal of Economics*, 117(1), 39-84.

[6] Boot, Arnoud, Stuart Greenbaum, and Anjan Thakor (1993). "Reputation and Discretion in Financial Contracting." *American Economic Review*, 83, 206-212.

[7] Dessein, Wouter (2000). "Control Allocations in Joint Undertakings: Balancing Formal and Real Authority," Working paper, University of Chicago.

[8] Dessein, Wouter (2002). "Authority and Communication within Organizations." *Review of Economic Studies*, 69, 811-838.

[9] Dewatripont, Mathias (2001). "Authority." Walras-Bowley Lecture presented at the North American Summer Meeting of the Econometric Society, College Park, Maryland, unpublished.

[10] Dewatripont, Mathias and Jean Tirole (1994). "A Theory of Debt and Equity: Diversity of Security and Manager-Shareholder Congruence." *Quarterly Journal of Economics*, 109, 1027-1054.

[11] Grossman, Sanford and Oliver Hart (1986). "The Costs and Benefits of Ownership: A Theory of Vertical and Lateral Integration." *Journal of Political Economy*, 94, 691-719.

[12] Halonen, Maja (1997). "A Theory of Joint Ownership," Working paper, University of Bristol.

[13] Hart, Oliver (1995). *Firms, Contracts and Financial Structure*. Oxford University Press.

[14] Hart, Oliver and Bengt Holmström (2002). "Vision and Firm Scope," Working paper, Harvard University and MIT.

[15] Hart, Oliver and John Moore (1990). "Property Rights and the Nature of the Firm." *Journal of Political Economy*, 98, 1119-1158.

[16] Hart, Oliver and John Moore (1994). "A Theory of Debt Based on the Inalienability of Human Capital." *Quarterly Journal of Economics*, 109, 841-879.

[17] Hart, Oliver and John Moore (1999a). "Foundations of Incomplete Contracts." *Review of Economic Studies*, 66, 115-138.

[18] Hart, Oliver and John Moore (1999b). "On the Design of Hierarchies: Coordination versus Specialization," Working paper: Harvard University and London School of Economics.

[19] Holmström, Bengt (1979). "Moral Hazard and Observability." *Bell Journal of Economics*, 10, 74-91.

[20] Holmström, Bengt (1982). "Moral Hazard in Teams." *Bell Journal of Economics*, 13, 324-340.

[21] Kreps, David, Paul Milgrom, John Roberts, and Robert Wilson (1982). "Reputation and Imperfect Information." *Journal of Economic Theory*, 27, 253-279.

[22] Legros, Patrick and Steven Matthews (1993). "Efficient and Nearly Efficient Partnerships." *Review of Economic Studies*, 60, 599-611.

[23] Legros, Patrick and Andrew Newman (1999). "Competing for Ownership," Working paper, London: ECARES and University College London.

[24] Maskin, Eric (1999). "Nash Equilibrium and Welfare Optimality." *Review of Economic Studies*, 66, 23-36.

[25] Maskin, Eric and John Moore (1999). "Implementation and Renegotiation." *Review of Economic Studies*, 66, 39-56.

[26] Maskin, Eric and Jean Tirole (1999). "Unforeseen Contingencies and Incomplete Contracts." *Review of Economic Studies*, 66, 83-114.

[27] Mirrlees, James (1999). "The Theory of Moral Hazard and Unobservable Behavior, Part I." *Review of Economic Studies*, 66, 3-22.

[28] Moore, John and Rafael Repullo (1988). "Subgame Perfect Implementation." *Econometrica*, 56, 1191-1220.

[29] Segal, Ilya (1999). "Complexity and Renegotiation: A Foundation for Incomplete Contracts." *Review of Economic Studies*, 66, 57-82.

[30] Sobel, Joel (1985). "A Theory of Credibility." *Review of Economic Studies*, 52, 557-573.

[31] Tirole, Jean (1999). "Incomplete Contracts: Where Do We Stand?" *Econometrica*, 67, 741-781.

[32] Watson, Joel (1999). "Starting Small and Renegotiation." *Journal of Economic Theory*, 85, 52-90.

7

Reputation Effects and the Limits of Contracting: A Study of the Indian Software Industry

Abhijit V. Banerjee
Esther Duflo

Abstract

This paper examines evidence of the role that reputation plays in determining contractual outcomes. We conduct an empirical analysis of the Indian customized software industry, using a data set we collected containing detailed information on 230 projects carried out by 125 software firms. We propose a model of the industry where reputation determines contractual outcomes. The evidence supports the view that reputation matters. *Ex ante* contracts, as well as the outcome after *ex post* renegotiation, vary with firms' characteristics plausibly associated with reputation. This holds after controlling for project, client, and firm characteristics.

1 Introduction

While the idea that there are severe limits to contracting and therefore reputation matters is now commonplace in economics,[1] little is known about the size of these effects. If these effects are shown to be large, they would imply a distinct view of the determinants of trade and growth, and, by implication, of policy: a view in which legal infrastructure and the availability of reputed firms could be as important as comparative advantage, human capital, and physical infrastructure.

This paper attempts to quantitatively assess the importance of reputation and, by implication, the seriousness of the limits on contracting, using data gathered from the Indian customized software industry. India is one of the largest exporters of software to the United States, but its legal infrastructure is widely seen as being quite primitive, limiting the scope for contracts. Contracts, however, play a vital role in the customized software industry since the structure of the industry invites holdups. The production process takes time — eight months on average — during which the firm commits a substantial

1. For an early expression of this view, see Fama [1980].

number of man-hours. The final product is typically quite specific to the client, so the client forgoes going to another firm. The client always keeps the property rights, and there is little general learning in the process of production.[2]

The extent to which contracts can protect, however, is limited by the fact that the desired end-product tends to be complex and difficult to describe ahead of time in a way that a court, especially an Indian court, would understand. At the outset, in most cases, neither the client nor the firm entirely understands what they are setting out to build. Disputes about the interpretation of the contract are not uncommon whenever there are cost overruns, *i.e.*, costs in excess of what was envisaged at the onset of the project. Both sides in these disputes accuse the other of failing to adhere to the letter of the contract, with the client claiming the software firm (hereafter: the firm) has not delivered what it had contracted to deliver, while the firm argues that the client has changed his demands. Given that the description of the product in the contract is highly incomplete, courts cannot be relied on to adjudicate correctly between these conflicting claims. In other words, contracts that target the source of the overrun are probably unenforceable. This is consistent with the fact that in the Indian industry we only observe fixed-price contracts (where the firm is supposed to absorb the entire overrun) and time and materials contracts (where the client is supposed to pay for all of it).

The basic hypothesis of this paper is that a role for reputation arises because contracts are limited in this way. We model reputation for being reliable: reliable firms and clients always pay for any overrun that they have generated, as long as the other side does the same. While this is what we often heard (many people told us "it was our fault and so we paid for it"), and it is consistent with the data (see Section 3), we recognize that other, related, forms of reputation are probably important in practice and that our empirical work cannot distinguish between them.

If all firms and clients were reliable, there would be no need for contracts about the sharing of overruns. However, it is usually impossible to be sure if the other side is reliable, hence the observation that all projects begin with either a fixed-price contract or a time and materials contract. While these contracts only protect one side from unreliable behavior by the other, that still dominates having no contract at all.[3] The choice of which side to protect depends on which side is more likely to be unreliable, *i.e.*, on the reputations of the two sides.[4] This generates correlations between reputation, the chosen contract, and contractual outcomes (such as the actual sharing of overrun) that we test in the empirical section.

2. In 90 percent of the cases we looked at, the platform and programing tools were known to the firm before starting the project.

3. The ineffectiveness of the Indian court system also limits the extent to which these contracts protect. The costlier, more corrupt, and slower the courts, the larger will be the concessions that the plaintiff will be willing to make in an out-of-court settlement. However, this is not to say that contracts are irrelevant. The renegotiated outcomes in our sample are indeed correlated with the initial contract. Anecdotal evidence suggests that some disputes do end up in court (at least one of the firms in our sample went to court). An Indian legal expert suggested that unless the plaintiff provides *prima facie* evidence that the court can interpret, the case has a chance of getting thrown out, which in this case amounts to upholding the written contract.

4. For an alternative view of what determines the choice between fixed-cost and time and materials contracts based on ease of renegotiation, see Bajari and Tadelis [1999].

The model suggested here is formally developed in Section 2. In Sections 3 and 4 we show that the model and its predictions are consistent with the observed facts. In particular, we find strong effects of reputation (measured in several different ways) on the choice of contracts and the contractual outcomes. Crocker and Reynolds' [1993] study of the procurement of airplane engines by the military is, to our knowledge, the only other paper that documents the effect of reputation (measured in their case by past disputes) on the choice of contracts (but not on the sharing of costs). The results of McMillan and Woodruff [1999] are also related. Using data from Vietnam and using several measures of trust including the length of the relationship and information from third parties, they show that interfirm trade credit is more likely when the delivering firm trusts its client.

2 A Model of the Software Industry

The model we propose in this section is an attempt to capture, in as simple a way as possible, the story of the industry told in the introductory section. The model adds endogenous contractual choice to a basic model of reputation formation along the lines of Diamond [1989].

2.1 Disagreements, Overrun, and Contracts

The client (C) wants the firm (F) to build a piece of software that will be worth V to the client (we will assume risk neutrality on both sides throughout, so that this is best thought of as a money payoff and the costs as money costs). In a world where the client can describe the product it wants perfectly and the firm also understands this description perfectly, the project should cost $\bar{y}$. We adopt the normalization that $\bar{y} = 0$. We assume, however, that in every real project the actual cost will be positive; *i.e.*, there will be overrun. One reason for this is that it is very costly for the client to describe *ex ante* exactly what it wants, and even if the description is perfect, it is too costly for the firm to understand it perfectly. Thus, total overrun will be the sum of overrun caused by the firm (y_F), and overrun caused by the client (y_C). We assume that all overrun is initially paid for by the firm.

The amounts of the overrun, y_F and y_C, are a result of choices made, respectively, by the firm and the client. Specifically, we assume that firms face a choice between a high level $\overline{y_F}$ and a low level $\underline{y_F}$. Likewise, the client faces a choice between $\overline{y_C}$ and $\underline{y_C}$.

Firms can reduce overrun by putting more effort into understanding what the client wants, by better management, and by assigning more able people to the project. Clients can reduce overrun by working more closely with the firm, and in particular, by being precise about what they want. Reducing overrun is therefore costly. The extra costs to the client and the firm from choosing a low level of overrun are, respectively, B_C and B_F. Assume that $\overline{y}_C - \underline{y}_C > B_C$ and $\overline{y}_F - \underline{y}_F > B_F$ so that it is always efficient to minimize overrun.

However, we will assume that both y_C and y_F are known only to the firm and its client. Third parties, such as the courts, only observe total overrun $(y_C + y_F)$.[5] Moreover, we restrict all contracts to being linear and additionally require that they do not involve throwing away any money. In other words, we only consider contracts where the client pays the firm an amount $P + (1 - s)(y_F + y_C)$, where P is a prespecified fixed payment and s is the share of the overrun borne by the firm ($s \in [0, 1]$) — and neither party makes any payments to third parties. Of particular interest to us will be two extreme contracts: the contract with $s = 1$ (corresponding to a fixed-price contract) and the contract with $s = 0$ (which corresponds roughly to a time and materials contract).[6] It is key to our analysis that neither of these contracts obviously dominates the other. The fundamental trade-off comes from the fact that s is one number that is being used to give incentives to both parties. A high s gives good incentives to the firm but not to the client, while a low s contract does the reverse. As a result, it is typically not possible to implement the first best.[7]

2.2 Norms, Courts, and Renegotiation

When the first best cannot be achieved by contractual means, it is possible to improve on the outcome if the behavior of the firms and the clients is at least partly norm-governed. Specifically, assume that there are two types of firms and two types of clients. Of these, one type of firm and one type of client observe a norm of being reliable. Reliable firms and clients pay for the overrun that they generate, as long as the other side is reliable, but act to maximize current profits otherwise. Assume by contrast that unreliable firms and clients are myopic and always act to maximize their current profits, although it is possible that this involves simulating reliability.

When a firm and a client are matched, they do not directly observe each other's types. Rather, on the basis of what it knows of the client (firm), the firm (client) puts a probability θ_C (θ_F) on the client's (firm's) reliability. θ_C and θ_F therefore measure reputation.

5. In other words, the fact that, say, two people were assigned to the project for fourteen weeks longer than originally planned is verifiable, but not whether it took that long because the firm had not understood what it had to do or because the client had changed his mind about what he wanted.

6. The correspondence is not exact because a time and materials contract typically pays a markup on the realized costs, rather than a fixed payoff. Similar results hold for that case but the exposition is somewhat more cumbersome.

7. This basic tension is very general. Our restriction to linear contracts, while vital in the discrete case we have chosen here, can be relaxed if we are prepared to go to the model where overrun varies continuously: the impossibility of implementing the first best in that case is a consequence of the results in Holmstrom [1982]. More intuitively, the fact that both sides can generate overrun but the courts cannot observe who was responsible generates a free-rider problem. This is what drives our model.

Our formulation leaves out one of the key ingredients of the standard reputation model, the type that Tirole [1996] calls opportunists who choose to be reliable, not out of inner compulsions but because it pays in the long run. However, note that in a reputational equilibrium this type is behaviorally indistinguishable from the true reliable type. Therefore, we can accommodate the possibility that a fraction of the reliable types are actually reliable by choice as long as we assume that there is some probability that unreliable behavior will become public and that in equilibrium no one contracts with those who are known to have been unreliable in the past (as in Kandori [1992] or Tirole [1996]). Introducing into our model opportunists who only sometimes behave reliably complicates the analysis but leaves the main results unchanged.

In our chosen setting, since the reliable firms and clients are going to be self-regulated, the function of the contract is to protect reliable clients against opportunism by unreliable firms and *vice versa*. When at least one side turns out to be unreliable, there is a dispute, and the contract becomes important. However, because going to court is costly, the contract is likely to be renegotiated. We assume that in the renegotiated outcome, the firm pays a share $s^*(s)$ of the overrun when there is a dispute. It is natural to assume that s^* is increasing in s. We also assume that s^* is bounded below by $\underline{s}^* > 0$ and above by $\bar{s}^* < 1$.[8] A higher s^* and a lower $\bar{s}^*$ correspond in a natural way to a less effective legal system.

The timing of the model is as follows: a firm and a client are matched and decide on a contract; the project is then carried out; people choose actions that lead to an overrun. At the end of the project, the overrun is observed, and the two parties decide whether or not to behave reliably. If either side is unreliable, there is a dispute, and the overrun is shared in the proportion $s^*(s)/(1-s^*(s))$.

2.3 Reputation Formation

There are several mechanisms by which reputation can evolve. First, in those cases where the firm and the client have contracted at least once before, the presumption is that both had behaved reliably so that they both now have a better reputation with the other.

Second, the age of the firm should be a source of reputation. We have already noted that in order for there to be a reputational equilibrium, there must be some probability that unreliable behavior becomes publicly known in the future. Once that happens, no one will want to contract with the guilty firm, and it will probably end up

8. Given that we have assumed risk neutrality, the natural interpretation for s^* is that it is the *expected* share of the overrun borne by the firm in the event of a dispute. The actual share will presumably vary according to the exact circumstances of the negotiation process, and, on occasion, may turn out to be 1 or 0.

going out of business. This selection process ensures that older firms (and clients) will typically be more reliable. This is reinforced by the fact that information is revealed over time, and therefore a firm that has been in the industry a long time and does not have any black marks against it, is more likely to be reliable.

Finally, firms may be able to establish a good reputation by demonstrating that they follow processes that, in principle, should reduce overrun. Process certification by outside agencies, such as ISO 9001 certification, is therefore another potential source of reputation.

2.4 Analysis of the Model

Firm Behavior. Reliable firms have only one choice, to choose between $\overline{y}_F$ and $\underline{y}_F$. Unreliable firms have the same choice, but in addition they can choose whether or not to mimic reliable firms in the current period. Clients face an exactly symmetrical choice. The following proposition gives sufficient conditions for there to be an equilibrium where reliable firms choose low overrun, and unreliable firms behave unreliably and choose high overrun.

CLAIM 1. The unique equilibrium behavior of reliable firms and clients is to choose $y_F = \underline{y}_F$ and $y_C = \underline{y}_C$, as long as $(\theta_C + \underline{s}^*(1-\theta_C))(\overline{y}_F - \underline{y}_F) > B_F$ and $(\theta_F + (1-\overline{s}^*)(1-\theta_F))(\overline{y}_C - \underline{y}_C) > B_C$. The unique equilibrium behavior of unreliable firms and clients is to choose $y_F = \overline{y}_F$ and $y_C = \overline{y}_C$, subsequently going into dispute, as long as $\overline{s}^*(\overline{y}_F - \underline{y}_F) < B_F$, $(1-\underline{s}^*)(\overline{y}_C - \underline{y}_C) < B_C$, and $\underline{y}_F$ and $\underline{y}_C$ are both sufficiently close to 0.

For these conditions to be jointly satisfied, θ_F and θ_C have to be high enough, and s^* must be sufficiently bounded away from both 0 and 1. If the first condition fails, *i.e.*, if either θ_F or θ_C is not large enough, it does not pay to be reliable as the other side is very likely to be unreliable. When $\overline{s}^*$ is very large, it implies that the contract is very effective in punishing unreliable behavior by firms and therefore even unreliable firms will behave reliably. The same holds when $\underline{s}^*$ is very small. In the rest of the formal analysis, we will assume that these conditions hold.

The optimal contract and the sharing of overrun. The firm proposing the contract in our model knows its own type, and as result the proposed contract can be used as a signaling device. A firm that plans to be unreliable will prefer a contract where it pays very little of the overrun. Therefore, by choosing to absorb most of the overrun, a firm may be able to signal that it is reliable. Given that we are in a signaling environment, we expect that there will be many equilibria. However, all such equilibria will involve pooling because in any separating equilibrium no one will contract with unreliable firms.

Among the set of pooling equilibria, we focus on contractual outcomes where the total joint surplus of a firm and a client who are both reliable is maximized. This is always a Bayesian-Nash equilibrium (sustained by the belief that only opportunists deviate). The fact that it is also Pareto optimal from the point of view of the reliable types makes it an obvious focal outcome.

This expression for joint surplus is

$$\begin{aligned} W(s, \theta_C, \theta_F) &= V - \theta_F \underline{y}_C - (1-\theta_F)(1-s^*(s))(\underline{y}_C + \bar{y}_F) \\ &\quad - \theta_C \underline{y}_F - (1-\theta_C)s^*(s)(\underline{y}_F + \bar{y}_C)\,. \end{aligned}$$

The third term in this expression gives the total surplus that is lost because in a pooling equilibrium a reliable client must allow for the possibility that the firm is unreliable, while the fifth term is the surplus that is lost because the firm must allow for the possibility that the client is unreliable.

From the linearity of this expression in s^*, it immediately follows that the optimal contract is always either a fixed-price or a time and materials contract (s is either 0 or 1). For any fixed level of client reputation, the more reputed the firm, the more likely it is that it is a time and materials contract.[9]

The expected share of the overrun paid by the average firm with reputation θ_F that works for a client of reputation θ_C, is $\theta_F\theta_C[\underline{y}_F/(\underline{y}_F + \underline{y}_C)] + (1-\theta_F\theta_C)s^*(s(\theta_F, \theta_C))$. Increasing θ_F has two effects on the expected share. First there is an effect through the choice of the contract. Second, keeping the choice of the contract fixed, there is a mechanical effect deriving from the fact that more reputed firms are more likely to behave reliably and keep their overrun under control. As a result, they end up paying a smaller share of the overrun as long as $s^* > [\underline{y}_F/(\underline{y}_F + \underline{y}_C)]$, which is likely for firms with low reputations since they face fixed-price contracts. However, note that for very reputed firms, as it is likely that $s^* < [\underline{y}_F/(\underline{y}_F + \underline{y}_C)]$, the net effect of an increase in reputation can be to increase their share of the overrun.

The mean overrun generated by a firm of reputation θ_F and a client of reputation θ_C is $\theta_F \underline{y}_F + (1-\theta_F)\bar{y}_F + \theta_C \underline{y}_C + (1-\theta_C)\bar{y}_C$. This is clearly decreasing in θ_F. Finally, the share of total overrun

9. The reader may feel that the result that the contracts are always at one or the other extreme is driven by the assumption of risk neutrality. This is partly true in the sense that if the two parties are sufficiently risk-averse a less extreme contract will be chosen. However, note also that s^* is always strictly between zero and one; the effective contract is never very extreme. Therefore, it may well be the case that the initial choice of an extreme contract is consistent with optimal risk sharing.

caused by the firm is $\theta_F\theta_C[\underline{y}_F/(\underline{y}_F+\underline{y}_C)] + \theta_F(1-\theta_C)[\underline{y}_F/(\underline{y}_F+\overline{y}_C)] + \theta_C(1-\theta_F)[\overline{y}_F/(\overline{y}_F+\underline{y}_C)] + (1-\theta_F)(1-\theta_C)[\overline{y}_F/(\overline{y}_F+\overline{y}_C)]$. Simple calculations show that this expression is decreasing in θ_F.

So far, our results describe the effect of increasing θ_F, keeping θ_C fixed. However, our data do not contain measures of the client's reputation. The same results, however, hold without conditioning for the client's reputation under two scenarios. The first is one where most clients have similar reputations. This is not implausible because most clients are well-established companies. Alternatively, we could assume that there is random matching. This may be plausible in at least some cases because clients have quite specific demands. Finding an Indian firm with the right specialization that can work on the required schedule may not always be easy, forcing the client to choose the one firm that, by chance, happens to be available at that time.[10] Under either of these scenarios we have

CLAIM 2. Firms with a better reputation are more likely to have time and materials contracts. In most cases they also pay for a smaller share of the overrun. There is less firm-generated overrun and less total overrun in contracts involving more reputable firms.

2.5 Discussion

Our model yields a number of clear-cut results, but only under rather stringent conditions. One key assumption was that all firms do similar projects. If firms in our model could choose their projects, low reputation firms would tend to gravitate toward projects with low $\overline{y}_C$ even at the cost of lower returns. This is because they have the most to lose if the client misbehaves.[11] This suggests that low reputation firms will tend to choose projects which are simple and well understood where the client does not have to do very much work to make clear what he wants. Firms that switch to a low $\overline{y}_C$ project should be *more willing* to accept a fixed-cost contract. Moreover, the switch to low $\overline{y}_C$ will tend to *raise* the fraction of the overrun generated by the firm, and therefore the firm will typically pay a *larger* part of the overrun. All of these effects go in the direction of our previous results. Total overrun may, however, no longer fall with reputation since low reputation firms choose low overrun projects.

Our model is also limited by the fact that, by assumption, contracts have no direct incentive effects. If the set of options faced by the firms and clients were less discrete, one would imagine that contracts would also have incentive effects. A high value of s would then

10. The random matching assumption is clearly indefensible in the case of repeat contracts. The fact that the client and the firm have agreed to work together again signals mutual respect. Compared with the initial match between them, both θ_C and θ_F should therefore be higher. The net effect is therefore potentially ambiguous. However, given that there are many more start-ups among firms than among clients, it is plausible the firm's reputation will improve by more than the client's reputation. In this case, repeat contracts will be more likely to be time and materials contracts, and the firm's share of the overrun in a repeated contract should be lower. For the case of first time matches, in a previous version of this paper we formalized an argument showing that, *ceteris paribus*, firms with low reputations will prefer to work with highly reputed clients. This is because they are particularly vulnerable to opportunistic behavior by the client. This kind of nonrandom matching reinforces our result that low reputation firms get fixed-price contracts and end up with a higher share of the overrun. However, it also weakens the relation between total overrun and the firm's reputation.

11. This is formally shown in a previous version of the paper.

have the additional effect of discouraging firms from generating very high levels of overrun. An incentive effect of this kind reinforces the correlation between low reputation firms and fixed-price contracts. However, it also means that low reputation firms do not necessarily generate more overrun than their more reputable counterparts. This, in turn, weakens the correlation between reputation and total overrun. It should also weaken the relation between reputation and the share of overrun that is *paid* by the firm. However, one would still expect this last correlation to be negative, as low reputation firms have fixed-price contracts and those who have fixed-price contracts pay for more of the overrun.

A generalized version of our basic model that allows for both project choice and the incentive effect of contracts would have the following predictions: 1) low reputation firms will choose projects that are simple and easy to define; 2) low reputation firms are more likely to face fixed-price contracts, and on average pay for a higher share of the overrun; and, 3) neither total overrun nor the overrun generated by the firm is necessarily correlated with its reputation.

The combination of the last two predictions is what distinguishes a model, like ours, that emphasizes incentive problems and reputation effects: low reputation firms in our model will face harsher terms *even if their actual performance (measured by overrun) is indistinguishable from that of high reputation firms.*[12] This is because what matters in this type of model is not what firms actually do, but rather, what they *could do*.

By contrast, theories where firms are paid based on performance, but not because of contracting problems — standard marginal product theories, for example — would predict a correlation between reputation and the share of overrun paid by the firm, *only if there was also a correlation between reputation and overrun caused by the firm* (which, in turn, suggests a correlation between reputation and total overrun).[13] Theories that give a central role to bargaining between the firm and the client, for example, can generate a correlation between reputation and the share paid by the firm if bargaining power is correlated with reputation, but would tend to predict the wrong correlation between contract type and reputation. Intuitively, a firm that has a lot of bargaining power will value having a fixed-cost contract less than a firm that is in weak bargaining position. Finally, risk-sharing-based theories would tend to predict the wrong correlation between reputation and the share of the overrun paid by the firm. Less reputed firms are typically smaller and have fewer assets, and should bear less of the risk (overrun).

12. There are of course other models within the general category of incentive/reputation-based models. For example, a model where the reputation is for quality of work rather than for reliability may have rather similar predictions.

13. One example of this class of theories would be one that says low reputation firms generate more overrun and therefore pay for them. An alternative would be the argument that low reputation firms set low estimates either deliberately or out of inexperience and end up paying more as a result.

3 • Descriptive Evidence

In this section and the following, we document that both the central assumptions and main implications of our model are consistent with what we observe in the industry. The data set used here was collected by interviews with the CEOs of 125 software firms in the three major centers of software production in India (Bangalore, Pune, and Hyderabad) in the winter of 1997–1998. We collected general information about each firm, and specific data about the last two projects completed by the firm. More information about the data collection process is presented in the Appendix.

3.1 Projects, Estimates, and Overruns

We focus in this paper on contracts for customized software projects. A *project* is a well-defined notion in the industry. It corresponds to a set of functions that the software must execute. These functions are (often loosely) described in the Request for Proposal (RFP) sent by the client when they first look for a firm. Most projects in the sample (75 percent) were for overseas clients. Common projects include the development of a customized application specific to the client, customization of a package, porting or reengineering of an existing solution, and testing of existing software. Seven percent of the projects in the sample were Y2K projects, and another six percent were other simple projects: data manipulation, web pages, and CAD projects.

In response to the client's RFP, several firms submit proposals. Then the client chooses one of these firms. Each proposal contains contractual terms and an *estimate*. Our understanding, based on descriptions in standard software management textbooks (*e.g.*, Pressman [1997]) and conversations with people in the industry, is that the estimate is supposed to be the firm's best guess as to how many hours will be needed to complete the project, *assuming that the firm's current understanding of the project is correct and that the firm adheres to its own productivity norms.*[14] The firm and the client understand that both these assumptions may be false. The project may take more effort than estimated either because the firm took the wrong direction on the project, or the client changed his demands, or because productivity in the firm was lower than it would normally be. This uncertainty is taken into account in the terms of the contract, but the estimate is still a useful benchmark.

We asked the firm what the initial estimate was for each project. Using a timeline representing the project (which we drew on

14. The software industry measures everything in the unit of man-hours. This reflects the fact that labor is the key input and all other inputs (computers, space, and phone time) are more or less linearly related to the number of employees.

a piece of paper as we conducted the interview), we then asked them to identify all the stages in the project when the estimate was revised and by how much (more details about the process are given in the Data Appendix). *Overrun* is defined to be the difference between the actual effort involved in completing the project and the estimate. Several different questions were asked about the level of the overrun, and we made sure that the respondent gave consistent answers to all the questions, probing him if there was an inconsistency. We are confident that the figure we obtained for the overrun is a reliable measure of the difference between actual cost and the estimate. It is, of course, possible that the estimate itself was manipulated. A high estimate would favor an unreliable firm and a low estimate an unreliable client, and moreover, the estimate could be used for signaling at the precontracting stage. However, the fact that the client gets several competing estimates and the fact that there are standard methods and computer packages (used in 69 percent of cases) for computing the estimate make it much less likely that a firm would get away with substantially manipulating this number (the evidence in Section 4 on the level of overrun also gives us some confidence in the way we use these numbers).

Descriptive statistics are presented in Table 1. Overruns are frequent (75 percent of the cases), large (23 percent of the estimate on average), and variable (the standard deviation is 30 percent). We asked the firms to report the reason for the overrun by asking them what exactly happened in as neutral a way as possible. Firms attribute, on average, 45 percent of the overrun to changes explicitly required by the client, a further 12.8 percent to delay in the client's response at critical points, 19.5 percent to their own misunderstanding of the specifications of the project, and 9.1 percent to internal problems in the firm (for example, the loss of the project's manager). According to this, the client is responsible for 58 percent of the overrun on average (changes and delays in providing critical inputs), and the firm for 29 percent (misunderstandings and internal problems).

3.2 Clients and Contracts

Clients fall into two categories, external and internal clients. An internal client can be the firm's mother company (an American firm or an Indian group), or a company with whom the firm has a very long-term and open-ended relationship. For example, some software firms have established "Off-shore Software Development Centers" (OSDC), for their foreign clients whereby the firm dedicates a part of its office and manpower to that client. Even in the

TABLE 1

Descriptive Statistics

	External projects			Internal projects
	Mean	Median	Standard deviation	Mean
	(1)	(2)	(3)	(4)
Number of observations	167			57
Panel A: Project characteristics				
Project size (man-months)	75	27	141	207
Application area is familiar to the firm	0.68	1	0.47	0.69
Platform is familiar to the firm	0.90	1	0.30	0.93
Programming tools are familiar to the firm	0.87	1	0.34	0.84
Y2K, CAD, Web pages	0.14	0	0.35	0.07
Panel B: Reputation				
Founded 1993 or later	0.43	0	0.50	0.57
ISO certification	0.19	0	0.39	0.14
Worked with the client in the past	0.41	0	0.49	0.83
Panel C: Software firms and clients				
Number of employees in the software firm	147	60	279	153
Client is a Fortune 500 company or an Indian group	0.55	1	0.50	0.28
Client is an Indian firm	0.22	0	0.42	0.01
Panel D: Overruns				
Project cost > estimate (overrun)	0.75	1	0.43	0.70
Project cost < estimate (underrun)	0.02	0	0.15	0.10
Total overrun (percent of project cost)	23	15	30	27
Percent of overrun due to the client:	58	50	43	58
– Changes	45	50	43	47
– Client's delay	13	0	26	11
Percent of overrun due to the firm:	29	0	43	11
– Ambiguity in specifications	20	0	34	20
– Internal difficulties	9	0	25	-9
Panel E: Contracts (proportion)				
Fixed-cost contracts	0.58	1	0.49	0.23
Mixed contracts	0.26	0	0.44	0.07
Time and material contracts	0.15	0	0.36	0.67
Panel F: Share of overrun paid by the firm (percent)				
All contracts	57	77	45	20
Fixed-cost contracts	66	100	44	45
Time and material contracts	28	0	39	8
Fixed-cost contracts, firm responsible	86	100	33	no obs.
Fixed-cost contracts, client responsible	61	100	46	45

case of internal clients, the work is defined in terms of projects and is governed by a contract. However, the scope for unreliable behavior in this type of relationship is presumably much more limited, since both parties share the control rights. We will therefore view this kind of relationship as a substitute for reputation. Except for a few very large internal projects, internal and external projects are similar in nature.[15] Firms with internal projects are on average smaller and more recently established than other firms. Most firms who work for internal clients also do some work for external clients. We will use this feature to contrast the features of internal and external contracts.

Consistent with the predictions of our model, we observe only three types of contracts. Time and material contracts are the least frequent (15 percent). Fixed-cost contracts are the most frequent (58 percent). Mixed contracts divide the project into a specification phase (which is the first and most open-ended part of the project, where the client's needs are analyzed to design the broad architecture of the piece of software), and an execution phase (design, coding, and testing). A separate contract (time and materials or fixed-price) is signed for each part. The most frequent configuration is a time and materials contract for the specifications, and a fixed-price contract for the execution.

As assumed in our model, contracts are frequently renegotiated, but do indeed matter for the final outcome. This is shown in Panel F of Table 1. Firms bear on average 57 percent of the overrun. When they have a fixed-price contract, they bear on average 66 percent of the overrun (the median is 100 percent). When they have a time and materials contract, they bear on average 26 percent of it (the median is 0 percent). The data are consistent with our premise that some firms tend to pay for their mistakes no matter what the contract was. Even with fixed-price contracts, firms pay more (86 percent) of the overrun when they are fully responsible for it than when the client is fully responsible for it (61 percent). The ordering is the same for time and materials contracts.

3.3 Reputation

As discussed in the theory section, we consider three measures of reputation: the age of the firm, the fact that the firm has previously worked with the client (41 percent of the contracts), and ISO certification (19 percent of the contracts). In addition, we contrast internal and external contracts among firms that do some internal contracts.

15. The difference in mean effort (207 man-months for internal projects, 75 man-months for external projects) is driven by a few very large internal contracts. The median efforts are similar in both cases (25 and 27 man-months, respectively).

Preliminary evidence suggests that the principal empirical implications of our model are not rejected by the data. In Figure 1 we plot the proportion of fixed-cost contracts as a function of the age of the firm. In Figure 2 we plot the average share of overrun that is paid by the firm. Both the proportion of fixed cost contracts and the firm's share of the overrun strongly decrease with the age of the firm, in particular in the first five years (which is consistent with the prediction that the marginal effect of reputation declines as reputation increases). Table 2 shows the proportion of fixed-cost contracts, the firm's share of the overrun, and other project characteristics for each type of firm, and the difference between low and high reputation firms. Standard errors of the means and the difference in means are presented in parentheses. In columns (1) to (3) we show the contrast between young firms (created in 1994 or after) and old firms (created in 1993 or before). Young firms are significantly more likely to have fixed-price contracts (the probability is 26 percent higher). They also, on average, bear substantially more of the overrun (19 percent more). These differences are significant at the 95 percent level of confidence. ISO-certified firms (columns (4) to (6)), by contrast, are no less likely to get fixed-price contracts nor to pay less overrun than other firms. Firms engaged in a repeated relationship with their client are 9 percent less likely than other firms to have fixed-price contracts (columns (7) to (9)), although the difference is not significant, and they pay significantly less of the overrun (20 percent less). Finally, firms that have internal contracts pay for more of the overrun when they deal with external clients than when they deal with internal clients. Almost half of their external contracts are fixed-price contracts, whereas only 23 percent of the internal

FIGURE 1

Proportion of Fixed Cost Contracts

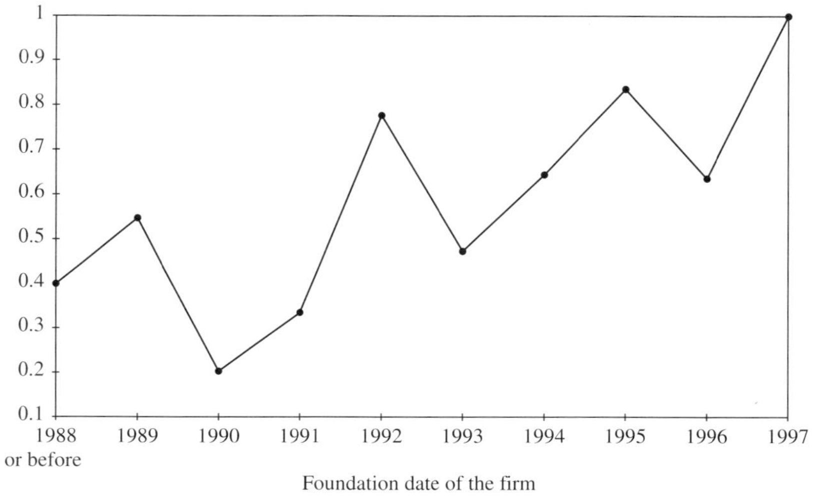

FIGURE 2

Share of Overrun Paid for by the Firm

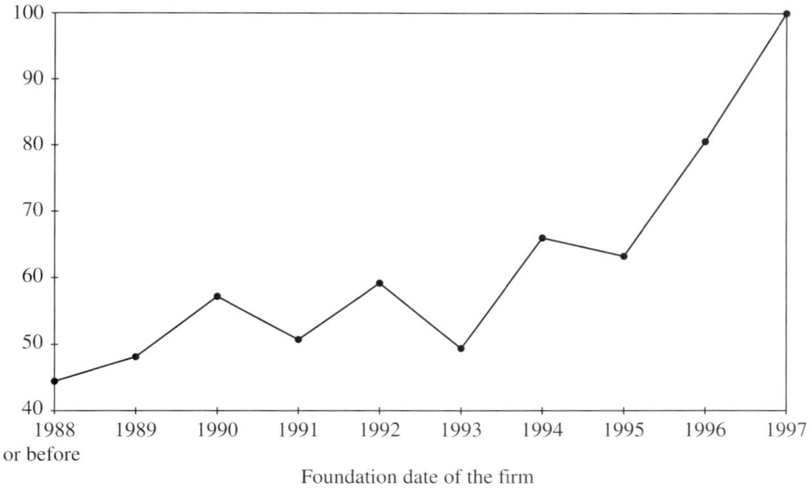

contracts are fixed-price contracts. Firms pay a much smaller share of the overrun (20 percent instead of 47 percent) in internal contracts than in external contracts.

This set of contrasts among the contracts and contractual outcomes of the different types of firms is not explained by obvious differences in firms' behavior or abilities, at least to the extent that these would be reflected in different overruns or different probabilities of delay.[16] In Table 2 we present the total overrun of the project, the total overrun due to the firm, and the proportion of projects that were delivered with a delay. None of the differences between high and low reputation firms are significant. If anything, total overruns and the probability of delay are somewhat smaller for young firms than for old firms, for non-ISO firms than for ISO firms, and for external contracts than for internal contracts.

We interpret these results as showing that reputation (except for ISO certification) does influence the way the overruns are shared between the client and the firm. To confirm this interpretation, we now turn to regressions estimates, which allow us to control for project, firm, and client characteristics which may have independent effects on both the contract and the outcome and may be correlated with our measures of reputation.

16. Delay is clearly an important index of the firm's performance. For simple projects where quality can be controlled relatively easily, clients are primarily concerned about delays (in 54 percent of the cases the deadline was extremely important or critical to the client). Delay is useful for us because it provides a check on the firm's performance that does not rely on the *estimate* which, as we have noted, might be subject to some manipulation.

TABLE 2

Descriptive Statistics, by Reputation

	External contracts									Firms that have internal projects		
	Firm foundation date			ISO 9001 certification			Relationship with the client			Type of project		
	> 1993	≤ 1993	Difference	No	Yes	Difference	New client	Repeated	Difference	External	Internal	Difference
	(1)	(2)	(3)	(4)	(5)	(6)	(7)	(8)	(9)	(10)	(11)	(12)
Proportion of fixed-cost contracts	0.73 (0.053)	0.47 (0.052)	0.26* (0.089)	0.59 (0.042)	0.53 (0.090)	0.061 (0.12)	0.62 (0.049)	0.53 (0.061)	0.087 (0.092)	0.45 (0.061)	0.23 (0.051)	0.22* (0.080)
Share of overrun paid for by the firm	68.6 (5.16)	49.3 (6.25)	19.4* (8.10)	56.9 (4.59)	57.8 (8.84)	-0.98 (10.4)	64.2 (4.94)	44.2 (6.73)	20* (8.27)	46.7 (6.36)	20.2 (5.82)	26.6* (8.67)
Mean of overrun (percent of initial estimate)	19.9 (2.84)	24.8 (2.65)	4.9 (5.16)	20.1 (1.89)	33.75 (6.10)	13.65 (8.64)	23.3 (2.59)	22.02 (2.86)	1.28 (4.84)	15.9 (2.55)	4.4 (-4.21)	-11.5 (5.92)
Overrun caused by the firm	7.52 (2.34)	7.03 (1.28)	0.49 (3.18)	6.97 (1.32)	10.9 (3.24)	-3.90 (4.24)	8.19 (1.81)	7.04 (1.49)	1.15 (3.39)	4.61 (1.64)	7.46 (2.86)	-2.85 (4.61)
Project late	0.15 (0.043)	0.23 (0.043)	-0.074 (0.062)	0.18 (0.03)	0.28 (0.081)	-0.10 (0.078)	0.22 (0.042)	0.17 (0.045)	0.06 (0.063)	0.18 (0.047)	0.20 (0.049)	-0.02 (0.068)

Standard errors are in parentheses. The standard errors of the differences in means are corrected for clustering at the firm level. An asterisk indicates that the difference is statistically different from 0 at the 95 percent level of confidence.

4 Evidence from Regressions

4.1 Choice of Contract

The theory suggests that there is a threshold, such that when the reputation of a firm crosses it, the optimal contract switches from time and materials to fixed-price contracts. In practice, this threshold should vary by firm, client, and project characteristics, and perhaps also in response to other environmental features. Therefore, the natural model to estimate is a discrete choice model. In our setting there are three kinds of contracts that can be ordered. Fixed-cost contracts give the most incentives to the firms, time and materials contracts give the most incentives to the clients, and mixed contracts are in between. We therefore assign a "1" to a fixed-price contract, a "2" to a mixed contract, and a "3" to a time and materials contract, and estimate an ordered probit model for the choice of contract.

Empirically, potential determinants of contract choice include not only reputation characteristics (a dummy for whether the firm was created after 1993, a dummy for whether the firm has worked with the client in the past, and a dummy for whether the firm is ISO certified) but also other variables potentially correlated with reputation, which may affect the choice of contract.

First, if firms and clients were risk-averse (in contrast to what we assume in the theory section), contracts would reflect risk-sharing motives. The contract may then depend on the client's and firm's size (as a proxy for their risk aversion). The inherent uncertainty of the project (which should be correlated with estimated project size, the complexity of the project, the degree to which the firm and the client are familiar with the project, etc.) should also influence the choice of contract. Since the client is generally much bigger than the firm, we might expect that characteristics which make the project riskier will also make it more likely that the chosen contract is a time and materials or a mixed contract.

Second, Crocker and Reynolds [1993] argue that fixed-price contracts are more likely when it is easier to draft an exhaustive list of requirements (a complete contract). Their empirical analysis confirms these predictions. Contracts tend to be fixed-price if the engine is well-known or the production cycle is short. In our context, this would also suggest that the contract is more likely to be a time and materials contract if the project is large and if the area of application or the platform is not familiar to the firm. We would also expect that extremely well-defined projects (such as CAD or Y2K projects) are more likely to have fixed-price contracts.

To summarize, denote by C_{ic} the type of contract obtained by firm i in contract c, by R_{ic} the vector of reputation variables, by X_{ic} the project characteristics, by Z_{ic} the firm's characteristics, and by M_{ic} the client's characteristics. We estimate the following model by ordered probit:[17]

$$C_{ic} = \alpha R_{ic} + \beta X_{ic} + \gamma Z_{ic} + \delta M_{ic} + \upsilon_i + w_{ic}. \qquad (1)$$

Results are presented in Table 3, columns (1) and (2). A negative coefficient on a variable indicates that the contract is moving away from time and materials toward fixed-price. Controlling for client and firm size, the client's country, and project characteristics, young firms are significantly more likely to have fixed-price contracts. Firms that work with a repeated client are more likely to have a time and materials contract, but the difference is not significant. ISO-certified firms are *more* likely to have a fixed-price contract, although this coefficient is not significant. These results confirm the descriptive statistics presented in Table 2.[18] In column (2) we focus on firms that have internal clients. When these firms work with an internal client, they are significantly more likely to have a time and materials contract than when they work with an external client.

Interestingly, project characteristics do not seem to influence the choice of contract. Firm and client size have no impact either. There is no strong evidence that risk-sharing or the difficulty in drafting the contract (as in Crocker and Reynolds [1993]) plays an important role in determining the contract.[19]

4.2 Share of the Overrun Paid by the Firm

A quantitative measure of the importance of reputation is obtained by estimating the effect of reputation on the share of the overrun that is actually paid by the firm. Our model predicts that reputation influences the share of the overrun paid by the firm both without conditioning on the contract, and potentially also after conditioning on the contract. We therefore run both regressions. Clearly, when we do not condition for the contract, we should control for all the characteristics that affect contractual choice. Once we condition on the contract, realized overrun and share paid by the firm are jointly determined. We focus on the estimation of a reduced form, as we do not have instruments for unpredicted overrun that would be necessary to estimate a structural model.

We therefore estimate the model using a random-effects specification model:

$$S_{ic} = \alpha R_{ic} + \beta X_{ic} + \gamma Z_{ic} + \delta M_{ic} + \lambda C_{ic} + \upsilon_i + w_{ic}, \qquad (2)$$

and its equivalent excluding C_{ic}.

17. The standard errors are corrected for firm-level grouping.

18. We have also interacted the fact of working for a repeat client with the age of the firm. Working with a repeat client makes it more likely that they have a time and materials contract, and this is not true for old firms. This suggests that old firms may have a strong enough reputation in the market to make specific bilateral relationships relatively unimportant.

19. This argument assumes that the project characteristics that we include in the regression are correlated with project risk and the difficulty of drafting a complete contract. We present later evidence that overrun is correlated with these characteristics. We also found (but to save space do not report) that the effort put into drafting the proposal (a measure of the difficulty to draft the contract) is correlated with these characteristics.

TABLE 3

Regression Results: Choice of Contracts and Share of Overrun Paid by the Firm

	Choice of contract Ordered probit		Share of overrun paid by the firm					
			Unconditional				Conditional	
			Random effect		Fixed effect		Random effect	Fixed effect
	(1)	(2)	(3)	(4)	(5)	(6)	(7)	(8)
Reputation								
Young firm	-0.69*		15*				9.0	
	(0.25)		(8.5)				(8.6)	
Repeated contract	0.22		-17*		-20		-15*	-19
	(0.24)		(8.8)		(16)		(8.7)	(17)
ISO-certified firm	-0.27		17				16	
	(0.32)		(13)				(13)	
Internal project		0.87*		-25*		-64*		
		(0.31)		(11)		(26)		
Contract								
Fixed-cost contract							13	12
							(9.4)	(25)
Time and material contract							-12	15
							(13)	(34)
Firm and client characteristics								
Number of employees (/100)	0.44	-0.44	-4.1	-2.4			-4.8	
	(0.98)	(1.1)	(7.7)	(5.0)			(4.5)	
Client is big	0.15	-0.18	-17	-13	-16	-40	16	-16
	(0.22)	(0.30)	(8.5)	(10)	(16)	(32)	(8.3)	(16)
Client is Indian	-0.43*	-0.76	13	23	-46*	14	9.3	-45*
	(0.27)	(0.63)	(9.5)	(18)	(20)	(41)	(9.5)	(21)
Project characteristics								
Estimated project size (man-months/10)	0.01	0.00	-0.12	0.35	-2.4	2.1	-0.13	-2.1
	(0.017)	(0.011)	(7.7)	(.38)	(1.9)	(2.6)	(0.76)	(2.0)
Area is familiar	0.08	0.09	-9.0	-4.0	18.9	-1.5	-6.3	16
	(0.25)	(.027)	(9.4)	(12)	(21)	(28)	(9.2)	(22)
Platform is familiar	0.60	0.20	26	1.9	48	61	29	49
	(0.48)	(0.59)	(20)	(12)	(35)	(74)	(19)	(36)
Y2K, data manipulation, etc.	-0.13	0.15	19	-4.8	-47		15	-41
	(0.32)	(0.35)	(17)	(25)	(36)		(16)	(39)

Standard errors (corrected for clustering at the firm level in columns (1) and (2)) are in parentheses. An asterisk indicates that the coefficient is significant at the 90 percent level of confidence.
All regressions include the following additional variables: number of employees squared, project size squared, and an indicator for whether tools are familiar to the firm. Sample in columns (1), (3), (5), (7), and (8) include all external projects (167 projects in 92 firms). Sample in columns (2), (4), and (6) include all projects of firms that do some internal work (88 projects in 58 firms).

The dependent variable of interest is measured only when there is an overrun.[20] We have also estimated a Heckman [1979] sample selection model, excluding the vector of project characteristics X_{ic} in equation (2). This exclusion is justified, as we have seen that they do not predict the type of contract. We do not report the results, which are very similar to the random-effects specification.[21]

Results are presented in columns (3), (4), and (7) of Table 3. Young firms pay 15 percent more of the overrun than old firms. Firms that work with a repeated client pay 17 percent less of the overrun than other firms. Both of these numbers are significant at the 90 percent level. ISO firms tend to pay more of the overrun than non-ISO firms. Firms pay 20 percent less of the overrun when they do internal projects. Bigger firms, firms that work with a foreign client, and firms that work for a big client (a Fortune 500 company, or an Indian group) pay less of the overrun. Conditional on the type of contract (column (7)), young firms pay more of the overrun (9 percent), but the difference is not significant. Firms that work with the client for the second time pay more of the overrun. The difference is as large as in the unconditional specification and remains significant. The fact that the age effect is small once we condition on the type of contract is not surprising. Once we control for contract type, the effect of age in our basic model comes from the fact that young firms generate more overrun (this is what we call the mechanical effect). In the more general model suggested in subsection 2.5, the correlation between age and firm-generated overrun disappears. As we will see, the data confirm the absence of such a correlation. The strong effect of repeat contracts, even after we control for the type of contract, is probably due to an effect that our model does not capture: in the real world, clients that have had a good experience with a firm are more likely to behave reliably since they want to retain the firm. In other words, reliability may be endogenous.

We use the fact that we have two observations for most firms to estimate a fixed-effects model. Fixed-effects wipe out both the effect of the age of the firm and the effect of whether it is an ISO firm, thus allowing us to look more closely at the effect of being in a repeated contract. Specifically, it allows us to check whether this effect is spuriously generated by the fact that better firms pay less of the overrun and are more likely to work again with the same client. It also gives us better estimates of the effect of internal contracts and other characteristics. Columns (5) and (8) present results for repeated contracts. Not surprisingly, the fixed-effects specification is much noisier than the random-effects specification. However, the point estimate of the effect of working with a repeated client is practically unaffected (– 20 percent instead of – 17 percent).[22] The effect of working with an internal client

20. In cases where there is a 0 or negative overrun, we could impute the sharing of the overrun predicted by the contract since in such cases the contract is never revised (in fact, 0 overrun often means a very small positive or negative overrun). The results are similar if we use this alternative variable. However, as we are interested in how large overruns are shared, it would be misleading to include the cases where there was very little overrun, because what happened in these cases does not necessarily tell us what would have happened if the overrun had been large.

21. We have also experimented with a double-sided tobit model, which takes into account the fact that the share of the overrun paid by the firm is bounded between 0 and 100 percent. The results are qualitatively similar; hence, we focus on the linear model.

22. The only coefficients affected are those of working with an Indian client and of doing Y2K projects, which become negative.

on the share of the overrun, shown in column (6), is *bigger* in the fixed-effects specification than in the random-effects specification.

4.3 Overruns and Project Characteristics

An alternative interpretation of our results could be that some characteristic of the firm, unobserved by us, but known to the client (say, the quality of the firm) is correlated both with the choice of contract (*e.g.*, good firms get time and materials contracts) and with our measures of reputation. However, as we have discussed in the theory section, this class of explanations would imply a correlation between the performance of the firm and its reputation. In contrast, our model, in its more general form, suggests that there can be a correlation between the contractual outcomes and the reputation of the firm, even in the absence of any link between the performance of the firm and its reputation.

Therefore, we estimate equations similar to equation (2) but with a measure of firm performance — such as total overrun (as a percentage of the initial estimate), overrun generated by the firm, and delay as the dependent variables. To save space, we report only random-effects estimates. Fixed-effects point estimates are similar.

Results are presented in columns (1) to (5) of Table 4. Neither client overrun nor overrun due to the firm is correlated with the reputation of the firm. They are not correlated with client and firm characteristics either, but are correlated with some of the project characteristics. Shorter projects have smaller overruns in percentage terms, as do projects where the platform is familiar to the firm and simple projects such as Y2K or CAD projects. The coefficients on reputation as well as those corresponding to firm, client, and project characteristics are similar irrespective of whether or not we control for the contract. Interestingly, in the cross section, total overrun (but not the overrun generated by the firm) seems to be bigger in fixed-cost contracts. If, perhaps as suggested by Crocker and Reynolds [1993], time and materials contracts were associated with less effort being put into the precontracting stage, one would have expected the opposite to hold. However, the association disappears in the fixed-effects regression. We also find that project delay is not systematically associated with reputation.

Finally, we examine whether the choice of projects is influenced by a firm's reputation. Once we control for size, young firms do not tend to do shorter projects (column (6)). However, consistent with our model, they do more Y2K projects (column (7)), and their projects are, according to their own assessment, simpler (column (8)).[23]

23. We asked the firms to provide all the metrics that were relevant to the project: line of codes, number of modules, of screens, etc. After this we asked them the following: taking everything into account, how would you rate the complexity of the project (on a scale of 1 to 5)? The dependent variable in column (8) is this subjective measure.

TABLE 4

Regression Results: Overruns and Project Characteristics

	Total overrun		Overrun due to the firm		Delay	Project size	Y2K	Subjective complexity
	Unconditional	Conditional	Unconditional	Conditional				
	Random effect	Random effect	Random effect	Random effect	Probit	Median regression	Probit	OLS
	(1)	(2)	(3)	(4)	(5)	(6)	(7)	(8)
Reputation								
Young firm	-0.48 (5.0)	-3.8 (5.0)	2.5 (3.4)	1.5 (3.5)	-0.28 (0.22)	-6.4 (5.4)	0.48* (0.29)	-0.42* (0.21)
Repeated contract	1.8 (4.9)	1.5 (4.8)	-0.92 (3.5)	-1.2 (3.5)	-0.2 (0.24)	-16.3* (5.4)	0.34 (0.30)	-0.07 (0.20)
ISO-certified firm	15 (7.9)	16 (7.7)	5.4 (5.4)	6.1 (5.5)	0.28 (0.37)	18* (8.5)	-0.52 (0.40)	0.08 (0.21)
Contract								
Fixed-cost contract		14* (5.4)		5.5 (3.9)				
Time and material contract		5.5 (7.5)		5.6 (5.4)				

Standard errors (corrected for clustering at the firm level in columns (5), (7), and (8)) are in parentheses.
An asterisk indicates that the coefficient is significant at the 90 percent level of confidence.
All regressions include the following additional variables: number of employees squared, project size squared, and indicator for whether tools are familiar to the firm.
Sample includes all external projects (167 projects in 92 firms).

	Total overrun		Overrun due to the firm		Delay	Project size	Y2K	Subjective complexity
	Unconditional	Conditional	Unconditional	Conditional				
	Random effect	Random effect	Random effect	Random effect	Probit	Median regression	Probit	OLS
	(1)	(2)	(3)	(4)	(5)	(6)	(7)	(8)
Firm and client characteristics								
Number of employees (/100)	-0.77*	-0.38	0.32	0.38	0.08	7.2*	0.23*	0.11*
	(0.24)	(0.24)	(1.7)	(1.7)	(0.13)	(2.4)	(0.11)	(0.066)
Client is big	0.88	0.43	1.8	1.3	-0.34	7.4	-0.05	0.11
	(4.8)	(4.8)	(3.4)	(3.4)	(0.23)	(5.3)	(0.24)	(0.17)
Client is Indian	4.1	2.8	-0.55	-0.78	0.07	-12*	-0.34	0.03
	(5.6)	(5.6)	(4.0)	(4.0)	(0.25)	(6.4)	(0.33)	(0.18)
Project characteristics								
Estimated project size (man-months)	0.11*	0.11*	0.04	0.04	0.01			
	(0.040)	(0.040)	(0.03)	(0.03)	(0.22)			
Area is familiar	-5.6	-5.9	-1.5	-1.6	0.08			
	(5.1)	(5.1)	(3.7)	(3.7)	(0.25)			
Platform is familiar	-20*	-18*	-12*	-12*	0.21			
	(10)	(10)	(7.4)	(7.5)	(0.58)			
Y2K, data manipulation, etc.	-13*	-13*	-9.41*	-8.8*	0.20			
	(7.2)	(7.1)	(5.1)	(5.1)	(0.32)			

Standard errors (corrected for clustering at the firm level in columns (5), (7), and (8)) are in parentheses.
An asterisk indicates that the coefficient is significant at the 90 percent level of confidence.
All regressions include the following additional variables: number of employees squared, project size squared, and indicator for whether tools are familiar to the firm.
Sample includes all external projects (167 projects in 92 firms).

5 • Conclusion

We set out in this paper to look for evidence that reputation plays an important role in determining contractual outcomes. We argue that the evidence strongly supports this view, although given that we do not directly observe people making use of reputation, and that there are important unobservables that might affect our estimates, some doubts clearly remain.

The conclusion that reputation matters is of course important, for it gives support to a range of theories that are based on limitations of contracting. Moreover, it might suggest part of the explanation as to why the Indian software industry is not much larger (Indian software exports were only worth 3.4 percent of the 1995 worldwide outsourcing business) despite its obvious labor-cost advantage[24] and the fact that it is a very labor-intensive industry. Reputation at the firm level is one possible reason. Most Indian firms are simply not trusted enough to be given important contracts. While our evidence cannot directly substantiate this view, the fact that reputation is important within the Indian industry suggests that it may also be important when an American client is deciding whether to go to a firm in India or to one in the United States. The industry clearly recognizes this. When we surveyed the firms, the association of software exporters and the government were actively supporting the firms to acquire ISO certification as a way of improving their reputation. As we show, and as they have come to realize, ISO certification is not an effective source of reputation. The association of software producers has now switched to recommending a competing standard (called SEI), specific to the software industry. Our results also suggest that the industry might benefit from the establishment of a credible system for rating firms modeled on credit rating systems, by making it possible for the market to efficiently aggregate all that is known about each firm.

Appendix: Data Collection

The data set used in this paper was collected by one of the authors during the period of November 15, 1997, to February 15, 1998. The survey instrument was developed after extensive conversations with members of the software industry in Bangalore during the preceding summer, and pretested on ten firms before the actual survey began. The sample frame was the list of firms belonging to the government-exporting organization (the Software Technology

24. The United States imports a very large number of Indian software professionals for short-term assignments at a cost of more than twice what they would earn in India.

Park). Almost all exporting firms belong to this organization. We excluded 100 percent wholly owned subsidiaries of large U.S. firms (Microsoft, AT&T, Hewlett-Packard, etc.), as well as the largest Indian firms (TCS, Wipro, Infosys). We interviewed half of the remaining firms. We picked the firms randomly (in alphabetical order, skipping over one firm at a time). We contacted the firms by telephone and arranged an appointment with the CEO, usually in the following week.

The response rate was excellent. No CEO whom we contacted refused to meet with us. In Bangalore, where we spent the longest period of time, all the interviews were arranged. In the other centers, we had to replace a few firms due to unavailability of the CEO or another senior person during the time we spent there. Although nonavailability is in principle not random, we believe that this was not a big enough problem to significantly affect the randomness of the sample. The total sample consisted of 125 firms and 230 contracts.

The interview was conducted with the CEO in most cases, or with another senior person in the firm. We collected general information about the firm, and specific information about the last two projects completed by the firm using a structured questionnaire, available on our web pages. The important limitation is that we could not collect precise information on the client, data profits, or price charged per man-months by the firm. The project managers involved in the two projects discussed were often present as well, or contacted by telephone for classifications. The interviews lasted from an hour to an hour and a half.

The first part of the questionnaire was straightforward and was answered by the respondent without any need for verification. The project-specific information was either recalled by the respondent or checked from records. The projects had been completed very recently, and the information we collected is part of the data routinely collected by the firms in the course of the project. They therefore had no difficulty answering these questions.

To facilitate the interview and obtain comparable answers from firm to firm at each interview, as we were conducting the interview we drew a timeline representing the different phases of the project (proposal, specifications, development). We used the timeline to ask them what the initial estimate was, when it was revised (after the specifications, at what point in the project), and what the actual effort was. Several questions can be used to determine the actual amount of the overruns. First, we asked them how the actual figure compared with the estimate (making sure whether they referred to the last estimate or the initial estimate), and the reasons for these changes. Second, we asked them separately whether there was any delay due to the client, any delay due to internal difficulty, and any request for changes (and when). In the course of asking these questions, we also asked them whether there was any overrun due to each of these reasons, and we made sure that the numbers corresponded to what they had told us before. If they did not, we probed until we reached consistency (which was usually easily done).

Acknowledgements. We thank Daron Acemoglu, Philippe Aghion, Susan Athey, Roland Bénabou, Mathias Dewatripont, David Genesove, Jonathan Guryan, Oliver Hart, Douglas Miller, Dilip Mookherjee, Ashok Rai, Emmanuel Saez, Andrei Shleifer, Jean Tirole, Richard Zeckhauser, and two referees for helpful comments, and Paul Joskow for encouragement and support. We acknowledge financial support from the National Science Foundation, the Alfred P. Sloan Foundation, the Shultz Fund, and the John D. and Catherine MacArthur Foundation. We are especially grateful to the software professionals in India, who patiently answered our many questions, and in particular to Mr. N. R. Narayana Murthy, from Infosys Technologies Limited, whose help and insights were crucial throughout this project.

REFERENCES

[1] Bajari, Patrick, and Steven Tadelis, "Incentives versus Transaction Costs: A Theory of Procurement Contracts," mimeo, Stanford University, 1999.

[2] Crocker, Keith, and Kenneth Reynolds, "The Efficiency of Incomplete Contracts: An Empirical Analysis of Air Force Engine Procurement," *RAND Journal of Economics*, XXIV (1993), 127-146.

[3] Diamond, Douglas W., "Reputation Acquisition in Debt Markets," *Journal of Political Economy*, XCVII (1989), 828-862.

[4] Fama, Eugene F., "Agency Problems and the Theory of the Firm," *Journal of Political Economy*, LXXXVIII (1980), 288-307.

[5] Heckman, James, "Sample Selection Bias as a Specification Error," *Econometrica*, XLVII (1979), 153-161.

[6] Holmstrom, Bengt, "Moral Hazard in Teams," *Bell Journal of Economics*, XIII (1982), 324-340.

[7] Kandori, Michihiro, "Social Norms and Community Enforcement," *Review of Economics Studies*, LIX (1992), 63-80.

[8] McMillan, John, and Christopher Woodruff, "Interfirm Relationships and Informal Credit in Vietnam," *Quarterly Journal of Economics*, CXIV (1999), 1285-1320.

[9] Pressman, Roger S., *Software Engineering, A Practitioner's Approach*, 4th edition (New York, NY: McGraw-Hill Companies, 1996).

[10] Tirole, Jean, "A Theory of Collective Reputations (with Applications to the Persistence of Corruption and to Firm Quality)," *Review of Economic Studies*, LXII (1996), 1-22.

8

Intrinsic and Extrinsic Motivation

Roland Bénabou
Jean Tirole

Abstract

A central tenet of economics is that individuals respond to incentives. For psychologists and sociologists, in contrast, rewards and punishments are often counterproductive, because they undermine "intrinsic motivation". We reconcile these two views, showing how performance incentives offered by an informed principal (manager, teacher, parent) can adversely impact an agent's (worker, child) perception of the task, or of his own abilities. Incentives are then only weak reinforcers in the short run, and negative reinforcers in the long run. We also study the effects of empowerment, help and excuses on motivation, as well as situations of ego bashing reflecting a battle for dominance within a relationship.

> Tom said to himself that it was not such a hollow world, after all. He had discovered a great law of human action, without knowing it — namely, that in order to make a man or a boy covet a thing, it is only necessary to make the thing difficult to attain. If he had been a great and wise philosopher, like the writer of this book, he would now have comprehended that Work consists of whatever a body is obliged to do, and that Play consists of whatever a body is not obliged to do.
>
> Mark Twain, *The Adventures of Tom Sawyer* (1876, Chapter 2).

1 • Introduction

Should a child be rewarded for passing an exam, or paid to read a book? What impact do empowerment and monitoring have on employees' morale and productivity? Does receiving help boost or hurt self-esteem? Why do incentives work well in some contexts, but appear counterproductive in others? Why do people sometimes undermine the self-confidence of others on whose effort and initiative they depend?

These questions will be studied here from a unifying perspective, emphasizing the interplay between an individual's personal motivation and his social environment. We shall thus model the interactions between an agent with imperfect self-knowledge and an informed principal who chooses an incentive structure, such as offering rewards and threatening punishments, delegating a task, or simply giving encouragement, praise, or criticism.

It is a central theme of economics that incentives promote effort and performance, and there is a lot of evidence that they often do (*e.g.* Gibbons (1997), Lazear (2000)). In other words, contingent rewards serve as "positive reinforcers" for the desired behaviour. In psychology, their effect is much more controversial. A long-standing paradigm clash has opposed proponents of the economic view to the "dissonance theorists", who argue that rewards may actually impair performance, making them "negative reinforcers", especially in the long run (see, *e.g.* Kruglanski (1978) for an account of this debate, and Deci, Koestner and Ryan (1999) for a recent and comprehensive meta-analysis of experimental results).

Indeed, a substantial body of experimental and field evidence indicates that extrinsic motivation (contingent rewards) can sometimes conflict with intrinsic motivation (the individual's desire to perform the task for its own sake). In a now classical experiment (see Deci, 1975), college students were either paid or not paid to work for a certain time on an interesting puzzle. Those in the no-reward condition played with the puzzle significantly more in a later unrewarded "free-time" period than paid subjects, and also reported a greater interest in the task. This experiment has since been replicated many times, with numerous variations in design (*e.g.* Wilson, Hull and Johnson, 1981) and in types of subjects. For instance, similar effects were found for high-school students in tasks involving verbal skills (Kruglanski, Friedman and Zeevi, 1971), and for preschool children in activities involving drawing with new materials (Lepper, Greene and Nisbett, 1973). In daily life, parents are quite familiar with what we shall call the "forbidden fruit" effect: powerful or salient constraints employed by adults to enforce the prohibition of some activity often decrease the child's subsequent internalization of the adults' disapproval.[1] Kohn (1993) surveys the results from a variety of programmes aimed at getting people to lose weight, stop smoking, or wear seat belts, either offering or not offering rewards. Consistently, individuals in "reward" treatments showed better compliance at the beginning, but worse compliance in the long run than those in the "no-reward" or "untreated controls" groups. Taken together, these many findings indicate a limited impact of rewards on "engagement" (current activity) and a negative one on "re-engagement" (persistence).

1. See, *e.g.* Lepper and Greene (1978). Relatedly, Akerlof and Dickens (1982) suggest that imposing stiffer penalties for crimes might be counterproductive, if it undermines individuals' "internal justification" for obeying the law.

A related body of work transposes these ideas from the educational setting to the workplace. In well-known contributions, Etzioni (1971) argues that workers find control of their behaviour via incentives "alienating" and "dehumanizing", and Deci and Ryan (1985) devote a chapter of their book to a criticism of the use of performance-contingent rewards in the work setting.[2] And, without condemning contingent compensation, Baron and Kreps (1999, p. 99) conclude that:

> There is no doubt that the benefits of [piece-rate systems or pay-for-performance incentive devices] can be considerably compromised when the systems undermine workers' intrinsic motivation.

Kreps (1997) reports his uneasiness when teaching human resources management and discussing the impact of incentive devices in a way that is somewhat foreign to standard economic theory. And indeed, recent experimental evidence on the use of performance-contingent wages or fines confirms that explicit incentives sometimes result in worse compliance than incomplete labour contracts (Fehr and Falk (1999), Fehr and Schmidt (2000), Gneezy and Rustichini (2000*a*)). Relatedly, Gneezy and Rustichini (2000*b*) find that offering monetary incentives to subjects for answering questions taken from an IQ test strictly decreases their performance, unless the "piece rate" is raised to a high enough level. In the policy domain, Frey and Oberholzer-Gee (1997) surveyed citizens in Swiss cantons where the government was considering locating a nuclear waste repository; they found that the fraction supporting siting of the facility in their community fell by half when public compensation was offered.

Our aim here will be twofold. First, we want to analyse the "hidden costs" of rewards and punishments from an economic and cognitive perspective, rather than just posit an aversive impact on motivation. Indeed, given that incentives work quite effectively in many instances, one needs to understand in what cases they should be used with caution. More generally, we seek to give a precise content to the loosely defined notions of intrinsic and extrinsic motivation, and to clarify when, in the terminology of Frey (1997), the latter should be expected to "crowd out" or "crowd in" the former. This information-based, strategic analysis distinguishes our approach from Frey's reduced-form treatment of these issues.

We consider an individual (the agent, "he") who faces uncertainty about his payoff from taking a particular action. The unknown variable could be a characteristic of the person himself, such as raw ability, of the specific task at hand (long-run return, how difficult or enjoyable it is to complete, etc.), or of the match between the two. Naturally, the agent will undertake the task only if he has sufficient confidence in his own ability to succeed, and in the project's net

2. See also Lepper and Greene (1978), Kohn (1993) and Frey (1997).

return. As a result, people with a stake in his performance have strong incentives to manipulate signals relevant to his self-knowledge. Given that effort and ability are usually complements in the production of performance, they will want to boost his self-confidence, as well as his interest in the task. Thus, in much of this paper, a principal (parent, spouse, friend, teacher, boss, colleague, etc., "she") has a vested interest in (derives a benefit from) the agent's undertaking and succeeding in the activity.

In many circumstances, both parties have private information about the agent's suitability to the task. The agent usually has better knowledge of his previous performances and of the relevant circumstances (his effort intensity, the idiosyncratic factors that may have come into play). He will often also receive privately signals about the attractiveness or unpleasantness of the task, either from third parties (friends tell him that school is not fun, while cigarettes are cool), from having performed similar ones in the past, or simply from his own experience as he starts carrying out the current one. The principal, on the other hand, often has complementary private information about the task or the agent's prospects from it. For example, a teacher or manager is better able to judge the difficulty of the subject or assignment, which, together with the agent's ability, conditions the probability of success. The principal may know better than the agent whether the task is attractive, in terms of either being enjoyable to perform, or having a high payoff for the agent. Last, while having less direct information about the agent's previous performances, she may be better trained at interpreting it due to her having performed the task herself, or having seen many others attempt it. As we shall discuss later on, the observation that others may have private information relevant to an individual's self-view underlies several fields of research in education and management. It is this type of private information that will be our focus.[3]

In the first part of the paper we thus study the *attributions* made by an agent when a principal with private information makes a decision, such as selecting a reward, delegating a task or more simply encouraging the agent, that impacts the latter's willingness to perform the task. As was pointed out by Cooley (1902), the agent should then take the principal's perspective in order to learn about himself. The agent's attribution of ulterior motivation to the principal, or, in economics parlance, his attempt to infer her private information from her decision, is what Cooley termed the "looking-glass self". The influence of the principal's decision on the agent's behaviour is then twofold: direct, through its impact on the agent's payoff from accomplishing the task (keeping information constant), and indirect, through his inference process. In analysing intrinsic and extrinsic motivation we thus adopt a cognitive approach, assuming that the

3. Delfgauw and Dur (2002), in contrast, focus on the more standard case where workers have private information about their own (dis)utility from working on the task, which they may then want to signal to, or conceal from, the employer.

individual seeks to extract from the words and deeds of those around him signals about what they know that concerns him.[4]

We first show that rewards may be only *weak reinforcers* in the short term and that, as stressed by psychologists, they may have *hidden costs*, in that they become negative reinforcers once they are withdrawn. The idea is that by offering low-powered incentives, the principal signals that she trusts the agent. Conversely, rewards (extrinsic motivation) have a limited impact on current performance, and reduce the agent's motivation to undertake similar tasks in the future. We then use the same logic to show that empowering the agent is likely to increase his intrinsic motivation. Similarly, help offered by others may be detrimental to one's self-esteem and create a dependence.

More generally, we conclude that explicit incentives may, but need not, be negative reinforcers; our analysis actually suggests when rewards and punishments work, and when they backfire. The "crowding out" case first requires that the agent be less knowledgeable in some dimension than the principal; this asymmetry of information is likely to be more important in some settings (education, health, new occupations) than in others (relatively standardized jobs). Furthermore, a sorting condition must hold, in that the principal must be more inclined to offer a reward when the agent has limited ability or the task is unattractive. Otherwise, there will be "crowding in". Thus, when concerned about a potential negative impact of rewards, one should first check whether the reward provider has private information about the task or the agent's talent. One should then, as the agent does, think through the provider's ulterior motivation and how her payoff from giving a contingent reward is affected by her knowledge.

In addition to low-powered incentives, we also investigate how the principal can sometimes use non-contingent payments (similar to "burning money") to signal her confidence in the agent's ability. While their short-term incentive effects differ, reducing the slope of the compensation schedule (the piece rate) and increasing its base part (the fixed salary) are two related ways in which the principal's confidence-management motive will be reflected in equilibrium contracts. Each has its domain of applicability (as we show), but both have similar effects on intrinsic, or long run, motivation, as well as on wage inequality. Indeed, by weakening the link (elasticity) between performance and compensation, both signalling strategies reduce earnings inequality across workers, in a Lorenz sense.

While most of the social psychology and human resource management literatures emphasize the necessity of boosting and protecting the self-esteem of one's personal and professional partners, people often criticize or downplay the achievements of their spouse,

4. We in fact focus on the polar case where individuals are fully rational and Bayesian. Although people surely make mistakes in processing information, we want the model to reflect the fact that they cannot constantly fool themselves, or others.

child, colleague, coauthor, subordinate or teammate. In the second part of the paper we consider several reasons why this may be, and formalize in more detail what is perhaps the most common one. We argue that such "ego bashing" may reflect *battles for dominance:* by lowering the other's self-confidence, an individual may gain real authority within the relationship, enabling her to steer joint decisions or projects in a preferred direction. This generally comes at a cost, however, namely the risk of demotivating the partner from seeking good projects, or from exerting effort at the implementation stage. We study this tradeoff, distinguishing two related forms of ego bashing: one is "by omission", where the principal omits to report news favourable to the agent; the other is active "disparaging", in which she explicitly belittles the agent. While both strategies lower the agent's self-confidence, the first one is reversible (the news can always be revealed later on), whereas the second is not. This is shown to have interesting implications for the timing of strategic disclosures of information (ego bashing and ego boosting) in situations where both the agent's initiative and joint control rights are at stake.

The paper is organized as follows. Section 2 provides a general introduction to the "looking-glass self" mechanism. Section 3 analyses the interplay of intrinsic and extrinsic motivation, focusing in particular on the hidden cost of rewards. Section 4 shows how the main insights carry over to other confidence-management strategies such as delegation, help and coaching. Section 5 studies the costs and benefits of ego bashing. Section 6 offers concluding remarks.

2 • The Looking-Glass Self

We begin here with a relatively general and abstract framework, then specialize it in the rest of the paper. Readers more interested in specific psychological and economic applications than in a unified presentation of the underlying mechanisms may want to proceed directly to Section 3.

There are two players, an agent (he) and a principal (she). The agent selects a continuous action or effort level e that impacts both his and the principal's utilities. The principal knows a parameter β, such as the difficulty of the task or the agent's ability to perform it, that affects the agent's payoffs from e. Thus informed, she selects a policy p (belonging to $\mathbb{R}$, for expositional simplicity) prior to the agent's choice of action; this may be a wage or contingent reward, help, surveillance, delegation, disclosure of information, or any other "extrinsic motivator" that can affect, directly or indirectly, the agent's behaviour. The agent's and the principal's payoffs are denoted

$U_A(\beta, e, p)$ and $U_P(\beta, e, p)$. Prior to his decision, the agent may also privately receive a signal σ that is informative about β. We shall assume for simplicity that this signal is redundant if one already knows the principal's information (β is a sufficient statistic for (β, σ)), but none of our main conclusions hinge on this assumption. What really matters is that the principal has information relevant to the agent's perception of himself or his task, and (for the specific "trust effect" discussed below) that the principal be uncertain about the agent's motivation. The timing of the game is as follows:

Stage 1: The principal learns the parameter β and selects a policy p.

Stage 2: After observing the policy chosen by the principal and learning σ, the agent chooses an action e.

Let us assume here (for notational simplicity) that the agent's optimal action e^* depends only on p and on his conditional expectation $\hat{\beta}(\sigma, p)$ of the unknown parameter.[5] The conditioning of $\hat{\beta}$ on p is the "looking-glass-self" phenomenon, whereby the agent tries to see through the principal's ulterior motives that led to p being selected. As long as the agent's participation in the relationship is not at stake, the principal's expected payoff from choosing a policy p when she has information β is thus

$$\mathrm{E}_\sigma[U_P(\beta, e^*(p, \hat{\beta}(\sigma, p)), p) \mid \beta].$$

Assuming differentiability (again for simplicity), the principal's choice of policy takes three effects into consideration:

$$\mathrm{E}_\sigma\left[\frac{\partial U_P}{\partial p} + \frac{\partial U_P}{\partial e} \cdot \frac{\partial e^*}{\partial p} + \frac{\partial U_P}{\partial e} \cdot \frac{\partial e^*}{\partial \hat{\beta}} \cdot \frac{\partial \hat{\beta}}{\partial p} \middle| \beta\right] = 0. \qquad (1)$$

The first term on the L.H.S. of (1) is the direct effect of p on the principal's payoff. For example, if the policy is a wage or bonus, as in the next section, this term is the direct cost of this compensation, keeping the agent's behaviour constant. The second term corresponds to the direct impact of p on the agent's behaviour. Thus, *ceteris paribus*, a bonus increases the incentive to exert effort. These two effects have been investigated in detail in the agency literature.

We shall be interested in the third, more novel effect, which corresponds to the principal's *confidence-management* motive. Whenever the principal's choice of policy is guided by private information, the agent will update his beliefs in reaction to the choice of p (term $\partial\hat{\beta}/\partial p$). The principal must then take into account how the agent's interpretation of her choice will affect his self-confidence — that is, his perceived prospects from undertaking the task. A particularly important issue is whether a higher level of self-confidence

5. More generally, it will depend on p and on the conditional distribution of β, given (σ, p).

affects the agent's decision making in a direction that the principal likes $((\partial U_P/\partial e)(\partial e^*/\partial\hat{\beta}) > 0)$ or dislikes $((\partial U_P/\partial e)(\partial e^*/\partial\hat{\beta}) < 0)$. Sections 3 and 4 will examine many common situations where the principal gains from boosting the agent's self-confidence. Section 5, on the other hand, will focus on cases where she may be reluctant to enhance the agent's self-confidence, or may even want to undermine it.

The confidence-management motive itself can itself arise through two channels, which we term the *profitability effect* and the *trust effect*. The former arises when the agent's type, on which the principal has private information, enters the *principal's objective function* in a way that would lead her to offer different policies to different agents, even if it did not affect anyone's effort level. This differential profitability of a given policy across types corresponds to a standard sorting condition; thus, for a one-dimensional policy it means that[6]

$$\frac{\partial}{\partial\beta}\left(\frac{\partial U_P/\partial p}{\partial U_P/\partial e}\right) \text{ has a constant sign.} \qquad (2)$$

Suppose, for instance, that an employer's expected profits are (proportionally) more sensitive to the employee's ability when the latter is empowered to make decisions than when he is closely monitored. The principal will then, *ceteris paribus*, delegate more to employees she thinks more highly of, and delegation will be seen as good news by employees. In contrast, no such profitability effect exists when the principal's private knowledge concerns the cost of accomplishing the task, or other aspects of it that bear solely on the agent's utility, and not on her own payoff.

The trust (or distrust) effect, on the contrary, arises when the principal's private information concerns a parameter, such as the cost or pleasure of accomplishing the task, that directly enters only in the *agent's incentive problem* — as envisioned by the principal. The issue here is how confident the principal is as to the agent's intrinsic motivation — that is, how she thinks the agent perceives the task and his suitability to it. A principal who has bad news about the agent's parameter β will be pessimistic about the agent's own signal σ, and may consequently fear that he will not be motivated enough to exert effort in the absence of added incentives. Providing stronger incentives, however, will at least partially reveal the principal's damaging information (compounding the signal σ). Thus, once again, extrinsic motivation may "crowd out" intrinsic motivation, and the optimal contract will be shaped by this tradeoff.

It is worth noting also that for the pure trust effect to operate, there must be some uncertainty (σ) on the part of the principal about the exact incentives perceived by the agent. Otherwise, the latter's response $\hat{\beta}(p)$ to any policy p would be perfectly predictable, and

6. In Section 3.2.2 we shall actually consider two-dimensional policies, consisting of a lump-sum payment and a performance-contingent bonus. We shall then use the general "implementability condition" (see, *e.g.* Fudenberg and Tirole (1991, pp. 258-260)) that extends the Spence-Mirlees sorting condition to multidimensional policies $p = (p_1, \ldots, p_n)$: $\sum_{i=1}^{n} \frac{\partial}{\partial\beta}\left(\frac{\partial U_P/\partial p_i}{\partial U_P/\partial e}\right)\left(\frac{dp_i}{d\beta}\right)$ must have a constant sign.

the principal would simply maximize $U_P(\beta, e^*(p, \hat{\beta}(p)), p)$. It is easily verified that, absent a profitability effect (*i.e.* when the expression in (2) is zero, *e.g.* when U_P is independent of β), the optimal policy is then completely independent of, and hence uninformative about, the agent's type β. It is quite reasonable to assume, however, that the agent does receive a private signal, causing the principal to worry (be uncertain) about his resulting motivation. As mentioned earlier, this may come from past personal experience, or from friends and brethren. Another important source of information is the agent's own initial perception as he starts performing the task: how he feels after a few weeks or months on the job, at school or in a diet programme; after reading a few chapters of a challenging book, a few minutes of working on a puzzle or painting a fence, etc. In many such real-world cases, the effort decision e should be interpreted as a continuation or "perseverance" decision — that is, whether or or not the agent will carry the task to completion.

To bring into sharper focus the trust and profitability effects, let us specialize our framework further. Many of our applications (*e.g.* bonuses, help, delegation) will share a common structure, where the principal's payoff function can be written as $U_P(\beta, e, p) = e\Lambda(\beta, p)$. In this formulation, the agent's equilibrium effort e is a zero-one decision of whether or not to undertake the task, and the function Λ is the principal's expected payoff when $e = 1$. The profitability effect is then governed by the sorting condition

$$\frac{\partial}{\partial\beta}\left(\frac{\partial U_P/\partial p}{\partial U_P/\partial e}\right) = \frac{\partial}{\partial\beta}\left(\frac{e\Lambda_p(\beta, p)}{\Lambda(\beta, p)}\right)$$

$$= e \cdot \frac{\partial^2 \ln U_P}{\partial\beta\partial p} \text{ has a constant sign,} \tag{3}$$

which is a simple form of complementarity.

To capture the pure trust effect, assume now that U_P, hence also Λ, does not depend on β at all. Then, under mild conditions on $U_A(\beta, e, p)$ and the conditional distribution $G(\sigma \mid \beta)$, the agent will work only when he receives a signal σ better than some threshold $\sigma^*(p)$, which depends on the policy p due to the looking-glass phenomenon. The principal's expected profits can then be written as $[1 - G(\sigma^*(p) \mid \beta)]\Lambda(p)$. One may then, intuitively, treat the agent's action threshold σ^* as the effort variable that the principal is trying to influence through her policy p, and look at a sorting condition for the "reduced-form" objective function $[1 - G(\sigma^* \mid \beta)]\Lambda(p)$. This yields

$$\frac{\partial}{\partial\beta}\left(\frac{\partial U_P/\partial p}{\partial U_P/\partial\sigma^*}\right) = \frac{\partial}{\partial\beta}\left(\frac{1 - G(\sigma^* \mid \beta)}{g(\sigma^* \mid \beta)}\right) \times \frac{\Lambda'(p)}{\Lambda(p)}.$$

The sign of this expression corresponds to a monotone likelihood ratio property (MLRP), that will be seen to play a key role in the trust effect. Intuitively, a principal who observes a "bad" β is worried that the agent will receive (or has received) a bad signal σ, so she feels compelled to offer him a higher p. This, in turn, is bad news for the agent.

3 • The Hidden Costs of Rewards

We shall now specialize the general framework to a more concrete model, where the interplay of intrinsic and extrinsic motivation can be more transparently and completely analysed. In demonstrating how the "looking-glass self" mechanism can make high-powered incentives schemes too costly for an optimizing principal to adopt, we shall first emphasize the trust effect, then show how the profitability effect can reinforce or counteract it. Finally, we shall relate the premises and results of our model to the relevant psychology literature, and argue that they accord rather well with it.

There may of course be still other sources for the hidden costs of rewards; let us mention here two fairly obvious ones. Concerning the engagement part, Condry and Chambers (1978, p. 66) suggest that "rewards often distract attention from the process of task activity to the product of getting a reward". As for the re-engagement part, these same authors argue that current rewards may decrease the individual's willingness to persist, because they orient activity toward performance rather than progress. In other words, Condry and Chambers offer what to economists is a familiar multitask interpretation: the individual is led by short-term rewards to sacrifice long-run payoffs.[7] Thus, subjects who are paid to solve problems typically choose easier ones than those who do not expect any payment. While this explanation is well taken, it does not apply uniformly. For instance, the individual may not be aware of future re-engagement opportunities, or may just not face any investment decision that crowds out current efficiency — as in the previously mentioned programmes involving weight loss, smoking, and seat belts. The multitask story can also not account for the evidence drawn from subjects' posterior reports about their intrinsic interest in the activity.

3.1 Task Attractiveness and the Trust Effect

This section describes the interplay between intrinsic and extrinsic motivation in a situation with only a trust effect. It formalizes the idea emphasized in the psychology literature that the subject finds the task less attractive when offered a reward.

7. For example, in Laffont and Tirole (1988) an agent exerts effort today both to reduce current operating cost and to increase future efficiency. Faced with a higher powered incentive scheme (a greater sensitivity of current reward to current cost level), the agent substitutes toward current cost reduction and sacrifices long-term investment. For a broader perspective on multitasking, see Holmström and Milgrom (1991). Condry and Chambers' argument follows a similar pattern, with the individual allocating his attention between the resolution of the current problem and a "deeper understanding" of the problem.

As before there are two players, an agent and a principal. The agent chooses whether to undertake an activity or task (exert effort) or not (exert no effort). His disutility or cost of effort is denoted $c \in [\underline{c}, \overline{c}]$. If the task is successful it yields direct payoffs $V > 0$ to the agent and $W > 0$ to the principal; if it fails, their gross payoffs are both equal to 0. Success requires effort, but effort is not sufficient for success: let $\theta \in (0, 1]$ denote the probability of success when the agent exerts effort.

Our focus in this paper is on the principal's superiority of information; in this section, the asymmetry concerns the cost that the agent will bear if he decides to undertake the task; that is, $\beta = c$.[8] With little loss of generality, we assume that the principal knows c perfectly. The agent knows that c is drawn from a cumulative distribution function $F(c)$ with a density $f(c)$ that has full support; he also learns a signal $\sigma \in [0, 1]$ with conditional distribution $G(\sigma \mid c)$ and positive density $g(\sigma \mid c)$. We assume that a higher σ is "good news", in the sense of the MLRP

$$\text{for all } \sigma_1 \text{ and } \sigma_2 \text{ with } \sigma_1 > \sigma_2, \ \frac{g(\sigma_1 \mid c)}{g(\sigma_2 \mid c)} \text{ decreasing in } c. \qquad (4)$$

In order to induce the agent to perform the task, the principal can offer a reward that is contingent on effort if she observes it, or on output if she does not. In the present context where the probability of success θ is common knowledge and both parties are risk-neutral, the former situation is equivalent to the latter, as is perhaps most easily seen for $\theta = 1$. We shall therefore focus the exposition on contracts where the principal selects a reward or *performance-based* "bonus" $b \leq W$, to be paid in case of success. In applications where the agent is paid just to carry out the task, successfully or unsuccessfully (*e.g.* paying a child to read a book, independently of whether it will turn out to be useful to him or his parents), one will remember that when e is observable a bonus scheme is equivalent to a *wage offer* of $w \equiv \theta b$, in exchange for the mere supply of effort. Note also that negative wages or bonuses are allowed (as in the Tom Sawyer illustration discussed below).[9]

We shall initially abstract from the agent's participation constraint, and normalize the non-contingent part of the contract to zero. As we show later on, this does not affect the results, since the agent's cost c has no effect on the principal's gain from inducing him to perform the task. The agent's net benefit in case of success is thus $V + b$ and the principal's is $W - b$, while both parties obtain 0 in case of failure. The stage-1 policy decision for the principal is thus the choice of a reward which we formalize as being a monetary one; but, in line with the psychology literature, b could with slight modifications be

8. Equivalently it could be V, as long as it is uncorrelated with the principal's payoff W. As explained earlier, the pure trust effect concerns private information of the principal that directly enters only in the agents' incentive problem.

9. Alternatively, rewards could be constrained to be non-negative (an assumption that makes sense when the agent can sabotage his observable performance without destroying V, or when V is a private benefit or learning experience from undertaking the task). Proposition 1, in what follows, would then still hold, as the non-negativity constraint affects only the *extent* to which the principal can reveal her information.

interpreted as working conditions, praise, friendliness or (minus) punishment.

Were the agent to know his cost c, he would choose to exert effort if and only if

$$\theta(V+b) \geq c\,.$$

Thus, when the agent has the same information as the principal, the reward is a positive reinforcer. In our model, however, only the principal observes c; the agent receives only a signal σ about c.

We shall now analyse the perfect Bayesian equilibria of this two-stage game. When offered a reward b, the agent updates his beliefs about c using the principal's equilibrium strategy. Let $\hat{c}(\sigma, b) \equiv \mathrm{E}[c \mid \sigma, b]$ denote the agent's (interim) assessment of the task's difficulty, that is, his expectation of the cost, conditional on his signal and the reward he is offered. This expectation is a weakly decreasing function of the signal σ. Letting $e \in \{0, 1\}$ denote the agent's effort, his utility is $U_A = [\theta(V+b) - \hat{c}(\sigma, b)]e$, and there exists a threshold signal $\sigma^*(b)$ in $[0, 1]$ such that:[10]

$$\hat{c}(\sigma, b) \leq \theta(V+b) \text{ if and only if } \sigma \geq \sigma^*(b)\,. \tag{5}$$

The principal's payoff if she offers the performance bonus b when her information is c is thus

$$\mathrm{E}_\sigma[U_P] = \theta[1 - G(\sigma^*(b \mid c))][W - b]\,, \tag{6}$$

which she maximizes over b.

Throughout the paper, we shall ignore "degenerate" equilibria where the principal receives zero regardless of her type because the agent exerts no effort whenever $b < W$. Such equilibria, when they exist, are supported by very pessimistic beliefs that a principal who offers any bonus below W must have really bad information, say, $c = \bar{c}$. Conversely, degenerate equilibria are ruled out when $\theta(V+W) > \bar{c}$: by offering a bonus slightly below W, the principal can ensure that the agent works.[11] Let us now denote by B the set of *equilibrium* bonuses; that is, $b \in B$ if and only if b is an equilibrium offer by the principal for some "type" c. Clearly, if b_1 and b_2 both belong to B, with $b_1 < b_2$, then

$$\sigma^*(b_1) > \sigma^*(b_2)\,. \tag{7}$$

If this inequality did not hold the principal could, regardless of her information about c, (weakly) increase the likelihood of effort while offering the lower wage. Therefore, b_2 could not be an equilibrium offer.

10. If $\mathrm{E}(c \mid 1, b) \geq \theta(V+b)$, one can define $\sigma^*(b) = 1$; if $\mathrm{E}(c \mid 0, b) \leq \theta(V+b)$, one can define $\sigma^*(b) = 0$.

11. Degenerate equilibria would also disappear if we assumed that the principal's information is an almost, but not totally, sufficient statistic for the agent's true cost c, in the sense that there is always a very small but positive probability that the agent's signal σ is so favourable that he undertakes the task regardless of the inference drawn from the bonus offer.

Proposition 1. *In equilibrium:*

(i) *Rewards are positive short-term reinforcers: if* $b_1 < b_2$, *then* $\sigma^*(b_1) > \sigma^*(b_2)$.

(ii) *Rewards are bad news, in that a confident principal offers a lower wage or bonus: if* b_1 *is a reward offered when the principal knows the task's difficulty to be* c_1, *and* b_2 *is offered when she knows it to be* $c_2 > c_1$, *then* $b_2 \geq b_1$.

(iii) *Rewards undermine the agent's assessment of the task's attractiveness: for all* (σ_1, σ_2) *and all equilibrium rewards* $b_1 < b_2$,

$$\mathrm{E}[c \mid \sigma_1, b_1] < \mathrm{E}[c \mid \sigma_2, b_2].$$

Future assessments of task attractiveness are also always reduced by an increase in the reward: the expectation of c conditional on σ, b, the action and the outcome is decreasing in b regardless of σ, the action and the outcome.

Proof. Part (i) has already been established. The proof of part (ii) rests on a standard revealed preference argument. Suppose that b_i is an optimal bonus when the principal has information c_i, $i = 1, 2$, and denote $\sigma_i = \sigma^*(b_i)$. Since b_i is optimal given c_i, it must be that

$$\theta[1 - G(\sigma_i \mid c_i)][W - b_i] \geq \theta[1 - G(\sigma_j \mid c_i)][W - b_j],$$

hence

$$\frac{1 - G(\sigma_1 \mid c_1)}{1 - G(\sigma_2 \mid c_1)} \geq \frac{W - b_2}{W - b_1} \geq \frac{1 - G(\sigma_1 \mid c_2)}{1 - G(\sigma_2 \mid c_2)}. \tag{8}$$

Since $c_2 > c_1$, the MLRP requires that $\sigma_1 \geq \sigma_2$. Hence $b_1 \leq b_2$ since $\sigma^*(\cdot)$ is decreasing. This establishes part (ii) which, in turn, implies that pooling occurs only over intervals.[12] Therefore, if the principal offers b_1 to types $[\underline{c}_1, \overline{c}_1]$ and $b_2 > b_1$ to types $[\underline{c}_2, \overline{c}_2]$, it must be that $\overline{c}_1 \leq \underline{c}_2$. This establishes part (iii) of the proposition. ■

Proposition 1 demonstrates the main idea of how the trust effect — the principal's expectation of what views the agent is likely to hold — gives rise to a conflict between extrinsic and intrinsic motivation, which in turn shapes the optimal contract.[13] It also has a number of interesting additional implications and extensions.

- *Forbidden fruits.* A higher reward is, in equilibrium, associated with a less attractive task; therefore, bonuses (or higher wages when effort is observable) reduce intrinsic motivation.

12. There is in fact no pure-strategy separating equilibrium. In such an equilibrium, the agent's behaviour would not depend on his signal. The principal's preference over bonuses that induce compliance with probability 1 will then be the same for all *c* (choose the lowest one), and so some pooling must necessarily occur.

13. Regarding part (iii), it might be objected that the undermining of the agent's view of the task's attractiveness has no consequence, as he will learn the cost *c* by doing the task anyway. Note first, however, that the agent may be discouraged from undertaking the task, and therefore not learn. Second, our parameter *c* may stand for the expected utility cost, while the realized cost also depends on a period-specific shock; the choice of bonus is then informative even when the agent exerts effort. Finally, there may be no learning by doing when the bonus signals the probability of success θ, or the long-run payoff *V* attached to it, and success is linked to a sequence of investments whose ultimate outcome is observed only with a delay.

Conversely, "forbidden fruits" are the most appealing.[14] Indeed, the optimal bonus could well be zero, perhaps even negative. A famous (literary) case is that of Tom Sawyer demanding bribes from other boys to let them paint a fence in his place:

> There was no lack of material; boys happened along every little while; they came to jeer, but remained to whitewash. . . . And when the middle of the afternoon came, from being a poor poverty-stricken boy in the morning, Tom was literally rolling in wealth. He had a nice, good, idle time all the while — plenty of company — and the fence had three coats of whitewash on it! If he hadn't run out of whitewash he would have bankrupted every boy in the village.[15]

- *Improper causal attributions.* While our analysis shows that the short-term incentive effect of rewards is reduced by their informational content, it also demonstrates how an outside observer might actually underestimate the power of these incentives. The probability of effort, $1 - G(\sigma^*(b) \mid c)$, and the probability of success, $\theta[1 - G(\sigma^*(b) \mid c)]$, are both decreasing in c, which is known only to the principal. Because c covaries positively with b in equilibrium, the observer who simply correlates b with outcomes may conclude that rewards are negative reinforcers *even in the short run*. The reason is that such unconditional correlations or regressions fail to take into account the fact that a principal seeking to induce compliance offers the highest incentives to the agents who would otherwise be the least likely to work.[16]
- *Robustness.* We have so far assumed that the bilateral relationship was not at stake, and have therefore ignored the agent's participation constraint. Let $\bar{U}$ denote his outside reservation utility, which we assume to be independent of the attractiveness of the task at hand. If $\theta(V+b) - E(c \mid \sigma^*(b), b) \geq \bar{U}$, the participation constraint is not binding. Otherwise, $\sigma^*(b)$ must be replaced by $\max\{\sigma^*(b), \sigma^{**}(b)\}$, where $\sigma^{**}(b)$ is defined by $\theta(V+b) - E(c \mid \sigma^{**}(b), b) = \bar{U}$. The proof of Proposition 1 is otherwise unaltered, and the conclusions therefore unchanged.
- *Immediate re-engagement effects.* The re-engagement effect may occur even if the agent does not undertake the same task repeatedly. First, the information conveyed by incentives on one task (say, math homework) spills over to correlated tasks (physics homework). Second, and more interestingly, rewards may have an *immediate* negative impact when performance measurement is state-contingent. Consider the same model as above, where the principal can initially threaten to punish the agent in case of poor performance or

14. A simple relabelling of actions extends our results to situations of conflicting interests, where the agent's success is the principal's failure. Suppose for instance that a parent threatens a child with an expected punishment $p \geq 0$ if he smokes. The punishment is (equally) costly to both. Let $W > 0$ and $V \gtrless 0$ denote the parent's and the child's payoffs from his *not* smoking (savings, long-term health benefits) and c the pleasure to be expected from smoking. Confronted with a signal σ positively correlated with c according to the MLRP, the child refrains from smoking if $E(c \mid \sigma, p) \leq V + p$, which occurs for $\sigma \leq \sigma^*(p)$; the parent chooses p to minimize $G(\sigma^*(p) \mid c)(W+p)$. The same reasoning as earlier shows that a stronger punishment signals a greater concern that smoking is likely to be attractive.

15. Mark Twain, *The Adventures of Tom Sawyer* (1876, Chapter 2).

16. In the two-type example developed in what follows (Proposition 3) for instance, the observer will see the agent working with positive probability (perhaps even a high probability) even when no reward is offered. From this he might be led to infer that rewards do not make much of a difference, and could thus perhaps be reduced or done away with. This would be a mistake, because in situations where the reward is actually given, it does have a significant impact on performance.

ative) up-front wage a, together with a bonus b in case of success.[20] Under symmetric information, the lump-sum transfer only enables the principal to tax the (high-ability) agent for the rent he derives from the activity. In a situation of private information, in contrast, the principal can use it to signal that she knows the agent to have a high probability of success. The intuition is akin to "burning money", in an amount that would wipe out any profits to be expected by inducing a low-ability agent to work, but would still leave the principal with a positive surplus if a high-ability agent undertook the task. As we shall see below, this is a form of what we termed the profitability effect.

There are, however, many equilibria in the multidimensional signalling game where a contract is a pair (a, b). We shall not attempt a complete analysis of the (potentially very large) equilibrium set, but rather limit ourselves to the two-type framework, which yields the key insights. Suppose therefore, as above, that the agent's ability can be either high or low, $\theta \in \{\theta_H, \theta_L\}$, and denote respectively by $G_H(\sigma)$ and $G_L(\sigma)$ the cumulative distribution functions of his signal σ in each case. We shall assume that

$$\theta_H G_H(\sigma) > \theta_L G_L(\sigma), \quad \text{for all } \sigma > 0. \tag{10}$$

This is essentially a limited informativeness condition, requiring that the signal's distribution does not vary too much with the underlying state. Its differentiable version, $-\partial \ln G(\sigma \mid \theta)/\partial \ln \theta < 1$, states that the elasticity of non-participation with respect to θ of an agent using any given cutoff rule σ must be less than one.[21]

Proposition 4. *In the two-type case, with limited informativeness, there is a unique separating perfect Bayesian equilibrium that satisfies the NWBR criterion. A principal who observes the agent to be of ability θ_k, $k \in \{L, H\}$, offers the contract (a_k, b_k), with $b_k = b_k^*$ and $a_L = 0 < c - \theta_L V = a_H$. The principal's expected utility is $U_P^L \equiv \theta_L(V + W) - c$ when $\theta = \theta_L$, and $U_P^H \equiv \theta_L V + \theta_H W - c$ when $\theta = \theta_H$. The agent's expected utility in each case is, respectively, 0 and $(\theta_H - \theta_L)V$.*

Proof. See the Appendix. ■

Thus, even with this more general class of contracts, it is still the case that a more high-powered incentive scheme — that is, a higher b and a lower a:

(i) is a positive reinforcer in the short-run, since it leads (low θ) agents to exert effort who otherwise would not have done so;

(ii) is bad news for the agent and permanently damages his self-confidence, no matter what the task's outcome turns out to be.

20. We thank an anonymous referee for prompting us to analyse the lump-sum payment case, and to more carefully discriminate between the trust and profitability effects.

21. It is, for example, satisfied by $G(\sigma \mid \theta) = 1 - e^{-\frac{\sigma}{\theta(1-\sigma)}}$ for all $\sigma \in [0, 1]$.

Souvorov (2003) shows that similar conclusions hold for all NWBR equilibria: under (10), the high type offers bonus $b_H^* = 0$ and the low type weakly mixes between b_H^* and b_L^*. Overall, these results highlight the workings of the profitability effect that comes into play when lump-sum payments (as opposed to conditional bonuses) are allowed: whereas $-(\partial U_P/\partial b)/(\partial U_P/\partial e) = e/(W-b)$ is independent of θ due to the multiplicative form of expected output, $-(\partial U_P/\partial a)/(\partial U_P/\partial e) = 1/(\theta(W-b))$ is decreasing in θ, meaning that a lump-sum transfer is an investment (in signalling) that has a higher rate of return when the agent is talented.[22] The complete specification of the contract will depend on the particular equilibrium that is played (*e.g.* contrast those of Propositions 3 and 4), but under the standard refinement used here, the basic result of a less performance-dependent compensation scheme for more able agents remains verified.

There are also some differences with the no-lump-sum-transfer case. First, bonuses are the same as under symmetric information, so in that sense, the informed-principal game leads to no distortion of incentives. Second, because of the fixed wage, the (high-ability) agent's utility is now higher than under symmetric information. Thus, the general weakening of performance-based compensation which is the model's main insight now takes the form of a lower *share* of contingent compensation in total compensation. In particular, it still implies that the distribution of rewards across a given population of agents will be *more equal*, in a Lorenz sense, due to the confidence-management problem.

It is worth commenting here on the *uses and limits of money-burning strategies*. Proposition 4 unveils an important new dimension of confidence management, and indeed, one often observes principals burning resources in such an effort — spending for instance considerable time trying to "convince" agents to attempt challenging tasks by giving them pep talks, encouragements, and similar unverifiable, soft information. At the same time, the money- or time-burning strategy can only be part of the overall story, for several reasons. First, the profitability effect to which it gives rise when the principal's private information is about θ does not occur when it is about the task's attractiveness (the cost c, or the ultimate reward V). As a result, one can show that the no-lump-sum equilibrium (the analogue to Proposition 3 for unknown c or V) remains a NWBR equilibrium when such transfers are allowed, provided the cutoff σ^* is not too high. Second, burning money is a non-contingent reward. In contrast, the psychology literature on intrinsic motivation mostly emphasizes the effects of contingent rewards, and the leading experimental case is that of a task of unknown attractiveness.[23] Yet another limitation of

22. Correspondingly, the implementability condition (see footnote 6) for the two-dimensional policy $p = (a, b)$ reduces to its component in a, which requires that $da/d\theta \geq 0$ in equilibrium. Another simple way to see that the role of lump-sum transfers here is to create a profitability effect is to observe that Proposition 4 applies unchanged when the agent does not receive any private signal ($G_H \equiv G_L$), in which case we saw in Section 2 that there can be no pure trust effect.

23. The experimental literature has also examined the effects of unconditional rewards on intrinsic motivation. Typically, none is found (*e.g.* Deci *et al.*, 1999). In these setups, however, the experimenter does not selectively give the lump sum to some subjects and not to others (a randomization is used, and subjects may not even be aware of differences in treatment). It is also generally not one where the experimenter can be thought to have a stake in the subject's performance, so he would again have no incentive to "burn money" to boost his motivation.

lump-sum transfers in a broader framework is that they tend to attract "undesirable types". This would be the case for example in our model if a fraction of the population were lazy — had a large cost of effort c — and if the principal was unable to distinguish between lazy and diligent types.[24]

In summary, our analysis distinguishing between the trust and profitability effects makes clear that low-powered incentives and burning money are two ways in which the principal's confidence-management motive will be reflected in equilibrium contracts — each with its own domain of applicability, but with similar effect on wage inequality and long-run motivation.

3.3 Back to the Debate

(a) *Relation to the Psychology Literature*

Let us now return to the hidden cost of rewards. Our approach, in the tradition of economics and cognitive psychology, focuses on the individual's beliefs and motivation. An alternative viewpoint, along the lines of the behaviourist school (Hull (1943), Skinner (1953)) would shun the inner process and posit a direct link from stimulus to response. The agent would then just be assumed to exhibit an instinctive, aversive reaction to being offered a contingent reward, or threatened with a punishment. Not surprisingly, we are not inclined to adopt such a "reduced form" approach. While individuals do not really compute perfect Bayesian equilibria when interpreting signals from their environment, there is a lot of evidence that they are quite sophisticated at (and definitely intent on) getting to the motives behind the words and deeds of the people with whom they interact.[25] Moreover, in the present context the information-based approach delivers two important benefits. First, it helps understand *why* the response to the stimulus is what it is. Second, it generates testable predictions as to *when* rewards may indeed have real costs, and when this view is likely to be a myth.

Thus, we have identified a class of interactions between a privately informed principal and an agent who attempts to infer her motives from the type of contracts offered to him, that have the following implications:

- Rewards impact intrinsic motivation. Whereas under symmetric information the intrinsic $(\theta V - c)$ and extrinsic (θb) motivations can be cleanly separated, under asymmetric information they cannot. When the agent is unsure about his ability, the intrinsic motivation $\hat{\theta}(\sigma, b)V - c$ decreases with

24. Another potential limitation on the use of lump-sum transfers (at least large ones) is that when agents are risk-averse, giving them a substantial lump-sum payment reduces their marginal utility of income, and can thus actually make it harder to motivate them to work.

25. With, naturally, some variations in the population. For example, adults usually have more experience in interpreting social signals than children, and the latter themselves exhibit different speeds of learning these skills.

the level of the bonus. Similarly, when he does not know how costly or exciting the task is, his perception of it, $\hat{c}(\sigma, b)$, is affected by the level of the wage or reward.

- A reward is a positive reinforcer in the short term, but always decreases future motivation.

These conclusions, as well as the underlying mechanisms, are well in line with an important branch of the social psychology literature. Indeed, the standard references on the hidden costs of rewards (Lepper *et al.* (1973), Deci (1975), Deci and Ryan (1985)) are based on self-perception and attribution theories, according to which individuals constantly reassess the reasons for their and others' behaviour. Both approaches emphasize the informational impact of rewards. As Deci (1975, p. 42) argues:

> Every reward (including feedback) has two aspects, a controlling aspect and an informational aspect which provides the recipient with information about his competence and self-determination.

Both views also stress the re-engagement effects of rewards. Thus Schwartz (1990), commenting on Lepper *et al.* (1973), argues:

> Reinforcement has two effects. First, predictably it gains control of [an] activity, increasing its frequency. Second, ... when reinforcement is later withdrawn, people engage in the activity even less than they did before reinforcement was introduced.

The tension between the short-term and long-term effects on motivation of offering a reward also suggests the following idea: once a reward is offered, it will be required — and "expected" — every time the task has to be performed again — perhaps even in increasing amounts.[26] In other words, through their effect on self-confidence, rewards have a *"ratchet effect"*. This irreversibility may explain people's (*e.g.* parent's) reluctance to offer them, even on occasions where they would seem like a small price to pay to get the current job done. Souvorov (2003) analyses this question using a two-period extension of the present model; an additional effect arises, namely that the agent now has a strategic incentive to appear demotivated (having a low σ), in order to be given a higher bonus in the future. Souvorov establishes three monotonicity properties. First, in each period a low type is offered a (weakly) higher bonus, meaning that Propositions 1-3 hold in a dynamic context as well. Second, for a given type, the bonus is (weakly) increasing over time, validating our earlier conjecture. Finally, for each given type, the initial bonus is lower when the principal is the same in both periods than if there are two different principals; the reason is that a long-lasting principal internalizes the fact that rewards are habit-forming.

26. The same task, or related tasks: see Frey, Fehr and Benz (2000) for experimental evidence showing that the crowding out of motivation may extend beyond the area of intervention.

Our results are also consistent with Etzioni's (1971) claim that workers find control of their behaviour via incentives "alienating" and "dehumanizing", with Kohn's (1993) argument that incentive schemes make people less enthusiastic about their behaviour, and with Deci and Ryan's 1985 view that rewards change the locus of causality from internal to external, making employees bored, alienated and reactive rather than proactive.

(b) Promised vs. ex post *Rewards*

Our analysis can also help clarify the difference between what we would label "promised" or "*ex ante*" contingent rewards, and "discretionary" or "*ex post*" rewards. Our model is about the *control* of behaviour through rewards: the principal selects a reward for a well-defined effort or performance *before* the agent's decision. The agent then rationally interprets the reward scheme as a signal of distrust or of a boring task.

By contrast, rewards that are discretionary (not contracted for) may well boost the agent's self-esteem or intrinsic motivation, because of a different learning effect: the worker or child learns from the reward that the task was considered difficult (and therefore that he is talented), or that the supervisor or parent is appreciative of, proud of, or cares about his performance — and therefore that it is worth repeating it. Giving *ex post* a bicycle to a hard-working child, or a special pay rise or early promotion to a productive assistant professor will not lead him to infer that his behaviour was controlled, because the principal was under no obligation (no commitment) to reward any particular outcome. And receiving the reward is good news, because the agent initially did not know how to interpret his performance. The reward then provides the agent with an indirect measure of his performance.[27]

(c) When Does Extrinsic Motivation Undermine Intrinsic Motivation?

The next point is alluded to in Deci (1975, p. 41):

> If a person's feelings of competence and self-determination are enhanced, his intrinsic motivation will increase. If his feelings of competence and self-determination are diminished, his intrinsic motivation will decrease.... We are suggesting that some rewards or feedback will increase intrinsic motivation through this process and others will decrease it, either through this process or through the change in perceived locus of causality process.

27. Consider an infinite-horizon extension of our model where, at the end of each period, agent and principal both observe whether the agent's effort was successful (which happens with a known probability $\theta \leq 1$), but only the principal knows whether the long-run payoffs that will ultimately be reaped from this success are high or low (*i.e.* $(W, V) \in \{(W_H, V_H), (W_L, V_L)\}$, with $W_H > W_L$ and $V_H > V_L$; this positive correlation may, but need not, reflect altruism). One can think of a parent and a child whose real payoffs to success on exams or test will come much later in life, in the form of a better career. There is then a natural (Bayesian perfect) reputational equilibrium where the principal gives a reward b^* in case of success *only* to high-payoff agents (hence rewards are good news); conversely, the agent works only if all previous successes were rewarded. The reward b^* is determined by the principal's incentive compatibility condition, namely $b^* = \delta(W_L - b^*)/(1-\delta) < \delta(W_H - b^*)/(1-\delta)$, where δ denotes her discount rate. The agent's hypothesized behaviour is optimal provided $V_L < c < V_H + b$.

Our economic analysis indeed unveils important necessary conditions for rewards to have a negative impact on self-confidence. The first is that the principal has *information* about the agent or the task that the agent does not. This may explain why the existence of hidden costs of rewards is less controversial in educational settings than in the workplace. Children have particularly imperfect knowledge of their selves and of their aptitudes in the quickly changing tasks which they face as they grow up (curriculum, sports, social interactions, etc.). In contrast, the structure of rewards in the workplace is often more anonymous: in most sectors, it is the same for all workers with the same "job description". The terms of this (contingent) contract still reflect information about the nature of the job, but much of it may already be publicly known.

The second key condition is the *sorting condition:* for rewards to signal a low ability or a boring task, it must be that the principal is comparatively more tempted to offer performance incentives under those circumstances. Conversely, consider the case of a manager who is promoted from a fixed-salary job and given the leadership of a new project or division, together with a pay-for-performance scheme. In this example (which is related to Section 4.1 below), the sorting condition works in the opposite direction: the contingent reward is associated with a *high* level of trust from the principal, demonstrated by a large "empowerment" effect, and should therefore boost the manager's self-confidence.

Another example in which the sorting condition works in the opposite direction, and rewards are long-term positive reinforcers, is when a task is subject to learning by doing and learning is more effective for a talented agent. By offering a reward, the principal is then really saying: "I know that you are talented. Encouraging you to try would make no sense if you were unable to learn by doing". That the sorting condition is needed in order for the principal to boost the agent's self-confidence is also demonstrated by the standard observations that the use of compliments to ingratiate oneself with a person may backfire, that parents often have a hard time motivating their children to work at school by telling them about their ability (θ), the rewards from education (V), and the pleasure of learning (c); and that depressed individuals often attribute ulterior motivation to those who try and comfort them.[28]

To sum up, before worrying about the negative impact of rewards, one should first check that the reward provider has private information about the task or the agent's talent (including as we have noted, a greater ability to interpret the agent's track record). One should then, as the agent does, think through the provider's ulterior

28. It would be interesting to assess in this light the evidence on the role of expectations. For example, teachers with initially over-optimistic expectations about their students lead to changes in the performances of the students which tend to confirm the expectations (Rosenthal and Jacobson (1968); see also Merton (1948) for a discussion of self-fulfilling prophecies). It seems, however, that while the students' behaviour changes, their self-confidence is unaffected (Darley and Fazio, 1980).

motivation and how her payoff from giving a contingent reward is affected by her knowledge.

(d) Retrospective Justification and Self-Perception

The same reasoning that held for inferences about the task's difficulty c obviously applies to the agent's payoff V from succeeding in it. Combined with imperfect memory, this result has an interesting implication for situations where currently available information provides only insufficient justification for a certain course of action.[29] Suppose that, at some later date, the agent again faces the choice of whether to undertake the same or a similar task; and that, come that time, he remembers only that he chose to engage in it, and the extrinsic incentives that were then offered, but not his intrinsic interest in the task (and the later observation of V). For instance, an individual engaged in a long-term project — writing a book, proving a theorem, running a marathon — may, at times, be seized by doubt as to whether the intellectual and ego-gratification benefits which successful completion is likely to bring will, ultimately, justify the required efforts. ("Why am I doing this?") He may then reflect that since he chose to embark on this project once again in spite of low financial and career incentives, the personal satisfaction enjoyed from previous completions (and which, at this later and perhaps somewhat stressful stage, he cannot quite recall) must have been significant. Hence it is worth persevering on the chosen path. The result that $\mathrm{E}[V \mid \sigma, b] > \mathrm{E}[V \mid b']$ for $b < b'$ can thus provide a formal explanation for this kind of *ex post* rationalization of one's *own* choices (Festinger and Carlsmith (1959), Bem (1967), Staw (1977)).

(e) Paternalism: Altruism Towards a Time-Inconsistent Agent

Another interesting class of situations for which our framework is relevant arises when an agent (child or adult) has time-inconsistent preferences, generating a divergence between *his own* short- and long-run interests. As a result of this "salience of the present", he may for instance shirk on homework or professional duties, fail to stick to a necessary diet or exercise regimen, or remain addicted to tobacco, drugs or alcohol. A well intentioned principal — parent or close friend — who takes the *long run* view of the agent's welfare will then have the exact same incentives as those we analyse here to manipulate the agent's perceptions of himself and of the tasks he faces — "for his own good".[30]

29. See Bénabou and Tirole (2002*a*) for a model of endogenously selective memory or awareness. The present argument requires only that memory be imperfect, especially with regard to one's past feelings and emotions (hedonic payoffs). For a framework where agents with imperfect recall make retrospective inferences about their own preferences from their past choices, see Bénabou and Tirole (2002*b*).

30. Formally, W in this case is equal to V/β, where $\beta < 1$ is the agent's quasi-hyperbolic discount factor; $1/\beta$ measures the salience of the effort cost c for the agent, at the time when he must incur it.

4 Other Confidence-Enhancement Strategies

4.1 Empowerment and Motivation

Section 3 showed that the principal may signal the agent's ability (high θ), the attractiveness of the task (low c) or its long-term payoff (high V) through the use of a low-powered incentive scheme. In the same spirit, we now investigate the use of delegation or empowerment to induce an agent to carry out the objectives of the principal (Miles, 1965). Intuitively, the principal demonstrates her confidence in the agent's ability (or, more generally, his intrinsic motivation) by delegating control of the task to him. This, in turn, makes it more likely that the agent exerts effort. The delegation vs. supervision problem is also interesting because it provides an example where the profitability and trust effects work in opposite directions, in contrast to the previous section where they reinforced each other.[31]

We shall abstract here from the explicit rewards that were our earlier focus ($a = b = 0$).[32] Let $\mathcal{W}_1(\theta)$ and $\mathcal{W}_0(\theta)$ denote the principal's expected payoff when she delegates ($d = 1$) and does not delegate ($d = 0$) to an agent with ability θ, and the agent exerts effort. The principal receives 0 if the agent does not try. As shown below, these reduced forms can be derived from a situation where the principal decides to either relinquish some control rights to the agent, or put in place a supervisor or monitoring technology. As earlier, we assume that the principal knows the agent's probability of success θ, while the latter receives a signal σ drawn from a cumulative distribution $G(\sigma \mid \theta)$, with density $g(\sigma \mid \theta)$ satisfying the MLRP. The agent's utility is, as usual, $\theta V - c_d$ for $d \in \{0, 1\}$ if he exerts effort, and 0 otherwise. We assume that $c_1 \le c_0$: *ceteris paribus*, the agent prefers delegation. The timing is as follows. At stage 1, the principal selects $d \in \{0, 1\}$. At stage 2, the agent decides whether to undertake the task; the principal's payoff is $\mathcal{W}_d(\theta)$ if he does, and 0 otherwise.

Assumption 1. For all $\theta \in [0, 1]$,

$$\frac{d}{d\theta}\left(\frac{\mathcal{W}_1(\theta)}{\mathcal{W}_0(\theta)}\right) > 0; \quad \text{moreover,} \quad \frac{\mathcal{W}_1(0)}{\mathcal{W}_0(0)} < 1 < \frac{\mathcal{W}_1(1)}{\mathcal{W}_0(1)}.$$

In words, an empowered agent is less likely to create damage to the principal when he is talented than when he is not. Furthermore, the principal does not want (*ceteris paribus*) to delegate the task to an inept agent ($\theta = 0$), and prefers to delegate the task to a very talented

31. The analysis given here is not based on the initiative effect studied in Aghion and Tirole (1997). There, an agent invests more in the acquisition of information about potential projects if he knows that the principal will not interfere too much with his suggestions. In Dessein (2002), the principal delegates so as to ensure that the decision taken will better reflect the agent's information than when the latter communicates it strategically and the principal decides. By delegating to the agent, the principal signals a greater *congruence* of their objectives. Salancik (1977) proposes yet another viewpoint, namely the "co-optation of personal satisfaction", related to our earlier discussion of retrospective justification: *"By having a person choose to do something, you create a situation that makes it more difficult for him to say that he didn't want to do it. And the ironic thing is that the more freedom you give him to make the decision, the more constraining you make his subsequent situation."*

32. In footnote 35, we will sketch how the results extend to contracts with lump sum or fixed wage payments $a \neq 0$. We shall continue to abstract from contingent rewards, however, as these were the main focus of the previous section. The constraint $b = 0$ could reflect, for instance, the fact that performance is not publicly verifiable.

one $(\theta = 1)$. This implies that there exists a θ^* in $(0, 1)$ such that, under symmetric information, it is efficient to delegate if $\theta > \theta^*$, and to monitor if $\theta < \theta^*$.

- *Example*: Suppose that the agent, when paying a cost $c_1 = c_0 = c$, comes up with a project. The project, in its initial form, will succeed if the agent is "good", and fail if he is "bad". The principal knows the probability θ that the agent is good. If the project is unmodified by the principal and is successful, the agent receives new job offers, with value V to him; he receives no such offer if the project fails, is modified, or if he does not even try. Success also yields a monetary payoff W to the principal. "Delegation" means transferring the control right to the agent, who will then implement his project without modification, resulting in expected payoffs $\theta V - c$ for himself and θW for the principal (both get 0 if the agent does not try). Alternatively, the principal may keep the control rights and pay a fixed monitoring cost C to supervise the agent's project. This enables her to discover along the way (and with some probability) if it is headed for failure, and to then modify it so as to make it successful. We assume that the principal is able, with probability x, to turn a failing project into a successful one, where $xW > C$. Payoffs are then still $\theta V - c$ for the agent (he gets no credit for a project modified by the principal since it would have failed otherwise), but now $(\theta + (1 - \theta)x)W - C$ for the principal. Thus

$$\mathcal{W}_d = [\theta + (1 - \theta)x(1 - d)]W - C(1 - d)$$

for $d \in \{0, 1\}$, and therefore Assumption 1 is satisfied, since

$$\frac{\mathcal{W}_1(\theta)}{\mathcal{W}_0(\theta)} = \frac{1}{1 - x + \dfrac{x - C/W}{\theta}}.$$

Assumption 1 corresponds to what we termed a profitability effect, which here pushes the principal towards giving greater autonomy to more able agents. The trust effect, on the other hand, works in the opposite direction: when σ is highly correlated with θ, the principal is very concerned about boosting the motivation of low-ability agents (offsetting the bad signals which they are likely to receive). Thus, if delegation is thought to be reserved for high-ability agents, she may want to in fact give it to some very low ability individuals as well. Moreover, when $c_1 < c_0$ delegation also involves an implicit "reward", in that it makes the task more pleasant to perform. Of course, in equilibrium the looking-glass-self principle will operate, and agents will (on average) correctly infer the principal's motivations in delegating or not delegating to them (*e.g.* rewards are bad news, as we showed earlier). Due to the conflict between the profitability and trust effects, however, Assumption 1 is generally not sufficient to make the informational content of delegation unambiguous, even though its effect on the agent's *effort* will be unequivocal. This additional result will require a second assumption:

Assumption 2. For all (σ_0, σ_1) with $\sigma_0 > \sigma_1$, the elasticity of the odds ratio $(1 - G(\sigma_0 \mid \theta))/(1 - G(\sigma_1 \mid \theta))$ with respect to θ is less than that of $\mathcal{W}_1(\theta)/\mathcal{W}_0(\theta)$.

This limited-informativeness condition imposes an upper bound on the trust effect arising from the correlation between the signals θ and σ received by the principal and the agent.[33] It implies that the profitability effect dominates in the agent's inference problem.

Proposition 5. *In equilibrium, under Assumption* 1:

(i) *Empowerment always increases the probability that the agent will exert effort (no matter what his type θ is).*

(ii) *There is more empowerment than under symmetric information: there exists a $\theta^{**} < \theta^{*}$ such that the principal delegates whenever $\theta > \theta^{**}$.*

(iii) *Suppose that Assumption* 2 *holds as well. Empowerment is then always good news for the agent about his ability, and permanently changes his attitude towards the task: for any signal σ, $\mathrm{E}[\theta \mid \sigma, d = 1] > \mathrm{E}[\theta \mid \sigma, d = 0]$.*

Proof. See the Appendix. ■

Proposition 5 and its premises are consistent with Pfeffer's (1994) observation that:

> When employees are subjected to close external monitoring or surveillance, they may draw the psychological inference that they are not trusted and thus not trustworthy, acting in ways that reinforce this perception.[34]

Note, finally, that while we have abstracted here from the use of fixed payments by the principal to signal her trust in the agent ("burning money"), the main insights and results conveyed by Proposition 5 are, once again, robust to allowing for lump-sum transfers.[35]

4.2 Help

Still assuming that the agent is unsure about his ability, suppose that the principal offers to contribute a level of help h (at private cost h) in case the agent decides to undertake the task. This help improves the probability of success, which is thus a function $P(\theta, h)$ with $P_\theta > 0$ and $P_h > 0$. The agent then undertakes the project if and

33. For example, with the conditional distribution $G(\sigma \mid \theta) = 1 - e^{\left(\frac{\sigma}{\sigma - 1}\right)/(\theta + k)}$ for $\sigma \in [0, 1]$, Assumption 2 amounts to imposing a lower bound on k.

34. Cited in Baron and Kreps (1999), who provide an illustration at Hewlett-Packard.

35. Suppose that there are two types, θ_H and θ_L, with frequencies f_H and f_L respectively, such that $W_1(\theta_L)/W_0(\theta_L) < 1 < W_1(\theta_H)/W_0(\theta_H)$ and $\theta_H V - c > 0 > \theta_L V - c$. Performance is non-verifiable, so the contract can only specify a fixed payment $a \geq 0$. If f_H is high enough that $(f_H\theta_H + f_L\theta_L)V - c > 0$, then $\{a = 0, d = 1\}$ constitutes a pooling equilibrium, in which the agent exerts effort. Since both types of principal then receive their maximum possible payoff, no intuitive-criterion type of reasoning could upset this equilibrium (we believe that it is in fact the only Cho-Kreps robust equilibrium in this case). When $(f_H\theta_H + f_L\theta_L)V - c < 0$, on the other hand, the Cho-Kreps robust equilibrium will involve separation or semi-separation via money burning, provided that $W_1(\theta_L) \leq W_1(\theta_H)$, so that one can find an $a_H > 0 = a_L$ such that $W_1(\theta_L) - a_H \leq W_1(\theta_H) - a_H$.

only if $\sigma \geq \sigma^*(h)$, where $\mathsf{E}[P(\theta, h) \mid \sigma^*(h), h]V = c$, and $\sigma^*(h)$ is a decreasing function. Ignoring rewards, the principal's payoff is

$$U_P = [1 - G(\sigma^*(h) \mid \theta)][P(\theta, h)W - h]. \tag{11}$$

The term in the second bracket is her expected payoff conditional on the agent's undertaking the task. Let us assume that the percentage increase in that payoff achieved by a higher level of help (the expected rate of return on investing in help) is smaller when the agent is talented than when he is untalented:

Assumption 3. For all θ and h, $\partial^2 \ln (P(\theta, h)W - h)/\partial\theta\partial h < 0$.

In other words, help makes more of a difference for weak agents than for strong ones.[36] We shall also use a limited-informativeness condition, similar to Assumption 2 earlier.

Assumption 4. For all (σ_0, σ_1) with $\sigma_1 > \sigma_0$ and (h_0, h_1) with $h_1 > h_0$, the elasticity of the odds ratio $(1 - G(\sigma_0 \mid \theta))/(1 - G(\sigma_1 \mid \theta))$ with respect to θ is less than that of $(P(\theta, h_1)W - h_1)/(P(\theta, h_0)W - h_0)$.

Following the steps in the proof of Proposition 5, one easily shows:

Proposition 6. *In equilibrium:*

(i) *Under Assumption 3, giving more help always decreases the probability that the agent exerts effort (his action threshold $\sigma^*(h)$ is increasing in h).*

(ii) *When Assumption 4 also holds, a high level of help is always bad news for the agent, permanently weakening his self-confidence with respect to his ability for the task.*

Proposition 6 may explain why help, like rewards or lack of delegation, can be detrimental to self-confidence. For example, depression, a recognized disorder of self-esteem (Bibring (1953)), is relatively common among individuals with "dependent" personality patterns — that is, individuals with backgrounds characterized by pampering and overprotection (Snyder, Higgins and Stucky, 1983, p. 233). Similarly, Gilbert and Silvera (1996) observe that a parent who finds dependence of his or her child gratifying may provide unnecessary assistance.

A sorting condition like the one assumed above seems quite appropriate when task performance is of a *zero-one* nature: graduating high school or passing an exam, getting a job or keeping it, etc. In other situations the sorting condition may be reversed, so that receiving help is a positive signal. This is likely to occur when the principal's payoff in case of success rises with the agents' ability, or with the level

36. This is again a profitability effect: since $-(\partial U_P/\partial h)/(\partial U_P/\partial e) = -e(\partial \ln (PW - h)/\partial h)$, Assumption 3 implies the standard sorting condition.

of help which was provided (a more helping principal gets more "credit").[37] One can think of situations such as joining a start-up firm, or contributing time and money to a political party or candidate. The two types of sorting conditions can be illustrated by the contrast between the case of a professor helping a student write a term paper or getting his or her thesis done (the professor's payoff is largely independent of the margin of success with which the student passes the hurdle), and that where the same professor coauthors a research paper with the student or with a younger faculty member (helping is then more attractive, the better the prospects for the paper's success due to the coauthor's talent).

4.3 Coaching

The use of encouragement, praise, strategies to minimize the effect of failures and the like, is a central theme in human resource management and education.[38] Successful coaches are viewed as those who build up others' confidence (Kinlaw, 1997).

(a) Encouragement

The usual complementarity between effort and talent makes it clear why even a selfish coach may gain by building up the agent's self-esteem. (Section 5 will nonetheless identify settings where coaches may have the reverse incentives, and bash agents' egos.) Formally, the principal's policy p here is the disclosure (or absence of disclosure) to the agent of hard private information about his ability. The release of a signal covarying positively (negatively) with θ boosts (lowers) the agent's self-confidence.

(b) Praise, Criticism and Excuses

Let us now turn to the coach's *ex post* assessment of the agent's performance. This assessment exercise is of course still forward looking, in that it is meant to improve the agent's future performances. Taking it for granted that the principal wants to boost the agent's self-esteem, it is interesting to note that, in some circumstances, reassurance can nonetheless have ambiguous consequences. Suppose that the agent failed. The principal may then try to convince him that the link from talent and effort to performance is rather random ("the jury was incompetent") or, relatedly, that the agent was discriminated against (*e.g.* racial prejudice by employers or educators, methodological bias by referees). Offering such excuses may sometimes prove self-defeating.[39] Indeed, if the noise

37. Formally, replacing W by $W(\theta)$ or $W(h)$ in the expected payoff $P(\theta, h)W - h$ (with $W' > 0$) tends to reverse the sorting condition, by generating a complementarity between θ and h.
38. For example, Korman (1970) emphasizes the positive role of one's self-image in the determination of work attitude and effort, and argues that managers should attempt to improve the employee's self-image.
39. See Snyder *et al.* (1983) for a broad discussion of excuses.

affecting the past performance is recurrent (*e.g.* the agent is likely to be discriminated again in the future if he has been in the past), then the excuse may discourage rather than encourage him. To illustrate this idea, suppose that there are two periods, $t = 1, 2$. The agent's payoff in period t is

$$(\varepsilon_t \theta V - c_t) e_t, \qquad (12)$$

where $e_t \in \{0, 1\}$ is the date-t effort, and $\varepsilon_t \in \{0, 1\}$ is the date-t noise, which is serially correlated: $\mu \equiv \Pr(\varepsilon_2 = \varepsilon_1) \geq 1/2$. At date t, the agent's current cost c_t of undertaking the task is drawn from a random distribution with conditional support $[0, \infty)$ (this is just to avoid possible indifferences in the principal's disclosure decision). Finally, to simplify computations we assume that $\theta = \theta_H \equiv 1$ with probability f_H, while $\theta = \theta_L < 1$ with probability $f_L = 1 - f_H$. The agent's expected talent will be denoted $\theta^e \equiv f_H \theta_H + f_L \theta_L$.

When the agent undertakes the task at date 1 (which he does when c_1 is low enough) and succeeds, this of course reveals that $\varepsilon_1 = 1$. When he fails, however, only the principal learns the realization of ε_1. More specifically, assume that if the agent faced a handicap ($\varepsilon_1 = 0$) the principal receives hard evidence of it, whereas if he faced no handicap she learns nothing. When the principal has evidence of a handicap, she decides whether or not to reveal it. For simplicity, ε_1 is the only piece of private information that the principal may hold; in particular, she has no information about θ.

At the end of period 1, the principal seeks to maximize the likelihood that the agent will undertake the date-2 task. Suppose that he has failed, but that the principal knows that he faced a handicap ($\varepsilon_1 = 0$). Will full disclosure occur in equilibrium? The agent's expected gross benefit from undertaking the date-2 task is $(1 - \mu)\theta^e$ if he is informed that $\varepsilon_1 = 0$, and $\mu \theta_L$ if he receives no such information (he then infers that his talent is low). Truthful disclosure is thus an equilibrium behaviour if and only if

$$\frac{\mu}{1 - \mu} \leq \frac{\theta^e}{\theta_L}. \qquad (13)$$

The principal trades off the benefit of boosting the agent's self-esteem by offering an excuse against the risk that this excuse may itself demotivate the agent. If external circumstances exhibit little serial correlation (μ is close to 1/2), or if self-esteem is badly affected by failure in the absence of an excuse (θ_L is very low), then in the unique equilibrium, the principal will want to disclose the excuse. When condition (13) does not hold, by contrast, the principal either does not provide any excuse, or plays a mixed strategy.[40]

40. More precisely, let $\tau \equiv \Pr(\varepsilon_1 = 0)$ and $\hat{\theta} \equiv [\tau/(\tau + (1 - \tau) f_L)]\theta^e + [(1 - \tau) f_L/(\tau + (1 - \tau) f_L)]\theta_L$. If $\mu/(1 - \mu) \geq \hat{\theta}/\theta_L$, the unique equilibrium involves no disclosure. With intermediate degrees of correlation, $\hat{\theta}/\theta_L < \mu/(1 - \mu) < \theta^e/\theta_L$, it involves a randomization between disclosing and not disclosing.

Straightforward variations on this model allow us to identify the costs and benefits of praise ("you succeeded even though ε was low") and criticism ("you failed even though ε was high"). Praise boosts the agent's self-esteem but makes him doubt his environment; criticism lowers it, and yet may not discourage him. For instance, minority parents who feel that their child is being discriminated against at school, or themselves at work, are often reluctant to convey these views to their child, for fear that he or she would lose faith in the school system and the returns to educational investment.

5 Undermining the Other's Ego

5.1 Possible Rationales

Our premise until now has been — as in much of the human resources and education literatures — that a person generally benefits from a higher self-esteem of her spouse, child, colleague, coauthor, subordinate, or teammate. Yet while boosting others' self-confidence is a pervasive aspect of social interactions, people also often criticize or downplay the achievements of their colleagues and relatives. The study in Sections 3 and 4 must therefore be part of a broader construct, in which the principal sometimes wants to repress the agent's ego. We first consider some simple potential motivations for such behaviours, then turn to a more interesting one.

(a) Direct Competition

A rather trivial reason arises when the two individuals are in direct competition (for a job, a mate, a discovery, a title, and so forth). The former is then directly hurt when the latter succeeds; in the context of our model, W is negative.[41]

(b) The Risk of "Coasting"

A basic premise in social psychology (and, consequently, our starting point in Section 3) is that the marginal payoff to an individual's effort is generally increasing in his ability. In certain situations, however, effort and ability are substitutes rather than complements, creating the risk that the agent may reduce effort when feeling more self-confident ("resting on his laurels"). This case arises in particular when the agent's private payoff from performance is of a "pass-fail" nature. For example, a pupil whose only ambition is to pass an exam may study less if he feels talented. Similarly, an individual who aims

41. See footnote 14 for the application of our basic model to punishments and other costly disincentives.

at little more than keeping his spouse and takes her for granted will not put much effort into remaining attractive to her.[42] The teacher or parent may then want to downplay the pupil's achievements, and the spouse may tell her partner that he is not so great after all.

In these examples, a high self-confidence reduces effort. In other examples, it may induce the wrong type of effort. For example, the agent may demonstrate excess initiative, selecting a new and risky path that he feels will pay off due to his talent, while the principal would have preferred a more conservative approach. There are probably many situations in which the principal's payoff as a function of the agent's self-confidence $\hat{\theta}$ is hill-shaped, as opposed to constantly increasing as posited in Section 3: an increase in the agent's self-esteem helps up to a point, beyond which it becomes hubris and starts hurting the principal.

(c) *Shadow Cost of Reputation*

A teacher or a manager who makes very complimentary comments to every pupil or employee may lose her credibility. As we already noted, when disclosing *soft* information to several agents the principal must realize that they will see through her ulterior motivation, and believe her only if she builds a reputation for not exaggerating claims. Refraining from boosting some agents' self-esteem may help her make more credible statements to the others.[43] A related tradeoff appears in Fang and Moscarini (2002), where a firm has private information about the ability of each of a continuum of workers.[44]

We now turn to, and analyse in more detail, what is probably the most common reason for restraining another person's ego.

5.2 Ego Bashing and Battles for Dominance

Many circumstances in private life or in the workplace are characterized by power relationships. Egos clash as individuals try to establish dominance over each other along some dimension (intellectual, physical). What matters in such situations is one's relative standing in the group, rather than any absolute standing. Shattering the other's self-confidence in the relevant dimension may then increase one's power in the relationship.

5.2.1 *Private Benefits from Dominance*

Consider a pair of individuals, 1 and 2, who must make a joint decision (they share the "formal control right" over it). Each comes with an idea or project, but only one of these can be selected.

42. A simple formalization of these two examples goes as follows. Suppose the agent aims at performance y_0 and gets no extra utility from $y > y_0$. Consider a deterministic technology $y = \theta e$ where θ is talent and e effort. Then $e = y_0/\theta$, and so self-confidence reduces effort.

43. This can be modelled either in a repeated-action setting or, more simply, by having the principal make simultaneous announcements to a large number of agents who each have ability θ_H or θ_L, with probabilities f_H and f_L. Whereas the principal could not credibly convey any information to a single agent (as long as $f_H\theta_H + f_L\theta_L < c/V < \theta_H$, she would always want to announce θ_H), the law of large numbers makes truth-telling an equilibrium where each compliment has a clear opportunity cost. (The equilibrium is supported by off-the-equilibrium path beliefs that a principal who declares more than a fraction f_H of agents to be talented must be babbling.) Because high-ability agents are the most productive, it is indeed optimal for the principal to reserve his praise for those types.

44. Workers observe all wage contracts (lump-sum plus bonus). Abilities are independently distributed, so by the law of large numbers the firm must convey bad news to some workers if it is to convey good news to others. Whereas under symmetric information it would give higher wages to the more able, it may then choose not to differentiate if the (motivation) costs of bad news exceeds the benefits of good ones. Fang and Moscarini show that this occurs in particular if most workers are overoptimistic about their ability.

Individual i's idea yields, in expectation, $\theta_i V + B$ to i and $\theta_i V$ to j, where θ_i is individual i's talent and $B > 0$ is a private benefit accruing to individual i when his point of view prevails. The existence of a private benefit is natural, since individuals are more likely to search for (or reveal) ideas that favour them; B could thus arise from the fact that i's favoured project is easier for him to carry out, has positive spillovers on to his other activities, or will bring him outside credit for having had the idea.

Let us assume for simplicity that θ_1 is common knowledge, whereas θ_2 can take either one of two values, θ_2^L and $\theta_2^H > \theta_2^L$, such that

$$\theta_2^H V + B > \theta_1 V > \theta_2^L V + B \quad \text{and} \quad \theta_1 V + B > \theta_2^H V. \tag{14}$$

We consider situations where individual 1 may have hard information about θ_2 that individual 2 himself does not have, for example some third-party's feedback about individual 2's earlier performances. In our terminology, individual 1 can thus be viewed as the principal and individual 2 as the agent, even though there is no hierarchy in terms of *a priori* control rights. For simplicity, we assume that the principal either has no information regarding θ_2, or else knows its true value. In the latter case, she can either disclose the information or conceal it. Formally, the principal receives a signal $s \in \{\varnothing, \theta_2\}$, where $\varnothing$ is uncorrelated with θ_2, and can report $r \in \{\varnothing, s\}$ to the agent. To fix ideas, suppose that two coauthors with different research styles, tastes or installed bases of contributions must make modelling choices, or decide what to emphasize. Individual 1 has private information on the popularity of individual 2's research agenda or preferred approach, about which she may have heard or read comments. She may then disclose the (good or bad) news to individual 2, or conceal them from him.

We rule out monetary transfers, again for simplicity. The timing is as follows:

Stage 1: The principal learns either nothing or learns θ_2. In the latter case, she chooses whether or not to disclose the information.

Stage 2: Both individuals come up with one idea each for a joint undertaking.

Stage 3: With probability 1/2 each, one of them is selected to make a take-it-or-leave-it offer, *i.e.* gets to choose which project will be implemented.

It is easy to see that when the principal learns that $\theta_2 = \theta_2^L$, she wants to convey this bad news to the agent, because in doing so she establishes dominance: by (14), even if the agent gets to propose the course of action he will then defer to the principal, which he would not do if he were more self-confident. By lowering the other's ego, individual 1 enjoys *real authority* despite sharing *formal authority* over decisions with individual 2. Similar ideas hold when monetary transfers between the two individuals are feasible, as long as talent-contingent outside options are available; again, the basic point is that the principal's bargaining power is enhanced when the agent's self-confidence is damaged.

The situation described above may still be viewed as a relatively tame and efficient version of the "battle of the egos", since the principal's lowering of the agent's self-confidence by revealing that $\theta_2 = \theta_2^L$ is Pareto-improving (introducing monetary transfers would thus not affect anyone's decision in this case). When this information is brought to him, individual 2 may feel disappointed, but should recognize that he is being saved from making a costly mistake.

The other state in which the principal is informed ($\theta_2 = \theta_2^H$) can, however, yield a much less harmonious and efficient outcome. Let $\bar{\theta}_2$ denote the agent's self-confidence conditional on $s \in \{\varnothing, \theta_2^H\}$, which is his information set when the principal reports no signal (since she always passes on any bad news). By (14), when the principal learns that $\theta_2 = \theta_2^H$ she cannot lose by concealing this favourable information. It actually pays to do so if

$$\bar{\theta}_2 V + B < \theta_1 V, \tag{15}$$

as a report of "no news" will then induce the agent to submit to her authority. The principal will thus censor positive signals about the agent's ability, and would even be willing to spend resources in order to prevent them from reaching him.[45] In contrast to the earlier case, her undermining of the agent's self-confidence (by omission) is now detrimental to the latter, and may even result in a lower total surplus (if $\theta_2^H > \theta_1$). This case corresponds well to that of a mediocre and insecure manager, who abstains from passing on to his subordinates positive feedback about their performance from higher-ups or customers, for fear that they may then challenge his authority and diminish his ability to shape decisions (an extreme case being going after his job).[46]

Proposition 7. *In the game described above, individual* 1 *bashes individual* 2*'s ego in order to establish dominance and acquire real authority. She does so both by disclosing bad news to individual* 2 *and by feigning ignorance when learning good news.*

One could further enrich the analysis to capture escalating "arguments" by allowing agent 2, in response to an attack on his ego, to seek costly counter-evidence, as well perhaps as information that reflects negatively on agent 1's ability.

45. When $\bar{\theta}_2 V + B > \theta_1 V$, there are multiple equilibrium disclosure behaviours, but a unique equilibrium payoff outcome: the agent always chooses his own project. The principal's ability to conceal information is then irrelevant in the state where $\theta_2 = \theta_2^H$.

46. There are also other reasons why individual 2 may resent having his ego undercut. First, he may be suffering from a general self-motivation problem (perhaps most relevant for later, more important tasks) due to time-inconsistent preferences, which results in his attaching negative value to information about his ego (Carrillo and Mariotti (2000), Bénabou and Tirole (2002*a*)). Second, the two agents may be involved in bargaining over how to share the surplus created by their joint project, and the revelation that $\theta_2 = \theta_2^L$ may hurt individual 2's bargaining position more than it helps him by making sure that the efficient project is selected.

5.2.2 *The Sequencing of Ego Bashing and Ego Boosting*

Ego bashing may also have costs for the principal. As shown earlier, the agent's lack of self-confidence can reduce his initiative in coming up with good projects initially, as well as his motivation for putting effort into the joint endeavour later on. The resulting tradeoff has interesting implications for situations where the principal can choose the timing of information revelation. Suppose that, as shown in Figure 1, she can release information either before or after the agent searches for a project. The principal thus first learns either the agent's true type (θ_2), or nothing $(\varnothing)$; if she has information she may then disclose it. Next, the agent decides whether to search for a project, and the principal learns whether she has one of her own. The agent finds a viable project if and only if he exerts effort, which involves a private cost c. As to the principal, for simplicity we assume that she has a relevant project of her own with exogenous probability $x < 1$. The principal's uncertainty about the existence of a good project is what may make it costly for her to lower the agent's ego early on. The remainder of the game is otherwise unchanged: the principal has a second chance to disclose her information if she has not done so yet, then both jointly select a project.

To focus on the more interesting parameter configurations, we assume that (14) and (15) are satisfied, as well as

$$(1-x)(\theta_2^L V + B) < c < (1-x)(\theta_2^H V + B) + \frac{x}{2}(\theta_2^H V + B - \theta_1 V). \quad (16)$$

The first inequality in (16) states that bad news destroys incentives for effort: the project of an agent who knows he has a low talent will matter only if the principal has no viable alternative, *i.e.* only with probability $1-x$. The second inequality, by contrast, means that a self-confident agent finds it optimal to conceive a project of his own. Having such a project makes a difference if either the principal has none (probability $1-x$), or if she has one but the agent ends up with the bargaining power (probability $x/2$).

Definition 1. Consider stage $t = 1$ (*ex ante*) or 2 (*ex post*), and denote by $r_t(\theta_2) \in \{\varnothing, \theta_2\}$ the principal's disclosure at date t when she knows the agent's type θ_2. We say that the principal: (i) engages in ego bashing if her strategy is (or is payoff-equivalent to) $r_t(\theta_2^L) = \theta_2^L$ and $r_t(\theta_2^H) = \varnothing$; (ii) engages in ego boosting if it is (or is payoff-equivalent to) $r_t(\theta_2^L) = \varnothing$ and $r_t(\theta_2^H) = \theta_2^H$; (iii) conceals her information if her strategy is (or is payoff-equivalent to) $r_t(\theta_2) = \varnothing$ for $\theta_2 \in \{\theta_2^L, \theta_2^H\}$.

Proposition 8. *The principal engages in ego bashing* ex post *(provided she has not yet disclosed the information).* Ex ante, *she*

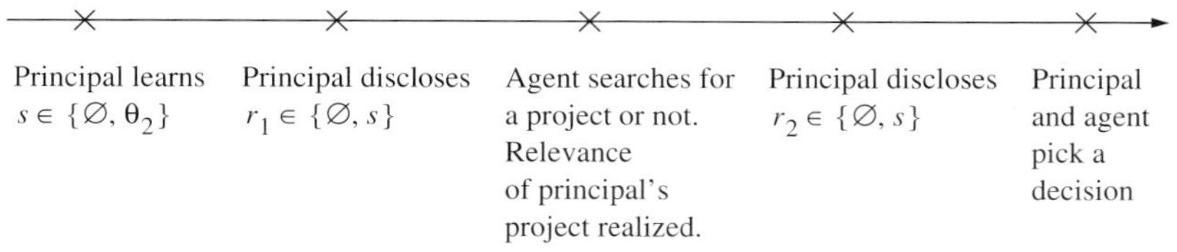

FIGURE 1

Timing of signals and reports

either engages in ego boosting, or refrains from disclosing information. Thus, good news tends to be revealed earlier than bad news; put differently, the relationship becomes more antagonistic over time.

Proof. See the Appendix. ■

To illustrate these results, one may think of a parent faced with his or her child's choice between different careers, or different sports. The parent may have information about the child's ability or value in some of these alternative activities — *e.g.* the family business. At the same time, there is always a chance (probability $1 - x$) that the parent's preferred choice will turn out not to be suited to the child anyway. The parent will then at first attempt to appear broad-minded (refrain from belittling the child's judgment or tastes), or even actively encourage him to explore alternatives. When coming close to a decision, however, the "father-knows-best" attitude will resurface, as long as the parent still has a credible alternative to the activity favoured by the child.

In the framework described by Figure 1, effort is related to the search for a project and comes before decision making. It is then quite natural that the early stage of the relationship be biased toward ego boosting, and the late stage toward ego bashing. Suppose, on the other hand, that the agent's effort relates to the implementation of a project rather than to its conception. With the choice of project coming first and the agent's effort second, it is clear that the timing of ego bashing and ego boosting is reversed: the principal tends to "beat up" on the agent at first, only to provide reassurance later on (if feasible), once the project has been selected and the principal wants the agent to be motivated.

We have emphasized here the obvious cost of ego bashing in terms of demotivation. Another cost may stem from individual 2's drawing more complex inferences about individual 1's preferences. Suppose that agent 2 cares not only about the project, but also about individual 1's altruism, friendship, or love towards him, over which he has incomplete information as well. Ego bashing may then be interpreted as individual 1 caring little about individual 2, and backfire.

Despite these costs, people may often be willing to belittle and criticize others in order to establish dominance. Because this can result in very inefficient outcomes, an interesting avenue for future research is how individuals and organizations try to limit the scope for such ego clashes. Let us, for now, content ourselves with a few thoughts in this regard. One possible strategy suggested by the model is to allocate formal control to individual 1. An example may be giving decision rights to parents until the children have reached a certain age. Another arrangement sometimes observed is the acceptance by individual 2 of individual 1's dominance (presumably because individual 2 also has private information about himself). Individual 2's "puppy dog" strategy may enable him to avoid ego clashes with individual 1. Another promising topic is the study of *institutional structures* and *personnel management strategies* designed to prevent excessive rivalry and ego clashes within organizations, and promote instead a cooperative interpersonal atmosphere.

6 Concluding Remarks

Psychologists, experts in human resource management and sociologists have long emphasized the central role played by intrinsic motivation in many social and economic interactions. In particular, they have called attention to the fact that explicit incentive schemes may sometimes backfire, especially in the long run, by undermining agents' confidence in their own abilities or in the value of the rewarded task. This side of social psychology has been largely neglected by economists.[47] The present paper has shown that these phenomena are often quite rational, and provided a formal analysis that helps reconcile the economic and the psychological views.

Several avenues of further research seem particularly interesting. The first one would combine the looking-glass self with the reverse form of signalling, namely self-presentation, in which the agent tries to signal his information to the principal.[48] The second avenue concerns the dynamics of motivation and its "management" in long-term relationships. Third, while our model already accommodates the possibility of altruism, friendship or love, it ought to be extended to allow for asymmetric information about such feelings. As noted earlier, each party would then draw from the other's behaviour subtle inferences not only about abilities and task characteristics, but also about how much the other cares about him or her. Finally, the analysis should be extended to groups. One hears frequent complaints about workplaces where egos loom large and clash too much to allow a pleasant and cooperative environment. More generally, the interactions between intrapersonal confidence-maintenance strategies, the looking-glass self, and self-presentation raise a fascinating set of questions (*e.g.* whether these strategies are mutually reinforcing), as well as issues of institutional design related to the optimal organization of educational and work environments.

47. With the previously noted exceptions of Frey (1997) and Kreps (1997).

48. For example, in the literatures on depression and on excuses, when the agent tries to lower the principal's expectations the latter's course of action is often a choice of whether to accept the stated reason and offer comfort, or to resist it. In so doing, the principal reveals information to the agent, that impacts his subsequent behaviour.

Appendix

Proofs of Propositions 3 and 4

We derive here equilibrium behaviour in the two-type case, first without and then with lump-sum payments. The agent's ability can be high, θ_H (probability f_H), or low, θ_L (probability f_L).

The conditional densities of his signal are denoted $g_H(\sigma)$ and $g_L(\sigma)$, and the MLRP simply means that g_H/g_L is increasing.

No Lump-Sum Payment (Proposition 3)

Consider an arbitrary perfect Bayesian equilibrium. From Propositions 1 and 2, the equilibrium is monotonic: if B_H and B_L denote the sets of bonuses that, in equilibrium, are offered with positive probability by a principal of type θ_H and θ_L respectively (*i.e.* one who knows that the agent has ability θ_H, or θ_L) then for any $(b, b') \in B_H \times B_L$, one must have $b \leq b'$. This, in turn, implies that: (i) $B_H \subseteq B_L$, or else the θ_L type could profitably deviate to some b that was strictly less than any b' in B_L, thus leading the agent to think that he had high ability with probability one, and thereby (weakly) improving motivation while saving on incentive costs; (ii) B_H has at most one element, or else, since $B_H \subseteq B_L$, monotonicity would be violated; (iii) $B_L \setminus B_H$ also has a unique element, because it cannot be optimal to offer one bonus that signals θ_L if a lower one has the same informational content and also induces effort.

In summary, there are at most two equilibrium bonuses: a pooling bonus b and (possibly) a higher bonus signalling type θ_L. The latter is then necessarily equal to b_L^*, since the low-type principal can always guarantee herself her complete information payoff by offering b_L^*, and no bonus that signals θ_L for sure will induce the agent to work if it is less than b_L^*.

An equilibrium is thus defined by three parameters: the pooling bonus $b < b_L^*$, the probability x^* that type θ_L selects b, and

$$\left(\frac{f_H g_H(\sigma^*)}{f_H g_H(\sigma^*) + f_L g_L(\sigma^*) x^*} \theta_H + \frac{f_L g_L(\sigma^*) x^*}{f_H g_H(\sigma^*) + f_L g_L(\sigma^*) x^*} \theta_L\right) V = c, \qquad \text{(A.1)}$$

which defines the agent's cutoff σ^*, with $\sigma^* \in (0, 1)$ by the full-support assumption.

Let us next show that there exists a unique equilibrium satisfying the NWBR criterion, and that it is such that $b = 0$. Consider, by contradiction, a pooling bonus $b > 0$, with associated cutoff σ. We will show that, for any $\hat{b} < b$, if a deviation to $\hat{b}$ elicits from the agent a response, described by a cutoff $\hat{\sigma}$, that results in weakly higher profits for a principal of type θ_L,

$$\theta_L[1 - G(\hat{\sigma} \mid \theta_L)](W - \hat{b}) \geq \theta_L[1 - G(\sigma \mid \theta_L)](W - b), \quad \text{(A.2)}$$

then this same deviation will be strictly preferred by a principal of type θ_H. This is obvious when $\hat{\sigma} \leq \sigma$, since a deviation to $\hat{b}$ then yields higher effort by the agent, at a lower cost for the principal (of any type). Suppose now that $\hat{\sigma} > \sigma$; we then have

$$\frac{W - b}{W - \hat{b}} \leq \frac{1 - G(\hat{\sigma} \mid \theta_L)}{1 - G(\sigma \mid \theta_L)} < \frac{1 - G(\hat{\sigma} \mid \theta_H)}{1 - G(\sigma \mid \theta_H)}, \quad \text{(A.3)}$$

where the first inequality obtains from (A.2) and the second follows from the MLRP, since $\theta_L < \theta_H$ and $\sigma < \hat{\sigma}$. Thus, if a deviation to $\hat{b}$ is profitable for type θ_L, then *a fortiori* it is strictly profitable for type θ_H. Hence, according to the NWBR criterion, when the agent is offered a $\hat{b} < b$ (say, $\hat{b} = b - \varepsilon$), he should believe that it emanates from type θ_H. Therefore, $b > 0$ cannot be part of a pooling equilibrium, and so it must be that $B = \{0, b_L^*\}$.

Next, note that when $\theta = \theta_L$ the principal must randomize between $b = 0$ and $b = b_L^*$: if she only played b_L^*, then $b = 0$ would induce compliance with probability 1, and would therefore be preferred to b_L^*. The equilibrium is thus described by two parameters: $x^* \in (0, 1]$, the probability that a principal observing $\theta = \theta_L$ selects bonus 0 (pools); and σ^*, the agent's cutoff signal for working when he is offered a zero bonus. These are given by

$$\theta_L(W - b_L^*) = \theta_L[1 - G_L(\sigma^*)]W, \quad \text{(A.4)}$$

expressing the principal's willingness to randomize when $\theta = \theta_L$, and equation (A.1), which can be rewritten as

$$\frac{g_H(\sigma^*)}{g_L(\sigma^*)} = x^*\left(\frac{f_L}{f_H}\right)\left(\frac{c/V - \theta_L}{\theta_H - c/V}\right). \quad \text{(A.5)}$$

By our assumptions on the likelihood ratio, for any $x^* > 0$ there exists a unique solution $\sigma^* = s(x^*)$ to (A.1), with $\sigma^* > 0$. Substituting into (A.4), the principal's net incentive to offer bonus 0 when $\theta = \theta_L$ and the agent expects her to randomize with probability x^* is

$$\theta_L[1 - G_L(s(x^*))]W - \theta_L(W - b_L^*). \quad \text{(A.6)}$$

This function is increasing in x^*, and negative at $x^* = 0^+$. So either it has a unique zero on $(0, 1)$, which then defines the principal's mixing strategy; or else it is non-positive on all of $(0, 1]$, in which case the principal's equilibrium strategy is $x^* = 1$, meaning that *no bonus is ever offered*. In both cases the equilibrium is unique. Note, finally, that the agent works only with probability $1 - G_H(s(x^*))$ when $\theta = \theta_H$, and with probability $1 - x^* G_L(s(x^*))$ when $\theta = \theta_L$. Thus, in either state of the world, he works less than under symmetric information (where $e = 1$ with probability one). ■

Lump-Sum Payments (Proposition 4)

In any separating equilibrium the agent always works; when $\theta = \theta_L$ he thus gets bonus b_L^* and no lump-sum payment. Denoting by (a, b) the contract he gets when $\theta = \theta_H$, let us show that when $\theta = \theta_L$ the principal must be indifferent between offering $(0, b_L^*)$ and (a, b). Clearly the θ_L-type principal cannot strictly prefer (a, b), and were she to strictly prefer $(0, b_L^*)$, the θ_H-type could profitably deviate to $(a - \varepsilon, b)$, for small $\varepsilon > 0$. According to NWBR this would still convince the agent that $\theta = \theta_H$, since for ε small enough the θ_L-type still prefers $(0, b_L^*)$ to $(a - \varepsilon, b)$ even when the agent works with probability 1 after being offered the latter contract. Next, as in the proof of Proposition 3, it is easy to show that $b = 0$: were $b > 0$, the principal could offer $b - \varepsilon$ and the agent would interpret this (according to NWBR) as a sure sign that $\theta = \theta_H$.

The NWBR separating equilibrium, if it exists, is thus necessarily defined by the contracts $(0, b_L^*)$ and $(a = c - \theta_L V, 0)$. Moreover, the limited-informativeness condition ensures that the NWBR criterion is indeed satisfied. Indeed, suppose that the principal deviates to a contract $(\hat{a}, \hat{b})$, and let $\hat{\sigma}$ define the agent's reaction to this offer. If this is weakly profitable for the θ_H type,

$$\theta_H(1 - G_H(\hat{\sigma}))(W - \hat{b}) - \hat{a} \geq \theta_H W - (c - \theta_L V),$$

then (10) implies that it is strictly profitable for the θ_L type,

$$\theta_L(1 - G_L(\hat{\sigma}))(W - \hat{b}) - \hat{a} > \theta_L W - (c - \theta_L V),$$

as long as either $b > 0$ or $\hat{\sigma} > 0$; when $\hat{b} = \hat{\sigma} = 0$ both types gain, equally. According to NWBR the agent should then interpret any such deviation as indicative of $\theta = \theta_L$, and shirk, so it cannot be profitable. ■

Proof of Proposition 5

For a given delegation policy $d \in \{0, 1\}$, the agent undertakes the task if and only if $\mathsf{E}[\theta \mid \sigma, d]V \geq c_d$. Therefore, there is a cutoff σ_d^* such that he exerts effort if and only if $\sigma \geq \sigma_d^*$. The principal then chooses $d \in \{0, 1\}$ so as to maximize $[1 - G(\sigma_d^* \mid \theta)]\mathcal{W}_d(\theta)$. Suppose first that $\sigma_1^* \geq \sigma_0^*$. Then, from the MLRP and Assumption 1:

$$\frac{d}{d\theta}\left[\left(\frac{1 - G(\sigma_1^* \mid \theta)}{1 - G(\sigma_0^* \mid \theta)}\right)\left(\frac{\mathcal{W}_1(\theta)}{\mathcal{W}_0(\theta)}\right)\right] > 0, \qquad \text{(A.7)}$$

and so the principal delegates if and only if $\theta \geq \tilde{\theta}$ for some $\tilde{\theta}$. This implies that delegation is good news: $\mathsf{E}[\theta \mid \sigma, 1] > \mathsf{E}[\theta \mid \sigma, 0]$ for all σ; in particular, $c_1 = \mathsf{E}[\theta \mid \sigma_1^*, 1] > \mathsf{E}[\theta \mid \sigma_0^*, 0] = c_0$, a contradiction. So it must be that $\sigma_1^* < \sigma_0^*$, meaning that (for given θ) the agent works more under delegation; hence part (i) of the proposition. As a result, for all $\theta > \theta^*$ we have $[1 - G(\sigma_1^* \mid \theta)]W_1(\theta) > [1 - G(\sigma_0^* \mid \theta)]W_0(\theta)$, so the principal strictly prefers to delegate. By continuity, this remains true on some interval $[\theta^{**}, \theta^*]$ with $\theta^{**} < \theta^*$. This proves part (ii). This property, however, does not necessarily make θ^{**} a cutoff such that delegation occurs if *and only if* $\theta > \theta^{**}$: indeed with $\sigma_1^* < \sigma_0^*$, the term in square brackets in (A.7) need no longer be increasing in θ (although it cannot be everywhere decreasing, otherwise the principal would delegate if and only if θ was above a cutoff $\hat{\theta}$, contradicting (ii)). When Assumption 2 holds, however, (A.7) again applies, implying that delegation occurs if and only if $\theta \geq \theta^{**}$, where $\theta^{**} < \theta^*$. This, in turn, ensures part (iii) of the proposition, and more generally implies that delegation raises the agent's posterior distribution about his ability, independently of his signal and of the task's outcome. ■

Proof of Proposition 8

Let us work by backward induction.

(a) Suppose that at $t = 2$ the principal knows the agent's type, but has not yet disclosed it. Let $y(\theta_2^L)$, $y(\varnothing)$ and $y(\theta_2^H)$ denote the equilibrium probabilities that the agent will stick to his own project when: (a) the principal also has a relevant project, but it is the agent who gets to make the selection; and (b) the agent was previously told $r_2 = \theta_2^L$, $\varnothing$ or θ_2^H respectively. From (14) and (15), we have

$$y(\theta_2^L) = 0 \leq y(\varnothing) \leq y(\theta_2^H) = 1. \qquad \text{(A.8)}$$

If $y(\varnothing) > 0$, it is clearly strictly optimal for the principal to disclose $\theta_2 = \theta_2^L$ *ex post.* In the absence of any news the agent will thus infer that $s \in \{\varnothing, \theta_2^H\}$, and condition (15) then implies that $y(\varnothing) = 0$ after all, a contradiction. The fact that $y(\varnothing) = 0 < 1 = y(\theta_2^H)$, in turn, makes it strictly optimal for the principal not to disclose that $\theta_2 = \theta_2^H$, when she has such news. Finally, when the principal knows that $\theta_2 = \theta_2^L$ she is indifferent between disclosing it and saying nothing, since $y(\theta_2^L) = y(\varnothing) = 0$ (this is why we allow for payoff-equivalence in the definition preceding Proposition 8). We may thus, without loss of generality, assume that she chooses to reveal the bad news.

(b) Let us now look at the principal's *ex ante* behaviour ($t = 1$) and the agent's subsequent effort decision. Let $z(\theta_2^L)$, $z(\varnothing)$ and $z(\theta_2^H)$ denote the probabilities that the agent searches for a project after hearing reports $r_1 = \theta_2^L, \varnothing$ and θ_2^H respectively. Equation (16) implies that

$$z(\theta_2^L) = 0 \leq z(\varnothing) \leq z(\theta_2^H) = 1. \quad \text{(A.9)}$$

Either $z(\varnothing) = 0$, and then we might as well assume that the principal reports $r_1(\theta_2^L) = \varnothing$ (if not, change her behaviour to $r_1(\theta_2^L) = \varnothing$ for sure; then $z(\varnothing) = 0$ *a fortiori*). Or else $z(\varnothing) > 0$, and then it is strictly optimal for the principal not to disclose θ_2^L *ex ante*, given that she can (and will) do it *ex post*.

Last, when $\theta_2 = \theta_2^H$ the principal faces a tradeoff if $z(\varnothing) < z(\theta_2^H)$. Disclosing the good news raises incentives for effort, but emboldens the agent in the *ex post* negotiation. It can be shown that depending on the values of the parameters, the principal may or may not disclose $\theta_2 = \theta_2^H$ in equilibrium. ■

Acknowledgements. The first version of this paper was titled "Self-Confidence and Social Interactions". We are grateful for helpful comments and discussions to Philippe Aghion, Mark Armstrong, Isabelle Brocas, Daniel Gilbert, Robert Lane, Marek Pycia, Gérard Roland, Julio Rotemberg, Ilya Segal, Anton Souvorov, participants at the Francqui conference on "The Economics of Contracts" (Brussels, 1999), participants at seminars at Harvard and Paris, and at the ISNIE 2002 Congress (Boston) and three anonymous referees. Bénabou gratefully acknowledges financial support from the National Science Foundation (SES-0096431) and the MacArthur Foundation, as well as the hospitality of the Institute for Advanced Study over the academic year 2002-2003.

REFERENCES

[1] Aghion, P. and Tirole, J. (1997), "Formal and Real Authority in Organizations", *Journal of Political Economy*, **105**, 1-29.

[2] Akerlof, G. and Dickens, W. (1982), "The Economic Consequences of Cognitive Dissonance", *American Economic Review*, **72** (3), 307-331.

[3] Baron, J. and Kreps, D. (1999) *Strategic Human Resources* (New York: John Wiley).

[4] Bem, D.J. (1967), "Self-Perception: An Alternative Interpretation of Cognitive Dissonance Phenomena", *Psychological Review*, **74**, 183-200.

[5] Bénabou, R. and Tirole, J. (2002*a*), "Self-Confidence and Personal Motivation", *Quarterly Journal of Economics*, **117** (3), 871-915.

[6] Bénabou, R. and Tirole, J. (2002*b*), "Willpower and Personal Rules" (CEPR Discussion Paper 3143).

[7] Bibring, E. (1953), "The Mechanism of Depression", in P. Greenacre (ed.) *Affective Disorders* (New York: International University Press).

[8] Carrillo, J. and Mariotti, T. (2000), "Strategic Ignorance as a Self-Disciplining Device", *Review of Economic Studies*, **66**, 529-544.

[9] Cho, I. K. and Kreps, D. (1987), "Signaling Games and Stable Equilibria", *Quarterly Journal of Economics*, **102**, 179-221.

[10] Condry, J. and Chambers, J. (1978), "Intrinsic Motivation and the Process of Learning", in M. Lepper and D. Greene (eds.) *The Hidden Cost of Reward: New Perspectives on the Psychology of Human Motivation* (New York: John Wiley).

[11] Cooley, C. (1902) *Human Nature and the Social Order* (New York: Scribner's).

[12] Darley, J. and Fazio, R. (1980), "Expectancy Confirmation Processes Arising in the Social Interaction Sequence", *American Psychologist*, **35**, 867-881.

[13] Deci, E. (1975) *Intrinsic Motivation* (New York: Plenum Press).

[14] Deci, E., Koestner, R. and Ryan, R. (1999), "A Meta-Analytic Review of Experiments Examining the Effects of Extrinsic Rewards on Intrinsic Motivation", *Psychological Bulletin*, **125** (6), 627-668.

[15] Deci, E. and Ryan, R. (1985) *Intrinsic Motivation and Self-Determination in Human Behavior* (New York: Plenum Press).

[16] Delfgauw, J. and Dur, R. (2002), "Signaling and Screening of Workers' Motivation" (Tinbergen Institute DP 2002-050/3).

[17] Dessein, W. (2002), "Authority and Communication in Organizations", *Review of Economic Studies*, **69** (4), 811-838.

[18] Etzioni, A. (1971) *Modern Organizations* (Englewood Cliffs, NJ: Prentice-Hall).

[19] Fang, H. and Moscarini, G. (2002), "Overconfidence, Morale and Wage-Setting Policies" (Mimeo, Yale University).

[20] Fehr, E. and Falk, A. (1999), "Wage Rigidity in a Competitive Incomplete Contract Market", *Journal of Political Economy*, **107** (1), 106-134.

[21] Fehr, E. and Schmidt, K. (2000), "Fairness, Incentives, and Contractual Choices", *European Economic Review*, **44** (4-6), 1057-1068.

[22] Festinger, L. and Carlsmith, J. (1959), "Cognitive Consequences of Forced Compliance", *Journal of Abnormal and Social Psychology*, **58**, 203-210.

[23] Frey, B. (1997) *Not Just for the Money — An Economic Theory of Personal Motivation* (Cheltenham, U.K.: Edward Elgar).

[24] Frey, B., Fehr, E. and Benz, M. (2000), "Does Motivation Crowding Out Spread Beyond the Area of Intervention? Experimental Evidence" (Mimeo, University of Zurich).

[25] Frey, B. and Oberholzer-Gee, F. (1997), "The Cost of Price Incentives: An Empirical Analysis of Motivation Crowding-Out", *American Economic Review*, **87** (4), 746-755.

[26] Fudenberg, D. and Tirole, J. (1991) *Game Theory* (Cambridge, MA: MIT Press).

[27] Gibbons, R. (1997), "Incentives and Careers in Organizations", in D. Kreps and K. Wallis (eds.) *Advances in Economic Theory and Econometrics*, Vol. II (Cambridge, U.K.: Cambridge University Press).

[28] Gilbert, D. and Silvera, D. (1996), "Overhelping", *Journal of Personality and Social Psychology*, **70**, 678-690.

[29] Gneezy, U. and Rustichini, A. (2000*a*), "A Fine is a Price", *Journal of Legal Studies*, **29** (1) (part 1), 1-17.

[30] Gneezy, U. and Rustichini, A. (2000*b*), "Pay Enough or Don't Pay at All", *Quarterly Journal of Economics*, **115** (3), 791-810.

[31] Holmström, B. and Milgrom, P. (1991), "Multi-Task Principal-Agent Analyzes: Incentive Contracts, Asset Ownership, and Job Design", *Journal of Law, Economics and Organization*, 7, 24-52 (special issue).

[32] Hull, C. L. (1943) *Principles of Behavior* (New York: Appleton-Century-Crofts).

[33] Kinlaw, D. (1997) *Coaching: Winning Strategies for Individuals and Teams* (U.K.: Gower Publishing).

[34] Kohn, A. (1993) *Punished by Rewards* (New York: Plenum Press).

[35] Korman, A. K. (1970), "Toward an Hypothesis of Work Behavior", *Journal of Applied Psychology*, **54**, 31-41.

[36] Kreps, D. (1997), "Intrinsic Motivation and Extrinsic Incentives", *American Economic Review*, **87** (2), 359-364.

[37] Kruglanski, A. (1978), "Issues in Cognitive Social Psychology", in *The Hidden Cost of Reward: New Perspectives on the Psychology of Human Motivation* (New York: John Wiley).

[38] Kruglanski, A., Friedman, I. and Zeevi, G. (1971), "The Effect of Extrinsic Incentives on Some Qualitative Aspects of Task Performance", *Journal of Personality*, **39**, 608-617.

[39] Laffont, J.-J. and Tirole, J. (1988), "Repeated Auctions of Incentive Contracts, Investment and Bidding Parity, With an Application to Takeovers", *Rand Journal of Economics*, **19**, 516-537.

[40] Lazear, E. (2000), "Performance, Pay and Productivity", *American Economic Review*, **90** (5), 1346-1361.

[41] Lepper, M. and Greene, D. (1978), "Overjustification Research and Beyond: Toward a Means-Ends Analysis of Intrinsic and Extrinsic Motivation", in *The Hidden Cost of Reward: New Perspectives on the Psychology of Human Motivation* (New York: John Wiley).

[42] Lepper, M., Greene, D. and Nisbett, R. (1973), "Undermining Children's Interest with Extrinsic Rewards: A Test of the 'Overjustification Hypothesis'", *Journal of Personality and Social Psychology*, **28**, 129-137.

[43] Merton, R. (1948), "The Self-Fulfilling Prophecies", *Antioch Review*, **8**, 193-210.

[44] Miles, R. (1965), "Human Relations and Human Resources", *Harvard Business Review*.

[45] Pfeffer, J. (1994) *Competitive Advantage Through People: Problems and Prospects for Change*, Chapter 4 (Boston: Harvard Business School Press).

[46] Rosenthal, R. and Jacobson, L. (1968) *Pygmalion in the Classroom* (Holt-Rinehart-Winston).

[47] Salancik, G. (1977), "Commitment and the Control of Organizational Behavior and Beliefs", in B. Staw and G. Salancik (eds.) *New Directions in Organizational Behavior* (Chicago: St. Clair Press).

[48] Schwartz, B. (1990), "The Creation and Destruction of Value", *American Psychologist*, **45**, 7-15.

[49] Skinner, G. F. (1953) *Science and Human Behavior* (New York: Macmillan).

[50] Snyder, C., Higgins, R. and Stucky, R. (1983) *Excuses: Masquerades in Search of Grace* (New York: John Wiley).

[51] Souvorov, A. (2003), "Addiction to Rewards" (Mimeo, GREMAQ, Toulouse).

[52] Staw, B. (1977), "Motivation in Organizations: Toward Synthesis and Redirection", in B. Staw and G. Salancik (eds.) *New Directions in Organizational Behavior* (Chicago: St. Clair Press).

[53] Wilson, T., Hull, J. and Johnson, J. (1981), "Awareness and Self-Perception: Verbal Reports on Internal States", *Journal of Personality and Social Psychology*, **40**, 53-71.

9

Detrimental Effects of Sanctions on Human Altruism

Ernst Fehr
Bettina Rockenbach

Abstract

The existence of cooperation and social order among genetically unrelated individuals is a fundamental problem in the behavioural sciences. The prevailing approaches in biology and economics view cooperation exclusively as self-interested behaviour — unrelated individuals cooperate only if they face economic rewards or sanctions rendering cooperation a self-interested choice. Whether economic incentives are perceived as just or legitimate does not matter in these theories. Fairness-based altruism is, however, a powerful source of human cooperation. Here we show experimentally that the prevailing self-interest approach has serious shortcomings because it overlooks negative effects of sanctions on human altruism. Sanctions revealing selfish or greedy intentions destroy altruistic cooperation almost completely, whereas sanctions perceived as fair leave altruism intact. These findings challenge proximate and ultimate theories of human cooperation that neglect the distinction between fair and unfair sanctions, and they are probably relevant in all domains in which voluntary compliance matters — in relations between spouses, in the education of children, in business relations and organizations as well as in markets.

Human societies are characterized by an unprecedented division of labour supported by a myriad of social and economic exchanges and compliance with social norms[1,2]. Norm compliance and the exchange of favours, goods and services pervade every aspect of human life. They shape the interactions in families, neighbourhoods, schools, firms, markets and politics. The crucial feature of any exchange is that the parties involved have to trust each other. If the exchange partners had doubts about the other's reliability most exchanges would not take place. In fact, much of the economic backwardness in the world can plausibly be explained by a lack of mutual confidence inhibiting cooperation in the production and the exchange of goods and services[3,4]. Yet, what ensures that exchange partners trust each other? In modern societies one solution is to conclude a legally enforceable contract that regulates all aspects of the exchange — in particular, the sanctions imposed on those who breach the contract. If the punishment for breaching the contract is large enough, it is in the self-interest of the involved parties to fulfil their obligations because otherwise they will be heavily punished.

For millennia, however, humans have not been able to rely on contracts because there were no impartial courts enforcing voluntary agreements. Even today it is typically not possible to regulate transactions in every detail, and frequently the courts are unable to verify who violated an agreement. Therefore, even in modern societies the overwhelming majority of all social and economic exchanges are not based on complete and legally enforceable contracts but on implicit agreements and social norms lacking explicitly specified sanctions for non-compliance[5,6]. In such situations there are ample opportunities for cheating the exchange partner to one's own advantage. It is the ubiquity of such cheating opportunities that renders altruistic cooperation important. Altruistic cooperators are willing to cooperate, that is, to abide by the implicit agreement, although cheating would be economically beneficial for them. Much recent research indicates that altruistic cooperation is an important behavioural force[7-11].

However, the prevailing theoretical approaches in biology[12-17] and economics[18,19] neglect costly altruistic behaviour that does not yield future economic benefits for the altruist. Individuals are supposed to do others a favour only if they can themselves reap direct[12,13] or indirect[14-17] future benefits from such others. Likewise, individuals are supposed to cheat on agreements unless they are sufficiently rewarded for compliance or sanctioned for non-compliance. This axiom of self-interested behaviour implies that the only remedy for the compliance problem lies in the provision of sufficient rewards or sanctions. Yet, if these incentives for cooperation undermine altruistic behaviour the remedy may do more harm than good because it aggravates the compliance problem[5,20-23]. Influential social scientists have hypothesized that economic incentives might undermine altruism[20,21] but so far it has been impossible to provide compelling evidence from uncontrolled field studies.

Capturing Trust and Altruistic Cooperation

We examine the question of how sanctions intended to prevent cheating affect human altruism in a sequentially played social dilemma experiment with real monetary stakes. In each trial of the experiment two mutually anonymous subjects are involved — one subject in the role of investor, the other one in the role of trustee. First, the investor has the chance of choosing a costly trusting action. Then the trustee is informed about the investor's action and he can honour the investor's trust by taking a costly cooperative action. The payoff rules of the experiment ensure that if the investor chooses a trusting action and the trustee responds cooperatively both players increase their monetary payoff. However, the trustee also has the option of not honouring the investor's trust. In this case the trustee saves the costs of cooperation but the investor is worse off than if he had not been trustful. Because a cooperative action is costly for the trustee, the trustee is tempted not to honour the investor's trust. Yet, if the investor expects that the trustee will not honour his trust the investor will not choose a costly trusting action in the first place. Thus, the subjects are caught in a dilemma because trust and cooperation is beneficial for both subjects but the trustee faces the temptation not to cooperate and, therefore, the investor is tempted not to trust.

To examine potential detrimental effects of sanctions on human altruism we implement two experimental conditions — an incentive condition and a trust condition. In the trust condition, cooperation of the trustee cannot be achieved by incentives because there are no rewards or sanctions available to the investor. The trustee's cooperation in this condition provides, therefore, a baseline measure of altruism because — in the absence of economic incentives — purely selfish trustees will never cooperate. In the incentive condition, the investor has the option of fining a trustee who has not cooperated sufficiently. The incentive condition informs us, therefore, whether there are detrimental effects of sanctions on the trustee's altruism. In particular, if the amount of cooperation is higher in the absence of the sanction that would be evidence of a detrimental effect.

The details of the trust condition are as follows. Both the investor and the trustee receive an endowment of ten money units (MUs). The investor has the option to trust his partner by sending between zero and ten MUs of his endowment to the trustee. The experimenter then triples any amount sent so that if the investor sends, say, 10 MUs the trustee receives 30 MUs. The tripling of the investment mimics a situation where the trustee has superior productive opportunities for the use of economic resources. If the investor transfers money to the trustee he also has to specify a "desired back-transfer" that can be any amount between zero and the tripled transfer. In the previous example, for instance, where the investor sent 10 and the trustee received 30 MUs, the desired back-transfer can be any amount between zero and 30 MUs. Once the investor has made his investment the trustee is informed about the amount sent and the desired back-transfer. Then the trustee has the option to cooperate by choosing the actual level of the back-transfer. The trustee is free to send any amount between zero and the tripled transfer — in our example, up to 30 MUs — back to the investor. The back-transfer is not tripled by the experimenter — if the trustee sends back, say, 8 MUs the investor receives exactly 8 MUs.

The final payoff of the investor is given by his endowment of 10 MUs minus the transfer to the trustee plus the actual back-transfer of the trustee. The payoff of the trustee is given by the endowment of 10 MUs plus the tripled transfer minus the actual back-transfer. Thus, if there is no trust and cooperation the investor's transfer and the trustee's back-transfer are zero. In this case, both earn just their endowment of 10 MUs. This is the predicted outcome if both subjects are fully selfish and the investor anticipates the trustee's selfishness. In the trust condition, a selfish trustee will never pay back anything and, therefore, a selfish investor, who anticipates the trustee's behaviour, will transfer nothing. Yet, trust and cooperation can render both subjects better off. If the investor trusts fully and sends 10 MUs and the trustee's actual back-transfer is 20 MUs the investor earns 20 MUs, and the trustee earns his endowment of 10 plus the tripled transfer of 30 minus the back-transfer of 20, which in total also gives 20 MUs.

The incentive condition is exactly identical to the trust condition except for one feature: the investor can impose a fine of four MUs on the trustee if less than the desired amount has been sent back. Yet, the investor can also refrain from imposing the fine. The trustee need not be fined even if he pays back less than the desired amount. At the time when the investor chooses the transfer and the desired back-transfer he also has to specify whether to impose a fine for the case that the trustee's actual back-transfer is lower than the desired one. Thus, when the trustee makes his decision in the incentive condition he knows whether the investor has chosen the fining option. To avoid evocative language the experimental instructions do not include value-laden terms like fine or punishment. Instead, the fine is described, more neutrally, as a deduction from the trustee's payoff. The fine affects only the trustee's payoff by reducing his earnings by 4 MUs in the case of an insufficient back-transfer. The fine does not affect the investor's payoff directly. However, the investor can use the fine to affect the trustee's back-transfer. In the incentive condition, a selfish trustee who does not face a fine will never pay back anything. Only if he faces a fine will he be ready to pay back up to 4 MUs. For instance, if the desired back-transfer is 3 MUs the trustee is better off by actually paying back 3 MUs instead of paying the fine of 4 MUs. Therefore, if the world were populated only by selfish subjects we should observe that all investors impose a fine and that only if a fine is imposed will the trustees pay back a positive amount. In such a world the available sanction would be used to enforce the cooperation of selfish trustees, and altruistic cooperation would be absent.

All the interactions in the experiment took place anonymously and each pair of subjects played the experiment only once. This means that repeated interactions[12,13] or reputation formation[14-17] cannot account for positive back-transfers. In the absence of a fine, positive back-transfers can, therefore, be characterized as altruistic cooperation. Likewise, if the investor imposes a fine, back-transfers exceeding the fine of 4 MUs represent altruistic cooperation because selfish trustees will never pay back more than 4 MUs.

Sanctions and Altruistic Cooperation

In our first experiment, 24 pairs of subjects participated in the trust condition and 45 pairs in the incentive condition. To examine the motives behind the investors' choices in more depth we later conducted an additional experiment with 50 pairs in the incentive condition. Figure 1 shows the behaviour of trustees in the two conditions of our first experiment. In contrast to the self-interest hypothesis the trustees paid back substantial amounts of money in all conditions. In addition, back-transfers were increasing in the investors' transfer, indicating the reciprocal nature of human altruism. This kind of altruism should not, however, be confused with the notion of "reciprocal altruism" as defined by Trivers[12]. In our experiment there are no repeated interactions so that trustees cannot hope to receive future rewards from their current altruistic acts. 19 of the 24 trustees (79%) in the trust condition paid back more than zero. 29 of the 45 trustees (64%) in the incentive condition paid back more than 4 MUs. This confirms that altruism is an important force in our setting. More

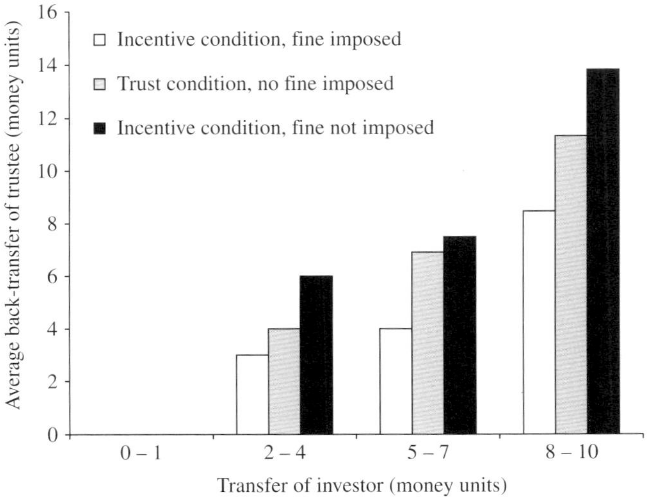

FIGURE 1

The average back-transfer of the trustees plotted as a function of the investors' transfers. In the trust condition and the incentive condition the back-transfers of the trustees increase with the investors' transfers — irrespective of whether the fine is imposed or not. If the investors impose a fine in the incentive condition, trustees reduce their back-transfers, indicating a detrimental effect of the incentive on altruistic cooperation. Trustees' back-transfers are highest if the investor deliberately refrains from imposing the fine.

importantly, however, there were striking differences in trustees' altruism across conditions (Fig. 1). For any interval of the investors' transfers the trustees' back-transfers were highest when the investor voluntarily refrained from the fine in the incentive condition and lowest when the investor imposed the fine. The back-transfers in the trust condition were always at an intermediate level. When the investor voluntarily refrained from the fine no trustee chose a back-transfer of zero and 47% (7 out of 15 subjects) chose a back-transfer of 15 MUs or more, yielding an average back-transfer of 12.5 MUs (Table 1). In contrast, if a fine was imposed, 33% (10 out of 30 subjects) paid back nothing and only 13% (4 out of 30 subjects) paid back 15 MUs or more, causing an average back-transfer of only 6 MUs. This difference in back-transfers is significant (Mann-Whitney test, $z = -2.988$, $P = 0.003$, two-tailed), providing a first indication that the imposition of the fine had detrimental effects on altruistic behaviour.

One reason for the higher back-transfers in the absence of fines could be that those investors who did not impose a fine transferred higher amounts to the trustees (Table 1). Investors who imposed a fine transferred 6.8 MUs on average whereas those who refrained from fining transferred 8.7 MUs (Mann-Whitney test, $z = -1.961$, $P = 0.050$, two-tailed). Trustees tended to pay back more money when they had received higher transfers (Fig. 1), so the higher back-transfers in the absence of the fine could be due to the higher transfers of the investors. To control for this effect we computed the actual back-transfer as a percentage of the tripled investment (Table 1). We find that if the fine was imposed the trustees paid back 30.3% of the tripled investment, and if investors voluntarily refrained from fining, significantly more, 47.6%, was paid back (Mann-Whitney test, $z = -1.930$, $P = 0.054$, two-tailed). A similar picture emerges if we examine how much the trustees paid back

TABLE 1

Average behaviour and payoffs of investors and trustees

	Trust condition	Incentive condition, fine chosen	Incentive condition, no fine chosen
Investment	6.5	6.8	8.7
Desired back-transfer as a percentage of tripled investment	59.9	67.4	63.7
Actual back-transfer	7.8	6.0	12.5
Actual back-transfer as a percentage of tripled investment	40.6	30.3	47.6
Actual back-transfer as a percentage of desired back-transfer	74.4	54.5	74.1
Investor's payoff	11.3	9.2	13.8
Trustee's payoff	21.8	22.4	23.5
Number of observations	24 pairs	30 pairs	15 pairs

relative to the desired back-transfer. If the fine was imposed the trustees paid back only 54.5% of the desired level whereas in the absence of the fine 74.1% of the desired level was paid back (Table 1).

The negative impact of sanctions on altruistic responses is also supported by a regression analysis, which controls for the investor's transfers and the desired back-transfers. Keeping these other factors constant, using the fine in the incentive treatment reduced the back-transfers significantly by 4.56 MUs ($t = 2.380$, $P = 0.020$, two-tailed). As a consequence, investors who did not use the fine earned significantly more money (Mann-Whitney test, $z = -2.283$, $P = 0.022$): 13.8 MUs in the absence of the fine and only 9.2 MUs when the fine was imposed (Table 1). The imposition of the fine reduced the back-transfers by 4.56 MUs, so it is tempting to assume that trustees who decided to pay back less than the desired amount — and hence had to pay the fine — reduced the back-transfer by the amount of the fine. This was, however, not the case. Those trustees who were actually fined paid back 2.94 MUs on average, whereas those who transferred back the desired amount, so that they did not have to pay the fine, paid back 9.5 MUs on the average. The median back-transfer of those who actually had to pay the fine was zero MUs.

Why do so many investors in the incentive treatment — two-thirds (30 out of 45) — threaten to sanction the trustee if the threat is associated with much lower back-transfers? We hypothesized that there are two potential reasons for this behaviour. First, preferences for strong reciprocity[24,25], which have been shown to prevail in many situations[8,9,11], could be the proximate cause. A strong reciprocator is willing to sacrifice resources for rewarding behaviour that is perceived as kind or fair and for punishing behaviour perceived as hostile or unfair, even if reciprocation is costly and provides no present or future material benefits whatsoever[24]. The variance in trustees' back-transfers is considerable, so the investor always faces the risk of being cheated. Therefore, strong reciprocators will impose a fine in case of malfeasance even if it reduces their overall earnings. Second, investors may simply not have anticipated the detrimental effects of the incentive on the back-transfers.

To discriminate between these two hypotheses we conducted a second experiment with 50 pairs of subjects in the incentive treatment. In this experiment, we informed the investors about the behaviour of the trustees in the first incentive treatment. We gave them two scatter diagrams that showed the trustees' back-transfers for every level of the investors' transfers. One diagram depicts the trustees' behaviour when they faced the fine, the other one shows trustees' behaviour in the absence of the fine. If the investors' preferences for fining were caused by false expectations about the effects of the fine they should change their decisions when informed about the true effects of the fine. This did, however, not occur. Again, roughly two-thirds of the investors (34 out of 50) preferred to fine the trustees in case of non-compliance. This suggests that the desire to punish cheaters is the reason for the frequent use of the fine.

Why Do Sanctions Reduce Altruistic Cooperation?

All the other qualitative findings observed in the first incentive treatment were also replicated in our second experiment. In particular, we again observed a sizeable increase in the back-transfers if the investors voluntarily waived the possibility of imposing the fine. How can we explain this behaviour by trustees? The notion of strong reciprocity can provide an answer to this question, too. First, refraining from the threat of fining, although the threat is available, could itself be perceived as a fair act, which induces the trustees to increase their cooperation. Second, attempts to use the sanction to enforce an unfair distribution of income may be perceived as hostile acts, inducing the trustees to reduce cooperation.

A back-transfer of two-thirds of the tripled transfer equalizes the trustee's and the investor's payoff. Therefore, we classified desired back-transfers of two-thirds or less of the tripled transfer as low, and desired back-transfers above two-thirds of the tripled transfer were classified as high. We find that for low desired back-transfers the imposition of the fine decreases the actual back-transfers in the incentive condition from 43% to 35.2% of the tripled transfer (Fig. 2). This is evidence that the fine itself diminishes altruistic responses but the effect is not significant (Mann-Whitney test, $z = -0.520$, $P = 0.603$, two-tailed). A significantly large effect occurs, however, if the fine is combined with high desired back-transfers. In this case, the imposition of the fine leads to back-transfers of only 22% of tripled investments whereas voluntarily refraining from fining elicits back-transfers of 60.1% (Fig. 2, Mann-Whitney test, $z = -2.262$, $P = 0.024$, two-tailed). In fact, if the fine is imposed and the desired back-transfers are high, 46% of the trustees give back nothing and the average back-transfers are only 3.82 MUs, which suggests that altruistic responses have largely vanished.

Previous research on "public good" experiments has shown that altruistic punishment is a highly effective means of enforcing cooperation[26]. Why do the sanctions in the public good context enhance cooperation but reduce cooperation in our context? Our

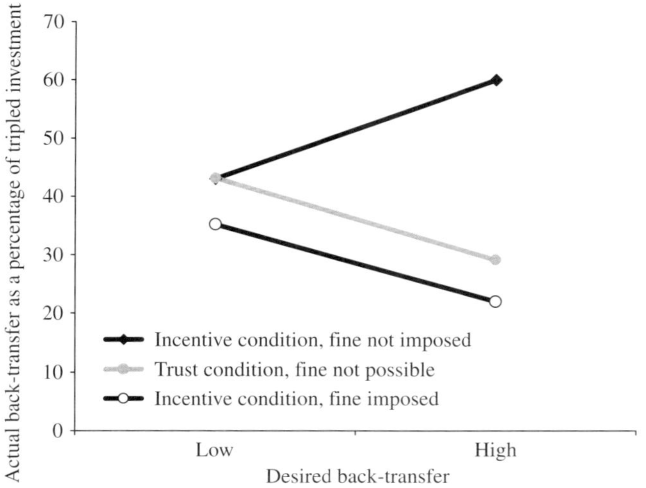

FIGURE 2

Actual back-transfer as a percentage of tripled investment plotted as a function of the investors' desired back-transfers. The desired back-transfer is categorized as low if, in the case that the trustee pays this back-transfer, the investor would earn the same or less than the trustee. It is categorized as high if the investor would earn more than the trustee. At low desired back-transfers the sanctioning threat reduces actual back transfers in the incentive treatment but the effect is not statistically significant. At high desired back-transfers the sanctioning threat has a large negative impact on the actual back-transfers in the incentive condition, indicating that if sanctions are used to achieve a distributional advantage they strongly undermine altruistic cooperation.

results suggest that the moral legitimacy of the sanction is a crucial factor. In the public good context the punishment of "free-riders" is an altruistic act that is considered as morally legitimate. Therefore, the disciplining effect of the sanctions is not undermined by a decline in altruistic cooperation. In the present context, punishment serves the punisher's self-interest and, if it is used to enforce an unfair payoff distribution in favour of the punisher, it decreases altruistic responses. This interpretation is also supported by the following fact. If the fine is imposed in the incentive condition the actual back-transfers as a percentage of tripled investments are significantly lower when the desired back-transfers are high than when the desired back-transfers are low (Mann-Whitney test, $z = -1.85$, $P = 0.064$, two-tailed).

In human societies, social order and cooperation rely on both the use of rewards and sanctions, which ensures the compliance of self-interested actors, and on the presence of people willing to perform altruistic acts. However, as our experiments indicate, sanctions intended to deter non-cooperation may backfire because they undermine altruistic cooperation. Whereas altruistically motivated sanctions for the benefit of the group enhance cooperative behaviour, sanctions that are imposed to enforce an unfair distribution of resources have the opposite effect. This is in contrast to prevailing approaches in economics, biology and behavioural ecology, which predict cooperation-enhancing effects of sanctions, regardless of the moral legitimacy or purpose of each sanction.

Our results, however, do not imply that economic incentives generally have negative motivational effects. There is evidence indicating that rewarding incentives and moralistic sanctions in repeated interactions have large positive effects on cooperation[27]. This suggests that economic incentives cause mainly negative effects on altruistic cooperation if they come in the form of sanctions and if they are associated with greedy or selfish intentions. We believe that these insights are important for everyone who needs the voluntary compliance of other people.

Methods

The experiments were conducted with 238 students at the University of Bonn. They took place in a large lunch room for students where we recruited subjects on the spot to participate in the experiment. At noon the lunch room is visited by hundreds of students from various disciplines. Each pair of subjects played the game just once and no subject could participate in the experiment for a second time. At registration, subjects received an instruction sheet (available from the authors upon request) that explained the rules of the game, the payoff structure, the random and anonymous matching with another student subject recruited at the same occasion, the conversion rate of experimental MUs into German Marks and the payment mode. Subjects were privately paid immediately after the experimental session. After having read the instructions, each subject was randomly assigned to one of two roles (investor or trustee) and anonymously matched with a subject in the other role. Investors received a blank decision sheet in which they had to fill in the transfer and the desired payback amounts. In the incentive condition, they additionally had to mark one of two options "no deduction" and "a deduction of 4 MUs" for the case where the trustee would pay back less than the desired amount. While making their decisions subjects were seated in a polling booth that we had brought to the lunch room. After an investor had made his three decisions a monitor checked whether all the necessary information was on the decision sheet. Then the monitor handed the decision sheet to the trustee with whom the investor was matched. The trustees had just one decision to make, namely, to specify the back-transfer to the investor. After completion the decision sheet was handed to the monitor who controlled for completeness and calculated the payoffs. Immediately after their game was over subjects were paid. Special care was taken to ensure the anonymity of the subjects and the privacy of the payment procedure. Each subject received a flat fee of DM3 (€1.53) for participation and each MU earned was rewarded with DM0.5 (€0.26). On average an investor earned DM8.45 (€4.32) and a trustee earned DM14.23 (€7.28). On average half an hour elapsed between registration and payment.

Acknowledgements. This paper is part of the European Network for the Development of Experimental Economics (ENDEAR). E.F. gratefully acknowledges support by the Ludwig Boltzmann Institut for the Analysis of Economic Growth, by the Swiss National Science Foundation and by the MacArthur Foundation Network on Economic Environments and the Evolution of Individual Preferences and Social Norms. B.R. gratefully acknowledges support by the Deutsche Forschungsgemeinschaft and the Ministerium für Wissenschaft und Forschung des Landes Nordrhein-Westfalen for providing the subject payments.

REFERENCES

[1] Smith, A. *The Wealth of Nations* (The Modern Library, New York, 1776).

[2] Durkheim, E. *De La Division Du Travail Social* (Presses Universitaires de France, Paris, 1902).

[3] Arrow, K. Gifts and exchanges. *Phil. Publ. Affairs* **1**, 343-362 (1972).

[4] Knack, S. & Keefer, P. Does social capital have an economic payoff? *Q. J. Econ.* **112**, 1251-1288 (1997).

[5] Bowles, S. *Economic Institutions and Behavior* (Princeton Univ. Press, Princeton, in the press).

[6] Milgrom, P. & Roberts, J. *Economics, Organization & Management* (Prentice Hall, Englewood Cliffs, 1992).

[7] Dawes, R. M. Social Dilemmas. *Annu. Rev. Psych.* **31**, 169-193 (1980).

[8] Fehr, E., Kirchsteiger, G. & Riedl, A. Does fairness prevent market clearing? *Q. J. Econ.* **108**, 437-460 (1993).

[9] Berg, J., Dickhaut, J. & McCabe, K. Trust, reciprocity and social history. *Games Econ. Behav.* **10**, 122-142 (1995).

[10] Andreoni, J. Cooperation in public goods experiments: kindness or confusion. *Am. Econ. Rev.* **85**, 891-904 (1995).

[11] Ostrom, E. A behavioral approach to the rational choice theory of collective action. *Am. Pol. Sci. Rev.* **92**, 1-22 (1998).

[12] Trivers, R. The evolution of reciprocal altruism. *Q. Rev. Biol.* **46**, 35-57 (1971).

[13] Axelrod, R. & Hamilton, W. D. The evolution of cooperation. *Science* **211**, 1390-1396 (1981).

[14] Nowak, M. A. & Sigmund, K. Evolution of indirect reciprocity by image scoring. *Nature* **393**, 573-577 (1998).

[15] Milinski, M., Semmann, D. & Krambeck, H. J. Reputation helps solve the "tragedy of the commons". *Nature* **415**, 424-426 (2002).

[16] Leimar, O. & Hammerstein, P. Evolution of cooperation through indirect reciprocity. *Proc. R. Soc. Lond. B* **268**, 745-753 (2001).

[17] Zahavi, A. The cost of honesty (further remarks on the handicap principle). *J. Theor. Biol.* **67**, 603-605 (1977).

[18] Mas-Colell, A., Whinston, M. D. & Green, J. R. *Microeconomic Theory* (Oxford Univ. Press, Oxford, 1995).

[19] Laffont, J. J. & Martimort, D. *The Theory of Incentives* (Princeton Univ. Press, Princeton, 2002).

[20] Titmuss, R. M. *The Gift Relationship* (Allen and Unwin, London, 1970).

[21] Frey, B. S. *Not Just For the Money. An Economic Theory of Personal Motivation* (Edward Elgar, Cheltenham, 1997).

[22] Bewley, T F. *Why Wages Don't Fall During A Recession* (Harvard Univ. Press, Cambridge, Massachusetts, 1999).

[23] Bohnet, I., Frey, B. S. & Huck, S. More order with less law: on contract enforcement, trust and crowding. *Am. Pol. Sci. Rev.* **95**, 131-144 (2001).

[24] Rabin, M. Incorporating fairness into game theory and economics. *Am. Econ. Rev.* **83**, 1281-1302 (1993).

[25] Gintis, H. Strong reciprocity and human sociality. *J. Theor. Biol.* **206**, 169-179 (2000).

[26] Fehr, E. & Gächter, S. Altruistic punishment in humans. *Nature* **415**, 137-140 (2002).

[27] Fehr, E. & Falk, A. Psychological foundations of incentives. *Eur. Econ. Rev.* **46**, 687-724 (2002).

10

The Economics of Career Concerns, Part II: Application to Missions and Accountability of Government Agencies

Mathias Dewatripont
Ian Jewitt
Jean Tirole

Abstract

The paper uses a simple multitask career concern model in order to analyse the incentives of government agencies' officials. Incentives are impaired by the agency pursuing multiple missions. A lack of focus is even more problematic in the case of fuzzy missions, that is when outsiders are uncertain about the exact nature of the missions actually pursued by the agency. Consequently agencies pursuing multiple missions receive less autonomy.

The paper further shows that professionalization creates a sense of mission for the agency, and that the specialization of officials raises their incentives. Last, the paper compares its predictions with the stylized facts on Government bureaucracies.

1 Introduction

What drives civil servants? Which goals do they pursue? What distinguishes Government agencies and private firms? To address these questions and others, this paper builds a simple multitask career concern model, and compares its predictions with the stylized facts on Government bureaucracies. Perhaps the most striking stylized facts, summarized in James Q. Wilson's celebrated survey of U.S. Government agencies (1989), are:

(a) *Differences between Government agencies and private firms.* In Chapter 7 of his book, Wilson stresses three key differences between Government agencies and private firms:

- *Preponderance of career concerns*: Financial incentives play a much more limited role in Government agencies than in the private sector.
- *Multiplicity and, possibly, fuzziness of objectives*: While private firms' managers can focus on profit maximization, Government

agencies pursue multiple goals. Furthermore, the set of goals to be pursued may not reflect a clear understanding between the agency and its principals.

- *Limited autonomy*: Government agencies have much less freedom in their managerial decisions than their private counterparts.

(b) *Mission setting*. Wilson warns against a lack of understanding concerning the set of desirable goals. He stresses the concomitant necessity of developing a sense of "mission". In his view, the organization must eschew "vague objectives" and define a set of "critical tasks" or "operational goals" (pp. 25, 32-34):[1] The "culture" of an organization is a way to see what these critical tasks are and how to deal with them (p. 93). A "mission" is a single culture that is widely and enthusiastically shared by the members of the organization (p. 99).

(c) *Focus*. Wilson emphasizes the incentive cost of the pursuance of multiple goals. He stresses the need for focusing on a subset of tasks even at the price of sacrificing other important tasks. This pursuit of focus may lead well-run agencies to resist being granted new tasks (in contrast to Leviathan theories of Government), as "conglomerate agencies rarely can develop a sense of mission; the cost of trying to do so is that few things are done well" (p. 371).

He provides examples of important tasks that have deliberately been neglected by those U.S. agencies, listed in Table 1, that have successfully developed a sense of mission: environmental issues and strategic planning by the Tennessee Valley Authority, environmental issues and education of the public by the National Forest Service, and rehabilitation of prisoners in Texas prisons.[2]

Examples of new tasks being resisted by agencies include the food stamp programme (helping the poor) by the Department of Agriculture, and supplementary programmes for people in need (poor, blind, disabled) by the Social Security Administration. In both cases, the new programmes implied missions remote from the agencies' core missions (namely, helping farmers and paying benefits to pensioners in a timely fashion, respectively).

(d) *Role of "professionals" and "narrow specialists" in creating a sense of mission*. Substituting "professionals", namely officials whose career concerns are at least partly determined by their professional environment, for "bureaucrats", whose career concerns are primarily internal, can help develop a sense of mission. For example, the massive hiring of engineers helped define the missions pursued by the Tennessee Valley Authority and the Department of Transportation (pp. 59-65). Similarly, the hiring of forestry experts was crucial in defining a mission for the National Forest Office.

1. For example, while the "education of children" is the objective of the school system, it has to be translated into a precise curriculum, examination methods, a system of discipline inside schools, and so forth.

2. Because neglected tasks can be quite important, we may want to create "advocates" for the associated causes. Our work differs from that of Dewatripont-Tirole (1999) on advocacy. In our paper, objectives are not *per se* incompatible, while the separation of tasks in the later paper results from an intrinsic conflict between goals (a success in one dimension comes at the expense of a poorer performance in another dimension.) An example of such intrinsic conflict mentioned by Wilson (p. 158) concerns the Immigration and Naturalization Service, which has found it hard to be simultaneously tough ("keep immigrants out") and nice ("let in necessary agricultural workers", "facilitate the entry of foreign tourists", and so forth).

TABLE 1

Agency	General objective	Mission
Tennessee Valley Authority	Regional planning	Produce electricity
Social Security Program	Administer social security	Pay benefits on time
Department of Agriculture	Feed the nation	Help farmers
National Forest Service[a]	"Promote" the pool of forests	Manage forests
Texas Prisons[b]	Containment and rehabilitation of prisoners	Control inmates
Department of Transportation	Improve the safety of driving	Improve car safety

[a] At the turn of the century, under the leadership of Gifford Pinchot.
[b] In the 1970s, under the leadership of George Beto.

(e) *Sense of mission and autonomy.* Finally, Wilson stresses the fact that agencies with a strong sense of mission are perceived to be more effective and are consequently given more freedom (p. 217). In this respect, professionalization can be a key ingredient to the preservation of one's autonomy. "The maintenance of some agencies depends so crucially on their appearing professional and nonpolitical that it would be foolhardy for an elected official to compromise that appearance" (p. 199).

To address these stylized facts, we extend Holmström's celebrated (1982) career concerns model to a multitask environment. In our view, an important distinction between a Government agency and a private company is that the former is instructed to pursue social welfare objectives while the latter is asked to maximize solely shareholder value. That is, the mandate of a Government agency is to internalize a number of externalities (employment, pollution, education, etc.) besides the monetary dimension of its activity. In a sense, an agency is the ultimate "stakeholder society". Agencies must therefore pursue goals that, unlike financial objectives, are hard to measure and therefore to reward directly. As will be shown in Section 3.3, this observation implies that agencies may operate more or less on a fixed budget and that career concerns are paramount in prodding officials to pursue the agencies' goals.

The key insight of the career concern model is that, even in the absence of monetary incentives, an agent of uncertain talent expends effort in order to convince the relevant "labour market" of her high talent; a high performance raises the perception of her ability and translates into future job opportunities within or outside the organization. In a companion paper (Dewatripont *et al.*, 1999), we investigate the properties of the career concerns model and derive general results on the relationship between information structures and incentive intensity. This paper in contrast derives specific organizational implications of the multitask career concern model. It first makes the following observation: in the presence of complementarity between effort and talent, multiplicity of equilibria can arise: market expectations about high or low effort can be self-fulfilling. In a multi-task context, this implies that the agent can end up focusing on the set of tasks the market expects her to focus on.

In our set-up, we obtain the following set of predictions:

- Expanding the set of tasks pursued by the agent typically reduces total effort. This can even lead to a collapse of effort if too many tasks are pursued because the link from performance to the market's inference about talent becomes too weak.
- Fuzzy mission equilibria, namely equilibria in which the market is uncertain about the nature of tasks pursued by the agent, typically involve less total effort than equilibria in which the market knows the effort allocation across tasks (while still not observing effort) because the uncertainty weakens the link from performance to the market's inference about talent.
- These two results imply that a principal who hires a "narrow specialist", whose talent is known to be low for all but a subset of tasks, can count on more effort and has less incentives to monitor the agent.
- Since effort in the career concern model is driven by talent uncertainty, the principal faces a tradeoff between the riskiness of overall performance and effort, a tradeoff which is not present in explicit incentive models.

The first three results nicely back Wilson's evidence. The first result predicts a positive correlation between "accountability" of an organization (its effort level) and its "focus". The second result says that accountability increases with the "clarity" of its mission. And the third result implies that "narrow professionals" are naturally more accountable, and thus are conferred more autonomy. Finally, the fourth result is a logical implication of our analysis and is consistent with Wilson's evidence, although it is not stressed by him. While in the explicit incentive model, reducing riskiness of operations typically raises effort, it does not in the career concern model; since agents work in order to "impress" the market about their talent, talent uncertainty raises effort. It thus pays the organization to specialize its members in subsets of tasks for which talent risk is positively correlated; the downside of this is that it may destabilize the overall performance of the organization. We feel that this tradeoff is a significant feature of government organizations, as opposed to explicit-incentive private firms, and one of the key insights of this paper.

The paper is organized as follows: Section 2 details the model, while Sections 3 to 6 look in turn at the four predictions just described. Finally, Section 7 concludes.

2 The Model

2.1 Description and Equilibrium

There are two parties, called the "agent" and the "market" (or the "organization", or the "principal"). The agent chooses an unobservable vector of "actions" or "efforts" $a = (a_1, \ldots, a_n)$ and incurs private cost $c(a)$. The market then observes a vector of observables or performance variables $y = (y_1, \ldots, y_m)$ and takes actions that result in benefit or reward t for the agent, whose utility is then

$$t - c(a).$$

The reward t reflects the market's expectation of an unknown parameter θ conditional on the observables y. As in the standard career concern model, θ will be referred to as the "agent's talent" and for most of the paper is taken to be a scalar. As in our companion paper, let $f(\theta, y \mid a)$ denote the joint density of talent and observables given effort vector a, and

$$\hat{f}(y \mid a) = \int f(\theta, y \mid a)\, d\theta,$$

denote the marginal density of the observables. The agent's reward for performance variables y and equilibrium actions a^* is thus

$$t = E(\theta \mid y, a^*) = \int \theta \frac{f(\theta, y \mid a^*)}{\hat{f}(y \mid a^*)}\, d\theta.$$

Let c_a and $\hat{f}_a$ denote the gradients with respect to efforts of the cost function and of the marginal distribution (we will use "primes" for derivatives in the scalar case), and suppose that the market anticipates equilibrium effort vector a^*. The agent chooses a so as to maximize her expected utility

$$\max E[E(\theta \mid y, a^*)] - c(a), \tag{2.1}$$

where the first expectation is with respect to performance and the second with respect to talent. As shown in our companion paper, this leads to:

Proposition 2.1 (Equilibrium condition). *In an equilibrium of the career concern model, the gradient of the cost function is equal to the covariance of talent and the likelihood ratio:*

$$\mathrm{cov}\left(\theta, \frac{\hat{f}_a}{\hat{f}}\right) = c_a(a^*)\,. \tag{2.2}$$

2.2 The Multi-Task Normal Model

This paper applies the analysis to multiple tasks in order to investigate the connection between effort incentives and the set of activities pursued by the agent. We undertake this analysis within a framework which, although specific, allows us to consider the additive-normal and multiplicative-normal models as special cases.

The multi-task normal model. Assume that performance concerning task $i \in \{1, \ldots, N\}$ is given by

$$y_i = \theta(\mu a_i + b) + \gamma a_i + \varepsilon_i,$$

where μ, γ and b are positive known constants, $a_i \geqq 0$ is effort expended on task i and, as earlier, θ and ε_i are independently distributed and

$$\theta \sim \mathcal{N}(\bar{\theta}, \sigma_\theta^2) \text{ and } \varepsilon_i \sim \mathcal{N}(0, \sigma_\varepsilon^2)\,.$$

Holmström's model is a special case of this model with $\mu = 0$ (and $b = \gamma = 1$). A positive μ depicts a complementarity between talent and effort.

We distinguish between the (exogenous) number of potential tasks (N) and the number of tasks actually pursued (n), that is the number of tasks for which $a_i > 0$. We assume complete symmetry of the different tasks in order not to introduce a technological bias in favour of a focus on specific tasks.

Unless otherwise stated, we will assume that the principal cares only about

$$Y = \sum_{i=1}^{N} y_i\,.$$

In this benchmark case, only $\hat{a}$ matters, not its distribution across individual tasks.[3] But of course, other objective functions can be entertained. For example, the principal might have a preference for the effort being split equally among the tasks for a given total effort.

In the same vein, we assume away any economies or diseconomies of scope, so the cost function can be written as a function, $c(\hat{a})$,

3. Note that an increase in the number of tasks brings about a mechanical bonus $\bar{\theta}b$ per new task, unless b is renormalized (equal to some constant divided by the number of tasks) when the number of tasks varies. Since this "mechanical bonus" plays no role in the analysis, which focuses on effort, we do not bother renormalizing b in this way.

of total effort $\hat{a} \equiv \sum_{i=1}^{N} a_i$. We assume $c' > 0$, $c'' > 0$, $c'(0) \geqq 0$. [The figures will be drawn for the quadratic cost function $c(\hat{a}) = (\hat{a}^2/2) + d\hat{a}$.]

The single-task case. To build intuition before embarking on the analysis of multiple tasks, let us first consider the case in which $N = 1$. We thus have a single-task, single-performance model, but where talent matters more, the higher the effort. In other words, talent matters little if the agent shirks, but makes an important difference if the agent "tries to make things happen". When talent and effort are complements, performance is more likely to be informative about talent, the higher the effort. It is then easy to envision the following self-fulfilling behaviours: If the market puts substantial weight on the agent's performance, the agent is induced to exert high effort, which in turn leads the market to pay much attention to the agent's performance. And conversely.[4] Specifically, Proposition 2.1 then yields

$$\frac{\bar{\theta}\mu + \gamma}{(\mu\hat{a} + b) + \dfrac{\sigma_\varepsilon^2}{(\mu\hat{a} + b)\sigma_\theta^2}} = c'(\hat{a}).$$

The marginal cost of effort (the right-hand side of this condition) is increasing in $\hat{a}$. The covariance between θ and the likelihood ratio (the left-hand side of this condition) depends on $\hat{a}$ only through its denominator, and this only when $\mu \neq 0$. Indeed, in the pure additive case $(\mu = 0)$, the signal-to-noise ratio is independent of effort. With a multiplicative effect $(\mu > 0)$ the derivative of the denominator of the covariance with respect to effort,

$$\mu\left[1 - \frac{\sigma_\varepsilon^2}{\sigma_\theta^2(\mu\hat{a} + b)^2}\right],$$

is increasing in $\hat{a}$. There exists a level of $\hat{a}$, call it $\tilde{a}$, such that this derivative is positive for all $\hat{a}$s larger than $\tilde{a}$. Depending on parameter values, $\tilde{a}$ is strictly positive or not. For example *ceteris paribus*, for σ_ε^2 small enough, the covariance between θ and the likelihood ratio is always decreasing in effort. To understand this, consider the pure multiplicative model without noise: $y = \theta\hat{a}$. For a given equilibrium effort a^*, the market estimates θ as y/a^*, so that a given increase in effort by the agent leads to a weaker upward revision of the market's estimate of talent.

For positive σ_ε^2, another effect goes however in the opposite direction: higher expected effort leads the market to give more weight

4. The multiplicity of equilibria in the career concerns model bears some resemblance with Arrow's (1973) theory of discrimination.

FIGURE 1

$\mu = 0$ (additive case)

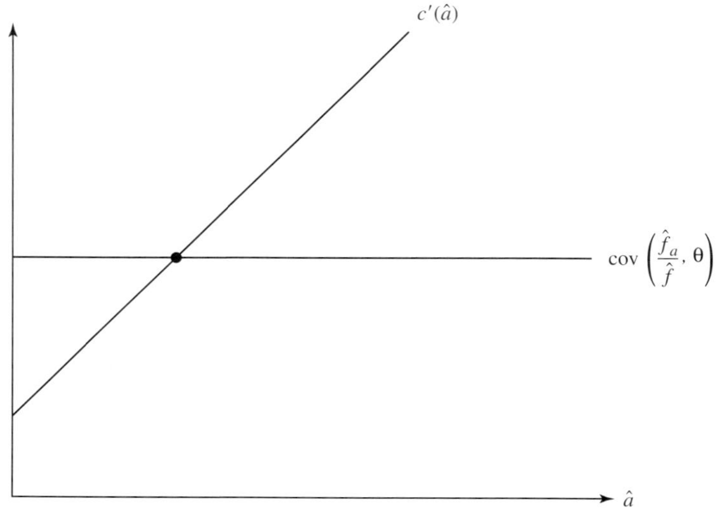

to talent relative to noise when observing good performance. Indeed, for $b = 0$ (pure multiplicative case), when the market expects $\hat{a} = 0$, it attributes good performance *solely* to good luck, which is not the case when it expects positive effort.

For low $\hat{a}$s, this second effect can dominate the first one for b small enough or $\sigma_\varepsilon^2/\sigma_\theta^2$ high enough. In any case, for $\hat{a}$s high enough, the first effect always dominates.

Figure 1 shows the unique equilibrium in the additive case. Figure 2 shows the unique equilibrium when $\mu > 0$ and b large or

FIGURE 2

$\mu > 0$; b large or $\sigma_\varepsilon^2/\sigma_\theta^2$ small (weak multiplicative element)

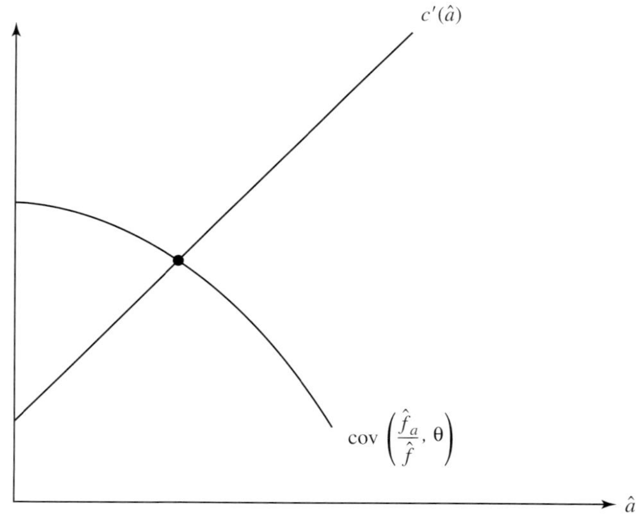

FIGURE 3

$\mu > 0$; b small or $\sigma_\varepsilon^2/\sigma_\theta^2$ large (strong multiplicative element)

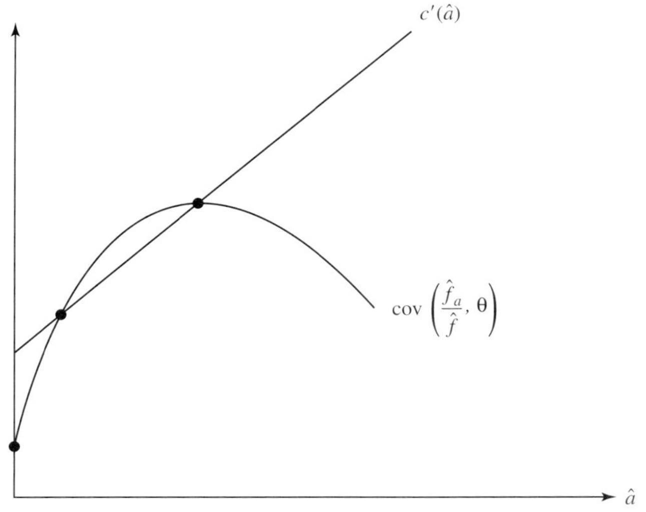

$\sigma_\varepsilon^2/\sigma_\theta^2$ low. Finally, the last case is depicted in Figure 3, where two stable equilibria may coexist (the intermediate one being unstable).

Remark. If performance y were verifiable, then, following Gibbons-Murphy (1992), one might ask whether career concerns and explicit incentives are complement or substitutes. For the additive-normal model with mean-variance preferences and linear explicit incentives, Gibbons and Murphy show that an increase in the discount factor (and thus in career concerns) leads to a reduction in the slope of the current explicit incentive scheme. Figure 3 suggests why with a multiplicative technology explicit and implicit incentives may become complements (see Dewatripont *et al.* (1997) for more detail). Suppose that the marginal cost curve, $c'(\hat{a})$, lies above, without intersecting the implicit incentive curve, $\text{cov}\ (\hat{f}a/\hat{f}, \theta)$. Then as the discount factor grows and the two curves come closer to each other, it may become optimal to boost explicit incentives so that the total (explicit plus implicit) incentive reaches the marginal cost curve. Explicit incentives increase effort and, when effort and talent are complements, induce the market to look more closely at performance. Through this channel explicit incentives reinforce career concerns, which may lead to a positive covariation of the two types of incentives.[5]

5. The complementarity between explicit and implicit incentive schemes arises both "globally", to affect the *set* of equilibria, as well as locally, in terms of the high effort equilibrium. The more spectacular effect of explicit incentive schemes is when they expand the equilibrium set to include a positive effort equilibrium. Similarly, in some cases, they can *reduce* the equilibrium set by knocking off the zero effort equilibrium. But there is also a local complementarity between explicit and implicit incentive schemes: in the high effort equilibrium, raising explicit incentives raises effort, which in turn raises the attention the market gives to performance, thereby providing further effort incentives to the agent.

3 Multiple Tasks, Missions and Focus

This section investigates the relationship between the *number* of tasks the agent pursues and total effort.

3.1 Analysis

3.1.1 *Observation of Aggregate Performance Only*

We first look at the case where only the total performance on a subset I of tasks

$$Y_I = \sum_{i \in I} y_i,$$

is observed by the market. The multi-task model then reduces to a single-task one. Whatever the set of tasks the agent could or would be allowed to work on, if the market only observes Y_I, the agent expends effort solely on the tasks included in I. How does total effort, $\hat{a}$, depend on I? If I includes n tasks,

$$Y_I = \theta(\mu\hat{a} + nb) + \gamma\hat{a} + \sum_{i \in I} \varepsilon_i.$$

We obtain[6]

$$\mathrm{cov}_n\left(\frac{\hat{f}_{\hat{a}}}{\hat{f}}, \theta\right) = \frac{(\bar{\theta}\mu + \gamma)}{(\mu\hat{a} + nb) + n\sigma_\varepsilon^2/[(\mu\hat{a} + nb)\sigma_\theta^2]}.$$

Positive equilibrium levels of effort are those which equate this covariance with $c'(\hat{a})$. An increase in n lowers the covariance between talent and the likelihood ratio, and thus equilibrium effort, in all three cases. The most interesting one concerns Figure 3 where, for n large enough, the high-effort equilibrium disappears, as shown in Figure 4.

In the (Holmström) additive-normal model, $\hat{a}$ decreases continuously with n, which may not be the case when a multiplicative effect is introduced: As Figure 4 demonstrates, there is then a maximum n, $\bar{n}$, that allows for the high-effort equilibrium; beyond that value, $\hat{a}$ can only be zero.

The reader can obtain intuition for why total effort decreases with n, by focusing on the pure additive ($\mu = 0$) and the pure multiplicative ($b = \gamma = 0$) cases. For notational simplicity, assume moreover $b = \gamma = 1$ in the pure additive case, and $\mu = 1$ in the pure multiplicative case.

6. Since all ε_is are uncorrelated, the distribution of Y_I is normal with mean $\bar{\theta}(\mu\hat{a} + nb) + \gamma\hat{a}$ and variance $\sigma_\theta^2(\mu\hat{a} + nb)^2 + n\sigma_\varepsilon^2$. Consequently,

$$\frac{\hat{f}_{\hat{a}}(Y_I)}{\hat{f}(Y_I)} = \frac{\left[(\theta - \bar{\theta})(\mu\hat{a} + nb) + \sum_{i \in I}\varepsilon_i\right][\bar{\theta}\mu + \gamma]}{\sigma_\theta^2(\mu\hat{a} + nb)^2 + \sigma_\varepsilon^2}.$$

FIGURE 4

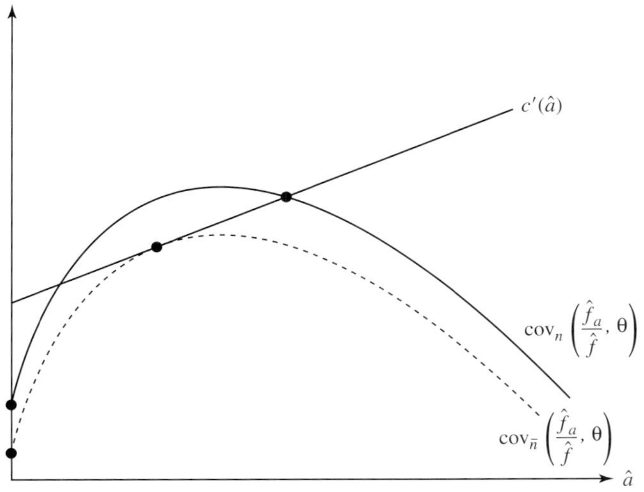

Consider first the "noiseless case", that is, $\sigma_\varepsilon^2 = 0$. In this case, the pure additive and the pure multiplicative models become, respectively

$$Y_I = \theta n + \hat{a},$$

$$Y_I = \theta \hat{a}.$$

Clearly, in the pure multiplicative case, changing n leaves $\hat{a}$ unchanged. Instead, in the pure additive case, incentives to expend effort go down, since the market infers the following θ from a performance Y_I given effort expectation $\hat{a}^*$

$$\frac{Y_I - \hat{a}^*}{n} = \theta + \frac{\hat{a} - \hat{a}^*}{n}.$$

There is moreover a second effect of an increase in n on effort, similar in both cases: the variance of $\sum_{i=1}^{n} \varepsilon_i$, namely $n\sigma_\varepsilon^2$, increases with n. In total, effort thus goes down when n increases.

Another interpretation goes as follows, in the pure additive case. Since, for $\mu = 0$ and $b = \gamma = 1$,

$$\text{cov}_n\left(\frac{\hat{f}_{\hat{a}}}{\hat{f}}, \theta\right) = \frac{1}{n + \sigma_\varepsilon^2/\sigma_\theta^2} = \left[\frac{\sigma_\theta^2}{\sigma_\theta^2 + \sigma_\varepsilon^2/n}\right]/n,$$

raising n increases the signal-to-noise ratio, since θ is multiplied by n while n *independent* errors appear in additive form; an increase in n further reduces the relative effect of effort $\hat{a}$ and talent θ on performance. While the first effect raises effort incentives — and this would be *less* the case if talent across tasks were not perfectly positively correlated — the second effect, which dominates overall, reduces effort incentives.

Let us summarize our results in the following:

Proposition 3.1 (Benefit from focus). *Consider the multitask normal model and assume that only the aggregate performance on n tasks entrusted to the agent is observable. The higher the number n, the lower the stable, positive equilibrium total effort. Furthermore, in the presence of a multiplicative effect* ($\mu > 0$) *and for* $c'(0) > 0$, *there is a value of n,* $\bar{n}$, *beyond which the high-effort equilibrium disappears altogether.*

How robust is Proposition 3.1? One could first object, in the additive case, to the fact that raising n raises the impact of talent on performance Y_I: if it means splitting the agent's total working time into more slices, it might make more sense to have, in the "noiseless" case

$$Y_I = \frac{\theta}{n} n + \hat{a} = \theta + \hat{a}.$$

However, in this case, Proposition 3.1 is again valid: for $\sigma_\varepsilon^2 = 0$, raising n leaves total effort unchanged, and for $\sigma_\varepsilon^2 > 0$, it reduces total effort.

More important for the result is the assumption that raising the number of tasks raises the amount of pure noise (captured here by $\sum_{i=1}^{n} \varepsilon_i$). We feel this assumption is appropriate whenever effort is about raising the *expectation* of performance without affecting its variance. This is why performance on each task has an exogenous additive risk component, and the agent's effort changes this riskiness *solely* through talent uncertainty. Relaxing this assumption could change the results: for example, changes in n would become irrelevant for total effort if we had

$$Y_I = (\theta + \hat{a})\varepsilon \text{ or } Y_I = \theta\hat{a}\varepsilon,$$

where ε would be independent of n. In reality however, effort is often not uncertainty-enhancing, so Proposition 3.1 is in our view quite general. Exploring conditions under which it might fail is however an interesting topic for further research.

Note also that the above analysis determines total effort $\hat{a}$, but says little about its distribution across tasks. In this benchmark case, neither the agent nor the principal care about this distribution. If, instead, one introduced just a tiny amount of economies of scope in the agent's cost function, $\hat{a}$ would be spread equally across all tasks whose performance is reported as part of Y_I. This will suit the principal whenever he has convex preferences across tasks.

3.1.2 *Disaggregated Performance Accounting*

A specificity of the above analysis is that it restricts public information to the observation of aggregate performance

$$Y_I = \sum_{i \in I} y_i .$$

A plausible alternative is to assume the observability of individual performances

$$S_I = \{y_i \mid i \in I\} .$$

Whenever I includes at least two elements and in the presence of multiplicative effects disaggregation may expand the multiplicity of equilibria: There may be a tendency for the agent to focus on the tasks the market expects her to focus on![7]

Proposition 3.2 (Disaggregated performance measurement). *Consider the multi-task normal model. In the pure additive case* $(\mu = 0)$, *the unique equilibrium effort* $\hat{a}^*$ *is the same whether aggregate* (Y_I) *or disaggregated* (S_I) *performance is observed. In the pure multiplicative case* $(b = 0)$, *the set of equilibria corresponding to the disaggregated information structure* S_I *is the union of the symmetric equilibrium sets for the aggregated information structures corresponding to subsets* $I' \subseteq I$, *that is to the observation of*

$$Y_{I'} = \sum_{i \in I'} y_i .$$

Proof. In the pure additive case, Y_I is a sufficient statistic for S_I as far as updating θ is concerned, so observing S_I or Y_I makes no difference. In the pure multiplicative case, when a_i is expected to be equal to 0, y_i is considered as pure noise and disregarded by the market, making $a_i = 0$ optimal for the agent. For each $I' \subseteq I$, there is thus an equilibrium where $a_i = 0$ for $i \notin I'$, and a_i is positive and constant across $is \in I'$, and where total effort is the same as that when only $Y_{I'}$ is observed. ■

Remark. Propositions 3.1 and 3.2 can be seen as corollaries of Proposition 5.1 of our companion paper (Dewatripont *et al.*, 1999). Consider a two-task problem. In the additive case $\mu = 0$, total effort is the same whether y_1 and y_2 or $y_1 + y_2$ is observed, and it is lower than if y_1 or y_2 is observed alone. Assume for example, without loss of generality, that $a_1 = \hat{a}$ when y_1 alone is observed, and consider the effect of making y_2 observable on top of y_1. Because y_2 is good news for θ conditional on y_1, condition (a) of the proposition holds. Moreover, since effort a_1 decreases y_2 conditional on y_1, condition (b) holds, and thus effort and news are oppositely ordered. By Proposition 5.1, the observability of y_2 thus reduces effort.

7. In the absence of economies of scope in the effort cost function, multi-task equilibria are in fact unstable: Were the market to put slightly more weight on any given task, the agent would "react" by concentrating her efforts solely on that task! On the other hand, the presence of economies of scope can ensure the local stability of the equilibria referred to in Proposition 3.2.

In contrast, in the pure multiplicative case $(b = \gamma = 0)$, assuming again $a_1 = \hat{a}$ when y_1 alone is observed, the observability of y_2 on top of y_1 preserves the equilibria that obtain when only y_1 is observed: If $a_2 = 0$ is anticipated, y_2 is pure irrelevant noise. On the other hand, there exist also equilibria with $a_1 = a_2$. What matters in the pure multiplicative case is the set of *market expectations about focus*. Instead, in the pure additive case, what matters is *observability of tasks*.

3.2 Interpretation

3.2.1 *Focus: Task Allocation or Information Systems?*

How should Proposition 3.1 be interpreted? One possibility is that the agent is allocated all *N* tasks, but that only the aggregate performance on subset *I* is made public. This set-up induces effort allocation only on subset *I*, and, the smaller the number of tasks included in *I*, the higher the total effort, which is the appropriate evaluation criterion.

Another interpretation is that *I* is the subset of tasks given to the agent. In this case, allocating more tasks to the agent brings an expected "mechanical" bonus $\bar{\theta}b$ for each additional task. However, focusing solely on effort remains the appropriate interpretation if one thinks of "dividing" the set of *N* tasks into subsets, one for each agent. In this interpretation, we identify a benefit of the division of labour, in terms of higher individual efforts.

Preferences over focus. Under either interpretation a principal interested in maximizing $Y = \sum_{i=1}^{N} y_i$ and thus indifferent with respect to the *distribution* of individual performances (the y_is) should thus try and induce focus. As for the agent, in the case of an exogenous date-1 financial compensation, she prefers a broad mission, so as to reduce effort: Indeed, she realizes she will fool no one by working in equilibrium, and sees a broad mission as a commitment not to expend effort. If, instead, the agent is able to obtain *ex ante* a wage equal to expected productivity, committing to a focused mission through the observability of a single y_i maximizes the agent's wage.

3.2.2 *Equilibrium Selection*

How should Proposition 3.2 be interpreted? In the pure additive case, things are simple, since the result of Proposition 3.1 is replicated. In contrast, the multiplicity of equilibria in the pure multiplicative case raises the question of equilibrium selection. Still, we can say that the result of Proposition 3.1 is "robust", if we are ready to assume that, when S_I is expanded, the equilibrium number of tasks with positive effort (weakly) rises. Equilibrium selection remains a challenge for game theory, and this paper cannot pretend to contribute to resolving this challenge. The above assumption is natural, and guarantees that focus remains at least weakly optimal for total effort, even in the pure multiplicative case. Note moreover that introducing an additive component for talent to performance would reinforce the positive impact of focus on effort.

3.2.3 *Career Concerns versus Explicit Incentives*

What results rely on career concerns, as opposed to pure explicit incentives? Proposition 3.1 would also hold in a simple linear explicit incentive scheme context with CARA preferences, since expanding I means more noise. In this sense, it is our "technological assumptions" which generate a benefit of focus in Proposition 3.1. Under explicit incentive schemes, the roles of θ and ε are more symmetric than under career concerns, as Section 6 will make clear.

In this section, the difference between career concerns and explicit incentives lies in Proposition 3.2:

- Under explicit incentive schemes, the multiplicity of equilibria is not a concern.
- In the additive case, which has a unique equilibrium, expanding S_I lowers total effort, while with pure explicit incentives, one can always disregard additional information, which is at best irrelevant.

The insights lead us to the following observations in terms of comparisons with the literature:

Relationship to the Holmström-Milgrom task exclusion result. Holmström and Milgrom (1991) show that it may be optimal to prevent an agent from pursuing tasks, the gains of which cannot be shared by the principal and which might induce a diversion of effort away from tasks that are more profitable to the principal. Our task exclusion result has a very different nature. Indeed, according to the logic of Diamond (1984)'s diversification result, adding more tasks could only benefit the principal under explicit incentives if performance measurements on all tasks were available. The Holmström-Milgrom result is linked to an asymmetry in measurement, while our result emphasizes the benefit from focus in a symmetric situation.

Implications for information aggregation. The implications of Proposition 3.2 depend on what is assumed concerning the principal's control of the agent's visibility to the market. Let us content ourselves with the case in which the principal has *full* control over the agent's visibility. That is, the principal selects the set I of tasks and further decides whether the aggregate performance (Y_I) or individual ones (S_I) are observable (in the same way a school decides on the topics followed by students and whether to release only their overall performance or a detailed account of their grades).

Together with Proposition 3.1, Proposition 3.2 then suggests that disaggregated performance measurement may be costly. Suppose that, under aggregate performance measurement, the principal would like the agent to focus on n^* tasks (n^* may exceed one if the marginal utility of performance for the principal on each task is decreasing, or if there are complementarities across tasks). If the principal releases individual performances on the n^* tasks, then she runs the risk that the agent focus on a subset of tasks. [There is actually another hazard, which will be discussed in Section 4; we have assumed that the labour market correctly anticipates which mission(s) are pursued in equilibrium by the agent. In the next section, we will label these "clear missions". Disaggregated performance accounting creates scope not only for a focus on a subset of missions but also for "fuzzy missions", that is situations in which the labour market is no longer sure which mission(s) the agent is pursuing.] Thus the implicit incentives model does not deliver the same conclusion in this respect as the explicit incentives paradigm, in which aggregation is generally detrimental and at best neutral (Holmström-Milgrom (1987) and Laffont-Tirole (1990)).[8]

3.3 Limited Monetary Incentives in Government

We have assumed that none of the dimensions of performance is contractible. This of course is rarely the case. In particular, an agency's cost is readily measured. One may wonder why monetary incentives are so limited within Government, and whether the possibility of providing agencies with monetary incentives alters our analysis. Our argument in the matter is a mere transposition of a standard one in the literature on multitask explicit incentives.[9]

Suppose, still in the framework of the multi-task normal model, that y_1 stands for (minus) the agency's cost, while $y_2, \ldots, y_N$ are still noncontractible. The principal designs an explicit incentive scheme based on the realization of y_1, perhaps subject to the agent's limited liability constraint. Consider an equilibrium allocation in which the agent exerts efforts a_1^* on task 1, a^* on task 2 through n and 0 on the other tasks (in the symmetric multitask normal model all efforts on pursued noncontractible tasks must be equal). Let w_1 denote the deriva-

8. Holmström and Milgrom (1987) consider a repeated moral hazard model in which the agent controls the drift of a Brownian process. They show that if the agent has constant absolute risk aversion, the optimal contract between the agent and the principal can be conditioned solely on (and be chosen linear in) the overall performance. Laffont and Tirole (1990) consider a multitask adverse selection problem. The agent's realized cost on task i depends on a (possibly task-specific) adverse selection parameter, her effort on the task, some observable variable (such as the quantity of good i), and possibly some additive task-specific noise. They derive conditions under which subcost observation is useless, that is under which the agent's reward can be based only on aggregate cost.

9. Holmström and Milgrom (1991) show that when efforts on different tasks are close substitutes in the agent's production function, no incentives should be provided on contractible tasks if the principal wants to promote effort on noncontractible tasks. Our argument is a straightforward application to implicit incentives of that in Holmström-Milgrom. [Holmström-Milgrom assume that the agent delivers an exogenous amount of effort in the absence of explicit incentives. We endogenize this amount through career concerns as in Laffont-Tirole (1991), who show that the incentive intensity of a cost centre should be reduced if incentives for another task, namely quality, are provided by reputational concerns and this other task becomes more valuable to the principal.]

tive of the expected y_1 - contingent wage with respect to a_1, measured at a_1^*. When efforts are perfect substitutes (the effort cost is $c(\sum_i a_i)$), the equilibrium conditions are

$$w_1 + \frac{(\bar{\theta}\mu + \gamma)(\mu a_{1_*} + b)}{(\mu a_1^* + b)^2 + (n-1)(\mu a_*^* + b)^2 + \sigma_\varepsilon^2/\sigma_\theta^2}$$

$$= \frac{(\bar{\theta}\mu + \gamma)(\mu a^* + b)}{(\mu a_1^* + b)^2 + (n-1)(\mu a^* + b)^2 + \sigma_\varepsilon^2/\sigma_\theta^2}$$

$$= c'(a_1 + (n-1)a^*).$$

We can now consider three possibilities: (i) Either $a^* = 0$. Then the agent focuses on the monetary task. The agency is then run as a *private firm*. (ii) Or $w_1 = 0$. In this case the equilibrium $a_1^* = a_2^* = \ldots = a_n^* = a^*$ can be obtained by offering the agency a *fixed budget*, as is assumed in this paper. (iii) Or else $w_1 > 0$ and $a^* > a_1^* \geqq 0$. This last possibility is however ruled out by the equilibrium conditions in the additive case ($\mu = 0$).

Proposition 3.3 (Budget-run agencies). *Suppose that only the cost performance of the agency can be contracted upon. Then in the additive case, the agency is run either as a private, cost-minimizing entity or as a fixed-budget agency.*

Proposition 3.3 of course describes an extreme case. In practice, some monetary cost-minimization incentives can be provided without abandoning the other tasks. But such incentives are in general likely to be limited and cost minimization will be pursued often more through tight monitoring of the agency.

4 Fuzzy Missions

The multitask analysis with disaggregated performance accounting of Section 3.1.2 focused on situations in which the market perfectly understands which missions the agent selects. But the market may be uncertain as to which mission the agent is actually pursuing. To the extent that the market is ignorant not only about the agent's level of effort but also about its allocation across tasks, the market needs to infer this allocation of effort from the agent's vector of performances in order to properly update its beliefs about the agent's talent. A "fuzzy mission" equilibrium is thus an equilibrium in which the market (perhaps imperfectly) learns about the mission(s) pursued by the agent from the vector of performances. Technically, the distinction between clear and fuzzy mission equilibria is similar to that between pure and mixed strategy equilibria.[10]

10. As in Myerson (1998), the mixed strategy here refers solely to a randomization over the allocation of effort, and not to a randomization over its level.

This section compares two situations in which the agent specializes in a single task. In the case of a clear mission, the market knows the agent specializes in task 1, say. By contrast, in a fuzzy mission equilibrium, the agent specializes in mission $i \in \{1, \ldots, n\}$ with probability $1/n$ and the market is not informed of the agent's choice. The key question then is whether the agent has more incentive to exert effort when the market knows the mission. Intuition suggests that fuzzy missions create a garbling of information and therefore generate less incentives than clear missions. And, indeed, the information structure in clear and fuzzy mission equilibria can be ordered in the Blackwell sense, since the information about the choice of mission is suppressed in the case of a fuzzy mission. Our companion paper however shows that regularity conditions are required for comparisons of information structures. These regularity conditions are satisfied for the following specification:

The no effort-no information multiplicative case

$$y_i = a_i\theta + \varepsilon_i, \quad \varepsilon_i \text{ logconcave idd}, \quad i = 1, \ldots, n.$$

$\theta \geqq 0$ with probability 1 and $\log \theta$ has a logconcave density.

Proposition 4.1 (Incentives in clear and fuzzy missions). *Assume disaggregated performance accounting.*

(i) *In the additive normal case, incentives are identical in fuzzy and clear mission equilibria.*

(ii) *In the no effort-no information multiplicative case, incentives are higher under a clear mission than under a fuzzy mission.*

The intuition for Proposition 4.1 (which is proved in the Appendix) is the following. First, in the additive model, $\sum_i y_i$ is a sufficient statistic about θ, and the market's inference about talent does not depend on the expected allocation of effort across tasks, just as in Proposition 3.2. In contrast, in the multiplicative case, inference about talent crucially depends on the market's expectation about the allocation of effort. In a mixed strategy equilibrium, the market infers from the vector of performance levels both a value for talent *and* an allocation of effort. This is why incentives for effort provision are lower: *good performance on a task the agent has focused on is attributed only partly to high talent since it is attributed only partly to high effort on that task.*

While derived under restrictive assumptions, Proposition 4.1 suggests that the scope for multiple missions creates a further hazard beyond the lack of focus. The incentive intensity is further impaired by the lack of understanding by the market of which missions are pursued by the agent. We conjecture that fuzziness is facilitated when agents are heterogeneous in a way that is not observed by the labour market, as is the case when some agents have an intrinsic preference for task 1 and others for task 2, say. Similarly, the generalization of our model to multidimensional talent and multiple labour markets may lead *a priori* identical agents to select different missions.

5 Focus, Professionalization and Autonomy

Our results show that in a multitask context in which the information about task performance cannot be suppressed, the agent may be too dispersed. To restore focus on a particular task j, the principal may wish to hire a "narrow specialist", able only to perform this task. In this case, it may be impossible to have equilibria where effort is positive on any task other than j. Note here that by "narrow specialist" we do not mean an agent who has a productivity on task j that is higher than that of other agents. The mere fact that it has a high cost of pursuing the other tasks is enough to eliminate a number of lower-effort equilibria and to ensure high effort for task j. In this respect, we can talk about *higher accountability of narrow specialists*.

This result is consistent with Wilson's account of the role of "professionals" in shaping the mission of agencies towards a subset of tasks in their potential agenda. In turn, our framework leads to another prediction detailed in Wilson: The higher degree of autonomy enjoyed by "professional" agencies.

Indeed, assume the agent can perform at most two tasks and consider the following timing:

Stage 1: The principal hires an agent, who is either a "bureaucrat" or a "professional". Both types of agent are identical except that the professional has zero productivity on one task.

Stage 2: At a cost k, the principal can "monitor" the agent, *i.e.* force the agent to focus on a particular task. If the principal does not monitor the agent, the agent freely selects her level of effort on each of the two tasks.

In this framework, professionalism creates focus, while the bureaucrat's incentive intensity may be impaired by the hazards studied in Sections 3 (lack of focus) and 4 (fuzziness). This may force the principal to engage in a costly monitoring of the bureaucrat, while no monitoring is required for the same outcome in the case of a professional.

To be certain, bureaucrats have a comparative advantage when there is uncertainty about the relative value of the tasks. Suppose that after the agent has been hired but prior to the principal's monitoring activity, the principal learns that one task is more valuable than the other. Then the principal can instruct the generalist bureaucrat to focus on the important task, while this may prove impossible if the wrong type of professional has been hired. We thus conclude that professionals are particularly effective when there is little uncertainty about organizational goals.

6 • The Tradeoff Between Talent Risk and Incentives Under Career Concerns

Let us now introduce task-specific productivity and ask how effort is related to the bundle of tasks given to the agent.

Consider the additive-normal model. Assume the following performance for task $i = 1, 2$

$$y_i = \theta_i + a_i + \varepsilon_i .$$

Let θ_i and ε_i be normally distributed

$$\theta_i \sim \mathcal{N}(\bar{\theta}, \sigma_\theta^2) \text{ and } \varepsilon_i \sim \mathcal{N}(0, \sigma_\varepsilon^2).$$

While ε_1 and ε_2 are independent and are independent of two dimensions of talent, the latter may be correlated (the case of perfect correlation was treated above). Assume that prospective employers care about

$$\theta_1 + \theta_2 .$$

What can we say about total effort $a_1 + a_2 = \hat{a}$ as a function of the correlation coefficient ρ between θ_1 and θ_2? We have

$$y_1 + y_2 = (\theta_1 + \theta_2) + \hat{a} + \varepsilon_1 + \varepsilon_2 ,$$

which has a normal distribution with mean $2\bar{\theta} + \hat{a}$ and variance $2(1+\rho)\sigma_\theta^2 + 2\sigma_\varepsilon^2$. This yields

$$\frac{\hat{f}_{\hat{a}}(y_1 + y_2)}{\hat{f}(y_1 + y_2)} = \frac{(\theta_1 + \theta_2 - 2\bar{\theta}) + (\varepsilon_1 + \varepsilon_2)}{2(1+\rho)\sigma_\theta^2 + 2\sigma_\varepsilon^2},$$

and

$$\text{cov}\left(\frac{\hat{f}_{\hat{a}}}{\hat{f}}, \theta_1 + \theta_2\right) = \frac{2(1+\rho)\sigma_\theta^2}{2(1+\rho)\sigma_\theta^2 + 2\sigma_\varepsilon^2}.$$

Consequently, equilibrium total effort will be higher, the higher the correlation between θ_1 and θ_2. Indeed, since the mean of $\theta_1 + \theta_2$ is kept constant, a higher ρ simply means a higher signal-to-noise ratio: The higher the initial uncertainty about talent relative to pure noise in performance, the higher the effort expended by the agent.

This observation has implications about *clustering of tasks* among agents. If one has to allocate N tasks in total to agents who can each do only n tasks, effort will be maximized by grouping tasks that require "similar" talents.

Assume for example that four tasks must be performed. Assumed two agents are hired, A and B, and each is given two tasks. The output in task i is

$$y_i = \theta_{iK} + a_i + \varepsilon_i,$$

for $K \in \{A, B\}$ if agent K is allocated to task i, has task-specific talent θ_{iK} and expends effort a_i on task i. Assume that the θ_{iK}s have identical mean $\bar{\theta}$ and variance σ_θ^2 and all ε_is have zero mean and variance σ_ε^2. Tasks 1 and 2, and 3 and 4 respectively, are related in that θ_{1K} and θ_{2K} are positively correlated and so are θ_{3K} and θ_{4K}; all other dimensions of talent are otherwise uncorrelated. Suppose further that, due to learning by doing, the market cares only about $\sum_{i \in I(K)} \theta_{iK}$, where $I(K)$ is the set of the two tasks allocated to agent K (say, the market will reemploy the agent in the same tasks tomorrow). Incentives are maximized by allocating tasks 1 and 2 to one agent and tasks 3 and 4 to the other.[11]

This "specialization result" is specific to the career concern paradigm: In a model where the agent cares solely about monetary incentives as in Holmström-Milgrom (1991), task allocation should reduce the total variance due both to pure noise and talent risk and, by doing so, effort can be increased, since the tradeoff between effort and risk has been improved (Diamond (1984)).

We believe that the positive correlation between effort and talent risk in career concern models, a feature which is reversed in explicit incentive scheme models, is a key insight that helps us understand the importance that scholars like Wilson have given to "focus" in explaining Government agencies' performance.

7 Concluding Remarks

This paper is a first step at providing a formal model of the relation between the objective function of Government agencies and

11. Of course, in a more general model, there are costs to creating focus by clustering related tasks in this way. First, suppose the principal's objective function exhibits complementarities between unrelated tasks: Instead of $\sum_{i=1}^{4} y_i$, it becomes $F(y_1 + y_2, y_3 + y_4)$ with $F_{1,2} > 0$. For $F_{1,2}$ sufficiently large, the principal will sacrifice incentives and reduce the risk of unmatched performances $(y_1 + y_2)$ and $(y_3 + y_4)$ by allocating unrelated tasks to agents. Second, risk averse agents will be concerned about the substantial wage risk attached to specialization. These costs however do not invalidate the basic insight of this section, namely the beneficial incentive effect of specialization.

their performance. A multitask career concern model provides a precise interpretation of concepts such as "missions" and their "focus" or "clarity". Our model moreover backs the sociological evidence that emphasizes the benefits of focused and clear missions in terms of agency performance. And it points to a fundamental tradeoff between their level and riskiness of performance.

Our feeling is that this paradigm can be fruitfully expanded, for example to a dynamic perspective where effort choices are repeated and where the evolution of mission design can be analysed. Another important extension will consider multiple labour markets when talent is multidimensional. For example, an official in a government agency may well behave differently, for example focus on different tasks, depending on whether she intends to pursue her career in politics, in the civil service, in a law firm or in academia. Last, in situations where there are either multiple equilibrium clear missions or fuzzy missions, it is important to understand how specific missions come about. Wilson (1989) for instance emphasizes the role of clear statements about missions and of charismatic leadership. A formal modelling of these selection mechanisms would substantially clarify Wilson's observations. Also, history matters, perhaps because of adaptive learning, learning by doing, or collective reputations. Again, future research should explain why we observe corporate cultures that are stable with respect to mission pursuit. All these issues could in fact usefully apply beyond Government agencies: several issues addressed here are clearly relevant for private firms, at least when they are confronted with difficulties of providing explicit incentives for certain jobs.

Appendix

Proof of Proposition 4.1

(ii) In the no effort-no information multiplicative case, the expected payoff conditional on outcome y in a fuzzy mission in which $a = (a_1, \ldots, a_n) = e_i = (0, \ldots, a^*, \ldots, 0)$ with probability $1/n$, $i = 1, \ldots, n$ can be written as

$$E^F = \sum_i E^i \cdot p_i$$

where $p_i = p_i(y)$ is the posterior probability that the agent specialized in the i-th task conditional on observing $y = (y_1, \ldots, y_n)$ and $E^i = E^i(\theta \mid y_i, a^*)$. Applying Bayes rule yields

$$p_i(y) = \frac{f_i}{\sum_j f_j} = \frac{f(y \mid e_i)}{\sum_j f(y \mid e_j)}$$

$$E^F - E^k = \sum_i (E^i - E^k) \cdot \frac{f_i}{\sum_j f_j}$$

and therefore the difference in marginal incentive (fuzzy minus clear) for an agent specializing in task k is given by

$$\int (E^F - E^k) f_{ak}\, dy = \int \sum_i (E^i - E^k) \cdot \frac{f_i f_k}{\sum_j f_j} \cdot \frac{f_{ak}}{f_k}\, dy\,.$$

Trivially, rewriting the above equation by relabelling the summation operators gives

$$\sum_k \int (E^F - E^k) f_{ak}\, dy = \int \sum_i \sum_k (E^k - E^i) \cdot \frac{f_i f_k}{\sum_j f_j} \cdot \frac{f_{ai}}{f_i}\, dy\,.$$

Changing the order of summation and adding to the previous equation, we obtain

$$2 \sum_k \int (E^F - E^k) f_{ak}\, dy = \int \sum_k \sum_i (E^i - E^k) \cdot \frac{f_i f_k}{\sum_j f_j} \left(\frac{f_{ak}}{f_k} - \frac{f_{ai}}{f_i} \right) dy$$

$$= \sum_k \sum_i \int (E^i - E^k) \cdot \frac{f_i f_k}{\sum_j f_j} \left(\frac{f_{ak}}{f_k} - \frac{f_{ai}}{f_i} \right) dy.$$

Hence, if for each $i,\ k\ =\ 1, \ldots, n$

$$\int (E^i - E^k) \cdot \frac{f_i f_k}{\sum_j f_j} \left(\frac{f_{ak}}{f_k} - \frac{f_{ai}}{f_i} \right) dy \leqq 0\,,$$

then clear missions provide greater incentives than fuzzy missions. This condition will certainly hold if the integrand is everywhere nonpositive.

Because $E[\theta \mid y_i, a_i]$ is nondecreasing in y_i, and $\hat{f}_a / \hat{f} \equiv \hat{f}_a(y_i \mid a_i) / \hat{f}(y_i \mid a_i)$ is nondecreasing in y_i, one sees that this is true for the no effort-no information multiplicative case since $(E^k - E^i)$ and $(f_{ak}/f_k - f_{ai}/f_i)$ always have the same sign. This proves part (ii) of the proposition. For part (i), notice that for the additive normal case, $\sum y_k$ is sufficient for θ regardless of which task the agent specializes in. It follows that inferences about θ are made from the equation $\sum y_k\ =\ n\theta + a + \sum \varepsilon_k$, regardless of the expected allocation of effort across tasks.

Acknowledgements. The authors are grateful to Patrick Bolton, Juan Carrillo, Patrick Rey and a referee for helpful comments. Mathias Dewatripont acknowledges support from contract P4/28 of the Interuniversity Poles of Attraction Programme of the Belgian Federal State (Prime Minister's Office, Federal Office for Scientific, Technical and Cultural Affairs). Ian Jewitt acknowledges support from the ESRC.

REFERENCES

[1] Arrow, K. (1973), "The Theory of Discrimination", in Ashenfelter, O. and Rees, A. (eds.) *Discrimination in Labor Markets* (Princeton: Princeton University Press).

[2] Dewatripont, M., Jewitt, I. and Tirole, J. (1997), "Missions and Accountability of Government Agencies" (Mimeo).

[3] Dewatripont, M., Jewitt, I. and Tirole, J. (1999), "The Economics of Career Concerns, Part I: Comparing Information Structures", *Review of Economic Studies*, **66**, 183-201.

[4] Dewatripont, M. and Tirole, J. (1999), "Advocates", *Journal of Political Economy* (forthcoming).

[5] Diamond, D. (1984), "Financial Intermediation and Delegated Monitoring", *Review of Economic Studies*, **51**, 393-414.

[6] Gibbons, R. and Murphy, K. (1992), "Optimal Incentive Contracts in the Presence of Career Concerns: Theory and Evidence", *Journal of Political Economy*, **100**, 468-505.

[7] Holmström, B. (1982), "Managerial Incentive Problems: A Dynamic Perspective", in *Essays in Economics and Management in Honor of Lars Wahlbeck* (Helsinki: Swedish School of Economics).

[8] Holmström, B. and Milgrom, P. (1987), "Aggregation and Linearity in the Provision of Intertemporal Incentives", *Econometrica*, **55**, 303-328.

[9] Holmström, B. and Milgrom, P. (1991), "Multi-Task Principal-Agent Analyses: Incentive Contracts, Asset Ownership and Job Design", *Journal of Law, Economics and Organization*, **7**, 24-52.

[10] Laffont, J.J. and Tirole, J. (1990), "The Regulation of Multi-Product Firms, I: Theory", *Journal of Public Economics*, **43**, 1-36.

[11] Laffont, J.J. and Tirole, J. (1991), "Provision of Quality and Power of Incentive Schemes in Regulated Industries", in Barnett, W., Cornet, B., d'Aspremont, C., Gabszewicz, J. and Mas Colell, A. (eds.) *Equilibrium Theory and Applications: Proceedings of the Sixth International Symposium in Economic Theory and Econometrics* (Cambridge: Cambridge University Press), pp. 161-196.

[12] Myerson, R. (1998), "Informational Origins of Political Bias Towards Critical Groups of Voters" (Mimeo, Northwestern University).

[13] Wilson, J.Q. (1989), *Bureaucracy: What Government Agencies Do and Why They Do It* (New York: Basic Books).

11

Regulatory Inertia

Antoine Faure-Grimaud
David Martimort

Abstract

Regulatory independence from political control enlarges the collusive opportunities between regulators and interest groups. This is costly for current politicians because deterring capture becomes harder. However, independence also constrains future governments. Whenever future and current governments have different preferences, independence creates a stabilization effect as both majorities find it more difficult to move policies toward their ideal points. Since deterring collusion links current and future policies, the current majority can strategically affect the choices of a future government: a commitment effect. We compare those effects and draw some conclusions for the design of the agency's legal status.

1 Introduction

A major puzzle of regulatory policies is to understand why they exhibit significant momentum and why it is so difficult for newly elected political principals to make an independent and long-lived bureaucracy implement their own regulatory policies. This article gives answers to these questions by analyzing the dynamic interactions between a regulatory agency, its political principals at different points in time, and the interest group it is supposed to regulate. It also adresses the choice of regulatory agencies' status by politically biased principals.

What are the costs and benefits of granting independence to a regulator for empowered politicians? Giving up control rights to a regulator by making him independent and not removable by future majorities opens new strategic possibilities for this regulator. Independence increases the scope for capture by the interest group that he is supposed to regulate. Knowing that he will not be dismissed by the future government allows an independent regulator to exchange favors with interest groups in a way that is not possible for short-lived regulators. This constrains the current majority in inducing policies closer to its own ideal point. However, the flip side of independence is that it also limits the future majority in exactly the same way. Independence makes it harder for a future majority to overrule the initial incentives and to make the regulator more responsive to its own preferences. As a result, an independent regulatory bureaucracy plays a moderating role in the political process by reducing the politically induced fluctuations of regulatory policies. This is a benefit for the current majority, because independence acts as a safeguard against being in the minority tomorrow.

Another related consequence of independence is that both current and future majorities have to collectively prevent long-term collusive behavior between the interest group and the independent regulator. This link between current and future policies can then be used strategically by the current majority to affect tomorrow's policy choices.

To make these points, we build a regulation model based on two main ingredients. The first one is asymmetric information between the political principals and the firm they want to control. Asymmetric information is key both to generate a nontrivial distribution of information rents in the economy and to justify the use of the regulator as a way of bridging this informational gap. Whenever information is asymmetric, the government faces a tradeoff between efficiency and rent extraction at the time of designing regulatory policies.[1] Second-best policies depend on the weight given to the regulated firm in its objective function. That the interest group and the agency share information not available to political principals creates scope for capture to preserve information rents.[2] This capture may take different forms that all reward the regulators in one way or the other for having taken a lenient stance vis-à-vis the sector they are supposed to regulate. For instance, regulators may benefit from in-kind favors or find attractive job opportunities in this sector when they leave the civil service. Capture thus creates a control problem between the government and its bureaucracy that is solved by contract.[3]

The second important ingredient of our model is the specification of the regulator's preferences. As has often been argued, bureaucrats are averse to political fluctuations and want to keep the same level of prestige, resources, and staff regardless of political changes.[4] To model this bureaucratic aversion to political fluctuations, we assume that the private benefits the bureaucrat receives from his relationship with the interest group is a concave function of the amount of bribes that he receives. A rationale for this assumption is that bribes can sometimes be detected by principals, and that the probability of detection increases with the size of the bribe. Although quite intuitive, this assumption on the technology of side contracting has striking

1. On this point, see Baron and Myerson (1982) and Laffont and Tirole (1993).

2. See Laffont and Tirole (1993) and Laffont and Martimort (1999) for models of regulatory capture.

3. There is a by now well-accepted literature in political science that, following Niskanen (1971), views the relationship between political principals (Congress or the presidency) and regulators as a principal-agent governed by a contract; see, for instance, Wood (1988), Brehm and Gates (1997), Wood and Waterman (1994), Banks and Weingast (1992), or Laffont (2000), among many others.

4. Moe (1990, p. 144) has, for instance, reported that "With one election or the demise of a committee chair, an agency's political world can suddenly shift from friendly to hostile. Bureaucrats have various means of insulating themselves from these and other sources of political uncertainty. They can promote further professionnalization and more extensive reliance on civil service... They can base decisions on technical expertise, operational expertise... They can try to monopolize the information necessary for effective political oversight."

implications in a dynamic context. As the rent-efficiency tradeoffs favored by political principals in power at different points in time differ, the regulatory stakes over which the regulator has some discretion change. Granting independence to a regulator opens the set of collusive possibilities: bribes can be smoothed over time to reduce the deadweight loss of side contracting. The set of regulatory policies that are robust to the threat of capture is thus significantly reduced compared to the case of affiliated regulators who must resort to short-term collusion.[5] As a result, new political principals, when they come to power, face more constraints than if they were dealing with their own appointees. Those constraints prevent them from implementing their ideal regulatory policies and constitute a brake on policy changes.

Even though he does not explicitly recognizes that independent regulators have more opportunities for being captured because of their long-term position, Dixit (1996, p. 81) has also informally stressed the fact that the capture of independent regulators is a serious concern and that political principals must adapt regulatory contracts accordingly: "[T]he independence of the agencies creates some new questions: how can these agencies be protected from capture by the very interest they are supposed to regulate? … [T]he Congress typical solution is to impose constraints on the actions of the agency: this often leads to micromanagement by Congress and the re-entry of politics." This is precisely the micromanagement perspective that we take in this article.

To understand more precisely how the capture of an independent agency is a source of regulatory inertia, it is useful to come back to the tradeoff faced by a political principal when designing a regulation robust to capture. By moving regulation away from efficiency, a political principal reduces the regulated firm's information rent, but by doing so he also reduces the regulator's discretion and the scope for capture. Low-powered incentives and large output distortions are best responses to the threat of collusion. Of course, political principals are more eager to implement such policies when collusion is easier, *i.e.*, when the marginal cost of transferring bribes is lower. Because of decreasing returns in the technology of side contracting, a political principal who is willing to redistribute more rent to the regulated firm faces fewer difficulties in fighting collusion, since the marginal cost for transferring bribes grows as regulatory stakes increase. In our dynamic context, the desire to insulate themselves from political fluctuations makes the independent regulator and the firm exchange a bribe that is an average between the regulatory stakes offered by different political principals at different points in time. As a result, the principal who is most eager to give up large information rents will now find it marginally harder to fight capture with an independent regulator than with an affiliated one. The reverse holds for a principal willing to give up less information rent. Through this first *stabilization effect*, each political principal moves his

5. The notion that regulatory capture is a significant constraint in the case of long-term relationships between long-lived regulators and the firms they are supposed to regulate has been stressed by Kahn (1988, vol. 2, p. 11) when he notes that agencies "become increasingly solicitous and protective of the interests of the companies they are supposed to regulate, resistant to changes, wedded to status quo."

own policy toward that of the other. Regulatory policies implemented at different points in time converge toward each other.

Time also introduces a fundamental asymmetry between the principals. Because he is acting first, a date-1 principal can use this intertemporal linkage between the regulatory policies to exert some leverage on the date-2 government. By choosing a policy close to one that he would be offering with an affiliated agency, the first-period government attracts the second-period policy toward that point. This is a *commitment effect* that favors the first-period constituency.

In a model with quadratic utility functions and technologies of side contracting, the commitment and the stabilization effects just compensate each other in the first period to leave unchanged the regulatory policy whether an independent or an affiliated agency is chosen. Instead, the second-period policy under independence significantly differs from its value with an affiliated agency and reflects a weighted average between the preferences of the first-period and second-period principals. We provide closed-forms formulas showing how the preferences of political principals are *de facto* aggregated over time.

We show that the first-period principal always prefers granting independence to the agency. This choice nevertheless results from a nontrivial tradeoff between facilitating capture and constraining future political principals so that the current majority's views are still represented in future policies. One important task is then to determine when this partisan choice conflicts with social welfare. Independence is the best institutional choice from a social welfare viewpoint when the future does not matter too much or, equivalently, when the weight of the first-period principal in social welfare is large enough.

Several contributions have stressed the view that delegation to an independent agency helps the government in a dynamic context when the latter has different policy choices *ex ante* and *ex post* because of a commitment problem and not, as here, because preferences change. Rogoff (1985) demonstrated that choosing a more inflation-averse central banker helps the government reduce his incentives to create surprise inflation. For environmental regulation, Spulber and Besanko (1992) argued that the executive chooses an agency having preferences that are noncongruent with his own to achieve credible commitment.

Applying the same idea to antitrust policy, Besanko and Spulber (1993) proved that antitrust agencies should put a greater weight on consumer surplus at the enforcement stage of merger policy. Finally, Calvert, McCubbins, and Weingast (1989) also discussed how the legislative and executive branches of the government collectively choose the preferences of an agency and how they design its control. One important weakness of this literature is that political principals can choose the preferences of the bureaucrats to whom they delegate regulatory discretion at the *ex ante* stage but cannot change those bureaucrats *ex post* even if they would like to do so. Instead, we assume that these preferences cannot be chosen. Bureaucrats come with their own preferences, and their choices can be influenced by various contracts either with political principals or with interest groups. What the legal status of the agency does then is to change the constraints faced by those contracts to make the bureaucracy more or less sensitive to political fluctuations.

Following McCubbins, Noll, and Weingast (1989), a sizable branch of the political science literature discusses how the structure and processes of administrative rules can be designed *ex ante* to control an agency and avoid policy drifts. This theory, as ours, starts from the observation that politicians and bureaucrats are in a principal-agent relationship, but it does not model explicitly why the policy implemented by an agency may differ from what the democratic coalition that enacts this agency would like it to be. By modelling explicitly the informational problem between politicians and bureaucrats and the scope for capture by private interests, we give firmer foundations to this bureaucratic drift.

Section 2 presents the model and its benchmark where bureaucrats are not captured. Section 3 discusses the policy outcomes with two affiliated regulators. Section 4 tackles the case of an independent long-lived agency and describes the collusion-proof allocations in this case. Section 5 characterizes the optimal regulatory contracts and isolates the sources of regulatory inertia. Section 6 offers comparative statics for some specific functional forms. Section 7 discusses the endogenous choice of the agency's legal status by the first-period principal. Section 8 concludes and discusses some possible extensions of our framework. Proofs are relegated to the Appendix.

2 The Model and its Benchmark

We consider a two-period relationship between two political principals, one holding office in each period, a regulator who can be either long-lived or short-lived, and a long-lived regulated firm in a three-tier hierarchical model of regulation à la Laffont and Tirole (1993). Time is indexed by a subscript i in $\{1, 2\}$. The political principal at date i, P_i, can be viewed as the elected legislative or executive branch of the government.[6] Once elected, a political principal maximizes the expected welfare of his own constituency.

Political principals delegate the task of collecting welfare-improving information to a regulator. The agency is either *affiliated* with a political principal or is *independent*. When affiliated, the regulator's

6. A whole branch of the political science literature discusses the relative importance of the legislative and the executive branches on the control of the bureaucracy (see, for instance, Weingast and Moran (1983)). We will unify those two branches in the spirit of most of the incentive-regulation literature.

tenure is the same as that of the political principal. This means that P_2, when he comes to power, renews the bureaucracy. When independent, the agency remains in office for both periods. As reported by Viscusi, Vernon, and Harrington (1995) for the United States, an independent regulatory commission at the federal level is made up of five or more members with staggered terms. Political principals thus have limited control of the bureaucracy, since they are able to appoint only a fraction of its members. Our approach can thus be viewed as a crude modelling of this setting, since we assume, first, that the agency is made up of a single bureaucrat and, second, that this bureaucrat has a longer tenure than the political principals, to capture the idea that all commissioners cannot be removed simultaneously at the discretion of the President when the agency is independent of the executive branch.

2.1 Information

The regulated firm has some private information about its marginal cost. This efficiency parameter θ is drawn once and for all at date 1 from a common knowledge distribution on $\Theta = \{\underline{\theta}, \bar{\theta}\}$ ($\Delta\theta = \bar{\theta} - \underline{\theta} > 0$) with respective probabilities ν and $1 - \nu$. The firm is efficient (respectively, inefficient) at both dates when $\theta = \underline{\theta}$ (respectively, $\theta = \bar{\theta}$).

The regulator gets a hard information signal σ on θ that is also known by the firm. The regulator observes with probability ε the firm's type if it is efficient. Otherwise, he observes nothing. Hence, $\sigma = \underline{\theta}$ with probability $\nu\varepsilon$ and $\sigma = \varnothing$ with probability $1 - \nu\varepsilon$. The affiliated regulator at date i, R_i, only learns σ when he comes into office.

2.2 Preferences

Let us denote by $\delta \in [0, \infty)$ the common discount factor of all agents. For ease of notations, it is useful to define $\beta = \frac{1}{1+\delta}$ in $]0, 1]$. β is the normalized weight on the first period's utility for all agents. It is a measure of the relative length of the first period.

Firm. Using this normalization, the regulated firm's intertemporal profit is $\beta u_1 + (1 - \beta)u_2$, where $u_i = t_i - \theta q_i$ is date-i profit, with t_i and q_i denoting respectively the transfer received from P_i and the firm's output at this date.

Independent regulator. The long-lived regulator (hereafter R) receives a transfer s_i from P_i. This transfer can be viewed as the share of the agency budget and resources that can be diverted by the regulator for his private use. It can also be viewed as a proxy for the private benefits, the prestige, or the size of the administrative staff that the regulator gets when holding office.[7] The regulator's intertemporal utility

7. Even though our focus on monetary incentives for the regulator makes the presentation of our model easier, our results are also robust when we replace monetary incentives by career concerns. We can, for instance, interpret s as the probability of being promoted to a higher position in the civil service times the benefits of this higher position.

can be written as $\beta s_1 + (1-\beta)s_2$, where, because of limited liability, wages must remain positive. If the regulator, say R_i, is affiliated to P_i, he receives only a wage s_i at date *i*.[8]

Political principals. Asymmetric information between the government and the firm introduces a well-known tradeoff between efficiency and extraction of the regulated firm's information rent. Following the partisan politics literature,[9] political principals holding office at different dates have different preferences regarding this tradeoff depending on whether they defend a more or less "pro-firm" constituency. Political principal P_i's per-period objective function is:[10]

$$SW_i = S(q_i) - s_i - t_i + \alpha_i u_i = S(q_i) - \theta q_i - s_i - (1-\alpha_i)u_i, \quad (1)$$

where $S(q)$ ($S'(\cdot) > 0$, $S''(\cdot) < 0$ with $S(0) = 0$) is the consumer net surplus derived from consuming q units of output and $\alpha_i < 1$ is the weight that the principal puts on the firm's utility. $|S''(\cdot)|$ is sufficiently large to always ensure strict concavity of the political principal's objective function with respect to outputs under both independent and affiliated agencies.[11] Moreover, $S(\cdot)$ satisfies the Inada conditions to always get strictly positive outputs in all circumstances.

As $\alpha_i < 1$, both political principals dislike giving up rents to firms. However, α_i changes over time, reflecting the election of new majorities.[12] For simplicity, the government is supposed to change for sure at date 2. To fix ideas, we focus on the case where P_1 is more concerned by rent extraction and less by efficiency than P_2, *i.e.*, $\alpha_1 < \alpha_2$. We can interpret $\Delta\alpha = \alpha_2 - \alpha_1$ as the degree of polarization in society.[13]

2.3 Regulatory Contracts

The *grand contract* GC_i between P_i, the regulator, and the firm consists of a budget for the regulator, a transfer, and an output target for the firm. There is no loss of generality in viewing such a regulatory contract as a direct mechanism $GC_i = \{(\underline{t}_i, \underline{s}_i, \underline{q}_i); (\bar{t}_i, \bar{s}_i, \bar{q}_i); (t_i, s_i, q_i)\}$. The first two vectors are offered when the regulator makes an uninformative report $\hat{\sigma}_i = \varnothing$ to P_i and the firm reports respectively being efficient and inefficient. The last vector is offered following an informative report by the supervisor, $\hat{\sigma}_i = \underline{\theta}$. Note that with σ_i being hard information, P_i knows for sure that the firm is efficient if $\hat{\sigma}_i = \underline{\theta}$. Everything thus happens as if the regulator first reports to the principal, and, if this report is uninformative, the firm reports its type to the political principal.

In the case of an independent regulator, two contractual restrictions are implicitly made above. First, GC_1 is not contingent on

8. Note that the regulator's preferences are the same whether he is affiliated or not and that he has no preferences *per se* on policies. Keeping preferences constant as one changes the institutional setting allows us to avoid any modeling bias in favor of one or the other of these institutions. Nevertheless, our framework could easily incorporate the possibility that the regulator has some policy preferences of his own. For instance, our results are robust to the case where the regulator's utility function places a positive weight on the information rent left to the regulated firm: $s_i + \gamma U_i$ for some $\gamma > 0$.

9. Baron (1988), Laffont (2000), and Boyer and Laffont (1999), among others, propose such models.

10. The agency has no weight in the principals' objective functions, capturing the fact that redistributing wealth to bureaucrats is not part of any government's objective. Alternatively, regulators represent a group without significant political power. The main insights of our analysis are robust to the case where parties' objective functions put the same positive (but less than one so that the regulator's rents are costly) weight on the regulator's utility.

11. The corresponding restriction on parameter values is made clear in Section 6, once we specify quadratic utility functions.

12. We take α_i as exogenous. However, this parameter can reflect the extent of the political pressure placed by the industry on the political principals themselves if one takes the view that capture is also a concern at the higher level of the government.

13. The effects we identify hereafter still hold when $\alpha_1 > \alpha_2$, with their directions being reversed.

the second-period output and regulatory reports. The fact that he will not be in power at date 2 prevents P_1 from imposing any regulation at date 2 and delaying payments until date-2 actions are taken.

Second, GC_2 does not depend on first-period output, transfers, and reports either. Consistent with the fact that the performance of a regulated industry is publicly released only after a lag, the past history of regulatory actions is unknown to P_2 when he offers his contract.[14]

Finally, note that the first-period grand contract GC_1 is observable by P_2 so that P_1 can use it as a leverage on future regulatory policies. Indeed, this first grand contract determinates the rent that the firm can get from regulation in the first period. It thus affects the overall benefit that the interest group may get from capturing the regulator if the latter has a long-term tenure. Through this intertemporal channel, the first-period policy affects the set of second-period regulatory policies that are robust to capture if the regulator is independent.

2.4 Capture

To keep its information rent, the firm bribes the regulator to make an uninformative report and hide from the political principal that it is efficient. Of course, to be accepted, such a side contract must give the regulator more than what he gets from reporting truthfully to his political principal.

An *affiliated* regulator is short-lived and may collude with the firm only after GC_i has been offered. This side contract stipulates a bribe τ_i exchanged when the regulator reports $\hat{\sigma}_i = \varnothing$ to P_i if he has observed that the firm is efficient.[15]

The technology for transforming bribes into private benefits for the regulator exhibits decreasing returns. It is at the margin easier to transfer small bribes than larger ones because, for instance, large bribes can be more easily be detected by the principal.[16] Transferring $\tau \geq 0$ units of bribes to the regulator only increases his utility by an amount $k(\tau)$ such that $k(\tau) < \tau$ with $k'(\cdot) > 0$, $k''(\cdot) < 0$, and $k(0) = 0$.

For technical reasons, we also assume that $k'(\tau) < k(\tau)/\tau \leq 1 - \alpha_2 < 1 - \alpha_1$ for all τ. The average transaction cost of side contracting is thus greater than the weight given to the firm's information rent in each principal's objective function. In other words, paying the regulator indirectly through bribes given by the firm is always more costly than paying him directly with a wage. This also justifies the use of the regulator as a more efficient source of information than any direct communication with the firm.

An *independent* regulator is instead long-lived. *A priori*, the set of collusive strategies with the firm contains all strategies available to

14. This assumption is made to abstract from the well-known ratchet effect (see Freixas, Guesnerie, and Tirole (1985) and Laffont and Tirole (1993)), although we discuss its possible implications in the Conclusion. We also assume that P_2 cannot make the regulator and the firm reveal their first-period reports, mainly because such a mechanism would trigger further collusion.

15. As in most of the collusion literature, we assume enforceability of the collusive long-term side contract. This assumption can be justified by appealing to "word of honor" or to more general reputational arguments. This allows us to characterize an upper bound on the benefits of collusion.

16. The assumption of convexity of the transaction costs is quite standard in the public choice literature (see, for instance, Congleton (1984)).

the affiliated regulator. However, the scope of collusion now expands. In particular, *long-term collusion* with the firm is now possible. With such a side contract, the regulator hides information from both principals and receives a profile of intertemporal bribes to which the firm can commit.

In a dynamic context, the convexity of transaction costs has a striking implication. Long-lived collusive partners facing changing political conditions want to smooth bribes over time in order to save on the intertemporal deadweight loss of collusion.

In our model, the regulator's desire to avoid political fluctuations is endogenized through this tendency for bribe smoothing.

Finally, note that transaction costs are independent of the agency's legal status. Only the set of collusive contracts changes with the institutional context.

2.5 Timing

We now describe the timing of the game with a long-lived bureaucracy.

(i) The firm discovers the value of θ.

(ii) Principal P_1 offers a grand contract GC_1 to both the regulator and the firm. The regulator and the firm both learn σ. If any of them refuses the contract, the game ends and those agents get their exogenous reservation payoffs, normalized to zero.

(iii) The collusion phase takes place.

(iv) The regulator reports $\hat{\sigma}_1$ to P_1. If this report is uninformative, the firm reports its information $\hat{\theta}_1$ directly to the principal. A transfer-quantity pair is implemented and the regulator and the firm are paid according to their reports.

(v) Principal P_2 gets elected. Knowing the first-period contract GC_1 but having not observed date-1 reports, P_2 offers a second-period contract GC_2 to both the current regulator and the firm. If any of them refuses the contract, the game ends.

(vi) The regulator reports $\hat{\sigma}_2$ to P_2. If it is uninformative, the firm reports its information $\hat{\theta}_2$ to the principal. A transfer-quantity pair is implemented and the regulator and the firm are paid according to their reports.

Because it does not obscure understanding, and the derivation of collusion-proof policies given below is rather intuitive, we describe the collusion phase between the long-lived regulator and the firm in more detail in the Appendix. With affiliated regulators, there are two such collusion phases, one with each regulator (the second being just after P_2 has been elected).

2.6 Asymmetric Information without Capture

As a benchmark, let us first consider the second-best regulatory policies that are implemented when a political principal P_i is empowered for a single period and the affiliated regulator is not captured and always reports truthfully. The regulator's wage being socially costly, a null payment is enough to obtain information in all states of nature. Indexing the solution by a superscript *SB*, we have $s_i^{SB} = \underline{s}_i^{SB} = \bar{s}_i^{SB} = 0$. Since the firm's information rent is costly from P_i's viewpoint, it is reduced to zero both when the firm is efficient and observed by the regulator, $u_i^{SB} = t_i^{SB} - \underline{\theta} q_i^{SB} = 0$, and when it is inefficient and unobserved, $\bar{u}_i^{SB} = \bar{t}_i^{SB} - \bar{\theta}\bar{q}_i^{SB} = 0$.

When the efficient firm is not observed by the regulator, the regulatory contract must induce the firm to tell the truth on its cost. The following incentive-compatibility constraint must thus be satisfied:

$$\underline{u}_i \geq \Delta\theta\bar{q}_i. \tag{2}$$

It is well known that this constraint is binding at the optimum so that $\underline{u}_i = \Delta\theta\bar{q}_i$. (See, for instance, Laffont and Martimort (2002).) Taking into account the expression of the information rents of the regulated firm as a function of outputs and transfers and replacing in the political principal's objective function, the optimal grand contract offered by P_i thus solves the following problem:

$$\max_{(\underline{q}_i, \bar{q}_i, q_i)} \quad SW(\underline{q}_i, \bar{q}_i, q_i) - \nu(1-\varepsilon)(1-\alpha_i)\Delta\theta\bar{q}_i,$$

where $SW(\cdot)$ denotes expected efficiency:

$$SW(\underline{q}_i, \bar{q}_i, q_i) = \nu\varepsilon(S(q_i) - \underline{\theta}q_i) + \nu(1-\varepsilon)(S(\underline{q}_i) - \underline{\theta}\underline{q}_i)$$
$$+ (1-\nu)(S(\bar{q}_i) - \bar{\theta}\bar{q}_i).$$

Whatever the exact preferences of the political principal, the efficient firm always produces the first-best output $q_i^{SB} = \underline{q}_i^{SB} = q^{FB}$, which is such that marginal gross surplus is equal to marginal cost:

$$S'(q^{FB}) = \underline{\theta}. \tag{3}$$

Since different political principals differ only in the social weight they give to the firm's information rent and since this rent does not depend on the efficient firm's output, different political principals agree on what this output should be.

The inefficient firm's output is instead downward distorted below the first best:

$$S'(\bar{q}_i^{SB}) = \bar{\theta} + \frac{\nu}{1-\nu}\Delta\theta(1-\alpha_i)(1-\varepsilon). \tag{4}$$

At the optimum, only the efficient firm gets a strictly positive information rent,

$$\underline{u}_i^{SB} = \Delta\theta\bar{q}_i^{SB}, \tag{5}$$

when the regulator has not observed its cost.

Outputs are downward distorted to limit the efficient firm's information rent. However, rent extraction is less of a concern when α_i is higher. The firm's rent increases with α_i. Under asymmetric information, second-best policies fluctuate with the identity of the principal in power. Because $\alpha_2 > \alpha_1$, the firm receives more information rent in the second period than in the first. If there is more congruence of interests between the interest group and the political principal, the firm gets a larger information rent.

It is easy to check that the same output and wage policies can also be implemented when a single independent and benevolent regulator holds office for both periods.[17] The legal status of the bureaucrat is irrelevant when capture is not an issue.

3 Capture with Affiliated Agencies

Regulator R_i now holds office for only one period. The only collusion with the firm runs for the current period. For such collusion, an efficient firm is ready to pay up to the information rent $\Delta\theta\bar{q}_i$ that it gets with an uninformative report ($\hat{\sigma}_i = \varnothing$) if an informed regulator hides his information from P_i. The private benefits that the regulator draws from colluding with the firm are reduced because of the transaction costs of side contracting. They are worth only $k(\Delta\theta\bar{q}_i)$.

The collusion-proofness principle holds in this context.[18] There is no loss of generality in having P_i offer a direct-revelation mechanism that is robust to the formation of the coalition between R_i and the firm. Indeed, because $k(\tau) < (1-\alpha_2)\tau < (1-\alpha_1)\tau$ for all τ, paying the affiliated regulator $k(\Delta\theta\bar{q}_i)$ to obtain hard information on the firm is always less costly from P_i's viewpoint than asking the firm directly for its type and giving up some information rent that has a cost $(1-\alpha_i)\Delta\theta\bar{q}_i$. The following collusion-proofness constraint must thus be satisfied at each date i:

$$s_i \geq k(\Delta\theta\bar{q}_i). \tag{6}$$

The optimal grand contract offered by P_i solves now the problem[19]

$$\max_{(\underline{q}_i, \bar{q}_i, q_i, s_i)} SW(\underline{q}_i, \bar{q}_i, q_i) - \nu\varepsilon s_i - \nu(1-\varepsilon)(1-\alpha_i)\Delta\theta\bar{q}_i$$

subject to (6).

17. The only slight modification comes from the firm's and the independent regulator's participation constraints, which state that their respective intertemporal utility over both periods has to be positive. There are many different ways of satisfying those constraints that do not affect the optimal outputs at each date and leave the first-period principal's intertemporal welfare unchanged.

18. See Tirole (1986) for a proof of this principle.

19. The fact that (6) is binding (as it is the case at the optimum) may introduce some nonconcavity in the principal's objective function with respect to output. To avoid these uninteresting technicalities, we have assumed that $|S''(\cdot)|$ is sufficiently large. In Section 6, we make this condition exact in the case of a quadratic surplus function and a quadratic technology of side contracting.

We index by a superscript A the optimal solution in the case of affiliated regulators.

Proposition 1. *The optimal collusion-proof dynamic regulation with affiliated agencies entails the following:*

(i) *The short-term collusion-proofness constraint* (6) *is binding.*

(ii) *The optimal output of the efficient firm is always equal to its first-best value:* $q_i^A = \underline{q}_i^A = q^{FB}$.

(iii) *The optimal output of the inefficient firm is downward distorted with respect to its second-best value* $\bar{q}_i^A < \bar{q}_i^{SB}$ *with*

$$S'(\bar{q}_i^A) = \bar{\theta} + \frac{\nu}{1-\nu}\,\Delta\theta((1-\alpha_i)(1-\varepsilon) + \varepsilon k'(\Delta\theta\bar{q}_i^A)). \quad (7)$$

(iv) *There is no linkage between date-*1 *and date-*2 *policies.*

Of course, P_i wants to reduce the regulator's wage as much as possible and the collusion-proofness constraint (6) is binding. Since the right-hand side of (6) is increasing with output, it is more costly to satisfy the collusion-proofness constraint as the regulatory stake $\bar{u}_i = \Delta\theta\bar{q}_i$ increases. The political principal wants to decrease the wage given to his affiliated regulator to make less costly the collusion-proofness constraint and does so by reducing output below its second-best value. Intuitively, the political principal reduces the regulator's discretion in manipulating information to prevent capture. The optimal regulatory package stipulates a small regulatory stake and a low wage for the regulator. This excessively low-powered incentive scheme looks like the bureaucratic rules often found in practice.[20]

It is already worth noticing that a decrease in the marginal transaction costs of side contracting (*i.e.*, making $k'(\cdot)$ greater) makes it marginally harder for the principal to fight collusion. As a result, output distortions are greater as $k'(\cdot)$ is increased. We will come back to this important point when we analyze the impact of the regulator's independence on the optimal policies.

Since $\alpha_1 < \alpha_2$, the first-period government implements a greater output distortion than the second-period one: $\bar{q}_1^A < \bar{q}_2^A$. These policies with affiliated regulators can be viewed as ideal points for the principals. If P_i could remain in power for both periods, he would choose policy $\bar{q}_i^A$ in each period.

With affiliated regulators, there is no intertemporal linkage between the regulatory policies on both dates. Regulatory policies reflect only the preferences of the current majority on what should be the rent-efficiency tradeoff. There is no institutional brake on the policy fluctuations induced by changes in the identity of the political principal.

20. Wilson (1989) has forcefully argued that government agencies are subject to constraints that limit their discretion.

4 Capture with an Independent Agency

4.1 The Stake of Long-Term Capture

As a preliminary step in the analysis of long-term capture, we first show that the regulator's independence makes it harder to prevent collusion with the interest group. To do so, it is useful to come back to the contracts obtained with affiliated agencies and check that they are indeed not robust to a long-term collusive agreement between the regulator and the firm. With those contracts, there exists a stake for long-term capture. Indeed, instead of exchanging bribes $\Delta\theta\bar{q}_1^A$ at date 1 and $\Delta\theta\bar{q}_2^A$ at date 2, suppose that the firm and the regulator exchange a constant bribe:

$$\tau^A = \Delta\theta(\beta\bar{q}_1^A + (1-\beta)\bar{q}_2^A)\,. \tag{8}$$

Note first that $\Delta\theta\bar{q}_2^A > \tau^A > \Delta\theta\bar{q}_1^A$ and thus the efficient firm makes a first-period loss that is exactly compensated by a second-period gain so that its intertemporal participation constraint is still satisfied. Hence, the firm is willing to collude.

Since the regulator's wages are obtained when the short-term collusion-proofness constraints (6) are binding in both periods, we have

$$\begin{aligned}\beta s_1^A + (1-\beta)s_2^A &= \beta k(\Delta\theta\bar{q}_1^A) + (1-\beta)k(\Delta\theta\bar{q}_2^A)\\ &< k(\Delta\theta(\beta\bar{q}_1^A + (1-\beta)\bar{q}_2^A))\,,\end{aligned}$$

where we use the strict concavity of $k(\cdot)$. Hence, the regulator prefers to receive a constant bribe τ^A and hide information in both periods rather than report truthfully to each political principal and receive the corresponding wages. When the transaction costs of side contracting are strictly convex, the pair of regulatory contracts implemented with affiliated agencies is not robust to long-term collusion. Political principals can no longer content themselves with preventing capture in any given period but must also curb the temptation of an independent regulator to take advantage of his long-term relationship with the firm to reach more valuable collusive deals.

4.2 Collusion-Proof Regulatory Policies

In this dynamic setting, once the first-period regulatory contract has been established, the long-lived interest group offers a side contract to the regulator anticipating the regulatory environment that will be designed by P_2 when he comes to power. In turn, this principal offers a regulatory contract anticipating that some profile of bribes may be exchanged between the long-lived regulator and the interest group. In offering these monetary transfers to the regulator, the interest group and the second-period principal are thus both willing to influence the choice of reports made by the regulator.[21] In the Appendix, we derive equilibria of this game such that collusion does not occur on the equilibrium path. When the firm's dominated strategies are eliminated, those equilibria have an intuitive characterization.

Proposition 2. *A pair of grand contracts* (GC_1, GC_2) *is collusion-proof if and only if it satisfies the following constraints:*

$$s_1 \geq k(\Delta\theta\bar{q}_1), \tag{9}$$

$$s_2 \leq (1-\alpha_2)\Delta\theta\bar{q}_2, \tag{10}$$

$$s_2 \geq k(\Delta\theta\bar{q}_2), \tag{11}$$

$$\beta s_1 + (1-\beta)s_2 \geq k(\Delta\theta(\beta\bar{q}_1 + (1-\beta)\bar{q}_2)). \tag{12}$$

For a fixed first-period regulatory environment stipulating a pair (s_1, q_1) satisfying (9) and thus preventing collusion over the first-period report only, conditions (10) to (12) define the set of second-period regulatory contracts which are robust to any manipulation of the second-period report. The first condition (10) simply means that the regulator's wage should be less costly from P_2's point of view than giving up information rent to the firm. It amounts to saying that P_2 does not find it worthwhile to let capture occur. Condition (11) means that the regulator's second-period wage is large enough to prevent any attempt by the firm to capture the regulator only for the second period. This yields the same short-term collusion-proofness constraint as for an affiliated regulator.

Finally, (12) means that the intertemporal wage of the regulator over both periods must be greater than the private benefit he draws from exchanging a constant bribe with the interest group equal to the average regulatory stake. It is intuitive that if this condition does not hold, the interest group can offer the constant bribe $\tau = \Delta\theta(\beta\bar{q}_1 + (1-\beta)\bar{q}_2)$ and, just as above, induce the regulator to hide informative reports from both P_1 and P_2.

Since both (10) and (11) must also hold with an affiliated regulator, the new collusion-proofness condition (12) captures how the regulator's independence puts more constraints on second-period policy than in the case where elected principals have all control rights on their bureaucracy and can appoint an affiliated agency. The independent regulator and the interest group can adopt whatever collusive strategies were available to the affiliated ones, but they can also reach more efficient agreements that significantly constrain future policies.

21. We are thus facing a common-agency game along the lines of Grossman and Helpman (1994), except for the existence of asymmetric information between the regulator and the second-period principal.

5 The Dynamics of Regulation

We solve the contractual game backward.[22] We first give some insights on how the first-period policies affect the problem of the second-period principal. Given a first-period grand contract, Proposition 2 presents the set of second-period contracts that are immune to collusion. Within this set, we select the best continuation from P_2's point of view as the solution to the following program:

$$\max_{(\underline{q}_2,\bar{q}_2,q_2,s_2)} \quad SW(\underline{q}_2,\bar{q}_2,q_2)-\nu\varepsilon s_2-\nu(1-\varepsilon)(1-\alpha_2)\Delta\theta\bar{q}_2$$

subject to (10), (11), and (12).

As expected, the long-term collusion constraint (12) potentially creates a link between the first- and second-period policies. The choice of the first-period regulatory wage s_1 affects which of these collusion-proof constraints bind. Let us remark here that a sufficiently low s_1 is such that only the long-term constraint (12) is binding, while a sufficiently high s_1 would result in only the short-term second-period constraint (11) being binding.[23]

Let us first illustrate which policy would be chosen by the second-period principal if only the long-term collusion-proofness constraint (12) binds. Solving P_2's maximization problem in that case yields an output distortion satisfying

$$S'(\bar{q}_2^r(\bar{q}_1)) = \bar{\theta}+\frac{\nu}{1-\nu}\Delta\theta[(1-\alpha_2)(1-\varepsilon) + \varepsilon k'(\Delta\theta(\beta\bar{q}_1+(1-\beta)\bar{q}_2^r(\bar{q}_1)))]. \tag{13}$$

What is apparent from (13) is the dependence of the second-period output choice on the first-period output.[24] Intuitively, $\bar{q}_2^r(\bar{q}_1)$ is the second-period output that P_2 would choose with an affiliated regulator if the marginal cost of collusion were $k'(\Delta\theta(\beta\bar{q}_1+(1-\beta)\bar{q}_2))$ instead of $k'(\Delta\theta\bar{q}_2)$. We look for equilibria such that $\bar{q}_1<\bar{q}_2^r(\bar{q}_1)$, and thus $\beta\bar{q}_1+(1-\beta)\bar{q}_2^r(\bar{q}_1)<\bar{q}_2^r(\bar{q}_1)$, which, together with the concavity of $k(\cdot)$, implies that $\bar{q}_2^r(\bar{q}_1)<\bar{q}_2^A$. Given that P_1 likes to see relatively low output levels, this already suggests that P_1 should not raise s_1 too much if he wants to shift the second-period regulatory policy toward his ideal point $\bar{q}_1^A$. Instead, when only the short-term

22. We look for an equilibrium such that P_1 offers an output $\bar{q}_1$ that is strictly less than the output $\bar{q}_2$ offered by P_2. This ranking is consistent with the policies described earlier when the regulators are affiliated.

23. Of course, both constraints may be binding for intermediate values of s_1.

24. This dependence can be formally illustrated by differentiating (13) with respect to $\bar{q}_1$ to obtain

$$\frac{\partial\bar{q}_2^r(\bar{q}_1)}{\partial\bar{q}_1} = \frac{\frac{\nu}{1-\nu}(\Delta\theta)^2\varepsilon\beta k''(\Delta\theta(\beta\bar{q}_1+(1-\beta)q_2^r(\bar{q}_1)))}{S''(\bar{q}_2^r(\bar{q}_1))-\frac{\nu}{1-\nu}(\Delta\theta)^2\varepsilon(1-\beta)k''(\Delta\theta(\beta\bar{q}_1+(1-\beta)q_2^r(\bar{q}_1)))}>0.$$

collusion-proofness constraint (11) binds, P_2 behaves as in the affiliated case and chooses $\bar{q}_2^A$. More generally, the second-period output choice $\bar{q}_2$ describes the whole interval $[\bar{q}_2^r(\bar{q}_1), \bar{q}_2^A]$, as s_1 varies.

Keeping these effects in mind, the policy choice for P_1 is governed by both his concern for the well-being of his constituency at date 1 but also at date 2 through the links just discussed. Formally, the optimal first-period grand contract now solves

$$\max_{(\underline{q}_1, \bar{q}_1, q_1, s_1)} \quad \beta[SW(\underline{q}_1, \bar{q}_1, q_1) - \nu\varepsilon s_1 - \nu(1-\varepsilon)(1-\alpha_1)\Delta\theta\bar{q}_1]$$

$$+ (1-\beta)[SW(\underline{q}_2, \bar{q}_2, q_2) - \nu\varepsilon s_2(s_1, \bar{q}_1) - \nu(1-\varepsilon)(1-\alpha_1)\Delta\theta\bar{q}_2(s_1, \bar{q}_1)]$$

subject to (6) for date 1,

$$s_2(s_1, \bar{q}_1) \geq k(\Delta\theta\bar{q}_2(s_1, \bar{q}_1)), \tag{14}$$

and

$$\beta s_1 + (1-\beta)s_2(s_1, \bar{q}_1) \geq k(\Delta\theta(\beta\bar{q}_1 + (1-\beta)\bar{q}_2(s_1, \bar{q}_1))), \tag{15}$$

where the latter two constraints are the collusion-proofness constraints at date 2 but rewritten with the corresponding second-period continuation output $\bar{q}_2(s_1, \bar{q}_1)$ and regulatory wage $s_2(s_1, \bar{q}_1)$ that are described in Proposition A1 in the Appendix. We index with a superscript I the outputs under independence.

Proposition 3. *The optimal first-period regulatory policy offered by P_1 with an independent regulator entails the following:*

(i) *The long-term collusion-proofness constraint* (12) *is binding and the short-term collusion-proofness constraint* (6) *at date* 1 *is slack in equilibrium.*

(ii) *The efficient firm's output is always equal to its first-best value:* $q_1^I = \underline{q}_1^I = \underline{q}^{FB}$.

(iii) *The inefficient firm's output $\bar{q}_1^I$ is downward distorted with respect to its second-best value $\bar{q}_1^I < \bar{q}_1^{SB}$, with*

$$S'(\bar{q}_1^I) = \bar{\theta} + \frac{\nu}{1-\nu}\Delta\theta\Bigg((1-\alpha_1)(1-\varepsilon) + \underbrace{\varepsilon k'(\Delta\theta(\beta\bar{q}_1^I + (1-\beta)\bar{q}_2^r(\bar{q}_1^I)))}_{\text{stabilization effect}}$$

$$\underbrace{+ (1-\varepsilon)\Delta\alpha\left(\frac{1-\beta}{\beta}\right)\frac{\partial\bar{q}_2^r(\bar{q}_1^I)}{\partial\bar{q}_1}}_{\text{commitment effect}}\Bigg). \tag{16}$$

(iv) *The inefficient firm's output at date* 2 *is* $\bar{q}_2^I = \bar{q}_2^r(\bar{q}_1^I)$.

It is obviously optimal for P_1 to reduce s_1 up to the point where the long-term collusion-proof constraint (12) binds: it reduces the wage cost at date 1 and allows P_1 to indirectly control P_2's policy. When binding, the long-term collusion-proofness constraint creates a strategic link between the regulatory policies chosen at dates 1 and 2. Preventing the long-term capture of the regulator can be viewed as a public good for both principals. By offering only a small first-period wage to the regulator, P_1 free-rides on the provision of this public good and makes it more likely that P_2 bears most of its cost. The long-term collusion-proofness constraint is then binding in P_2's program. If it is so, reducing $\bar{q}_1$ also reduces the average collusion stake $\Delta\theta(\beta\bar{q}_1 + (1-\beta)\bar{q}_2)$. From P_2's viewpoint, collusion thus becomes more costly at the margin than with an affiliated regulator, since transaction costs of side contracting are convex.

P_2 is thus forced to distort $\bar{q}_2$ downward by more than what he would do with an affiliated regulator. Doing so, P_2 implements a policy that comes closer to what P_1 would do himself.

Comparing the right-hand sides of (7) (for $i = 1$) and (16), we can isolate two different effects that characterize the differences between the affiliated and the independent cases.

The stabilization effect. By paying a small first-period wage, P_1 forces P_2 to bear most of the cost of preventing long-term collusion and to distort $\bar{q}_2$ toward his own ideal point. By doing so, P_1 exerts the maximal leverage on the second-period policy.

As for P_2, what matters now for P_1's ability to assess the marginal cost of deterring collusion is the average collusion stake determined by outputs in both periods. P_2 being less reluctant than P_1 to give up information rents, this average collusion stake is greater than what P_1 would offer to an affiliated regulator. Transaction costs of side contracting being convex, exchanging higher bribes decreases the marginal cost of preventing capture from P_1's viewpoint. P_1's incentives to reduce output in the first period are lower than with an affiliated regulator. This tendency to increase first-period output is thus precisely the opposite of what P_2 faces, since the latter wants to reduce output below what he offers to an affiliated regulator. Regulatory policies are thus stabilized. Intuitively, this stabilization effect implies that the independent bureaucrat forces the political principals to adopt regulatory budgets and economic regulations that are less sensitive to their preferences.

The commitment effect. Through the stabilization effect above, the second-period policy is directly linked to the first-period one. P_1 can thus use this link to exert some leverage on future regulation. With an independent regulator, we have already seen that decreasing $\bar{q}_1$ makes it harder at the margin for P_2 to prevent collusion, and this pushes $\bar{q}_2$ down. If P_1 strategically reduces $\bar{q}_1$, he reduces the rent left to the firm not only at date 1 but also at date 2. This induces a distribution of information rents that better fits his preferences.

Contrary to the stabilization effect, this commitment effect is asymmetric. Because he plays first, only P_1 can influence P_2's policy. This commitment effect creates some extra momentum pushing the second-period policy toward P_1's ideal policy.

Summing both effects. From P_1's viewpoint, the commitment and the stabilization effects go in opposite directions. The first effect pushes first-period output up because the first-period policy is "attracted" by P_2's ideal point. On the contrary, the second effect pushes the first-period policy down to "attract" the second-period policy. Instead, from P_2's viewpoint, both effects reinforce each other. For a given first-period output, the stabilization effect pushes date-2 policy toward P_1's ideal point. When the commitment effect is now taken into account, there is an extra reduction in the second-period output that pushes it even further toward P_1's ideal point.

6 • Comparative Statics

To get more precise conclusions on the respective sizes of the stabilization and the commitment effects, we now specify some functional forms. Let us first assume that surplus is quadratic, $S(q) = \mu q - (\lambda/2)q^2$ for some μ and λ such that equilibrium outputs always remain positive. Second, let us also assume that transaction costs are quadratic, $k(\tau) = k\tau - (r/2)\tau^2$ for values of r such that regulatory stakes (and thus possible bribes) remain within the range $[0, k/r]$, where $k(\cdot)$ is increasing. We assume that $k \leq 1 - \alpha_2$ so that each political principal finds it less costly to use the regulator than to directly ask the firm for its type in the case of affiliated regulators. To ensure concavity of both principals' objective function with both an independent and an affiliated regulator, we finally assume that $y = \lambda/[\varepsilon r(\nu/(1-\nu))\Delta\theta^2] > 1$.[25]

Proposition 4. *Assume quadratic utilities. We have the following:*

(i) *The optimal output offered by a second-period government for an inefficient firm is smaller with an independent agency than with an affiliated agency,* $\bar{q}_2^I = \bar{q}_2^r(\bar{q}_1^I) < \bar{q}_2^A$.

(ii) *The optimal output offered by a first-period government for an inefficient firm is the same with an independent and with an affiliated agency,* $\bar{q}_1^I = \bar{q}_1^A$.

25. To reinforce the generality of the following results, note that this quadratic model can be viewed as a good second-order approximation of any specification of the utility functions and transaction-cost technologies when $\Delta\theta$ is small enough. The policies we derive here and those obtained with general surplus and transaction-cost functions would differ only in terms of order of magnitude above $\Delta\theta^2$.

(iii) *Average output is shifted downward with an independent regulator,* $\beta\bar{q}_1^I + (1-\beta)\bar{q}_2^I < \beta\bar{q}_1^A + (1-\beta)\bar{q}_2^A$.

(iv) *The variance of policy* $\beta(1-\beta)(\bar{q}_2 - \bar{q}_1)^2$ *diminishes with independence:* $\bar{q}_2^A - \bar{q}_1^A = \Delta q^A > \Delta q^I = \bar{q}_2^I - \bar{q}_1^I$.

With our quadratic specifications, the commitment effect and the stabilization effect just compensate each other in the first period so that the corresponding output is independent of the legal status of the agency. As a result, the distribution of policies over time also has a reduced mean to better fit P_1 's strong preferences for rent extraction. Granting political independence to the agency is a way for P_1 to commit to move policies in both periods toward his ideal policy. Independence of the agency stabilizes political fluctuations over time, but it also shifts downward the intertemporal distribution of outputs around a lower mean.

By the mere design of the legal status of the agency and its first-period mandate, P_1 incorporates the preferences of his own constituency into future policies even if those policies are run by another political principal who has different preferences on the rent-efficiency tradeoff. Today's majority sees its own preferences represented in the policies chosen by tomorrow's majority. This leads to a significant regulatory inertia.

To better highlight this effect, it is worth identifying $\bar{q}_2^I$ with the optimal policy that would have been chosen by a fictitious second-period principal having preferences on the rent-efficiency tradeoff given by a parameter α_2' and dealing with an affiliated agency. With our quadratic specification of preferences, this identification leads immediately to

$$\alpha_2' = \left(\frac{\beta}{y-1+\beta}\right)\alpha_1 + \left(\frac{y-1}{y-1+\beta}\right)\alpha_2. \tag{17}$$

Hence, the modified preferences of the second-period principal are a weighted average of his own preferences and those of the first-period principal. As the first period lasts relatively longer (*i.e.*, as β gets larger), the weight on the first-period principal's preferences increases and the second-period policy looks more like the first-period one. A first-period principal finds it easier to incorporate his own preferences into future policies when he remains in power for a longer period. Through the political process, an implicit collusion takes place between P_1 and the independent regulator. It then becomes harder for a new majority to get effective control on the independent bureaucracy that pursues its initial mandate.

Our model fits nicely with the evidence reported by some political scientists. In their important work on the articulation between elected political principals and the bureaucracy, Wood and Waterman (1994, p. 143) argued that

> when political principals create a bureaucracy to implement a legitimated public policy, they establish a contract between current democratic principal and the new bureaucracy. The terms of this contract are contained in the legal authority, mission statement, constraints and design of the new agency. As the new agency develops through time, the terms of this original contract are altered through changing law and new legal interpretations. However, these are often marginal adjustments to the original contract between past democratic principals and the bureaucracy. Bureaucracy remains bounded by law, administrative constraints and structural incentives.

The same authors (p. 145) also reckon that "bureaucracies represent past democratic coalitions against future majorities… Thus, bureaucracies perform an integrative function for U.S. democracy. They blend demands from past democratic coalitions with those from current democratic coalitions to produce a policy output at a consistent level." Equation (17) shows how this aggregating procedure takes place and what its main determinants are.

In particular, it is also worth noting that as transaction costs become more convex (*i.e.*, as r gets larger or y smaller while still keeping the constraint $y > 1$), the incentives of the firm and the regulator for smoothing bribes over time become stronger. Long-term collusion is much more efficient than a pair of short-term side contracts, and preventing long-term capture is much more costly than preventing short-term capture. This exacerbates the link between today's and tomorrow's policy, and it makes the second-period principal look more like the first-period one.

7 Endogenous Design of the Agency's Legal Status

We can now move one step back and ask whether P_1 would propose to enact legislation granting political independence to the agency and, more generally, what consequences this legal status would hold for the welfare of various groups in society.

7.1 Choice of the Legal Status by the First-Period Principal

As discussed in Section 5, granting political independence to an agency presents some benefits for P_1 because it gives him some effective leverage on future policies. However, it also opens new strategic possibilities for collusion between this long-lived regulator and the interest group. This increases the regulatory wage bill paid by P_1's constituency. Indeed, for a given pair of outputs $\bar{q}_1$ and $\bar{q}_2$, preventing the long-term collusion hurts both principals since $k(\cdot)$ is concave and a new costly long-term collusion-proofness constraint must be satisfied. Independence is associated with an increase in the wage bill needed to control the regulator. *A priori*, it is not clear which of those two effects dominates.

The next proposition shows that in our quadratic example, the leverage effect always dominates and ensures that independence is the most preferred legal status from P_1's viewpoint.

We denote by SW_1^A (respectively, SW_1^I) the intertemporal welfare of P_1's constituency with affiliated agencies (respectively, an independent agency).

Proposition 5. *Assume quadratic utilities. Then for all* $\beta \in)0, 1]$, P_1 *always prefers an independent agency to a sequence of affiliated agencies. Moreover, the difference in* P_1*'s intertemporal expected welfare between the two organizations is*

$$SW_1^I - SW_1^A = \frac{\beta(1-\beta)\nu\Delta\alpha^2(1-\varepsilon)^2}{2r\varepsilon(y-1)(y-1+\beta)} \geq 0. \tag{18}$$

The main conclusion of our analysis is that a biased political principal voluntarily gives up independence to the agency to constrain future political principals. *De facto*, the first-period principal and the independent agency are thus implicitly colluding against the second-period principal.

The preferences of the first-period principal remain somewhat incorporated into the policy outcome implemented in the future, and this inertia gives some long-lasting effect to the first-period optimal policy.

Finally, looking at the right-hand side of (18), we note that a greater degree of political polarization ($\Delta\alpha$ larger) and a greater cost uncertainty ($\Delta\theta$ larger) both increase the benefits of independence. Indeed, these parameters exacerbate the principals' conflict on the amount of information rents left to the firm and the fluctuations that the political game induces on regulatory policies.

When β goes to zero, the first-period principal has almost no leverage on the future policy, which is close to its value with affiliated regulators, and hence the benefit of independence vanishes. Similarly, when β is close to one, the second period does not count much, and again the benefit of independence disappears.

7.2 Impact on the Interest Group

Taking now the perspective of the interest group, we have the following result:

Proposition 6. *For all* $\beta \in)0, 1]$, *independence of the agency hurts the regulated firm.*

Since average output is reduced under independence, the firm's expected information rent is lower than with affiliated agencies. Even though, *a priori*, the newly opened strategic possibilities between the long-lived regulator and the firm increase the costs of ensuring collusion-proofness from the principals' collective viewpoint, their collective response to the threat of capture makes the regulatory policies significantly more stringent, and this definitively hurts the firm. This conclusion would be reversed if the first-period principal was less concerned about rent extraction than the second-period one. In this case, independence shifts output and rent up toward P_2's ideal policy, and this unambiguously favors the regulated firm. More generally, the interest group is better off when the legal status of the agency is chosen by the government that is the least adverse to his interests.

7.3 Impact on the Regulator(s)

We now compare the total wage bill paid to regulator(s) under either affiliated agencies and independence.

Proposition 7. *For all* $\beta \in)0, 1]$, *independence of the agency hurts the bureaucracy:* $\beta s_1^A + (1 - \beta)s_2^A > \beta s_1^I + (1 - \beta)s_2^I$.

Once the reactions of both principals to the threat of collusion are taken into account, independence of the agency reduces the average output and its variance. The first effect reduces the regulatory stakes in both periods and tends to reduce the intertemporal wage bill of the regulator. The variance effect tends, on the contrary, to increase this wage bill. Overall, the first effect dominates, so that the independent regulator would like to commit himself *ex ante* to behave as an affiliated regulator in both periods. Even though, *ex post*, *i.e.*, after the first-period policy has been chosen, a long-term collusion between the interest group becomes a desirable strategy, the regulator ends up being hurt by the strategic policy choice made by P_1.

It should be stressed that this conclusion depends on the sequencing. If P_1 is less eager to extract information rent than P_2, the average output is greater under independence, and this unambiguously increases the regulator's bill, making him prefer independence.

7.4 Impact on Social Welfare

The question we want to address here is whether the independence of the agency is a good or a bad thing from a social welfare perspective. In other words, we wonder whether the regulator is a good defender of social welfare in a world where political principals pursue their own biased objectives. To measure social welfare, we assume that a social planner would maximize the same kind of objective function as each principal except that α_i is now replaced in both periods by $\hat{\alpha} = \beta\alpha_1 + (1-\beta)\alpha_2$. Hence the planner, if he were empowered, would maximize a weighted average of both principals' objective functions with a weight proportional to the length of the period where each is in power.

Let us denote by $\hat{SW}^I - \hat{SW}^A$ the social welfare difference between the case of independent and affiliated agencies. Since the only difference between this planner and the biased principal P_1 comes from the weight they respectively put on the efficient firm's information rent, we immediately obtain

$$\hat{SW}^I - \hat{SW}^A = [SW_1^I - SW_1^A]$$
$$+ [\nu(1-\varepsilon)\Delta\alpha\Delta\theta(1-\beta)(\beta q_1^I + (1-\beta)q_2^I - (\beta q_1^A + (1-\beta)q_2^A))].$$

The planner's assessment of the benefit of independence is the sum of P_1's own assessment (the first bracketed term) plus a new term characterizing the conflict of interest between P_1 and the planner on the intertemporal distribution of information rents left to the firm (the second bracketed term). Taking into account that $\bar{q}_1^I = \bar{q}_1^A$ and that $\bar{q}_2^I < \bar{q}_2^A$, we observe that the second bracketed term above is negative. Indeed, the delegation to an independent agency leads to a bias toward the preferences of P_1, and thus there is not enough output being produced and less information rent left to the firm with respect to what a planner would also like.

Proposition 8. *Assume quadratic utilities. Then the social planner prefers an independent agency to a sequence of affiliated agencies if and only if $\beta > 1/2$. Moreover, the difference in intertemporal social welfare between the two organizations is*

$$\hat{SW}^I - \hat{SW}^A = \frac{\beta(1-\beta)\left(\beta - \frac{1}{2}\right)\nu\Delta\alpha^2(1-\varepsilon)^2}{2r\varepsilon(y-1)(y-1+\beta)}. \tag{19}$$

When the future matters a lot in the social planner's objective function, *i.e.*, β close to zero, the planner wants to protect the interests of the future majority against the expropriation that occurs if the current majority chooses an independent agency. Hence, the planner prefers the affiliated regulators. On the other hand, when the present matters a lot, the weight on the preferences of the current majority dominates in the planner's objective function, and the latter prefers to choose an independent agency. In this case, there is enough congruence of interests between the biased first-period political principal and the social planner to ensure that delegating the choice of the agency's legal status to this first-period principal is socially optimal.

8 Concluding Remarks

We have investigated the origins of regulatory inertia in a dynamic model stressing the complex relationship between a captured bureaucracy and its biased political principals at different points in time. We have also analyzed the incentives of a first-period principal to grant independence to this agency to strategically constrain his successors, and the consequences of this institutional choice on social welfare and the distribution of rents in the economy.

Let us now briefly investigate how our results could be extended.

8.1 More Than Two Periods

Successive principals who alternate in power are still willing to influence future policies, and this would lead to a more complex aggregation of the preferences of past democratic coalitions into future policies. Those principals all want to take advantage of the commitment effects to constrain their successors. One can conjecture that the commitment abilities of successive principals might somewhat compensate each other and that only the stabilization effect could remain in the long run. "Middle-of-the-road" policies close to the socially optimal ones are very likely to be implemented, with political changes having very little impact on actual policies and with lots of autonomy (interpreted as an increase in the scope for capture) left to the bureaucracy. This gives a cynical view of bureaucrats as *de facto* defenders of the social welfare even though they are captured. Bureaucrats do not have preferences that are *a priori* aligned with those of a social planner, but their desire to insulate themselves from short-term political pressures nevertheless moves policies closer to those that the planner prefers. This tendency of bureaucrats to identity themselves as defenders of public interests has been noticed by several sociologists of the state, such as Nordlinger (1981) and Skocpol (1985).

8.2 Information Structure

To avoid the technical complexities associated with the ratchet effect, we have assumed that the outcome of the first-period regulatory policy was not known by the second-period political principal. The consideration of imperfect information revelation might reinforce our findings, at least, with the sequence of political principals used in the text. If first-period reports are known by P_2, both the regulator and the firm would hide information from P_1 in order to preserve some rent in the second period.

A partial revelation of the efficient firm's type in the first period tends to be favorable to this firm later on, since a second-period principal who does not observe full revelation becomes more pessimistic on the firm's type. If so, P_2 is less concerned by rent extraction, which is analogous to an increase in α_2. As $\alpha_1 < \alpha_2$, imperfect information revelation increases the conflict of interests between the first- and second-period political principals. Therefore, the bureaucracy's desire for stabilized policies is exacerbated, possibly leading to stronger stabilization and commitment effects. Note nevertheless that the ratchet effect reduces this conflict of interests if instead P_2 is the first-period political principal. The stabilization and the commitment effects are then reduced but still exist.

8.3 Fluctuations in the Cost of Public Funds

Our methodology could also shed some lights on the resistance to changes in regulatory policies when shocks other than political ones affect the rent-efficiency tradeoff of the government. Consider, for instance, exogenous economic shocks like increases in the state deficit that affect its budget constraint at different points in time. Because of those shocks, the cost of public funds may vary, with a higher cost being associated with a hardening of the budget constraint. As the social cost of the budget allocated to regulatory policies varies over time, the tradeoff between efficiency and rent extraction that a given political principal is willing to implement at different dates may change. Here also, the principal may be willing to tie his hands against his anticipated future incentives to expand or contract the size of regulation by giving up independence to an agency.

8.4 Endogenous elections

Our modelling of the second-period election has been very crude, since we assumed that the identity of the political principal changes for sure at this date. Adding some randomness to the outcome of this election is a straightforward extension of our framework, as long as this randomness is exogenous. If there is only a probability p (respectively, $1-p$) that P_2 (respectively, P_1) is elected, the weight of his policy in the intertemporal collusive stake is $(1-\beta)p$, and some political uncertainty in the second period exacerbates regulatory inertia. However, new interesting feedback is likely to emerge when one endogenizes the probabilities that each principal gets elected. The stabilization effects induce convergence of policies and thus increase political competition for voters whose preferences lie between those of P_1 and P_2.

Appendix

Proofs of Propositions 2–6 and 8 follow.

Proof of Proposition 2. For a given first-period regulatory contract (*i.e.*, a given $(s_1, \bar{q}_1)$), we describe the collusive game with an independent regulator. The collusion phase takes place at stage 3 between an independent regulator and the interest group; we suppose that the regulator has learned $\sigma = \underline{\theta}$, and we describe this phase in detail below.

(iii)(a) The firm makes a collusive (and secret) offer to the regulator. This contract stipulates a positive bribe τ_i to the regulator if he hides information at date i and reports $\hat{\sigma}_i = \varnothing$, and zero otherwise. Note that this side contract may entail four different configurations of reports over both periods, namely $(\hat{\sigma}_1, \hat{\sigma}_2) = (\varnothing, \varnothing)$, $(\hat{\sigma}_1, \hat{\sigma}_2) = (\varnothing, \underline{\theta})$, $(\hat{\sigma}_1, \hat{\sigma}_2) = (\underline{\theta}, \varnothing)$, and $(\hat{\sigma}_1, \hat{\sigma}_2) = (\underline{\theta}, \underline{\theta})$. Therefore, taking into account the fact that bribes are zero when $(\hat{\sigma}_1, \hat{\sigma}_2) = (\underline{\theta}, \underline{\theta})$ (interpreting this as the absence of collusion), we will write a side contract as a triplet $\{(\tau_1, \tau_2); \hat{\tau}_1; \hat{\tau}_2\}$, where the three different components correspond respectively to $(\hat{\sigma}_1, \hat{\sigma}_2) = (\varnothing, \varnothing)$, $(\hat{\sigma}_1, \hat{\sigma}_2) = (\varnothing, \underline{\theta})$, and $(\hat{\sigma}_1, \hat{\sigma}_2) = (\underline{\theta}, \varnothing)$. The firm commits to such a side contract. Also, in any long-term collusive agreement, we assume that the regulator receives the benefit from collusion (in both periods) only after his second-period report.[26]

(iii)(b) The regulator decides which manipulation he makes, if any. If the regulator's reports are uninformative, the firm reports its information $\hat{\theta}_i$ directly to P_i.

Given that P_1 has already chosen his regulatory instruments, the firm and P_2 act in fact as two principals who are both willing to influence the regulator's decision to report the truth or not. When the efficient firm makes its offer, it knows that the regulator is informed about its type, and it anticipates the regulatory contract that will be

26. One can imagine that the collusive partners use a risk-neutral third party to post a bond that is worth his first-period net benefit from manipulating the first-period report. The third party then releases this money at date 2 only if the regulator still continues to hide the informative signal from P_2.

offered by P_2. We denote by $(s_2^e, \bar{q}_2^e)$ this expectation. On the other hand, P_2 does not observe the side contract and forms beliefs on which side contract is signed. Since first-period reports are not observed by P_2, P_2 does not know whether the side contract stipulates a truthful report at date 1 or not. We denote by $\hat{\tau}_2^{2e}$ P_2's expectation about bribe exchanges for a manipulation $(\underline{\theta}, \varnothing)$ and by (τ_1^e, τ_2^e) P_2's expectations about bribes exchanges for a manipulation $(\varnothing, \varnothing)$. Note that in any pure-strategy equilibrium, P_2's beliefs have point mass on $\{(\tau_1^e, \tau_2^e); \hat{\tau}_1^e, \hat{\tau}_2^e\}$.

Because the game is of incomplete information, we look for its perfect Bayesian equilibria (PBE). Thanks to the fact that first-period reports are not observed, there is no scope for updating P_2's beliefs about which side contract has been signed following a first-period report. Nevertheless, P_2's offer will depend on how he expects the regulator to react to any unexpected offer he may make. Consistent with a PBE, following any such offer, the regulator's behavior remains sequentially optimal: he hides information from P_2 if he finds it optimal to do so following any P_2's offer. We are interested in characterizing equilibria of this game where collusion does not occur. This means that the preferred reports of the regulator should always be $(\underline{\theta}, \underline{\theta})$.

To do so, we start by characterizing the best-response functions of the second-period players.

The regulator's behavior. The regulator refuses to collude whenever his wage exceeds the bribes he can get by manipulating information. This yields the following constraints:

$$s_1 \geq k(\hat{\tau}_1), \tag{A1}$$

$$s_2^e \geq k(\hat{\tau}_2), \tag{A2}$$

$$s_2^e \geq \frac{\beta}{1-\beta}(k(\tau_1) - s_1) + k(\tau_2). \tag{A3}$$

This last equation takes into account that the net benefit of date-1 manipulation accrues only at date 2 and must be counted in date-2 money.

Note that the regulator's decision not to collude on the second-period report can change if P_2 deviates and makes an unexpected offer $(s_2, \bar{q}_2) \neq (s_2^e, \bar{q}_2^e)$. Refusing to collude in that second period is then sequentially optimal when

$$s_2 \geq k(\hat{\tau}_2), \tag{A4}$$

$$s_2 \geq \frac{\beta}{1-\beta}(k(\tau_1) - s_1) + k(\tau_2). \tag{A5}$$

P_2's behavior. To avoid collusion in the second period, P_2 must offer a wage s_2 such that both manipulations $(\underline{\theta}, \varnothing)$ and $(\varnothing, \varnothing)$ are prevented. Again, $\hat{\tau}_2^e$ and (τ_1^e, τ_2^e) denote the bribes that P_2 expects under either of these manipulations. P_2's payoff is maximum when the wage he offers is the minimal one satisfying both (A4) and (A5) for those bribes. It is

$$s_2 = \max\left\{\frac{\beta}{1-\beta}(k(\tau_1^e) - s_1) + k(\tau_2^e);\ k(\hat{\tau}_2^e)\right\}. \tag{A6}$$

P_2 does not deviate by inducing collusion when it is less costly to pay this wage than to leave a costly information rent to the efficient firm:

$$\max\left\{\frac{\beta}{1-\beta}(k(\tau_1^e) - s_1) + k(\tau_2^e);\ k(\hat{\tau}_2^e)\right\} \le (1-\alpha_2)\Delta\theta\bar{q}_2. \tag{A7}$$

The firm's behavior. In any equilibrium without collusion, F should not want to deviate and offer a side contract $\{(\tau_1, \tau_2); \hat{\tau}_1; \hat{\tau}_2\}$, which induces a manipulation of reports.

We now compute the maximal payoff of the firm for any possible nontruthful deviations $(\hat{\sigma}_1, \hat{\sigma}_2) \neq (\underline{\theta}, \underline{\theta})$. Denote by $U(\hat{\sigma}_1, \hat{\sigma}_2)$ the intertemporal rent of the efficient firm under any of these configurations. Of course, $U(\underline{\theta}, \underline{\theta}) = 0$, since truthful reports are followed by full rent extraction by the principal holding office at any date. In any equilibrium where collusion does not occur, we must thus have $U(\hat{\sigma}_1, \hat{\sigma}_2) = 0 \quad \forall(\hat{\sigma}_1, \hat{\sigma}_2) \neq (\varnothing, \varnothing)$.

Let us first consider the case where the side contract induces the manipulation $(\hat{\sigma}_1, \hat{\sigma}_2) = (\varnothing, \varnothing)$. Taking as fixed the expectations of the regulator and the firm on the wage s_2^e offered by P_2, the side contract induces manipulations in both periods if

$$\beta s_1 + (1-\beta)s_2^e \le \beta k(\tau_1) + (1-\beta)k(\tau_2), \tag{A8}$$

$$\beta s_1 + (1-\beta)k(\hat{\tau}_2) \le \beta k(\tau_1) + (1-\beta)k(\tau_2), \tag{A9}$$

$$\beta k(\hat{\tau}_1) + (1-\beta)s_2^e \le \beta k(\tau_1) + (1-\beta)k(\tau_2). \tag{A10}$$

The best of such deviations is obtained when (A9) and (A10) are relaxed as much as possible, *i.e.*, when $\hat{\tau}_1 = \hat{\tau}_2 = 0$ and then only (A8) matters. The maximal payoff obtained with such a deviation is thus

$$U(\varnothing, \varnothing) = \max_{(\tau_1, \tau_2)} \beta(\Delta\theta\bar{q}_1 - \tau_1) + (1-\beta)(\Delta\theta\bar{q}_2^e - \tau_2)$$

subject to (A8).

Solving this problem yields a constant bribe $\tau_1 = \tau_2 = k^{-1}(\beta s_1 + (1-\beta)s_2^e)$ and $U(\varnothing, \varnothing) = \Delta\theta(\beta q_1 + (1-\beta)q_2^e) - k^{-1}(\beta s_1 + (1-\beta)s_2^e)$. Inducing the regulator to report $(\varnothing, \varnothing)$ is thus dominated from F's viewpoint by inducing $(\underline{\theta}, \underline{\theta})$ when

$$\Delta\theta(\beta q_1 + (1-\beta)q_2^e) - k^{-1}(\beta s_1 + (1-\beta)s_2^e) \le 0 . \qquad \text{(A11)}$$

Let us now consider the case where the side contract induces the report $(\hat{\sigma}_1, \hat{\sigma}_2) = (\underline{\theta}, \varnothing)$. This is the case when

$$\beta s_1 + (1-\beta)s_2^e \le \beta s_1 + (1-\beta)k(\hat{\tau}_2), \qquad \text{(A12)}$$

$$\beta k(\tau_1) + (1-\beta)k(\tau_2) \le \beta s_1 + (1-\beta)k(\hat{\tau}_2). \qquad \text{(A13)}$$

$$\beta k(\hat{\tau}_1) + (1-\beta)s_2^e \le \beta s_1 + (1-\beta)k(\hat{\tau}_2). \qquad \text{(A14)}$$

The best of such deviations is obtained when (A13) and (A14) are relaxed as much as possible, and this is the case for $\tau_1 = \tau_2 = \hat{\tau}_1 = 0$. Only (A12) matters then. We thus have

$$U(\underline{\theta}, \varnothing) = \max_{\hat{\tau}_2} (1-\beta)(\Delta\theta\bar{q}_2^e - \hat{\tau}_2)$$

subject to (A12).

Solving this problem yields $\hat{\tau}_2 = k^{-1}(s_2^e)$ and $U(\underline{\theta}, \varnothing) = (1-\beta)(\Delta\theta\bar{q}_2^e - k^{-1}(s_2^e))$. Inducing $(\underline{\theta}, \varnothing)$ is thus dominated by $(\underline{\theta}, \underline{\theta})$ when

$$\Delta\theta\bar{q}_2^e - k^{-1}(s_2^e) \le 0 . \qquad \text{(A15)}$$

Finally, let us now consider the case where the side contract induces the report $(\hat{\sigma}_1, \hat{\sigma}_2) = (\varnothing, \underline{\theta})$. Proceeding exactly as above, we find that $\hat{\tau}_1 = k^{-1}(s_1)$ and $U(\varnothing, \underline{\theta}) = \beta(\Delta\theta\bar{q}_1 - k^{-1}(s_1))$. Inducing the report $(\varnothing, \underline{\theta})$ is dominated by $(\underline{\theta}, \underline{\theta})$ when

$$\Delta\theta\bar{q}_1 - k^{-1}(s_1) \le 0 . \qquad \text{(A16)}$$

Equilibrium characterization. In equilibrium, expectations must be correct. An equilibrium where collusion does not occur is thus a vector $\{(s_2, \bar{q}_2); (\tau_1, \tau_2); \hat{\tau}_1; \hat{\tau}_2\}$ that satisfies inequalities (A1), (A4), (A5), (A6), (A7), (A11), (A15), and (A16) taken for correct expectations. Rewriting these constraints accordingly, they become

$$s_2 \ge \max\,\{k(\hat{\tau}_2), k(\Delta\theta\bar{q}_2)\}, \qquad \text{(A17)}$$

$$s_1 \ge \max\,\{k(\hat{\tau}_1), k(\Delta\theta\bar{q}_1)\}, \qquad \text{(A18)}$$

$$\beta s_1 + (1-\beta)s_2 \ge \max\,\{k(\Delta\theta(\beta\bar{q}_1 + (1-\beta)\bar{q}_2)), \beta k(\tau_1) + (1-\beta)k(\tau_2)\}, \qquad \text{(A19)}$$

$$s_2 = \max\left\{\frac{\beta}{1-\beta}(k(\tau_1)-s_1)+k(\tau_2);\, k(\hat{\tau}_2)\right\}, \tag{A20}$$

$$\max\left\{\frac{\beta}{1-\beta}(k(\tau_1)-s_1)+k(\tau_2);\, k(\hat{\tau}_2)\right\} \le (1-\alpha_2)\Delta\theta\bar{q}_2, \tag{A21}$$

$$\beta s_1 + (1-\beta)s_2 \ge k(\Delta\theta(\beta\bar{q}_1+(1-\beta)\bar{q}_2)), \tag{A22}$$

$$s_2 \ge k(\Delta\theta\bar{q}_2), \tag{A23}$$

$$s_1 \ge k(\Delta\theta\bar{q}_1). \tag{A24}$$

There are many possible equilibria to this game. To refine among those equilibria, we follow Grossman and Helpman (1994) and define a *truthful schedule* for the firm if F gets the same payoff, *i.e.*, zero, for all actions $(\hat{\sigma}_1, \hat{\sigma}_2)$ it may induce even the nonequilibrium ones. In this case, F does not play any dominated strategy. In our context, this implies $\hat{\tau}_2 = \Delta\theta\bar{q}_2$, $\hat{\tau}_1 = \Delta\theta\bar{q}_1$, and $\tau_1 = \tau_2 = k(\Delta\theta(\beta\bar{q}_1+(1-\beta)\bar{q}_2))$. Simplifying the set of constraints above then yields constraints (10) to (12). ■

Proof of Proposition 3 *(continuation contract).* To make the description of the continuation contract offered by P_2 easier, let us denote by $\hat{\bar{q}}_2(s_1, \bar{q}_1)$ the solution to

$$\beta s_1 + (1-\beta)k(\Delta\theta\bar{q}_2) = k(\Delta\theta(\beta\bar{q}_1+(1-\beta)\bar{q}_2)).$$

For a given pair $(s_1, \bar{q}_1)$, $\hat{\bar{q}}_2(s_1, \bar{q}_1)$ is the value of the second-period output that ensures that both collusion-proofness constraints (11) and (12) are as costly from P_2's point of view. With this output, it costs the same for P_2 to prevent long-term collusion having started at date 1 or short-term collusion starting at date 2 only.

Proposition A1. Fix the first-period regulatory contract, the continuation contract offered by P_2 for date 2 is such that

(i) The optimal output of the efficient firm is always equal to its first-best value $\underline{q}_2(s_1, \bar{q}_1) = q_2(s_1, \bar{q}_1) = \underline{q}^{FB}$.

(ii) The optimal output of the inefficient firm $\bar{q}_2(s_1, \bar{q}_1)$ is downward distorted with respect to its value with an affiliated agency $\bar{q}_2(s_1, \bar{q}_1) \le \bar{q}_2^A$. Moreover, we have

Regime 1. If $\hat{\bar{q}}_2(s_1, \bar{q}_1) \le \bar{q}_2^r(\bar{q}_1)$, then $\bar{q}_2(s_1, \bar{q}_1) = \bar{q}_2^r(\bar{q}_1)$ and the output implemented at the continuation contract depends on $\bar{q}_1$. The regulator's wage at date 2 is

$$s_2(s_1, \bar{q}_1) = \frac{1}{1-\beta}(k(\Delta\theta(\beta\bar{q}_1+(1-\beta)\bar{q}_2^r(\bar{q}_1))) - \beta s_1).$$

Regime 2. If $\bar{q}_2^A \geq \hat{\bar{q}}_2(s_1, \bar{q}_1) \geq \bar{q}_2^r(\bar{q}_1)$, then $\bar{q}_2(s_1, \bar{q}_1) = \hat{\bar{q}}_2(s_1, \bar{q}_1)$ and the output implemented at the continuation contract depends on both $\bar{q}_1$ and s_1. Moreover, it is increasing in s_1. The regulator's wage at date 2 is

$$s_2(s_1, \bar{q}_1) = \frac{1}{1-\beta}(k(\Delta\theta(\beta\bar{q}_1 + (1-\beta)\hat{\bar{q}}_2(s_1, \bar{q}_1))) - \beta s_1)$$

$$= k(\Delta\theta\hat{\bar{q}}_2(s_1, \bar{q}_1)).$$

Regime 3. If $\hat{\bar{q}}_2(s_1, \bar{q}_1) \geq \bar{q}_2^A$, then $\bar{q}_2(s_1, \bar{q}_1) = \bar{q}_2^A$ and the output implemented at the continuation contract is the same as with an affiliated agency. The regulator's wage at date 2 is

$$s_2(s_1, \bar{q}_1) = k(\Delta\theta\bar{q}_2^A).$$

In any solution to P_2's problem, it must be that either (11), (12), or both constraints are binding, since P_2 wants to reduce as much as possible the wage s_2 offered to a regulator when he reveals his informative signal.

Observe that when $\bar{q}_2 \leq \hat{\bar{q}}_2(s_1, \bar{q}_1)$, (11) implies (12), and (11) is thus the harder collusion-proofness constraint to satisfy. Inserting the corresponding value of s_2 into P_2's concave objective function and optimizing with respect to the inefficient firm's output over the set of relevant outputs yields $\bar{q}_2(s_1, \bar{q}_1) = \min(\hat{\bar{q}}_2(s_1, \bar{q}_1), \bar{q}_2^A)$. Of course, the optimization still results in the first-best output being offered to the efficient firm.

Observe also that when $\bar{q}_2 \geq \hat{\bar{q}}_2(s_1, \bar{q}_1)$, (12) now implies (11), and (12) is thus the harder collusion-proofness constraint to satisfy.

Inserting the corresponding value of s_2 into P_2's objective function and optimizing with respect to inefficient firm's output over the set of relevant outputs now yields $\bar{q}_2(s_1, \bar{q}_1) = \max(\hat{\bar{q}}_2(s_1, \bar{q}_1), \bar{q}_2^r(\bar{q}_1))$.

Note now that P_2's objective function is continuous in s_1 and that $\bar{q}_2^r(\bar{q}_1) < \bar{q}_2^A$. Hence, starting from a value s_1 satisfying (11) at date 1, three successive regimes must be considered when s_1 increases:

Regime 1. $\hat{\bar{q}}_2(s_1, \bar{q}_1) \leq \bar{q}_2^r(\bar{q}_1)$, then $\bar{q}_2^r(\bar{q}_1)$ is the optimal second-period output. (12) is the only binding collusion-proofness constraint. A second-period output in Regime 1 obtains when $\hat{\bar{q}}_2(s_1, \bar{q}_1) \leq \bar{q}_2^r(\bar{q}_1)$, and it is worth $\bar{q}_2^r(\bar{q}_1)$ with associated regulatory wage $s_2 = [1/(1-\beta)](k(\Delta\theta(\beta\bar{q}_1 + (1-\beta)\bar{q}_2^r(\bar{q}_1))) - \beta s_1)$.

Regime 2. $\bar{q}_2^A \geq \hat{\bar{q}}_2(s_1, \bar{q}_1) \geq \bar{q}_2^r(\bar{q}_1)$, then $\hat{\bar{q}}_2(s_1, \bar{q}_1)$ is the optimal second-period output, which is at a kink of P_2's objective function. Both (11) and (12) are binding. A second-period output in Regime 2 is obtained when $\bar{q}_2^A \geq \hat{\bar{q}}_2(s_1, \bar{q}_1) \geq \bar{q}_2^r(\bar{q}_1)$, and it is worth $\hat{\bar{q}}_2(s_1, \bar{q}_1)$ with associated $s_2 = [1/(1-\beta)] (k(\Delta\theta(\beta\bar{q}_1 + (1-\beta)\hat{\bar{q}}_2(s_1, \bar{q}_1))) - \beta s_1) = k(\Delta\theta\hat{\bar{q}}_2(s_1, \bar{q}_1))$.

Regime 3. $\bar{q}_2^A \leq \hat{\bar{q}}_2(s_1, \bar{q}_1)$, then $\bar{q}_2^A$ is the optimal second-period output. (11) is the only binding collusion-proofness constraint. A second-period output in Regime 3 is obtained when $\bar{q}_2^A \leq \hat{\bar{q}}_2(s_1, \bar{q}_1)$, and it is worth $\bar{q}_2^A$ with associated regulatory wage $\underline{s}_2^* = k(\Delta\theta\bar{q}_2^A)$.

As can be easily seen, (11) at date 1 is (or can be) satisfied in all regimes above.

Fix $\bar{q}_1$; as s_1 continuously increases, all possible second-period outputs for an inefficient firm belong to the nonempty interval $[\bar{q}_2^r(\bar{q}_1), \bar{q}_2^A]$. Moreover, this whole interval is covered and, in any case, output is downward distorted with respect to the second-best value.

Note that for $\bar{q}_2 \leq \hat{\bar{q}}_2(s_1, \bar{q}_1)$, (11) is binding and, by assumption, $k'(\tau) \leq k(\tau)/\tau < 1 - \alpha_2$ for all τ and thus $k(\Delta\theta\bar{q}_2) < (1-\alpha_2)\Delta\theta\bar{q}_2$. Hence, for such outputs, it is less costly to pay the regulator for having information than to pay the firm. (10) is satisfied. Now define

$$f(x) = (1-\alpha_2)\Delta\theta x - \frac{k(\Delta\theta(\beta\bar{q}_1 + (1-\beta)x)) - \beta s_1}{1-\beta}.$$

We have $f'(x) = \Delta\theta((1-\alpha_2) - k'(\Delta\theta(\beta\bar{q}_1 + (1-\beta)x))) > 0$ again by assumption on the technology of collusion $k(\cdot)$. Since $f(\hat{\bar{q}}_2(s_1, \bar{q}_1)) = (1-\alpha_2)\Delta\theta\hat{\bar{q}}_2(s_1, \bar{q}_1) - k(\Delta\theta\hat{\bar{q}}_2(s_1, \bar{q}_1)) > 0$, we have $f(\bar{q}_2) > 0$ for all $\bar{q}_2 > \hat{\bar{q}}_2(s_1, \bar{q}_1)$, and thus it is less costly to satisfy the collusion-proofness constraint (12) than to obtain information directly from the firm for all such $\bar{q}_2$. Hence, paying the regulator is less costly than letting collusion occur for $\bar{q}_2 \geq \hat{\bar{q}}_2(s_1, \bar{q}_1)$.

The optimal first-period contract. The proof proceeds through several steps.

Step 1: optimization with respect to s_1. We first fix $\bar{q}_1$ and we optimize over all s_1, knowing that P_2 offers a collusion-proof contract for β small enough. As has been shown in the proof of Proposition A1, varying s_1 amounts to varying $\bar{q}_2 \in [\bar{q}_2^r(\bar{q}_1), \bar{q}_2^A]$. Moreover, one can describe this whole interval while still satisfying (6) at date 1. Note also that for s_1 sufficiently large, $\bar{q}_2^A$ is implemented by P_2 for any s_1.

For all these $\bar{q}_2$, (12) is binding and one can substitute $\beta s_1 + (1-\beta)s_2$ by $k(\Delta\theta(\beta\bar{q}_1 + (1-\beta)\bar{q}_2))$ into P_1's intertemporal payoff. P_1 now chooses s_1 (satisfying (6) at date 1), and thus indirectly $\bar{q}_2$, to solve the following simplified problem:

$$\max_{\{\bar{q}_2 \in [\bar{q}_2^r(\bar{q}_1), \bar{q}_2^A]\}} SW_1^I(\bar{q}_1, \bar{q}_2),$$

where $SW_1^I(\bar{q}_1, \bar{q}_2) = \beta((1-\nu)(S(\bar{q}_1) - \bar{\theta}\bar{q}_1) - \nu(1-\varepsilon)(1-\alpha_1)\Delta\theta\bar{q}_1)) + (1-\beta)((1-\nu)(S(\bar{q}_2) - \bar{\theta}\bar{q}_2) - \nu(1-\varepsilon)(1-\alpha_1)\Delta\theta\bar{q}_2) - \nu\varepsilon k(\Delta\theta(\beta\bar{q}_1 + (1-\beta)\bar{q}_2))$ and where it has been taken into account that the second-period rent left to the efficient agent is $\Delta\theta\bar{q}_2$.

The partial derivative of $SW_1^I(\bar{q}_1, \bar{q}_2)$ with respect to $\bar{q}_2$ is

$$(1-\beta)((1-\nu)(S'(\bar{q}_2) - \bar{\theta}) - \Delta\theta(\nu(1-\varepsilon)(1-\alpha_1) - \nu\varepsilon k'(\Delta\theta(\beta\bar{q}_1 + (1-\beta)\bar{q}_2))),$$

which, because $\alpha_2 > \alpha_1$, is inferior to

$$(1-\beta)((1-\nu)(S'(\bar{q}_2) - \bar{\theta}) - \Delta\theta(\nu(1-\varepsilon)(1-\alpha_2) - \nu\varepsilon k'(\Delta\theta(\beta\bar{q}_1 + (1-\beta)\bar{q}_2))) < 0,$$

where the last inequality comes from the fact that $\bar{q}_2 \geq \bar{q}_2^r(\bar{q}_1)$ on the relevant interval of outputs. Hence, $SW_1^I(\bar{q}_1, \bar{q}_2)$ is decreasing over the relevant interval for $\bar{q}_2$ and is thus maximum for $\bar{q}_2^r(\bar{q}_1)$.

Step 2: optimization with respect to $\bar{q}_1$. It is clear that no distortion is implemented on the production of the efficient agent. We can now optimize over $\bar{q}_1$ knowing that $\bar{q}_2^r(\bar{q}_1)$ is implemented at date 2. P_1's simplified problem writes as

$$\max_{\{\bar{q}_1\}} SW_1^I(\bar{q}_1, \bar{q}_2^r(\bar{q}_1)).$$

The solution to this problem yields $\bar{q}_1^I$ as an implicit solution to (16).

Both the commitment and the stabilization effects are positive, and thus $\bar{q}_1^I < \bar{q}_1^{SB}$.

Step 3: values of regulatory transfers. There exists a whole range of transfers s_1 that satisfy (6) at date 1, and such that given this value of s_1, both (12) and (11) are satisfied with (6) being slack. All these transfers can be part of an equilibrium implementing $\bar{q}_2^r(\bar{q}_1)$ at date 2. All these equilibria yield the same intertemporal welfare to P_1. A focal equilibrium may be the one that maximizes P_2's second-period welfare, *i.e.*, the one with the highest s_1. In this equilibrium, transfers are given by

$$s_2^I = k(\Delta\theta\bar{q}_2^r(\bar{q}_1^I))$$

and

$$s_1^I = \frac{k(\Delta\theta(\beta\bar{q}_1^I + (1-\beta)\bar{q}_2^r(\bar{q}_1^I))) - (1-\beta)k(\Delta\theta\bar{q}_2^r(\bar{q}_1^I))}{\beta} > k(\Delta\theta\bar{q}_1^I),$$

where the last inequality comes from the fact that $k(\cdot)$ is concave. ■

Proof of Proposition 4. Under independence, we first observe that $\bar{q}_2^r(\bar{q}_1)$ is now the solution to the following linear equation:

$$\mu - \lambda\bar{q}_2^r(\bar{q}_1) = \bar{\theta}$$

$$+ \frac{\nu}{1-\nu}\Delta\theta((1-\varepsilon)(1-\alpha_2) + \varepsilon(k - r\Delta\theta(\beta\bar{q}_1 + (1-\beta)\bar{q}_2^r(\bar{q}_1)))). \quad \text{(A25)}$$

This immediately yields $\dfrac{\partial\bar{q}_2^r(\bar{q}_1)}{\partial\bar{q}_1} = \dfrac{\beta}{y-1+\beta}$. Inserting this value into (16) yields

$$\mu - \lambda\bar{q}_1^I = \bar{\theta} + \frac{\nu}{1-\nu}\Delta\theta\Big((1-\varepsilon)(1-\alpha_1) + \varepsilon(k - r\Delta\theta(\beta\bar{q}_1^I$$

$$+ (1-\beta)\bar{q}_2^r(\bar{q}_1^I))) + (1-\varepsilon)\Delta\alpha\frac{1-\beta}{y-1+\beta}\Big). \quad \text{(A26)}$$

From (A25) and (A26), we deduce that

$$\Delta q^I = \bar{q}_2^r(\bar{q}_1^I) - \bar{q}_1^I = \frac{\nu\Delta\theta\Delta\alpha(1-\varepsilon)}{(1-\nu)\lambda}\left(\frac{y}{y-1+\beta}\right) > 0.$$

Inserting this expression of Δq^I into (A25), we obtain

$$\mu - \lambda\bar{q}_2^I > \bar{\theta} + \frac{\nu}{1-\nu}\Delta\theta((1-\varepsilon)(1-\alpha_2) + \varepsilon(k - r\Delta\theta\bar{q}_2^I))$$

and $\bar{q}_2^A > \bar{q}_2^I$.

Inserting this expression of Δq^I into (A26) yields

$$\mu - \lambda\bar{q}_1^I = \bar{\theta} + \frac{\nu}{1-\nu}\Delta\theta((1-\varepsilon)(1-\alpha_1) + \varepsilon(k - r\Delta\theta\bar{q}_1^I)),$$

i.e., $\bar{q}_1^I = \bar{q}_1^A$.

Under affiliated agencies, we first observe that $\bar{q}_i^A$ is the solution to the following linear equation:

$$\mu - \lambda\bar{q}_i^A = \bar{\theta} + \frac{\nu}{1-\nu}\Delta\theta((1-\varepsilon)(1-\alpha_i) + \varepsilon(k - r\Delta\theta\bar{q}_i^A)). \quad \text{(A27)}$$

This immediately yields

$$\Delta q^A = \bar{q}_2^A - \bar{q}_1^A = \frac{\nu\Delta\theta\Delta\alpha(1-\varepsilon)}{(1-\nu)\lambda}\left(\frac{y}{y-1}\right).$$

Hence $\Delta q^A > \Delta q^I$, since $y/(y-1) > y/(y-1+\beta)$, which is always true for all $\beta > 0$. ■

Proof of Proposition 5. Since for both an independent and an affiliated regulator, and for both principals, the efficient firm always produces efficiently, the choice of the best legal status from P_1's point of view can be seen just by comparing simplified welfare expressions (*i.e.*, allocative efficiency when the firm is inefficient minus the cost of implementing this allocation in terms of both information rents and regulatory wages). We denote by $SW_1^A = SW_1^A(\bar{q}_1^A, \bar{q}_2^A)$ this reduced-form welfare when agencies are affiliated. Formally, we have

$$\begin{aligned} SW_1^A(\bar{q}_1^A, \bar{q}_2^A) &= \beta((1-\nu)(S(\bar{q}_1^A) - \bar{\theta}\bar{q}_1^A) - \nu(1-\varepsilon)(1-\alpha_1)\Delta\theta\bar{q}_1^A) \\ &\quad + (1-\beta)((1-\nu)(S(\bar{q}_2^A) - \bar{\theta}\bar{q}_2^A) - \nu(1-\varepsilon)(1-\alpha_1)\Delta\theta\bar{q}_2^A) \\ &\quad - \nu\varepsilon(\beta k(\Delta\theta\bar{q}_1^A) + (1-\beta)k(\Delta\theta\bar{q}_2^A)). \end{aligned}$$

The modified welfare with an independent agency writes instead as $SW_1^I(\bar{q}_1^I, \bar{q}_2^I)$.

Note that, ideally, P_1 would also like to implement $\bar{q}_1^A$ at date 2. Using the quadratic specifications, we have

$$\begin{aligned} A &= SW_1^A(\bar{q}_1^A, \bar{q}_2^A) - SW_1^A(\bar{q}_1^A, \bar{q}_1^A) \\ &= -\frac{(1-\beta)\varepsilon(1-\varepsilon)^2 r\nu^3\Delta\theta^4\Delta\alpha^2}{2\lambda^2(1-\nu)^2}\frac{y^2}{y-1} < 0. \end{aligned} \tag{A28}$$

Note that we can write

$$SW_1^I = SW_1^I(\bar{q}_1^I, \bar{q}_2^I) = SW_1^A(\bar{q}_1^A, \bar{q}_2^I) + C,$$

where

$$C = \nu\varepsilon(\beta k(\Delta\theta\bar{q}_1^I) + (1-\beta)k(\Delta\theta\bar{q}_2^I) - k(\Delta\theta(\beta\bar{q}_1^I + (1-\beta)\bar{q}_2^I))).$$

C represents the difference in agency costs to prevent collusion with the regulator between the affiliated agency case and the independent agency case if the outputs of the independent case are implemented. This is a negative number by the fact that $k(\cdot)$ is concave.

With quadratic specifications,

$$\begin{aligned} C &= -\frac{\nu\varepsilon r\Delta\theta^2\beta(1-\beta)}{2}(\Delta\bar{q}^I)^2 \\ &= -\frac{r\Delta\theta^4\beta(1-\beta)\nu^3\varepsilon(1-\varepsilon)^2\Delta\alpha^2}{2(1-\nu)^2\lambda^2}\left(\frac{y^2}{(y-1+\beta)^2}\right). \end{aligned} \tag{A29}$$

We also have

$$B = SW_1^A(\bar{q}_1^A, \bar{q}_2^I) - SW_1^A(\bar{q}_1^A, \bar{q}_1^A)$$
$$= -\frac{(1-\nu)}{2}\left(\lambda - \frac{\varepsilon r\nu\Delta\theta^2}{1-\nu}\right)((1-\beta)(\bar{q}_2^I - \bar{q}_1^A)^2).$$

Simplifying yields

$$B = -\frac{(1-\beta)\varepsilon(1-\varepsilon)^2 r\nu^3\Delta\theta^4\Delta\alpha^2}{2\lambda^2(1-\nu)^2}\left(\frac{y^2(y-1)}{(y-1+\beta)^2}\right). \quad \text{(A30)}$$

Finally, we have

$$SW_1^I - SW_1^A = B - A + C$$
$$= \frac{\beta(1-\beta)r\nu^3\Delta\theta^4\Delta\alpha^2\varepsilon(1-\varepsilon)^2}{2\lambda^2(1-\nu)^2}\left(\frac{y^2}{(y-1)(y-1+\beta)}\right),$$

and, after simplifications, we find (18). ■

Proof of Proposition 6. Let us denote by C^A (respectively, C^I) the intertemporal regulatory wage bill under affiliated agencies (respectively, independence). We have

$$C^A = \beta\left(k\Delta\theta\bar{q}_1^A - \frac{r}{2}(\Delta\theta\bar{q}_1^A)^2\right) + (1-\beta)\left(k\Delta\theta\bar{q}_2^A - \frac{r}{2}(\Delta\theta\bar{q}_2^A)^2\right)$$

and

$$C^I = k\Delta\theta(\beta\bar{q}_1^A + (1-\beta)\bar{q}_2^I) - \frac{r}{2}(\Delta\theta(\beta\bar{q}_1^A + (1-\beta)\bar{q}_2^I))^2$$
$$= k\Delta\theta(\beta\bar{q}_1^A + (1-\beta)\bar{q}_2^I)$$
$$- \frac{r}{2}\Delta\theta^2(\beta\bar{q}_1^A + (1-\beta)(\bar{q}_2^I - \bar{q}_2^A) + (1-\beta)\bar{q}_2^A)^2.$$

After computations, we get

$$C^A - C^I = (1-\beta)\Delta\theta(\bar{q}_2^A - \bar{q}_2^I)\left[k - r\Delta\theta\left(\beta\bar{q}_1^A + (1-\beta)\frac{(\bar{q}_2^I + \bar{q}_2^A)}{2}\right)\right],$$

which is positive because $\bar{q}_2^A > \bar{q}_2^I$, and the bracketed term is positive because by assumption $\frac{k}{r}$ is greater than the possible bribes. ■

Proof of Proposition 8. Straightforward computations.

Acknowledgements. We thank seminar participants in Brussels, Paris, and at the Universities of Montréal, Québec, Toronto, Toulouse, and Barcelona. We are grateful to Mark Armstrong, Jacques Lawarrée, Raymond Deneckere, and a referee for their comments on an earlier version. All errors are ours.

REFERENCES

[1] Banks, J.S. and Weingast, B.R. "The Political Control of Bureaucracies Under Asymmetric Information." *American Journal of Political Science*, Vol. 36 (1992), pp. 509-524.

[2] Baron, D. "Regulation and Legislative Choice." *RAND Journal of Economics*, Vol. 19 (1988), pp. 467-477.

[3] —— and Myerson, R.B. "Regulating a Monopolist with Unknown Costs." *Econometrica*, Vol. 50 (1982), pp. 911-930.

[4] Besanko, D. and Spulber, D.F. "Contested Mergers and Equilibrium Antitrust Policy." *Journal of Law, Economics and Organization*, Vol. 9 (1993), pp. 1-29.

[5] Boyer, M. and Laffont, J.-J. "Toward a Political Theory of the Emergence of Environmental Incentive Regulation." *RAND Journal of Economics*, Vol. 30 (1999), pp. 137-157.

[6] Brehm, J. and Gates, S. *Working, Shirking, and Sabotage: Bureaucratic Response to a Democratic Public*. Ann Arbor, Mich.: University of Michigan Press, 1997.

[7] Calvert, R.L., McCubbins, M.D., and Weingast, B.R. "A Theory of Political Control and Agency Discretion." *American Journal of Political Science*, Vol. 33 (1989), pp. 588-611.

[8] Congleton, R.D. "Committees and Rent-seeking Effort." *Journal of Public Economics*, Vol. 25 (1984), pp. 197-209.

[9] Dixit, A.K. *The Making of Economic Policy: A Transaction-Cost Politics Perspective*. Cambridge, Mass.: MIT Press, 1996.

[10] Freixas, X., Guesnerie, R., and Tirole, J. "Planning Under Incomplete Information and the Ratchet Effect." *Review of Economic Studies*, Vol. 52 (1985), pp. 173-191.

[11] Grossman, G.M. and Helpman, E. "Protection for Sale." *American Economic Review*, Vol. 84 (1994), pp. 833-850.

[12] Kahn, A.E. *The Economics of Regulation: Principles and Institutions*. Cambridge, Mass.: MIT Press, 1988.

[13] Laffont, J.-J. *Incentives and Political Economy*. New York: Oxford University Press, 2000.

[14] —— and Martimort, D. "Separation of Regulators Against Collusive Behavior." *RAND Journal of Economics*, Vol. 30 (1999), pp. 232-262.

[15] —— and ——. *The Theory of Incentives: The Principal-Agent Model*. Princeton, N.J.: Princeton University Press, 2002.

[16] —— and Tirole, J. *A Theory of Incentives in Regulation and Procurement*. Cambridge, Mass.: MIT Press, 1993.

[17] McCubbins, M., Noll, R., and Weingast, B. "Structure and Process, Politics and Policy: Administrative Arrangements and the Political Control of Agencies." *Virginia Law Review*, Vol. 75 (1989), pp. 431-482.

[18] Moe, T. "The Politics of Structural Choice: Toward a Theory of Public Bureaucracy." In O.E. Williamson, ed., *Organization Theory: From Chester Barnard to the Present and Beyond*. New York: Oxford University Press, 1990.

[19] Niskanen, W.A. *Bureaucracy and Representative Government*. Chicago: Aldine Atherton, 1971.

[20] Nordlinger, E. *On the Autonomy of the Democratic State*. Cambridge, Mass.: Harvard University Press, 1981.

[21] Rogoff, K. "The Optimal Degree of Commitment to an Intermediate Monetary Target." *Quarterly Journal of Economics*, Vol. 100 (1985), pp. 1169-1189.

[22] Skocpol, T. "Bringing the State Back In: Strategies of Analysis in Current Research." In P. Evans, D. Rueschemeyer, and T. Skocpol, eds., *Bringing the State Back In*. New York: Cambridge University Press, 1985.

[23] Spulber, D.F. and Besanko, D. "Delegation, Commitment, and the Regulatory Mandate." *Journal of Law, Economics and Organization*, Vol. 8 (1992), pp. 126-154.

[24] Tirole, J. "Hierarchies and Bureaucracies: On the Role of Collusion in Organizations." *Journal of Law, Economics and Organization*, Vol. 2 (1986), pp. 181-214.

[25] Viscusi, W.K., Vernon, J.M., and Harrington, J.E. *Economics of Regulation and Antitrust*, 2d ed. Cambridge, Mass.: MIT Press, 1995.

[26] Weingast, B.R. and Moran, M.J. "Bureaucratic Discretion or Congressional Control? Regulatory Policymaking by the Federal Trade Commission." *Journal of Political Economy*, Vol. 91 (1983), pp. 765-800.

[27] Wilson, J.Q. *Bureaucracy: What Government Agencies Do and Why They Do It*. New York: Basic Books, 1989.

[28] Wood, B.D. "Principals, Bureaucrats, and Responsiveness in Clean Air Enforcements." *American Political Science Review*, Vol. 82 (1988), pp. 213-234.

[29] —— and Waterman, R.W. *Bureaucratic Dynamics: The Role of Bureaucracy in a Democracy*. Boulder, Colo.: Westwiew Press, 1994.

12

Collusion and Group Lending with Adverse Selection

Jean-Jacques Laffont

Abstract

In an environment with correlated returns, this paper characterizes optimal lending contracts when the bank faces adverse selection and borrowers have limited liability. Group lending contracts are shown to be dominated by revelation mechanisms which do not use the *ex post* observability of the partners' performances. However, when collusion between borrowers under complete information is allowed, group lending contracts are optimal in the class of simple revelation mechanisms (which elicit only the borrower's own private information) and remain useful with extended revelation mechanisms.

1 Introduction

The development of group lending through the Grameen Bank and similar institutions has attracted the interest of all those who believe that lending to the poor is a necessary step to exit the vicious circles of underdevelopment. The empirical evaluation of the success of these new ways of lending to entrepreneurs who have no collateral is still subject to debates (see Khandker *et al.*, 1995; Morduch, 1999; Pitt and Khandker, 1996).

Theorists have proposed various explanations for the new opportunities provided by group lending (see Ghatak and Guinnane, 1999 for a review). In this paper, we restrict our attention to group lending as an instrument to improve discrimination between entrepreneurs of different types (adverse selection).

Ghatak (2000) and Armendariz de Aghion and Gollier (2000) have argued that group lending triggers a peer selection effect among entrepreneurs who know each other. For independent types, they show how the knowledge of the types in the group which vary with the different regroupings (for example, in a group of two: two good types or two bad types or one good and one bad type) makes discrimination possible. When entrepreneurs do not know each other, with independent types, group lending brings no improvement (Laffont and N'Guessan, 2000).

In this paper, we propose a simple model to study the role of group lending in discrimination when collusion between borrowers is possible.

We consider exogenously fixed potential pairs of *ex ante* identical entrepreneurs who carry projects with correlated returns. Each entrepreneur, when he discovers his type, revises his beliefs about the type of his partner, but he does not observe his partner's type. At this point in time, he cannot switch to another partner and draw again his type. When correlation becomes perfect, we have the situation where agents know each other.

Through this modeling, we leave aside the issue of endogenous regrouping to focus on two questions: first, what is the relative power of group lending (for which a successful entrepreneur's repayment depends on the success or failure of his partner) in the class of all possible lending mechanisms? Second, what are the optimal collusion-proof lending contracts and how do the group lending contracts perform from the point of view of collusion?

The model with correlated types is presented in Section 2. The optimal individually incentive-compatible contracts are obtained in Section 3. The place of individual contracts and group lending contracts in the class of individually incentive-compatible mechanisms is explained in Section 4. Section 5 shows that the group lending contracts are in fact optimal when a certain type of group incentive constraints are taken into account. Section 6 considers more general revelation mechanisms and shows that group lending contracts remain useful in this context. Section 7 concludes.

2 • The Model

There is a continuum of pairs of entrepreneurs, each entrepreneur being associated with a good or a bad project. A good (resp. bad) project returns h when it is successful, *i.e.* with probability $\overline{p}$ (resp. $\underline{p}$ with $\overline{p} > \underline{p}$), for one unit of investment. For simplicity we consider only projects of size 1.

A pair of entrepreneurs represents a local set of investment opportunities. For simplicity again, we take the case of a group of two entrepreneurs, but, at the cost of more complex notation, it could be a group of any size. However, the size of the group is here exogenous, and we do not raise the issue of the optimal number of entrepreneurs in a group.

Let p_i in $\{\underline{p}, \bar{p}\}$ be the type of entrepreneur i's project, or, for brevity, the type of the entrepreneur. It is private information of the entrepreneur.[1] The types in a pair, (p_1, p_2), are jointly distributed according to the distribution function

$$\pi_{11} = \Pr(p_1 = \underline{p} \text{ and } p_2 = \underline{p})$$

$$\pi_{12} = \Pr(p_1 = \underline{p} \text{ and } p_2 = \bar{p}) = \pi_{21} = \Pr(p_1 = \bar{p} \text{ and } p_2 = \underline{p})$$

$$\pi_{22} = \Pr(p_1 = \bar{p} \text{ and } p_2 = \bar{p}).$$

Let $\rho = \pi_{11}\pi_{22} - \pi_{12}\pi_{21}$, be a measure of the correlation of types that we assume to be positive $(\rho > 0)$. The positive correlation of returns is the most natural one, as the productivity of investments is often affected by common shocks such as weather or local business conditions.

Entrepreneurs are risk neutral[2] and have no wealth. They must borrow to invest and they can only reimburse their loan if their project is successful. The lender is a monopolistic bank which has a cost of funds r and which maximizes expected profit. We assume that under complete information, all loans are socially valuable because the expected profit from a bad type project is greater than the entrepreneur's opportunity cost $\underline{p}h - r - \underline{u} > 0$, when $\underline{u}$ is the status quo utility level of an entrepreneur outside the relationship with the bank. Efficiency calls for all projects to be financed.[3]

3 Optimal Contracts

The bank considers the natural groups of entrepreneurs which are the pairs of entrepreneurs with correlated projects and exploits the fact that the structure of correlation is common knowledge. For notational convenience let us refer to type $\underline{p}$ (resp. $\bar{p}$) as type 1 (resp. 2). From the revelation principle, there is no loss of generality in restricting the offer of contracts to two four-uples, $(x_{11}, x_{12}, x_{21}, x_{22})$, $(y_{11}, y_{12}, y_{21}, y_{22})$, where x_{ij} is the repayment of an entrepreneur who has announced that he is of type i when his partner has announced that he is of type j, and when both have succeeded; similarly y_{ij} is the repayment of a successful entrepreneur when his partner has not succeeded, and with the same announcements.[4]

1. We consider a case of pure adverse selection. It would certainly be interesting to extend the model to situations where the verifiability of the level of production is an issue and enforcement of contracts is imperfect.
2. To assume risk neutrality may appear inappropriate in this context. However, the assumption of limited liability at zero wealth will play a role similar to risk aversion given that there is no *ex post* moral hazard dimension in the entrepreneurs' activity.
3. In our framework with a monopolistic bank, it is the interesting case to consider. If only the good type projects were socially valuable, the bank would offer contracts which are only accepted by the good type entrepreneurs and would leave them no rent. Efficiency would always be achieved. Note also that with our stochastic structure, competition of banks would always lead to efficiency and group lending would be irrelevant.
4. It can easily be proved that all entrepreneurs of a given type receive or do not receive a loan, *i.e.* there is no gain to expect from stochastic loan contracts. We focus also without loss of generality on symmetric solutions.

At a truthful Bayesian Nash equilibrium, the participation and incentive constraints of type $\underline{p}$ and $\bar{p}$ are, respectively, (see Appendix A):

$$\pi_{11}(h-\underline{p}x_{11}-(1-\underline{p})y_{11})+\pi_{12}(h-\bar{p}x_{12}-(1-\bar{p})y_{12}) \geq \frac{u}{\underline{p}}(\pi_{11}+\pi_{12}) \quad (1)$$

$$\pi_{21}(h-\underline{p}x_{21}-(1-\underline{p})y_{21})+\pi_{22}(h-\bar{p}x_{22}-(1-\bar{p})y_{22}) \geq \frac{u}{\bar{p}}(\pi_{21}+\pi_{22}) \quad (2)$$

$$\pi_{11}(h-\underline{p}x_{11}-(1-\underline{p})y_{11})+\pi_{12}(h-\bar{p}x_{12}-(1-\bar{p})y_{12}) \geq \pi_{11}(h-\underline{p}x_{21}-(1-\underline{p})y_{21})+\pi_{12}(h-\bar{p}x_{22}-(1-\bar{p})y_{22}) \quad (3)$$

$$\pi_{21}(h-\underline{p}x_{21}-(1-\underline{p})y_{21})+\pi_{22}(h-\bar{p}x_{22}-(1-\bar{p})y_{22}) \geq \pi_{21}(h-\underline{p}x_{11}-(1-\underline{p})y_{11})+\pi_{22}(h-\bar{p}x_{12}-(1-\bar{p})y_{12}). \quad (4)$$

Furthermore, we have the wealth constraints:

$$x_{ij} \leq h;\ y_{ij} \leq h \text{ for all } i, j. \quad (5)$$

The bank's expected profit is, for a pair of entrepreneurs:

$$\pi_{11}[2\underline{p}^2x_{11}+2\underline{p}(1-\underline{p})y_{11}] + 2\pi_{12}[\underline{p}\bar{p}(x_{12}+x_{21})+\underline{p}(1-\bar{p})y_{12}+(1-\underline{p})\bar{p}y_{21}] + \pi_{22}[2\bar{p}^2x_{22}+2\bar{p}(1-\bar{p})y_{21}]-2r.$$

The average profit for the continuum of entrepreneurs is:

$$\pi_{11}\underline{p}[\underline{p}x_{11}+(1-\underline{p})y_{11}] + \pi_{12}[\underline{p}(\bar{p}x_{12}+(1-\bar{p})y_{12})+\bar{p}(\underline{p}x_{21}+(1-\underline{p})y_{21})] + \pi_{22}\bar{p}[\bar{p}x_{22}+(1-\bar{p})y_{22}]-r. \quad (6)$$

We note that both in the objective function of the bank and in the constraints, the entrepreneurs' payments enter only through the expected terms $X_{11} = \underline{p}x_{11}+(1-\underline{p})y_{11}$, $X_{12} = \bar{p}x_{12}+(1-\bar{p})y_{12}$, $X_{21} = \underline{p}x_{21}+(1-\underline{p})y_{21}$, $X_{22} = \bar{p}x_{22}+(1-\bar{p})y_{22}$. The wealth constraints are obviously less constraining when $x_{ij} = y_{ij}$ for all i, j. Thus, we can rewrite the bank's program as:

$$\max_{(X_{ij})} \pi_{11}\underline{p}X_{11} + \pi_{12}(\underline{p}X_{12} + \bar{p}X_{21}) + \pi_{22}\bar{p}X_{22} - r \quad i, j = 1, 2$$

s.t.

$$\pi_{11}(h - X_{11}) + \pi_{12}(h - X_{12}) \geq \frac{u}{\underline{p}}(\pi_{11} + \pi_{12}) \tag{7}$$

$$\pi_{21}(h - X_{21}) + \pi_{22}(h - X_{22}) \geq \frac{u}{\bar{p}}(\pi_{21} + \pi_{22}) \tag{8}$$

$$\pi_{11}(h - X_{11}) + \pi_{12}(h - X_{12}) \geq \pi_{11}(h - X_{21}) + \pi_{12}(h - X_{22}) \tag{9}$$

$$\pi_{21}(h - X_{21}) + \pi_{22}(h - X_{22}) \geq \pi_{21}(h - X_{11}) + \pi_{22}(h - X_{12}) \tag{10}$$

$$X_{ij} \leq h \text{ for all } i, j. \tag{11}$$

We first show that if the correlation of types is high enough, the optimal pairing contracts are efficient and leave no rent to entrepreneurs.

Proposition 1. *When the correlation is high enough (π_{12} small enough), the optimal contracts of the bank are efficient.*

Proof. See Appendix B.

The logic here is the one of Crémer and McLean (1988). Using the correlation of types, the bank can design rewards and penalties which, because entrepreneurs are risk neutral, both induce truthful revelation of types by entrepreneurs and make participation constraints binding. Indeed, the correlation of types doubles the degrees of freedom in the construction of revelation mechanisms. In our two-type environment, we have now four transfers X_{ij} instead of two for independent types. The incentive constraints can be satisfied with 2 degrees of freedom, so that we have 2 degrees of freedom left to saturate the Bayesian participation constraints.

Here, we find $X_{11} = X_{21} < X_{12} = X_{22}$, *i.e.* the payment of an entrepreneur is independent of his own type and greater when he is paired with a good type. We do not need to condition contracts on the production level of the partner, but only on announcements (and on the agent's production level because of limited wealth). Difficulties may arise from wealth constraints, but this does not occur for a correlation of types high enough.

To explore the effects of binding wealth constraints, we consider a special case of correlation which can be characterized by a single number (This case corresponds to the constraint $\pi_{11} = \pi_{22}$):

$$\pi_{11} = \pi_{22} = \frac{1}{2} - \varepsilon; \quad \pi_{12} = \pi_{21} = \varepsilon; \quad \rho > 0 \Leftrightarrow \varepsilon < \frac{1}{4}.$$

Then, Proposition 1 holds always if the wealth constraints are not binding, *i.e.* if (see Appendix B):

$$\varepsilon < \varepsilon^* = \frac{\underline{p}}{2(\bar{p} + \underline{p})}.$$

Proposition 2. *When* $\pi_{11} = \pi_{12}$*, the wealth constraint becomes binding for* $\varepsilon > \varepsilon^*$*. Then, the solution is*

$$X_{12} = X_{22} = h$$

$$X_{11} = X_{21} = h - \frac{u}{\underline{p}} \frac{\pi_{11} + \pi_{12}}{\pi_{11}}.$$

Then, the good type obtains a rent

$$R = \left(\frac{\varepsilon}{\frac{1}{2} - \varepsilon} \frac{\bar{p}}{\underline{p}} - 1 \right) u. \tag{12}$$

This opens the possibility that offering a contract not accepted by the bad type might be better. Indeed, the bank prefers to offer only a contract to the good type with no rent if

$$\underline{\pi}(\underline{p}h - r - u) < \bar{\pi} R, \tag{13}$$

i.e. if the expected profit made with type $\underline{p}$ entrepreneurs is less than the expected rent which must be given up to type $\bar{p}$ when a contract accepted by both types is offered.

When the correlation is high, it is possible by using two payments (one when the partner announces he is good, one when he announces he is bad) to discriminate between types and extract all the information rents. This is achieved despite the pooling nature of the optimal contract.

When the correlation of types is small, the bank asks the successful entrepreneur to pay his whole gain h when his partner announces he is a bad type and must give up a rent to the good type because it is not possible to exploit sufficiently the correlation of types. It shows one limit of yardstick competition[5] especially in developing countries where limited liability constraints are particularly severe.

5. See Shleifer (1985) and Auriol and Laffont (1992).

4 Restricted Contracts

4.1 Individual Contracts

The bank may design individual contracts. An entrepreneur randomly chosen has a probability $\underline{\pi} = \pi_{11} + \pi_{12}$ (resp. $\bar{\pi} = \pi_{21} + \pi_{22}$) of being of type $\underline{p}$ (resp. $\bar{p}$).

The bank has two possible strategies, either to offer contracts which are accepted by both types of entrepreneurs (Regime 1), or to offer a contract which is only accepted by a good type (Regime 2). We obtain immediately:

Proposition 3. *If*

$$\underline{\pi}(\underline{p}h - r - u) > \bar{\pi}\,\frac{\bar{p} - \underline{p}}{\underline{p}}\,u,$$

Regime 1 holds. The bank offers a pooling contract which gives a loan to all entrepreneurs for a reimbursement $x = h - \frac{u}{\underline{p}}$ when the project is successful.

If

$$\underline{\pi}(\underline{p}h - r - u) < \bar{\pi}\,\frac{\bar{p} - \underline{p}}{\underline{p}}\,u,$$

Regime 2 holds. The bank offers a contract accepted only by type $\bar{p}$ entrepreneurs with a reimbursement $x = h - \frac{u}{\bar{p}}$ when the project is successful.

In Regime 1, an entrepreneur of type $\bar{p}$ has an expected rent

$$\bar{p}\left(h - \left(h - \frac{u}{\underline{p}}\right)\right) - u = \frac{\bar{p} - \underline{p}}{\underline{p}}\,u.$$

Regime 1 is preferred by the bank if the expected profit to be realized with type $\underline{p}$ entrepreneurs, $\underline{\pi}(\underline{p}h - r - u)$, exceeds the expected rent,

$$\bar{\pi}\left(\frac{\bar{p} - \underline{p}}{\underline{p}}\right)u$$

that must be given up in Regime 1 to type $\bar{p}$ (in contrast to Regime 2 where no rent need to be given to these entrepreneurs), because of the presence of type $\underline{p}$.

In Regime 1, the allocation of loans is efficient, and the good type entrepreneurs are able to obtain a rent despite the monopolistic structure of banking. In Regime 2, the allocation of loans is inefficient since the valuable projects of type $\underline{p}$ are not financed, but the good type entrepreneurs obtain no rent.

Individual contracts are of course dominated by the optimal contracts. In the case $\pi_{11} = \pi_{22}$, from Eqs. (12) and (13), lending to both types occurs less often than with the efficient contract since for $\varepsilon < 1/4$, $\frac{\varepsilon}{1/2 - \varepsilon} < 1$.

4.2 Group Lending Contracts

A group lending contract is characterized, for any entrepreneur, by two possible payments when he is successful: X if his partner is also successful and Y if his partner is not successful.[6]

There is no incentive constraint and participation constraints write:

$$\pi_{11}\underline{p}[\underline{p}(h-X)+(1-\underline{p})(h-Y)]+\pi_{12}\underline{p}[\bar{p}(h-X) + (1-\bar{p})(h-Y)] \geq u(\pi_{11}+\pi_{12}) \tag{14}$$

$$\pi_{21}\bar{p}[\underline{p}(h-X)+(1-\underline{p})(h-Y)]+\pi_{22}\bar{p}[\bar{p}(h-X) + (1-\bar{p})(h-Y)] \geq u(\pi_{21}+\pi_{22}). \tag{15}$$

Using the notations of Section 3, we observe that:

$$X_{11} = X_{21} - \underline{p}X + (1-\underline{p})Y \tag{16}$$

$$X_{12} = X_{22} = \bar{p}X + (1-\bar{p})Y. \tag{17}$$

Let $\underline{X}^* = X_{11} = X_{21}$ and $\bar{X}^* = X_{12} = X_{22}$ the payments in the optimal pairing contracts of Section 3. From Eqs. (16) and (17), we can implement those payments with

$$X = \frac{(1-\underline{p})\bar{X}^* - (1-\bar{p})\underline{X}^*}{\bar{p}-\underline{p}}$$

$$Y = \frac{\bar{p}\underline{X}^* - \underline{p}\bar{X}^*}{\bar{p}-\underline{p}}.$$

6. Offering a menu of group lending contracts would bring no improvement.

It remains to be seen when the limited liability constraints become binding. In the example $\pi_{11} = \pi_{21} = (1/2) - \varepsilon$, $\pi_{12} = \pi_{21} = \varepsilon$, Y is always less than h and

$$X \leq h \quad \text{iff} \quad \varepsilon < \frac{1}{2}\left(1 - \frac{1}{\underline{p} + \bar{p}}\right).$$

As expected, this condition is always more stringent than the one obtained for the optimal contract since

$$\frac{\underline{p}}{2(\bar{p} + \underline{p})} > \frac{1}{2}\left(1 - \frac{1}{\underline{p} + \bar{p}}\right).$$

When ε is too large, $X = h$ and

$$Y = h - \frac{u}{\underline{p}} \frac{1}{(1 - \underline{p}) + 2\varepsilon(\underline{p} - \bar{p})}$$

with a rent for the good type.[7]

Proposition 4. *The optimal group lending contracts are efficient if correlation is high enough but are not always optimal.*

A striking feature is that contrary to the practice of Grameen Banks, the payments required from a successful entrepreneur are higher when his partner is successful than when he fails.[8] This is because we have assumed a positive correlation of types. Payments must differ to use the correlation for rent extraction. The positive correlation implies that it is better to extract more in more likely events. To rationalize in our model with adverse selection the practice of Grameen Bank's contracts for which an additional payment is required when a partner fails, we would need to assume negative correlation of types. We do not argue that negative correlation is a good rationalization of Grameen Bank contracts. We rather draw the conclusion that, for the type of model considered here, such rationalization must be looked for elsewhere for example as an attempt to solve moral hazard or enforcement problems.[9]

Alternatively, we may consider a different model with adverse selection. So far, we have consider what Ghatak (2000) calls the De Meza and Webb (1987)[10] setup in which entrepreneurs differ in their probability of success, but obtain the same payoff h when they succeed. The advantage of this setup is that the observability of success does not enable the bank to infer the type of the entrepreneur.

He also considers (as well as Armendariz de Aghion and Gollier, 2000) the Stiglitz and Weiss (1981) setup where expected revenues are identical $\underline{ph} = \bar{p}\bar{h}$, which requires $\bar{h} < \underline{h}$, *i.e.* a good type

7. Of course, loans to good types only occur in similar circumstances as in Section 3, Eq. (13) with the proper definition of the rent.

8. Note that this feature creates an incentive for an entrepreneur to make his partner's project unsuccessful.

9. See Laffont and Rey (2000) for moral hazard and Laffont and N'Guessan (2001) for enforcement.

10. See also Besanko and Thakor (1987).

(in terms of probability of success) obtains less when he succeeds. To avoid the inference of the type *ex post*, the authors must make the additional (and questionable) assumption that the bank observes if the entrepreneur succeeds but not proceeds $\underline{h}$ or $\bar{h}$. As Ghatak (2000) shows, the results obtained are then very different. In Appendix C, we briefly adapt our analysis to this setup to explain why one can then conclude that the repayment can be greater if the partner fails than if he succeeds (let us call that the "Grameen Bank property").

Considering the more general case where $\underline{h} = h + \delta$, $\bar{h} = h$ we see that this result holds[11] if

$$\delta > \frac{u(\bar{p} - \underline{p})}{\underline{p}\bar{p}},$$

which is always true in the Stiglitz-Weiss case $\left(\delta > \frac{h(\bar{p} - \underline{p})}{\underline{p}}\right)$.

The intuition is as follows. Payments are higher when the partner fails if and only if one can extract more in the optimal mechanism from an entrepreneur paired with a bad type than from an entrepreneur paired with a good type. This last result is purely driven by the desire to make binding both participation constraints. When both types have the same expected revenue $\underline{p}(h + \delta) = \bar{p}h$, one can extract more when paired with a bad type than a good type because:

- for a good type who reimburses more often, this is a less likely event because of positive correlation;
- for a bad type, it is on the contrary more likely, but it is compensated by the fact that he pays less often.

When the two types have the same payoff when they succeed, this is not possible, because the more likely payment he has to make breaks his participation constraint if the one of the good type is binding.

Thus, the driving force is not that a higher payment, when paired with an unsuccessful partner, weakens the incentive constraint through a self-selection mechanism, since incentive constraints are irrelevant here.

Suppose one imposes, in the De Meza-Webb framework, that payment, if the partner fails, is higher, than if he succeeds and that we allow for a menu of group lending contracts X_1, Y_1 for type $\underline{p}$ and X_2, Y_2 for type $\bar{p}$ with $Y_1 \geq X_1$ and $Y_2 \geq X_2$. Then, we obtain:

Proposition 5. *If we allow for a menu of group lending contracts constrained to* $Y_i \geq X_i$, $i = 1, 2$, *then the optimal menu is such that* $X_1 = Y_1$ *and* $Y_2 > X_2$.

11. See Appendix C.

Proof. See Appendix D.

Under the constraint of the Grameen Bank property, the menu of group lending contracts yields a self-selection effect since good types are willing to pay more if their partner fails, because it is less likely due to the positive correlation.

Thus, it appears that the self-selection effect discussed in the literature (Ghatak, 2000; Armendariz de Aghion and Aghion, 2000) occurs in our monopolistic setting only when group lending contracts are constrained to be of the "Grameen Bank" type. It is therefore not a justification of Grameen Bank contracts, but the reverse. The self-selection effect is a second-best response to the "Grameen Bank" constraint.

5 Collusion Under Complete Information

Let us first assume that entrepreneurs may collude when they play the revelation mechanism offered by the bank but after having accepted the offer of the bank. Accordingly, the participation constraints remain the interim individual participation constraints. Furthermore, we assume that entrepreneurs always share their private information after having accepted the bank's contract, and that a ringmaster organizes the collusion. More precisely, we have the following timing:[12]

Entrepreneurs obtain their private information	Bank offers mechanism G	Entrepreneurs accept or reject G	Entrepreneurs share information	An uninformed ringmaster offers a collusion contract G	$G \circ S$ is played

Because entrepreneurs share information, individual incentive constraints are dominant strategy incentive constraints

$$h - \underline{p}x_{11} - (1 - \underline{p})y_{11} \geq h - \underline{p}x_{21} - (1 - \underline{p})y_{21} \qquad (18)$$

$$h - \bar{p}x_{12} - (1 - \bar{p})y_{12} \geq h - \bar{p}x_{22} - (1 - \bar{p})y_{22} \qquad (19)$$

$$h - \underline{p}x_{21} - (1 - \underline{p})y_{21} \geq h - \underline{p}x_{11} - (1 - \underline{p})y_{11} \qquad (20)$$

$$h - \bar{p}x_{22} - (1 - \bar{p})y_{22} \geq h - \bar{p}x_{12} - (1 - \underline{p})y_{12}. \qquad (21)$$

When internal transfers are available within the coalition, collusion-proof constraints simplify to, for a pair $(1, 1)$:

$$2(h - \underline{p}x_{11} - (1 - \underline{p})y_{11}) \geq 2h - \underline{p}x_{ij} - (1 - \underline{p})y_{ij} - \underline{p}x_{ji} - (1 - \underline{p})y_{ji} \quad \text{for all } i, j, \qquad (22)$$

12. We are not taking into account the financial constraints in the collusive side-contracts proposed by the ringmaster. This exaggerates the threat of collusion, but it is of no relevance for the results we present below. Furthermore, it can be justified if investors have hidden wealth they can use in their side-contracting (but could not be used as collateral).

for a pair (1, 2):

$$\underline{p}(h-\bar{p}x_{12}-(1-\bar{p})y_{12})+\bar{p}(h-\underline{p}x_{21}-(1-\underline{p})y_{21})$$

$$\geq \underline{p}(h-\bar{p}x_{ij}-(1-\bar{p})y_{ij})+\bar{p}(h-\underline{p}x_{ji}-(1-\underline{p})y_{ji}) \quad \text{for all } i, j, \tag{23}$$

for a pair (2, 2):

$$2(h-\bar{p}x_{22}-(1-\bar{p})y_{22})\geq 2h-\bar{p}x_{ij}$$

$$-(1-\bar{p})y_{ij}-\bar{p}x_{ji}-(1-\bar{p})y_{ji} \quad \text{for all } i, j. \tag{24}$$

If we proceed as in Section 3 and do not distinguish payments according to the success or failure of the partner, *i.e.* $X_{ij} = x_{ij} = y_{ij}$ for all i, j, incentive constraints imply

$$X_{11} = X_{21} = X_{22} = X_{12}.$$

We are then back immediately to the individual contracts of Section 4.1.

Suppose, on the contrary, that we keep the flexibility of $x_{ij} \neq y_{ij}$.

Dominant strategy incentive constraints imply

$$\underline{p}x_{11}+(1-\underline{p})y_{11} = \underline{p}x_{21}+(1-\underline{p})y_{21} \tag{25}$$

$$\bar{p}x_{22}+(1-\bar{p})y_{22} = \bar{p}x_{12}+(1-\bar{p})y_{12}, \tag{26}$$

and the collusion-proof constraints reduce to

$$\underline{p}x_{11}+(1-\underline{p})y_{11}\leq \underline{p}x_{12}+(1-\underline{p})y_{12} \tag{27}$$

$$\bar{p}x_{22}+(1-\bar{p})y_{22}\leq \bar{p}x_{21}+(1-\bar{p})y_{21} \tag{28}$$

$$\underline{p}x_{21}+(1-\underline{p})y_{21}\leq \underline{p}x_{22}+(1-\underline{p})y_{22} \tag{29}$$

$$\bar{p}x_{12}+(1-\bar{p})y_{12}\leq \bar{p}x_{11}+(1-\bar{p})y_{11}, \tag{30}$$

with the wealth constraints:

$$x_{ij}\leq h \quad \text{for all } i, j$$

$$y_{ij}\leq h \quad \text{for all } i, j.$$

With the interim participation constraints and the incentive constraints, we have eight constraints and also eight variables. Furthermore, we have the wealth constraints.

Imposing

$$x_{11} = x_{12} = x_{21} = x_{22} = X$$

$$y_{11} = y_{12} = y_{21} = y_{22} = Y$$

enables us to satisfy all individual and coalition incentive constraints, and also to extract all the rents if

$$h - \frac{\underline{p}\pi_{11} + \bar{p}\pi_{12}}{\pi_{11} + \pi_{12}} X - \frac{(1-\underline{p})\pi_{11} + (1-\bar{p})\pi_{12}}{\pi_{11} + \pi_{12}} Y = \frac{u}{\underline{p}}$$

$$h - \frac{\underline{p}\pi_{21} + \bar{p}\pi_{22}}{\pi_{21} + \pi_{22}} X - \frac{(1-\underline{p})\pi_{21} + (1-\bar{p})\pi_{22}}{\pi_{21} + \pi_{22}} Y = \frac{u}{\bar{p}}.$$

The determinant of this system is $(\underline{p} - \bar{p})\rho$ which is non-null as soon as there is some correlation. We can find X and Y which solve the system.

In the case $\pi_{11} = \pi_{22} = (1/2) - \varepsilon$, $\pi_{12} = \pi_{21} = \varepsilon$, we obtain:

$$X = h - \frac{u}{\underline{p}\bar{p}} \left[\frac{(1-2\varepsilon)(\bar{p} + \underline{p}) - 1}{1 - 4\varepsilon}\right]$$

$$Y = h - \frac{u}{\underline{p}\bar{p}} \left[\frac{(1-2\varepsilon)(\bar{p} + \underline{p})}{1 - 4\varepsilon}\right] < h.$$

with

$$X < h \text{ if } \varepsilon < \frac{1}{2}\left(1 - \frac{1}{\underline{p} + \bar{p}}\right).$$

We obtain (for $\underline{p} + \bar{p} > 1$):

Proposition 6. *The optimal collusion-proof contract is the optimal group lending contract if correlation is high enough.*[13]

The intuition for this result is simply the following: announcement contracts are not robust to collusion, while contracts which depend on the production of the partner are robust to collusion (since we assumed that production is verifiable). Furthermore, for a

[13] In the limit for $\varepsilon = 0$, it may seem that it is as if the bank was facing a single agent. This is true for incentive constraints, but we have here two participation constraints that the bank can saturate because, by observing the success or failure of both projects, it still has 2 degrees of freedom.

His (Bayesian) participation constraint is:

$$\frac{\pi_{11}}{\pi_{11}+\pi_{12}}\underline{p}(h-\underline{p}x_{11}-(1-\underline{p})y_{11}) + \frac{\pi_{12}}{\pi_{11}+\pi_{12}}\underline{p}(h-\bar{p}x_{12}-(1-\bar{p})y_{12}) \geq u$$

hence Eq. (1) and similarly for Eq. (2).

Indeed, with probability $\underline{p}$, he obtains h. With probability $\frac{\pi_{11}}{\pi_{11}+\pi_{12}}$, he will be paired with a type $\underline{p}$ partner. In this case, his partner succeeds with probability $\underline{p}$ and he must reimburse x_{11}. His partner fails with probability $(1-\underline{p})$ and he must then reimburse y_{11}. With probability $\frac{\pi_{12}}{\pi_{11}+\pi_{12}}$, he will be paired with a type $\bar{p}$ partner who succeeds with probability $\bar{p}$ (in which case, he pays x_{12}) and fails with probability $(1-\bar{p})$ (in which case he pays y_{12}) and similarly for type $\bar{p}$.

His (Bayesian) incentive constraint is

$$\begin{aligned}&\frac{\pi_{11}}{\pi_{11}+\pi_{12}}\underline{p}(h-\underline{p}x_{11}-(1-\underline{p})y_{11}) + \frac{\pi_{12}}{\pi_{11}+\pi_{12}}\underline{p}(h-\bar{p}x_{12}-(1-\bar{p})y_{12})\\ &\geq \frac{\pi_{11}}{\pi_{11}+\pi_{12}}\underline{p}(h-\underline{p}x_{21}-(1-\underline{p})y_{21}) + \frac{\pi_{12}}{\pi_{11}+\pi_{12}}\underline{p}(h-\bar{p}x_{22}-(1-\bar{p})y_{22})\end{aligned}$$

hence, Eq. (3) and similarly for Eq. (4).

Appendix B. Proof of Propositions 1 and 2

Proposition 1

Constraints (7)–(10) are binding if:

$$\begin{bmatrix} -\pi_{11} & \pi_{12} & 0 & 0 \\ 0 & 0 & -\pi_{21} & -\pi_{22} \\ -\pi_{11} & -\pi_{12} & \pi_{11} & \pi_{12} \\ \pi_{21} & \pi_{22} & -\pi_{21} & -\pi_{22} \end{bmatrix} \begin{bmatrix} X_{11} \\ X_{12} \\ X_{21} \\ X_{22} \end{bmatrix} = \begin{bmatrix} (\pi_{11}+\pi_{12})(\frac{u}{\underline{p}}-h) \\ (\pi_{21}+\pi_{22})(\frac{u}{\bar{p}}-h) \\ 0 \\ 0 \end{bmatrix} = \begin{bmatrix} a \\ b \\ 0 \\ 0 \end{bmatrix}$$

The determinant of this system is $\Delta = -\rho^2$.

Solving the system we obtain:

$$X_{11} = X_{21} = \frac{b\pi_{12} - a\pi_{22}}{\rho} = h - \frac{u}{\underline{p}} - \frac{u}{\rho}\,\pi_{12}(\pi_{12} + \pi_{22})\,\frac{\bar{p} - \underline{p}}{\bar{p}\,\underline{p}}$$

$$X_{12} = X_{22} = \frac{a\pi_{21} - b\pi_{11}}{\rho} = h - \frac{u}{\bar{p}} - \frac{u}{\rho}\,\pi_{21}(\pi_{11} + \pi_{12})\,\frac{\bar{p} - \underline{p}}{\bar{p}\,\underline{p}}.$$

These payments satisfy the limited liability constraint if π_{12} is close enough to zero. Then, both entrepreneurs are indifferent between lying or telling the truth about their type and no rent is given up. They are rewarded if their partner is bad and punished if he is good.

Proposition 2

As π_{12} increases, we reach the boundary h for X_{12}.

For example, if $\pi_{11} = \pi_{22} = (1/2) - \varepsilon$ and $\pi_{12} = \pi_{21} = \varepsilon$, the boundary is reached for

$$\varepsilon^* = \frac{\underline{p}}{2(\bar{p} + \underline{p})}.$$

For $\varepsilon > \varepsilon^*$, the solution entails $X_{12} = X_{22} = h$, hence, the constraints:

$$\pi_{11}(h - X_{11}) \geq \frac{u}{\underline{p}}(\pi_{11} + \pi_{12}) \tag{A.1}$$

$$\pi_{21}(h - X_{21}) \geq \frac{u}{\bar{p}}(\pi_{21} + \pi_{22}) \tag{A.2}$$

$$\pi_{11}(h - X_{11}) \geq \pi_{11}(h - X_{21}) \tag{A.3}$$

$$\pi_{21}(h - X_{21}) \geq \pi_{21}(h - X_{11}). \tag{A.4}$$

From Eqs. (A.3) and (A.4), $X_{11} = X_{21} = X$.

We can expect the bad type's participation constraint to be binding

$$X = h - \frac{u}{\underline{p}}\,\frac{\pi_{11} + \pi_{12}}{\pi_{11}}$$

with an expected rent for the good type:

$$\left[\frac{\pi_{21}(\pi_{11} + \pi_{12})}{\pi_{11}(\pi_{21} + \pi_{22})}\,\frac{\bar{p}}{\underline{p}} - 1\right]u.$$

In the special case, this is positive if ε is larger than ε^*.

Appendix C. Characterization of the Condition for the "Grameen Bank Property" to Hold

Consider the more general model in which type $\bar{p}$ obtains h when he succeeds and type $\bar{p}$ obtains $h+\delta$. If $\delta = 0$, we have the De Meza and Webb (1987) model; if δ is such that $(\bar{p}h = \underline{p}(h+\delta))$, we have the Stiglitz and Weiss (1981) model.

The analysis of optimal contracts and optimal individual contracts is exactly the same as in the text. Consider the optimal contract $(X_{11}, X_{12}, X_{21}, X_{22})$ for which participation and incentive constraints bind. They solve now (see Appendix B):

$$\begin{bmatrix} -\pi_{11} & -\pi_{12} & 0 & 0 \\ 0 & 0 & -\pi_{21} & -\pi_{22} \\ -\pi_{11} & -\pi_{12} & \pi_{11} & \pi_{12} \\ \pi_{21} & \pi_{22} & -\pi_{21} & -\pi_{22} \end{bmatrix} \begin{bmatrix} X_{11} \\ X_{12} \\ X_{21} \\ X_{22} \end{bmatrix} = \begin{bmatrix} (\pi_{11}+\pi_{12})(\frac{u}{\underline{p}} - h - \delta) \\ (\pi_{21}+\pi_{22})(\frac{u}{\bar{p}} - h) \\ 0 \\ 0 \end{bmatrix},$$

i.e.

$$\underline{X}^* = X_{11} = X_{21} = \frac{1}{\rho}\left[[\pi_{21}+\pi_{22}]\left(\frac{u}{\bar{p}} - h\right)\pi_{12} - (\pi_{11}+\pi_{12})\left(\frac{u}{\underline{p}} - h - \delta\right)\pi_{22}\right]$$

$$\bar{X}^* = X_{12} = X_{22} = \frac{1}{\rho}\left[[\pi_{11}+\pi_{12}]\left(\frac{u}{\underline{p}} - h - \delta\right)\pi_{21} - (\pi_{22}+\pi_{12})\left(\frac{u}{\underline{p}} - h\right)\pi_{11}\right].$$

The associated group lending contract is such that (see Section 4.2):

$$X = \frac{(1-\underline{p})\bar{X}^* - (1-\bar{p})\underline{X}^*}{\bar{p}-\underline{p}}; \quad Y = \frac{\bar{p}\,\underline{X}^* - \underline{p}\bar{X}^*}{\bar{p}-\underline{p}}.$$

Note that

$$Y - X = \frac{\underline{X}^* - \bar{X}^*}{\bar{p}-\underline{p}}.$$

Thus, the "Grameen Bank property" holds if one can extract more when paired with a bad type than with a good type ($\underline{X}^* > \overline{X}^*$), which reduces to

$$\delta > \frac{u(\bar{p} - \underline{p})}{\underline{p}\bar{p}}.$$

In particular, for the Stiglitz-Weiss setup for which $\delta = \frac{h(\bar{p} - \underline{p})}{\underline{p}}$, this inequality becomes $\bar{p}h > u$ which holds since all projects are socially valuable. For the De Meza-Webb setup ($\delta = 0$), it cannot hold.

Appendix D. Proof of Proposition 5

Allowing for a menu of group lending contracts X_1, Y_1, X_2, Y_2 with the constraint $Y_1 \geq X_1$, $Y_2 \geq X_2$, the bank's problem can be rewritten (with $\Delta_1 = Y_1 - X_1$; $\Delta_2 = Y_2 - X_2$):

$$\max\ (2\pi_{11} + \pi_{12})\underline{p}Y_1 + (2\pi_{22} + \pi_{21})\bar{p}Y_2 - (2\pi_{11}\underline{p}^2 + \pi_{12}\underline{p}\bar{p})\Delta_1$$
$$- (2\pi_{22}\bar{p}^2 + \pi_{21}\underline{p}\bar{p})\Delta_2,$$

s.t.

$$(\Delta_2 - \Delta_1)a + Y_1 - Y_2 \geq 0$$

$$(\Delta_1 - \Delta_2)b + Y_2 - Y_1 \geq 0$$

$$b\Delta_1 - Y_1 \geq c$$

$$a\Delta_2 - Y_2 \geq d$$

$$Y_1 \leq h, \quad Y_2 \leq h, \quad \Delta_1 \geq 0, \quad \Delta_2 \geq 0,$$

for

$$a = \frac{\pi_{21}\underline{p} + \pi_{22}\bar{p}}{\pi_{21} + \pi_{22}}$$

$$b = \frac{\pi_{11}\underline{p} + \pi_{12}\bar{p}}{\pi_{11} + \pi_{12}}$$

$$c = -h + \frac{u}{\underline{p}}$$

$$d = -h + \frac{u}{\bar{p}}.$$

Then, it is easy to see that the optimal solution entails

$$Y_2 = h \text{ and } X_2 = h - \frac{u}{\underline{p}a}$$

$$\Delta_1 = 0 \text{ with } X_1 = Y_1 = -c$$

$$Y_2 = h \text{ and } X_2 = h - \frac{u}{a\underline{p}}.$$

Appendix E. Proof of Proposition 7

Let us denote $x = X_{11} = X_{22}$.

To bind both participation constraints, we need

$$X_{12} = -\frac{\pi_{11}}{\pi_{12}}x + \frac{\pi_{11} + \pi_{12}}{\pi_{12}}\left(h - \frac{u}{\underline{p}}\right)$$

$$X_{21} = -\frac{\pi_{22}}{\pi_{21}}x + \frac{\pi_{21} + \pi_{22}}{\pi_{21}}\left(h - \frac{u}{\bar{p}}\right).$$

The constraint

$$\frac{X_{12} + X_{21}}{2} \geq X_{22} = X_{11}$$

writes now as

$$x \leq h - (\pi_{11} + \pi_{12})\frac{u}{\underline{p}} - (\pi_{21} + \pi_{22})\frac{u}{\bar{p}}.$$

The constraint

$$\frac{\underline{p}X_{12} + \bar{p}X_{21}}{\underline{p} + \bar{p}} \leq X_{11} = X_{22}$$

writes now as

$$x \geq h - \frac{u}{\underline{p}(\pi_{11} + \pi_{12}) + \bar{p}(\pi_{21} + \pi_{22})}.$$

These inequalities are compatible if

$$\underline{p}^2 + \bar{p}^2 + \underline{p}\bar{p}\left[\frac{(\pi_{11} + \pi_{12})^2 + (\pi_{21} + \pi_{22})^2 - 1}{(\pi_{11} + \pi_{12})(\pi_{22} + \pi_{21})}\right] \leq 0.$$

However, the left-hand side equals

$$\underline{p}^2 + \bar{p}^2 - 2\underline{p}\bar{p} = (\bar{p} - \underline{p})^2 > 0 \quad \text{if } \bar{p} > \underline{p}\,.$$

Acknowledgements. I thank Abhijit Banerjee, Tim Besley, Oliver Hart, Guido Friebel, Patrick Rey, Ilya Segal and Jean Tirole and two referees for helpful comments.

REFERENCES

[1] Armendariz de Aghion, B., Gollier, C., 2000. Peer group formation in an adverse selection model. *Economic Journal* 110, 632-643.

[2] Auriol, E., Laffont, J.J., 1992. Regulation by duopoly. *Journal of Economics and Management Strategy* 1, 503-533.

[3] Besanko, D., Thakor, A., 1987. Collateral and rationing: sorting equilibria in monopolistic and competitive credit markets. *International Economic Review* 28, 671-689.

[4] Crémer, J., McLean, R., 1988. Full extraction of the surplus in Bayesian and dominant strategy auctions. *Econometrica* 56, 1247-1258.

[5] De Meza, D., Webb, D., 1987. Too much investment: a problem of asymmetric information. *Quarterly Journal of Economics* 102, 281-292.

[6] Ghatak, M., 2000. Screening by the company you keep: joint liability lending and the peer selection effect. *Economic Journal* 110, 601-631.

[7] Ghatak, M., Guinnane, T., 1999. The economics of lending with joint liability: theory and practice. *Journal of Development Economics* 60, 195-228.

[8] Khandker, S., Khalily B., Khan Z., 1995. Grameen Bank: performance and sustainability. World Bank, Discussion Paper 306, Washington, DC.

[9] Laffont, J.J., N'Guessan, T.T., 2000. Group lending with adverse selection. *European Economic Review* 44, 773-784.

[10] Laffont, J.J., N'Guessan, T.T., 2001. Group contracting and enforcement. *Journal of Institutional and Theoretical Economics* 157, 487-498.

[11] Laffont, J.J., Rey P., 2000. Collusion and Group Lending with Moral Hazard, mimeo IDEI.

[12] Morduch, J., 1999. The microfinance promise. *Journal of Economic Literature* 37, 1569-1614.

[13] Pitt, M., Khandker S., 1996. Household and intrahousehold impact of the Grameen Bank and similar targeted credit programs in Bangladesh. World Bank, Discussion Paper 320, Washington, DC.

[14] Shleifer, A., 1985. A theory of yardstick competition. *Rand Journal of Economics* 16, 319-327.

[15] Stiglitz, J., Weiss, A., 1981. Credit rationing in markets with imperfect information. *American Economic Review* 71, 393-410.

13

Financial Contracting Theory Meets the Real World: An Empirical Analysis of Venture Capital Contracts

Steven N. Kaplan
Per Strömberg

Abstract

We compare the characteristics of real world financial contracts to their counterparts in financial contracting theory. We do so by studying the actual contracts between venture capitalists (VCs) and entrepreneurs. The distinguishing characteristic of VC financings is that they allow VCs to separately allocate cash flow rights, board rights, voting rights, liquidation rights and other control rights. We describe and measure these rights. We then interpret our results in relation to existing financial contracting theories. We also describe the interrelation and the evolution across financing rounds of the different rights.

1 • Introduction

There is a large academic literature on the principal-agent problem in financial contracting.[1] The papers in this literature often begin with a situation in which an investor negotiates with an entrepreneur over the financing of a project or company. Despite the large volume of theory, relatively little empirical work exists that compares the characteristics of real world financial contracts to their counterparts in financial contracting theory.[2] In this paper, we attempt to inform theory by describing in detail the contracts between VCs and entrepreneurs. We compare the actual contracts to the assumed and predicted ones in different financial contracting theories.

In doing this, we assume that VCs are real world entities who closely approximate the investors of theory. VCs invest in entrepreneurs who need financing to fund a promising venture. VCs have strong incentives to maximize value, but, at the same time, receive few or no private benefits of control. Although they are intermediaries, VCs typically receive at least 20% of the profits on their portfolios.[3]

1. For a recent summary, see Hart (2001). Extensive theoretical overviews can be found in Allen and Winton (1995), Harris and Raviv (1992) and Hart (1995).
2. For earlier, related work, see Sahlman (1990), Gompers (1998), Black and Gilson (1998) and Baker and Gompers (1999, 2000). Kaplan and Strömberg (2001) discuss other ways that

We study 213 VC investments in 119 portfolio companies by 14 VC firms. Each VC firm provided the contractual agreements governing each financing round in which the firm participated. The VC firm also provided (if available) the company's business plan, internal analyses evaluating the investment, and information on subsequent performance.

We find that VC financings allow VCs to separately allocate cash flow rights, board rights, voting rights, liquidation rights, and other control rights. These rights are often contingent on observable measures of financial and non-financial performance. In general, board rights, voting rights, and liquidation rights are allocated such that if the firm performs poorly, the VCs obtain full control. As performance improves, the entrepreneur retains/obtains more control rights. If the firm performs very well, the VCs retain their cash flow rights, but relinquish most of their control and liquidation rights.

We also report that it is common for VCs to include non-compete and vesting provisions that make it more expensive for the entrepreneur to leave the firm, thus mitigating the potential hold-up problem between the entrepreneur and the investor.

Finally, the cash flow incentives, control rights and contingencies in these contracts are used more as complements than as substitutes. Ventures in which the VCs have voting and board majorities are also more likely to make the entrepreneur's equity claim and the release of committed funds contingent on performance milestones.

Our results have the following implications. First, cash flow rights matter in a way that is consistent with the principal-agent theories of Holmström (1979), Lazear (1986) and others. For example, the entrepreneur's equity compensation function is more sensitive to performance when incentive and asymmetric information problems are more severe.

Second, the allocation of control rights between the VC and the entrepreneur is a central feature of the financial contracts. This strongly suggests that despite the prevalence of contingent contracting, contracts are inherently incomplete. This finding gives support to the incomplete contracting approach pioneered by Grossman and Hart (1986) and Hart and Moore (1990).

Third, cash flow rights and control rights can be separated and made contingent on observable and verifiable measures of performance. This is most supportive of theories that predict shifts of control to investors in different states, such as Aghion and Bolton (1992) and Dewatripont and Tirole (1994).

venture capitalists (VCs) mitigate principal/agent problems.

3. See Gompers and Lerner (1999).

Fourth, the widespread use of non-compete and vesting provisions indicates that VCs care about the hold-up problem explored in Hart and Moore (1994).

Finally, we think our descriptive results suggest fruitful avenues for future theoretical research.

The paper proceeds as follows. Section 2 describes our sample. Section 3 describes the VC contracts. Section 4 compares the empirical results in Section 3 and additional cross-sectional analyses to the assumptions and predictions of financial contracting theories. Section 5 presents additional descriptive information regarding the contracts that should be of use to future theory. Section 6 summarizes and discusses our results.

2 Sample

We analyse 213 VC investments in 119 portfolio companies by 14 VC partnerships.

2.1 Description

To obtain this sample, we asked each VC to provide detailed information on as many of their portfolio company investments as they were willing to provide. For each of these companies, the VCs provided the documents that include all the financing terms, the firm's equity ownership — investors, founders, management, etc. — and any contingencies to future financing. The VCs also provided (if available) the portfolio company's business plan at the time of the financing, the VC's internal analysis of the investment, and the subsequent portfolio company financial performance.

Before we present our results, it is worth pointing out that while we have a great deal of data, we do not have complete data on every financing round. As a result, the number of observations varies across our analyses according to the availability of the relevant information.

Table 1 presents summary information. Panel A indicates that we have 213 investments in 119 portfolio companies by 14 VC firms. 98 of the 213 investments are the first VC financing rounds.

The VCs commit a median of $4.5 million in equity in each financing round. Not all of the committed financing is released to the company immediately, however. The VCs disburse a median $3.6 million at the time the round closed. The difference between committed financing and the amount that is released at the closing is particularly large for first VC financing rounds.[4]

4. We consider a financing round as a set of contracts agreed to on a particular date that determines the disbursement of funds from a VC to a company. A new financing round differs from the contingent release of funds in that the price and terms of the financing are not set in advance.

D. Liquidation Rights and Redemption Rights

	All rounds, N = 213			*First VC rounds only, N = 98*		
	% of obs.	Mean	(Med.)	% of obs.	Mean	(Med.)
VC liq. rights < cumulative investment	1.5%			1.1%		
VC liq. rights = cum. investment	27.3%			29.0%		
VC liquidation rights > cum. investment	71.2%			69.9%		
Cumulative accruing dividend rate	43.8%	0.081	(0.080)	48.9%	0.079	(0.080)
Participating preferred stock	40.5%			30.8%***		
Common/Conv. plus straight preferred	7.5%			10.2%		
Other cases with liq. rights > inv.	2.4%			2.1%		
Non-VC liq. rights senior or par to VC/VC cumulative investment	49.8%	0.167	(0.000)	38.9%***	0.116	(0.000)**
Founder claims sen. or par to VC/Cum. inv.	34.3%	0.059	(0.000)	24.5%***	0.092	(0.000)**
VC has redemption/put rights	78.7%			81.7%		
Among firms with redemption/put rights only:						
Maturity, years		4.87	(5.00)		5.28	(5.00)***
Redemption includes cumul. div.	54.0%			59.2%		
Redemption at fair market value	12.9%			18.4%**		
Other redemption > cum. investment	9.8%			6.6%		
VC gets board control and/or right to sell company upon failed redemption	31.9%			38.2%		

E. Other terms

	All rounds, N = 213			*First VC rounds only, N = 98*		
	% of cases	Mean	(Med.)	% of cases	Mean	(Med.)
Automatic conversion provisions	95.2			92.6		
Auto. conv. price/round price		3.6	(3.0)		4.4	(3.0)%***
Any anti-dilution protection	94.7			91.0**		
Full ratchet	21.9			24.7		
Weighted average	78.1			75.3		
Founder vesting	41.2			48.0*		
Founder non-compete clauses	70.4			71.2		
Founder non-compete, excl. California	73.5			78.4		

Post-round allocations of rights for 213 investments in 119 portfolio companies by 14 venture capital partnerships. Investments were made between 1987 and 1999. VC allocations are aggregated over all claims from VCs present in a particular round. Founders include the founding management team. Others include employees and non-VC investors. In *Panel A*, VC%, founders% and other% are, respectively, the percentage of residual cash flow rights (*i.e.* fully diluted equity) owned by the VCs, the founders, and others. Minimum VC ownership if management meets all performance and vesting milestones or contingencies. Max founders and employees vesting occurs if non-performance based management stock and options vest. Maximum VC ownership occurs if management does not meet performance milestones and stock and options do not vest. In *Panel B*, normal board is the board at the completion of the financing. Adverse state board is the board that will result if the portfolio company performs poorly or reaches an adverse state. VC seats are board seats that are reserved for VCs. Founder seats are board seats that are reserved for or controlled by the founders/entrepreneurs. Outsider seats are board seats that are to be filled by individuals mutually agreed upon by the VCs and the founders/entrepreneurs. % seats to cash flow is the fraction of board seats divided by the fraction of residual cash flow rights held by the VCs, founders and others. The % seats to cash flow excludes observations where cash flow rights are zero. In *Panel C*, minimum (maximum) VC votes represents the minimum (maximum) votes the VCs control based on subsequent management performance and vesting milestones or contingencies. % VC, % Founder and % Neither control are, respectively, the percentage of instances in which voting control is held by the VCs, the founders, or neither. % Votes to Cash Flow is the fraction of votes divided by the fraction of residual cash flow rights held by the VCs, Founders and Others. The % Votes to Cash Flow excludes observations where cash flow rights are zero. In *Panel D* liquidation rights are the proceeds accruing to the party upon a liquidation or bankruptcy. The mean and median dividend rates are over observations that have cumulative accruing dividends, while mean and median fractions of non-VC senior or par claims are over all observations. In *Panel E*, conversion price is the IPO or sale price per share of common stock at which the venture capital securities automatically convert into common stock. Round price is the price per share of common stock at which the securities issued in the current round convert or are priced. If a company subsequently issues equity at a lower price per share than the current round: under a full ratchet provision, the conversion price on the current round drops to the new issue price; under a weighted-average provision, the conversion price of the current round declines to a value between the current round and the new issue price. First VC rounds differ from subsequent rounds at the 1%***; 5%**, and 10%* levels.

Panel A also indicates that there are state-contingencies built into the cash flow rights. The VC stake is a median of 4.2% (average of 8.8%) lower under full vesting and good performance compared to the minimum vesting, bad performance state. State-contingencies are significantly greater in first VC rounds compared to subsequent ones, with a median of 8.0% (average 12.6%).

3.3 Board and Voting Rights

The rights to control or make corporate decisions are provided in board rights and in voting rights. The board is generally responsible for (1) hiring, evaluating, and firing top management; and (2) advising and ratifying general corporate strategies and decisions. Certain corporate actions are governed or subject to shareholder votes. These vary across firms, but sometimes include large acquisitions, asset sales, subsequent financings, election of directors, or any other actions stipulated by contract.

Board rights and voting rights can be different from cash flow rights and from each other. The difference is achieved in a number of ways including unvested stock options (which do not have votes), non-voting stock, contracts specifying a change in equity ownership at the IPO (*i.e.* at the point when the VC has pre-committed to giving up most control rights), or explicit contracting on the right to exercise votes depending on performance targets. Board rights, in turn, can be separated from voting rights through explicit agreements on the election of directors. Different securities also can have different rights to elect directors. Panels B and C of Table 1 describe board and voting rights in our sample.

3.3.1 *Board Rights*

We distinguish between three kinds of board members — VCs, founders, and outsiders. VC seats are board seats that are reserved for or controlled by VCs. Founder seats are board seats that are reserved for or controlled by the founders/entrepreneurs. Outsider seats are board seats that are to be filled by individuals mutually agreed upon by the VCs and the founders/entrepreneurs.

We also distinguish between normal board rights that reflect the board rights or composition at the completion of the financing from adverse state board rights that reflect board rights or composition if the portfolio company performs poorly or reaches an adverse state.

Panel B reports that boards have an average of and a median of six members. These boards are appreciably smaller than those of public companies. Overall, the VC has the majority of the board seats in 25% of the cases, the founders in 14% of the cases, and neither in 61% of the cases. VC board control is less common for first VC rounds.

State-contingent board provisions (*i.e.* the VC gets control of the board in the bad state) are present in 18% of the cases. This provides an important example of state-contingent control rights that do not occur simply in case of default on a debt payment. This state-contingency result and those that follow are important in light of several of the financial contracting theories we describe in Section 4.

3.3.2 *Voting Rights*

Panel C of Table 2 reports post-round voting rights. Voting rights measure the percentage of votes that investors and management have to effect corporate decisions.

In panel C, minimum (maximum) VC votes represents the minimum (maximum) votes the VCs control based on subsequent management performance and stock vesting milestones or contingencies. VC%, Founder%, and Neither% control are, respectively, the percentage of instances in which voting control is held by the VCs, the founders, or neither. Switch in control indicates the percentage of instances in which voting control can switch based on subsequent performance.

Panel C indicates that VCs have a voting majority in 53% of all financings in the minimum contingency case and in 41% of first VC rounds. In the maximum VC vote contingency cases, VCs control a voting majority in 69% of all financings and 61% of first VC rounds.

Voting control also is commonly state-contingent. In 18% of all financings and 25% of first VC financings, voting control switches depending on state-contingencies.

We also measure the degree to which voting and cash flow rights are separated by the fraction of votes to cash flow. VCs hold a significantly higher fraction of votes than cash flow rights compared to the founder, while both VCs and founders hold more votes than others, such as employees.

3.4 Liquidation Cash Flow Rights

The residual cash flow rights discussed in the previous section describe how the cash flow rights of the company are divided in the good state of the world, when the value of the venture is sufficiently high and after senior claims have been paid off. In contrast, when the value of the venture is low, the cash-flow rights go to the senior claims, which we call the liquidation cash flow rights. In this subsection and in panel D of Table 2, we describe the liquidation cash flow rights in VC financings.

First, VCs have claims that in liquidation are senior to the common stock claims of the founders. This is true in all but one of the financings. In that financing, the VC bought common stock.

Second, the claims of the VCs in liquidation are typically at least as large as the original investments. Panel B indicates that this is true in more than 98% of the financings.

Even though most of the financings give liquidation claims to the VCs, there are some cross-sectional differences in how strong these are for different deals. One common way of making the liquidation rights stronger is to make the preferred dividends cumulative (rather than non-cumulative). Even though these are dividends that do not have to be paid out, they accumulate and are added to the liquidation claim. Cumulative preferred dividends are present in 43.8% of our financings.

Another common way that VCs strengthen liquidation rights is to use either participating convertible preferred stock or a combination of common and straight preferred stock. These are present in 48% of our deals. In both of these cases, the VC receives not only a senior liquidation claim up to the face value of the preferred (plus the accumulated dividend, if present) but also shares whatever value is left after the senior claim has been paid off with the common stock.

3.5 Redemption Rights

Optional redemption and put provisions also are commonly used to strengthen the liquidation rights of the VC's investment. After some period of time, these provisions give the VC the right to demand that the firm redeem the VC's claim, typically at liquidation value (or occasionally, at the maximum of the liquidation value and "fair market value"). This is very similar to the required repayment of principal at the maturity of a debt claim. Without this provision, the liquidation right loses much of its bite because there are no other contracted payments for the firm to default on. Unlike a debt claim, however, the company cannot force the VC to exercise the redemption right. Panel D indicates that redemption provisions are present in 78.7% of our financings with a typical maturity of 5 years.

3.6 Other Terms

VC financings include a number of additional terms and conditions. Bartlett (1995), Gompers (1998), Levin (1998) and Sahlman (1990) detail many of these. In this section, we describe several of the terms and conditions that we believe are relevant to the financial contracting theories.

3.6.1 *Automatic Conversion*

Securities in VC financings often include automatic conversion provisions in which the security held by the VCs automatically converts into common stock under certain conditions. These conditions relate almost exclusively to an initial public offering (IPO) and require a minimum common stock price, dollar amount of proceeds, and/or market capitalization for the company.[9]

As Black and Gilson (1998) argue, the effect of these provisions is to require the VCs to give up their superior control, board, voting, and liquidation rights if the company attains a desired level of performance. Upon such performance, the VCs retain only those rights associated with their ownership of common stock. If the company does not deliver that performance, the VCs retain their superior control rights. This provides the entrepreneur an incentive to perform in addition to the monetary incentive.

Panel E of Table 2 indicates that an automatic conversion provision is present in 95% of the financing rounds. The financing rounds that included an automatic conversion provision required that the company complete an IPO at an IPO stock price a median 3.0 times greater than the stock price of the financing round. The ratio is significantly higher in first VC rounds.

It is worth emphasizing that at the median ratio of 3.0, the VCs are not willing to give up control unless they triple their money. Over a 4-year horizon, this works out to a return of 31% per year.

3.6.2 *Anti-Dilution Protection*

VC financings also frequently include anti-dilution protection that protects the VC against future financing rounds at a lower valuation than the valuation of the current (protected) round. In the extreme case, known as full ratchet protection, the protected security receives a claim to enough additional shares in the subsequent financing to reduce the price of the protected issue to the price of the new issue. In a convertible issue, this is accomplished by decreasing the conversion price on the protected issue to the conversion price of the new issue. The other common type of anti-dilution protection is the weighted average ratchet. Under a weighted average ratchet, the reduction in the conversion price (or common stock price) of the protected issue is a function of the existing shares, the new shares issued and the conversion price of the new issue.

9. Unlike Gompers (1998), who analysed 50 contracts for one specific VC firm, we never observe automatic conversion contingent on profit or sales benchmarks, and conclude that these are probably quite rare.

Panel E indicates that almost 95% of the financings include anti-dilution protection. About 78% of these financings utilize the weighted average method rather than the full ratchet method.

3.6.3 *Vesting and Non-Compete Clauses*

The inalienability of human capital theories of Hart and Moore (1994) assume that the entrepreneur cannot contractually commit to stay with the firm. Even though it is not possible to write enforceable contracts that compel the entrepreneur to stay with a firm, there are contractual provisions that make it more costly for the entrepreneur to leave. In real-world contracts, two methods are commonly used to make it costly for the entrepreneur to leave the firm.

First, the entrepreneur's shares can vest over time. This means that the company receives or can buy back any unvested shares for some low value if the entrepreneur leaves. The earlier the entrepreneur leaves, the more shares are unvested. Second, the VCs can require the entrepreneur to sign a non-compete contract that prohibits him from working for another firm in the same industry for some period of time if he leaves. Both of these provisions improve the bargaining power of the VCs if the entrepreneur tries to hold up the VCs.

Panel E shows that the VC financings commonly utilize both founder vesting and non-compete clauses. Founder vesting is used in almost 41% of financing rounds. Such vesting is more frequent in first VC financings (48%). Non-compete clauses are used in approximately 70% of the financings.

3.7 Contingencies

Different theories make different assumptions concerning what it is and is not possible to write contracts on. For example, some financial contracting theories — see Hart and Moore (1998) — assume that the entrepreneur and outside investors can observe firm output, but cannot write contracts on that output because output cannot be verified in court.

Panel A of Table 3 reports the extent and nature of contracts between VCs and entrepreneurs that are contingent. Contracts may be contingent on subsequent financial performance, non-financial performance, actions, dividend payments, future security offerings, or continued employment. Contingencies may affect cash flow rights, voting rights, board rights, sale rights, liquidation rights, redemption rights, or future funding. Panel B reports specific examples of these contingencies.

A. Percentage of rounds with contingent contracts

	Cash flow rights	Voting rights	Board rights	Right to force sale	Liquidation, or dividend amount	Redempt. rights	Release of committed funds	Any rights
Contingent on financial performance	8.0% [11.2]*	5.6% [7.1]	0.5% [1.0]	1.4% [2.0]	3.3% [2.0]	0.5% [1.0]	4.2% [7.1]*	17.4% [22.4]*
Contingent on non-financial perform	6.1 [6.1]	4.2 [3.1]	0.0 [0.0]	0.0 [0.0]	0.0 [0.0]	0.0 [0.0]	3.3 [5.1]	8.9 [11.2]
Contingent on actions	1.9 [2.0]	0.5 [0.0]	0.5 [1.0]	0.0 [0.0]	0.0 [0.0]	0.5 [0.0]	8.9 [12.2]	11.3 [14.3]
Contingent on default on dividend or redemption payment	5.2 [6.1]	5.2 [6.1]	19.2 [21.4]	1.4 [2.0]	2.8 [1.0]	0.5 [0.0]	0.0 [0.0]	27.7 [29.6]
Contingent on future securities offerings or "fair market value"	8.9 [13.3]**	7.5 [9.2]	0.0 [0.0]	3.8 [5.1]	11.7 [16.3]*	0.9 [1.0]	0.9 [1.0]	21.1 [27.6]**
Any of the above	18.8 [23.5]*	15.5 [16.3]	19.2 [22.4]	6.1 [8.2]	15.5 [19.4]	2.3 [2.0]	14.6 [20.4]**	52.6 [60.2]**
Contingent on founder remaining with firm	44.6 [51.0]*	40.4 [48.0]**	– –	0.0 [0.0]	0.0 [0.0]	0.0 [0.0]	0.9 [1.0]	40.8 [51.0]*
Any contingent contracting	52.6 [61.2]**	50.7 [58.2]**	19.2 [22.4]	6.1 [8.2]	15.5 [19.4]	2.3 [2.0]	14.6 [20.4]**	72.8 [79.6]**

Contingencies for 213 investments in 119 portfolio companies by 14 venture capital partnerships. Investments were made between 1987 and 1999. Table measures the extent to which venture capital contracts include contingencies based on observable and verifiable characteristics or states. The numbers in the table are the percentage of all rounds that exhibit a certain type of contingent contracting. The numbers in brackets are the corresponding percentages of first VC financings only. The "Contingent on future securities offerings or 'fair market value'" group excludes anti-dilution and automatic conversion provisions. First VC rounds differ from subsequent rounds at the 1%***; 5%**, and 10%* levels.

B. Examples of contingencies

Type of contingency	Examples
1. Contract contingent on financial measures of performance	• VC dividend on preferred shares, payable in common stock, is suspended if revenue and operating profit goals attained (CF, VO) • Founder (VC) receives options if revenue/earnings goal (not) attained (CF) • VC can only vote for all owned shares if realized EBIT below threshold value, in which case VC gets voting control (VO) • If net worth below threshold, VC will get three more board seats (BD) • Founder has veto power against sale of company for three years, as long as company achieves at least 80% of revenues and profits before tax relative to business plan (FS) • VC liquidation value multiple of net operating cash flow or net earnings (LI) • If earnings are below threshold, VC is allowed to redeem shares (RD) • Committed funds paid out when achieves projected net revenue (ST)
2. Contract contingent on non-financial measures of performance	• Employee shares vest when release of second major version of the product that incorporates significant new functionality, FDA approval of new drug, new corporate partnership found, or patents approved (CF, VO) • VC gets fewer shares if secures distribution agreement within 3 months (CF, VO) • Founder gets options when company secures threshold number of customers who have purchased the product and give positive feedback (CF) • Committed funding paid out when new clinical tests completed, new strategic partnership completed, or patent approved (ST)

Type of contingency	Examples
3. Contract contingent on meeting dividend of redemption payment	• If company cannot pay dividend in cash, it has to be paid in common stock (CF, VO) • If company fails to redeem preferred stock, VC elects majority of board (BD) • If company fails to pay out certain fraction of revenue as a dividend, VC elects majority of board (BD) • If company fails to redeem preferred stock, VC has the right to select an investment banker to assist in the sale of the business (FS) • If company fails to redeem preferred stock, cumulative dividend will be increased (LI)
4. Contract contingent on certain actions being taken	• Founder gets equity when VP of sales and marketing hired, or acquires certain technology (CF, VO) • VC gets board majority if company fails to recruit a CEO within 9 months (BD) • VC has option to redeem preferred stock until new CEO hired acceptable to VC (RD) • Committed funding paid out subject to new business plan for entering new markets completed and approved by board, new key executives or CEO hired, certain company acquired, or company starts to develop new facilities (ST)
5. Contract contingent on offering of securities	• Founder ownership increasing non-linear function of share price obtained in sale or IPO (CF) • VC receives dividend in stock, canceled upon IPO of minimum value, or if company manages to raise minimum amount of new funding above minimum price per share (CF, VO) • VC warrants expire if company manages to raise alternative funds where proceeds and price of securities exceed threshold (CF) • If no IPO has occurred within 5 years, VC has right to force a sale of company (FS) • VC can redeem preferred shares after IPO at a value that increases the later the IPO date (LI) • VC can redeem shares at fair market value (LI)
6. Contract contingent on founder staying with firm	• Founder loses unvested shares if employment terminated (CF, VO) • Founder loses voting rights (but keeps cash-flow rights) for shares if terminated for cause (VO) • Committed funding paid out under the condition that founder still employed (ST)

Contingencies for 213 investments in 119 portfolio companies by 14 venture capital partnerships. Investments were made between 1987 and 1999. Table gives examples of contingencies based on observable and verifiable characteristics or states. Examples include contingent residual cash flow rights (CF), voting majority (VO), board control (BD), right to force a sale (FS), liquidation or dividend cash flow rights (LI), redemption rights (RD), and release of committed financing (ST).

TABLE 3

Contingencies and the contracting space

Panel A indicates that almost 73% of the financings explicitly include some type of contingency. In particular, over 17% of financings are contingent on financial performance; almost 9% on non-financial performance; and 11% on actions. The panel also shows that in almost 15% of the financings, the VCs provide only a portion of the total funding commitment at the closing or signing of the financing. Additional funding is contingent on subsequent performance and actions. For example, in two financings, the VC provided only 5% of its total commitment at closing with the rest being contingent.[10]

Panel B reports specific examples of contingencies. In one financing round, the VCs contractually obtain voting control from the entrepreneur if the firm's EBIT — earnings before interest and taxes — falls below a mutually agreed upon amount. In another financing round, VCs obtain board control if a firm's net worth falls below a threshold. These examples indicate that VCs are able to write (and presumably enforce) contracts in which control rights are contingent on subsequent financial performance independently of cash flow rights.

10. About 55% of these contingencies (excluding vesting) specify a specific time horizon, which is typically 12-18 months from the initial closing, but in a few cases 5 years or more.

Panel B.2 shows that financing rounds include contingencies based on subsequent non-financial performance. In one instance, share vesting is contingent on product functionality or performance. In several others, vesting is contingent on FDA or patent approvals.

Panel B.4 describes financing rounds that include contingencies based on certain actions being taken. For example, in different rounds, the disbursal of committed funding is contingent on hiring new executives, developing new facilities, and completing a new business plan. Presumably, these actions are both observable and verifiable.

Overall, Table 3 generates two strong results. First, investors (VCs) commonly write contracts in which control rights are contingent on subsequent measures of financial performance, non-financial performance, and actions. Second, there is a great deal of variation in the contingencies in these contracts. By looking at the contingencies, we also obtain examples of managerial actions that the VC is trying to induce or avoid. We discuss these issues in more detail in Kaplan and Strömberg (2002).

3.8 Summary

We make several general observations concerning the descriptive results in this section.

First, VC financings allow VCs to separately allocate cash flow rights, board rights, voting rights, liquidation rights, and other control rights.

Second, while VCs use convertible securities most frequently, they also implement the same allocation of rights using combinations of multiple classes of common stock and straight preferred stock. Furthermore, VCs make frequent use of participating convertible preferred which is the equivalent of a position of preferred stock and common stock rather than a position of convertible preferred.

Third, rights are allocated such that if the company performs poorly, the VCs obtain full control. As company performance improves, the entrepreneur retains/obtains more cash flow rights and control rights. If the company performs very well, the VCs relinquish most of their control and liquidation rights.

Fourth, it is common for VCs to include non-compete and vesting provisions aimed at mitigating the potential hold-up problem between the entrepreneur and the investor. The vesting provisions are more common in early stage financings where it is more likely that the hold-up problem is more severe.

Finally, cash flow rights, control rights, voting rights, and future financings are frequently contingent on observable measures of financial and non-financial performance. These state contingent rights are more common in first VC and early stage financings.

4 Relation to Financial Contracting Theories

In this section, we interpret our results relative to financial contracting theories. We focus on three general classes of theories: (1) classical principal-agent; (2) control theories; and (3) debt theories. We consider the extent to which the contract provisions we have examined are consistent with the assumptions and predictions of the theories. We augment this discussion and analysis with cross-sectional regressions when appropriate. We conclude this section by discussing the results for the general classes of theories in relation to more recent VC specific theories.

4.1 Allocation of Cash Flow Rights and Pay-Performance Incentives

4.1.1 *Theoretical Predictions*

The first set of theories deals with the allocation of cash flow rights between the VC and entrepreneur. The classical principal-agency approach, pioneered by Holmström (1979), assumes that the agent's effort is unobservable to the principal. Signals, such as firm output or profits, however, are correlated with effort and can be contracted on. The optimal incentive contract ensures that the agent puts in enough effort by making the agent's compensation dependent on the outcome of the signals. In the basic model, and in the absence of risk-aversion, the investor maximizes the sensitivity of the agent's compensation to the signal. Moreover, it is in the investor's interest to make the entrepreneur's compensation contingent on as many verifiable signals correlated with effort as possible (the "Informativeness Principle" of Holmström (1979); see also Harris and Raviv (1979), Innes (1990)).

The result that the entrepreneur's pay-performance sensitivity should be maximized may not hold if the entrepreneur is risk averse or if multitasking problems exist. Compensation contingent on performance is costly because a risk-averse entrepreneur requires a higher level of compensation to offset the extra risk. Prendergast (1999) mentions several potentially testable predictions: (1) entrepreneurs who are more risk averse will have less pay performance sensitivity. (2) Noisier performance signals impose more risk on the entrepreneur, making pay performance sensitive compensation more expensive. Less noisy performance measures should be given relatively higher weight in compensation. (3) The higher the positive effect on performance for a given effort by the entrepreneur, the higher the pay-performance sensitivity should be. (4) If entrepreneurs differ in ability, performance sensitive contracts will be relatively more attractive to better entrepreneurs (holding risk-aversion constant). This gives rise to selection effects (see Lazear, 1986). Investors can screen out entrepreneurs by offering high-powered compensation contracts because only high-ability entrepreneurs will accept such contracts. Hence, the higher the asymmetric information regarding the ability of the entrepreneurs, the higher the pay performance sensitivity in the contracts offered by the investor.

Multi-tasking models (Holmström and Milgrom (1991), Baker (1992)) assume that there are several activities for which the entrepreneur needs to exert effort. This leads to a problem of potential "gaming", where the entrepreneur will only exert effort in the activity whose signal is most rewarded in the compensation contract. As a result, overall incentives have to be muted in the optimal compensation contract, and the principal will tend to rely more on subjective performance evaluation. This suggests that compensation should be less dependent on performance and more dependent on subjective performance measures in situations with gaming potential.

4.1.2 *Empirical Results*

The descriptive analysis of cash-flow rights in Table 2 seems largely consistent with both the assumptions and predictions of the classical principal agent approach. In our financings, the entrepreneur gets a large fraction of equity in the firm and the entrepreneur's equity stake increases with performance. Moreover, Table 3 shows that the contracts often condition the entrepreneur's equity compensation on a multitude of financial and non-financial signals, consistent with the "Informativeness Principle".

To test the models, we would ideally plot the entrepreneur's compensation as a function of the venture's value, and examine what independent variables determine the shape of this function. The pay-performance sensitivity of the founder's compensation is increasing both in the function's slope — the fraction of the value promised to the entrepreneur at a given value — and its convexity — the increase in the fraction of the value given to the entrepreneur as value increases.

Because it is hard to capture these aspects in one single measure and no measure is perfect, we examine several. First, we look at the percentage of the residual cash flow rights allocated to the founder (FRCFs). This captures the compensation function slope given that the venture is worth more than the liquidation claims. This percentage, unfortunately, is not ideal, because it is also potentially a function of the (unobservable) quality of the entrepreneur.

Second, we look at the change in the fraction of FRCFs as a function of vesting. As this fraction becomes more state-contingent, the compensation function becomes more convex and the pay-performance sensitivity increases. We separate contingencies into the sensitivity due to performance vesting — financial or non-financial — and the sensitivity due to time vesting of the founders' shares. This is a relevant separation in theory as time vesting can be interpreted as a form of subjective performance evaluation. With time vesting, the founder's compensation is contingent on the board's decision to retain the founder, rather than on explicit benchmarks. This might be expected to be more likely when multi-tasking is present.[11] We measure the change in FRCFs both on an absolute scale and relative to the level of the FRCF. We think the relative change in FRCF is more indicative of incentives because it measures the fraction of the founders' equity that is at risk, therefore, controlling for unobservable quality.

Third, we look at the degree to which the founder has claims to the liquidation proceeds. Giving the founder part of the liquidation cash flow rights lowers the convexity of the compensation function and leads to lower pay performance sensitivity.

The key independent variables in our analyses are pre-revenue, repeat entrepreneur, and months since the first VC round. Pre-revenue equals one if the company had no revenues at the time of financing, and zero otherwise. It seems likely that uncertainty and asymmetric information are greater for pre-revenue firms. It also is arguable that incentive problems are more severe for early stage ventures since the entrepreneur's effort is relatively more important. As Myers (2000) assumes, this likely would be the case of the development of a new technology or concept. Once the technology or concept has been created or validated, the founders are more replaceable with outsiders.

Repeat entrepreneur takes the value of one if the founders previously founded a company that was either taken public or acquired by a public company, and zero otherwise. This provides a measure of the extent to which VC may have prior information on the quality of the founders. Such information reduces the likelihood of adverse selection and the uncertainty of the venture.[12] If this is important, we would expect repeat entrepreneurs to have lower powered incentives. On the other hand, repeat entrepreneur also is likely to be correlated with higher outside wealth and lower risk

11. This also is a prediction from the control theory of Hart and Moore (1994) that we describe in the following section. Vesting makes it more costly for the founder to leave the company which mitigates a potential hold-up problem.

12. We use the company business plan, the VC analysis, and company web sites to obtain this information.

aversion. If repeat entrepreneur measures differences in risk aversion, we would expect repeat entrepreneurs to have higher powered incentives.

Months since the first VC financing round is another measure of asymmetric information. VC uncertainty about management quality and asymmetric information should be highest in the first VC financing round and should decrease thereafter.

Table 4 presents the results of our cross-sectional regression analyses. The regressions include controls for industry volatility, industry research and development (R&D), industry size, company location, and VC.[13] We also control for the amount of funds invested by the VC by including in the accumulated VC investment as a control variable.[14] Finally, we attempt to include a control for performance. Although we have incomplete data on accounting performance, we have more complete data on financing terms. Accordingly, we measure performance based on the annual return on the securities since the initial investment. When the company performs poorly, the VCs will pay less for the securities acquired in the round. A problem with using this return as an independent variable is that the round price is endogenous and related to the percentage of equity allocated to the VC in the round. To address this, we include dummies for whether the return is in the upper or lower quartile rather than including the return directly.

The first regression in Table 4 examines the determinants of the fraction of equity (cash flow rights) allocated to the entrepreneur. The only significant result is that as the VC-entrepreneur relationship progresses, the founder's equity stake declines. This is consistent with classical principal agent theory — lower powered incentives are required as asymmetric information declines. This also may be a function of the need to provide newly hired managers with equity incentives as the company grows.

The second and third regressions of Table 4 analyse the determinants of absolute and relative sensitivity to explicit performance benchmarks. Explicit performance-based equity compensation is used more in pre-revenue ventures, less for repeat entrepreneurs, and earlier in VC-founder relationships. All three of these results are consistent with asymmetric information and moral hazard models where pay performance sensitivity increases when uncertainty about venture quality is higher. The negative coefficient on repeat entrepreneur suggests that repeat entrepreneur picks up information effects rather than risk aversion effects. Also, the negative coefficient on the return variable indicates that the use of explicit performance benchmarks increases with poor performance.

13. The table provides a more detailed description of the control variables in the regressions.

14. Because this is potentially endogenous, we instrument this variable with median industry capital expenditures and yearly time fixed effects using two-stage least squares.

TABLE 4

Determinants of founder cash-flow incentives

	% Founder residual cash flow rights (FRCF), best case	% FRCF sensitivity, performance benchmarks	Relative % FRCF sensitivity, performance benchmarks	% FRCF sensitivity, vesting	Relative % FRCF sensitivity, vesting	Founder has liquidation CF rights (logit)
Sample	All, $N = 189$	All, $N = 189$	All, $N = 188$	All, $N = 189$	All, $N = 188$	All, $N = 163$
Constant	–	–	–	–	–	–
Pre-revenue	-3.68 (3.17)	1.61 (0.63)**	4.74 (1.69)***	8.47 (2.33)***	23.62 (6.04)***	0.06 (0.56)
Repeat entrepr.	6.14 (3.76)	-0.67 (0.47)	-2.20 (1.24)*	-0.06 (2.30)	1.96 (7.09)	1.78 (0.62)***
Mos. since 1st VC round	-0.70 (0.12)***	-0.06 (0.03)**	-0.13 (0.06)**	-0.063 (0.06)	-0.37 (0.20)*	0.028 (0.013)**
VC cum. invest (instrumented)	3.67 (2.79)	1.13 (0.67)*	3.20 (1.72)*	-0.37 (1.76)	3.51 (5.38)	–
Return	-1.35 (2.44)	-0.81 (0.36)**	-2.34 (1.02)**	0.08 (1.01)	1.86 (3.36)	0.25 (0.44)
Ind. volatility	-2.57 (2.36)	-0.45 (0.38)	-2.03 (0.93)**	4.16 (1.69)**	10.76 (4.19)**	0.012 (0.38)
Ind. R&D/sales	35.0 (37.6)	-20.1 (11.2)*	-69.4 (31.4)**	23.4 (21.7)	17.48 (67.66)	-6.74 (5.76)
Industry size	1.53 (1.20)	0.68 (0.28)**	2.43 (0.81)***	-0.72 (0.75)	-0.34 (2.42)	-0.094 (0.20)
California	1.86 (3.55)	-2.02 (0.70)***	-6.61 (1.91)***	-1.82 (2.36)	-19.01 (7.01)***	-0.99 (0.58)*
Midwest	12.9 (4.30)***	-0.44 (0.89)	-0.55 (2.17)	-2.40 (2.06)	-20.91 (6.89)***	-0.67 (0.58)
North-east	4.67 (4.00)	-1.21 (0.93)	-4.78 (2.29)**	-1.42 (2.09)	-10.16 (7.13)	-1.63 (0.60)***
χ^2/F-test, location [P-value]	3.70 [0.03]**	6.18 [0.002]***	6.23 [0.002]***	0.08 [0.92]	0.95 [0.38]	2.49 [0.29]
VC dummies	Yes	Yes	Yes	Yes	Yes	Yes
χ^2/F-test, VC [P-value]	2.30 [0.02]**	2.72 [0.008]***	2.94 [0.004]***	1.67 [0.11]	0.84 [0.57]	8.94 [0.18]
Adj. / Ps. R2	0.31	0.33	0.40	0.27	0.30	0.22

OLS and two-stage least squares regressions of founder cash-flow incentives on various independent variables for 213 investments in 119 portfolio companies by 14 venture capital partnerships. Investments were made between 1987 and 1999. % Founder residual cash flow rights (FRCF), best case is the % of cash flow rights owned by founders if they meet all time and performance vesting milestones. % FRCF sensitivity, performance (time vesting) benchmarks is the difference in founders equity if they meet performance (time vesting) benchmarks. Relative % FRCF sensitivity, performance (time vesting) benchmarks are the corresponding measures as a percentage of the founder's equity stake in the best case. Pre-revenue takes the value of one if the venture has no revenues at the time of financing, and zero otherwise. Repeat entrep. takes the value of one if the founder's previous venture was able to go public or was sold to a public company. Industry volatility is the value-weighted volatility of the log stock return for the venture's industry according to the Fama and French (1997) industry classification. Industry R&D/sales is the aggregate R&D expense to sales for public firms in the venture's three-digit SIC industry according to COMPUSTAT. Industry size is equal to log sales, in millions, in the venture's four-digit SIC industry according to the 1997 U.S. census. VC cumulative investment is instrumented using two-stage least squares with industry capital expenditures to sales as well as year dummies. Return takes the value of minus one if the ratio of per share round price to first round price is in the lowest quartile, one if it is in the highest quartile, and zero otherwise. White (1980) robust standard errors are in parentheses. Asterisks indicate statistical significance at the 1%***; 5%**, and 10%* levels. In the fourth regression, 29 observations (corresponding to two specific VCs) had to be dropped due to collinearity.

The results imply economically meaningful effects. The relative (absolute) sensitivity to explicit performance benchmarks is 4.7% (1.6%) greater in pre-revenue companies and 2.2% (0.7%) lower when repeat entrepreneurs are present. These compare to mean values for relative and absolute sensitivities of 3.5% and 1.1%, respectively.

The fourth and fifth regressions analyse the determinants of absolute and relative pay performance sensitivity due to time vesting. Time vesting is significantly higher for pre-revenue ventures and, in the relative regressions, for early VC-founder relationships. The relative and absolute sensitivities to time vesting for pre-revenue companies are large at 23.6 and 8.5%, respectively. Again, this is supportive of asymmetric information and moral hazard models.

Interestingly, the signs on the industry ratios are opposite the ones in the performance benchmarks regressions. The contracts in high volatility, high R&D, and smaller, presumably less established industries seem to use time vesting rather than explicit performance benchmarks to induce pay-performance sensitivity. One interpretation, consistent with theory, is that these are environments where explicit performance signals are noisier measures of true performance. Because of this, explicit performance benchmarking will be more costly, both because of managerial risk-aversion as well as multi-tasking or gaming problems.

Finally, in the sixth regression, we use a logit specification to analyse the determinants of founder liquidation rights.[15] While pre-revenue is not significant, both repeat entrepreneur and months since first VC round are positive and significant. Hence, when the founder has been successful in the past, and as the VC learns more about the firm over time, the founder has more liquidation rights. Again, this is consistent with less pay-for-performance as asymmetric information declines. Again, this result is not consistent with repeat entrepreneur as a measure of (less) risk aversion.

The results in Table 4 control for VC and location fixed effects. The use of performance benchmarks varies significantly among VCs. Also, explicit performance benchmarks are used significantly less in California ventures. Hence, contract design may be affected by different contracting "styles" for different VCs and markets.

To sum up, the regressions in Table 4 are largely supportive of classical principal agent theories and their screening implications. As uncertainty about the quality of the venture and the founder increases, the VC increases the pay performance sensitivity by making the founder's cash flow compensation increasingly convex in performance through more explicit performance compensation, more time vesting, and fewer liquidation cash flow rights. Also, as explicit

15. The logit regression excludes observations for VCs that did not allocate founder liquidation rights in any of their investments. The results are qualitatively similar when we exclude the VC dummies and include all observations.

performance signals become noisier measures of true performance, the contracts substitute explicit performance benchmarks with more vesting and lower liquidation cash flow rights.

4.2 Control Theories: Cash Flow Verifiable but Not Actions

4.2.1 *Theoretical Predictions*

Board rights and voting rights give the controlling party the right to decide on any action that is not pre-specified in the original contract. Such rights are valuable in an incomplete contracting world, when it is not feasible or credible to specify all possible actions and contingencies in an *ex ante* contract. Incomplete contracting and control rights were introduced by Grossman and Hart (1986) and Hart and Moore (1988, 1990).[16] These theories change the traditional principal-agent model assumptions by assuming that actions are observable, but not verifiable. Output and monetary benefits may or may not be contractible. As a result, control rights that determine who chooses which action to take will be important.

Two important papers that take this approach are Aghion and Bolton (1992) and Dewatripont and Tirole (1994). In Aghion and Bolton (1992), the project yields both monetary benefits that are verifiable and transferable to outside investors, and private benefits or actions that are non-verifiable and go only to the entrepreneur. The magnitude of these benefits, in turn, depends on what (non-verifiable) action is taken with respect to the project. This introduces a conflict of interest. Aghion and Bolton (1992) show that as the external financing capacity of the project increases (*i.e.* the higher the profitability of the project and the lower the conflicts of interest), control moves from more investor control to more entrepreneur control. In particular, for projects with high external financing capacity, the entrepreneur should always have control. As external financing capacity decreases, there should be state-contingent control similar to a debt contract that transfers control to investors only in bad states of the world. Finally, for projects with low external financing capacity, the investor should always be allocated control.

Dewatripont and Tirole (1994) build on Aghion and Bolton (1992) by focusing on the optimal correlation between control rights and cash flow rights. In their model, the entrepreneur always prefers to take the riskier action (*e.g.* continuing the project), even though it will be *ex post* optimal to take the less risky action (*e.g.* liquidate the project) when the project is doing badly. They show that when performance is poor, the party in control should have a cash flow claim that is concave in performance (such as debt), while when

16. Also, see Hart (1995) and Hart (2001) for an overview of these theories.

performance improves more control should be transferred to a holder of a convex cash flow claim (such as equity).

4.2.2 *Empirical Results*

The extensive use of control rights in our sample is broadly consistent with the assumptions and predictions of these theories. State-contingent board and voting control rights also are common features in our contracts. This contracting is more elaborate than that in ordinary debt contracts that only give liquidation rights in case of default on a promised payment. As Table 3 shows, control can be made contingent on financial performance or on non-financial events independently of the division of cash-flow rights. These results are broadly consistent with Aghion and Bolton (1992). We now examine the predictions of these theories in more detail by analysing the cross-section.

The control theories predict that as agency problems and financial constraints become more severe, the contracts should change from entrepreneur control to state-contingent control to full VC control. We interpret the situation where neither the VC nor the founder is in control as similar to state-contingent control. For example, in boards where outside, jointly appointed, board members are pivotal, it seems plausible that these members will vote with the VC as founder performance declines. On the other hand, we assume that when the VC explicitly gets control in the bad state, through a default board provision or state-contingent voting control, the VC has relatively more control compared to cases where the outsiders are pivotal. Therefore, for a given financing round, we let the board/voting control variables equal zero if the founder always controls a majority of the seats/votes, one if neither the VC nor the founder has a majority of the seats/votes in the bad state, two if the VC controls a majority in the bad state only, and three if the VC controls a majority of the seats/votes in the good and bad states.[17]

The first two regressions presented in Table 5 use ordered logits to analyse board rights and voting rights, respectively. VCs are more likely to have board and voting control in pre-revenue ventures, as the time since the first financing round increases, and in industries with higher volatility and more fixed assets. VCs are more likely to have board control when returns are high and less likely to have voting control with repeat entrepreneurs.

The coefficients are economically as well as statistically significant. For example, VC voting control (group 3) is almost 30% more likely in pre-revenue companies while the other three states are each roughly 10% less likely. VC voting control is 20% less likely in companies with a repeat entrepreneur while neither control in the bad state (group one) is 10% more likely.

17. The classification of the situation in which neither party is in control in the bad state is arguably ambiguous. We have run alternative regressions (not in the table) in which we classify these situations as entrepreneur control (0) or with the VC control in the bad state (2). Our results are qualitatively identical.

TABLE 5

Determinants of control allocations

	Degree of VC board control (ordered logit)	Degree of VC voting control (ordered logit)	Ln auto. conv. price/round price (2SLS)
Observations	All rounds N = 182	All rounds N = 192	All rounds N = 158
Constant	–	–	–
Pre-revenue	0.81 (0.39)**	1.27 (0.43)***	0.24 (0.10)**
Repeat entrepr.	0.07 (0.50)	-0.83 (0.47)*	-0.25 (0.12)**
Months since 1st VC round	0.066 (0.012)***	0.066 (0.014)***	-0.005 (0.005)
VC cum. invest (instrumented)	–	–	-0.084 (0.088)
Return	0.58 (0.35)*	0.24 (0.32)	-0.36 (0.12)***
Ind. volatility	0.63 (0.29)**	0.87 (0.35)**	0.071 (0.074)
Ind. fixed assets	6.25 (2.51)**	5.54 (3.18)*	-0.67 (0.81)
Industry size	-0.08 (0.17)	-0.29 (0.19)	-0.090 (0.049)*
California	-0.45 (0.48)	-0.74 (0.52)	-0.24 (0.13)*
Midwest	0.44 (0.49)	-1.36 (0.53)**	-0.27 (0.12)**
North-east	1.14 (0.47)**	-1.35 (0.50)**	-0.20 (0.14)
χ^2/F-test, location	$\chi^2(2)$ = 9.6***	$\chi^2(2)$ = 1.8	$F(2, 138)$ = 0.12
[P-value]	[0.01]	[0.42]	[0.89]
VC dummies?	Yes	Yes	Yes
χ^2/F-test, VC [P-value]	$\chi^2(7)$ = 20.1*** [0.01]	$\chi^2(7)$ = 11.8* [0.11]	$F(8, 138)$ = 1.26 [0.27]
Adj. / Ps. R2	0.17	0.17	0.57
Ord. logit cut-offs:			
Cut-off group 1	2.91	1.19	
Cut-off group 2	6.12	2.72	
Cut-off group 3	6.90	3.53	

Two-stage least squares and ordered logit regressions of VC board control, voting control, and automatic conversion provisions on various independent variables for 213 investments in 119 portfolio companies by 14 VC partnerships. Investments were made between 1987 and 1999. The degree of board and voting control variables take the value of 0 if the founder always has control, 1 if neither the VC nor the founder has control, 2 if the VCs have control only in the bad state, and 3 if the VCs always have control. Pre-revenue takes the value of one if the venture has no revenues at the time of financing, and zero otherwise. Repeat entrepr. takes the value of one if the founder's previous venture was able to go public or was sold to a public company. Industry volatility is the value-weighted volatility of the log stock return for the firm's industry according to the Fama and French (1997) industry classification. Industry fixed assets is the median fixed to total assets for all (public as well as closely held) firms in the venture's four-digit SIC industry according to Onesource. Industry size is equal to log sales, in millions, in the venture's four-digit SIC industry according to the 1997 U.S. census. VC cumulative investment is instrumented using two-stage least squares with industry capital expenditures to sales as well as year dummies. Return takes the value of minus one if the ratio of per share round price to first round price is in the lowest quartile, one if it is in the highest quartile, and zero otherwise. White (1980) robust standard errors are in parentheses. Asterisks indicate statistical significance at the 1%***; 5%**, and 10%* levels.

These results indicate that when the uncertainty about the venture and the quality of the founder is higher, the VC is allocated more control. In contrast, VC control increases as the VC-entrepreneur relationship progresses. Although the uncertainty about the venture should decrease over time, the VC also invests more funds. The founder's stake declines over time as the VC receives more control and cash flow rights in exchange for the additional funds invested.[18] This is consistent with Aghion and Bolton (1992) who predict that the investor should be allocated more control as the financing constraint becomes more binding.

Of the other industry characteristics, the amount of fixed to total assets is significantly positively related to VC voting control.[19] One explanation for this is that such companies are less reliant on the intangible human capital of the original founder, making intervention by the VC more efficient.

The last regression uses the price at which the VC's securities are automatically converted into common equity as a measure of VC control. The lower this price is, the more states in which the VC has pre-committed to give up its control and liquidation rights. As a dependent variable, we normalize the automatic conversion price by dividing by the round price and then taking logs.

The automatic conversion price is higher for pre-revenue ventures and lower for repeat entrepreneurs. Again, this is supportive of the prediction that as uncertainty about the quality of venture increases, the VC demands more control. Among the other industry controls, the automatic conversion price is lower for ventures in larger, more established industries. Finally, as one might expect almost by construction, the relative automatic conversion price decreases as the round price increases (as measured by return). As with cash flow rights, the degree of board and voting control varies significantly across different VCs. Also, the degree of board control is higher in the companies based in the Northeast U.S.

Together, the results imply that for ventures with greater initial uncertainty about viability, the VC receives more board and voting control, and demands stronger performance (through the automatic conversion price) before ceding control. This is broadly consistent with Aghion and Bolton (1992). When uncertainty is high, conflicts are more likely to arise between the VC and the founder regarding issues whether the manager should be replaced or the business should be continued. Hence, the VCs need to be allocated control in more states in order for their investment to be *ex ante* profitable.

4.3 Debt Theories and the Allocation of Liquidation Rights

4.3.1 *Theoretical Predictions*

Many financial contracting theories predict that the investor should hold a debt-like claim. As mentioned in Section 4.1.1, the secu-

18. When we include the log accumulated VC financing in the ordered logit regression, it is strongly positive and significant. The months since first VC round variable is still significant. The amount of financing is endogenous, and cannot be instrumented in an ordered logit framework, hence, we do not include this specification in the table. We have also run 2SLS regressions on the difference between the fraction of VC and founder votes or board seats, instrumenting log VC investment with year dummies. Log VC financing is positive and all other results are similar.

19. When we replace fixed to total assets with R&D to sales, the coefficient is negative. Because the two variables are highly negatively correlated, we do not include both simultaneously in the regressions. The result does not change when we include cumulative VC investment. We do not include it in the reported regression because it is endogenous to VC control and cannot be instrumented in the ordered logit framework.

rity design theories based on classical principal agent theory (such as Innes, 1990) show that giving investors a senior claim is useful for incentive purposes as it makes the manager's residual claim more sensitive to performance. Similarly, signaling theories such as Myers and Majluf (1984) and Duffie and Demarzo (1999), show that in an asymmetric information setting, the manager can signal that success is more likely by offering the investor a senior claim that receives all of the value in case of failure. According to these models, VC liquidation rights should be stronger when there is greater uncertainty about venture quality and founder ability.

Apart from seniority, however, the other important characteristic of debt is the ability to take control and liquidate the firm when performance is bad. This can be interpreted as another way of allocating the investor state-contingent control. One criticism, however, of this explanation for debt — see Hart (1995) — is that changes in control in Aghion and Bolton (1992) do not necessarily coincide with default on a contracted payment, which is a central feature of real-world debt contracts. This feature of debt can be derived in a model where not only actions, but also profits and cash flows are non-observable or non-verifiable. In this world, there is no way to stop the entrepreneur from stealing the firm's profits.

There are two main strands to this literature, which we denote "stealing models". Costly state verification (CSV) models — *e.g.* Townsend (1979) and Gale and Hellwig (1985) — assume that profits are completely unobservable, unless a verification cost is paid. The other strand — *e.g.* Hart and Moore (1998), Bolton and Scharfstein (1990) and Fluck (1998) — assumes that profits are observable but not verifiable to outsiders and courts. The optimal financial claim in both approaches is a debt-like claim in which (1) the entrepreneur promises a fixed payment to the investor; and (2) the investor takes control of the project and liquidates the assets if the payment is not made. Hence, these theories are consistent both with the seniority and the default aspects of debt contracts. Bolton and Scharfstein (1990) also show that withholding future funding can play a role similar to demanding repayment in forcing liquidation.

In these models, the value investors can realize when they seize assets limits the liquidation claim that can be promised to outside investors. Hence, liquidation claims should be greater when assets are more tangible and when the founder's human capital is less crucial. Because the liquidation threat always exists in the stealing models, there are no cross-sectional predictions regarding the investor's ability to force liquidation in the bad state. Given that the models rely on the assumption of non-verifiability of cash flow, however, one possible prediction would be where cash flow is harder to verify, the ability to liquidate should be more important and we should observe stronger VC liquidation rights.

4.3.2 *Empirical Approach*

In Section 3, we showed that the allocation of liquidation rights is an important feature of the venture contracts. First, in all of our observations but one, the VC is senior to common equity in liquidation. The seniority of the VC claim is consistent with classical moral hazard theories, signaling and screening theories, as well as the "stealing" theories. Second, consistent with the "stealing theories", the VCs do have some power to liquidate upon default on a contracted payment.

We note, however, that "stealing" theories do not explain a number of our results including the allocation of residual cash-flow rights and the frequent contingent contracting on financial performance measures. Such features are ruled out by assumption because cash flow is not verifiable.[20,21]

In Table 6 we analyse the cross-sectional determinants of VC liquidation rights in more detail. In the first regression, we analyse the determinants of the size of the VC's liquidation claim. We use a dummy variable that equals one if the liquidation claim exceeds the VC's cumulative investment (through cumulative dividends, participating preferred, etc.) and zero otherwise.[22] Because the VC's liquidation claim varies little between rounds, we report results using the first financing round for each firm. The results with the full sample are almost identical. Overall, the results are weak. There is no evidence that the VC's liquidation claim is larger when asymmetric information problems are more severe, because volatility, pre-revenue, and repeat entrepreneur are not significant. Collateral value, measured as fixed to total assets, is not significant either. Only the debt capacity of the venture, measured as the industry median long-term debt ratio, is related to the VC liquidation claim.

The remaining regressions of Table 6 analyse the VC's ability to liquidate. We first analyse whether redemption rights are present in the VC contracts. Again the results are weak. In the second regression, redemption rights are unrelated to the pre-revenue and the repeat entrepreneur variables.

Even though redemption rights are the part of the VC contracts that most resemble debt, there are other ways that a VC can force a liquidation of badly performing firms. The most important mechanism is through staging of the investment.[23] We distinguish between two different forms of staging: *ex ante* (or within-round) and *ex post* (or between-round) staging.

20. They are still consistent with the control theory of Aghion and Bolton (1992). See Hart (2001).

21. There are "stealing" models that explain the use of outside equity. In the models of outside equity financing in Myers (2000) and Fluck (1998), the liquidation right is replaced by the right to fire management. This occurs if dividends are too low. Here it is essential, that outside equity investors have this right, which in turn implies that they need to control a majority of the board/votes. Moreover, in these models, the firm has to pay out dividends. Both of these assumptions are frequently violated in our venture capital financings. In a significant fraction, the VC lacks board/voting control. Moreover, few ventures pay any cash dividends.

22. Separate regressions on cumulative dividends and participating preferred stock generate similar results.

23. See Bolton and Scharfstein (1990). Neher (1999) provides a model of staging based on Hart and Moore (1998).

TABLE 6

Determinants of VC redemption rights, staging, and liquidation claims

	VC liq. claim > cum. invest. (logit)	VC has redemption rights (logit)	Months until next fin. round (2SLS)	Months until next fin. round (OLS)	% of funds up front (2SLS)	% of funds up front (2SLS)	% of funds up front (OLS)
Observations	1st firm observ. $N = 108$	1st firm observ. $N = 106$	All observ. $N = 164$	1st firm obs. $N = 98$	All observ. $N = 191$	All observ. $N = 191$	1st firm obs. $N = 98$
Constant	–	–	–	14.7 (7.8)*	–	103.9 (20.8)***	92.6 (30.4)***
Pre-revenue	-0.20 (0.75)	-0.32 (0.63)	-0.10 (1.10)	-1.81 (1.23)	-0.30 (3.87)	-3.69 (3.62)	-4.50 (5.19)
Repeat entrepreneur	0.28 (0.98)	-0.83 (0.81)	4.39(1.86)**	2.36 (1.39)*	3.58 (3.69)	7.69 (3.50)**	9.83 (5.91)*
Months since 1st VC round	–	–	-0.003 (0.034)	–	0.21 (0.08)**	0.28 (0.11)**	–
Investment in round (instr.)	–	–	1.86 (1.85)	–	-3.37 (3.33)	-4.24 (4.22)	–
Return	–	–	-0.30 (1.11)	–	6.36 (3.25)*	6.55 (3.14)**	–
Ind. volatility	-0.06 (0.52)	-0.20 (0.62)	-0.37 (0.89)	-1.39 (0.86)	-1.72 (2.72)	-3.65 (2.83)	-4.56 (4.37)
Ind. fixed assets	-3.75 (4.94)	-3.80 (5.08)	5.87(9.98)	–	-17.1 (30.4)	-56.7 (33.4)*	-24.8 (44.4)
Ind. LT debt to assets	11.84 (5.29)**	5.14 (4.33)	-20.8 (7.1)***	-10.7 (4.9)**	-68.2 (32.4)**	-69.2 (30.9)**	-107.2 (33.9)***
Industry size	-0.33 (0.31)	-0.20 (0.35)	0.91 (0.57)	0.62 (0.66)	1.47 (1.75)	2.59 (2.02)	0.65 (0.79)
California	-2.41 (1.06)**	-1.93 (0.91)**	1.50 (1.43)	–	7.23 (4.39)	–	–
Midwest	-1.04 (0.87)	-0.50 (1.21)	-0.90 (1.61)	–	4.67 (6.16)	–	–
North-east	-3.41 (1.18)***	-2.66 (0.92)***	1.77 (1.78)	–	5.56 (5.01)	–	–
χ^2/F-test, location	$\chi^2(3) = 9.59$** [0.02]	$\chi^2(3) = 11.36$*** [0.01]	$F(2, 143) = 1.56$ [0.21]	–	$F(2, 170) = 0.37$ [0.90]	–	–
VC dummies	Yes	Yes	Yes	No	Yes	No	No
χ^2/F-test, VC dummies	$\chi^2(8) = 6.32$ [0.61]	$\chi^2(8) = 9.85$ [0.28]	$F(8, 143) = 1.57$ [0.14]	–	$F(8, 170) = 3.50$ [0.00]***	–	–
Adj./Ps. R2	0.25	0.23	0.19	0.10	0.39	0.29	0.24

Regressions of degree of VC liquidation rights on various independent variables for 213 investments in 119 portfolio companies by 14 VC partnerships. Industry LT debt to assets is the median ratio of long-term debt to assets for public firms in the venture's three-digit SIC industry according to COMPUSTAT. For remaining variable definitions, see Table 5, above. Investments were made between 1987 and 1999. White (1980) robust standard errors are in parentheses. Asterisks indicate statistical significance at the 1%***; 5%**, and 10%* levels.

In an *ex ante* staged deal, part of the VC's committed funding is contingent on financial or non-financial performance milestones. This essentially gives the VC the right to liquidate the venture in the bad state of the world. Even many VC financings are not explicitly staged *ex ante*, most of them are implicitly staged *ex post*, in the sense that even when all the funding in the round is released immediately, future financing will be needed to support the firm until the IPO. By providing less funding in a given round, and hence shortening the time until the next financing round, the VC increases the ability to liquidate the venture if performance is unsatisfactory.[24] *Ex ante* staging within a given round, however, arguably makes this liquidation right stronger and more explicitly related to performance.

The fourth and fifth regressions in Table 6 analyse between-round staging by explaining the time until the next financing round. The repeat entrepreneur dummy is positively related to the time between rounds, indicating that previously successful founders receive more funding in a given round, reducing the VC's liquidation threat. In contrast with Gompers (1995), most of our industry variables are insignificant.[25] The exception is the industry long-term debt ratio, which is negative and significant. Hence, the use of between-round staging seems to be complementary with the use of debt in the industry.

The three final regressions address *ex ante* staging by analyzing the fraction of funds committed in a given round that are provided up front. Repeat entrepreneurs receive more of their funding up front, although the variable is not significant when VC dummies are included. Again, the use of *ex ante* staging is positively related to industry debt. In addition, when the round return is higher, more funds are provided up front and are less contingent on performance. The coefficient on the time since the first VC round is negative, showing that *ex ante* staging is more common in earlier rounds.

To sum up, our results on liquidation rights and claims are mixed. The results on redemption rights and staging, although somewhat weak, at least suggest that the VCs increase their ability to liquidate when dealing with less proven entrepreneurs. There does not seem to be any strong relation between liquidation rights and the tangibility of assets or with the degree to which cash flows are uncertain and hard to verify. However, the strength of VC liquidation rights and claims increases with industry debt. To the extent that industry debt is a better measure of collateral than tangible assets, this result is consistent with the stealing theories.

4.4 Venture-Capital Specific Theories

While the theories analysed above are general financial contracting models, a number of recent theoretical papers focus specifi-

24. Gompers (1995) analyses *ex post* staging, using VE data. Time between financing rounds decreases with industry R&D intensity and market-to-book ratios; it increases with industry tangible asset ratios.

25. None of the measures Gompers (1995) uses — the fixed asset ratio, R&D to sales, or market to book ratio — are significant in our regressions. Part of this could be an issue of power, however, since Gompers has a larger sample.

cally on venture capital contracts. Most of these papers try to explain the use of convertible securities in venture capital financings (based on the results in Sahlman, 1990).

The first group of theories is motivated by empirical evidence that, apart from the mere provision of funds, VCs exert substantial effort in monitoring and aiding their portfolio companies.[26] Motivated by this observation, these theories, including Casamatta (2000), Dessi (2001), Inderst and Müller (2001), Renucci (2000), Repullo and Suarez (1998) and Schmidt (1999), model the VC-entrepreneur relationship as a double moral-hazard problem, where both the entrepreneur and the VC have to be given incentives to provide costly effort.

Consistent with our empirical evidence, these models predict that both the entrepreneur and the VC should be allocated residual cash flow rights.

These theories have more mixed success in explaining the liquidation cash flow rights that come with the convertible preferred securities. In Repullo and Suarez (1998) the optimal contract calls for giving the initial VC investors a warrant-like claim. This avoids inefficient liquidations for projects that turn out to be marginally profitable after the first round of financing. This intuition is inconsistent with our findings because the liquidation rights that come with a convertible or participating preferred in practice would worsen the inefficient liquidation problem in their model.

In the models of Casamatta (2000), Dessi (2001), Renucci (2000), and Inderst and Müller (2001), VC liquidation rights emerge as part of the optimal contract, but only for parts of the parameter space. For example, in Casamatta (2000), only as the external financing constraint becomes more binding does the VC's claim resemble a convertible and the entrepreneur's resemble common stock. For low levels of external financing need, the entrepreneur gets a convertible and the VC common stock.[27] Given that (1) VCs are allocated liquidation cash flow rights in our sample (212 out of 213 financings), and (2) that liquidation claims do not vary much with our proxies for the severity of the agency problem (see Table 6), the cross-sectional predictions do not seem consistent with the data.[28]

Schmidt's (1999) theory relies heavily on the VC contract being a standard convertible security, rather than participating preferred or a combination of straight preferred and common. Given the widespread use of participating preferred in particular (39% of our sample), this is a serious shortcoming of Schmidt's model.

A second theoretical approach, represented by Cornelli and Yosha (1998), motivates convertible securities as a way of stopping the entrepreneur from manipulating interim performance.[29] In their

26. See Hellman and Puri (2002) and Kaplan and Strömberg (2001, 2002).

27. Similarly, in Inderst and Müller (2001) VCs only get convertibles when there is low competition among VC funds, and in Dessi (2001) convertibles are only optimal under very specific assumptions regarding collusion between the VC and entrepreneur against uninformed third-party investors.

28. Still, there are two observations that give some support to Casamatta's (2000) model. First, as we show in Table 8, below, the strength of the VC's liquidation claim increases in later financing rounds, *i.e.* as the VC invests additional funds. Second, empirical evidence on angel financings (see *e.g.* Wong, 2001) shows that angel investments are smaller in magnitude and more likely to involve common stock.

29. The intuition of their model is somewhat similar to the risk-shifting motivation for convertibles of Green (1984) and Brennan and Schwartz (1982).

model, entrepreneurs have the incentive to manipulate interim performance signals upward to secure additional rounds of VC financing. A properly designed convertible contract avoids this problem by making conversion undesirable for the entrepreneur (*i.e.* by setting a low conversion price). Because a high performance signal increases the probability of a VC conversion that dilutes the entrepreneur's equity stake, the entrepreneur will refrain from such manipulation. Although the use of convertibles is consistent with our evidence, the model relies on the convertible contract maturing before the true performance of the venture is revealed. Because the real-world convertibles we observe have infinite maturity (in the sense that they cannot be called by the company), and typically only convert at a successful IPO or sale, this explanation does not seem consistent with our data. Moreover, our observation that VC residual cash flow rights decrease with interim performance signals goes against the model's predictions.

A third theoretical approach, represented by Berglöf (1994) and Hellman (2001), derives convertibles as a way to avoid inefficient venture exit decisions. In Berglöf's model, convertibles enable VCs and entrepreneurs to capture a maximum amount of rents when selling the venture to third-party buyers. The convertibles give control rights to the entrepreneur in the good state which enables him to get fully compensated for his private benefits, and control to the VC in the bad state which compensates the VC from being expropriated by the new majority owners after the sale. Although Berglöf's prediction of the allocation of control rights is consistent with our evidence, the allocation of cash flow rights is not. His model predicts that all cash flow rights are allocated to the VC, and hence does not capture the fact that cash flow rights are also allocated based on firm performance. Moreover, the expropriation assumption is questionable in that it relies on the VC staying as a minority shareholder after a trade sale.

Building on Aghion and Bolton (1992), Hellman (2001) argues that convertibles solve a conflict between the VC and the entrepreneur regarding exit choice. The conflict arises because a minimum amount of equity has to be given up to the entrepreneur in the case of an IPO, while no such restriction exists in a trade sale, making VCs prefer trade sales *ceteris paribus*. The optimal contract calls for leaving control with the entrepreneur as long as the VC breaks even, and allocating cash flow rights to the VC, subject to leaving the minimum stake to the entrepreneur in the case of an IPO. The model is successful in explaining a number of features of VC contracts, such as participating preferred (which will be optimal when the financing constraint is tight), automatic conversion at an IPO (which is necessary to guarantee the entrepreneur's minimum IPO share), and transfer of control from the entrepreneur to the VC as the financing constraint tightens (as in Aghion and Bolton). Moreover, if we assume that the financing constraint tightens in later financing rounds (as more funds are invested), the finding in Table 2 that both the use of participating preferred and VC control increase in later rounds is consistent with Hellman's predictions. One shortcoming, however, similar to that of the double moral-hazard models, is that VCs are predicted to hold only common stock for parts of the parameter space. Still, Hellman (2001) shows that by augmenting Aghion and Bolton with a role for cash flow incentives (which Hellman models in reduced form by the minimum entrepreneur IPO stake), a number of features of the VC contracts can be explained simultaneously.

5 Complexity of Real World Contracts: Complementarity and Dynamics

In the previous section, we examined venture capital contracts in the light of standard financial contracting theories. It appears that real world contracts are more complex than the theories predict. First, control rights, cash flow incentives and liquidation rights are all used simultaneously. Moreover, control rights are multidimensional, with several different types of control being allocated between VCs and entrepreneurs, and switching gradually with performance. Second, the contractual relationship between the VCs and the entrepreneurs evolves; each new round involves a new set of contract terms with previous contracts potentially being renegotiated. In this section, we describe these features in more detail in order to provide stylized facts for future theoretical work.

5.1 Complementarity and Substitutability of Contract Provisions

We use cluster analysis to divide the contracts into five generic groups to analyse the simultaneous use of different governance mechanisms — pay-performance compensation, board and voting control, and liquidation rights. The hierarchical cluster method[30] we use forms groups that maximize the Euclidian distance between matrices of dummy variables measuring twelve main contractual characteristics for the companies in each group. Although cluster analysis is a somewhat subjective methodology because it depends on the number of groups and input variables used, the results using different specifications are qualitatively similar. We restrict the sample to first VC financing rounds when available (89 cases) or, otherwise, from second round investments when available (seven cases) in order to purge the comparison from effects due to the subsequent evolution of the contracts.

30. See Aldenderfer and Blashfield (1984) for details on this procedure.

Cluster:	1 – max VC control	2	3 – no party in control	4	5 – max fndr control	Kruskal-Wallis χ^2
Founder residual cash flow rights, %:	$N = 14$	$N = 29$	$N = 17$	$N = 20$	$N = 16$	statistic (4 d.f.)
Total equity in best case	24.4 (24.0)	25.8 (24.9)	44.6 (45.5)	46.3 (42.1)	52.0 (55.1)	39.2***
Sensitivity, benchmarks	4.54 (0.00)	1.12 (0.00)	0.90 (0.00)	0.36 (0.00)	2.49 (0.00)	12.2**
Sensitivity, vesting	5.61 (4.64)	6.36 (2.35)	23.6 (25.0)	-2.23 (0.00)	-2.67 (-0.69)	40.5***
Voting control (% of cases):						
VC always in control	92.9	89.7	0.0	5.0	12.5	69.6***
Fndr always in control	0.0	0.0	0.0	60.0	50.0	42.2***
Control state-contingent	0.0	3.5	100.00	0.0	18.8	75.3***
VC votes/CF, best case	1.14 (1.12)	1.14 (1.12)	1.15 (1.12)	1.18 (1.16)	1.17 (1.17)	1.6
Fndr votes/CF, best case	1.12 (1.15)	0.96 (1.04)	1.13 (1.12)	1.16 (1.13)	1.12 (1.09)	10.9**
Board control (% of cases):						
VC always in control	100.00	0.0	5.9	5.0	0.0	81.5***
Fndr always in control	0.0	3.5	0.0	0.0	93.8	81.4***
Outside directors pivotal	0.0	65.5	88.2	70.0	6.2	41.7***
Control state-contingent	0.0	31.0	5.9	25.0	0.0	13.2**
VC seats/CF, best case	1.13 (1.05)	0.67 (0.65)	1.21 (1.08)	1.32 (1.12)	1.23 (1.10)	40.2***
Fndr seats/CF, best case	1.07 (0.92)	1.85 (1.28)	1.14 (0.85)	0.92 (0.92)	1.34 (1.12)	16.1***
VC liquidation rights (% of cases):						
Redemption rights	85.6	89.7	76.5	80.0	75.0	2.2
liq. claim > cum. investment	71.4	89.7	52.9	45.0	81.2	14.4***
Investment of VC funds:						
Investment commitment	20.1 (12.4)	7.09 (6.00)	2.95 (2.30)	3.21 (2.24)	3.77 (3.00)	25.1***
$m % of funds released up front	54.6 (50.0)	73.3 (70.0)	97.6 (100)	97.6 (100.0)	90.6 (100.0)	29.9***
Number of VCs in syndicate	3.6 (3.0)	3.7 (4.0)	3.0 (2.0)	1.8 (2.0)	1.9 (2.0)	21.8***
Relative auto. conv. price:	3.14 (3.00)	5.30 (4.32)	5.13 (5.00)	3.8 (3.0)	3.30 (3.00)	5.7
Contingent contracting on (% of cases):						
Financial performance	28.6	34.5	23.5	0.0	37.5	9.4*
Non-financial performance	14.3	20.7	17.6	0.0	0.0	7.8*
Actions	35.7	24.1	5.9	0.0	0.0	14.9***
Default on redemp./dividend	28.6	41.4	11.8	40.0	18.8	6.3
Securities issues/valuations	50.0	17.2	29.4	20.0	37.5	6.3
Founder staying with firm	57.1	55.2	94.1	5.0	6.2	41.0***
% Pre-revenue ventures	64.3	58.6	62.5	35.0	25.0	8.7*

Table compares mean (median) frequencies and values of various contract provisions and firm characteristics between five clusters of portfolio companies. Data is taken from first VC financing rounds when available (89 cases) otherwise from second round investments (seven cases). 23 firms where data on first or second round investments were not available were excluded from the sample. Clusters are obtained from a hierarchical cluster analysis maximizing between-group variation measured by Euclidian distance with respect to the following 12 dummy variables: (1) founder cash-flow rights depend on performance benchmarks; (2) founder cash-flow rights depend on vesting; (3) VC has voting majority; (4) founder has voting majority; (5) voting majority is state-contingent; (6) VC controls board; (7) founder controls board; (8) neither VC nor founder controls board; (9) board majority is state-contingent; (10) VC has redemption rights; (11) VC financing commitment is staged *ex ante;* (12) VC liquidation claim is larger than investment commitment. Asterisks indicate jointly statistically significant differences between clusters at the 1%***; 5%**; and 10%* levels, using a Kruskal-Wallis χ^2 test.

TABLE 7

Complementarity and substitutability of contractual provisions

Table 7 reports the results. The order of the five clusters increases in the degree of residual cash-flow rights given up by the founder. The ordering also corresponds roughly to the degree of board and voting control allocated to the VC, with cluster 1 (5) being the firms with the most (least) VC control. The first three clusters exhibit the highest degree of VC control and also contain a significantly higher fraction of pre-revenue firms. Hence, the first three clusters are presumably associated with a higher degree of uncertainty regarding the viability of the venture.

We make a number of observations regarding the interplay among the different rights. First, voting and board control are positively correlated. When VCs control the board (cluster 1), they typically also have a voting majority; when founders control the board (cluster 5), the founder group tends to control a voting majority. Not surprisingly, these two control mechanisms are more complements than substitutes. Also, cash flow rights and control rights largely go together. The fraction of equity held by the founder is significantly higher for cluster 5 compared to cluster 1.

Second, although voting, board and residual cash flow rights are correlated, the correlation is far from perfect. Cluster 2 firms have VC voting control, but no or only state-contingent board control; cluster 4 firms exhibit a high fraction of founder voting control without board control. This further supports the result that control is more multi-dimensional and continuous than most financial contracting theories assume.[31] Moreover, the fraction of votes and board seats relative to cash flow rights vary between clusters and are typically different from one. In general, the VC and founder hold more control rights relative to their residual cash flow rights, at the expense of third parties such as employees.

Third, the founder's pay performance sensitivity, measured by the convexity induced by performance benchmarks and vesting, is lower when the founder controls the venture. In cluster 1, the founder's cash flow rights are reduced by roughly 20% if performance benchmarks are not met, and by another 20% upon leaving the firm; in contrast, the pay performance convexity of clusters 4 and 5 is close to zero.[32] Hence, high-powered cash flow compensation and VC control are largely complementary.[33] The firms in cluster 3 represent an intermediate case, with founder residual cash flow rights dependent on vesting, but not on explicit performance benchmarks. In addition, neither the VC nor the entrepreneur has control, with state-contingent voting control and outside directors pivotal in the board. This type of contract turns out to be particularly common in pre-revenue, R&D ventures.[34] One potential explanation could be that these ventures are particularly dependent on the skills of the original founder,

31. One exception is Kirilenko (2001).

32. In clusters 4 and 5, the sensitivity to vesting is even slightly negative. This is due to vesting of employee and other managers. If these do not vest the founder ends up with a higher fraction of the residual cash flow rights.

33. See also Baker and Gompers (1999) who analyse equity ownership of IPO firms. They find that CEOs of VC-backed firms hold a smaller fraction of total equity but have a higher elasticity to performance due to options.

34. The R&D to sales ratio is significantly higher for this group compared to the others (significant at the 5%-level using a Mann-Whitney test). We have omitted R&D to sales from the table due to space considerations.

increasing potential hold-up problems along the lines of Hart and Moore (1994). The high degree of vesting makes it costly for the founder to leave the firm prematurely, mitigating the hold-up threat during the time the venture is most dependent on his or her skills. The open control, in turn, protects the entrepreneur from being held up by the VC, since outside board members are unlikely to vote to replace the founder unless performance is truly inferior.

Fourth, liquidation claims and redemption rights are largely independent and not systematically related to control rights and residual cash flow rights.

Fifth, the size of the VC commitment and the release of funds are related to control. For firms in clusters 1 and 2, where the VCs have the most control, the total commitment of VC funds is higher, with a large fraction contingent on milestones. Hence, VC control is complementary with *ex ante* staged, longer-term contracts that give the VC a greater ability to force the firm into liquidation by withholding funds.

Sixth, the degree to which contracts are written contingent on actions and performance differs across clusters. Non-financial performance, actions, and founder employment contingencies are more common in the clusters where the VC is in control. Moreover, these ventures are more often pre-revenue, where the future performance uncertainty is the highest. Hence, in the ventures where observability and verifiability problems might be expected to be particularly severe, we observe the highest degree of contracting on events that the incomplete contracting literature describes as non-verifiable. The examples in Table 3 suggest, however, that some of these actions and non-financial performance measures might indeed be difficult to verify objectively.

There are two possible explanations for the complementarity between VC control and contingencies. Because the contingencies may be difficult to verify, the VC will only be comfortable using them when the VC has control and, therefore, a greater ability to decide whether the contingency is met.[35] An alternative interpretation is that because of the large uncertainty and difficulty in writing all contingencies, control is given to the VC. To keep the VC from taking too much advantage of that control, some contingencies are written that protect the entrepreneur.

5.2 Dynamic Evolution of Contracts

So far we have largely ignored the fact that different financing rounds for the same company are related. Accordingly, in Table 8, we report cash flow rights, voting rights, board rights, liquidation rights, and other terms as a function of the financing round. We distinguish

35. This suggests that there is the possibility of the VC behaving opportunistically towards the founder in interpreting the contracts. It is likely that the reputational concerns of the VC mitigate such problems.

between financings in which future financing is contingent on performance (*ex ante* staging) and those that are not. Finally, to control for the fact that we do not have complete observations of all financing rounds for every firm, the last column shows changes in terms between rounds where we have observations for two consecutive VC financings.

Table 8 indicates that founders' cash flow, voting, and board rights decline over financing rounds while VC rights increase. The degree of state-contingent control also decreases over time in favour of more VC control. The results for board rights are similar, although the rate at which VCs increase their board control is slower. The increase in VC cash flow and control rights over financing rounds is consistent with the VC demanding more equity and control as compensation for providing additional funding. Hence, a less successful venture will see control being transferred from the founder to the VC through two mechanisms: through explicit state-contingent control, specified *ex ante* in the contracts in a given round, and through dilution of control as the VC has to provide additional subsequent financing. The table also shows that while the use redemption rights does not change much over time, the size of the VC liquidation claims (relative to VC investment) does increase somewhat between rounds.

Comparing the *ex ante* staged rounds with the other first round observations, we observe some interesting differences. Naturally, these contracts commit a significantly larger amount of financing, of which on average half is released subject to future performance. Consistent with the cluster analysis, the VCs are significantly more often in control, both in terms of votes and board seats, and more future contingencies are specified in advance. We believe that the choice between *ex ante* staged, longer-term contracts, vs. short term, "*ex post*" staged contracts, is an interesting issue for future research.

Finally, we also provide evidence that contract terms are sometimes renegotiated. In about 30% of subsequent financing rounds (34 cases), some contractual rights from a previous financing round are renegotiated as a part of the new contract. The most commonly renegotiated terms are the automatic conversion price (typically increasing it; 11 cases) and the VC liquidation claim (changing dividends or participation; 10 cases). Other renegotiated terms include changing the redemption maturity, waiving funding milestones, or changing vesting provisions and performance benchmarks (each present in five cases).[36] Since our data are incomplete, these numbers likely underestimate the frequency of renegotiation.[37] This gives additional support to the incomplete contracting theories which rely heavily on the presence of bargaining and renegotiation (see *e.g.* Hart, 1995). The fact that contractual provisions are not always enforced does not necessarily imply that they are irrelevant. Even in those instances, the initial contracts are likely to be important in determining the outside options for any subsequent bargaining over rights in later rounds.

36. Note that a renegotiation may involve several different provisions.

37. In particular, for the *ex ante* staged financings, we usually have data from the initial contracting stage only and do not know whether some terms were subsequently renegotiated.

TABLE 8

Evolution of contracts over time

Mean (median)	Round 1 *Ex ante* staging	Round 1 No *ex ante* staging	Round 2	Round 3	Round 4+	Average change between two consecutive rounds
	$N = 34$	$N = 64$	$N = 50$	$N = 31$	$N = 34$	$N = 90$
Founder residual cash flow rights, %:						
Total equity in best case	30.8 (30.3)[1]	44.0 (41.1)[1]	25.7 (21.1)	23.6 (21.3)	21.5 (16.0)	-10.2 (-7.7)***
Sensitivity, benchmarks	2.81 (0.00)	1.21 (0.00)	0.42 (0.00)	0.43 (0.00)	0.63 (0.00)	-0.38 (0.00)
Sensitivity, vesting	7.02 (3.21)	8.68 (0.00)	4.12 (0.00)	2.31 (0.00)	4.24 (0.00)	-3.69 (0.00)***
Voting Control (% of cases):						
VC always in control	64.7[1]	28.1[1]	61.2	61.3	70.6	19.1 (0.00)***
Fndr always in control	8.82[5]	28.1[5]	8.2	3.2	0.0	-9.00 (0.00)***
Control state-contingent	17.6	28.1	14.0	9.7	8.8	-11.1 (0.00)**
VC votes/CF, best case	1.13 (1.09)	1.16 (1.13)	1.16 (1.14)	1.13 (1.10)	1.18 (1.14)	0.00 (0.01)
Fndr votes/CF, best case	0.98 (1.05)[5]	1.20 (0.99)[5]	1.09 (1.10)	1.13 (1.10)	1.09 (1.10)	0.01 (-0.01)
Board control (% of cases):						
VC always in control	23.5[1]	4.76[1]	27.3	34.5	54.6	11.0 (0.00)***
Fndr always in control	8.8	21.3	11.4	6.9	6.1	-8.75 (0.00)**
Outside directors pivotal	41.2[5]	63.9[5]	54.6	55.2	33.3	2.50 (0.00)
Control state-contingent	26.5[5]	9.68[5]	6.8	3.5	6.1	-4.94 (0.00)**
VC seats/CF, best case	1.00 (0.87)[5]	1.13 (1.00)[5]	0.88 (0.84)	0.91 (0.78)	0.97 (0.90)	-0.11 (-0.07)***
Fndr seats/CF, best case	1.41 (0.96)	1.20 (0.99)	1.90 (1.29)	2.17 (1.52)	2.69 (1.13)	0.49 (0.27)***
VC Liquidation rights (% of cases):						
Redemption rights	84.4	80.3	71.4	71.0	88.2	-1.11 (0.00)
Liq. claim > cum. investment	72.7	67.2	62.5	69.0	87.9	4.71 (0.00)**

Mean (median)	Round 1 *Ex ante* staging	Round 1 No *ex ante* staging	Round 2	Round 3	Round 4+	Average change between two consecutive rounds
	N = 34	N = 64	N = 50	N = 31	N = 34	N = 90
Investment of VC funds:						
Investment commitment, $m	12.5 (6.7)[1]	3.69 (3.0)[1]	6.3 (5.4)	7.4 (6.2)	7.2 (5.3)	2.01 (1.17)***
% of funds released up front	50.1 (51.8)[1]	100.0 (100)[1]	88.4 (83.9)	90.0 (100)	95.6 (100)	0.75 (0.00)
Number of VCs in syndicate	3.0 (2.0)	2.6 (2.0)	4.8 (4.5)	6.4 (6.0)	6.6 (5.0)	1.59 (1.00)***
Relative auto. conv. price:	5.1 (4.1)	4.0 (3.0)	3.3 (2.8)	2.7 (2.5)	9.7 (2.2)	2.03 (-0.43)***
Contingent contracting on (% of cases):						
Financial performance	41.2[1]	12.5[1]	14.0	6.5	17.6	-5.56 (0.00)
Non-financial performance	23.5[1]	4.7[1]	8.0	6.5	5.9	-2.22 (0.00)
Actions	32.4[1]	4.7[1]	14.0	6.5	2.9	1.11 (0.00)
Default on redemp./dividend	35.3	26.6	30.0	12.9	32.3	-3.33 (0.00)***
Securities issues/valuations	38.2[10]	21.9[10]	16.0	16.1	14.7	2.22 (0.00)
Founder staying with firm	58.8	42.2	42.0	29.0	29.4	0.00 (0.00)
Round involves renegotiation of prev. terms (% of cases):	–	–	30.0	29.0	26.5	–

Contract terms by financing round for 213 investments in 119 portfolio companies by 14 venture capital partnerships. Investments were made between 1987 and 1999. For first financing rounds, we distinguish rounds where part of the committed financing is contingent (*ex ante* staging) from rounds where all funds are released upon the initial closing (no *ex ante* staging). Significant differences between *ex ante* and no *ex ante* staging are indicated at the 1%[1]; 5%[5]; and 10%[10] levels, using a Mann–Whitney test. The last column shows changes in allocations between two consecutive rounds using the sample of observations where this information is available. Significant changes between rounds are indicated at the 1%***; 5%**; and 10%* levels, using a Wilcoxon test.

6 Conclusion

In this paper, we have compared the characteristics of real world financial contracts between VCs and entrepreneurs to their counterparts in financial contracting theory. The distinguishing characteristic of VC financings is that they allow VCs to separately allocate cash flow rights, board rights, voting rights, liquidation rights, and other control rights. We describe and measure these rights. We then interpret our results in relation to existing financial contracting theories. Overall, the theories do rather well, particularly, the classical principal agent theories (*e.g.* Holmström, 1979) and control theories (*e.g.* Aghion and Bolton, 1992).

Still the results suggest there is room for additional theory. Our results clearly show that real world contracts are more complex than existing theories predict. For example, Section 5 indicates that the allocations of cash flow and control rights and the use of contingencies are related in systematic ways. We hope that these results and others in the paper provide stylized facts for future theory.

Acknowledgements. This research has been supported by the Kauffman Foundation, by the Lynde and Harry Bradley Foundation and the Olin Foundation through grants to the Center for the Study of the Economy and the State, and by the Center for Research in Security Prices. Alejandro Hajdenberg, Hwagyun Kim, Peter Lang, Lena Mercea, and Konstantin Semyonov provided excellent research assistance. James Dow (the editor) and two anonymous referees were extremely helpful in improving the paper. Amar Bhide, Francesca Cornelli, Mathias Dewatripont, Doug Diamond, Ron Gilson, Paul Gompers, Rick Green, Oliver Hart, Thomas Hellman, Bengt Holmström, Randy Kroszner, Josh Lerner, John Moore, Stew Myers, Rick Ruback, David Scharfstein, Jeremy Stein, Luigi Zingales, and seminar participants at Alberta, Arizona State, Carnegie Mellon, the CEPR Summer Symposium, CIAR, the International Francqui Conference on the Economics of Contracting, Duke, Illinois at Urbana-Champaign, Maryland, Minnesota, the NBER Summer Institute, North Carolina, NYU, Princeton, Stanford, the Stockholm School of Economics, Texas, Utah Winter Finance Conference, Washington University, Wharton, and Wisconsin provided helpful comments. We are grateful to the venture capital partnerships for providing data. Ted Meyer was particularly helpful.

REFERENCES

[1] Aghion, P. and Bolton, P. (1992), "An Incomplete Contracts Approach to Financial Contracting", *Review of Economic Studies*, **77**, 338-401.

[2] Aldenderfer, M. and Blashfield, R. (1984), *Cluster Analysis* (Newbury Park, CA: SAGE Publications Inc.).

[3] Allen, F. and Winton, A. (1995), "Corporate Financial Structure, Incentives, and Optimal Contracting", in R. Jarrow, V. Maksimovic and W. T. Ziemba (eds.), *Handbooks in Operations Research and Management Science, Volume 9: Finance* (North-Holland).

[4] Baker, G. (1992), "Incentive Contracts and Performance Measurement", *Journal of Political Economy*, **100**, 598-614.

[5] Baker, M. and Gompers, P. (1999), "An Analysis of Executive Compensation, Ownership, and Control in Closely Held Firms" (Working Paper, Harvard Business School).

[6] Baker, M. and Gompers, P. (2000), "The Determinants of Board Structure and Function in Entrepreneurial Firms" (Working Paper, Harvard Business School).

[7] Bartlett, J. (1995), *Equity Finance: Venture Capital, Buyouts, Restructurings and Reorganizations* (New York: John Wiley & Sons).

[8] Berglöf, E. (1994), "A Control Theory of Venture Capital", *Journal of Law, Economics and Organization*, **10**, 247-267.

[9] Black, B. and Gilson, R. (1998), "Venture Capital and the Structure of Capital Markets: Banks Versus Stock Markets", *Journal of Financial Economics.*

[10] Bolton, P. and Scharfstein, D. (1990), "A Theory of Predation Based on Agency Problems in Financial Contracting", *American Economic Review*, **80**, 94-106.

[11] Brennan, M. and Schwartz, E. (1982), "The Case for Convertibles", *Continental Bank Journal of Applied Corporate Finance.*

[12] Casamatta, C. (2000), "Financing and Advising: Optimal Financial Contracts with Venture Capitalists" (Working Paper, Université de Toulouse).

[13] Cornelli, F. and Yosha, O. (1998), "Stage Financing and the Role of Convertible Debt" (Working Paper, London Business School).

[14] Dessi, R. (2001), "Start-up Finance, Monitoring and Collusion" (Working Paper, IDEI, University of Toulouse).

[15] Dewatripont, M. and Tirole, J. (1994), "A Theory of Debt and Equity: Diversity of Securities and Manager–Shareholder Congruence", *Quarterly Journal of Economics*, **109**, 1027-1054.

[16] Duffie, D. and Demarzo, P. (1999), "A Liquidity Based Model of Security Design", *Econometrica*, **67**, 65-99.

[17] Fama, E. and French, K. (1997), "Industry Costs of Equity", *Journal of Financial Economics*, **43**, 153-193.

[18] Fluck, Z. (1998), "Optimal Financial Contracting: Debt Versus Outside Equity", *Review of Financial Studies*, **11** (2), 383-418.

[19] Gale, D. and Hellwig, M. (1985), "Incentive-compatible Debt Contracts: The One-period Problem", *Review of Economic Studies*, **52**, 647-663.

[20] Garmaise, M. (2000), "Informed Investors and the Financing of Entrepreneurial Projects" (Working Paper, University of Chicago).

[21] Gompers, P. (1995), "Optimal Investment, Monitoring, and the Staging of Venture Capital", *Journal of Finance*, **50**, 1461-1490.

[22] Gompers, P. (1998), "An Examination of Convertible Securities in Venture Capital Investments" (Working Paper, Harvard Business School).

[23] Gompers, P. and Lerner, J. (1999), *The Venture Capital Cycle* (Cambridge, MA: MIT Press).

[24] Green, R. (1984), "Investment Incentives, Debt, and Warrants", *Journal of Financial Economics*, **13**, 115-136.

[25] Grossman, S. and Hart, O. (1986), "The Costs and Benefits of Ownership: A Theory of Vertical and Lateral Integration", *Journal of Political Economy*, **94**, 691-719.

[26] Harris, M. and Raviv, A. (1979), "Optimal Incentive Contracts with Imperfect Information", *Journal of Economic Theory*, **20**, 231-259.

[27] Harris, M. and Raviv, A. (1992), "Financial Contracting Theory", in J. Laffont (ed.) *Advances in Economic Theory: Sixth World Congress*, Vol. II (Cambridge, UK: Cambridge University Press).

[28] Hart, O. (1995), *Firms, Contracts, and Financial Structure* (Oxford: Oxford University Press).

[29] Hart, O. (2001), "Financial Contracting", *Journal of Economic Literature*.

[30] Hart, O. and Moore, J. (1990), "Property Rights and the Nature of the Firm", *Journal of Political Economy*, **98**, 1119-1158.

[31] Hart, O. and Moore, J. (1994), "A Theory of Debt Based on the Inalienability of Human Capital", *Quarterly Journal of Economics*, **109**, 841-879.

[32] Hart, O. and Moore, J. (1998), "Default and Renegotiation: A Dynamic Model of Debt", *Quarterly Journal of Economics*, **113**, 1-41.

[33] Hellman, T. (2001), "IPOs, Acquisitions and the Use of Convertible Securities in Venture Capital" (Working Paper, Stanford University).

[34] Hellman, T. and Puri, M. (2002), "Venture Capital and the Professionalization of Start-up Firms: Empirical Evidence" *Journal of Finance* (forthcoming).

[35] Holmström, B. (1979), "Moral Hazard and Observability", *Bell Journal of Economics*, **10**, 74-91.

[36] Holmström, B. and Milgrom, P. (1991), "Multitask Principal Agent Analyses: Incentive Contracts, Asset Ownership, and Job Design", *Journal of Law, Economics, and Organization*, **7**, 24-92.

[37] Inderst, R. and Müller, H. (2001), "Competition and Efficiency in the Market for Venture Capital" (Working Paper, University of Mannheim).

[38] Innes, R. (1990), "Limited Liability and Incentive Contracting with Ex-ante Action Choices", *Journal of Economic Theory*, **52**, 45-67.

[39] Kaplan, S. and Per Strömberg (2000), "Financial Contracting Theory Meets the Real World: Evidence From Venture Capital Contracts?" (Working Paper No. 7660, National Bureau of Economic Research).

[40] Kaplan, S. and Per Strömberg (2001), "Venture Capitalists as Principals: Contracting, Screening, and Monitoring", *American Economic Review Papers and Proceedings*, **91** (2), 426-430.

[41] Kaplan, S. and Per Strömberg (2002), "Characteristics, Contracts, and Actions: Evidence from Venture Capitalist Analyses" (Working Paper, University of Chicago).

[42] Kirilenko, A. (2001), "Valuation and Control in Venture Finance", *Journal of Finance*, **56**, 565-588.

[43] Lazear, E. (1986), "Salaries and Piece-rates", *Journal of Business*, **59**, 405-431.

[44] Lerner, J. (1994), "The Syndication of Venture Capital Investments", *Financial Management*, **23**, 16-27.

[45] Levin, J. (1998), *Structuring Venture Capital, Private Equity and Entrepreneurial Transactions* (Aspen Law and Business Series, Aspen Publishers).

[46] Myers, S. (2000), "Outside Equity", *Journal of Finance*, **55**, 1005-1037.

[47] Myers, S. and Majluf, N. (1984), "Corporate Financing and Investment Decisions when Firms Have Information that Investors Do Not Have", *Journal of Financial Economics*, **XIII**, 187-221.

[48] Neher, D. (1999), "Staged Financing: An Agency Perspective", *Review of Economic Studies*, **66**, 255-274.

[49] Prendergast, C. (1999), "The Provision of Incentives in Firms", *Journal of Economic Literature*, **37**, 7-63.

[50] Renucci, A. (2000), "Optimal Contracts between Entrepreneurs and Value-enhancing Financiers" (Working Paper, University of Toulouse).

[51] Repullo, R. and Suarez, J. (1999), "Venture Capital Finance: A Security Design Approach" (Working Paper, CEMFI).

[52] Sahlman, W. (1990), "The Structure and Governance of Venture Capital Organizations", *Journal of Financial Economics*, **27**, 473–521.

[53] Schmidt, K. (1999), "Convertible Securities and Venture Capital Finance" (Working Paper, Universität München).

[54] Sorensen, O. and Stuart, T. (2001), "Syndication Networks and the Spatial Distribution of Venture Capital Investments", *American Journal of Sociology*, **106**, 1546-1588.

[55] Townsend, R. (1979), "Optimal Contracts and Competitive Markets with Costly State Verification", *Journal of Economic Theory*; **21**, 265-293.

[56] White, H. (1980), "A Heteroscedasticity-Consistent Covariance Matrix Estimator and a Direct Test for Heteroscedasticity", *Econometrica*, **48**, 817-838.

[57] Wong, A. (2001), "Angel Financing" (Working Paper, University of Chicago).

14

Testing for Asymmetric Information in Insurance Markets

Pierre-André Chiappori
Bernard Salanié

Abstract

The first goal of this paper is to provide a simple and general test of the presence of asymmetric information in contractual relationships within a competitive context. We also argue that insurance data are particularly well suited to such empirical investigations. To illustrate this claim, we use data on contracts and accidents to investigate the extent of asymmetric information in the French market for automobile insurance. Using various parametric and nonparametric methods, we find no evidence for the presence of asymmetric information in this market.

1 Introduction

In the last 20 years, contract theory has developed at a rapid pace. But, until recently at least, empirical applications have lagged behind.[1] One striking illustration, for instance, is that although we can precisely describe the kind of problems that may arise from the presence of adverse selection within a competitive setting and even formulate detailed policy recommendations for alleviating these problems, we can hardly provide a list of markets in which adverse selection has empirically been shown to matter.

This lag between theory and empirical applications probably has several explanations. One is the scarcity of adequate data sets that offer a large sample of standardized contracts for which performances are recorded.[2] However, insurance offers a promising field for empirical work on contracts. In such fields as automobile, housing, or even life and health insurance, contracts are highly standardized and can be exhaustively described by a small set of variables. A large company typically covers hundreds of thousands (or even millions) of clients. In many cases, the company's files contain all the relevant information. Finally, the empirical counterpart of the client's

1. This is not to deny that important steps have recently been made in some directions. For instance, the econometrics of auctions has evolved in a very promising way (see, *e.g.*, Laffont, Ossard, and Vuong 1995; Florens, Hugo, and Richard 1997). Also, several papers have tried to estimate econometric models based on core contract theory. A nonexhaustive list includes Joskow (1990), Wolak (1994), Wunsch (1994), Slade (1996), and Dalen and Gomez-Lobo (1997). Salanié (1997, chap. 8) discusses some of this work. Finally, several recent papers provide direct tests of adverse selection, including works by Ausubel (1998), Cardon and Hendel (1998), and Toivanen and Cressy (1998).

"performance" is the occurrence of an accident and possibly its cost; again, this is precisely recorded in the company's files. Thus most predictions of contract theory can be tested here in a detailed way, using standard econometric tools.[3]

The first purpose of this paper is to prove this point by providing a simple and general test of the presence of asymmetric information in the contractual relationship. Our basic claim, following Chiappori (1994), is that the theoretical notion of asymmetric information (whether adverse selection or *ex ante* moral hazard) implies, in statistical terms, a positive correlation between two (conditional) distributions. This test, simple as it may be, is surprisingly robust. It does not rely on specific functional forms; neither does it require particular assumptions on preferences, technology, or the nature of the equilibrium.

The second goal of the paper is to provide an empirical application of the technique. We apply our test to a French survey of automobile insurance contracts and find that, when observables are adequately taken into account, there remains no evidence of asymmetric information in the sample we consider. This conclusion is in sharp contrast with those of other studies, for instance, Puelz and Snow (1994); we discuss in detail the reasons that may explain this difference.

1.1 What Does Theory Predict?

In this paper, we focus on exclusive contracts. That is, we consider only markets in which the insurer can impose an exclusive relationship. This allows firms to implement nonlinear and, in particular, convex price schedules, which are typically needed under asymmetric information.[4] In this context, the literature on adverse selection in a competitive setting builds on the seminal contribution of Rothschild and Stiglitz (1976). The numerous extensions that can be found in the literature suggest that some of their results may be overturned in slightly different settings. On the other hand, we believe that three conclusions are fairly robust: (1) Under adverse selection, observationally equivalent agents are likely to be faced with menus of contracts, among which they are free to choose. (2) Within the menu, contracts with more comprehensive coverage are sold at a higher (unitary) premium. (3) Within the menu, contracts with more comprehensive coverage are chosen by agents with higher accident probabilities.

The first prediction holds for various types of adverse selection; that is, agents may differ in their risk, as in Rothschild and Stiglitz's paper, but also in their wealth, preferences, risk aversion, and so forth.[5] Also, it is essentially qualitative and is unlikely to generate very powerful tests. Testing prediction 2 would require an explicit model of the firm pricing policy. This is a difficult task that in any case would necessitate strong assumptions on the technology.

2. However, the work of Murphy (1986) and Chiappori, Salanié, and Valentin (1999) shows that it is sometimes possible to circumvent the lack of recorded performances.
3. Chiappori and Salanié (1997) argue for the use of insurance data in more detail.
4. Chiappori (in press) surveys the literature on insurance under adverse selection and emphasizes the empirical implications of competition under exclusive and nonexclusive contracts.
5. When differences are not related to actuarial risk, fair pricing leads to identical contracts for all individuals. However, if either imperfect competition or transaction costs are introduced, then competition results in differentiated contracts.

On the other hand, prediction 3 suggests a very simple test: a positive correlation between coverage and frequency of accidents should be observed on observationally identical agents. In fact, this prediction turns out to be surprisingly general and to extend to a variety of more general contexts.

1. It does not depend on the firm's pricing policy; as such, it does not rely on specific assumptions on technology (such as linearity, absence of fixed costs, absence of loading, absence of cross-subsidies, etc.). It applies even when the firm's pricing policy is suboptimal.
2. Similarly, its validity does not depend on specific assumptions on preferences. In particular, the single crossing property is not required. As a consequence, (*a*) it is robust to the introduction of moral hazard, as studied by Chassagnon and Chiappori (1997). In their paper, the mere definition of "lower risk" is complex because riskiness is endogenous to the proposed contracts; agents of a given type may be more or less risky depending on the contract they face. Still, it can be shown that *ex post* (equilibrium) accident probabilities are higher for contracts entailing more comprehensive coverage. (*b*) Also, it remains valid in the multidimensional adverse selection case studied by Villeneuve (1996), where agents differ by their risk *and* their risk aversion (even though profits may in that case be positive in equilibrium).
3. It remains valid when agents differ not only by the probability of an accident but also by its severity, if some monotone likelihood ratio property holds (see Landsberger and Meilijson 1996).
4. Even more important is the fact that this property still holds in a dynamical setting. The literature on repeated adverse selection clearly indicates that partial pooling may occur, especially during the initial stages, and that revelation mechanisms are much more complex.[6] But the basic intuition remains valid.

A key remark, however, is that prediction 3 does not imply anything as far as pricing *across* risk classes is concerned. The self-selection issue applies only *within* such classes, that is, to observationally identical agents. In all that follows, we restrict ourselves to this situation. The empirical translation is that the probability distributions we shall consider will be conditional on all observables; our main goal will be to test for a positive correlation between (conditional) laws governing the choice of a contract on the one hand and the occurrence of an accident on the other hand.

6. Typically, "low-risk" individuals will be proposed contracts with higher deductibles *and* a stronger proportion of experience rating; see Dionne and Doherty (1994).

Section 2 deals with the empirical distinction between adverse selection and moral hazard. Section 3 surveys the empirical literature and particularly the paper by Puelz and Snow (1994). The empirical application is presented in Section 4, and Section 5 provides some concluding remarks.

2 Adverse Selection *versus* Moral Hazard: An Empirical Puzzle

Models other than that of Rothschild and Stiglitz (1976) may yield prediction 3. For instance, the choice of contract could be determined by totally different factors (say, preferences or risk aversion) that, by coincidence, turn out to be positively correlated with risk. But, of course, this explanation is in fact very close to the initial story; the difference is more a matter of interpretation than of structure. Agents certainly know their preferences better than the insurance company. If, in addition, preferences are correlated with risk, then agents indeed have a better knowledge of their risk, although in a somewhat indirect way.

A more convincing alternative relies on moral hazard. If this is prevalent, then agents who (for whatever reason) choose contracts with comprehensive coverage will have less incentive to reduce accident probability through prevention. The final consequence will be a positive correlation between the choice of a contract with a smaller deductible and *ex post* riskiness. But, of course, causality is reversed here. Agents do not select a particular contract because their accident probability is low; on the contrary, their accident probability is low because the contract they are facing provides adequate incentives.

Our paper will concentrate on testing prediction 3 of the Rothschild-Stiglitz model, without checking whether it holds because of adverse selection or moral hazard. Although the general problem of distinguishing between adverse selection and moral hazard from insurance data is left for future research,[7] in Section 4 below we offer a simple test that exploits the specifics of the French experience rating system.

3 Empirical Issues

A basic reference of the empirical literature on adverse selection is provided by the work of Puelz and Snow (1994).[8] Using individual data from an automobile insurer in Georgia, they build a two-equation model that predicts different estimates for the competing models of adverse selection in insurance markets. They conclude

7. An ideal situation for testing moral hazard occurs when a given set of agents experience a sudden and exogenous change in the incentive structure they are facing. See, *e.g.*, the analysis of the Quebec regulatory reform by Dionne and Vanasse (1996). The "natural experiment" approach is all the more convincing when there exists a reference sample for which incentives did not change; this is exploited in Chiappori, Durand, and Geoffard (1998) and Chiappori, Geoffard, and Kyriazidou (1998). Similar ideas may on some occasions apply even in the absence of a proper natural experiment. In principle, any context in which similar individuals are facing different incentive schemes can do — provided, of course, that the selection into the various schemes is exogenous and not related to risk-relevant characteristics. See Cardon and Hendel (1998) as well as Sec. 4 below. Finally, investigating the dynamics of the relationship provides a very strong test (see Chiappori and Heckman 1999).

8. See also Dahlby (1983,1992) and Boyer and Dionne (1989) for early references.

that their findings support the Rothschild-Stiglitz model. They first estimate a pricing equation of the form

$$P_i = g(D_i, X_i, \varepsilon_i),$$

where P_i and D_i are the premium and the deductible in the contract chosen by individual i, the X_i are individual-specific exogenous variables, and ε_i is an econometric error term. The second equation describes the individual's choice of deductible. The decision depends on his "price of deductible" $\hat{g}_D$,[9] as estimated from a third regression using instrumental variables and on his (unobserved) accident probability π_i. Since his accident probability is unobservable, it is proxied by a dummy variable RT_i that equals one if the individual had an accident and zero otherwise. This leads to an equation of the form

$$D_i = h(\hat{g}_{Di}, RT_i, X_i, \eta_i),$$

where η_i is another error term. The Rothschild-Stiglitz model predicts that higher risks buy better coverage, that is, a lower deductible, so that h should decrease in RT.

Puelz and Snow specify their first equation as a linear model and estimate it by ordinary least squares. Since there are only three levels of deductible in their data set, they estimate their second equation (again linear) by ordered logit. Their estimates exhibit the decreasing relationship predicted by Rothschild and Stiglitz, although as evidenced by their table 3, the choice of deductible does not vary much (*ceteris paribus*) with the risk type.

There are, however, several flaws in the Puelz-Snow approach that cast some doubts on the validity of their results. A first one is related to the choice of their risk type variable RT_i. While the expectation of this dummy variable clearly is π_i, this procedure introduces a measurement error into the second equation. In linear models, the estimates would be biased toward zero, which would reinforce the conclusion of Puelz and Snow. In an ordered logit, it is not clear which way the bias goes.

A more damning criticism of Puelz and Snow's work is that they use highly constrained functional forms. They rely on a set of only about 20 variables (we shall use 55 in our application, even though we consider a homogeneous subsample of "young" drivers). This implies that their estimates may suffer from omitted variables bias. Moreover, their functional forms are linear. Assume, for instance, that individual i has constant absolute risk aversion σ_i. Then we easily derive the individual's choice of deductible

$$D_i = \frac{1}{\sigma_i} \log \frac{1 - \pi_i}{\pi_i} \frac{-\hat{g}_{Di}}{1 + \hat{g}_{Di}},$$

9. This estimate is clearly negative since no rational insured would pay a higher premium for a higher level of the deductible.

which is highly nonlinear. In fact, applying the Puelz-Snow procedure to data generated by a *symmetric* information model according to this formula may well result in the kind of negative estimates they get, simply because the accident term in fact captures some of the omitted nonlinearities. Dionne, Gouriéroux, and Vanasse (1997) indeed show that Puelz and Snow's results may be spurious. To do this, they include the predicted probability of accident $\hat{\pi}_i$ in the right-hand side of the second equation (for the choice of deductible).[10] Note that now the impact of $\hat{\pi}_i$ (if any) has nothing to do with adverse selection since $\hat{\pi}_i$ is, by construction, a function of only the observed variables. They show that this completely breaks the results of Puelz and Snow: the variable *RT* is not significant any more.

Finally, the data set used by Puelz and Snow comprises individuals of various ages and driving records; nothing is done in their paper to control for this source of heterogeneity. Two problems arise at this point. One is heteroskedasticity. Presumably, the distribution of the random shocks, and especially of η_i, will depend on the driver's seniority. Within a nonlinear model such as the ordered logit, this will bias the estimation. The second and more disturbing problem relates to the estimation of adverse selection. Insurers typically observe past driving records; these records are highly informative on probabilities of accident and, as such, are used for pricing. These variables, however, are omitted in Puelz and Snow's regressions. This omission generates a bias that indeed tends to overestimate the level of adverse selection: the corresponding information is treated by the econometrician as being private, whereas it is in fact common to both parties.

This remark clearly suggests that the tests should consider drivers with similar seniority and moreover control for driving experience. The introduction of this variable, however, is quite delicate because it is (obviously) endogenous. Various strategies can be considered, but, ideally, panel data would be required (see Chiappori and Heckman 1999). In our application, we shall circumvent this problem by using only data on beginners.

4 Implementation and Results

This section contains the heart of the paper. We first present the French car insurance system and our data set. Then we specify our econometric methods and present results on beginning drivers. Since our results are negative, we then turn to more senior drivers, for whom the results are equally negative.

10. This is perfectly legitimate since $\hat{\pi}_i$ is just a particular nonlinear function of the observables.

4.1 Car Insurance in France

French law stipulates that all cars must be insured at the *responsabilité civile* (RC) level, a liability insurance that covers damage inflicted to other drivers or their cars. Every car insurance company offers this coverage, along with other noncompulsory coverage. The most typical other contract is *assurance tous risques* (TR), which also indemnifies damage to the insured's car (or driver), for which he or she is held responsible. Comprehensive insurance contracts are differentiated by the value of the deductible (which may be fixed or proportional).

All insurers are required by law to apply a uniform experience rating system, the "bonus/malus." At any date t, the premium is defined as the product of a basic amount, which is freely defined by firms but cannot be related to past experience, and a "bonus" coefficient, the evolution of which is strictly regulated. Precisely, if the bonus coefficient is b_t at the beginning of the period, the occurrence of an accident implies a 25 percent increase $(b_{t+1} = 1.25b_t)$, whereas no accident during the year results in a 5 percent decrease $(b_{t+1} = .95b_t)$; in addition, several special rules are imposed.[11] Moreover, insurance companies are allowed to overprice contracts by young drivers (less than three years of insurance); the surcharge is limited to 140 percent of the basic rate and must decrease by half every year in which the insured has not had an accident.

The law of the single price does not hold very well in the data: even for the RC guarantee, which is quite homogeneous, there are large variations in premia that do not appear to be justified by variations in insured/car characteristics. The following orders of magnitude may still be useful. For the average insured in our sample, the RC premium is about 3,000 francs; the average car costs about 50,000 francs, and the probability of an accident in a given year is about 10 percent (very few drivers — fewer than 2 percent — have more than one accident in a given year). The TR premium is at least twice as expensive, and that multiple is still higher for high-price cars. Therefore, the decision of buying the RC or the TR contract is an important one.

4.2 The Data: Concentrating on Young Drivers

The French federation of insurers (FFSA), which groups 21 companies that together have 70 percent of the French automobile insurance market, conducted in 1990 a survey of its members. The sampling rate was 1/20. The resulting data sets consisted of 41 variables on 1,120,000 contracts and 25 variables on 120,000 accidents, covering the year 1989. After a previous team merged them and cleaned

11. In the French system, b_t cannot exceed 3.5 and cannot go below 0.5. Also, b_t cannot be larger than one if no accident occurred for the last two years.

them up, we chose to concentrate on a data set of 20,716 "young" drivers, that is, all drivers who obtained their driver's license in 1986, 1987, or 1988.[12] For each driver, we have all the variables that are used by insurance companies to price their contracts — age, sex, profession, year of driver's license, age and type of the car, use of the car, and area — plus the characteristics of the contract and the characteristics of the accident if one occurred. There are several variables in most of these categories, so that our data set is fairly rich.

Concentrating on young drivers has several advantages. One is that the heteroskedasticity problem is probably much less severe on a sample of young drivers since the drivers' experience is much more homogeneous than in a population in which different seniority groups are mixed up. More important, concentrating on young drivers avoids the problems linked to experience rating and the resulting bias mentioned at the end of Section 3.

A final issue is the distinction between an accident and a claim. Since our data set comes from insurance companies, it relates to claims, not to accidents. But whether an accident, once it has occurred, becomes a claim (*i.e.*, is declared to the insurance company) is the individual's decision. This decision is in turn influenced by the nature of the contract. Obviously, an accident that is not covered will not be declared. This "*ex post* moral hazard" effect typically generates a correlation between the type of contract and the probability of a claim even in the absence of any *ex ante* moral hazard (*i.e.*, even when the *accident* probability is not affected by the type of contract). Still, it is essential to distinguish between them, if only because the welfare consequences are very different.[13] Our solution is to discard all accidents in which only one automobile was involved. Whenever two cars are involved, a declaration is much more likely to be made in any case.[14]

4.3 The Procedures

As explained in the Introduction, we want to test the conditional independence of the choice of better coverage and the occurrence of an accident, where "conditional" means conditional on all variables observed by the insurer. To do this, we shall use two parametric methods and three nonparametric methods.

4.3.1 *A Pair of Probits*

We define here our notation. Let $i = 1, \ldots, n$ denote individuals. The term X_i is the set of exogenous variables for individual i (these variables will be constants and dummy variables in our

12. Following the tradition in the French insurance industry, we call "young" the recent drivers, most, but not all, of whom are also young in age.

13. A limitation of insurance coverage may be welfare increasing when it reduces accident probability, much less so when its only effect is to discourage victims from filing a claim, unless, of course, the technology of the insurance industry (say, the presence of fixed costs) makes the processing of small claims especially inefficient.

14. In principle, the two drivers may agree on some bilateral transfer and thus avoid the penalties arising from experience rating. Such a deal is, however, quite difficult to implement between individuals who meet randomly, will probably never meet again, and cannot commit in any legally enforceable way (since declaration is compulsory according to insurance contracts). We follow the general opinion in the profession that such bilateral agreements can be neglected. An alternative solution is to concentrate on accidents with bodily injuries, since in that case declaration is compulsory by law (see, *e.g.*, Levitt and Porter 1998). However, this drastically reduces the number of accidents.

application). Also, let w_i denote the number of days of 1989 in which individual i was insured. We now define two 0-1 endogenous variables: (1) $y_i = 1$ if i bought (any form of) comprehensive coverage (a TR contract); $y_i = 0$ if i bought only the minimum legal coverage (an RC contract); (2) $z_i = 1$ if i had at least one accident in which he was judged to be at fault; otherwise (no accident or i not at fault) it is zero.

These definitions call for two remarks. First, there are many different comprehensive coverage contracts on offer, with (say) different levels of deductible. Ideally, these contracts should be treated separately and not bundled together as we do here. However, this would greatly complicate the model.[15] Second, we separate accidents in which the insured is at fault and those in which he is not. The reason is that if the insured has an accident in which another driver is to blame, any information on his risk type may not be conveyed. Also, we do not exploit the further information linked to drivers who had several accidents in 1989; again, there are very few of these cases.

We now set up two probit models, one for the choice of coverage and one for the occurrence of an accident. Let ε_i and η_i be two independent centered normal errors with unit variance. Then

$$y_i = \mathbf{1}(X_i\beta + \varepsilon_i > 0)$$

and

$$z_i = \mathbf{1}(X_i\gamma + \eta_i > 0).$$

We first estimate these two probits independently, weighing each individual by the number of days under insurance w_i. Then we can easily compute the generalized residuals $\hat{\varepsilon}_i$ and $\hat{\eta}_i$. For instance, $\hat{\varepsilon}_i$ is given by

$$\hat{\varepsilon}_i = E(\varepsilon_i \mid y_i) = \frac{\phi(X_i\beta)}{\Phi(X_i\beta)}\, y_i - (1 - y_i)\, \frac{\phi(X_i\beta)}{\Phi(-X_i\beta)},$$

where ϕ and Φ denote the density and the cumulative distribution function (cdf) of $N(0, 1)$. Now define a test statistic by

$$W = \frac{\left(\sum_{i=1}^{n} w_i \hat{\varepsilon}_i \hat{\eta}_i\right)^2}{\sum_{i=1}^{n} w_i^2 \hat{\varepsilon}_i^2 \hat{\eta}_i^2}.$$

The general results in Gouriéroux *et al.* (1987) imply that under the null of conditional independence $\operatorname{cov}(\varepsilon_i, \eta_i) = 0$, W is distributed asymptotically as a $\chi^2(1)$. This provides us with a test of the symmetric information assumption.

15. In addition, deductibles are in any case quite small. In expected terms, the difference between the various levels of deductible available in our sample is negligible when compared to that between comprehensive and partial coverage, on which we concentrate here. Experience rating is more important, but, by law, experience rating schemes are identical across firms.

To implement this procedure, we first need to choose what exogenous variables to include in X_i. The most contentious variable here is the past driving record, as represented by the bonus/malus coefficient (defined above). If we exclude this variable, then we neglect some of the insurer's information and our test will be biased. If we include it, it may also be biased since this variable is likely to be correlated with η_i. As indicated above, our solution is to focus in a first step on drivers who have no past driving record, or "beginners." In our data, this refers to drivers who obtained their driver's license in 1988. There are 6,333 of them in our sample. As for the other exogenous variables, we chose to include those that, according to the insurers, are most relevant: thus we have dummy variables for sex (1), make of car (7), performance of the car (5), type of use (3), type of area (4), age of driver (8), profession of driver (7), age of car (11), and region (9). This gives us 55 exogenous variables plus a constant. They all are clearly observed by insurers since the insurers built this data set themselves.

4.3.2 *A Bivariate Probit*

Estimating the two probits independently is appropriate under conditional independence, but it is inefficient under the alternative. For this reason, we also estimate a bivariate probit in which ε_i and η_i are still distributed as $N(0, 1)$ but have a correlation coefficient ρ, which we also estimate. This will allow us to test $\rho = 0$ but also to get a confidence interval for ρ.

4.3.3 *A χ^2 Test*

The two parametric procedures presented above rely on a fairly large number of exogenous variables, as compared to those in Puelz and Snow (1994), for instance. However, the functional forms involved are still relatively restrictive since the latent models are linear and the errors are normal. It is quite possible, for instance, that the data-generating process is driven by cross effects or even more complicated nonlinear functions of the exogenous variables. Then our results would be biased in unpredictable ways. To remedy this, we adopt here a fully nonparametric procedure based on χ^2 tests for independence.

Let x_i be a set of m exogenous 0-1 variables. Then we can define 2^m "cells" in which all individuals have the same values for all variables in x_i. In each cell, we compute a two by two table generated by the values of y_i and z_i, as in table 1. For $j = 0, 1$, define $N_{j.} = N_{j0} + N_{j1}$, $N_{.j} = N_{0j} + N_{1j}$, and $N_{..} = N_{.0} + N_{.1}$. Now consider the test statistic

$$T = \sum_{j,k=0,1} \frac{[N_{jk} - (N_{j.}N_{.k}/N_{..})]^2}{N_{jk}}.$$

This is the well-known χ^2 test for independence. If y_i and z_i are independent in the cell we consider, then T is asymptotically distributed as a χ^2 (1).

TABLE 1

Testing Independence

Population	$z_i = 0$	$z_i = 1$
$y_i = 0$	N_{00}	N_{01}
$y_i = 1$	N_{10}	N_{11}

Thus we face a collection of $M = 2^m$ statistics. There are many ways to use these data to derive a test for conditional independence. We shall use three different approaches. The first one is to do a Kolmogorov-Smirnov test on the empirical cdf $\hat{F}_M$. Let F denote the cdf of a χ^2 (1). Under conditional independence, the test statistic

$$K = \sqrt{M} \sup_x \left| \hat{F}_M(x) - F(x) \right|$$

converges to a distribution that is tabulated in statistics textbooks. As the Kolmogorov-Smirnov test is known to have limited power, we complement this by two other tests. Our second approach is to reject independence in a cell if the value of T for that cell is greater than 3.84, which is the 5 percent critical value for a $\chi^2(1)$. Then we count the number of rejections, which is distributed as a binomial $B(M, 0.05)$ under conditional independence. We shall also report the value of the statistic S generated by adding up the T values for all cells. This is distributed as a $\chi^2(M)$ under conditional independence.

To implement this procedure, we first need to select the exogenous variables in x_i. Letting $x_i = X_i$ would clearly not do since our total population is much smaller than 2^{55}. More generally, we face a trade-off between better conditioning (and thus a large number of cells) and not too small populations in each cell (to apply asymptotic results). To resolve this dilemma, we again rely on the insurer's experience. This tells us that six variables are highly relevant: (*a*) the sex of the driver, (*b*) the make of his car, (*c*) the size of his car, (*d*) whether the car is used in a city, (*e*) the age of the driver, and (*f*) the age of the car. Thus we construct six 0-1 variables to get x_i. This will give us 64 cells.

4.4 Results on Beginners

First turn to our pair of independently estimated probits. Since we have 112 estimated coefficients, it would be impractical to comment on them all.[16] We are not really interested in their values or significance levels anyway, since what matters to us is the value of the

16. No fewer than 25 coefficients are (individually) significant at the usual 5 percent level. To quote a simple example, men who drive old Japanese cars are less likely to buy comprehensive coverage. On the other hand, only the constant is significant in the probit on accident frequency. Insurers tell us that this is a standard result for beginning drivers. However, as expected, younger people have more accidents.

test statistic W. This turns out to be very small, at 0.46. Thus we are very far from rejecting conditional independence.

The bivariate probit gives us a similar message. Our estimate for ρ actually is slightly negative, at -0.029. However, its estimated standard error is 0.049, so that again we cannot reject conditional independence. Moreover, we can compute a 95 percent confidence interval for ρ: it is $[-0.125, 0.067]$, so that even if ρ is not actually zero, it is bound to be very small.

Turning to our nonparametric procedure, we compute a value of $K = 0.63$ for the Kolmogorov-Smirnov statistic. This is much below the 5 percent critical value, which is 1.35. Moreover, we obtain only five rejections out of our 64 cells. This corresponds to a 15 percent p-value for $B(64, 0.05)$, so that again, we cannot reject independence. It is interesting to look at the cells in detail. The average cell has about 100 individuals, but there is a large dispersion of cell sizes: the smallest cell has six individuals, there are five more with fewer than 20 individuals, and the largest cell has 373. Fortunately, the rejections are not in the smallest cells, so that our procedure seems reasonably reliable. The only anomaly occurs in a large cell (315 individuals) in which independence is very strongly rejected $(T = 13.4)$. However, splitting the cell according to a seventh criterion (type of income) leads to more reasonable values for T. Summing up all T values leads to a test statistic of $S = 69.3$, and the 5 percent critical value for a $\chi^2(64)$ is 87.5.

Thus all our procedures give the same, somewhat surprising, result: asymmetric information seems to be at most a negligible phenomenon in the market for automobile insurance, at least for young drivers.

4.5 Results on More Senior Drivers

Our results so far indicate that beginners have no informational advantage over insurers. This can be interpreted by saying that when signing their first contract, young drivers have very little driving experience and thus do not really know whether they will turn out to be good drivers or not. However, one can imagine that after a couple of years, they will learn something about their driving ability. If they get this information by having accidents, then the insurer will learn at the same pace. However, they may learn that they are bad drivers even if they manage to stay out of trouble. For instance, a driver who has several "near misses" will eventually know more than the insurer about his risk type. Thus it is quite possible that adverse selection emerges endogenously in the market for automobile insurance since drivers who avoid accidents may obtain an informational advantage over the insurer.

Fortunately, our data also allow us to test this model since we have data for relatively senior drivers, who obtained their driver's license in 1986, and we also know their bonus/malus, which sums up how many accidents they had in the past. Given the French legal bonus/malus system, we know that any driver who has had at least one accident since 1986 will have a bonus/malus coefficient greater than 100 (the reference level) in 1989. Thus we can focus on those drivers who got their license in 1986 and had a bonus/malus no greater than 100 in 1989. There are two caveats in this procedure. First, it is quite possible that a driver who got his license in 1986 started driving only in 1989; we have no way to check this from the data. Second, as discussed in subsection 4.6 below, French insurers appear to take some liberty with the bonus/malus system; in particular, some beginners start with the (favorable) coefficient of their father, who presumably is a good customer. Thus someone who has a bonus/malus lower than 100 in 1989 may actually have had an accident before 1989. Unfortunately, we do not have data on the history of individuals to sort out these two difficulties. We just hope that they are not too severe.

Here we apply our three procedures to the data set consisting of all drivers who obtained their license in 1986 and started 1989 with a bonus/malus no greater than 100. There are 6,802 such individuals.

After estimating the two probits independently, we compute a test statistic $W = 0.25$. Thus again, there is no way we can reject conditional independence. Estimating the bivariate probit yields the same conclusion: the estimated ρ is 0.024, with estimated standard error 0.057 and 95 percent confidence interval $[-0.888, 0.136]$. Finally, the nonparametric procedure leads to only one rejection of independence, which of course is much below the 5 percent critical value. The value of the statistic S is 59.3, again much smaller than the critical value. The Kolmogorov-Smirnov test gives the same message, as $K = 0.82$.

Thus all our tests consistently give us evidence against the presence of asymmetric information. This holds for both "exogenous" asymmetric information as in the preceding subsection and the less usual endogenously evolved form that we tested here.

4.6 A Specific Test for Moral Hazard

As argued in the Introduction, distinguishing between adverse selection and moral hazard is a difficult task when only static data are available. We suggest there that the dynamics of contracts, especially through experience rating, could provide tests in which adverse selection and moral hazard generate opposite predictions. However, such tests require panel data, which are not available at the moment.

In this subsection, we describe a test that, while requiring only cross-sectional data on beginners, keeps part of the flavor of the previous ideas. This test is based on a peculiarity of the French regulation. In the bonus/malus system described earlier, a young driver should in principle start with a bonus coefficient equal to one (*i.e.*, pay the standard premium corresponding to his profile). As it turns out, however, a significant proportion of young drivers (19.5 percent in our sample) started instead with the minimum possible coefficient, namely .5, which implies a 50 percent reduction in the premium. After discussing this apparent anomaly with several insurers, we realized that this reduction could be explained by a constraint that limits the implementation of the bonus system. Many young drivers face a simple choice. If the car they drive is declared as their personal belonging, they will pay whatever premium the insurance company will charge a young driver. However, they may also declare the car as belonging to one of their parents; the parent is then allowed to lend them the car, at an extra cost that reflects the extra premium required for a young driver. This allows young drivers to benefit from their parents' bonus coefficient. Since a high proportion (more than two-thirds) of the drivers in our total sample (all seniorities included) do benefit from the maximum reduction ($b_t = .5$), this constitutes a potentially serious problem.[17] It was explained to us that, in such a case, insurance companies may sometimes simply replicate the parents' bonus in the child's policy.

It is easy to see that any driver, whatever her risk, will be more tempted to buy comprehensive coverage if her bonus coefficient goes from one to .5. The data confirm this: running a probit on the choice of comprehensive coverage with an added explanatory variable that equals one if and only if the bonus is .5 shows that this new variable has a positive and significant coefficient. A more interesting question is whether this reduction has an impact on accident probabilities. Three possible stories can be considered: (1) Assume, first, that the parents' performances are positively correlated with the child's. Then the 50 percent bonus signals a better driver and should be *negatively* correlated with accident probability. (2) A second possibility is that the parents' performances are uncorrelated with the child's, and there is no moral hazard. Then the 50 percent bonus is allocated randomly and should not matter for accident probabilities. (3) Finally, assume that parents' and child's performances are uncorrelated but there is some moral hazard. Then we are facing a kind of natural experiment, as some drivers face a different incentive scheme for exogenous reasons. Since the marginal cost (to the insured) of an accident is increasing with the bonus coefficient, one should expect

17. It is not totally clear why not all young drivers use this opportunity. We were told that a typical insurance company will be reluctant to accept such a deal unless the father is a good customer and that, in addition, many young drivers prefer to own their car.

that a lower bonus coefficient decreases incentives and thus leads to *larger* accident probabilities.

We hence reestimated the probit on accident frequency with the additional variable. We found that its coefficient is negative and significant, which rejects the moral hazard hypothesis. We also computed our χ^2 (1) test for independence of the residuals of the two probits. This is again very low, so that adverse selection does not seem to be present either.

5 Conclusions

5.1 Misspecification and Spurious Correlation: An Asymmetric Danger

A lesson of this paper, as compared to the earlier literature, is that conditioning on observables is a rather delicate task. It requires large samples and numerous variables. It is quite easy, in particular, to mistakenly conclude that adverse selection does exist; this is likely to occur, for instance, whenever the various nonlinearities existing in either the pricing schedule or the accident probability have not been properly taken into account. We believe, in particular, that the use of simple, linear functional forms (such as logit or probit) should be restricted to homogeneous populations. In our empirical work, we restrict our attention to a sample of "young" drivers and find no evidence of adverse selection.

A second claim is that the problem we just evoked does not arise in a symmetric way. While the omission of some variables can obviously generate spurious correlations between contract choices and accident frequency, it is much more difficult to figure how it could hide some actual relationship. In other words, we believe that a negative conclusion, like the one we get, is probably much more robust than any positive finding could be. This claim should, however, be qualified. In fact, as our final result on the effect of the bonus coefficient clearly suggests, it may be the case that some variable that is observed by the insurers but somehow is not recorded in our data set influences contract choice and riskiness in opposite directions, and that it cancels out a conditional dependence in our estimates. However, such a situation seems unlikely because (i) our procedures include a large number of explanatory variables and are used on a relatively homogeneous subsample, and (ii) it would require an exact cancellation between the effect of the omitted variable and the adverse selection residual effect, which seems implausible.

5.2 Adverse Selection: Risk or Preferences?

Our main finding is that, although unobserved heterogeneity on risk is probably very important, there is no correlation between unobservable riskiness and contract choice. In other words, when choosing their automobile insurance contracts, individuals behave as though they had no better knowledge of their risk than insurance companies. This interpretation is fully consistent with the view generally shared by French automobile insurers, namely that the information at the company's disposal is extremely rich and that, in most cases, the asymmetry, if any, is in favor of the company.[18] This is, we believe, the most natural interpretation of our results: we do not find evidence of (risk-related) adverse selection because this phenomenon does not exist (or only to a very limited extent) in the market under consideration. A surprising consequence is that many variables that one might believe to be correlated with risk appear to be in fact irrelevant. A typical example is income. Insurance companies do not ask any question about income (which, incidentally, suggests that the datum they have — mainly the brand of the car — is a good enough proxy). As a result, income acts as an omitted variable in both our regressions. Since it is hard to believe that income is not correlated with the partial versus full coverage decision,[19] it must be the case that it is uncorrelated with accident probabilities, at least after one controls for all observables. Another striking example is annual mileage. This information is obviously available to the driver. Insurers, on the other hand, do not use it in general, although conditioning on actual mileage would not raise major technical problems.[20] This fact, by itself, suggests that the issue may not be crucial. Insurers believe that the mileage variable is very correlated with such proxies as area of residence or type of use (salespeople, for instance, have special contracts).

Another disturbing implication of our results is that moral hazard is not important either in this context. Two caveats should, however, be introduced. One is that, to some extent, moral hazard is taken care of through deductible and experience rating. If the effort associated with careful driving is not too costly, these tools may be sufficient. In addition, as argued above, we consider only accidents involving several drivers; this restriction is needed to avoid the "accident versus claim" bias. Insofar as moral hazard (or adverse selection, for that matter) is particularly strong for accidents involving only one driver (say, being careful is especially important when exiting one's own garage), we cannot detect it.

This does not mean, however, that asymmetric information is absent in this particular relationship, but rather that it takes a different

18. To quote the chief executive officer of a major company: "The really risky clients are those who believe they are first-class drivers!"

19. The sign of this effect is not clear. While the kind of "peace of mind" that insurance buys could be thought of as a normal good, there is strong empirical evidence that risk aversion decreases with wealth.

20. The client could be asked to declare *ex ante* what his mileage will be. The key point is that this declaration will be cross-checked only if an accident occurs, which is easy (since an expert will see the car in any case). Actually, after the survey had been completed, one firm (Mutuelles du Mans) did introduce a contract contingent on mileage. This contract was successful, but by no means overwhelmingly so.

form. While theoretical models concentrate on one particular source of adverse selection — the individual's better knowledge of her risk — the empirical relevance of this exclusive emphasis is not always guaranteed. Risk is not the only possible source of informational asymmetry and probably not the most important one. There are good reasons to believe that individuals know better their own preferences and particularly their level of risk aversion — an aspect that is often disregarded in theoretical models. The presence of preference-related adverse selection would explain both the existence of menus of contracts offered to clients and the absence of correlation between their choice and their accident probability. An extreme version of this is the so-called cherry-picking story. Assume that individuals have different risk aversions and that more risk-averse drivers tend to both buy more insurance and drive more cautiously; this would even suggest a *negative* correlation between insurance coverage and accident frequency.

Appealing as it may be, the cherry-picking story raises several questions. First, the link between higher risk aversion and higher prevention efforts is not direct, especially when a comprehensive insurance contract is available.[21] More important, the nature of the competitive equilibrium is more complex. Assume that heterogeneity occurs between low-risk but highly risk-averse drivers and high-risk but less risk-averse ones. Without loading, partial coverage just cannot be used as a signaling device. If full coverage contracts attract more risk-averse individuals, then the zero-profit equilibrium condition would indeed require their unit price to be lower (reflecting lower accident probability). But such a feature obviously violates revelation constraints.[22] As a result, equilibrium would be pooling, and no menu will be offered. This intuition, however, does not hold in the presence of loading. In a recent paper, de Meza and Webb (1999) study a model with moral hazard and adverse selection on risk, in the presence of loading. They show that equilibria can be either pooling or semipooling. In the latter case, their model implies a negative correlation between full coverage and accidents, although the correlation may be small. Whether additional tests can be designed in order to distinguish the cherry-picking story from the simplest explanation (adverse selection is simply absent) is still an open question.

5.3 Prospects for Future Work

As argued above, the absence of adverse selection is perhaps less surprising in the case of young drivers since they are likely to have a very imprecise perception of their potential riskiness. The question, at that point, is whether learning can be expected to modify

21. Jullien, Salanié, and Salanié (1999) study this issue and exhibit sufficient conditions for more risk-averse individuals to behave more cautiously. This, however, requires partial (or no) insurance. In any moral hazard model, full insurance is always associated with minimum effort and maximum risk, whatever risk aversion may be. Insurance is indeed partial in the French case (mainly because of experience rating), although the cost left to the insured remains small.

22. Note that the argument would be different in a principal-agent model because the insurance company could then exploit its monopoly power to charge *higher* rates to low-risk/high-risk aversion individuals, thus discriminating on their higher willingness to pay for insurance. This suggests that the cherry-picking argument might hold in a noncompetitive framework. This requirement probably excludes the example of automobile insurance but may apply in different contexts.

this situation and, more precisely, whether the driver's experience allows her to learn about her true ability faster than the insurance company. Our test in Section 4.5 on drivers with three years' seniority seems to point to the contrary. However, it may be that the effect exists for more senior drivers. If this is the case, then *theoretical models of asymmetric learning* should be further developed. This is an area left for future research (however, see de Garidel [1997]).

Another possible development lies in discriminating between adverse selection and moral hazard. Our simple test of Section 4.6 is only a first step in that direction. We believe, however, that exploiting dynamic data is the more promising route. An immediate consequence of the experience rating system is that, at least for fairly good drivers, the marginal cost (in dollars) of an accident increases with the number of past accidents. In a pure moral hazard setting, it follows that incentives are stronger the more accidents the driver had in the past. In other words, everything equal, the accident probability, conditional on past experience, should decrease with the number of past accidents. In an adverse selection setting, on the contrary, any accident signals a "risky" driver and thus increases the perceived probability of future accidents. Thus it should be possible to test between adverse selection and moral hazard if panel data are available. This point is further developed in Chiappori and Heckman (1999).

Finally, we should stress that our results are specific to the automobile insurance market. There are good reasons to believe that asymmetric information is much more relevant in other markets. While Cawley and Philipson (1997) do not find evidence for adverse selection on a sample of life insurance contracts, Cardon and Hendel (1998) conclude that moral hazard (although not adverse selection) is present in health insurance. Anecdotal evidence and preliminary studies also suggest that both adverse selection and moral hazard are important in unemployment mortgage insurance. Finally, it should be noted that government regulation can introduce adverse selection when it forbids the insurer to condition the contract on some observables. Whether automobile insurance markets entail adverse selection in more heavily regulated states or countries is an interesting and still open question.

Acknowledgements. We thank Christian Gouriéroux, Igal Hendel, Bo Honore, Steven Levitt, Costas Meghir, Ariel Pakes, Quang Vuong, and especially Jim Heckman, Georges Dionne, and an anonymous referee for useful comments and suggestions. Financial support from the French federation of insurance companies (FFSA) is gratefully acknowledged. Errors are strictly ours.

REFERENCES

[1] Ausubel, Laurence. "Adverse Selection in the Credit Card Market." Manuscript. College Park: Univ. Maryland, 1998.

[2] Boyer, Marcel, and Dionne, Georges. "An Empirical Analysis of Moral Hazard and Experience Rating." *Rev. Econ. and Statis.* 71 (February 1989): 128-34.

[3] Cardon, James H., and Hendel, Igal. "Asymmetric Information in Health Insurance: Evidence from the National Health Expenditure Survey." Manuscript. Princeton, N.J.: Princeton Univ., 1998.

[4] Cawley, John, and Philipson, Tomas. "An Empirical Examination of Information Barriers to Trade in Insurance." Manuscript. Chicago: Univ. Chicago, 1997.

[5] Chassagnon, A., and Chiappori, Pierre-André. "Insurance under Moral Hazard and Adverse Selection: The Case of Pure Competition." Manuscript. Paris: Département et Laboratoire d'Économie Théorique et Appliquée, 1997.

[6] Chiappori, Pierre-André. "Théorie des contrats et économétrie de l'assurance: Quelques pistes de recherche." Working Paper no. 94-01. Paris: Département et Laboratoire d'Économie Théorique et Appliquée, Chaire d'économie et d'économétrie de l'assurance, 1994.

[7] ——. "Econometric Models of Insurance under Asymmetric Information." In *Handbook of Insurance*, edited by Georges Dionne. London: Kluwer, in press.

[8] Chiappori, Pierre-André; Durand, Franck; and Geoffard, Pierre-Yves. "Moral Hazard and the Demand for Physician Services: First Lessons from a French Natural Experiment." *European Econ. Rev.* 42 (May 1998): 499-511.

[9] Chiappori, Pierre-André; Geoffard, Pierre-Yves; and Kyriazidou, Ekaterini. "Cost of Time, Moral Hazard, and the Demand for Physician Services." Manuscript. Chicago: Univ. Chicago, 1998.

[10] Chiappori, Pierre-André, and Heckman, James J. "Testing for Moral Hazard Using Dynamic Data." Manuscript. Chicago: Univ. Chicago, Dept. Econ., 1999.

[11] Chiappori, Pierre-André, and Salanié, Bernard. "Empirical Contract Theory: The Case of Insurance Data." *European Econ. Rev.* 41 (March/April 1997): 943-50.

[12] Chiappori, Pierre-André; Salanié, Bernard; and Valentin, Julie. "Early Starters versus Late Beginners." *J.P.E.* 107 (August 1999): 731-60.

[13] Dahlby, Bev G. "Adverse Selection and Statistical Discrimination: An Analysis of Canadian Automobile Insurance." *J. Public Econ.* 20 (February 1983): 121-30.

[14] ——. "Testing for Asymmetric Information in Canadian Automobile Insurance." In *Contributions to Insurance Economics*, edited by Georges Dionne. London: Kluwer, 1992.

[15] Dalen, Dag Marten, and Gomez-Lobo, Andres. "Estimating Cost Functions in Regulated Industries Characterized by Asymmetric Information." *European Econ. Rev.* 41 (April 1997): 935-42.

[16] de Garidel, T. "Pareto Improving Asymmetric Information in a Dynamic Insurance Market." Discussion Paper no. 266. London: London School Econ., Financial Management Group, 1997.

[17] de Meza, David, and Webb, D. "The Timid and the Reckless: Risk Preference, Precautions and Overinsurance." Manuscript. London: London School Econ., 1999.

[18] Dionne, Georges, and Doherty, Neil A. "Adverse Selection, Commitment, and Renegotiation: Extension to and Evidence from Insurance Markets." *J.P.E.* 102 (April 1994): 209-35.

[19] Dionne, Georges; Gouriéroux, Christian; and Vanasse, Charles. "The Informational Content of Household Decisions, with an Application to Insurance under Adverse Selection." Discussion Paper no. 9701. Paris: Centre de Recherche en Économie et Statistique, 1997.

[20] Dionne, Georges, and Vanasse, Charles. "Une évaluation empirique de la nouvelle tarification de l'assurance automobile au Québec." Manuscript. Quebec: Univ. Montreal, 1996.

[21] Florens, Jean-Pierre; Hugo, Marie-Anne; and Richard, Jean-Francois. "Game Theory Econometric Models: Application to Procurements in the Space Industry." *European Econ. Rev.* 41 (April 1997): 951-59.

[22] Gouriéroux, Christian; Monfort, Alain; Renault, Eric; and Trognon, Alain. "Generalised Residuals." *J. Econometrics* 34 (January/February 1987): 5-32.

[23] Joskow, Paul L. "The Performance of Long-Term Contracts: Further Evidence from Coal Markets." *Rand J. Econ.* 21 (Summer 1990): 251-74.

[24] Jullien, Bruno; Salanié, Bernard; and Salanié, François. "Should More Risk-Averse Agents Exert More Effort?" *Geneva Papers Risk and Insurance Theory* 24 (June 1999): 19-28.

[25] Laffont, Jean-Jacques; Ossard, Herve; and Vuong, Quang. "Econometrics of First-Price Auctions." *Econometrica* 63 (July 1995): 953-80.

[26] Landsberger, Michael, and Meilijson, Isaac. "Extraction of Surplus under Adverse Selection: The Case of Insurance Markets." *J. Econ. Theory* 69 (April 1996): 234-39.

[27] Levitt, Steven, and Porter, Jack. "Estimating the Effect of Alcohol on Driver Risk Using Only Fatal Accident Statistics." Manuscript. Chicago: Univ. Chicago, 1998.

[28] Murphy, Kevin J. "Incentives, Learning, and Compensation: A Theoretical and Empirical Investigation of Managerial Labor Contracts." *Rand J. Econ.* 17 (Spring 1986): 59-76.

[29] Puelz, Robert, and Snow, Arthur. "Evidence on Adverse Selection: Equilibrium Signaling and Cross-Subsidization in the Insurance Market." *J.P.E.* 102 (April 1994): 236-57.

[30] Rothschild, Michael, and Stiglitz, Joseph E. "Equilibrium in Competitive Insurance Markets: An Essay on the Economics of Imperfect Information." *Q.J.E.* 90 (November 1976): 629-49.

[31] Salanié, Bernard. *The Economics of Contracts: A Primer*. Cambridge, Mass.: MIT Press, 1997.

[32] Slade, Margaret E. "Multitask Agency and Contract Choice: An Empirical Exploration." *Internat. Econ. Rev.* 37 (May 1996): 465-86.

[33] Toivanen, Otto, and Cressy, Robert. "Is There Adverse Selection on the Credit Market?" Manuscript. Cambridge: Massachusetts Inst. Tech., 1998.

[34] Villeneuve, Bertrand. "Essais en économie de l'assurance." Ph.D. dissertation, Département et Laboratoire d'Économie Théorique et Appliquée, 1996.

[35] Wolak, Frank A. "An Econometric Analysis of the Asymmetric Information, Regulator-Utility Interaction." *Annales d'Économie et de Statistique*, no. 34 (April-June 1994), pp. 13-69.

[36] Wunsch, Pierre. "Estimating Menus of Linear Contracts for Mass Transit Firms." Manuscript. Louvain-la-Neuve: Centre Operations Res. and Econometrics, 1994.

15

The Macroeconomics of Labor and Credit Market Imperfections

Etienne Wasmer
Philippe Weil

Abstract

Credit market imperfections influence the labor market and aggregate economic activity. In turn, macroeconomic factors have an impact on the credit sector. To assess these effects in a tractable general-equilibrium framework, we introduce endogenous search frictions, in the spirit of Peter Diamond (1990), in both credit and labor markets. We demonstrate that credit frictions amplify macroeconomic volatility through a financial accelerator. The magnitude of this general-equilibrium accelerator is proportional to the credit gap, defined as the deviation of actual output from its perfect credit market level. We explore various extensions, notably endogenous wages.

Labor market frictions and wage rigidities are not the only deviation from the Arrow-Debreu paradigm. Modern economies are plagued with a variety of informational imperfections in financial markets. These imperfections, which may stem from moral hazard, adverse selection, and search externalities, are relevant not only for corporate finance — an area in which they have extensively been studied — but also for macroeconomics. This is, of course, the foundation of the credit channel view of the transmission of monetary policy: new businesses, having poor access to credit markets, are the primary victims of monetary contractions.[1]

Beyond monetary issues, the financial sector plays a crucial role in the determination of economic activity. On the one hand, finance contributes, in a Schumpeterian view of growth, to the development of new sectors and products. Note, however, that the causality between finance and macroeconomic activity might run in reverse. For instance, Joan Robinson (1952, p. 86), cited by Ross Levine (1997), suggests that "where enterprise leads, finance follows."[2] On the other hand, financial intermediation generates macroeconomic volatility. In particular, Nobuhiro Kiyotaki and John Moore (1997) and Bernanke *et al.* (1999) argue that a "financial

1. See, for instance, Ben S. Bernanke and Mark Gertler (1989) and Gertler and Simon Gilchrist (1994).
2. There have been several attempts to clarify empirically the links between finance and growth. Robert G. King and Levine (1993) examine cross-country evidence on the role of financial intermediaries in capital accumulation. Raghuram G. Rajan and Luigi Zingales (1998) argue that causality goes both ways, but establish that the growth of employment due to the number of establishments is twice as large as the growth due to existing firms. This suggests that financial intermediaries indeed mitigate informational asymmetries, and thus contribute to growth.

accelerator" amplifies macroeconomic fluctuations as the value of collateral varies over the cycle.

The objective of this paper is to build a simple macroeconomic model of credit and labor market imperfections which sheds light, in a tractable way, on the interaction between macroeconomic activity and finance, and to demonstrate the existence of a *financial accelerator* based on the general-equilibrium feedback between credit and labor markets. To that effect, we develop a theory of job creation and job destruction in an environment in which new entrepreneurs have no wealth of their own, and must raise funds on *imperfect* credit market before they enter the labor market to search for workers.

To introduce credit market imperfections, we use a modelling strategy that has proved tractable and fruitful in thinking about the macroeconomics of labor markets: search theory. We focus on the credit and labor rationing that arises, when agents are imperfectly aware of economic opportunities, from the stochastic matching between creditors and borrowers, and between workers and entrepreneurs. Thus, we take a leaf from the macro-labor literature, and follow, in the credit market, the lead taken by Christopher A. Pissarides (2000) in the labor market. Accordingly, we model capital market imperfections and labor market imperfections in a perfectly symmetric way, and summarize at an abstract level the properties of the credit and labor matching processes by a pair of matching functions.

The benefit of our symmetric, search-theoretical formalization is that it eschews the microeconomic detail associated, often at the cost of substantial complexity, with macroeconomic models that introduce credit market imperfections through moral hazard and/or adverse selection.[3]

Several pieces of empirical evidence can be adduced for our formalization of credit markets imperfections. David G. Blanchflower and Andrew J. Oswald (1998) report that raising capital constitutes the principal difficulty encountered by potential entrepreneurs. For instance, 20 percent of the respondents of the 1987 U.K. National Survey of the Self-Employed report that *where* to get finance was the biggest obstacle to self-employment.[4] On top of that, 51 percent of the participants in the British Social Attitudes Survey who say they failed to become self-employed report, over the period 1983-1986, that lack of capital or money was the main culprit.[5] Since 40 to 60 percent of jobs are held in small firms (less than 100 employees),[6] a theory of job creation and unemployment must deal with difficulties in *locating* credit. Furthermore, Mitchell A. Petersen and Rajan (2002) document how "information closeness" impinges on the efficiency of credit markets. In addition, the survey of Levine (1997, p. 715) indicates that "the durability of the bank-borrower relationship is valuable." We

3. See, for instance, Joseph E. Stiglitz and Andrew Weiss (1981) for microeconomic foundations, and Carl Shapiro and Stiglitz (1984), or Philippe Aghion *et al.* (1999), for macroeconomic applications.

4. Blanchflower and Oswald (1998), Table 8.

5. Blanchflower and Oswald (1998), Table 6.

6. These numbers are based on industry and market services. See OECD (1994).

take this as evidence of match specificity which is most simply modeled as the outcome of a search-matching process. Finally, Giovanni Dell'Ariccia and Pietro Garibaldi (2000) argue that matching models of the capital market are a promising way to rationalize the empirical evidence on gross credit flows.

Our symmetrical model of credit and labor market imperfections is parsimonious, yet rich. It enables us to show, in a framework reminiscent of IS/LM, that financial imperfections increase volatility, in the sense that they magnify the response of the economy to exogenous shocks. This amplification mechanism is not based, as it is in Bernanke *et al.* (1999) or Kiyotaki and Moore (1997), on fluctuations in the value of collateral, but instead on a general-equilibrium interaction: the state of the credit market affects the state of the labor market, but the state of the labor market itself affects the state of the credit market. We summarize this interaction by providing a simple measure of the financial accelerator, which depends on the *credit gap*, defined as the percent deviation of actual output from the level that would prevail absent credit market imperfections.

Beyond our basic framework, we extend the model to endogenous wages and to endogenous destruction. In the former case, the equilibrium outcome is crucially affected by the institutional arrangement that govern bargaining between financiers, entrepreneurs, and workers — the central organizational problem of capitalism. We establish, for instance, that financiers and bankers have a common incentive to inflate the firm's debt beyond what is strictly necessary in order to decrease the wage that will ultimately be negotiated between entrepreneurs and workers,[7] but that incentive compatibility considerations limit the use of debt as a strategic variable. In the latter extension, we establish that endogenous job destruction generates financial fragility, in the spirit of Wouter J. den Haan *et al.* (2003).

The paper is organized as follows. Section 1 introduces the model. Section 2 presents the model and derives the long-run equilibrium with exogenous wages. Section 3 highlights the existence of a financial accelerator. Section 4 extends the basic model by examining the effects of endogenous wages, and of endogenous destruction. The conclusion summarizes and outlines directions for future research.

1 The Model

In this section, we first describe the three types of agents in our economy. We then characterize optimal behavior during the four stages of the life of a firm.

7. See Stephen G. Bronars and Donald R. Deere (1991) and Enrico C. Perotti and Kathryn E. Spier (1993).

1.1 Entrepreneurs, Workers, and Financiers

There are three types of agents: entrepreneurs, workers, and financiers. Entrepreneurs have ideas but they cannot work in production, and have no capital of their own. Workers, who have neither entrepreneurial skills nor capital, toil on the production line, and transform the entrepreneurs' ideas into output. Finally, financiers have access to the financial resources required for the concretization of the entrepreneurs' ideas, but have no ideas and cannot work on the production line.[8] In the real world, there is a bit of the entrepreneur, the worker, and the financier in each agent, and people can choose in which activity they want to specialize. In our model, however, this is not the case, and entrepreneurship, working, and financing are assigned, for simplicity, to mutually exclusive and exogenously assigned types of agents.

Entrepreneurs and Workers. — Producing output in a firm requires a team of one entrepreneur and one worker. There are labor market frictions, so that entrepreneurs and workers cannot meet easily. An entrepreneur must search for the worker that will enable him to carry out his idea. We adopt the now standard device of Pissarides (2000), and subsume the process of matching workers to firms (which in principle involves heterogeneity, together with informational difficulties) into a simple constant-returns-to-scale technology $h(\mathcal{U}, \mathcal{V})$ that "produces" a flow of matches between firms and workers with two "inputs:" job vacancies $\mathcal{V}$ posted by firms, and available (*i.e.*, unemployed) workers $\mathcal{U}$.[9] Measuring *labor market tightness* (from the point of view of firms) by the index $\theta = \mathcal{V}/\mathcal{U}$, the instantaneous probability that an entrepreneur will find a worker is thus

$$\frac{h(\mathcal{U}, \mathcal{V})}{\mathcal{V}} = h(\theta^{-1}, 1) \equiv q(\theta).$$

The tighter the labor market, the less probable it is that an entrepreneur meets an available worker $(q'(\theta) < 0)$.

Financiers and Entrepreneurs. — Since an entrepreneur must expend resources to search for a worker *before* production even starts, the entrepreneur must be able to finance his recruitment efforts. Traditional models of the labor market, such as Pissarides (2000), focus solely on labor market frictions, and thus assume away credit market frictions. As a result, entrepreneurs have no problem whatsoever financing their search for a worker, whether they finance it on their own, or borrow the cost of posting vacancies on a perfect capital market. But if credit markets are imperfect, an entrepreneur with an idea but without any capital will encounter some impediments when he turns to credit markets to find the funds required to post a vacancy.[10]

8. We will hereafter interchangeably refer to financiers or bankers.
9. We impose, as usual, that marginal products in matching are positive but decreasing: $h_1 > 0$, $h_2 > 0$, $h_{11} < 0$, $h_{22} < 0$. Because of homogeneity, there is no scope for on-the-job search.
10. This sequencing also captures the well-documented fact that financiers often play a crucial role in the composition of the management team of a firm, and that they thus have an essential role to play in production. Studying the reverse sequencing — labor search, *then* credit search — is interesting only in cases where credit frictions are relatively unimportant (*e.g.*, the start-ups in the Silicon Valley where skilled labor was much scarcer than venture capital). Accordingly, we focus exclusively in this paper on the "credit search, then labor search" model.

We could try, in line with the rest of the literature,[11] to describe in detail the microeconomic nature of these credit market frictions. Instead, we note that credit markets frictions do not differ much from those encountered in labor markets: moral hazard, heterogeneity, and specificity are the hallmark of both credit and labor markets imperfections. As a result, we chose to describe credit market frictions symmetrically to the way we model labor market frictions, and introduce a credit market matching function.[12]

Formally, let $\mathcal{B}$ be the number of bankers looking for entrepreneurs, and denote by $\mathcal{E}$ the number of entrepreneurs looking for financing. Each of these $\mathcal{E}$ entrepreneurs is searching for one the $\mathcal{B}$ available bankers.

The flow of loan contracts successfully signed between financiers and entrepreneurs is determined by the constant-returns-to-scale credit market matching function $m(\mathcal{B}, \mathcal{E})$.[13] From the point of view of firms, *credit market tightness* can be measured by $\phi = \mathcal{E}/\mathcal{B}$. Equivalently, $1/\phi$ is an index (for firms) of the *liquidity* of the credit market.[14]

The instantaneous probability that an entrepreneur/borrower will find a suitable financier is thus

$$\frac{m(\mathcal{B}, \mathcal{E})}{\mathcal{E}} = m(\phi^{-1}, 1) \equiv p(\phi),$$

which is decreasing in credit market tightness $(p'(\phi) < 0)$.

1.2 Four Stages in the Life of a Firm

The life of a firm can be decomposed into four successive stages of stochastic length: fund raising, recruitment, creation, and destruction.

- *Fund-raising*. In stage 0, prospective entrepreneurs are looking, at a flow search cost c, for a bank willing, in exchange for future repayments, to finance the posting of a job vacancy. In line with the assumption that entrepreneurs have no wealth, the cost c is assumed to be nonpecuniary, *e.g.*, a private sweat cost reflecting the time it takes an entrepreneur to find a financier. At the same time, financiers are searching for clients at a flow search cost k. The probability of a match, and of moving on to the recruitment stage, is $p(\phi)$.
- *Recruitment*. In stage 1, entrepreneurs have found a financier and are looking (at a flow search cost γ borrowed from their financier) for the worker that will enable them to start operating their firm. The probability that an entrepreneur meets a worker, and that the financing stage ends, is $q(\theta)$. The

11. See, for instance, Roger Farmer (1985) or Ricardo J. Caballero and Mohamad Hammour (1998).

12. Dell'Ariccia and Garibaldi (2000) and den Haan *et al.* (2003) also represent credit market frictions using a matching function, but they do not focus on the labor market. Den Haan *et al.* (2003) investigate the average distance between borrowers and lenders, and justify credit matching functions by the relevance of geographical considerations in financing decisions. Finally, Petersen and Rajan (2002) argue empirically that the IT revolution and the Internet have substantially affected the geography of financial relationships, a fact which again is consistent with the existence a credit market matching function.

13. We impose $m_1 > 0$, $m_2 > 0$, $m_{11} < 0$, $m_{22} < 0$.

14. Our concept of liquidity is the *willingness* of financiers to part from their resources to lend them to firms. It is similar to the notion of liquidity used in stock markets. There are of course other (more aquatic ...) meanings of liquidity studied in the literature — such as the *volume* of funds available for lending. For a leading analysis of liquidity as the availability of financial instruments able to transfer wealth across periods, see Bengt Holmstrom and Jean Tirole (1998).

repayment ρ that the entrepreneur will make to the entrepreneur once the firm starts operating is negotiated between the financier and the entrepreneur.

- *Creation*. In stage 2, the firm has found a worker and is generating exogenous flow output y. It uses this output to pay its workers an exogenous wage ω,[15] and to pay back to its financier a flow amount ρ as long as the productive unit operates.
- *Destruction*. In the final stage 3, the match between firm and worker is destroyed. We assume that destruction is exogenous — *i.e.*, that the transition from stage 2 to 3 occurs with a probability s.[16]

Throughout, we assume that their are no commitment problems for financiers, firms, or workers. All agents are risk neutral, with discount rate $r > 0$. Output, as well as wages and all search costs, are assumed for simplicity to be constant through time.[17]

The Value of a Bank. — Call B_i, $i = 0, 1, 2, 3$, the value of a bank in the fund-raising, recruitment, creation, and destruction phases. Focusing for the moment on long-run equilibria (we will discuss the short run below), the Bellman equations describing the evolution of the steady-state values of the bank over these four stages are:

$$rB_0 = -k + \phi p(\phi)(B_1 - B_0), \quad (1)$$

$$rB_1 = -\gamma + q(\theta)(B_2 - B_1), \quad (2)$$

$$rB_2 = \rho + s(B_3 - B_2). \quad (3)$$

The financier suffers a cash outflow k in the fund-raising stage while it is looking for a client. It pays out a flow γ in the recruitment stage, while it finances the entrepreneur's posting of a job vacancy. Once the firm is created, the bank enjoys a cash inflow ρ that corresponds to the repayment by the firm of its debt. We assume, for simplicity, that the destruction of the match between firm and worker with probability s entails a loss of the specificity of all matches, so that $B_3 = B_0$.[18]

The Value of an Entrepreneur. — Let E_i, $i = 0, 1, 2, 3$, denote the steady-state value of an entrepreneurial unit in the fund-raising, recruitment, creation, and destruction phases. It evolves as follows:

$$rE_0 = -c + p(\phi)(E_1 - E_0), \quad (4)$$

$$rE_1 = q(\theta)(E_2 - E_1), \quad (5)$$

$$rE_2 = y - \omega - \rho + s(E_3 - E_2). \quad (6)$$

15. We study in subsection 4.1 what happens when the wage is instead negotiated between entrepreneurs and workers.
16. We introduce endogenous destruction in subsection 4.2.
17. Were output and wages to grow exogenously at a common rate, search costs (which represent the opportunity cost of time) would have to grow at the same rate. It is thus straightforward to extend our model to allow for balanced growth.
18. An alternative formulation would impose $B_3 = B_1$, so that the value of the bank remains positive after the dissolution of the match between firm and worker. This would substantially complicate the model without affecting its main insights. This is similar to what happens in labor matching models when, in spite of free entry, the value of firms remains positive after the destruction of the match when there is, say, a fixed capital stock.

The entrepreneur expends a flow sweat cost c in the first stage, nothing during the recruitment phase (the cost of posting a job vacancy is borne by the financier), and receives a cash flow $y - \omega - \rho$ in the operating stage (output net of wage and financial costs). We again assume that destruction with probability s of the match between firm and worker destroys all specificity, so that $E_3 = E_0$.[19]

1.3 Bargaining Between the Financier and the Entrepreneur

The contract between financier and entrepreneur is negotiated when they meet. The terms of the contract are (i) that the bank will finance the recruitment cost of the entrepreneur (γ per unit of time) for as long as it takes to find a worker, and that, in exchange, (ii) the entrepreneur will repay the financier a constant amount ρ per unit of time as long as the firm operates.[20] Note that we refer to this financial contract as a "loan" although it has equity-like aspects. The return to the financier depends on how quickly the firm finds a worker and on how long the firm will operate.

Financier and entrepreneur share the surplus of their relationship according to a generalized Nash bargaining rule

$$r = \arg\max (B_1 - B_0)^{\beta}(E_1 - E_0)^{1-\beta},$$

where $\beta \in (0, 1)$ measures the bargaining power of bankers in the credit relationship.[21] It follows that the stipulated loan repayment ρ must satisfy

$$\beta(E_1 - E_0) = (1 - \beta)(B_1 - B_0). \tag{7}$$

2 Equilibrium

Assume it is costless to set up a bank or a firm in stage 0. Free entry of financiers and entrepreneurs on the credit and labor market then ensures that, in equilibrium:[22]

$$B_0 = 0 \quad \text{and} \quad E_0 = 0. \tag{8}$$

2.1 Equilibrium Credit Market Tightness

From the fund-raising stage value functions (1) and (4), it follows from reading period 0 Bellman equations backwards in time that

$$B_1 = \frac{k}{\phi p(\phi)}, \tag{9}$$

19. This assumption is symmetrical to the condition $B_3 = B_0$ we imposed above, and is subject, *mutatis mutandis*, to the caveat of footnote 18.

20. An alternative to this loan contract would be a loan schedule that would make repayment to the financier contingent on accumulated debt and on the time it took the entrepreneur to find a worker. This alternative contract would force us to introduce *ex post* heterogeneity between entrepreneurs — which we want to avoid.

21. In a Rubinstein game of alternating offers and counteroffers, the parameter β reflects the relative impatience of the negotiating parties.

22. These free-entry conditions are very convenient to obtain closed-form solutions. They are not necessarily realistic and may not hold if entry is associated to a fixed cost, or if agents are heterogenous. In either case, the simplicity of the solutions we exhibit here would be lost.

while

$$E_1 = \frac{c}{p(\phi)}. \tag{10}$$

In a less liquid credit market (higher ϕ), the equilibrium value of a (matched) financier is lower, while the value of a (matched) firm is higher — as financiers have to search less and firms more when there are more firms relative to banks.

Since the surplus of the banking relationship is split between financier and entrepreneur according to the sharing rule (7), we immediately have:

Proposition 1. *In equilibrium, the tightness of the credit market is*

$$\phi^* = \frac{1-\beta}{\beta}\frac{k}{c}.$$

Proof. Substitute (9) and (10) into (7). ■

The lower the flow cost k for financiers looking for a suitable lender, and the higher the flow cost c for entrepreneurs searching for a banker, the lower ϕ^* (*i.e.*, the higher the number of available financiers relative to the number of entrepreneurs raising funds). Moreover, the less profitable the sharing of the surplus of the credit relationship is to the bank (low β), the tighter the credit market (higher ϕ^*). Remarkably, ϕ^*, and hence the equilibrium value of the financier and of the entrepreneur, is constant in equilibrium, and depends only on technological (c and k) and institutional (β) features of the credit market. This feature, which is built by design into the model by our assumptions, allows for a convenient recursive solution.

2.2 Equilibrium Financial Contract

Banker and entrepreneur split the expected present discounted value of output, net of wages, that the firm will generate once it starts operating. The stronger the bargaining power of the bank relative to the firm, the larger the equilibrium repayment of the firm to the financier in the production stage:

Proposition 2. *In equilibrium, the repayment flow from entrepreneur to financier is*

$$\rho = \beta(y-\omega) + (1-\beta)(r+s)\gamma/q(\theta).$$

Proof. The proof is by forward substitution of the Bellman equations. From equations (9) and (10), the Bellman equations in the recruitment stage, (2) and (5), imply that, in equilibrium,

$$B_1 = \frac{-\gamma + q(\theta)B_2}{r + q(\theta)}, \tag{11}$$

and

$$E_1 = \frac{q(\theta)E_2}{r + q(\theta)}. \tag{12}$$

Similarly, the "exit" equations $B_3 = B_0 = 0$ and $E_3 = E_0 = 0$ imply, from equations (3) and (6), that,

$$B_2 = \frac{\rho}{r + s}, \tag{13}$$

and, from equations (5) and (6), that

$$E_2 = \frac{y - \omega - \rho}{r + s}. \tag{14}$$

By forward substitution of (13) into (11), and of (14) into (12), we find, using the (equilibrium) Nash bargaining condition $\beta E_1 = (1 - \beta)B_1$, that the value of ρ must be the one given in the proposition. ■

Once multiplied by the discount factor $q/[(r+q)(r+s)]$, the equilibrium Nash bargaining loan contract described in Proposition 2 can be interpreted as stipulating that the expected present discounted value of repayments from the entrepreneur to the financier is a weighted average of the expected present discounted value of the firm's output net of wages, and of the expected present discounted value of the loan made by the financier to the entrepreneur, with weights given by the respective bargaining power of financier and entrepreneur.

The stronger the bargaining power of the financier in the credit contract negotiation (*i.e.*, the larger β), the larger the share of the expected present discounted value of output net of wages that he can extract from the entrepreneur, and the further away the value of the firm's repayment from the expected present discounted value of what it has borrowed. Finally, note that, since $q'(\theta) < 0$, the entrepreneur on average repays more when labor markets are tight — for it takes on average longer for the firm to find a worker in a tight labor market.

Should we conclude from Proposition 2 that our model predicts that the equilibrium loan contract depends on the state of the labor market θ but not on the tightness of the credit market? No, because, as we shall now see, equilibrium θ itself depends on ϕ^*.

2.3 Equilibrium Labor Market Tightness

In a free-entry equilibrium, the expected search costs that financiers and entrepreneurs incur by entering the credit market must equal the expected benefits that they will eventually derive from forming a financial relationship. Therefore:

Proposition 3. *Equilibrium credit market tightness* $\phi^* = [(1-\beta)/\beta](k/c)$ *and labor market tightness* θ^* *are the solution to the pair of equations*

$$\frac{k}{\phi p(\phi)} = b\,\frac{q(\theta)}{r+q(\theta)}\left\{\frac{y-\omega}{r+s}-\frac{\gamma}{q(\theta)}\right\}, \tag{15}$$

$$\frac{c}{p(\phi)} = (1-\beta)\,\frac{q(\theta)}{r+q(\theta)}\left\{\frac{y-\omega}{r+s}-\frac{\gamma}{q(\theta)}\right\}. \tag{16}$$

Proof. Equations (9) and (10) provide us with backward-looking expressions for B_1 and E_1 that depend solely on ϕ: it is these expressions that we read on the left-hand side of equations (15) and (16). Now, forward substitutions of equation (13) into (11), and of equation (14) into (12) give us two alternative formulas B_1 and E_1 that depend on the endogenous parameters ρ and θ. Substituting ρ out of these formulas using Proposition 2, we get alternative expressions for B_1 and E_1 that depend only on θ: we find these expressions on the right-hand side of equations (15) and (16). Equilibrium requires that the backward and forward expressions for B_1 and E_1 coincide — whence Proposition 3. ■

To understand this proposition, note that the total surplus value of a job vacancy (to both the banker and the entrepreneur) is expected present discounted value of output net of wages and search costs,[23] *i.e.*,

$$V(\theta) = \frac{q(\theta)}{r+q(\theta)}\left\{\frac{y-\omega}{r+s}-\frac{\gamma}{q(\theta)}\right\}. \tag{17}$$

Using equations (9) and (10), the equilibrium conditions (15) and (16) are just another way of writing $B_1 = \beta V(\theta)$ and $E_1 = (1-\beta)V(\theta)$ or that, as described, the surplus $V(\theta)$ is split in proportions β and $1-\beta$ between banker and entrepreneur.

As depicted in Figure 1, equation (15) defines an upward-sloping iso-value ($B_0 = 0$) locus BB in (θ, ϕ) space with a vertical asymptote at $\bar{\theta}$ defined as the unique solution to the equation $V(\theta) = 0$. If

23. See Pissarides (2000).

FIGURE 1

Equilibrium Credit and Labor Tightness

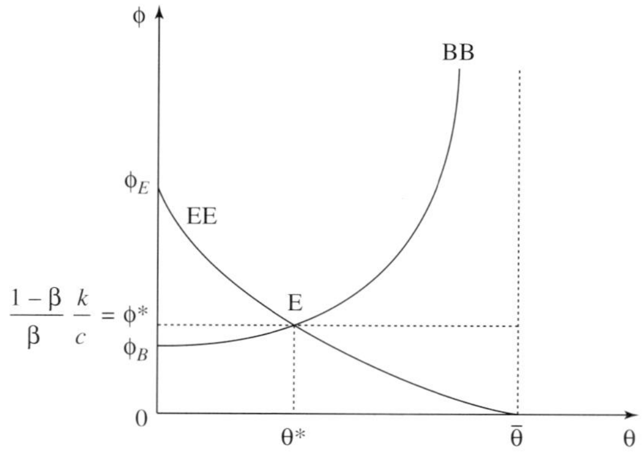

FIGURE 2

More Efficient Credit Matching

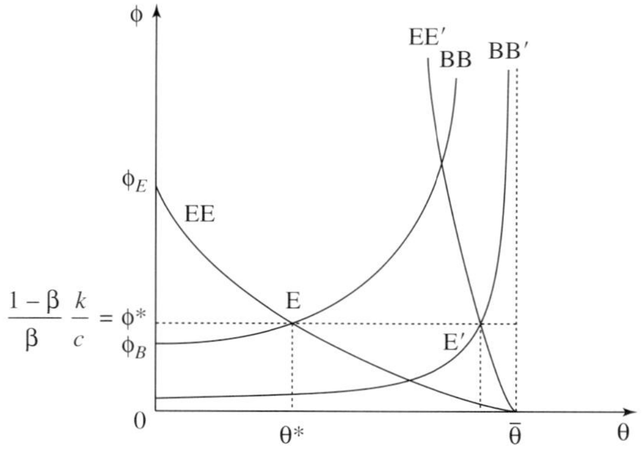

the expected cost of entry for a bank is higher because the credit market is looser (*i.e.*, there are many financiers chasing few entrepreneurs), zero profits can only be maintained by more slack in the labor market (*i.e.*, more vacancies relative to unemployment), which shortens the expected duration of the recruiting stage. Similarly, equation (16) defines a downward-sloping iso-value ($E_0 = 0$) locus EE in (θ, ϕ) space, depicting the trade-off for the entering firm between a tighter credit market (which raises the expected cost of searching for a bank) and a looser labor market (which lowers the expected cost of finding a worker). Consistent with Proposition 2, the BB and EE loci intersect at $\phi^* = [(1-\beta)/\beta][k/c]$. Moreover, Figure 1 shows that existence and uniqueness of equilibrium are easy to guarantee.[24]

As credit markets become more efficient in matching borrowers and lenders [this can be modeled as an increase in the matching probability $p(\phi)$ at all levels of ϕ], the BB curve shifts down and to the right. As a result, θ^* rises, but equilibrium ϕ^* remains unchanged as long as c and k remain unchanged and positive. Figure 2, which illustrates these features, therefore suggests that policies that shift the EE curve to the right are more effective in raising θ^*

24. Let ϕ_B be such that $k/[\phi_B p(\phi_B)] = \beta(y-\omega)/(r+s)$, and ϕ_E be such that $c/[p(\phi_E)] = (1-\beta)(y-\omega)/(r+s)$. Figure 1 shows that a necessary and sufficient condition for existence and uniqueness of equilibrium is $\phi_B < \phi_E$. We assume that this restriction on the parameters of the model is satisfied.

the stronger credit frictions are. We elaborate on this remark in the next section.

In the limit, as credit matching becomes instantaneous $[p(\phi) = +\infty$ for all $\phi]$, equilibrium labor market tightness tends to $\bar{\theta}$, so that $V(\bar{\theta}) = 0$. This is nothing but the Pissarides (2000) free-entry condition for firms in the absence of credit frictions. Our framework thus nests the Pissarides equilibrium without credit market frictions. How does θ^* compare with $\bar{\theta}$? The answer is provided by inspection of Figure 1, or more formally by:

Corollary 1. *Credit market imperfections lower equilibrium labor market tightness:* $\theta^* < \bar{\theta}$.

Proof. From either equation (15) or (16), and using Proposition 1, equilibrium labor market tightness satisfies

$$\gamma/q(\theta^*) = \gamma/q(\bar{\theta}) - \frac{c}{1-\beta}\left[p\left(\frac{1-\beta}{\beta}\frac{k}{c}\right)\right]^{-1} < \gamma/q(\bar{\theta}). \tag{18}$$

Since $q'(\cdot) < 0$, it follows that $\theta^* < \bar{\theta}$. ■

These results about equilibrium labor market tightness translate directly into statements about equilibrium unemployment and gross output, since unemployment declines and gross output rises when θ rises.[25] The EE/BB curves drawn in Figure 1 are thus reminiscent of IS/LM, although they rest on very different theoretical foundations: on the horizontal axis, gross output rises with θ, while on the vertical axis ϕ is a measure of the tightness of credit markets.

One might be tempted at this stage to argue that the result that credit frictions raise equilibrium unemployment relative to the Pissarides model is not surprising, and that all we have done is to prove that credit frictions shift the labor demand curve to the left, resulting in more equilibrium unemployment. But the mechanism at work in our model is much richer and subtler. Credit market frictions reduce the number of financiers. This discourages entry by firms, who find it harder to finance themselves. The reduced number of firms in turn discourages financiers from entering the credit market, as it is more difficult for banks to find an entrepreneur. This discourages entry by firms, which discourages entry by financiers, and so on. Hence, rather than an inward shift in the labor demand curve, what is really at work here is a *financial accelerator* stemming from general-equilibrium effects. As in Bernanke *et al.* (1999), credit markets frictions "amplify and propagate shocks to the macroeconomy." To be sure, the nature of the amplification mechanism in our double search model is different from the collateral/net worth effects at the

25. See subsection 2.4 for a proof.

heart of Kiyotaki and Moore (1997) or Bernanke *et al.* (1999). Ours is based on the general-equilibrium interaction between credit and labor markets, while theirs rests on the equilibrium link between current and future credit markets. But both mechanisms point out that a general-equilibrium analysis of the impact of credit frictions, rather than the study of shifts in the labor demand curve, is required to assess the effectiveness of economic policy. We return to this theme in Section 3.

2.4 A Beveridge Curve Representation

To characterize the effects of credit market imperfections on job vacancies and unemployment, we can represent equilibrium as the intersection of the Beveridge curve and of the ray representing equilibrium labor market tightness in the $(\mathcal{U}, \mathcal{V})$ plane.

Let u denote the unemployment rate. Normalize the mass of workers to 1, so that $u = \mathcal{U}$. In steady state, flows in and out of the unemployment pool must equilibrate, so that

$$s(1-u) = \theta q(\theta)u . \tag{19}$$

As a result, u is decreasing in θ, and so is gross output $(1-u)y$. Since $\theta = \mathcal{V}/u$, the equation of the Beveridge curve is $u = s/[s+(\mathcal{V}/u)q(\mathcal{V}/u)]$, which can be shown, given our assumptions, to be decreasing and convex. Now, we know that in the equilibrium with credit market imperfections $\mathcal{V} = \theta^* u$ while $\mathcal{V} = \bar{\theta}u$ in the Pissarides equilibrium without credit frictions. Equilibrium job vacancies and unemployment with and without credit frictions are thus determined in Figure 3 by the intersections W and P of the Beveridge curve with these two rays from the origin.

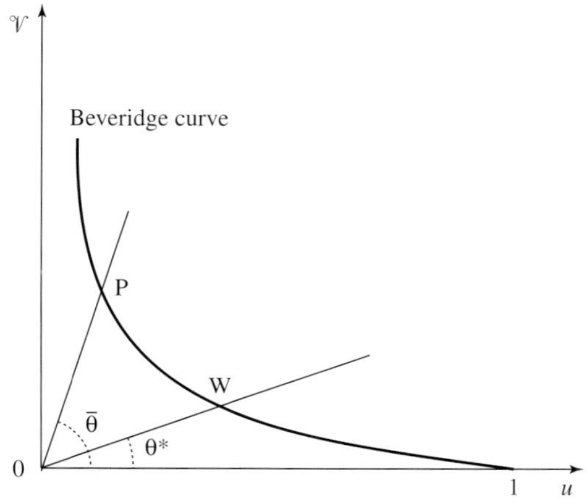

FIGURE 3

Beveridge Curve
Notes: P = Pissarides equilibrium; W = equilibrium with credit market imperfections.

3 A Financial Accelerator

We have suggested above that credit market frictions amplify shocks in the economy. We now document in two ways the existence in our model of a financial accelerator. First, we return to the long-run equilibrium described in the previous section and describe, both qualitatively and quantitatively, how this accelerator operates. Second, we establish that macroeconomic volatility is amplified even further in the short run (*i.e.*, before entry by banks takes place) by credit market frictions.

3.1 The Long Run

We first show that the amplitude of the response of shocks to search costs and profits is magnified by the existence of credit market frictions. We will exhibit this long-run financial accelerator graphically, and then quantify its magnitude.

Qualitative Comparative Statics. — Let us look first at the effect on equilibrium of higher search costs for banks, of lower search costs for firms, and of improved firms' net output.

Higher Search Costs for Banks. — What happens if the banks' search cost k rises? Inspection of equations (15) and (16) reveals that the BB curve shifts up and to the left (for any given level θ, a higher k induces exit by financiers and raises ϕ), while the EE curve stays put (firms entry decisions are not directly affected by k). As a result, the credit market tightens and the labor market slackens. The economic mechanism underlying this result is the following: higher search costs make some financiers exit the credit market. This induces some firms to exit, which lowers θ and mitigates the tightening of the credit market — through a move along the EE curve. If we think of higher search costs for banks as being induced by tighter monetary policy or more restrictive credit conditions, these comparative statics are quite similar qualitatively to that associated with contractionary monetary policy in the IS/LM model.

Lower Credit Search Costs for Entrepreneurs. — What happens if the firm's fund-raising cost goes down? Lower credit search cost c for firms induces entry of new entrepreneurs at any given level of credit market tightness: the EE curves shifts out and to the right. The banks' entry decisions are not directly affected by c, so that BB does not move.

In equilibrium, entry of new firms tightens both the credit and labor markets (a move along the BB curve), but the tightening of the credit market is mitigated by the entry of new financiers trying to take advantage of the increase in the number of entrepreneurs looking for credit.

FIGURE 4

Increase in Net Output $y - \omega$

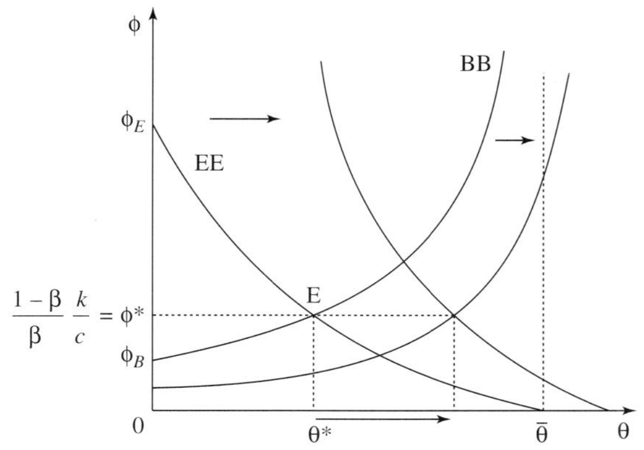

Improvement in the Firm's Profits. — Imagine output net of wages $y - \omega$ increases. This improved profitability directly affects the entry decisions of *both* firms and financiers by raising the size of the surplus that entering banks and firms will eventually split. As a result, for any given credit tightness ϕ, more firms are willing to search when $y - \omega$ is higher, so that the EE curve shifts out and to the right. At the same time, for any given labor market tightness, more financiers are willing to search when $y - \omega$ is high, so that the BB curve shifts down and to the right. Figure 4 depicts the equilibrium: credit market tightness is ultimately unchanged,[26] but the labor market tightens and unemployment declines.

Examination of Figure 2 shows that the effect of these cost or profit shocks on θ is amplified by credit market frictions as we move away from the Pissarides equilibrium. The magnitude of the financial accelerator thus depends on the strength of credit market frictions.

Measuring the Financial Accelerator. — To get a quantitative feeling for the size of the effects we have been discussing, we now log-linearize the main equations of the model around equilibrium. We proceed under the simplifying assumption that the discount rate r is zero.[27]

Labor Market Tightness. — Call

$$\Pi = (y - \omega)/(r + s) = (y - \omega)/s$$

the expected present discount value of output net of wages at the time the firm meets its worker. Denote by $\hat{x}$ the proportional deviation of a variable x from its equilibrium value x^*, *i.e.*, $\hat{x} = (x - x^*)/x^*$. Call ε and η the elasticities of the credit and labor matching functions at equilibrium:

$$\eta \equiv -\frac{q'(\theta^*)\theta^*}{q(\theta^*)}, \quad \varepsilon \equiv -\frac{p'(\phi^*)\phi^*}{p(\phi^*)}.$$

26. This is a result of Proposition 1.
27. The generalization to the case $r > 0$ is uninstructive.

Under the assumptions we have made on the matching functions, $\varepsilon \in (0, 1)$ and $\eta \in (0, 1)$. Elementary algebraic manipulations of equation (15), using Proposition 1,[28] tell us how equilibrium labor market tightness responds to changes in c, k, γ, and Π when $r = 0$:

$$\hat{\theta} \approx \frac{1}{\eta}\{(1+\mu)\hat{\Pi} - \mu[\varepsilon\hat{k} + (1-\varepsilon)\hat{c}] - \hat{\gamma}\}, \tag{20}$$

where

$$\mu = \frac{B_1}{\beta\Pi - B_1} = \frac{q(\theta^*)}{q(\bar{\theta})} - 1 \geq 0 \tag{21}$$

is a measure of credit market tightness — *i.e.*, a measure of the departure of equilibrium labor market tension from the Pissarides model. The coefficient μ ranges from 0 when $\theta^* = \bar{\theta}$ (no credit frictions) to $+\infty$ when credit frictions go to infinity and θ^* goes to zero. We conclude that:

- The elasticity of equilibrium labor market tightness with respect to the *present discounted value of net output* is $(1+\mu)/\eta > 1$. Credit market frictions thus *amplify* by a factor $1+\mu$ the effect of changes in profits on labor market tightness relative to the Pissarides case $(\mu = 0)$. The coefficient μ is thus a measure of the *financial accelerator.*
- The elasticity of θ^* with respect to the *search cost of banks k* is $-\mu\varepsilon/\eta$, while its elasticity with respect to the credit search cost of firms is $-\mu(1-\varepsilon)/\eta$. Both elasticities are negative: credit frictions slacken the labor market. These elasticities are larger in absolute value the tighter the credit market.
- The elasticity of θ^* with respect to the labor search cost γ is exactly the same, $-1/\eta$, as in the Pissarides model.

Unemployment. — Using equation (19), the unemployment rate and employment rate $e = 1 - u$ respond to changes in θ according to:

$$\hat{u} \approx -(1-u^*)(1-\eta)\hat{\theta}, \tag{22}$$

$$\hat{e} \approx -(1-e^*)(1-\eta)\hat{\theta}. \tag{23}$$

As in the Pissarides model, the proportional effect of labor market tightness on the (un)employment rate thus depends on the level of employment — a reflection of the convexity of the Beveridge curve. A similar result of course holds for gross output per head, which is proportional to $1-u$.

Now note that, for $\bar{\theta}$ close to θ^*, a first-order Taylor expansion of equation (21) around θ^* yields $\mu \approx \eta\hat{\theta}^*$. Combining this approximation with equation (23) hence provides us with a way to

28. Alternatively, we could use both (15) and (16).

quickly gauge empirically the magnitude of the financial accelerator close to the Pissarides equilibrium:

$$\mu \approx \frac{1-\eta}{\eta}\frac{1}{1-e^*}\hat{e}. \tag{24}$$

Now $\hat{e}$ is the percentage decline in the equilibrium employment rate (equivalently, in gross output per head) that is due to credit frictions. Call it the *credit gap*. For moderate credit frictions, the financial accelerator is thus proportional to the credit gap. The coefficient of proportionality equals 10, for instance, if the elasticity of the labor matching function is $\eta = 0.5$, and the employment rate is 90 percent. As a result, if the credit gap is 7 percent, the financial accelerator μ equals 70 percent, implying that the financial accelerator amplifies, say, the elasticity of equilibrium labor market tension with respect to profit shocks by 70 percent relative to the Pissarides equilibrium.[29]

Excess Return. — Finally, define the internal rate of return of loans to firms, as the interest rate R that equalizes the expected present discounted value of the loan $\gamma/[R+q(\theta^*)]$ and the expected present discounted repayment on the loan $\{q(\theta^*)/[R+q(\theta^*)]\}\{\rho/(R+s)\}$. Using Proposition 2, we find that

$$R-r = \beta(r+s)\mu. \tag{25}$$

The excess return $R-r$ on business loans is increasing in β (the share of the bank) and in μ (credit market imperfections). Credit market imperfections affect the excess return on commercial paper by increasing the duration of the (costly) first stage, and by increasing the cost of credit (and therefore μ). Furthermore, an increase in the destruction probability s increases R by decreasing the expected length of the repayment period.

Numerical Evaluation. — To get a feel for the equilibrium levels predicted by our model, we adopt the following parameterizations for matching functions:

$$q(\theta) = q_0\theta^{-\eta}$$

$$p(\phi) = p_0\phi^{-\varepsilon},$$

where q_0 and p_0 are (scale) measures of the intensity of the matches in labor and credit markets.

Table 1 reports equilibrium unemployment rates in four different cases that correspond to possible combinations of "high" and "low" credit and labor market frictions.[30] Traditional explanations (based solely on labor market imperfections) must rely on a high degree of mismatch on the labor market, as measured by q_0, to

29. Formula (24) relates two obviously endogenous variables, and is only provided for back-of-the-envelope calculations. A proper equilibrium computation is performed in the next subsection.

30. We assume $\beta = 0.5$ and $c = k = 0.35$, so that $\phi^* = 1$. Furthermore, we specify $\gamma = 1.5$, $y = 1$, $s = 0.15$, $r = 0.05$, $\eta = \varepsilon = 0.5$, and $\omega = 0.66$.

explain high unemployment: they are captured by the southwestern cell of Table 1. The northeastern cell of Table 1 suggests an alternative perspective: high unemployment might result from the combination of moderate labor *and* moderate credit frictions.

TABLE 1

Equilibrium Unemployment

u (percent)	**Credit** $p_0 = +\infty$	$p_0 = 1$
Labor		
$q_0 = 1.5$	5.6	9.3
$q_0 = 1.1$	9.9	16.0

This exercise confirms the macroeconomic relevance of intermediation or financial costs, already documented by Pierfederico Asdrubali *et al.* (1996), and suggests that credit costs are a good way to improve the calibration of the matching model.[31]

Consistent with our earlier back-of-the-envelope computations based on equation (24), the financial accelerator μ, equals 0.74, so that the elasticities of tightness to profits Π, search costs c or k, and γ are respectively, using (20), 3.4, -1.74, and -2. The internal rate of return on loans to the firms is 22.4 percent a year, *i.e.*, an excess return of 17.4 percent over the riskless rate $r = 5$ percent. In other terms, the internal rate of return on loans is 17.4 percent higher than it would be absent credit market imperfections — which we view again as an improvement over standard calibrations.

3.2 The Short Run: Overshooting

We have so far only discussed equilibria in which free entry of banks or firms drives down to zero the value of yet inactive financiers or entrepreneurs. In these equilibria, which can be viewed as describing long-run outcomes, financial liberalization, modeled as a policy that lowers the search cost k of banks, always has unambiguous expansionary effects: lower search costs for banks attract more financiers into credit; this attracts more entrepreneurs, which reduces equilibrium unemployment.

What if, by contrast, we lived in a short run in which the total number of banks were fixed and did not respond to improved profit incentives? If the free entry of banks that is at the heart of the expansionary long-run effects of a lower k is blocked, lowering k simply increases the value of existing banks B_0, instead of attracting more banks. This strengthens the bargaining power of existing banks in

31. See Monika Merz (1995), and Harold L. Cole and Richard Rogerson (1999) for more on calibration issues. For the parameters of the northeastern cell of the table, it takes about one year to find a credit line, and eight months to recruit a worker. Total pecuniary credit costs, excluding the sweat cost for the entrepreneur of finding a financier, represent 7 percent of total discounted output $y/(r+s)$. Equivalently, flow pecuniary costs $\mathcal{B}k$ represent 5.3 percent of annual GDP.

their negotiation with firms (as entrepreneurs are now facing a given number of banks that have more favorable outside options). As a result, the equilibrium repayment from firms to banks rises when k falls. This deterioration of the firms' financial condition leads some entrepreneurs to leave the credit market. This in turn must result in *higher* unemployment in the short run.

It is easy to confirm formally that, as a result of financial liberalization, the unemployment rate *overshoots* its long-run value: a lower k first raises, but then eventually lowers equilibrium unemployment.[32] This rationalizes the belief that financial liberalization might generate short-run volatility, and reinforces the message that an understanding of the effects of financial imperfections requires going beyond demand and supply. The mechanism at play is straightforward, and it is at the heart of the economics of imperfect markets: reducing the incumbents' costs when, in the short run, all barriers to entry have not yet been removed, only increases the incumbents' rents. Consequently, financial reform raises short-run unemployment when there are still obstacles to entry in the banking sector.

4 Extensions

We now demonstrate, by exploring possible extensions and applications, that our basic framework is well-suited to study two macroeconomic questions at the junction of labor and financial economics. What are the effects of financial imperfections on bargained wages and on the incentives of entrepreneurs to recruit suitable workers? What happens when a firm experiences episodes of negative cash flows?

4.1 Endogenous Wage

We have assumed up to now that the wage paid to workers was exogenous. We now examine what happens when, more generally and perhaps more realistically, the wage is negotiated between workers and entrepreneurs.

Endogenous wages gives rise to "ménage à trois" between workers, entrepreneurs, and bankers. How the final output of the firm is split between its three partners, and which institutional arrangements are put in place to organize their conflicting interests, is the central problem of capitalist economies. Our model provides a simple framework in which to think about the macroeconomic impact of various arrangements — a theme often associated with Marxian economics.

We show that the fact that entrepreneurs and bankers meet before entrepreneurs and workers does affect financial and wage

32. As long as there is free entry in the entrepreneurial sector, there is of course no such contrast between long-run and short-run effects of decreasing the search cost c of entrepreneurs.

bargaining. The parties who bargain first (the financier and the entrepreneur) anticipate in their financial dealings the later arrival of workers in the firm. Debt thus becomes a strategic instrument that financiers and entrepreneurs can use to reduce the wage that workers will eventually negotiate with their employer.[33] However, we argue that incentive compatibility considerations limit, in practice, the use of debt as a strategic variable.[34]

Sequential Bargaining. — There are now two types of contracts in our economy: loan contracts negotiated between financiers and entrepreneurs, and wage contracts bargained between entrepreneurs and workers. Consistent with the necessity for an entrepreneur to find a banker before she can look for a worker, these contracts are negotiated *sequentially*. The loan contract is struck in stage 1, when financier and entrepreneur meet. The wage contract is then negotiated in stage 2 when entrepreneur and worker find each other.

Entrepreneurs and workers take as given the loan contract which was written before they met. Bankers and entrepreneurs know that the result of their financial bargaining will influence the terms of the eventual labor contract.

Wage Bargaining. — We proceed backwards, and start with a description of wage bargaining between entrepreneur and worker, *given* the terms of the financial contract ρ struck earlier between the entrepreneur and his financier.

Let W denote the value for a worker of being employed, U the value of being unemployed, and b unemployment benefits. Then W and U satisfy the following steady-state Bellman equations:

$$rW = \omega + s(U - W), \tag{26}$$

$$rU = b + \theta q(\theta)(W - U), \tag{27}$$

since $\theta q(\theta)$ is the probability that an unemployed worker will get out of the unemployment pool by finding a job. Assume that entrepreneur and worker share the surplus $(E_2 - E_0) + (W - U)$ generated by their relationship according a general Nash bargaining rule.[35] Then

$$\omega = \arg\max\ (E_2 - E_0)^{1-\alpha}(W - U)^{\alpha},$$

where $\alpha \in (0, 1)$ measures the bargaining power of workers in the labor relationship. This enables us to establish:

Proposition 4. *The wage schedule in any individual firm is given by*

$$\omega = \alpha(y - p) + (1 - \alpha)rU.$$

33. The use of debt as a device to decrease the share of workers has been studied empirically and formalized theoretically by Bronars and Deere (1991) and Perotti and Spier (1993). The existence of this problem is recognized by Caballero and Hammour (1998) but assumed away by the assumption of block bargaining (workers against bankers and entrepreneurs).

34. Another limit, which we do not explore here because it would take us too far into contract theory, is the possibility that workers might refuse to work in a highly levered firm paying too low wages. This might induce the firm's bankers to accept *ex post* a debt reduction. The anticipation of this renegotiation might constrain *ex ante* the use of debt as a strategic variable.

35. As in the exogenous wage section (see footnote 18), we make the assumption that the relation between banker and entrepreneur is destroyed in case of a separation between entrepreneur and worker. Alternative specifications are possible (*e.g.*, an outside option of E_1 instead of E_0), but they have the unappealing feature that the bank would continue to finance the firm's job search beyond a breakdown of the wage negotiation. It is thus in the interest of the bank to commit *ex ante* to dissolve its relationship with the firm should the latter fail to hire a worker after a match — whence our assumption that the fallback option of the firm is E_0. In any case, both assumptions (E_0 or E_1) lead to similar qualitative results.

Proof. Using the free-entry condition $E_0 = 0$, the first-order condition for optimal surplus sharing is $\alpha E_2 = (1-\alpha)(W-U)$. Substituting equations (6), (26), and (27) into this first-order condition yields the expression in the proposition. ■

The larger the firm's output net of repayment to the financier, the larger the wage. The more pleasant the prospect of unemployment looks to the worker (*i.e.*, the larger U), the larger the wage must be. If workers have all the bargaining power $(\alpha = 1)$, they extract all the surplus of the relationship by claiming what is left of output once the financier has been repaid $(\omega = y - \rho)$. If workers have no bargaining power, they are just paid the annuity value of the utility they would get if they were unemployed $(\omega = rU)$.

We will need below the following characterization of the effect of the repayment ρ on the wage contract in the firm:

Corollary 2. *A unit increase in repayments to the firm's financier decreases the wage by* α *(i.e.,* $\partial\omega/\partial\rho = -\alpha$*).*

The more the entrepreneur has promised to repay its financier, the smaller the total surplus that remains available to the firm and its worker. Since the workers get all the surplus when they have all the bargaining power $(\alpha = 1)$, it is in such a case that an increased repayment to the banker affects them most.

We obtain an alternative characterization of the optimal wage contract by using equations (26) and (27) to compute U in Proposition 4. This yields:

Corollary 3. *The optimal wage contract is:*

$$\omega = \alpha_\theta(y-\rho) + (1-\alpha_\theta)b, \tag{28}$$

where $\alpha_\theta \equiv \alpha[r+s+\theta q(\theta)]/[r+s+\alpha\theta q(\theta)]$.

The weight α_θ increases from α to 1 when θ rises from 0 to ∞: increased labor market tightness improves the workers' outside options, and raises their share α_θ of output net of repayment to the financier. In the limit, when $\theta = +\infty$, the workers' outside option is the same as their current net value, and they capture all the surplus $(\alpha_\theta = 1)$.

Loan Bargaining. — Since the loan contract between financier and entrepreneur is written before the entrepreneur meets his worker, banker and entrepreneur take into account the effect of the bargain they strike now on the later negotiation between entrepreneur and worker. While it is still true that $\rho = \arg\max\,(B_1 - B_0)^\beta(E_1 - E_0)^{1-\beta}$, the outcome of bargaining is now given by

Proposition 5. *The financial contract between financier and entrepreneur is*

$$\rho = \beta_\alpha(y-\omega) + (1-\beta_\alpha)(r+s)\gamma/q(\theta), \tag{29}$$

where $\beta_\alpha \equiv \beta/[1-\alpha(1-\beta)] > \beta$.

Proof. Using Corollary 2 to track the effect of ρ on the firm's future wage, the first-order condition for optimal sharing of the surplus is, using the exit conditions $B_0 = E_0 = 0$:

$$(1-\beta_\alpha)B_1 = \beta_\alpha E_1. \tag{30}$$

The expression in the proposition follows immediately, using equations (2), (3), (5), and (6). ■

The equilibrium Nash-bargaining loan contract is formally similar to the one described by Proposition 5 in the exogenous wage case. However, it is now the higher *effective* bargaining power β_α of the banker that matters for the equilibrium outcome. For instance, when $\alpha = \beta = 0.5$, β_α equals 2/3, which represents a nonnegligible increase in the effective bargaining power of financiers.

Equilibrium. — Since sequential financial and wage bargaining effectively reinforces the hand of the banker in financial negotiations, we should expect the credit market to be *less tight* in the equilibrium with endogenous wages. Indeed, we have:

Proposition 6. *When wages are endogenous, equilibrium credit market tightness is*

$$\phi_\alpha^* = \frac{1-\beta_\alpha}{\beta_\alpha}\frac{k}{c} < \frac{1-\beta}{\beta}\frac{k}{c} = \phi^*. \tag{31}$$

Proof. By straightforward analogy with the proof of Proposition 1. ■

Equilibrium credit market tightness is denoted ϕ_α^* to emphasize its dependence, in the endogenous wage case, on the parameter α that governs the sharing of the surplus between entrepreneurs and workers.

For any α, the credit market is less tight when the wage is endogenous than when it is exogenous. A higher α has two effects. First, a size-of-the-cake effect. When workers have more bargaining power, there is less remaining surplus to be shared by bankers and entrepreneurs. However, as in the case of exogenous wages, size-of-the-cake effects, which affect entry margins for financiers and entrepreneurs equally, are irrelevant for the determination of equilibrium credit market tightness. Second, a distributive effect that tilts the allocation of output, net of wages, in favor of bankers to the detriment of entrepreneurs (see Proposition 5). Proposition 6 shows that only the latter effect matters for equilibrium credit market tightness. Indeed, if α were equal to zero, we would have $\beta_\alpha = \beta$ and $\phi^*_\alpha = \phi^*$ as the distributive effect would then disappear.

We now compute the equilibrium labor market tightness θ^*_α:

Proposition 7. *Equilibrium labor market tightness* θ^*_α *and credit market tightness* $\phi^*_\alpha = [(1-\beta_\alpha)/\beta_\alpha][k/c]$ *are the solution to the pair of equations:*

$$\frac{k}{\phi p(\phi)} = \beta_\alpha(1-\sigma_\theta)\frac{q(\theta)}{r+q(\theta)}\left(\frac{y-b}{r+s}-\frac{\gamma}{q(\theta)}\right),$$

$$\frac{c}{p(\phi)} = (1-\beta_\alpha)(1-\sigma_\theta)\frac{q(\theta)}{r+q(\theta)}\left(\frac{y-b}{r+s}-\frac{\gamma}{q(\theta)}\right)$$

with $\sigma_\theta \equiv [\alpha_\theta(1-\beta_\alpha)]/[1-\alpha_\theta\beta_\alpha]$.

Proof. Similar to the proof of Proposition 3. ■

Using this proposition, equilibrium wage and financial contracts can in turn be computed from Corollary 3 and Proposition 5.

Debt as a Strategic Variable? — We have so far assumed that entrepreneurs borrow exactly γ per unit of time, and repay the corresponding ρ. However, since increasing the value of ρ is a way to decrease the share of workers in the wage bargaining problem, it is in the interest of both bankers and firms to *use debt as a strategic variable to expropriate workers*, and to stipulate a flow loan larger than γ and, accordingly, a repayment larger than the ρ we have computed above. It is therefore natural to wonder whether the cash flow from financier to entrepreneur might rise, beyond γ, up to the point where wages have been reduced to their reservation level b.[36] We now show, by contradiction, that this is ruled out if we introduce incentive compatibility considerations.

Suppose that the debt of the firm is so high that the negotiated wage rate equals its reservation level: $\omega = b$. From Corollary 3, this can only occur, since $\alpha_\theta > \alpha > 0$, if $y - \rho = b$. But then equation (14) implies the value of the firm in stage 2 is zero:

$$E_2 = \frac{y-\omega-\rho}{r+s} = 0,$$

as the wage bargained between firms and workers is indeed reduced to its reservation level b only if the surplus shared in stage 2 is zero. Financier and entrepreneur can achieve this reduction by raising the

36. This reasoning of course presupposes either that the entrepreneur has consumed right away the resources lent to him by the financier above and beyond what was needed to search for a worker, or, if she has not, that he has protected them to exclude them from the negotiation with the workers.

payment the entrepreneur receives from the financiers above the search cost γ, so that output net of repayment to the financier, $y - \rho$, equals b.

Notice, however, the value of the firm in stage 1 is strictly positive as, by equation (10),

$$E_1 = \frac{c}{p(\phi_\alpha^*)} > 0 . \qquad (32)$$

We therefore conclude that $E_2 - E_1 < 0$ if the financier and the entrepreneur use debt strategically to bring down the wage to zero: the firm suffers a capital loss when moving from stage 1 to stage 2.

While we have assumed so far full commitment of all agents, we should however not forget that debt usually has disincentive effects that must be taken into consideration as soon as one starts analyzing strategic behavior. In that respect, a situation in which $E_2 - E_1 < 0$ provides no incentive to the entrepreneur to ever actually hire a worker. In other words, if debt is so high that it reduces E_2 to zero, the entrepreneur prefers to remain in stage 1, and to forever pocket the positive difference between what the entrepreneur lends her, call it z, and the labor search cost γ.

To foreclose this temptation, we should impose the incentive compatibility constraint

$$E_2 - E_1 \geqq 0 .$$

Combining this constraint with the stage 1 Bellman equation[37]

$$rE_1 = z - \gamma + q(\theta)(E_2 - E_1) ,$$

and using equation (32), we conclude, not surprisingly, that banks ration the credit they extend to firms:

$$z \leqq \gamma + rcp(\phi^*) .$$

What do we learn from all this? First, that the strategic use of debt by bankers and entrepreneurs to expropriate workers is a real possibility: banks might indeed lend to firms more than what is required to finance a job search. In that respect, it is both remarkable and reassuring that our stylized model of credit and labor market imperfections, once extended to include an endogenous wage, replicates the results of Perotti and Spier (1993) on the strategic use of corporate debt. Second, that the possibility to expropriate workers never reduces them to their reservation wage. We have indeed established this would require so much debt that the firm would lose any incen-

37. This Bellman equation is the generalization of equation (5) when the amount z lent by the financiers differs from the labor search cost γ.

tive to actually hire a worker, start producing, and repay its bank. Finally, that the strategic use of corporate debt, while theoretically plausible, probably does not amount to much in practice, as the difference $z - \gamma = rcp(\phi^*)$ is very small relative to γ for any sensible values of the parameters.[38]

4.2 Endogenous Destruction

We have assumed until now rather rudimentary production and destruction processes: output y is constant, and destruction occurs exogenously at rate s. Fortunately, our results readily generalize to a richer stochastic environment that yields interesting insights into the endogenous destruction of firms and their financial fragility.

Maintain, for simplicity, the assumption that wages ω are exogenous, but imagine that the output of a firm is governed by the following random process:[39]

- When a firm starts producing in stage 2, its initial output is y^0. All firms start with the same y^0.
- With Poisson arrival rate $\lambda > 0$, the output of a firm then idiosyncratically jumps to another level y, with y drawn randomly from a distribution with cumulative distribution $G(\cdot)$.[40]

Destruction or Refinancing? — If a firm were operating in *all* states of nature until it gets destroyed exogenously at rate s, computing the present discount value of its output, net of wages, would be as simple a matter as it was in Section 2. However, the firm does *not* operate, when output is random, in all states of nature: the financier and the entrepreneur optimally agree to dissolve their match, and close down the firm, if, and as soon as, the total surplus of the match between the bank and the firm becomes negative. Thus, there are two sources of destruction of the firm. An exogenous source, at rate s, that represents outside forces impinging on the firm's viability. Plus an endogenous source, which we must still characterize formally, that captures the optimal dissolution of firms in "bad" states of nature.[41]

The novelty introduced by stochastic changes in productivity is that there are now states of nature in which the firm operates in spite of negative output net of wages $(y - \omega < 0)$. These are states in which the financier has committed to inject new liquidity in the firm — to help it ride out of a temporary negative cash flow period — because the value of the match between bank and firm is still positive. However, as we shall see below, some of these states with positive total surplus are *financially fragile*, in the sense that the banker would nevertheless like *ex post* to close down the firm, but is restrained by his prior commitment to keep it in operation. We must

38. With $p_0 = 1$, $\alpha = 0.5$ and for the calibration parameters of footnote 30, $rcp(\phi^*)$ is only equal to 0.8 percent of the search cost γ — a negligible quantity. Assuming, as we have done earlier, that z equals γ, is thus not a drastic oversimplification.

39. See Dale T. Mortensen and Pissarides (1994).

40. We can allow output to be negative if we think of y as output *net* of operating costs other than wages or financial costs.

41. Destruction, whether exogenous or endogenous, is thus always efficient in our scenario.

therefore determine for which values of y the firm is closed down, when it is refinanced, and when it is financially fragile.

Viability Cutoff Rule and Equilibrium. — The value functions of banks and entrepreneurs add up to the total surplus S_i of their relationship in stage i, with $i = 1, 2, 3$. In stage 2 (which is crucial for destruction), the total surplus $S_2(y)$ depends on the state of nature y, and satisfies

$$rS_2(y) = y - \omega + s[S_3 - S_2(y)] \\ + \lambda \int \{\max [S_2(y'), S_3] - S_2(y)\} dG(y'). \qquad (33)$$

The relationship generates total flow profits $y - \omega$. The match is exogenously destroyed with intensity s, generating a capital gain (or loss, if negative) equal to $S_3 - S_2(y)$. In addition, with intensity λ, output reaches a new level y', and the match generates a capital gain which equals $\max [S_2(y'), S_3] - S_2(y)$ since the match is endogenously destroyed in states of nature in which $S_2(y') < S_3$.

Assume, as in Section 1, that the termination of the relationship leads to the loss of the specificity of the entrepreneur-banker relationship, so that $B_3 = B_0$ and $E_3 = E_0$. Together with the free-entry conditions $B_0 = E_0 = 0$, this implies that $S_3 = B_3 + E_3 = 0$. As a result, inspection of equation (33) reveals that $S_2(y)$ is linear in y, and can be written as

$$S_2(y) = \frac{y - y^d}{r + s + \lambda},$$

with the cutoff point y^d solving the equation $S_2(y) = 0$ or, from equation (33),

$$y^d = \omega - \lambda \int_{y^d}^{\infty} S_2(y')\, dG(y') < \omega. \qquad (34)$$

This defines a *viability rule*: banker and entrepreneur agree to keep the firm in operation for values of y above y^d for which output is sufficient to generate a positive total surplus.[42] In states where $y \in [y^d, \omega)$, the bank injects additional liquidity $\omega - y > 0$ in the firm to keep it alive.[43] As a result, the value of the firm in stage 2, $E_2(y)$, is always positive, since the entrepreneur receives (as long as the firm operates) additional liquidity in bad states of nature, and makes positive flow profits in good states.

In their financial negotiation in stage 1, financiers and entrepreneurs agree on how to share the total surplus of their relationship, given the total surplus $S_2(y^0)$ that their relationship will generate at

42. If $y^0 < y^d$, the economy is not viable *ex ante*: firms do not get the funds required to proceed to the recruiting stage, and no output is ever produced. We henceforth rule out that case.

43. This feature is already present in Mortensen and Pissarides (1994), but it is irrelevant in their perfect capital market setup.

the very beginning of stage 2. Hence, the equations of the BB and EE curves of the economy with endogenous destruction are the same as in the economy with exogenous destruction [equations (15) and (16)], but with $S_2(y^0)$ replacing the term $(y-\omega)/(r+s)$. The intersection of these modified BB and EE curves determines equilibrium credit market tightness — which remains, as before, equal to $\phi^* = [(1-\beta)/\beta](k/c)$ — and equilibrium labor market tightness θ^*. The latter depends on the initial profitability y^0 of firms, and on the restrictiveness of the viability cutoff rule y^d. The larger y^0 or the smaller y^d, the larger θ^* and the lower equilibrium unemployment.

Financial Fragility. — We now show that a salient feature of the equilibrium with endogenous destruction we have just described is that the financier would like *ex post* to renege on his commitment to refinance the firm in states of nature $y \in [y^d, \omega)$ if y ends up at the bottom of that range.

Consider the stage 2 Bellman equation of the bank in states of nature where $y < \omega$:

$$rB_2(y) = y - \omega + s[B_3 - B_2(y)] + \lambda \int_{-\infty}^{y^d} \{B_3 - B_2(y)\}\, dG(y')$$

$$+ \lambda \int_{y^d}^{\infty} \{B_2(y') - B_2(y)\}\, dG(y'). \tag{35}$$

The bank injects $\omega - y$ in the firm. The firm is destroyed with exogenous intensity s. With intensity λ, output changes to a new level y'. If y' is below y^d, the firm is closed down and the bank is left with B_3. Otherwise, it makes a capital gain $B_2(y') - B_2(y)$.

With our assumption that $B_3 = B_0$ and free entry, equation (35) implies that $B_2 < 0$ when $y < \omega$, in addition,

$$y < \omega - \lambda \int_{y^d}^{\infty} B_2(y')\, dG(y') \equiv y^B. \tag{36}$$

Now, comparing this expression with equation (34), we conclude that

$$y^B - y^d = \lambda \int_{y^d}^{\infty} [S_2(y') - B_2(y')]\, dG(y')$$

$$= \lambda \int_{y^d}^{\infty} E_2(y')\, dG(y') > 0.$$

The inequality follows from the remark above that the value of the firm in stage 2, $E_2(y)$, is positive in all states of nature, even when $y < \omega$.[44]

44. Note that this result does not depend on the shape of the financial contract.

This means that some of the states of nature in which the bank has contracted to refinance the firm because the total surplus is *positive* $(y > y^d)$ can also be states in which the value of the bank is *negative* $(y < y^B)$. Were it not for its prior commitment not to do so when $y > y^d$, the bank would therefore prefer *ex post* to sever its relationship with the firm when $y < y^B$.[45]

In these states, firms are *financially fragile*, as their survival hangs solely on the strength of the bank's prior commitments (or on its reputation).[46] Any weakening of these commitments would entail the destruction of some, or all, of these financially fragile firms.

5 Conclusion

This paper has built a simple macroeconomic model of credit and labor market imperfections based on matching frictions. Its main feature is the derivation of a *financial accelerator* that results from the general-equilibrium feedback between credit and labor markets.

Our paper leaves open a number of questions, both theoretical and empirical. First, what would happen if liquidity not only meant *willingness* to lend, but also existence of sufficient financial resources to finance economic activity? Second, can we build upon our model to generate a theory of growth and business cycles? Finally, what empirical evidence could be adduced to back up our claim that the combination of moderate credit frictions and moderate labor frictions is enough to explain high unemployment?

Answering the first question would require us to close our model differently (liquidity would need to assume a more traditional meaning of financial "water" flowing in and out of the economy). Doing so, although no simple matter, would enable us to study whether the economy generates enough liquidity in the face of shocks to finance itself without outside intervention,[47] and would generate a mechanism for the propagation and transmission of shocks over time.

Second, endogenous growth could be introduced in our model by assuming that new entrepreneurs, instead of using an existing technology, are the engine of technological innovation. Accordingly, finance would become an essential input into long-run growth.

Finally, the search for additional cross-sectional empirical evidence on credit frictions figures prominently on our research agenda.[48] Most importantly, we would like to understand further the

45. To ensure that the bank *initially* signs a contract with the firm, we must thus reinforce our previous condition $y^0 > y^d$ (which ensures a positive surplus) to require that, in addition, $y^0 > y^B$.
46. For an alternative view of financial fragility, see den Haan *et al.* (2003).
47. This is one of the main question asked by Holmstrom and Tirole (1998).
48. A cross-country extension of the data set compiled for the United States by Dell'Ariccia and Garibaldi (2003) on gross credit flows would help us provide additional corroboration of our results.

contribution of differences in the fluidity of regional credit markets to the sometimes persistently divergent unemployment experiences of areas that share, within the same country, identical labor market institutions. This might ultimately help to understand why deregulation of labor markets at the margin has not produced in Europe its expected effects on employment.

Acknowledgements. We are grateful to anonymous referees for their useful comments and suggestions. We thank the Belgian Fonds national de la recherche scientifique for financial support.

REFERENCES

[1] Aghion, Philippe; Bacchetta, Philippe and Banerjee, Abhijit. "Capital Markets and the Instability of Open Economies," in Pierre-Richard Agénor, Marcus Miller, David Vines, and Axel Weber, eds., *The Asian financial crisis: Causes, contagion and consequences*. Cambridge: Cambridge University Press, 1999, pp. 167-90.

[2] Asdrubali, Pierfederico; Sorensen, Bent E. and Yosha, Oved. "Channels of Interstate Risk Sharing: United States 1963-1990." *Quarterly Journal of Economics*, November 1996, *111*(4), pp. 1081-110.

[3] Bernanke, Ben S. and Gertler, Mark. "Agency Costs, Net Worth, and Business Fluctuations." *American Economic Review*, March 1989, *79*(1), pp. 14-31.

[4] Bernanke, Ben S.; Gertler, Mark and Gilchrist, Simon. "The Financial Accelerator in a Quantitative Business Cycle Framework," in John B. Taylor and Michael Woodford, eds., *Handbook of macroeconomics*, Vol. 1C. Amsterdam: North-Holland, 1999, pp. 1341-93.

[5] Blanchflower, David G. and Oswald, Andrew J. "What Makes an Entrepreneur?" *Journal of Labor Economics*, January 1998, *16*(1), pp. 26-60.

[6] Bronars, Stephen G. and Deere, Donald R. "The Threat of Unionization, the Use of Debt, and the Preservation of Shareholder Wealth." *Quarterly Journal of Economics*, February 1991, *106*(1), pp. 231-54.

[7] Caballero, Ricardo J. and Hammour, Mohamad. "Improper Churn: Social Costs and Macroeconomic Consequences." National Bureau of Economic Research (Cambridge, MA) Working Paper No. 6717, September 1998.

[8] Cole, Harold L. and Rogerson, Richard. "Can the Mortensen-Pissarides Matching Model Match the Business-Cycle Facts?" *International Economic Review*, 1999, *40*(4), pp. 933-59.

[9] Dell'Ariccia, Giovanni and Garibaldi, Pietro. "Gross Credit Flows." Centre for Economic Policy Research (London) Discussion Paper No. 2569, 2000.

[10] ——. "Gross Credit Flows." Mimeo, IGIER, Milano, 2003.

[11] den Haan, Wouter J.; Ramey, Garey and Watson, Joel. "Liquidity Flows and Fragility of Business Enterprises." *Journal of Monetary Economics*, September 2003, *50*(6), pp. 1215-41.

[12] Diamond, Peter. "Pairwise Credit in Search Equilibrium." *Quarterly Journal of Economics*, May 1990, *105*(2), pp. 285-319.

[13] Farmer, Roger. "Implicit Contracts with Asymmetric Information and Bankruptcy: the Effect of Interest Rates on Layoffs." *Review of Economic Studies*, July 1985, *52*(3), pp. 427-42.

[14] Gertler, Mark and Gilchrist, Simon. "Monetary Policy, Business Cycles, and the Behavior of Small Manufacturing Firms." *Quarterly Journal of Economics*, May 1994, *109*(2), pp. 309-40.

[15] Holmstrom, Bengt and Tirole, Jean. "Private and Public Supply of Liquidity." *Journal of Political Economy*, February 1998, *106*(1), pp. 1-40.

[16] King, Robert G. and Levine, Ross. "Financial Intermediation and Economic Development," in Colin Mayer and Xavier Vives, eds., *Capital markets and financial intermediation*. Cambridge, MA: Cambridge University Press, 1993, pp. 156-89.

[17] Kiyotaki, Nobuhiro and Moore, John. "Credit Cycles." *Journal of Political Economy*, April 1997, *105*(2), pp. 211-48.

[18] Levine, Ross. "Financial Development and Economic Growth: Views and Agenda." *Journal of Economic Literature*, June 1997, *35*(2), pp. 688-726.

[19] Merz, Monika. "Search in the Labor Market and the Real Business Cycle." *Journal of Monetary Economics*, November 1995, *36*(2), pp. 269-300.

[20] Mortensen, Dale T. and Pissarides, Christopher A. "Job Creation and Job Destruction in the Theory of Unemployment." *Review of Economic Studies*, July 1994, *61*(3), pp. 397-415.

[21] OECD. "Job Study." Paris, OECD, 1994.

[22] Perotti, Enrico C. and Spier, Kathryn E. "Capital Structure as a Bargaining Tool: The Role of Leverage in Contract Renegotiation." *American Economic Review*, December 1993, *83*(5), pp. 1131-41.

[23] Petersen, Mitchell A. and Rajan, Raghuram G. "Does Distance Still Matter? The Information Revolution in Small Business Lending." *Journal of Finance*, December 2002, *57*(6), pp. 2533-70.

[24] Pissarides, Christopher A. *Equilibrium unemployment theory*, 2nd Ed. Cambridge, MA: MIT Press, 2000.

[25] Rajan, Raghuram G. and Zingales, Luigi. "Financial Dependence and Growth." *American Economic Review*, June 1998, *88*(3), pp. 559-86.

[26] Robinson, Joan. *The rate of interest, and other essays*. New York: Macmillan, 1952.

[27] Shapiro, Carl and Stiglitz, Joseph E. "Equilibrium Unemployment as a Worker Discipline Device." *American Economic Review*, June 1984, *74*(3), pp. 433-44.

[28] Stiglitz, Joseph E. and Weiss, Andrew. "Credit Rationing in Markets with Imperfect Information." *American Economic Review*, June 1981, *71*(3), pp. 393-410.

16

Banking Crises and Bank Rescues: The Effect of Reputation

Jenny Corbett
Janet Mitchell

Abstract

This paper focuses on bank rescue packages and on the behavior of troubled banks in light of rescue offers. A puzzling feature of experience with banking crises is that in many cases policy authorities make offers of bank rescue, and banks are reluctant to accept these offers. We study situations in which regulators have decided to offer bank rescue plans, and we show that a combination of factors, including bankers' reputational concerns, can explain banks' potential reluctance to accept offers of recapitalization.

1 Introduction

In the 1980s and 1990s banking-sector problems, frequently escalating to crisis level, have become common. Lindgren *et al.* (1996) estimated that in the decade and a half to the early 1990s over 130 countries experienced some degree of financial difficulty. Of these, thirty-six countries were judged to have experienced a banking crisis. Importantly, these countries were not all developing and emerging market economies. After the Asian crisis of 1997 to 1998 several large Asian countries can now be added to the list.

Despite the frequency with which banking crises occur, relatively few formal analyzes of regulatory responses to crises have been undertaken. This paper focuses on bank rescue packages and on the behavior of troubled banks in light of rescue offers.

Much of the literature on bank regulatory policy suggests that bank rescues are inefficient and can worsen banking-sector problems. The whole tenor of prompt-corrective-action type regulation is to avoid having to bail out inadequately capitalized banks (see Bentson and Kaufman 1997) and it may well be that this is a first-best policy response. In many cases of systemic banking crises, however, it is already too late for this type of policy response.[1] Policymakers are

1. We are not suggesting that recapitalization is a substitute for PCA and improved bank regulation. Once the short-term systemic crisis has been dealt with the usual first-best policy advice would apply.

faced with the need to recapitalize banking systems to avoid credit crunches and premature liquidations of performing projects, along with nonperforming, if many banks become insolvent. This is the main reason that IMF advice frequently sanctions bank-restructuring packages which involve an element of bank recapitalization.

It is a puzzling fact, however, that in many cases policy authorities make offers of bank rescue plans, yet banks are reluctant to accept these offers. In recent years Thailand and Japan stand out as examples where government offers of recapitalization have been received unenthusiastically by private banks. Yet the failure to get banks to recapitalize, and to restructure and write off nonperforming loans, has been one reason for poor performance in the real economy in both cases. On the other hand Norway, Sweden, and Korea provide examples where recapitalization was achieved quite swiftly. This paper offers an explanation for these international differences that differs from potential explanations suggested by the existing literature.

We analyze a situation in which regulators have decided to offer bank rescue plans, and show that a combination of factors, including the quality of the bank supervisory system and bankers' reputational concerns, can explain banks' potential reluctance to accept offers of recapitalization. The analysis rests on the idea that there is asymmetric information between banks and regulators and between banks and the market regarding the amount of bad debts on banks' balance sheets. Banks may (and regularly do) hide the amount of bad debt on their balance sheets by rolling over and rescheduling loans that are in default. Banks' rollovers of defaulting loans not only disguise the banks' true financial states but also may exacerbate banking-sector problems and impose costs on the real economy. In these circumstances it is less costly to have banks accept recapitalization.[2] We show, however, that there may be equilibria in which banks have incentives to reject recapitalization and continue with loan rollovers. Banks' willingness to accept a government offer of recapitalization will depend upon the terms of the offer, but it will also depend upon the effect on banks' reputations. The reputational effect may itself be a function of whether other banks are accepting recapitalization.

This paper is related to two areas of literature. One set of papers to which the paper is indirectly related addresses the policy-maker's decision on when and whether to close a bank, assuming *symmetric* information between banks and regulators (and all other outsiders) regarding the financial health of the bank at the point where the regulator must make the closure decision.[3] (See, for example, Boot and Thakor 1993; Mailath and Mester 1994; Dreyfus, Saunders, and Allen 1994; Rochet and Tirole 1996.) While the assumption of symmetric information is probably realistic for the case of an individual bank in difficulty, we believe it is less so in the case of widespread

2. Krueger and Tornell (1999) point out that a lesson from Mexican experience is that "recovery is not possible unless the banking system has been 'fixed'. If there are sizeable portions of banks' portfolios that are nonperforming, the banks themselves cannot extend new loans at reasonable rates."

3. This is the theoretical literature which underpins the design of policies like PCA.

banking-sector problems, or when a crisis is brewing. In the latter case authorities often have to decide whether to allow for bank rescues before undertaking detailed investigations of the potentially troubled banks in the banking system. In many recent crises the decision to create an independent financial supervisory agency with the power to investigate banks' books has been part of a package of bank-restructuring policies which also included the offer of recapitalization, so that detailed examination of banks could not have preceded the recapitalization offer.[4]

This paper is more closely related to a second, small set of papers studying regulatory response to troubled banks in the presence of *asymmetric* information. (See Mitchell 1998a, 1998b, and Aghion, Bolton, and Fries 1998.)[5] These papers, like ours, focus on banks' treatment of their nonperforming loans. By establishing the incentives for banks to roll over nonperforming loans, this literature complements abundant anecdotal evidence of this practice.[6] Mitchell (1998a) shows that when regulators adopt a laissez-faire policy toward troubled banks and when managers of insolvent banks would lose private benefits if the bank's insolvency were discovered, then insolvent banks will roll over their defaulting loans in order to hide their insolvency.[7]

An obvious policy question is whether regulators can induce accurate revelation by banks of their bad loans by offering to recapitalize banks (assuming that the bank managers who accept the recapitalization are not dismissed). Mitchell (1998b) analyzes a regulator's offer of bank rescues, and its effect on banks' revelation of nonperforming loans, when the rescue offer occurs in response to a situation labeled "too many to fail." Although insolvent banks will have the incentive to reveal their bad loans, solvent but troubled banks may roll over their bad loans in the expectation of being rescued. Aghion, Bolton, and Fries (1998) show that if insolvent banks are recapitalized and bank managers not dismissed, solvent banks have an incentive to overstate their levels of bad debt (through excessive liquidation of loans in default) in order to qualify for recapitalization.

Yet, no paper in the literature provides a potential explanation for the problem observed in practice that too few, rather than too many, banks may come forward to accept the government's recapitalization offer. Although some anecdotal evidence suggests that some unsuccessful recapitalization programs have failed because the conditions imposed on banks were too stringent (for example, in Thailand), other anecdotal evidence suggests that this is not the only source of reluctance to accept recapitalizations. Our proposed explanation relates to banks' reputational concerns.

Some empirical examples help to illustrate both the relevance of the question as to why banks might refuse rescue offers and the plausibility of our proposed explanation. First, in order for banks to refuse

4. In the Swedish banking crisis of the early 1990s, the Bank Support Authority was established once the authorities made the decision to allow rescues of troubled banks. Concomitantly, a procedure was devised for soliciting information regarding the amount of loan defaults on the balance sheets of any bank requesting assistance. In Japan the Financial Supervisory Agency, whose staff of bank inspectors is considerably larger than the former supervision team at the Ministry of Finance, was established late in the crisis to administer the recapitalization program. Banks requesting assistance are required to submit detailed accounts to the Financial Reconstruction Commission which are subsequently made public. None of this account information was previously available.

5. O'Hara (1993) and Rajan (1994) model banks' treatment of bad loans under the assumption of asymmetric information between insiders and outsiders; however, the contexts are quite different from this paper. Dewatripont and Tirole (1994) also assume asymmetric information between regulators and banks; however, they do not endogenize the bank's choice or analyze the regulator's bank closure decision.

6. For example, Corbett (1999) provides a revealing quote from Lindgren *et al.*: "In addition, owners and managers of unsound banks have incentives to show loans as performing in order not to lose their bank." In an IMF discussion of "risky" assumptions that analysts often make when working with economies where there is no strong tradition of private ownership, Roulier (1997) notes, that "bank

a rescue offer, they must have a choice about whether to accept the offer. This requires that recapitalization is offered to the banks rather than imposed. In countries where banking sectors consist largely of state-owned banks, recapitalization may be more likely to be imposed upon banks, provided that regulators are fully aware of the banks' problems. Yet, even here banks may have a choice as to how much recapitalization they apply for, especially when recapitalization is linked to the restructuring of loans or to transfers of loans to a hospital bank. (This was the case, for example, in the Hungarian bank consolidation program.) In the cases of Mexico, Japan, Thailand, Malaysia, and Korea, privately owned banks were at the core of the recapitalization program. In Mexico, Japan and Thailand banks could voluntarily apply for programs while in Korea and Malaysia some coercion seems to have been applied (see Athukorala 1999 and Smith 1999).

A second key observation is that in several cases where banks do have a choice, they are reluctant to apply for recapitalization. McQuerry (1999) notes that in Mexico fewer banks than expected participated in the first-round recapitalization program offered after the 1994 currency crisis. She cites a report commissioned by the Mexican government that attributed banks' reluctance to participate to the fact that the market considered participation by banks as a sign of weakness. In Japan several offers of recapitalization since 1995 have met with very limited take-up. Of a Japanese package offered in March 1998 less than 8 percent was taken up. Moreover, anecdotal evidence suggests that government pressure had to be applied to stronger banks to participate in order for weaker banks not to suffer reputational damage. An even more substantial package offered in early 1999 also had low take-up and ultimately was accepted only when all the major banks applied together, submitting all their requests on exactly the same day. This strongly suggests that reputational effects should not be ignored. Another telling example is provided by Thailand, where only a tiny proportion of the available recapitalization package has been used and almost all major banks have rejected government funds.

Finally, numerous country studies of banking crises note the constantly moving target of bad-loan reporting in all countries and document changing official definitions, together with variable disclosure standards, as the cause. The timing of recapitalization offers and the subsequent revisions of estimates of bad loans in many cases (Japan is a well-documented example) suggest that regulators have incomplete information when recapitalization is offered.[8]

Our model shows that reputational concerns can have implications for the circumstances and conditions under which banks will accept recapitalization offers. This leads to some implications about

managers still function under incentives that encourage rolling over rather than collecting bad debts."

7. Troubled but solvent banks may also roll over loans in Mitchell (1998b) and Rajan (1994).

8. McQuerry (1999) also notes that although the Mexican government reacted swiftly to the crisis by proposing recapitalization and restructuring programs, "the absence of an established regulatory oversight agency made it virtually impossible for the authorities to discern the breadth of the crisis."

policy design. We find that even when conditions accompanying a recapitalization program are very "soft," banks may refuse to accept the plan. In order to compensate bankers for the negative reputational effects of accepting the plan, regulators may have to offer large amounts of recapitalization that are unrelated to the degree of the bank's insolvency. Regulators who are constrained in the amount of recapitalization that they can offer may be unable to undertake rescues.

Bank supervisory systems help to allay the consequences of bankers' reputational concerns. Specifically, if the probability of detecting banks who reject rescue offers and attempt to hide their bad debt is high enough, the regulator can induce troubled banks to accept rescue plans (and reveal their nonperforming loans) with less recapitalization than if the probability of detection is low. Thus, a strong bank supervisory system aids the regulator who opts for bank rescues. This result also suggests an explanation for international differences in banks' willingness to accept rescue offers.

We also derive results relating to the conditions accompanying rescue plans. Whereas the regulator must avoid punishing bankers who accept rescue plans, the regulator will want to impose costs on bankers who reject rescue plans but who later perform poorly. By imposing tough conditions on banks that reject rescue plans rather than on banks that accept plans, the regulator can induce banks to accept plans with smaller amounts of recapitalization. A final result relating to rescue plans is that even when the regulator takes account of bankers' reputational concerns in designing a rescue plan, rejection of the plan may occur in equilibrium.

The paper proceeds as follows. Section 2 of the paper sets out the model, which bears some similarity to the model of Rajan (1994). Section 3 analyzes bank responses to rescue offers for the case of a single bank. Much of the intuition of the model comes through in this section. Section 4 analyzes bank responses in the model with two banks and investigates how a bank's willingness to accept a rescue plan is influenced by other banks' performance. Section 5 discusses the regulator's optimal choice of rescue plan, given banks' reputational concerns. Section 6 concludes.

2 Model Description

Several of the basic elements of the model resemble features of the model of Rajan (1994). We consider an economy with banks (of identical size), many potential borrowers, and a public market, which could be the labor market for bank managers or the stock or bond market.[9] The probability that banks experience loan defaults is a function of the state of the world, which we take to be the severity

9. There is no explicit difference made between the utility function of bank managers and owners of banks. The reputation term in the utility function can be taken to be the manager's labor market reputation or some element of utility (such as bonuses) tied to the banks' reputation (that is, stock market value). Alternatively the utility function may be taken to refer to shareholder's utility, in which case the reputation term could be taken to be the stock market valuation itself. As will become evident below our interpretation is more appropriately applied to managers than to owners.

of the banking crisis, and of the banker's type (ability). The possible states of the world are a "nonsevere" crisis n or a severe crisis s. Loan defaults may occur in either state of the world; however, the probability that a bank has loan defaults is greater when the crisis is severe than when it is nonsevere. A nonsevere crisis may be thought of as a situation in which problems arise in the banking sector, but the problems have not become widespread enough to be labeled a severe crisis.

Banks' abilities, or types, are denoted by H (high) or L (low). A bank's type determines the state-dependent probability that it will suffer loan defaults. There are three possible levels of default: no default; a medium level of default; and a high level of default. Our assumptions on default levels as a function of the state of the world and the bank's type are illustrated in the following table.

	Nonsevere Crisis	**Severe Crisis**
High type	No default	Medium default
Low type	Prob. θ: No default	Prob. θ: Medium default
	Prob. $1-\theta$: Medium default	Prob. $(1-\theta)$: High default

These assumptions on default imply that more banks face loan defaults in a severe crisis than in a nonsevere crisis, and low-type banks may be severely distressed in a severe crisis. In the nonsevere crisis the only bank with default is the low type, which experiences a medium level of default with probability $(1-\theta)$. In the severe crisis the only bank with a high level of default is a low type. For expositional simplicity our assumptions on loan defaults are stylized. Our results are robust to changes in these assumptions. For example, allowing for a different probability $\hat{\theta}$ that a low type has medium level of default in a severe crisis or allowing for a probability $\tilde{\theta}$ that the high type has a high level of default in a severe crisis would not alter significantly the major results of the model; however, these changes would significantly complicate the algebra. We note in the discussion of our results differences that would occur with differing model specifications.

The bank observes the state of the world, its type, and the loan defaults in its portfolio.[10] Information on the type and the level of loan defaults is private to the bank. Information on the state of the world is also private to banks; outsiders, including the regulator, do not initally observe the state of the world although they have a prior on this variable.

Assume that all banks initially have outstanding loans with face value B and liabilities of L. Our assumptions on default translate into balance sheet values in the following way. If a bank has a loan in

10. We assume, like Rajan, that each individual bank has a portfolio that is diversified enough to be able to discern the severity of the crisis by observing the defaults in its own portfolio.

the amount of B in its portfolio and has no default, then it has a current net worth (or current balance sheet value) of $B - L$. We will refer to this level of current net worth as "high." When the bank has a medium level of default, its current net worth is $\hat{B} - L$, where $0 < \hat{B} < B$. When the bank has a high level of default, its current net worth is $-L$.

The banker with defaulting loans may choose either to reveal the default (for example, by invoking bankruptcy procedures against the defaulters or writing off the loan) or to hide the default (by rolling over or refinancing the defaulting loan). If the bank "succeeds" in hiding the default, it is able to report high current net worth $(B - L)$, which is the same level of net worth as it would have reported if the borrower had not been in default. On the other hand, if the bank's attempt to hide default "fails," the bank must write off the loan and report the current net worth stated above.[11]

Assumption 1. *When a bank with default attempts to hide its defaulting loans, it will "succeed" with probability a and "fail" with probability $(1 - a)$.*

We interpret the variable $(1 - a)$ to be the probability that the bank's attempt to hide loan defaults is detected by prudential supervisors.[12] This variable is a measure of the "effectiveness" of bank supervision. Since the value of a plays a critical role in the equilibrium conditions in our model, this variable allows for comparison of the results across economies with differing qualities of supervisory institutions. It also introduces possible explanations for observed international differences in banks' acceptance of rescue plans.

We assume that when a bank with a medium level of default attempts rollover of defaulting loans, it will succeed with positive probability a. In contrast, we assume that a bank with a high level of default is already so insolvent that even if it attempts to hide its bad loans it will become illiquid and its financial distress will be discovered in the current period; therefore, rollover will fail with certainty. The following assumption reflects these ideas.

Assumption 2. *$a > 0$ for banks with a medium level of default; $a = 0$ for banks with a high level of default.*

Although a bank that rolls over or refinances defaulting loans may succeed in hiding the default in the current period, the attempt to hide default is assumed to lower expected future recovery on the loans relative to the amount that would have been obtained if the loans had been immediately revealed and dealt with. The lower expected future loan recovery translates into lower bank net worth in the future period relative to the case where loan defaults were immediately confronted. For example, postponing liquidation of the

11. We employ the term "current net worth" rather than current earnings because what is ultimately important in banking crises is the bank's balance sheet, rather than its income statement. As will be seen below, bank recapitalization offered through a rescue plan improves the bank's balance sheet and also enters positively in the banker's utility function.

12. In addition to the motivation of hiding loan defaults, banks may roll over or refinance bad loans in an attempt to gamble for resurrection. Success in the latter would imply that by waiting, the bank has succeeded in being repaid enough on its defaulting loans to avoid insolvency. In principle, the probability of success in gambling for resurrection should be different from the probability of bank supervisors detecting the rolling over of loans. We abstract in this paper from the probability of success in gambling for resurrection and focus on the latter probability. Nevertheless, in a manner consistent with models of gambling for resurrection, we assume that rolling over defaulting loans results in a lower expected future net worth for the bank.

defaulting borrower can result in a lower liquidation value since the borrower has more time to dissipate the firm's assets. Thus, even if the bank has rolled over the loan and succeeded in reporting high net worth in the current period (that is, its deception was not detected), the bank bears a cost c_b next period through lower expected future net worth, where the subscript b indicates that the cost is a direct cost for the bank.

Yet, despite the reduction in the bank's future net worth caused by loan rollovers, the banker may still decide to hide loan defaults because of his current private reputational concerns. The banker's reputation is defined to be proportional to the market's belief about the bank's type. The market updates its prior regarding the bank's type after observing the bank's current net worth. Thus, if the banker's expected gain in reputational benefits from hiding default (and succeeding in reporting high current net worth) exceeds the future costs generated by loan rollovers, then the banker will hide defaulting loans.

We now introduce into the model a bank regulator, who offers (or not) to rescue and recapitalize banks on the basis of his prior about the state of the world. We define a rescue plan to be an offer by the regulator to banks (that can show evidence of loan defaults) of some level of recapitalization, possibly with some other conditions imposed. Because information on loan defaults and the state of the world is private to banks, the regulator knows neither the state of the world nor the true state of banks' balance sheets when he decides whether to offer a rescue package. Banks' responses to the rescue offer, together with the realization of their current net worths, will convey information about the state of the world and about each bank's financial distress. The feature of banking crises that we are intending to capture with this assumption is the observation discussed above that regulators often make the decision to allow bank rescues once a banking crisis is perceived to be severe enough; however, because of problems of asymmetric information, the decision to allow for bank rescues often occurs before regulators know the exact level of default on individual banks' balance sheets and even before they know which banks will ultimately need to be recapitalized.[13]

A banker's acceptance of a rescue offer automatically reveals the bank's defaulting loans.[14] In order for a bank to hide its loan defaults, it must reject the regulator's rescue offer. Yet, in certain circumstances the regulator (as well as other outsiders) is able to detect that a bank has attempted to hide its loan defaults. This occurs when the bank rejects the regulator's rescue offer, rolls over defaulting loans, but rollover "fails." The regulator may in this case impose an additional cost c_p on the bank, where the subscript p indicates the possibility that

13. The assumption that the regulator does not know the severity of the crisis is not critical to our results, although it does simplify the model by allowing us to abstract from any learning by the market of the severity of the crisis from the amount of recapitalization offered by the regulator to banks. What is important is that the regulator does not know which banks are distressed. It is possible to show that even when the regulator knows the state of the world (but not the financial situation of any given bank) the amount of recapitalization offered in equilibrium will be the same across states of the world. The extent to which in practice the regulator or the market has more information regarding banks' financial states has been an issue of debate in the literature. Empirical studies have yielded conflicting answers to this question.

14. It is possible (and even suggested by Japanese experience) that banks may choose to reveal only a portion of their loan defaults when accepting an offer of recapitalization. For simplicity, we consider in this paper only the case where banks' acceptance of a rescue offer reveals the total amount of default.

this cost is a private cost for the banker. For example, the cost c_p may represent a direct cost imposed by the regulator on "deceitful" banks (for example, fines) or it may represent the loss of private benefits to bankers who lose control (for example, through nationalizations) or to bankers who lose their jobs or are more heavily monitored in the future. The maximum level of the cost c_p can be expected to vary across countries and is related, in part, to powers given to regulators in dealing with troubled banks. For example, U.S. regulators have the power to bar bankers from the sector for life.[15] This implies that c_p is very high for the United States. In other countries where regulators have less power and/or bankers have strong connections to the government, c_p may be close to zero.[16]

Consider the situation in which a bank has defaulting loans and the regulator has made a rescue offer. If the bank wishes to reveal its loan defaults, it will accept the rescue offer. On the other hand, if the bank wishes to hide its defaults, it must reject the rescue offer. Thus, the bank's possible actions may be described as $\{Re, A\}$, where *Re* denotes "reject" and *A* denotes "accept" and where reject is synonymous with hiding default and accept is synonymous with revealing.

What information does the market have? When it observes "reject" and *B*, it does not know whether the bank is a high type and the state is *n*; whether the bank is a low type, the state is *n*, and rollover succeeded; or whether the bank is a high type, the state is *s*, and rollover succeeded. When the market observes "accept" and $\hat{B}$, then it knows that the bank has a medium level of default and has not rolled over its loans. However, the market does not know whether the bank is a low type in state *n* or state *s*, or whether the bank is a high type in state *s*. When the market observes accept and 0, it knows that the bank is a low type and that the state is *s*.

The timing of events is as follows.

Period 0

Banks make a loan

Period 1

State of the world realized and loan defaults occur
Regulator offers rescue plan
Banks accept or reject the plan
If bank with default rejects plan, current net worth is high with probability *a*
Report of current net worth realized and observed by market
Market updates bank's reputation

Period 2

Future loan repayments and costs (c_b and c_p) realized

15. We thank Alton Gilbert for pointing this out to us.
16. Some observers have expressed the opinion that Thailand may fall into the latter category.

In period 0 the bank makes a loan. In period 1 banks observe the state of the world, and each bank observes its level of defaulting loans. The regulator then makes a rescue offer (or not). Since the regulator does not observe the state of the world, his rescue offer conveys no information to the market about the state of the world. Banks then announce whether they accept or reject the rescue plan. If a bank with default rejects the plan, it will "succeed" with rollover with probability a. After success or failure of rollover has been realized, the bank's reported current net worth is announced. The market then updates the bank's reputation. In period 2 the bank's future net worth (reflecting the ultimate repayment of defaulting loans) and costs associated with hiding default are realized.

Notation and Additional Assumptions:

1. π is the market's (and the regulator's) initial prior regarding the probability that the crisis is severe.
2. p is the market's initial prior regarding the probability that a bank is a high type.
3. The market updates p via Bayesian updating (when possible). The posterior in the case of high current net worth $(B - L)$ is labeled p^+; the posterior with medium current net worth $(\hat{B} - L)$ is p^m; the posterior with low current net worth $(-L)$ is p^0.
4. R is the amount of recapitalization offered in a bank rescue plan.
5. $Ec = c_b + (1 - a)c_p$ represents the expected costs of rolling over loans.

2.1 The Banker's Objective Function

Bank managers have an objective function which is a weighted sum of the bank's expected net worth and a term containing the bank's reputation. The general form of the banker's expected utility is given by

$$U = (1 - \gamma) \cdot (\textit{exp. net worth}) + \gamma \cdot Ep \tag{1}$$

where $\gamma < 1$ is the weight placed on reputation, and Ep represents the banker's expected reputation. For simplicity, we assume no discounting. The term expected net worth is defined to be the expected future net worth of the bank, including any recapitalization offered by the regulator through a rescue plan, and where future net worth reflects any costs associated with hiding default. Expected future bank net worth for each of the differing possible cases is:

Bank with no default: $B - L$

Bank with medium level of default which accepts rescue plan: $\hat{B} + R - L$

Bank with medium level of default which rejects rescue plan: $\hat{B} - Ec - L$

Bank with high level of default which accepts rescue plan: $R - L$

Bank with high level of default which rejects rescue plan: $-L - c_b - c_p$

Three features of these cases are worth noting. First, the bank with a medium level of default has a future expected net worth of $\hat{B} - L$ if it accepts a plan (reveals its default), and therefore takes an action such as using a bankruptcy proceeding against its defaulters. This bank has a future expected net worth of something less than $\hat{B} - L$ if it rejects the plan and attempts to hide its default. The fact that the cost c_b is positive implies that hiding default is inefficient. Second, the bank with a medium level of default may be either solvent or insolvent but still liquid. We assume that if a bank with a medium level of default is insolvent, it is able to remain liquid for at least the current period. It is, in fact, a common feature of banking that banks may actually become insolvent long before they are illiquid.[17] Finally, because a bank with a high level of default that rejects a rescue plan is discovered with certainty (Assumption 2), its expected cost of rollover is greater than that for the bank with a medium level of default that rejects the plan. The expected cost of rollover for the former bank is $c_b + c_p$, whereas for the latter this cost is $Ec = c_b + (1 - a)c_p$.

It is worth commenting on the implicit assumption that whereas the banker who successfully rolls over bad loans enjoys a reputational benefit in period 1, the banker suffers no reputational cost in period 2 when its ultimate net worth turns out to be less than $B - L$.[18] This assumption is made, as in Rajan, in order to capture the notion that bankers' short-term reputational concerns can affect their behavior in response to defaulting loans, despite the long-term costs of this behavior. It would be straightforward to modify the assumptions to explicitly guarantee that banks which succeed with rollover in period 1 cannot be separated in period 2 from banks that had no defaulting loans on their balance sheets in period 1. One such assumption could be that the market does not observe the bank's period-2 net worth until period 3. If bankers either heavily discount period 3 or leave the bank at the end of period 2, no additional reputational costs will enter the banker's utility function.

Our analysis proceeds by backward induction. In sections 3 and 4 we characterize the effects of differing rescue plans on bank

17. For example, many of the failed Savings and Loans in the U.S. Savings and Loans crisis were liquid up until the date on which they were closed.

18. Note that bankers still suffer the cost c_b in period 2, which can be defined to include costs of maintaining deposits once depositors have discovered that the bank had defaulting loans. We discuss depositor behavior in section 6.

behavior. In this part of the analysis we take the terms of rescue plans (that is, the amount of recapitalization offered and the cost c_p) to be exogenous, and we identify necessary and sufficient conditions for rescue plans to succeed, that is, to be accepted by banks with default on their balance sheets. In order to illustrate the basic intuition, we present in the next section a model with only one bank.

3 • The Model with One Bank

Our analysis focuses on pure-strategy equilibria. We derive the equilibrium conditions for the bank's choice of strategy in the face of the regulator's offer of recapitalization and the market's updating of the bank's reputation. The method consists of examining the bank's incentive compatibility constraints with differing combinations of strategies and identifying the range of parameter values for which the incentive compatibility conditions are satisfied.

We first note a feature that is common to all equilibria.

Lemma 1. *The bank with a high level of default will always accept a rescue plan.*

Proof. See appendix.

The above lemma implies that in every equilibrium the low-type bank with a high level of default in a severe crisis will accept a rescue plan. In addition, the high-type bank will always reject the plan in the nonsevere crisis, since it has no loan defaults. Every equilibrium will thus involve rejection of the plan by the high type in a nonsevere crisis and acceptance of the plan by the low type with high default in a severe crisis. Equilibria must therefore be distinguished by the action taken by the low-type bank with default in the nonsevere crisis and by the bank with medium default in the severe crisis.

We define an equilibrium in the one-bank model by a set of strategies (σ_n, σ_s), where $\sigma \in \{A, Re\}$ and σ_n refers to the strategy that the low-type bank chooses when it has default in the nonsevere crisis, and σ_s refers to the strategy that the bank with a medium level of default chooses in the severe crisis. (It is straightforward to verify that low-type banks with medium default in a severe crisis choose the same strategy in equilibrium as high-type banks with medium default.)

One question that we address is whether the equilibrium strategies σ_n and σ_s can differ. We first consider equilibria of the form (Re, Re) and (A, A). We link existence of these equilibria to the strength of banking supervision, the costs of rollover, and the level of recapitalization offered by the regulator. We then show that the equilibrium (Re, A) does not exist and (A, Re) exists only for a limited range of parameter values. Finally, we characterize the pure-strategy equilibria in the one-bank model.

3.1 Equilibrium (Re, Re)

Suppose that the nonsevere crisis occurs. (Recall that the severity of the crisis is unobservable by the market.) The only bank that can have default in the nonsevere crisis is the low type. The expected utility for the bank with default if it rejects the plan is

$$\begin{aligned} U(Re \mid (Re, Re)) = {} & (1-\gamma) \cdot (\hat{B} - L - Ec) \\ & + \gamma[ap^{+}(Re \mid (Re, Re), \pi) \\ & + (1-a)p^{m}(Re \mid (Re, Re), \pi)] \end{aligned} \tag{2}$$

where $p^{+}(Re \mid (Re, Re), \pi)$ represents the bank's updated reputation when it rejects the plan and succeeds in reporting high current net worth, given that the market expects banks with default in each state of the world to reject the plan. The term $p^{m}(Re \mid (Re, Re), \pi)$ represents the bank's reputation when it rejects the plan, rollover fails, and it must report a current net worth consistent with a medium level of default. The values of the reputation terms are given in the appendix.

The bank's expected utility if it accepts the plan is

$$U(A \mid (Re, Re)) = (1-\gamma)(R + \hat{B} - L) + \gamma p^{m}(A \mid (Re, Re), \pi) \tag{3}$$

The market cannot calculate $p^{m}(A \mid (Re, Re), \pi)$ by Bayes' rule, since a bank's acceptance of a rescue plan is off the equilibrium path. We must specify the market's out-of-equilibrium belief in this case. We assume that the market assigns a value to $p^{m}(A \mid (Re, Re), \pi)$ by calculating the probability that the bank is a high type given that it has accepted the plan.[19] This gives

$$p^{m}(A \mid (Re, Re), \pi) = \frac{p\pi}{p\pi + (1-p)[(1-\pi)(1-\theta) + \pi\theta]}$$

which is equal to $p^{m}(Re \mid (Re, Re), \pi)$.

The incentive compatibility constraint for the bank with default in the nonsevere crisis is given by

$$Ec + R \leq \frac{\gamma}{(1-\gamma)} a[p^{+}(Re \mid (Re, Re), \pi) - p^{m}(Re \mid (Re, Re), \pi)]. \tag{4}$$

19. We have shown in an earlier version of this paper that a more extreme assumption on out-of-equilibrium beliefs, such as the assumption that $p^{m}(A \mid (Re, Re), \pi) = 0$, further strengthens the results of this section.

Now suppose that the crisis is severe. The expected utility of the bank with medium default if it rejects the plan is given by

$$U(Re \mid (Re, Re)) = (1-\gamma)(\hat{B} - L - Ec) + \gamma[ap^{+}(Re \mid (Re, Re), \pi) + (1-a)p^{m}(Re \mid (Re, Re), \pi)], \qquad (5)$$

where $p^{+}(Re \mid (Re, Re), \pi)$ and $p^{m}(Re \mid (Re, Re), \pi)$ are defined as above. This expected utility is identical to that of the low-type bank with default in the nonsevere crisis [equation (2)]. Similarly, the bank's expected utility if it accepts the plan is identical to the analogous utility for the low type with default in the nonsevere crisis [equation (3)]. Thus, the incentive compatibility constraints of banks with medium default in each state of the world are identical.

Consider the IC constraint (4). This constraint implies that if the costs due to rollover are low enough and if the amount of recapitalization offered is low enough, the bank will reject the plan. It is clear that a necessary condition for this constraint to be satisfied is that the right-hand side is positive. The assumptions of the model guarantee that $p^{+}(Re \mid (Re, Re), \pi) \geq p^{m}(Re \mid (Re, Re), \pi)$, with strict inequality for all $\pi < 1$; thus the right-hand side is strictly positive for all $\pi < 1$. Define the following critical value, equal to the right-hand side of IC constraint (4).

$$c^{re}(a) \equiv \frac{\gamma}{(1-\gamma)} a[p^{+}(Re \mid (Re, Re), \pi) - p^{m}(Re \mid (Re, Re), \pi)]. \qquad (6)$$

A necessary condition for the equilibrium (Re, Re) to exist is that $Ec + R \leq c^{re}(a)$. It is straightforward to verify that $c^{re}(a)$ is increasing in a. Thus, the higher is the probability of success with rollover or, equivalently, the weaker is bank supervision, the larger the range of values $Ec + R$ for which the equilibrium (Re, Re) will exist.

3.2 Equilibrium (A, A)

As in the case of the (Re, Re) equilibrium, the incentive compatibility constraints are identical for the bank with default in the nonsevere crisis and the bank with default in the severe crisis. The expected utility for a bank with default if it accepts the plan is given by

$$U(A \mid (A, A)) = (1-\gamma)(R + \hat{B} - L) + \gamma p^{m}(A \mid (A, A), \pi) \qquad (7)$$

where the value of $p^m(A \mid (A, A), \pi)$ is given in the appendix. If the bank rejects the plan, its expected utility is

$$U(Re \mid (A, A)) = (1-\gamma)(\hat{B} - L - Ec) + \gamma[ap^+(Re \mid (A, A), 0) + (1-a)p^m(Re \mid (A, A), \pi)]. \quad (8)$$

When the bank rejects the plan and reports high current net worth, the market believes that the state is n and sets $\pi = 0$ in updating the bank's reputation. On the other hand, $p^m(Re \mid (A, A), \pi)$ cannot be computed via Bayes' rule, since rejecting the plan and having current net worth consistent with a medium level of default is off the equilibrium path. We assume, in a manner analogous to section 3.1, that the market assigns a value to $p^m(Re \mid (A, A), \pi)$ by computing the probability that the bank is a high type given that it rejects the plan and has a medium level of default. The values of the reputation terms are given in the appendix. It is easily verified that $p^m(Re \mid (A, A), \pi) = p^m(A \mid (A, A), \pi)$.

The bank's IC constraint is given by

$$Ec + R \geq \frac{\gamma}{(1-\gamma)} a[p^+(Re \mid (A, A), 0) - p^m(A \mid (A, A), \pi)]. \quad (9)$$

This constraint states that banks with default will accept the plan if the sum of the expected costs of rollover and recapitalization are high enough. Define the following critical value, equal to the right-hand side of the above constraint.

$$c^A(a) = \frac{\gamma}{(1-\gamma)} a[p^+(Re \mid (A, A), 0) - p^m(A \mid (A, A), \pi)]. \quad (10)$$

A necessary condition for the equilibrium (A, A) to exist is that $Ec + R \geq c^A(a)$. It is easily verified that $c^A(a)$ is increasing in a.

3.3 Characterization of Equilibria in the One-Bank Model

We characterize here the pure-strategy equilibria in the one-bank model. The following proposition describes equilibria with state-independent strategies for banks with medium default.

Proposition 1. (i) *For every a, there exist values $c^{Re}(a)$ and $c^A(a)$, with $c^A(a) > c^{Re}(a)$, such that an equilibrium (A, A) exists if*

$Ec + R \geq c^A(a)$ and an equilibrium (Re, Re) exists $Ec + R \leq c^{Re}(a)$; (ii) as a increases, the equilibrium (A, A) becomes less likely and the equilibrium (Re, Re) becomes more likely.

Proof. See appendix.

Part (i) of the above proposition summarizes the discussion of the previous subsections, which pertain to pure-strategy equilibria. For values of $Ec + R \in (c^{Re}(a), c^A(a))$ equilibria are in mixed strategies. Part (ii) of the proposition illustrates the link between the strength of banking supervision and the willingness of banks to accept rescue plans. The weaker is banking supervision (that is, the higher is a), the greater the region of the parameter space for which banks will reject rescue plans and the smaller the region for which banks will accept rescue plans. This being said, the level of recapitalization offered by the regulator can also play an influential role in inducing acceptance of a rescue plan. More precisely, we may state the following corollaries.

Corollary 1. *Let $R^A(a) = c^A(a) - Ec$. The equilibrium (A, A) exists for all $R \geq R^A(a)$.*

Corollary 2. *$R^A(a)$ is increasing in a.*

These corollaries indicate that for every value of a there is a minimum level of recapitalization $R^A(a)$ such that the regulator can always induce banks to accept the rescue plan by offering a level of recapitalization that is at least as large as $R^A(a)$. Thus, a regulator who is unconstrained in the amount of recapitalization offered to banks can always induce banks to accept a rescue plan and reveal their default. Corollary 2 states that the minimum recapitalization $R^A(a)$ necessary to induce acceptance of rescue plans is increasing in a. The weaker the level of banking supervision, the greater the amount of recapitalization that is necessary to induce banks to accept a rescue plan.

The above corollaries illustrate how recapitalization can compensate banks for the negative reputational effect of revealing default and induce them to accept a plan. Interestingly, the expression for $R^A(a)$ implies that the amount of recapitalization required to generate an equilibrium (A, A) is unrelated to the amount necessary to bring an insolvent bank to solvency. This is due to the assumption that banks with medium default can remain liquid in period 1 even though they may be insolvent, which allows banks to reject a rescue plan without fear of bank closure if they succeed in hiding their default. Bankers' reputational concerns may force the regulator to offer an amount of recapitalization that is well above the amount necessary to restore solvency to the bank.

We now address the possibility of existence of equilibria where the strategies chosen by banks with medium default differ across the states of the world.

Proposition 2. (i) *Equilibria of the form* (Re, A) *do not exist;* (ii) *Equilibria of the form* (A, Re) *exist for a restricted range of parameter values.*

Proof. See appendix.

The above proposition states that it is impossible to have an equilibrium where banks with default reject the plan in the nonsevere crisis and accept the plan in a severe crisis. In contrast, it is possible for a limited range of pairs (Ec, R) to have an equilibrium where banks accept the plan in a nonsevere crisis and reject in the severe crisis. This equilibrium exists only for a range of values of Ec. Moreover, for each value of Ec in this range, there is only one value of R for which the equilibrium can exist. Finally, the necessary and sufficient condition for existence of this equilibrium is $Ec + R = \frac{\gamma}{(1-\gamma)}\left[\frac{p}{p+(1-p)\theta}\right]$, which is greater than $c^A(a)$. In order for this equilibrium to exist, the sum $Ec + R$ must exceed the value necessary for existence of the (A, A) equilibrium. Thus, for all parameter values for which the equilibrium (A, Re) exists, the equilibrium (A, A) also exists.

It is worth pointing out that equilibria derived in this and the next section are actually continuation equilibria; that is, they are equilibria *given* some choice of c_p and R by the regulator. We show in the proposition below that the amount of recapitalization required for existence of the equilibrium (A, Re) exceeds the minimum amount of recapitalization necessary to induce an equilibrium (A, A). This result is shown in section 5 to imply that the continuation equilibrium (A, Re) cannot be an equilibrium when we allow the regulator to choose R and c_p.

Proposition 3. *Suppose that* $Ec < \frac{\gamma}{(1-\gamma)}\left[\frac{p}{p+(1-p)\theta}\right]$. *Define* $\hat{R}(a) = \frac{\gamma}{(1-\gamma)}\left[\frac{p}{p+(1-p)\theta}\right] - Ec$. *Then,* $\hat{R}(a) > R^A(a)$.

Proof. Straightforward.

The above proposition implies that the regulator can induce banks with medium default to accept the plan with a lower level of recapitalization than that required for existence of an equilibrium (A, Re). Since we show in section 5 that the regulator always prefers the lower level of recapitalization, we ignore the equilibrium (A, Re) in the remaining discussion.

The results of this section suggest some possible explanations for international differences in bank behavior in banking crises. Given our interpretation of $(1 - a)$ as the probability that prudential monitoring will detect the existence of rollover of defaulting loans in banks' portfolios (thus rollover will "fail"), our results suggest that in banking systems where prudential regulation is strong (that is, a is low), regulators can induce troubled banks to reveal their default by offering a rescue package with less government financial support than would be necessary if prudential regulation were weak. In contrast, in banking systems with less well developed prudential regulation, regulators are disadvantaged by banks' reputational concerns. Regulators may be required to offer large amounts of recapitalization in order to induce banks to accept rescue offers and to reveal the default on their balance sheets. This suggests the possibility that a vicious circle can arise: weak banking supervision increases the probability of occurrence of a banking crisis; once a banking crisis develops, banks may be unwilling to reveal their bad loans unless offered a large amount of recapitalization. Yet, regulators in countries with insufficiently strong supervisory institutions who also face constraints on the amount of recapitalization that can be paid to banks may be unable to induce troubled banks to accept rescue plans.

Another parameter that can be linked to international differences in financial systems and regulation, and therefore, to differences in banks' reactions to rescue offers, is c_p, the cost that the regulator may impose on the banker who rejects the plan, then reports low current net worth. If c_p is high enough, the incentive compatibility constraint for the equilibrium (A, A) can be satisfied, and the regulator can induce the bank to accept a plan with only negligible recapitalization. Strikingly, this result implies not only that the regulator must refrain from imposing punishment on bankers who accept rescue plans [as pointed out by Aghion, Bolton, and Fries (1999)] but also that the regulator may want to impose punishment on bankers who reject rescue plans then exhibit poor performance. We show in section 5 that any rescue plan chosen by the regulator will always impose the maximum level of c_p. As far as we are aware, the potential importance of applying punishment to banks who do not accept rescue offers and then perform poorly has not been recognized in analyses of policy responses to banking crises.

Our results relating to equilibria in the one-bank model resemble those that can be obtained in the absence of a rescue plan (see Rajan). Nevertheless, two differences stand out. First, the bank's response to the regulator's rescue offer conveys information to outsiders concerning the bank's strategy with respect to its bad loans. This information, in addition to the bank's current net worth, can be used by the market to update its prior on the severity of the crisis, which is then used in updating the bank's reputation. In the absence of a rescue offer outsiders observe only the bank's current net worth; therefore, they obtain no direct information regarding the bank's strategy. Second, the regulator who offers a rescue plan can impose the cost c_p on a banker who rejects the plan then reports low current net worth. This cost, which does not exist in the model in which the regulator is absent, increases the probability of the bank's revealing its defaulting loans. These features lead to the result that the mere offer of a rescue plan, even one with very little recapitalization, motivates banks to reveal their default more often (that is, for a larger range of parameter values) than when no rescue plan is offered.

4 • Two-Bank Model

We consider in this section a model with two banks, which permits us to study the interaction of banks' strategies. In this model banks' strategies become interdependent due to the fact that the market takes into account Bank 2's accept/reject decision and current performance when updating its belief about Bank 1's type, given the latter's accept/reject decision and current performance. Implicitly, the market uses Bank 2's performance to update its prior on the state of the world and then applies the updated prior on the state when it updates Bank 1's reputation. The market similarly takes into account Bank 1's performance when updating its belief about Bank 2's type. Thus, when a bank is deciding whether to accept or reject a plan, it must take into account the other bank's expected behavior and performance given the state of the world and the effects of this performance on the market's updating of the original bank's reputation.

As in the previous section, one of the questions of interest is whether the equilibrium strategy chosen by a bank with default in a nonsevere crisis can differ from the strategy chosen by a bank with default in a severe crisis. It is indeed reasonable to suspect that in the two-bank model the strategies chosen by banks in each state may differ. A natural conjecture, that is also suggested by the two-bank model of Rajan, is that banks with default might be more willing to reveal their bad loans in a severe crisis than in a nonsevere crisis. Since other banks are more likely to have default in a severe crisis, the market will revise upward its prior on the severe crisis; therefore, the reputational effects of revealing loan defaults will be less unfavorable. We do find that an equilibrium exists whereby banks with default accept the plan in a severe crisis whereas banks with default reject the plan when the crisis is nonsevere.

The timing of the two-bank model is as follows.

Period 0

Banks make a loan

Period 1

State of the world realized and loan defaults occur

Regulator offers rescue plan

Banks simultaneously announce acceptance or rejection of the plan

If a bank with default rejects the plan, its current net worth is high with probability a

Current net worth realized by both banks and observed by market

Market updates both banks' reputations

Period 2

Future loan repayments and costs (c_b and c_p) realized

As before, we focus on equilibria in pure strategies. We consider equilibria that are symmetric in Bank 1 and Bank 2's strategies; that is, equilibria in which Bank 1 will adopt the same strategy if it is a high type as will Bank 2 if it is a high type. In order to simplify the algebra, we make two minor changes of assumption. First, we set $\gamma = 1/2$, so that terms involving γ drop out of the incentive compatibility conditions. Second, we assume that in a severe crisis low-type banks have a high level of default with certainty. Our assumptions on default are illustrated in the following table.

	Nonsevere Crisis	Severe Crisis
High type	No default	Medium default
Low type	Prob. θ: No default	High default
	Prob. $(1-\theta)$: Medium default	

Each of these changes is made for expositional purposes only. The change in our assumptions on default greatly simplifies the expressions for the reputation terms and the proofs of our results. All of our results nevertheless hold for the default assumptions analyzed in section 3.[20]

As in the previous section all equilibria in the two-bank model have the characteristic that banks with high default accept the plan and banks with no default reject the plan. Our definition of an equilibrium is therefore analogous: an equilibrium is a pair of strategies (σ_n, σ_s) chosen by banks with medium default in the nonsevere and severe crises, respectively, with $\sigma \in \{Re, A\}$. In contrast to the one-bank model, however, the incentive compatibility conditions associated with a given strategy are not identical across states of the world.

20. Proofs of our results for the assumptions used in section 3 are available upon request.

This is due to the fact that Bank 2's expected performance enters into the reputation terms for Bank 1, and Bank 2's expected performance is a function of the state of the world. Thus, Bank 1's optimal strategy is indirectly a function of the state of the world, and two incentive compatibility conditions must be satisfied for each equilibrium to exist.

For purposes of illustration we consider the equilibrium (Re, Re). In this equilibrium banks with default in the nonsevere crisis reject the plan, as do banks with default in the severe crisis. Suppose that the crisis is nonsevere. The only bank with default in this state of the world is the low type. If this bank rejects the plan, its expected utility is

$$\begin{aligned} U_n^L(Re) = {} & \hat{B} - L - Ec \\ & + [p + (1-p)\theta]\{ap^{1+}(Re \mid (Re, Re), \pi^{2+}(Re)) \\ & + (1-a)p^{1m}(Re \mid (Re, Re), \pi^{2+}(Re))\} \\ & + (1-p)(1-\theta)\{a[ap^{1+}(Re \mid (Re, Re), \pi^{2+}(Re)) \\ & + (1-a)p^{1+}(Re \mid (Re, Re), \pi^{2m}(Re))] \\ & + (1-a)[ap^{1m}(Re \mid (Re, Re), \pi^{2+}(Re)) \\ & + (1-a)p^{1m}(Re \mid (Re, Re), \pi^{2m}(Re))]\} \end{aligned} \tag{11}$$

where $p^{1+}(Re \mid (Re, Re), \pi^{2+}(Re))$ represents Bank 1's updated reputation when it rejects the plan and reports high current net worth, given that the market expects banks' strategies to be (Re, Re) and given that Bank 2 also rejects the plan and has high current net worth. The term $p^{1m}(Re \mid (Re, Re), \pi^{2+}(Re))$ represents Bank 1's updated reputation when it rejects the plan and rollover fails, given that Bank 2 has rejected the plan and reported high current net worth. Bank 1 does not know Bank 2's type. With probability $[p + (1-p)\theta]$ Bank 2 will have no default and will reject the plan and report high current net worth. With probability $(1-p)(1-\theta)$ Bank 2 will have default, in which case it will reject the plan and report high current net worth with probability a and medium current net worth with probability $(1-a)$. Expressions for the reputation terms appear in the appendix.

If Bank 1 deviates from the expected strategies and accepts the plan, its expected utility is given by

$$\begin{aligned} U_n^L(A) = {} & (\hat{B} - L + R) \\ & + [p + (1-p)\theta][p^{1m}(A \mid (Re, Re), \pi^{2+}(Re))] \\ & + (1-p)(1-\theta)\{ap^{1m}(A \mid (Re, Re), \pi^{2+}(Re)) \\ & + (1-a)p^{1m}(A \mid (Re, Re), \pi^{2m}(Re))\} \end{aligned} \tag{12}$$

where $p^{1m}(A\,|\,(Re, Re), \pi^{2+}(Re))$ represents Bank 1's updated reputation given that it accepts the plan and given that Bank 2 rejects the plan and reports high current net worth. Note that each of the reputation terms in the above expression is off the equilibrium path; therefore, we have to make assumptions about out-of-equilibrium beliefs. We make an assumption similar to that of section 3. For the term $p^{1m}(A\,|\,(Re, Re), \pi^{2+}(Re))$ we assume that the market computes the probability that Bank 1 is a high type, given that it accepts the plan and given that Bank 2 rejects the plan and reports high current net worth. It is easily verified that $p^{1m}(A\,|\,(Re, Re), \pi^{2+}(Re)) = p^{1m}(Re\,|\,(Re, Re), \pi^{2+}(Re))$. Similarly, $p^{1m}(Re\,|\,(Re, Re), \pi^{2m}(Re)) = p^{1m}(A\,|\,(Re, Re), \pi^{2m}(Re))$.

Using these observations, we may write the low-type bank's IC constraint in the nonsevere crisis as

$$\begin{aligned} Ec + R \leq [p + (1-p)\theta]a\{&p^{1+}(Re\,|\,(Re, Re), \pi^{2+}(Re)) \\ &- p^{1m}(Re\,|\,(Re, Re), \pi^{2+}(Re))\} \\ &[(1-p)(1-\theta)]a\{[ap^{1+}(Re\,|\,(Re, Re), \pi^{2+}(Re)) \\ &+ (1-a)p^{1+}(Re\,|\,(Re, Re), \pi^{2m}(Re))] \\ &- [ap^{1m}(Re\,|\,(Re, Re), \pi^{2+}(Re)) \\ &+ (1-a)p^{1m}(Re\,|\,(Re, Re), \pi^{2m}(Re))]\}. \end{aligned} \quad (13)$$

Now suppose that the crisis is severe. When the high-type bank rejects the plan, its expected utility is

$$\begin{aligned} U_s^H(Re) = \hat{B} - Ec - L + p\{&a[ap^{1+}(Re\,|\,(Re, Re), \pi^{2+}(Re)) \\ &+ (1-a)p^{1+}(Re\,|\,(Re, Re), \pi^{2m}(Re))] \\ &+ (1-a)[ap^{1m}(Re\,|\,(Re, Re), \pi^{2+}(Re)) \\ &+ (1-a)p^{1m}(Re\,|\,(Re, Re), \pi^{2m}(Re))]\} \\ &+ (1-p)(1-ac_p). \end{aligned} \quad (14)$$

With probability p Bank 2 will have a medium level of default and will reject the plan. In this case with probability a Bank 2 will succeed in reporting high current net worth. With probability $(1-p)$ Bank 2 will be a low type and has a high level of default. In this case Bank 2 will accept the plan, in which case the market knows that the crisis is severe and that Bank 1 is a high type. The regulator, however, now knows that Bank 1 rolled over its defaulting loans. Therefore, even in the case where Bank 1 succeeded with rollover and was able to report a high current net worth, the regulator can impose the cost c_p on the bank. This explains the appearance of the term $-(1-p)ac_p$ in addition to the inclusion of $(1-a)c_p$ in the definition of Ec.

When the bank accepts the plan, its expected utility is

$$\begin{aligned} U_s^H(A) &= R + \hat{B} - L + p\{ap^{1m}(A \mid (Re, Re), \pi^{2+}(Re)) \\ &\quad + (1-a)p^{1m}(A \mid (Re, A), \pi^{2m}(Re))\} \\ &\quad + (1-p)\cdot 1. \qquad (15) \end{aligned}$$

The incentive compatibility constraint for the high type in the severe crisis can be expressed, after some rearrangement, as

$$\begin{aligned} Ec + R \le pa\{&a[p^{1+}(Re \mid (Re, Re), \pi^{2+}(Re)) \\ &- p^{1m}(Re \mid (Re, Re), \pi^{2+}(Re))] \\ &+ (1-a)[p^{1+}(Re \mid (Re, Re), \pi^{2m}(Re)) \\ &- p^{1m}(Re \mid (Re, Re), \pi^{2m}(Re))]\} - (1-p)ac_p. \qquad (16) \end{aligned}$$

A necessary condition for the equilibrium (Re, Re) to exist is that the right-hand side of each incentive compatibility constraint is positive. It turns out that with our assumptions on default in this section, there exist parameter values for which this necessary condition is not satisfied; that is, for which the right-hand side of at least one of the IC constraints is negative. This results from the fact that for certain combinations of parameter values (namely, π and θ) a bank's reputation is actually lower when it rejects the plan and reports high current net worth than when it accepts the plan or than when it rejects the plan and reports medium current net worth. In this case the right-hand side of the constraint becomes negative.

That the bank's reputation may be higher when it reveals default than when it rejects the plan and reports high current net worth may appear counterintuitive; however, the explanation is logical. In the severe crisis all banks have default, but only the high type has a medium level of default. Therefore, if the market's prior π on the severe crisis is high enough (and if the value of θ is "large enough" so that low types have medium default with only low probability in the nonsevere crisis), then revelation of a medium level of default signals good news about the bank's type. In this situation, high-type banks have an incentive to accept the plan in the severe crisis. However, the low-type bank with default in the nonsevere crisis may now also have an incentive to accept the plan.

Note that with the assumptions on default used in the model of section 3, this situation does not arise; the right-hand side of the each of the above IC constraints is always positive. The explanation follows from the fact that as θ increases, the low-type bank has a larger probability of having a medium level of default in the severe crisis, which offsets the corresponding decrease in the probability of the low type having medium default in a nonsevere crisis. A medium level of default no longer signals good news about the bank's type.

A higher reputation associated with revelation versus nonrevelation of default by high-type banks in severe crises is consistent with the practice sometimes observed whereby the healthier banks are the first to reveal and write off bad loans during a crisis, and they improve their reputations by doing so.[21] In our model, a lowering of the probability that the low type has a medium level of default in the severe crisis relative to its probability of having no default in the nonsevere crisis has the effect of improving the high type's ability to signal its type by revealing its default when it has loan defaults. As a consequence, the region of the parameter space for which banks will accept the plan increases.

4.1 Characterization of Equilibria in the Two-Bank Model

We first describe pure-strategy equilibria (Re, Re) and (A, A). Discussion of these equilibria applies to parameter values for which the equilibrium (Re, Re) may exist; that is, for which the right-hand side of the both incentive compatibility constraints in the (Re, Re) equilibrium are positive.

Proposition 4. *There exist critical values $c^{RR}(a)$ and $c^{AA}(a)$, with $c^{AA}(a) > c^{RR}(a)$, such that an equilibrium (Re, Re) exists if $c^{RR}(a) > 0$ and $Ec + R \leq c^{RR}(a)$; and an equilibrium (A, A) exists if $Ec + R \geq c^{AA}(a)$.*

Proof. See appendix.

The description of equilibria (Re, Re) and (A, A) is similar to that for the one-bank model, with the principal difference being that in the two-bank model the critical value $c^{RR}(a)$ is the minimum of the critical values implied by each of the incentive compatibility conditions for the equilibrium (Re, Re); and the critical value $c^{AA}(a)$ is the maximum of the critical values implied by each of the incentive compatibility conditions for the equilibrium (A, A).

We now turn to the possibility of equilibria where the strategies differ in each state of the world. The following proposition dem-

21. See Gibson (1999) for a model in which the same result occurs. Good banks can use loan-loss disclosures to signal information about their quality to markets. Gibson also supplies empirical evidence of this phenomenon for the United States and Japan.

onstrates that the only pure-strategy equilibrium in which banks with default in the nonsevere crisis will adopt a different strategy from banks in the severe crisis is the equilibrium (Re, A). In this equilibrium banks with default reject the plan when the crisis is nonsevere; however, they accept the plan when the crisis is severe. This implies that regulators will not be able to successfully rescue banks unless the crisis is severe.

Proposition 5. (i) *There exists a critical value* $c^{RA}(a)$ *such that an equilibrium* (Re, A) *exists if* $c^{RA}(a) > 0$ *and* $Ec + R \leq c^{RA}(a)$; (ii) *the equilibrium* (A, Re) *does not exist.*

Proof. See appendix.

The intuition associated with the equilibrium (Re, A) is that, given the market's beliefs, a high-type bank in the severe crisis can signal its type by accepting the plan, since it knows that Bank 2 will accept the plan and the market will believe that the crisis is severe. On the other hand, if Bank 1 rejects the plan when Bank 2 accepts, the market is not sure of the state of the world, and Bank 1 loses its ability to signal its type. The incentive compatibility constraint for acceptance of the plan by the high type in the severe crisis is thus always satisfied. In contrast, the bank with default in the nonsevere crisis cannot perfectly fool the market by accepting the plan, since Bank 2 will always reject the plan in the nonsevere crisis. Hence, if $Ec + R$ is low enough, the bank with default in the nonsevere crisis has the incentive to reject the plan.

What can we say about the occurrence of the equilibrium (Re, Re) versus the equilibrium (Re, A)? In the equilibrium (Re, Re) the incentive constraint for the high type is more binding than the IC constraint for the low type. A necessary and sufficient condition for existence of this equilibrium is that $Ec + R \leq$ right-hand side (16). In addition, the IC constraint for the high type in the equilibrium (Re, Re) requires a lower value of $Ec + R$ than the IC constraint for the low type in the equilibrium (Re, A). Thus, $c^{RR} < c^{RA}$. The equilibrium (Re, A) exists for a larger range of parameter values than does the equilibrium (Re, Re). For all values of $Ec + R$ for which the equilibrium (Re, Re) exists, the equilibrium (Re, A) also exists.

Proposition 5 shows that it is impossible in equilibrium for banks with default in the severe crisis to reject a plan if banks in the nonsevere crisis accept the plan. This result arises again from the fact that it is always easier to induce a bank with medium default in the severe crisis to accept a plan than a bank with medium default in the nonsevere crisis. Hence, if the sum $Ec + R$ is high enough to induce banks to accept the plan in the nonsevere crisis, then this sum will be too large to be compatible with rejection of the plan by the high-type bank in the severe crisis.

In summary, the interaction of banks' strategies in this model motivates banks to accept plans more readily in a severe crisis than in a nonsevere crisis. This leads to the possibility of equilibria where, although banks with default reject the plan in the nonsevere crisis, banks with default in the severe crisis will accept the plan. Regulators who wish to offer bank rescues may not be successful in doing so until the banking crisis is severe.

5 The Optimal Rescue Plan

The analysis of the previous sections has taken the conditions of rescue plans — that is, the values of R and c_p — as given. On the basis of this analysis we may make some tentative observations regarding the conditions of rescue plans that would be chosen by the regulators when they take into account the effects of reputation on banks' willingness to accept rescue plans. In this section we discuss aspects of the regulators' choice of rescue plan, without undertaking a comprehensive analysis of this choice.

We take as given that regulators who have decided to offer banks rescue plans perceive some expected benefit V from the rescue of a troubled bank. One might expect that the value of V increases with the regulator's belief π that the banking crisis is severe and as the negative externalities associated with multiple bank failures increase. Consider a regulatory objective function with the following simple form:

$$W(c_p, R) = \max \{I_A[V - g(R)], 0\}$$

where V is the expected benefit associated with the rescue of a troubled bank; I_A is an indicator function which takes on a value of 1 if the bank accepts the rescue offer and 0 otherwise; $g(R)$ is the cost function associated with recapitalization. We assume that $g(\cdot)$ is nondecreasing in the amount of recapitalization R offered to the bank. Note that the indicator function I is a function of all of the parameters identified in sections 3 and 4 that influence banks' willingness to accept rescue plans: the state of the world, the amount of recapitalization offered in the plan, the expected costs of rollover c_b and c_p, and the reputation formed in the market.

The regulator's problem is to choose c_p and R, subject to constraints on the maximum feasible values of these variables, to maximize the above objective function. The maximum feasible value of c_p, which we will denote by $\bar{c}_p$, is determined by the financial system and existing regulatory institutions. The regulator may also face a constraint

$\bar{R}$ on R, if the amount of recapitalization that can be offered is subject to a budgetary limit.

For simplicity we consider the regulator's choice in the context of the one-bank model. We then note how the results would differ in the two-bank model. A first result follows immediately.

Proposition 6. *The regulator will choose* $c_p = \bar{c}_p$ *in any rescue plan.*

The analysis of sections 3 and 4 has identified the unambiguously positive effect of the cost c_p on banks' willingness to accept rescue plans. Moreover, imposing the cost c_p in a rescue plan has no effect on the regulator's cost function; therefore, the regulator chooses the maximum level. This result leads to some additional observations. If $\bar{c}_p$ is sufficiently high to induce the bank to accept the plan with certainty (that is, to induce the (A, A) equilibrium), then the regulator will offer a rescue plan with only negligible recapitalization. If, on the other hand, $\bar{c}_p$ is sufficiently low that the bank will reject a plan with no recapitalization, then the regulator must consider offering a positive level of R.

Now consider the level of recapitalization $R^A(a) = c^A(a) - Ec$, defined in section 3.2 as the minimum level of recapitalization required to induce the bank to accept a rescue plan with certainty. Denote by $R^A(a, \bar{c}_p)$ this minimum level of recapitalization when $c_p = \bar{c}_p$. We take $R^A(a, \bar{c}_p)$ to be equal to 0 if $\bar{c}_p$ is sufficiently high to induce the bank to accept a plan with no recapitalization. We now define another level of recapitalization: $R^{re}(a, \bar{c}_p) = c^{re}(a) - Ec$, where $c^{re}(a)$ is defined in section 3.1 and where we use $\bar{c}_p$ in the definition of Ec. $R^{re}(a, \bar{c}_p)$ represents the maximum amount of recapitalization such that the equilibrium (Re, Re) exists. That is, if $R^{re}(a, \bar{c}_p) > 0$, then any rescue plan with $R < R^{re}(a, \bar{c}_p)$ will be rejected with certainty. We may now state a second, immediate result.

Proposition 7. *Let* R^* *be the optimal amount of recapitalization offered in a rescue plan. Then,* $R^{re}(a, \bar{c}_p) \leq R^* \leq R^A(a, \bar{c}_p)$, *with* $R^* = R^A(a, \bar{c}_p)$ *when the regulator wishes for the bank to accept the plan with certainty.*

This proposition states that the regulator never offers a rescue plan with an amount of recapitalization less than $\max\,[R^{re}(a, \bar{c}_p), 0]$, since this rescue plan would be rejected with certainty. This also implies that if the regulator faces a constraint on the amount of recapitalization that can be offered and if $\bar{R} < R^{re}(a, \bar{c}_p)$, then no rescue plan will be offered. The proposition also implies that the regulators never offer a rescue plan with a level of capitalization that exceeds

$R^A(a, \bar{c}_p)$, since a plan with $R^A(a, \bar{c}_p)$ will be accepted with certainty. If the regulator chooses to offer a rescue plan that induces the equilibrium (A, A), then he will offer exactly $R^A(a, \bar{c}_p)$. Recall that this level of recapitalization may be zero if $\bar{c}_p$ is sufficiently high.

There may nevertheless exist circumstances in which the regulator chooses a level of recapitalization that is strictly less than $R^A(a, \bar{c}_p)$. Recall from section 3.3 that for values of $Ec + R$ such that $c^{Re}(a) < Ec + R < c^A(a)$, no pure strategy equilibria exist; equilibria are in mixed strategies. For each value of $Ec + R$ in this range, there is some positive probability that the bank will accept the plan (otherwise, an equilibrium in pure strategies would exist). Consider a value $\hat{R}$ such that $c^{Re}(a) < Ec + \hat{R} < c^A(a)$. Assume that the probability that the bank accepts the plan in the mixed-strategy equilibrium induced by $\hat{R}$ is equal to λ. The regulator's expected utility from offering a rescue plan with $\bar{c}_p$ and $\hat{R}$ is given by begin

$$\lambda[V - g(\hat{R})].$$

With probability λ the bank accepts the plan and the regulator's utility will equal $V - g(\hat{R})$; with probability $(1 - \lambda)$ the bank will reject the plan and the regulator's utility will equal zero. In order to decide whether to offer the rescue plan with $\hat{R}$ rather than $R^A(a, \bar{c}_p)$, the regulator must compare $\lambda[V - g(\hat{R})]$ with $V - g(R^A(a, \bar{c}_p))$. If the costs of offering $R^A(a, \bar{c}_p)$ in recapitalization are high enough or if the probability λ is high enough, the regulator's utility will be higher with the rescue plan with $\hat{R}$. In this case the regulator will choose to offer the lower amount of recapitalization $\hat{R}$, knowing that with some probability the bank will reject the plan. The optimal level of recapitalization will be the value R^* in the range $R^{re}(\bar{c}_p) \le R^* \le R^A(a, \bar{c}_p)$ which maximizes the regulator's expected utility.

Now consider the model with two banks. The results of the above discussion also apply to this model, with the additional result that there exist levels of recapitalization that generate the pure-strategy equilibrium (Re, A) in which banks will reject the plan if the crisis is nonsevere and accept the plan if the crisis is severe. Similarly to the case of mixed-strategy equilibria discussed above, it can be shown that the optimal level of recapitalization offered in the rescue plan may be one that generates the equilibrium (Re, A). In this case, only if the crisis is severe will banks be willing to accept the plan.

In summary, when the regulator takes into account banks' reputational concerns, the optimal rescue plan will involve imposition of the maximum feasible value of c_p on banks that reject rescue plans, then report loan defaults. In addition, the level of recapitalization offered in the optimal rescue plan may be low enough so that with positive probability the plan will be rejected. Banks' reputational concerns can result in the equilibrium rejection of optimal rescue plans.

6 Conclusion

This paper models bank behavior during banking crises when asymmetric information exists between banks and outsiders regarding the extent of bad loans on banks' balance sheets. We show that asymmetric information creates the incentive for banks to roll over their nonperforming loans in an attempt to disguise their financial states. Although a regulator may be able to combat this incentive by offering a "soft" rescue package, reputational concerns by bankers may cause them to reject rescue offers and to continue with loan rollovers. In order to induce banks to accept rescue plans and to address their problem loans, regulators may be forced to offer amounts of recapitalization that well exceed the amount necessary to restore banks to solvency. This "extra" recapitalization serves to compensate bankers for the reputational harm caused by the revelation of bad loans that accompanies acceptance of a rescue offer. If regulators are constrained in the amount of recapitalization that they can offer, they may be unable to induce banks to accept rescue plans and to reveal their bad loans, or they may have to wait until the banking crisis is severe (and more banks become distressed) before banks are willing to accept rescues.

In addition to offering a potential explanation for several observed cases in which banks have refused offers of rescue in banking crises, our model yields some insight into the link between bank supervisory institutions that are in place *ex ante* and the policy options that are available to regulators *ex post*, once a crisis has occurred. In countries with strong supervisory systems, regulators can induce banks to accept rescue plans with lower amounts of recapitalization than if the supervisory system were weak. This suggests the possibility of a vicious circle arising in countries with weak supervisory institutions, whereby weak banking supervision increases the probability of occurrence of a banking crisis, but once a banking crisis develops banks are unwilling to reveal their bad loans unless offered a large amount of recapitalization.

A novel policy implication of our analysis is that the optimal rescue plan imposes a cost on banks that *reject* rescue offers and then exhibit poor performance. By committing to imposing a punishment on banks that reject rescue offers and then are discovered to be in poor financial shape, the regulator can induce troubled banks to accept a rescue offer with less recapitalization than in the absence of such a commitment. If this cost is high enough, the regulator can induce banks to accept rescue plans with only negligible recapitalization. This result points to an informational role that is served by bank rescue offers in our model. An offer of rescue forces a bank to take an explicit stand with respect to the presence of bad loans on its balance sheets. The bank's acceptance or rejection of a rescue offer conveys information to bank outsiders — which they would not otherwise receive — about the severity of the banking crisis, the bank's type, and its treatment of nonperforming loans. This creates the possibility of punishing banks who attempt to hide their nonperforming loans and are discovered. The ultimate effect of the increase in information generated by the offer of a rescue plan is to induce banks to reveal their defaulting loans more often than in the absence of rescue offers.

Yet, banks may still decide to reject rescue offers. Even when the regulator takes into account bankers' reputational concerns in designing a rescue offer, rejection of the rescue offer may occur in equilibrium. For example, it is possible that high costs of recapitalization may result in an optimal plan in which the regulator offers an amount of recapitalization that will be accepted by banks only if the crisis is severe enough. If the crisis is less severe, banks will reject the offer.

To this point our discussion and analysis have ignored depositor behavior. We can now address this issue. Like the market, depositors do not observe the state of the world or the bank's type. When a bank rejects a rescue plan in period 1 and succeeds, depositors are unaware of the bank's true financial state. However, one might reasonably assume that depositors do observe the true financial state of the bank in period 2. Therefore, even if a bank with loan defaults has succeeded in hiding the defaults in period 1, depositors will observe the bank's true net worth in period 2 and can decide to exit the bank. This would impose an additional cost on the bank which rolled over its defaulting loans in period 1, and this cost could easily be added into the parameter c_b of our model. Thus, the more sensitive are depositors to the bank's solvency, the greater the costs to banks of rolling over nonperforming loans.

Similar observations apply to the parameter c_p in our model. We have described this parameter as a cost imposed by the regulator on troubled banks that have rejected rescue plans and then are discovered by the regulator. In this case depositors, too, immediately discover not only the bank's defaulting loans but also the fact that the bank attempted to deceive outsiders by hiding these loans. Depositors may react to this deception by immediately withdrawing their funds, which could act as an increase to c_p. This increase would have the effect of increasing banks' willingness to accept rescue plans. Thus, in countries where discipline exercised by depositors is strong enough, banks may be willing to accept rescue plans with only small amounts of recapitalization. Discipline exercised by depositors complements the discipline exercised by the regulatory system.

Appendix: One-Bank Model

Proof of Lemma 1

Only low-type banks have a high level of default. If the bank with high default accepts the plan, its expected utility will be

$$U(A) = (1-\gamma)(R-L) + \gamma p^0(A). \tag{A.1}$$

Since acceptance of the plan and revelation of a high level of default signal the bank's type with certainty, the market assigns a value of 0 to the reputation term $p^0(A)$, which is the conditional probability that the bank is a high type. The bank's expected utility in the case where it rejects the plan will be

$$U(Re) = -(1-\gamma)(L + c_b + c_p) + \gamma p^0(Re) \tag{A.2}$$

where we note that $p^0(Re)$ is also zero since this bank never succeeds with rollover. Since $U(A) > U(Re)$, the low-type bank will always choose to accept the plan when it has a high level of default. ■

Reputation Terms for Equilibrium (Re, Re)

$$p^+(Re \mid (Re, Re), \pi)$$
$$= \frac{p[(1-\pi)+\pi a]}{p[(1-\pi)+\pi a] + (1-p)(1-\pi)[\theta + (1-\theta)a] + (1-p)\pi\theta a}$$

and

$$p^m(Re \mid (Re, Re), \pi)$$
$$= \frac{p\pi(1-a)}{p\pi(1-a) + (1-p)(1-a)[(1-\pi)(1-\theta)+\pi\theta]}$$
$$= \frac{p\pi}{p\pi + (1-p)[(1-\pi)(1-\theta)+\pi\theta]}$$

Reputation Terms for Equilibrium (A, A)

$$p^+(Re \mid (A, A), 0) = \frac{p}{p + (1-p)\theta}$$

$$p^m(A \mid (A, A), \pi) = \frac{p\pi}{p\pi + (1-p)[(1-\pi)(1-\theta)+\pi\theta]}$$

Proof of Proposition 1

Part (i) of the proposition summarizes the discussion of the subsections 3.1 and 3.2. Part (ii) of the proposition follows from two observations: (1) $Ec = c_b + (1-a)c_p$ is decreasing in a; and (2) $c^{Re}(a)$ and $c^A(a)$ are increasing in a. Thus, for given values c_b and R, as a increases, $Ec + R$ decreases and $c^{Re}(a)$ and $c^A(a)$ increase. This implies that the region of values of $Ec + R$ over which an equilibrium (Re, Re) exists increases with increasing a and the region of $Ec + R$ over which an equilibrium (A, A) exists decreases with a. ■

Proof of Proposition 2

(i) *Conditions for an equilibrium* (Re, A): In this equilibrium the market assumes that the crisis is nonsevere (sets $\pi = 0$ in updating the bank's reputation) when the bank rejects a plan. Similarly, the market assumes that the crisis is severe when the bank accepts a plan.

Two IC conditions must be satisfied in order for this equilibrium to exist.

Nonsevere crisis:

$$\begin{aligned} U(Re \mid (Re, A)) \\ &= (1-\gamma)(\hat{B} - L - Ec) + \gamma\{ap^+(Re \mid (Re, A), 0) \\ &\quad + (1-a)[p^m(Re \mid (Re, A), 0)]\}, \end{aligned} \tag{A.3}$$

where the last argument of $p^+(Re \mid (Re, A), 0)$ indicates that the market infers that the state of the world is n when the bank rejects the rescue plan.

$$p^+(Re \mid (Re, A), 0) = \frac{p}{p + (1-p)[\theta + (1-\theta)a]}$$

and

$$p^m(Re \mid (Re, A), 0) = 0 .$$

The bank's expected utility if it accepts the plan is

$$U(A \mid (Re, A)) = (1-\gamma)(R + \hat{B} - L) + \gamma p^m(A \mid (Re, A), 1) . \tag{A.4}$$

When the bank accepts the plan, the market assumes that the state is s; therefore, it sets $\pi = 1$ when updating the bank's reputation.

$$p^m(A \mid (Re, A), 1) = \frac{p}{p + (1-p)\theta}$$

The IC constraint for state n is

$$Ec + R \leq \frac{\gamma}{(1-\gamma)}[ap^+(Re \mid (Re, A), 0) - p^m(A \mid (Re, A), 1)] \tag{A.5}$$

That $p^+(Re \mid (Re, A), 0) \le p^m(A \mid (Re, A), 1)$ implies that the right-hand side of this constraint is negative, and the constraint cannot be satisfied. Hence, the equilibrium (Re, A) does not exist.

(ii) *Conditions for an equilibrium with* (A, Re) : *Nonsevere crisis*: The bank's expected utility from accepting the plan is

$$U(A \mid (A, Re)) = (1-\gamma)(R + \hat{B} - L) + \gamma[p^m(A \mid (A, Re), 0)]. \quad \text{(A.6)}$$

When the bank accepts the plan, the market believes that the state is n, in which case $p^m(A \mid (Re, A), 0) = 0$.

The bank's expected utility from rejecting the plan is

$$U(Re \mid (A, Re)) = (1-\gamma)(\hat{B} - L - Ec) + \gamma[ap^+(Re \mid (A, Re), \pi) + (1-a)p^m(Re \mid (A, Re), 1)]. \quad \text{(A.7)}$$

When the bank rejects the plan, then has high current net worth, the market cannot tell whether the state is n and the bank has no default or whether the state is s. The market's prior π on the state remains unchanged.

$$p^+(Re \mid (A, Re), \pi) = \frac{p[(1-\pi) + \pi a]}{p[(1-\pi) + \pi a] + (1-p)[(1-\pi)\theta + \pi\theta a]} = \frac{p}{p + (1-p)\theta}.$$

When the bank rejects the plan, and then reports medium current net worth, the market believes that the state is s. In this case

$$p^m(Re \mid (A, Re), 1) = \frac{p}{p + (1-p)\theta}.$$

The IC condition is

$$R + Ec \ge \frac{\gamma}{(1-\gamma)}[ap^+(Re \mid (A, Re), \pi) + (1-a)p^m(Re \mid (A, Re), 1)]$$

or

$$R + Ec \ge \frac{\gamma}{(1-\gamma)}\left[\frac{p}{p + (1-p)\theta}\right]. \quad \text{(A.8)}$$

Severe crisis: The bank's expected utilities are as follows:

$$U(Re \mid (A, Re)) = (1-\gamma)(\hat{B} - L - Ec) + \gamma[ap^+(Re \mid (A, Re), \pi) + (1-a)p^m(Re \mid (A, Re), 1)]. \quad \text{(A.9)}$$

$$U(A \mid (A, Re)) = (1-\gamma)(R + \hat{B} - L) + \gamma[p^m(A \mid (A, Re), 0)]. \quad \text{(A.10)}$$

The IC condition is

$$Ec + R \leq \frac{\gamma}{(1-\gamma)}\left[\frac{p}{p+(1-p)\theta}\right]. \tag{A.11}$$

Comparison of the two IC constraints implies that each must be satisfied with equality in order for the equilibrium to exist. ■

Appendix: Two-Bank Model

Reputation Terms for Equilibrium (Re, Re)

$$p^{1+}(Re \mid (Re, Re), \pi^{2+}(Re)) = \frac{p(1-\pi)[p+(1-p)(\theta+(1-\theta)a)] + p\pi p a^2}{(1-\pi)[p+(1-p)(\theta+(1-\theta)a)]^2 + p\pi p a^2},$$

$$p^{1m}(Re \mid (Re, Re), \pi^{2+}(Re)) = \frac{p\pi p a}{p\pi p a + (1-p)(1-\pi)(1-\theta)[p+(1-p)(\theta+(1-\theta)a)]}$$

$$p^{1+}(Re \mid (Re, Re), \pi^{2m}(Re)) = \frac{p(1-\pi)[(1-p)(1-\theta)] + p\pi p a}{[p+(1-p)(\theta+(1-\theta)a)](1-\pi)[(1-p)(1-\theta)] + p\pi p a}$$

$$p^{1m}(Re \mid (Re, Re), \pi^{2m}(Re)) = \frac{p\pi p}{p\pi p + (1-p)^2(1-\pi)(1-\theta)^2}.$$

Proof of Proposition 4

Equilibrium (Re, Re)

The IC constraints are provided in the text.

Define c^{1re} = right-hand side of IC constraint (13).

Define c^{2re} = right-hand side of IC constraint (16). Define $c^{RR}(a) = \min\,[c^{1re}, c^{2re}]$. Then necessary and sufficient conditions for existence of this equilibrium are: (1) $c^{RR}(a) > 0$ and (2) $Ec + R \leq c^{RR}(a)$.

Equilibrium (A, A)

Nonsevere crisis; low type

$$U_n^L(A) = R + \hat{B} - L + [p+(1-p)\theta]p^{1m}(A \mid (A, A), \pi^{2+}(Re)) + (1-p)(1-\theta)p^{1m}(A \mid (A, A), \pi^{2m}(A)). \tag{A.12}$$

When Bank 2 rejects the plan and has high current earnings, the market knows that the state is n; therefore, $p^{1m}(A \mid (A, A), \pi^{2+}(Re)) = 0$.

$$p^{1m}(A \mid (A, A), \pi^{2m}(A)) = \frac{p\pi p}{p\pi p + (1-p)^2(1-\pi)(1-\theta)^2}.$$

$$\begin{aligned} U_n^L(Re) = {} & \hat{B} - Ec - L \\ & + [p + (1-p)\theta][ap^{1+}(Re \mid (A, A), \pi^{2+}(Re)) \\ & + (1-a)p^{1m}(Re \mid (A, A), \pi^{2+}(Re))] \\ & + (1-p)(1-\theta)[ap^{1+}(Re \mid (A, A), \pi^{2m}(A)) \\ & + (1-a)p^{1m}(Re \mid (A, A), \pi^{2m}(A)) \end{aligned} \tag{A.13}$$

Note that $p^{1m}(Re \mid (A, A), \pi^{2+}(Re)) = 0$ for the same reason that $p^{1m}(A \mid (A, A), \pi^{2+}(Re)) = 0$.

The low type's incentive compatibility constraint is

$$\begin{aligned} Ec + R \geq {} & [p + (1-p)\theta]ap^{1+}(Re \mid (A, A), \pi^{2+}(Re)) \\ & + (1-p)(1-\theta)]a[p^{1+}(Re \mid (A, A), \pi^{2m}(A)) \\ & - p^{1m}(Re \mid (A, A), \pi^{2m}(A))]. \end{aligned} \tag{A.14}$$

Note that

$$\begin{aligned} & p^{1+}(Re \mid (A, A), \pi^{2+}(Re)) \\ & = p^{1+}(Re \mid (A, A), \pi^{2m}(A)) = \frac{p}{p + (1-p)\theta} \end{aligned}$$

since the market knows that the state is n when it observes a bank reject a plan. We may rewrite the IC constraint as

$$\begin{aligned} Ec + R \geq {} & ap^{1+}(Re \mid (A, A), \pi^{2+}(Re)) \\ & - (1-p)(1-\theta)ap^{1m}(Re \mid (A, A), \pi^{2m}(A))]. \end{aligned} \tag{A.15}$$

Severe crisis; high type

$$U_s^H(A) = R + \hat{B} - L + p[p^{1m}(A \mid (A, A), \pi^{2m}(A)) + (1-p)]$$

$$\begin{aligned} U_s^H(Re) = {} & \hat{B} - Ec - L + p[ap^{1+}(Re \mid (A, A), \pi^{2m}(A)) \\ & + (1-a)p^{1m}(Re \mid (A, A), \pi^{2m}(A))] + (1-p)(1 - ac_p) \end{aligned}$$

The high type's IC constraint is

$$Ec + R \geq p[ap^{1+}(Re \mid (A, A), \pi^{2m}(Re)) + (1-a)p^{1m}(Re \mid (A, A), \pi^{2m}(A))] - (1-p)ac_p. \quad \text{(A.16)}$$

Define $c^{1A}(a)$ = right-hand side of IC constraint (A.15). Define $c^{2A}(a)$ = right-hand side of IC constraint (A.16). Define $c^{AA}(a) = \max[c^{1A}(a), c^{2A}(a)]$. A necessary and sufficient condition for the existence of the equilibrium (A, A) is that $Ec + R \geq c^{AA}(a)$. ■

Proof of Proposition 5, Part (i): Equilibrium (Re, A)

Severe crisis; high-type bank. Consider Bank 1 and suppose that it is a high type. This bank's expected utility when it accepts the plan is given by

$$U_s^H(A) = R + \hat{B} - L + p\{p^{1m}(A \mid (Re, A), \pi^{2m}(A))\} + (1-p)p^{1m}(A \mid (Re, A), \pi^{20}(A)). \quad \text{(A.17)}$$

With probability p Bank 2 is a high type and accepts the plan, in which case $p^{1m}(A \mid (Re, A), \pi^{2m}(A))$ will be Bank 1's updated reputation. Given that acceptance of a plan by both banks signals to the market that the crisis is severe (since banks with default reject the plan in a nonsevere crisis), the market knows that Bank 1 is a high type. Hence, $p^{1m}(A \mid (Re, A), \pi^{2m}(A)) = 1$. With probability $(1-p)$ Bank 2 is a low type and will accept the plan and report a high level of default. In this case, too, the market will know that Bank 1 is a high type and will also assign a value of 1 to Bank 1's updated reputation. Thus, we may reexpress Bank 1's expected utility when it accepts the plan as

$$U_s^H(A) = R + \hat{B} - L + 1. \quad \text{(A.18)}$$

Bank 1's expected utility if it rejects the plan is given by

$$U_s^H(Re) = \hat{B} - L - Ec + p[ap^{1+}(Re \mid (Re, A), \pi^{2m}(A)) + (1-a)p^{1m}(Re \mid (Re, A), \pi^{2m}(A))] + (1-p)(1-ac_p). \quad \text{(A.19)}$$

Neither of the reputation terms $p^{1+}(Re \mid (Re, A), \pi^{2m}(A))$ or $p^{1m}(Re \mid (Re, A), \pi^{2m}(A))$ can be calculated via Bayes' rule. We follow the method discussed earlier in assigning expressions for these terms. $p^{1+}(Re \mid (Re, A), \pi^{2m}(A))$ is calculated as the probability that

Bank 1 is a high type given that it rejects the plan and has high current net worth and given that Bank 2 accepts the plan and has medium current net worth.

$$p^{1+}(Re \mid (Re, A), \pi^{2m}(A)) =$$
$$\frac{p[\pi pa - (1-\pi)(1-p)(1-\theta)]}{p[\pi pa + (1-\pi)(1-p)(1-\theta)] + (1-p)(1-\pi)[\theta + (1-\theta)a][(1-p)(1-\theta)]}$$

Also,

$$p^{1m}(Re \mid (Re, A), \pi^{2m}(A)) = \frac{p\pi pa}{p\pi p + (1-p)^2(1-\pi)(1-\theta)^2}.$$

The high type's incentive compatibility constraint is

$$\begin{aligned} Ec + R \geq p\{&ap^{1+}(Re \mid (Re, A), \pi^{2m}(A)) \\ &+ (1-a)p^{1m}(Re \mid (Re, A), \pi^{2m}(A))\} - p - (1-p)ac_p. \end{aligned} \quad \text{(A.20)}$$

The expression inside the brackets in the right-hand side of (A.20) is less than 1; therefore, $p\{\cdot\}$ is less than p. The right-hand side of (A.20) is negative, and this incentive compatibility constraint is always satisfied.

Nonsevere crisis; low-type bank. Suppose that Bank 1 is a low type and has default. If it rejects the plan, its expected utility will be given by

$$\begin{aligned} &U_n^L(Re) \\ &= \hat{B} - L - Ec + [p + (1-p)\theta]\{ap^{1+}(Re \mid (Re, A), \pi^{2+}(Re)) \\ &\quad + (1-a)p^{1m}(Re \mid (Re, A), \pi^{2+}(Re))\} \\ &\quad + (1-p)(1-\theta)\{a[ap^{1+}(Re \mid (Re, A), \pi^{2+}(Re)) \\ &\quad + (1-a)p^{1+}(Re \mid (Re, A), \pi^{2m}(Re))] \\ &\quad + (1-a)[ap^{1m}(Re \mid (Re, A), \pi^{2+}(Re)) \\ &\quad + (1-a)p^{1m}(Re \mid (Re, A), \pi^{2m}(Re))]\}. \end{aligned} \quad \text{(A.21)}$$

When the market observes both banks reject the plan, it assumes that the state is n; thus, when Bank 1 rejects the plan and rollover fails, the market knows that the bank is a low type and assigns a value of zero to $p^{1m}(Re \mid (Re, A), \pi^{2+}(Re))$ and to $p^{1m}(Re \mid (Re, A), \pi^{2m}(Re))$. In addition,

$$\begin{aligned} p^{1+}(Re \mid (Re, A), \pi^{2+}(Re)) &= p^{1+}(Re \mid (Re, A), \pi^{2m}(Re)) \\ &= \frac{p}{p + (1-p)[\theta + (1-\theta)a]}. \end{aligned}$$

Using these observations we may rewrite the low type's expected utility when it rejects the plan as

$$U_n^L(Re) = \hat{B} - L - Ec + ap^{1+}(Re \mid (Re, A), \pi^{2+}(Re)) . \quad \text{(A.22)}$$

If Bank 1 accepts the plan, its expected utility is

$$\begin{aligned} U_n^L(A) = & \ (\hat{B} + R - L) \\ & + [p + (1-p)\theta][p^{1m}(A \mid (Re, A), \pi^{2+}(Re))] \\ & + (1-p)(1-\theta)\{ap^{1m}(A \mid (Re, A), \pi^{2+}(Re)) \\ & + (1-a)p^{1m}(A \mid (Re, A), \pi^{2m}(Re))\}. \end{aligned} \quad \text{(A.23)}$$

We note that $p^{1m}(A \mid (Re, A), \pi^{2+}(Re))$ and $p^{1m}(A \mid (Re, A), \pi^{2m}(Re))$ cannot be computed by Bayes' rule. We follow the procedure described earlier for computing these values.

$$p^{1m}(A \mid (Re, A), \pi^{2+}(Re)) = \frac{p^2 \pi a}{p^2 \pi a + (1-p)(1-\pi)(1-\theta)[p + (1-p)[\theta + (1-\theta)a]]}.$$

$$p^{1m}(A \mid (Re, A), \pi^{2m}(Re)) = \frac{p^2 \pi}{p^2 \pi + (1-p)^2(1-\pi)(1-\theta)^2}.$$

The low type's IC constraint is

$$\begin{aligned} & Ec + R \\ & \quad \le [p + (1-p)\theta]\{ap^{1+}(Re \mid (Re, A), \pi^{2+}(Re)) \\ & \quad - p^{1m}(A \mid (Re, A), \pi^{2+}(Re))\} \\ & \quad + [(1-p)(1-\theta)]\{a[p^{1+}(Re \mid (Re, A), \pi^{2+}(Re)) \\ & \quad - p^{1m}(A \mid (Re, A), \pi^{2+}(Re)) \\ & \quad - (1-a)p^{1m}(A \mid (Re, A), \pi^{2m}(Re))]\}. \end{aligned} \quad \text{(A.24)}$$

A necessary condition for this constraint to be satisfied is that the right-hand side is positive. It can be shown that the right-hand side is positive for values of π and θ "low enough" and for values of a high enough, therefore, the IC constraint will be satisfied for values of a high enough and for values of $Ec + R$ low enough. Thus, sufficient conditions for the equilibrium (Re, A) to exist are that a be high enough and that $Ec + R$ be less than the right-hand side of constraint A.24. An example of parameter values for which the right-hand side is positive is $p = .6 \ \pi_0 = .5 \ \theta = .3 \ a = .9$.

Proof of Proposition 5, Part (ii) Equilibrium (A, Re)

Nonsevere Crisis; Low-type bank. When the low type accepts the plan, its expected utility is

$$U_n^L(A) = R + \hat{B} - L + (p + (1-p)\theta)p^{1m}(A \mid (Re, A), \pi^{2+}(Re)) + (1-p)(1-\theta)p^{1m}(A \mid (A, Re), \pi^{2m}(A)), \quad \text{(A.25)}$$

where both of the reputation terms equal zero. Acceptance of the plan signals to the market that the crisis is nonsevere, in which case only the low type can have default. We may thus rewrite the expected utility as

$$U_n^L(A) = R + \hat{B} - L.$$

When the low type rejects the plan, its expected utility is

$$\begin{aligned} U_n^L(Re) = {} & \hat{B} - Ec - L \\ & + [p + (1-p)\theta]\{ap^{1+}(Re \mid (A, Re), \pi^{2+}(Re)) \\ & + (1-a)p^{1m}(Re \mid (A, Re), \pi^{2+}(Re))\} \\ & + [(1-p)(1-\theta)]\{ap^{1+}(Re \mid (A, Re), \pi^{2m}(A)) \\ & + (1-a)p^{1m}(Re \mid (A, Re), \pi^{2m}(A))\} \end{aligned} \quad \text{(A.26)}$$

where

$$p^{1+}(Re \mid (A, Re), \pi^{2+}(Re)) = \frac{p(1-\pi_0)[p + (1-p)\theta] - p^2\pi_0 a^2}{(1-\pi_0)[p + (1-p)\theta]^2 + p^2\pi_0 a^2}.$$

When the market observes that both banks reject the plan and one bank has a medium level of default, the market assumes that the crisis is severe; therefore, $p^{1m}(Re \mid (A, Re), \pi^{2+}(A)) = 1$. When the market observes one bank reject the plan and report high current net worth and the other bank accept the plan, it assumes that the crisis is nonsevere. Thus,

$$p^{1+}(Re \mid (A, Re), \pi^{2m}(A)) = \frac{p}{p + (1-p)\theta}.$$

We must define the out-of-equilibrium belief for the term $p^{1m}(Re \mid (A, Re), \pi^{2m}(A))$. We follow the procedure described above.

$$p^{1m}(Re \mid (A, Re), \pi^{2m}(A)) = \frac{p\pi p}{p\pi p + (1-p)^2(1-\pi)(1-\theta)^2}.$$

The IC constraint for the low type is

$$
\begin{aligned}
&Ec + R \\
&\quad \geq [p + (1-p)\theta]\{ap^{1+}(Re \mid (A, Re), \pi^{2+}(Re)) \\
&\quad + (1-a)\} + [(1-p)(1-\theta)]\{ap^{1+}(Re \mid (A, Re), \pi^{2m}(A)) \\
&\quad + (1-a)p^{1m}(Re \mid (A, Re), \pi^{2m}(A))\}. \qquad \text{(A.27)}
\end{aligned}
$$

Severe crisis; high type. When the high type rejects the plan, its expected utility is

$$
\begin{aligned}
U_S^H(Re) = \hat{B} - Ec - L + p\{a[ap^{1+}&(Re \mid (A, Re), \pi^{2+}(Re)) \\
&+ (1-a)p^{1+}(Re \mid (A, Re), \pi^{2m}(Re)) \\
&+ (1-a)[ap^{1m}(Re \mid (A, Re), \pi^{2+}(Re)) \\
&+ (1-a)p^{1m}(Re \mid (A, Re), \pi^{2m}(Re))]\} \\
&+ (1-p)(1-ac_p). \qquad \text{(A.28)}
\end{aligned}
$$

We note that $p^{1+}(Re \mid (A, Re), \pi^{2m}(Re)) = 1$. In addition,

$$
p^{1m}(Re \mid (A, Re), \pi^{2+}(Re)) = p^{1m}(Re \mid (A, Re), \pi^{2m}(Re)) = 1 .
$$

We may thus rewrite the expected utility given that the high type rejects the plan as

$$
\begin{aligned}
U_S^H(Re) = \hat{B} - Ec - L + p\{a[ap^{1+}&(Re \mid (A, Re), \pi^{2+}(Re)) \\
&+ (1-a)] + (1-a)\} - (1-p)(1-ac_p). \qquad \text{(A.29)}
\end{aligned}
$$

When the high type accepts the plan, its expected utility is

$$
\begin{aligned}
U_S^H(A) = \hat{B} - Ec - L + p[ap^{1m}&(A \mid (A, Re), \pi^{2+}(Re)) \\
&+ (1-a)p^{1m}(A \mid (A, Re), \pi^{2m}(Re))] + (1-p)1 \qquad \text{(A.30)}
\end{aligned}
$$

where $p^{1m}(A \mid (A, Re), \pi^{2+}(Re)) = 0$, and where $p^{1m}(A \mid (A, Re), \pi^{2m}(Re))$ is calculated in a similar manner to the reputation term $p^{1m}(Re \mid (A, Re), \pi^{2m}(A))$ above. (It is easily verified that these two terms are equal.) Using these observations, we may rewrite the high type's expected utility as

$$
U_S^H(A) = \hat{B} - Ec - L + p(1-a)p^{1m}(A \mid (A, Re), \pi^{2m}(Re)) + (1-p) .
$$

The IC constraint for the high type is

$$\begin{aligned} &Ec + R \\ &\quad \le p\{a^2 p^{1+}(Re \mid (A, Re), \pi^{2+}(Re)) + a(1-a) + (1-a)\} \\ &\quad - p(1-a)p^{1m}(A \mid (A, Re), \pi^{2m}(Re)) - (1-p)ac_p. \end{aligned} \tag{A.31}$$

In order to show that the equilibrium (A, Re) does not exist, it suffices to demonstrate that the right-hand side of IC constraint (A.27) is greater than the right-hand side of IC constraint (A.31); hence, that the two IC constraints are inconsistent.

Lemma 2. *The IC constraint (A.31) is inconsistent with the IC constraint (A.27).*

Proof. Observe that $p^{1+}(Re \mid (A, Re), \pi^{2+}(Re)) > p$ and $p^{1+}(Re \mid (A, Re), \pi^{2m}(A)) > p$. Using this observation, we can identify a necessary condition for constraint (A.27) to be satisfied:

$$\begin{aligned} &Ec + R \\ &\ge ([p + (1-p)\theta + (1-p)(1-\theta)]ap + (1-a)\{p + (1-p)\theta) \\ &+ (1-p)(1-\theta)p^{1m}(Re \mid (A, Re), \pi^{2m}(A))\} \end{aligned} \tag{A.32}$$

or

$$\begin{aligned} &Ec + R \\ &\quad \ge (ap + (1-a)p + (1-a)(1-p)\theta) \\ &\quad + (1-a)(1-p)(1-\theta)p^{1m}(Re \mid (A, Re), \pi^{2m}(A)). \end{aligned} \tag{A.33}$$

A necessary condition for the IC constraint (A.31) to be satisfied is that

$$\begin{aligned} &Ec + R \\ &\quad \le ap\{ap^{1+}(Re \mid (A, Re), \pi^{2+}(Re)) + (1-a)\} + p(1-a) \\ &\quad \le ap + p(1-a). \end{aligned} \tag{A.34}$$

Conditions (A.33) and (A.34) are inconsistent since the right-hand side of (A.33) is greater than the right-hand side of (A.34). Hence, the IC constraints (A.31) and (A.27) cannot simultaneously be satisfied. ■

Acknowledgements. The authors thank Erik Berglof, Patrick Bolton, Arnoud Boot, Aleix Calveras, Mathias Dewatripont, Xavier Freixas, Rafael Repullo, Bruce Smith, Andrew Winton, and an anonymous referee for many valuable comments. They are especially grateful to Patrick Legros for many long and helpful conversations.

REFERENCES

[1] Aghion, Philippe, Patrick Bolton, and Stephen Fries. "Optimal Design of Bank Bailouts: The Case of Transition Economics." *Journal of Institutional and Theoretical Economics* 155 (March 1999), 51-79.

[2] Athukorala, P. "The Malaysian Experiment." Conference paper from Reform and Recovery in East Asia: The Role of the State and Economic Enterprise, Canberra: ANU, 1999.

[3] Benston, G., and G. Kaufman. "FDICIA after Five Years: A Review and Evaluation." *Journal of Economic Perspectives* 11 (1997), 139-59.

[4] Boot, Arnoud W., and Anjan Thakor. "Self-Interested Bank Regulation." *American Economic Review* 83 (May 1993), 206-12.

[5] Corbett, Jenny. "Japan's Banking Crisis in International Perspective." In *Finance, Governance, and Competitiveness in Japan*, edited by M. Aoki and G. Saxonhouse. Oxford: Oxford University Press, 1999.

[6] Dewatripont, Mathias, and Jean Tirole. *The Prudential Regulation of Banks*. Boston: MIT Press, 1994.

[7] Dreyfus, J.-F., A. Saunders, and L. Allen. "Deposit Insurance and Regulatory Forebearance: Are Caps on Insured Deposits Optimal?" *Journal of Money, Credit, and Banking* 26 (1994), 412-38.

[8] Gibson, Scott. "On the Information Content of Bank Loan-Loss Disclosures: A Theory and Evidence from Japan." *International Review of Finance*, 1999.

[9] Krueger, A., and A. Tornell. "The Role of Bank Restructuring in Recovering from Crises: Mexico,1995-98." National Bureau of Economic Research Working Paper 7042, 1999.

[10] Lindgren, C.-J., et al. *Bank Soundness and Macroeconomic Policy*. Washington: International Monetary Fund, 1996.

[11] Mailath, George, and Loretta Mester. "When Do Regulators Close Banks: When Should They?" *Journal of Financial Intermediation* 3 (1994), 272-99.

[12] McQuerry, Elizabeth. "The Banking Sector Rescues in Mexico." Federal Reserve Bank of Atlanta *Economic Review* 84:3 (1999), 14-29.

[13] Mitchell, Janet. "The Problem of Bad Debts: Cleaning Banks' Balance Sheets in Economies in Transition." Center for Economic Policy Research Discussion Paper no. 1977, London, 1998a.

[14] ——. "Strategic Creditor Passivity, Regulation, and Bank Bailouts." Center for Economic Policy Research Discussion Paper no. 1780, London, 1998b.

[15] O'Hara, Maureen. "Real Bills Revisited: Market Value Accounting and Loan Maturity." *Journal of Financial Intermediation*, 1993.

[16] Rajan, Raghuram. "Why Bank Credit Policies Fluctuate: A Theory and Some Evidence." *Quarterly Journal of Economics* 109 (May 1994), 399-442.

[17] Rochet, J.-C., and Jean Tirole. "Interbank Lending and Systemic Risk." *Journal of Money, Credit, and Banking* 28 (November 1996, Part 2), 733-62.

[18] Roulier, Richard. "Governance Issues and Banking System Soundness." In *Banking Soundness and Monetary Policy*, edited by Charles Enoch and John H. Green. Washington: International Monetary Fund, 1997.

[19] Smith, H. "The State, Banking, and Corporate Relationships: Korea and Taiwan." Conference paper from Reform and Recovery in East Asia: The Role of the State and Economic Enterprise, Canberra: ANU, 1999.

17

Soft Budget Constraints and Banking in Transition Economies

Erik Berglof
Gérard Roland

Abstract

In this paper, we focus on soft budget constraints for enterprises that are financed by banks in transition economies and analyze several theoretical models as variants of a basic sequential model. Despite various transmission channels for soft budget constraints, all models share the same sequential structure in which soft budget constraints arise due to the endogenous lack of credibility for liquidating a project instead of refinancing it. All also have the same property that refinancing is optimal *ex post* for the decision maker. Hence, mechanisms for hardening the budget constraint require endogenously restoring the credibility of liquidation.

1 • Introduction

Soft budget constraints were one of the most important incentive problems in socialist economies (Kornai, 1980). Hardening budget constraints has therefore, not surprisingly, been one of the main challenges of reforms in transition economies. To tackle the problem governments have, for example, drastically reduced subsidies to state-owned enterprises and promoted the role of banks in enterprise financing. These measures have delivered positive results. The literature points to strong evidence of harder budget constraints in several transition economies (Pinto and van Wijnbergen, 1994; Grosfeld and Nivet, 1997; Bonin and Schaffer, 1995; and Schaffer, 1998).

Despite this progress and the shift from government to bank financing of state-owned enterprises, soft budget constraints remain an important problem, albeit to varying degrees across the countries in transition. Perhaps the most convincing evidence comes from Romania where the correlation between bank lending to enterprises and arrears has strengthened over time (Perotti and Carare, 1997). Other observations suggestive of soft budget constraints in banks are the growth of bad loans on banks' balance sheets in several transition economies and repeated episodes of bank bailouts in, for example, Hungary, the Czech Republic, and Bulgaria (Anderson and Kegels, 1997). In addition, increasing tax arrears of enterprises in some countries indicate continued softness on the side of government (Schaffer, this volume).

The transition experience has shown that soft budget constraints are associated not only with centrally planned economies. A growing literature on soft budget constraints has also demonstrated that the phenomenon is multifaceted. This should not come as a surprise to anyone following the corporate finance literature, in which many contributions over the past two decades have tried to understand the complexity of firms' budget constraints and financial discipline in the market-economy context. Both the transition and the corporate finance literature have identified a number of sources and channels of transmission, or propagation, of soft budget constraints. The objective of this article is to present a simple, unifying framework for surveying these contributions and comparing their policy implications.

A fundamental problem with the discussion of soft budget constraints in the context of centrally planned, or transition, economies has been the lack of formalization of the concept. For an interesting discussion of the conceptual issues and some related measurement problems, see Schaffer (1998). Janos Kornai, who originally coined the term, thought of it as a general phenomenon, closely associated with the notion of paternalism. In his own formalization (Kornai and Weibull, 1983), the government simply bails out loss-making firms and thus undermines *ex ante* incentives. Understanding the phenomenon of paternalism, in particular its underpinnings in political economy, is worthwhile in its own right, but the recent literature has shown that paternalism is not a necessary, nor a sufficient, condition for soft budget constraints.

The early literature on transition is dominated by debates over macroeconomic stabilization. This body of work is also characterized by the relative neglect of institutions; hardening of budget constraints is perceived as a purely exogenous action chosen by policymakers. However, this view does not specify how hard budget constraints are to be enforced credibly. A fundamental contribution to the understanding of the mechanism of soft budget constraints has been provided by Dewatripont and Maskin (1995). Their key insight is that an agent may have a soft budget constraint because it is *ex post* optimal for the investor to bail him out instead of liquidating his activity since any prior funds invested in the firm are sunk costs. More broadly, the Dewatripont-Maskin model helps us understand soft budget constraints as a more general dynamic commitment problem where an agent can fail to take an efficient action, or can undertake an inefficient action, because he knows that he will receive additional finance. Hardening of budget constraints thus means creating conditions for a credible commitment not to refinance an agent.

This paper considers several contributions to the theoretical literature on soft budget constraints and banking in transition economies.[1] The objective is to analyze both similarities and differences between these models in the analysis of the causes of soft budget constraints in enterprises financed by banks. We reconstruct these contributions as variants of a basic sequential model of soft budget constraints. Each variant implies one or more specific sources of the soft budget constraint in bank-firm relations in transition economies. Our list is far from exhaustive, but we identify five different origins of soft budget constraints: (1) the *ex post* benefit of refinancing, (2) a high cost of liquidation when there are strong interdependencies between enterprises, (3) the poor quality of competing projects as an alternative to refinancing existing loans, (4) the incentive to remain passive, hide bad loans, and gamble for resurrection when there is deposit insurance, and (5) rent-seeking activities of banks to exploit the softness of government. In each case, we analyze both the sources of the soft budget constraint and the mechanisms for hardening budget constraints. Despite the differences in sources of and channels for soft budget constraints, all models share the same sequential structure. Soft budget constraints arise due to the endogenous lack of credible commitment to liquidate a project instead of refinancing it. The models also have in common that harder budget constraints are achieved by restoring endogenously the credibility of the liquidation threat.

We develop these various sources by using extensions and modifications of the same basic model introduced in Section 2. Section 3 extends this model by including interactions between firms to allow for trade arrears. In Section 4, we introduce entry of firms to analyze the competition for funds between old and new loans. Section 5 analyzes soft budget constraints in the context of a three-tier hierarchy of government, banks, and firms. We look first at the possibility that *ex post* recapitalization of banks leads to gambling for resurrection which, in turn, makes budget constraints to firms soft. Section 6 explains how banks can promote soft budget constraints for firms to prevent their liquidation so as to extract subsidies from the government. Section 7 concludes with a summary and policy implications.

1. The focus in this survey is on the literature related to banking. We should also mention that there is a rich body of work discussing soft budget constraints more generally (for a recent contribution on the relationship between privatization and soft budget constraints, see Debande and Friebel (1997)).

2 • The Basic Model of Soft Budget Constraints

Our basic model is a modified version of the Dewatripont-Maskin model due to Qian and Roland (1993). We start with a government-firm relation to characterize soft budget constraints under socialism in a two-period setting. At the beginning of period 1, firms draw n projects (normalized to 1 without loss of generality) and submit them to the government. Projects are of two types, either good in proportion α or poor in proportion $(1-\alpha)$. Project types are unknown to the government *ex ante*, and all have start-up cost of 1 monetary unit. At the end of period 1, good projects yield a gross monetary, and taxable, return of R_g and deliver private benefits $B_g > 0$ to the firm's management. Poor projects yield the same outcome *only* if the firm exerts high effort so that B_g is the private benefit net of effort. Effort is assumed to be a binary choice variable (high or low), but we allow for mixed strategies. If the firm exerts low effort, then the project yields zero return after one period. The government can then choose to liquidate the firm's assets, in which case it gets a liquidation value L while the manager has a net private benefit of 0. The government can also refinance the loan, injecting an additional monetary unit to get, at the end of period 2, a gross return R_p, while the firm gets a private benefit of B_p. For simplicity, we assume no discounting. The timing and structure of the game is depicted in Fig. 1.

FIGURE 1

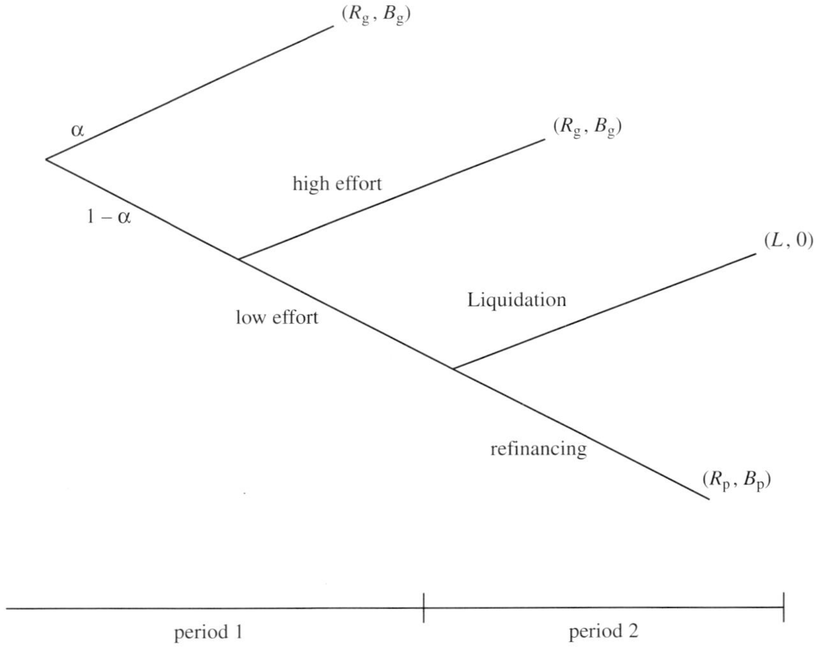

We assume that the government maximizes the net returns to investment plus the private benefits of firms. This incorporates the idea that the government may care about the loss of jobs for political reasons. All monetary returns are assumed to go back to the government as repayment for the initial loan. Firms are thus solely interested in maximizing their total net private benefits.

The firm is said to have a soft budget constraint if it gets refinanced. If the prospect of refinancing causes the firm not to exert high effort in situations when the prospect of liquidation would, there is an incentive problem. In other words, the absence of a credible commitment to hard budget constraints can create a moral hazard problem at the level of the firm. The difference with the Dewatripont-Maskin model is that, in the latter, the choice variable is whether or not to submit a project. In their model, there is no effort decision in firms. The moral hazard version seems to fit better the reality of transition in which firms must undertake restructuring efforts, but it gives the same qualitative results. Under what conditions will there be soft budget constraints? Will poor projects be financed and if so, what costs would this entail for the government? The answers are given in the following proposition:

Proposition 1. *If $B_p > B_g$ and $L < R_p + B_p - 1$, firms will have soft budget constraints and exert low effort. All projects will be financed if $\alpha > \alpha^S = 2 - R_p - B_p / R_g + B_g - R_p - B_p + 1$, and no projects will be financed otherwise. Refinancing poor projects is inefficient if $R_p + B_p < 2$.*

Proof. If $R_p + B_p > L + 1$, then it is *ex post* optimal for the government to refinance. If $B_p > B_g$, then firms prefer to choose low effort if they know they will be refinanced. If soft budget constraints are expected, the expected net return to lending is $\alpha(R_g + B_g - 1) + (1 - \alpha)(R_p + B_p - 2)$, which is positive as long as $\alpha > \alpha^S = 2 - R_p - B_p / R_g + B_g - R_p - B_p + 1$. Since there is asymmetric information, all projects are financed when $\alpha > \alpha^S$, but none are financed under that threshold. There is a loss of $2 - R_p - B_p$ on each poor project. ■

Proposition 1 captures the idea that soft budget constraints are related to government paternalism. The government takes the private benefits of the firm insiders into account in its decision to liquidate or to refinance. However, paternalism is not a necessary condition for soft budget constraints. An interesting feature of the Dewatripont-Maskin framework is that profit-maximizing banks are also faced with the soft budget constraint problem; soft budget constraints are thus not necessarily confined to socialism as the following proposition shows:

Proposition 2. *Firms will have soft budget constraints and low effort if* $B_p > B_g$ *and* $L < R_p - 1$. *Projects will be financed if* $\alpha > \alpha^B = 2 - R_p/R_g - R_p + 1$. *Financing of poor projects is inefficient for banks if* $R_p < 2$.

Proof. If $R_p > L + 1$, then it is *ex post* optimal for banks to refinance. If refinancing is assured and $B_p > B_g$, then firms prefer to choose low effort. When soft budget constraints are expected, the expected net return to lending is $\alpha(R_g - 1) + (1 - \alpha)(R_p - 2)$, which is positive if $\alpha > \alpha^B = 2 - R_p/R_g - R_p + 1$. Banks lose $2 - R_p$ on each poor project. ■

Note that if the bank could credibly commit to liquidate a poor project, the firm would always choose high effort since $B_g > 0$. Soft budget constraints are here due to a general dynamic commitment problem.

Transfer of lending activities to profit-maximizing banks may thus lead to hardening of budget constraints if $R_p - 1 < L < R_p + B_p - 1$. However, there may still be soft budget constraints if $L < R_p - 1$. The model shows that the soft budget constraint problem may persist after banking reform (*i.e.*, when banks are profit-maximizing), and even after the privatization of firms, if the liquidation value L is low enough. The liquidation value is related to the level of collateral; in transition economies collateral is scarce due partly to the absence of private wealth under socialism, partly to poorly functioning markets for liquidated assets. Consequently, soft budget constraints in banks should be an important problem in these economies. We could even go one step further. The model predicts soft budget constraints to be widespread since the existence of sunk costs drives a wedge between *ex ante* efficiency and *ex post* efficiency. We should thus observe soft budget constraints as a very general phenomenon. Judging from the empirical evidence, soft budget constraints are not as pervasive as suggested by this analysis. We will come back to this question in Section 4.

Another important parameter in the model that plays a crucial role in what follows is α, the proportion of good loans. The lower α is, the higher the efficiency losses from soft budget constraints are. When α falls below α^B, lending basically stops because it has a negative expected return. In what follows, we will assume that $\alpha > \alpha^B$.

In this section, the basic source of soft budget constraints is that the *ex post* benefits of bailing out are higher than the benefits of liquidation. Soft budget constraints are possible even though they involve an inefficiency because the initial investment is sunk. Soft budget constraints are likely if firms are state-owned and the government exhibits paternalism, *i.e.*, when the benefits of bailing out a particular firm go beyond the pure monetary return and include the welfare of its employees. Low levels of collateral, as in transition economies, further reduce financial discipline.

In the context of this model, the main mechanism for hardening budget constraints found in the literature is the decentralization of credit. Dewatripont and Maskin (1995) and Povel (1995) show that if refinancing requires funds from an outside bank, inefficiencies in bargaining between banks may make refinancing less attractive.[2]

In the remainder of the paper, we explore basic extensions and slight alterations of this model to account for important phenomena observed in economies in transition.

3 Trade Arrears and Soft Budget Constraints

We introduce interactions between firms to explore the issue of trade arrears between firms and its relationship to soft budget constraints. Trade arrears were an important phenomenon in the beginning of transition. After price liberalization, many firms became insolvent and could not pay their suppliers so that payment arrears began to accumulate. *De facto*, many suppliers were lending to their clients. These trade arrears effectively worsened the financial situation of good firms which were themselves brought into a difficult financial situation. These spillover effects tended to create a too many to fail problem for banks, forcing them to bail out bad loans in order to prevent generalized insolvency of firms which could put banks themselves in a difficult position. In many countries this problem subsided as the government refrained from intervention and levels of interenterprise credits stabilized, but several transition economies, notably Russia, Bulgaria, and Romania, have experienced partial government bailouts of interenterprise arrears, leading to expectations of future capital infusions, implying a continued soft budget constraint of enterprises.

We model enterprise arrears by incorporating a simplified version of the model in Perotti (1993). Specifically, let θ be the proportion of firms with poor projects that exert effort and restructure. This form of restructuring may be seen as defensive restructuring since, unlike strategic restructuring, it does not require outside investment.[3] Among those firms that do not restructure, let λ be the proportion of projects that the bank decides to liquidate. Thus, $(1-\alpha)(1-\theta)\lambda$ projects get liquidated. To capture the possibility of interaction between projects, assume that healthy firms, *i.e.*, firms with good

2. In the Dewatripont-Maskin model, this is due to an agency problem in monitoring between the bank that refinances and the bank that made the initial investment. In Povel's model, banks play a war of attrition at the renegotiation stage.

3. On defensive and strategic restructuring, see Grosfeld and Roland (1996).

projects or firms that have restructured, have supplier-customer relationships with firms with poor projects. We modify the basic model by assuming that the gross return to loans in those firms decreases in relation ω to the proportion of liquidated projects in the total number of projects. Thus the liquidation of some firms, due to their insolvency, may affect the financial situation of other firms. As a consequence of this assumption, the return to both the good and the restructured projects is $R_g(1-\omega(1-\alpha)(1-\theta)\lambda)$.

These interactions between firms due to the trade arrears of insolvent firms give rise to a problem for the bank. A "tough" liquidation policy may spill over to healthy firms causing their financial situation to deteriorate and, eventually, worsening the bank's own situation.

The bank's expected profit as a function of θ and λ is given by

$$\Pi(\lambda, \theta) = (\alpha + (1-\alpha)\theta)R_g(1-\omega(1-\alpha)(1-\theta)\lambda) + (1-\alpha)(1-\theta)[\lambda L + (1-\lambda)(R_p - 1)],$$

where λ is chosen by the banks after firms' choice of θ. Otherwise, the timing is the same as in the previous model.

The externality reduces the liquidation value of a loan for the bank. We can rewrite $\Pi(\lambda, \theta)$ as

$$\Pi(\lambda, \theta) = (\alpha + (1-\alpha)\theta)R_g + (1-\alpha)(1-\theta)[\lambda(L-\omega) + (1-\lambda)(R_p - 1)] \quad (1)$$

We thus have the following proposition.

Proposition 3. *If $\omega > L + 1 - R_p$, firms have soft budget constraints, and if $\omega < L + 1 - R_p$, they have hard budget constraints.*

Proof. Obvious. ■

The basic message is that the stronger that trade links between firms with different projects are, the softer the bank will tend to be in order to avoid spillover effects from a tough but self-defeating liquidation policy. By bailing out firms banks make it possible for the latter to pay their suppliers.

The model can be extended to obtain multiple equilibria, and in particular a "too many to fail" result with multiple equilibria, as in Perotti's analysis. Firms that exert effort and restructure, by doing so, reduce their trade links with traditional state-owned enterprises. We call this "restructuring with redeployment". In effect, ω, instead of being a constant, is then assumed to be a negative, continuous, and differentiable function of θ, $\omega(\theta)$, with $d\omega/d\theta < 0$. The following proposition concerns restructuring with redeployment:

Proposition 4. *If* $\omega(1) < L + 1 - R_p < \omega(0)$, *there are multiple and symmetric equilibria:*

(i) *two pure strategy equilibria with* (a) *a soft budget constraint equilibrium where firms do not restructure and banks refinance and* (b) *a hard budget constraint equilibrium where all firms restructure; and*

(ii) *a mixed strategy equilibrium with partial restructuring* $\theta^* \in (0, 1)$ *and partial liquidation* $\lambda^* \in (0, 1)$.

If $L + 1 - R_p < \omega(1)$, *there is a unique equilibrium with soft budget constraints. If* $\omega(0) < L + 1 - R_p$, *there is a unique equilibrium with hard budget constraints.*

Proof. Take Eq. (1) with $\omega(\theta)$ replacing ω. Taking the derivative of $\Pi(\lambda, \theta)$ with respect to λ yields $L - \omega(\theta) - R_p + 1$. If $\omega(1) < L + 1 - R_p < \omega(0)$, there exists a value θ^* for which $L - \omega(\theta^*) - R_p + 1 = 0$. Since $d\omega/d\theta < 0$, above θ^*, the bank will strictly prefer to liquidate and below θ^*, it will strictly prefer to refinance. Firms face a coordination problem: the only two pure Nash equilibria of this coordination game are $\theta = 0$ or $\theta = 1$. Indeed, firms prefer to restructure whenever $B_g > (1 - \lambda)B_p$. For all $\theta < \theta^*$, $\lambda = 0$. For any $0 < \theta < \theta^*$, because $B_g > B_p$, firms would like to deviate and restructure less unless $\theta = 0$. For all $\theta > \theta^*$, $\lambda = 1$. For any $\theta^* < \theta < 1$, because $B_g > 0$, firms would like to deviate unless $\theta = 1$. If $\theta = \theta^*$, then the bank is indifferent between any $\lambda \in [0, 1]$. For θ^* to be an equilibrium, λ^* must be such that $B_g = (1 - \lambda^*)B_p$.

If $L + 1 - R_p < \omega(1)$, $L + 1 - R_p < \omega(\theta)$ for any θ. In other words, banks will always want to refinance regardless of the restructuring policy of firms. If $\omega(0) < L + 1 - R_p$, $\omega(\theta) < L + 1 - R_p$ for any θ. In other words, banks will never want to refinance. ■

The interesting insight here is that the marginal benefit of liquidation $L - \omega(\theta) - R_p + 1$ increases with the extent of restructuring. When firms restructure, it becomes credible for the bank to liquidate *ex post* and this leads to hardening of budget constraints. However, when firms do not restructure, the marginal benefit of liquidation is the lowest or its cost the highest. Therefore the bank will have an incentive to be soft.

To summarize the results of this section, the sources for soft budget constraints are dependencies between firms of the old state sector and a lack of restructuring driven by expectations of bailout under conditions of low restructuring. A mechanism for hardening budget constraints can be provided only if there is a focal point making firms expect general restructuring; this, in turn, leads to the selection of the hard budget constraint equilibrium. Unfortunately, the lack of a good theory of focal points or equilibrium selection makes it harder to draw clear-cut policy conclusions. As is commonly the case with multiple equilibria, there is no convincing reason to select one equilibrium over the other.

4 • Soft Budget Constraints, Entry, and Credit Crunches

We turn to another extension of the basic model set up in Section 2 based on Berglöf and Roland (1997). In particular, we study the effect of entry and the competition between old loans to poor projects seeking refinance and new loans. The only change is the addition of another period to the model, specifically a period 0 before period 1. We assume that, at the beginning of period 0, the bank finances a unit mass of projects. Enterprises with poor projects decide during that period on their effort level, given their expectation of future bailout. At the beginning of period 1, the bank faces the problem of using the proceeds from period 0 investment to finance either new projects or refinance poor projects. We assume that the supply of new projects is perfectly elastic to create the strongest contrast with Section 2; there are more new projects than funds to finance them.

An important difference compared to the basic model is that the proportion of good projects in period 1, denoted β, is not necessarily the same as in period 0 because of the entry of new projects. New entry is a characteristic aspect of transition; there is no reason to believe that the quality of projects is the same during the early phases of transition as it was under socialism. Enterprises with poor projects financed in $t = 1$ decide on their effort level during period 1. We assume that at the beginning of period 2, no new projects are generated. The only decision for banks is whether to refinance poor projects using revenues generated by the investments in period 1. If projects are refinanced, they generate revenues during period 2, which is terminal.

We assume that $2 > R_p > 1$, *i.e.*, the returns from refinancing are higher than the cost of refinancing but lower than the total investment into the project. In that case poor projects are *ex ante* nonprofitable, but they are always refinanced *ex post* in period 2. Given that the bank has an incentive to refinance poor projects in period 2, enterprises with poor projects know they have soft budget constraints and thus choose low effort in period 1. The expected net return to a new project financed in period 1 is then $\beta(R_g - 1) + (1 - \beta)(R_p - 2)$.

It is instructive to contrast the decision of the bank in period 2 sketched above with its decision in period 1 when the bank can choose to allocate its revenues between refinancing existing projects and funding new projects. The bank's choice in period 1 determines whether the budget constraints of enterprises with poor projects funded in period 0 are hard or soft, and this in turn affects the enterprise's incentives in period 0. Indeed, if the bank prefers to put all its revenues from period 0 into new lending, enterprises are better off choosing high effort in period 0 as long as $B_g > 0$. However, if $B_p > B_g$, enterprises will always prefer low effort if they expect to be refinanced.[4] If the bank prefers to refinance existing projects before making new loans, enterprises will choose low effort. The following proposition indicates the conditions for hard or soft budget constraints to prevail.

Proposition 5. *For* α *given, and if* $2 > R_p > 1$, *enterprises have hard budget constraints in period* 1 *if* β *is greater than* $\hat{\beta} = 1/R_g - R_p + 1$, *and soft budget constraints otherwise.*

Proof. The expected net return from new lending is $\beta(R_g - 1) + (1 - \beta)(R_p - 2)$ and the expected net return from refinance is $R_p - 1$. The condition follows immediately from comparing both expressions. Given the assumption that the supply of new projects is perfectly elastic, the bank will use all its funds in period 1 to finance new projects if the return of the latter is higher. If $B_g > 0$, enterprises prefer to provide high effort. In the opposite case, available funds will be used to bail out existing projects before financing new ones. If $B_p > B_g$, enterprises prefer low effort. ■

The conditions for hard budget constraints have an intuitive explanation. The higher the proportion of good projects β in the entire cohort to be financed at $t = 1$ that are related to new entry and the higher the difference in returns between good projects and refinancing of poor projects (*i.e.*, the higher $R_g - R_p$), the more likely budget constraints are to be hard. A low quality of average loan projects and a low variance in returns between good and poor projects will soften budget constraints. Indeed, banks will prefer recouping money on bad loans to financing new projects, many of which are likely to be poor projects, if they receive insufficient compensation from good projects. This sheds light on the persistence of soft budget constraints in transition economies.

4. The latter condition must be changed if, when the firm chooses high effort in period 0, it draws a project that is selected in period 1 with a positive probability.

By contrast, when projects are of high enough average quality, hard budget constraints will obtain. As stated above, the nature of sunk costs of existing loans advanced by Dewatripont and Maskin is quite general and does not relate exclusively to phenomena in transition economies. It is thus a puzzle why we do not observe more soft budget constraints in banking sectors of all economies. Proposition 5 proposes an answer: banks may prefer funding new loans to refinancing old projects if the quality of new projects is high enough; hence, competition from other projects serves as a credible commitment to terminate loans on poor projects.

Note that if we made the model more realistic by allowing for investment in new projects in period 2 and extended the model to more periods, our result would only be strengthened. Proposition 5 assumes that budget constraints will always be soft in period 2. This may not be the case in the presence of new lending opportunities. By backward induction, hard budget constraints in the future will increase the relative return to new projects, as compared to refinancing old projects, thereby further hardening budget constraints today.

Proposition 5 has an immediate corollary.

Corollary. *Less new projects are financed in period* 1 *if enterprises have soft budget constraints.*

Proof. Indeed, under hard budget constraints, total net returns to the bank are $(\beta R_g + (1-\beta)(R_p - 1))R_g - 1$. However, under soft budget constraints, total net returns are $(\beta R_g + (1-\beta)(R_p - 1))(\alpha R_g - (1-\alpha)) + (1-\alpha)R_p - 1$. Comparing the funds available in period 1 for new projects, R_g under hard budget constraints and $(\alpha R_g - (1-\alpha))$ under soft budget constraints, it is clear that $(\alpha R_g - (1-\alpha)) < R_g$. ■

The lower the quality α of old loans, the bigger the credit crunch under soft budget constraints. This corollary is interesting because, early in the transition period, findings by Dittus (1994) that banks had cut drastically the allocation of credit to enterprises led to the conclusion — perhaps premature — that banks had hardened the budget constraints of enterprises. Our model shows not only that soft budget constraints and credit crunches are not necessarily inconsistent, but that soft budget constraints can coexist and even lead to a credit crunch with respect to new loans.

To summarize the results of this section, the source of soft budget constraints is the poor quality of new projects. The sunk cost of early investment drives a wedge between the return on new loans and the return on refinancing poor loans, making it possible that the latter is higher than the former. The key parameter leading to hardening of budget constraints is β, the quality of new loans. In Berglöf and Roland (1997), we show that investments in screening activities, allowing the bank to avoid financing part of the bad projects, increase β and thus harden budget constraints. Interestingly, in contrast to the results of Dewatripont and Maskin, smaller banks may be softer than bigger banks. Due to economies of scale, small banks may have to refrain from screening, whereas large banks can afford the fixed investments in screening activities.

5 Bank Passivity and Gambling for Resurrection

Starting with this section, we make the analysis of soft budget constraints and banking in transition more complex by adding another tier to the analysis, *i.e.*, a game between the government and the banks. The government may be tempted to bail out banks under certain conditions; banks have indeed been bailed out in several transition economies. Hungary, for example, experienced four bailouts in as many years. Most recently, Bulgaria went through a major recapitalization of its entire banking sector. Bailouts of banks affect their incentives to harden budget constraints of enterprises. In other words, the soft budget constraints of banks may lead to soft budget constraints for firms. We start the analysis by incorporating a simplified version of the basic model of bank passivity due to Mitchell (1997).

Take again the bank-firm model of Section 2 and make the following modifications. Assume that when a poor project is refinanced, there is a probability q that it generates return R_p for the bank and a probability $(1-q)$ that it generates a liquidation value $L_s < L$. In both cases, the project yields private benefits B_p.[5] The firm's incentives thus remain unchanged but the bank's incentives may change, depending on its relationship with the government.

We thus add on top of the game between the bank and enterprises a game between the government and the bank. The government can decide to monitor the bank to detect whether, as a creditor, it is active in filing for bankruptcy, *i.e.*, whether it chooses to liquidate poor projects or tries to remain passive. The reason the bank may want to remain passive is that limited liability shelters it from the downside risk of refinancing bad projects; the bank may choose to "gamble for resurrection". The government must decide *ex ante* on a detection probability D at a cost $C(D)$ assumed to be a

5. Note that one does not need to assume that refinancing takes place. The model may be simply reinterpreted by assuming that the bank can decide to roll over the loan as in Mitchell (1997), leading to $R_p - 1$ with probability q or to $L_s - 1$ with probability $(1-q)$.

FIGURE 2

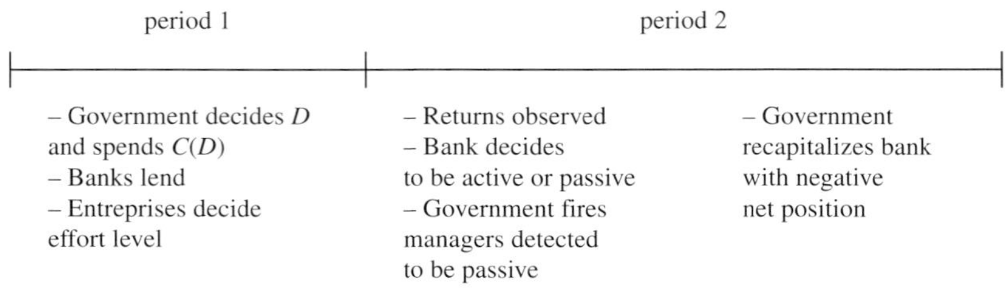

convex function of D. Detection takes place after the bank decides to refinance or not. If the bank is detected being passive, the government can fire the bank management. To make this threat credible, we assume that the government can commit to firing management, *e.g.*, by writing it into the banking law.

The timing of the game is as follows. In period 1, the government decides on D and spends $C(D)$. The bank lends to finance projects, and enterprises with poor projects decide on their effort level. In period 2, returns are observed and the bank decides to be active or passive, *i.e.*, whether to liquidate or not, and chooses a level of activity $a \in [0, 1]$. Directly afterward, the government monitors and fires passive bank managers. At the end of the period, the government recapitalizes banks by injecting capital K to be determined endogenously; due to deposit insurance, a negative net position of the bank must be covered by the government (see Fig. 2).

The government's optimization problem is to minimize $C(D) + K$ subject to the constraint that at the end of period 2, the sum of K and the bank's net position be nonnegative.[6] The bank's payoff is $\max\{0, \pi\} + \rho$ where π is the net return from lending and ρ is the private benefit of managing the bank. The net return from lending may be negative, but the bank's losses will be covered. Thus, $K = \max\{-\pi, 0\}$ and bank management loses ρ if it is fired. Firing management does not change the bank's financial position; by assumption, when passivity is detected, it is too late to undo the bank's refinancing decision.

Even though we have a three-tier hierarchy, the analysis can concentrate on the government-bank relationship. The following lemma characterizes enterprise behavior:

Lemma. *Firms have soft budget constraints if and only if* $(1 - a)B_p \geq B_g$.

Proof. Obvious. ■

Firms have hard budget constraints only if the bank is sufficiently active; they have soft budget constraints otherwise. Firm

6. Note that the objective function of government is not equivalent to social welfare. However, efficiency enters directly via the concern for recapitalization. Bank passivity and soft budget constraints of firms create the need for recapitalization costs that the government wants to avoid.

behavior affects the financial position of the bank. Thus, if firms have hard budget constraints, the bank's payoff will be

$$-1 + R_g + \rho .$$

If firms do not exert effort, then the bank's payoff is

$$a[\max\{-1 + \alpha R_g + (1-\alpha)L, 0\} + \rho]$$
$$+ (1-a)(1-D)[q(\alpha R_g + (1-\alpha)(R_p - 1) - 1) + \rho] .$$

With probability q passive banks are lucky, in which case they get the returns from the good loans αR_g and the net returns from refinancing $(1-\alpha)(R_p - 1)$ minus the initial credit expenditure of 1. With probability $(1-q)$ they are unlucky with refinancing and realize they ended up throwing good money after bad. Their position then becomes $\alpha R_g + (1-\alpha)(L_s - 1) - 1$, which can be negative if α is not too big and L_s is sufficiently small. The government's payoff when firms have soft budget constraints is

$$-C(D) - a\max\{0, 1 - \alpha R_g - (1-\alpha)L\}$$
$$-(1-a)\max\{0, (1-q)(1 - \alpha R_g + (1-\alpha)(1-L_s))\} . \quad (5.1)$$

The amount of recapitalization depends directly on a, not on D, but a itself depends on D. If firms have hard budget constraints, the government's payoff is $-C(D^H)$.

We assume that $1 - \alpha R_g + (1-\alpha)(1-L_s) > 0$ so that recapitalization is necessary when banks are passive. To simplify the analysis we also assume that $1 - \alpha R_g - (1-\alpha)L < 0$, *i.e.*, that the bank does not need to be recapitalized when it is active.[7] The more important assumption is that $L_s - 1 < L$ so that the government payoff increases with bank activity.

With $D \geq 0$, the bank will prefer $a = 1$ if

$$-1 + \alpha R_g + (1-\alpha)L + \rho > (1-D)[q(\alpha R_g + (1-\alpha)(R_p - 1) - 1) + \rho],$$

which is equivalent to

$$D > \tilde{D} = \frac{(1-\alpha)[q(R_p - 1) - L] - (1-q)(\alpha R_g - 1)}{q(\alpha R_g + (1-\alpha)(R_p - 1) - 1) + \rho} .$$

The banks' decision is thus mainly based on the expected benefits of gambling for resurrection given the existence of deposit insurance and the potential punishment of being fired if caught being passive. Note that $d\tilde{D}/d\rho < 0$ so that the higher the private benefit the

7. See Mitchell (1997) for a complete analysis of different cases.

lower the detection probability necessary to dissuade the bank from gambling for resurrection. This is the incentive effect related to the threat of being fired. Note also that $d\tilde{D}/d\alpha < 0$. The higher α is, the higher the bank's loss from good loans in case of recapitalization and the lower the net expected gain from refinancing of bad loans is.

Proposition 6. *Hard budget constraints obtain if* $C(\tilde{D}) < (1-q)(1-\alpha R_g + (1-L_s))$*; otherwise budget constraints are soft.*

Proof. Note first that for any $D < \tilde{D}$, banks choose $a = 0$. The government's optimal choice in that range is then $D = 0$. As soon as $D = \tilde{D}$, banks choose $a = 1$. The government then never gains from choosing $D > \tilde{D}$. The government's choice is binary: whether to incur cost $C(\tilde{D})$ leading to hard budget constraints and no recapitalization, or to not monitor banks, thereby accepting soft budget constraints of firms and recapitalization of banks *ex post*.

Whether hard budget constraints obtain or not depends thus on the costs of effective monitoring *versus* the potential costs of recapitalization. As expected, the cost of recapitalization decreases with α. In transition economies both the costs of monitoring and those of recapitalization are expected to be high. However, if the cost of recapitalization is sufficiently important, the government will want to eliminate soft budget constraints in banking.

Another solution is to reduce directly the incentives for banks to engage in gambling for resurrection by injecting capital equal to C up front at the opportunity cost of government funds, denoted $\lambda(C)$. The level of capital infusion $\tilde{C}$ necessary to preclude the bank from gambling for bailout is given by

$$\tilde{C} - 1 + \alpha R_g + (1-\alpha)L + \rho$$
$$= q(\alpha R_g + (1-\alpha)(R_p - 1) - 1 + \tilde{C}) + \rho, \quad (5.2)$$

where the left-hand side is the return from being active, and the right-hand side is the return from being passive. Banks will strictly prefer to be active for

$$C \geq \tilde{C} = \frac{1-\alpha}{1-q}[q(R_p - 1) - L] - (\alpha R_g - 1).$$

The question remains whether such a policy can be in the interest of government. *Ex ante* capitalization will never be in the interest of the government if $\tilde{C} + \lambda(\tilde{C}) > K$. As can be easily seen, when q increases, $\tilde{C}$ increases and $K = (1-q)(1-\alpha R_g + (1-\alpha)(1-L_s))$ decreases so that $\tilde{C}$ may be bigger than K. On the other hand, $\tilde{C}$ may be much smaller than K for low levels of q. Under those conditions, when $\tilde{C} + \lambda(\tilde{C}) < C(\tilde{D})$, recapitalization achieves hard budget constraints at a lower cost than monitoring. ■

This section has shown that soft budget constraints can arise in enterprises even when refinancing of poor projects *per se* is not optimal. Protection against downside risk may lead the bank to gamble for resurrection by rolling over credits and avoiding liquidation; in this sense insurance leads to creditor passivity and soft budget constraints. Naturally, this behavior is more likely when banks are poorly capitalized. Knowing this, the government can engage in monitoring and thus increase the banks' costs of passivity. Recapitalization *ex ante* may be a cheaper way of hardening budget constraints.

6 Gambling for Bailout and Rent-Seeking by Banks

In the previous section, banks gambled because they were insured against downside risks. However, banks can also trigger bailouts or, more generally, extract rents from the government. They can do so by exploiting the softness of government, which, unlike the banks, cares not only about the verifiable revenues but also about the private benefits of employees. These types of games between governments and banks are an important feature of transition (for an interesting discussion, see Anderson and Kegels (1997)). In this section we analyze such a game along the lines developed in Berglöf and Roland (1995).

The most important modification of the basic model developed in Section 2 is the assumption that the bank is not interested in refinancing *per se*, *i.e.*,

$$L > R_{\mathrm{p}} - 1 .$$

This small alteration of the model is conceptually another important departure from the basic framework of Dewatripont and Maskin (1995) in which softness stems from the fact that previous investments are sunk costs at the time of the refinancing decision. In the following, softness arises because banks can extract subsidies from the government.

We assume that at $t = 0$, the government injects an initial capital of 1 in the bank at a gross cost $\lambda(1)$ (assumed to be greater than 1 to include the distortionary costs associated to its financing). A unit mass of projects can be financed by the bank, but the bank may choose to finance only k projects and keep reserves $E = 1 - k$. At $t = 1$, the point of refinancing, the government can give a subsidy S at a cost $\lambda(S)$. The subsidy to the bank is paid after a verifiable commitment from the bank that it will bail out firms. By assumption, the government cannot recover the returns from refinancing; its only instrument is to inject capital. However, since the government maximizes the total welfare, *i.e.*, the welfare of both banks and firms, it is willing to pay the subsidy if

$$(1 - \alpha)k(R_p + B_p - 1) > \lambda(S).$$

The government is willing to inject money to finance all projects *ex ante* because the net expected benefit to government is bigger than the expected cost:

$$\alpha(R_g + B_g) + (1 - \alpha)(R_p + B_p - 1) - 1 \geq \lambda(1) + \lambda(1 - \alpha - \alpha R_g).$$

Moreover, the bank's liquidity position can be observed perfectly by the government. The subsidy will cover the extra liquidity needed to bail out the poor projects exactly, *i.e.*,

$$S = k[(1 - \alpha) - \alpha R_g] - (1 - k),$$

where $(1 - \alpha)k$ is the cost of refinancing, $\alpha k R_g$ is the verifiable revenues generated by the good projects, and $(1 - k)$ is the initial capital contribution by the government net of the investment. Banks will be interested in obtaining a subsidy if the gain from this subsidy is bigger than the loss due to the refinancing obligation. We have the following lemma.

Lemma. *$S - (1 - \alpha)k(1 + L - R_p) \geq 0$ is a necessary condition for the firms to have soft budget constraints.*

The first question we ask is if $k = 1$, will budget constraints be soft or hard? The following proposition answers this question.

Proposition 7. *If $k = 1$, there exists an α^H such that if $\alpha \leq \alpha^H = R_p - L/R_p - L + R_g$, budget constraints will be hard.*

Proof. Using the above Lemma and the expression for the optimal subsidy, we have that $S = (1 - \alpha) - \alpha R_g \geq (1 - \alpha)(1 + L - R_p)$, which implies that $\alpha \leq \alpha^H = R_p - L/R_p - L + R_g$. ■

In the following we assume $R_p - L > 0$ so that soft budget constraints may occur with low α. Precisely, in case $\alpha < \alpha^H$, the bank may set aside (or be forced to set aside) reserves $E = 1 - k$ and finance only k projects. The more reserves the bank has, the less it will be interested in rent-seeking. The bank will be indifferent between hard and soft behavior if

$$(1-\alpha)k - \alpha k R_g - E = (1-\alpha)k(1+L-R_p),$$

which implies reserves

$$E = k((R_p - L) - \alpha(R_p + R_g - L)).$$

Given an initial capital infusion of 1, the bank faces the following tradeoff. It can opt for either soft budget constraints and a bailout or hard budget constraints and choose $k < 1$ so as to commit credibly not to seek a bailout.

In case of soft budget constraints the profit of the bank is

$$\Pi_s = (1-k) + k(\alpha R_g - (1-\alpha)) + S + (1-\alpha)kR_p = (1-\alpha)kR_p.$$

Clearly, $d\Pi_s/dk > 0$ so that $k = 1$, which implies

$$\Pi_S = (1-\alpha)R_p.$$

When budget constraints are hard, bank profit is

$$\Pi_H = k(R_g - 1).$$

To ensure hard budget constraints the bank will need to determine k^H such that, for α given

$$k^H = \frac{1}{1+(R_p - L) - \alpha(R_p + R_g - L)}.$$

Since $dk/d\alpha > 0$, the lower is the quality of projects α, the higher is the level of reserves needed to ensure hard budget constraints.

Hard budget constraints obtained by setting such minimum reserves yield higher profits to the bank if the following inequality is satisfied,

$$\frac{(R_g - 1)}{1+(R_p - L) - \alpha(R_p + R_g - L)} > (1-\alpha)R_p,$$

which is equivalent to

$$(R_g - 1) > (1-\alpha)R_p[1+(R_p - L) - \alpha(R_p + R_g - L)].$$

For $\alpha = 1$, it is clear that this inequality is satisfied. For $\alpha = 0$, given that $R_p - L < 1$ and $1 + R_p - L < 2$, it is not obvious that

$R_g - 1 > 2R_p$. So we may have $\Pi_H < \Pi_S$ for low α. The right-hand side of the inequality $(1-\alpha)R_p[1+(R_p-L)-\alpha(R_p+R_g-L)]$ is a convex curve declining in α. For the bank, being hard yields higher returns but on less projects.

What then is optimal for the government? Under soft budget constraints its payoff is

$$-\lambda(1)-\lambda(1-\alpha-\alpha R_g)+\alpha B_g+(1-\alpha)(R_p+B_p)$$

and under hard budget constraints

$$-\lambda(1+(R_p-L)-\alpha(R_p+R_g-L))+(R_g+B_g).$$

We have the following proposition:

Proposition 8. *The government prefers soft budget constraints and bailouts over hard budget constraints and a credit crunch when the following inequality is satisfied:*

$$\lambda(1+(R_p-L)-\alpha(R_p+R_g-L))-\lambda(1)-\lambda(1-\alpha(R_g+1))$$
$$>(R_g+B_g-R_p-B_p)+\alpha(B_g-R_p-B_p).$$

Evaluating this inequality at $\alpha = 0$ and $\alpha = 1$ shows that both equilibria are possible. Obviously, the payoffs to hard budget constraints increase in the liquidation value L.

So far we have assumed implicitly that the government cannot observe the quality of bank portfolios, but only the overall proportion of good and bad projects and the bank's liquidity. If the government could identify the bad loans in bank portfolios, it could withdraw bad loans from the bank and refinance them, *e.g.*, by transferring loans to a specialized government institution. Such hospital agencies have been set up in many transition economies to clean up bank portfolios and to avoid subsidizing the bank for refinancing bad projects; if all the bad loans are withdrawn, this will be more costly than a bailout in terms of subsidies. The bailout will cost $(1-\alpha)-\alpha R_g < (1-\alpha)$. Indeed, when all bad loans are transferred to the hospital agency, the cost in terms of subsidies is always higher. The reason is that the government will have to pay the full cost of refinancing, not only the shortfall after the bank's own funds have been used as in a bailout.

Assume instead that only h projects are transferred to the hospital bank. The subsidy will now be

$$S(h) = (1-\alpha)-h-\alpha \mathrm{R}_g.$$

In essence, the government should withdraw an amount sufficient to make rent-seeking unprofitable for the bank. In order to discourage the bank from gambling for bailout, it must be that

$$S(h) - (1-\alpha)h(1-R_p) \leq (1-\alpha)L,$$

which is equivalent to

$$h \geq \frac{(1-\alpha)(1-L)+\alpha R_g}{1+(1-\alpha)(1-R_p)}.$$

The government will thus set $h = [(1-\alpha)(1-L)+\alpha R_g]/[1+(1-\alpha)(1-R_p)]$ to get hard budget constraints. As expected the share of loans that must be transferred to the hospital agency decreases in liquidation value and increases in the verifiable revenues from both good and poor projects. For $\alpha = 0$, h is a positive number in the interval $(0, 1)$. For $a = 1$, there is no need for a hospital agency; budget constraints will be hard in any case.

7 Concluding Remarks

This paper considers some contributions to the theoretical literature on soft budget constraints in enterprises having a focus on banking during economic transition. However, the soft budget constraint is not confined to bank lending or only to centrally planned economies and economies in transition. Indeed, soft budget constraints reflect a universal dynamic commitment problem that is potentially present in any form of finance and in any financial system. This paper identifies several sources of and transmission channels for soft budget constraints in enterprises and proposes mechanisms for improving financial discipline.[8] The variety of mechanisms available for hardening budget constraints may explain why financial discipline during economic transition is not worse, as the empirical evidence validates, and also why soft budget constraints were so pervasive under socialism. The list also suggests important complementarities between different aspects of reform. For example, investments in screening are likely to strengthen the effects of new entry.

When looking at the similarities and differences between the various models, it is striking that the models of Sections 2 through 4 are all variants of the basic Dewatripont-Maskin model even though they exhibit different channels for the soft budget constraints. In all cases, soft budget constraints arise because of the sunk cost nature of the initial investment. It is profitable *ex post* to refinance loans that are not profitable *ex ante*. The three-tier models of Sections 5 and 6 are different. In the Mitchell model, soft budget constraints arise

8. Aghion *et al.* (1996) also analyze banking in transition but with a focus on the incentives of banks to reveal information. The bank can hide the real amount of bad loans initially. If the government is too tough, the bank will underdeclare; if the government is too lenient, the bank will exaggerate the amount of bad loans. Truthful revelation can be obtained via a nonlinear pricing scheme for purchasing the bad loans.

because bank incentives are distorted due to limited liability and to imperfect monitoring of bank behavior. Hence, banks have an added incentive to refinance when compared with the situation in the Dewatripont-Maskin two-tier framework. In the rent-seeking model of Section 6, the bank has no intrinsic interest in refinancing a loan but it can extract subsidies by exploiting the softness of government.

In the Dewatripont-Maskin two-tier framework, the difference between the *ex ante* inefficiency of future refinancing and the *ex post* benefit of refinancing is crucial to characterizing soft budget constraints. Without *ex ante* inefficiency, refinancing would not be wasteful; without the *ex post* benefit to refinancing, the rationale for soft budget constraints would be missing. At the same time, the *ex ante* inefficiencies and the *ex post* benefits all accrue only to the bank, *i.e.*, the sole investor. In the models of Sections 5 and 6, the bank benefits because it is able to shift part of the costs of refinancing to the government. In both models, refinancing is optimal from the perspective of the decision maker, namely the bank in Mitchell's case and the government in the rent-seeking model. In Mitchell's model, refinancing may not be socially optimal *ex post* because the bank's objective diverges from social efficiency due to the existence of deposit insurance. In the rent-seeking case, the government chooses to subsidize the bank to prevent the loss of private benefits that would result from the liquidation of firms.

Despite their differences, all the models share the same common sequential structure and have the same property that refinancing is optimal *ex post* according to the decision maker's criterion. Enterprises provide low effort if they expect rationally to be refinanced. Hard budget constraints are obtainable by imposing institutional rules that curb the bank's incentive to refinance. We hope that our paper provides a useful framework for organizing empirical verification of the sources of and transmission channels for soft budget constraints and leads to a better understanding of the persistence and disappearance of soft budget constraints in transition economies.

REFERENCES

[1] Aghion, Philippe, Bolton, Patrick, and Fries, Stephen, *Financial Restructuring in Transition Economies*, Discussion Paper 96111. Tilburg: Center for Economic Research, Tilburg Univ., 1996.

[2] Anderson, Ron, and Kegels, Chantal, *Financial Development of Post-Socialist Economies: The Main Issues*. Mimeo, Université Catholique de Louvain, 1997.

[3] Berglof, Erik, and Roland, Gérard, "Bank Restructuring and Soft Budget Constraints in Financial Transition." *J. Jpn. Int. Econom.* **9**, 4:354-375, Dec. 1995.

[4] Berglof, Erik, and Roland, Gérard, "Soft Budget Constraints and Credit Crunches in Financial Transition." *Eur. Econom. Rev.* **41**, 3-5:807-817, April 1997.

[5] Bonin, John, and Schaffer, Mark, *Banks, Firms, Bad Debts and Bankruptcy in Hungary 1991-94*. Centre for Economic Performance Discussion Paper 234. London: London School of Economics, 1995.

[6] Debande, Olivier, and Guido Friebel, *Privatization and Managerial Efficiency,* The Davidson Institute Working Paper Series, No. 39. Univ. of Michigan Business School, 1997.

[7] Dewatripont, Mathias, and Maskin, Eric, "Credit and Efficiency in Centralized and Decentralized Economies." *Rev. Econom. Studies* **62**, 4:541-555, Oct. 1995.

[8] Dittus, Peter, *Corporate Governance in Central Europe: The Role of Banks,* Economic Papers, no. 42. Basel: Bank for International Settlements, Monetary and Economic Department, 1994.

[9] Grosfeld, Irena, and Nivet, Jean-Francois, *Firm's Heterogeneity in Transition: Evidence from a Polish Panel Data Set.* Mimeo, DELTA, 1997.

[10] Grosfeld, Irena, and Roland, Gérard, "Defensive and Strategic Restructuring in Central European Enterprises." *J. Transf. Econom. Soc.* **3**, 4:21-46, Fall 1996. [Also as Discussion Paper. 1135. Center for Economic Policy Research, 1996].

[11] Kornai, János, *Economics of Shortage.* Amsterdam: North Holland, 1980.

[12] Kornai, János, and Weibull, Jörgen, "Paternalism, Buyers' and Sellers' Market." *Math. Soc. Sci.* **6**, 2:153-169, Nov. 1983.

[13] Mitchell, Janet, *Strategic Creditor Passivity, Regulation, and Bank Bailouts,* The Davidson Institute Working Paper Series, No. 46. Univ. of Michigan Business School, 1997.

[14] Perotti, Enrico, "Bank Lending in Transition Economies." *J. Bank. Fin.* **17**, 5:1021-1032, Sept. 1993.

[15] Perotti, Enrico, and Carare, Octavian, *The Evolution of Bank Credit Quality in Transition: Theory and Evidence from Romania.* Mimeo, Univ. of Amsterdam, 1997.

[16] Pinto, Brian, and van Wijnbergen, Sveder, *Ownership and Corporate Control in Poland: Why State Firms Defied the Odds.* Mimeo, International Finance Corporation, 1994.

[17] Povel, Paul, *Multiple Banking as a Commitment Not to Rescue,* LSE Financial Markets Group Discussion Paper 206. London: London School of Economics, 1995.

[18] Qian, Yingyi, and Roland, Gérard, *Regional Decentralization and the Soft Budget Constraint: The Case of China,* Discussion Paper 1013. Centre for Economic Policy Research, 1994.

[19] Schaffer, Mark E., "Do Firms in Transition Economies Have Soft Budget Constraints? A Reconsideration of Concepts and Evidence." *J. Comp. Econ.* **26**, 1:80-103, March 1998.

18

Blocks, Liquidity, and Corporate Control

Patrick Bolton
Ernst-Ludwig von Thadden

Abstract

The paper develops a simple model of corporate ownership structure in which costs and benefits of ownership concentration are analyzed. The model compares the liquidity benefits obtained through dispersed corporate ownership with the benefits from efficient management control achieved by some degree of ownership concentration. The paper reexamines the free-rider problem in corporate control in the presence of liquidity trading, derives predictions for the trade and pricing of blocks, and provides criteria for the optimal choice of ownership structure.

1 Introduction

The recent incomplete contracting approach in corporate finance has considerably improved our understanding of how small firms determine their capital structure. The basic setting considered in this line of research is one where a founder-manager seeks funding from one or several financiers. The main premise is that the founder-manager, in her dealings with the financiers, is primarily concerned with maintaining her private benefits of control. For small firms these are often quite large relative to the financial returns. Thus, for a small firm the problem of determining the financial structure often reduces to the problem of how to obtain funding while giving away as little control as possible to the financiers. Of course, most financiers insist on some form of protection, so that the final compromise reached in most financial contracts for small firms is one resembling a debt contract (or a venture capital contract), which protects the founder-manager's control as long as the firm is performing adequately.[1]

This perspective for small firms does not extend naturally to large firms because the private benefits of control of the managers for

1. For a recent discussion of this literature see Hart (1995).

large firms are likely to be small relative to the firm's monetary returns, so that protection of these benefits is not an overriding consideration. Moreover, large firms tend to have more dispersed ownership and therefore less effective investor control. If anything, the main control problem for large firms seems to be how to get investors or shareholders to exert more control. Indeed, this is the problem on which the recent literature on corporate governance has focused.[2]

Interestingly, there is little variation across nations in the capital structure of small firms, but for large firms the problem of inducing more effective investor control has been tackled very differently. In broad terms, there have been two different responses. In the United States and the United Kingdom primarily, share-ownership in large firms is widely dispersed, turnover is high, and investor control is often exerted through the threat of takeovers. In other countries, share-ownership is more concentrated, turnover is much lower, and control is exerted, if at all, by the largest shareholders (or debtholders). Three countries that exemplify this latter type of financial system are Germany, France, and Japan.[3]

When evaluating the differences of these two types of systems, it is important to realize that the issue is not whether ownership concentration per se is desirable or not. The issue rather is how often and at what points in a firm's life ownership should be concentrated. One alternative for the design of ownership structure is persistent ownership concentration, wherein a large blockholder is expected to exercise control of management continuously; the other is ownership dispersion, with reliance on secondary market trading to create concentration whenever necessary for intervention in managerial decision making. This paper develops a framework in which the costs and benefits of the two systems — dispersed ownership combined with a takeover mechanism on the one hand, and large controlling blocks (or "noyaux durs"), on the other — can be evaluated. The benefits of dispersion are mainly greater market liquidity and better risk-diversification.[4]

Several empirical studies have documented that the liquidity of a stock is larger the larger the market capitalization of the firm. The explanations usually given for this finding relate in one way or another to the presence of transactions costs, which limit market participation.[5] Thus, for example, if market makers face set-up costs, the number of market makers dealing in a stock will be increasing — and, therefore, liquidity will be increasing — in the market capitalization of that stock. Similarly, if market participants face information asymmetries, the number of investors willing to invest in information acquisition in a particular stock will be increasing in the anticipated gains from trade and, hence, in the stock's market capitalization.

2. Surveys of recent research on corporate governance can be found in Kojima (1995) and Shleifer and Vishny (1997). For a discussion of the recent policy debate on corporate governance see also *The Economist* (1994).

3. For a description of the main differences between the financial systems of the United States and the United Kingdom, on the one hand, and of Germany, France, and Japan, on the other, see Franks and Mayer (1994) and Kojima (1995).

4. The model we develop focuses on the liquidity benefits of dispersion. We abstract from risk-diversification issues mostly to keep the model tractable. For an analysis of the impact of risk sharing on corporate control see Admati, Pfleiderer, and Zechner (1994).

5. See, for example, Demsetz (1968), Merton (1987), Pagano (1989), and Allen and Gale (1994).

This argument immediately implies that when a firm decides to set up a controlling block, it reduces the number of shareholders who can participate in the trading of the firm's stock and, therefore, it effectively reduces the market capitalization, and hence the liquidity, of its stock. This is the principal mechanism relating concentration and liquidity in our model.

Besides limited market participation by potential shareholders, the model builds on two other key assumptions. First, in the spirit of Shleifer and Vishny (1986), it is assumed that some degree of ownership concentration improves control of management and, therefore, can increase firm value. There is a large body of cross-sectional evidence in support of this assumption,[6] but there are also well-known counterexamples. These include cases of large owners who have managed their companies for very long periods (Johnson *et al.* (1985)), or of management-affiliated blockholders who allow management to dilute share value away from other shareholders (Wruck (1989), Slovin and Sushka (1993)). We are aware of these cases, but we do not consider them in this paper.

Second, it is assumed that by exercising control a shareholder incurs net private costs. This assumption may appear more restrictive than the first one, in light of some of the empirical evidence on the pricing of corporate control transactions. Barclay and Holderness (1989), for example, find that large blocks of shares mostly trade at a premium, which, they argue, results from private benefits accruing to the blockholder. As we discuss in Section 3, however, the empirical evidence on block pricing reflects several different elements, of which the costs of controlling management are only one.[7] Indeed, our main justification for focusing on the costs rather than the benefits of control is empirical. If private benefits of control were, in general, more important than private costs, corporate governance would be a relatively minor problem; the real problem would be to select among the bidders for large blocks of shares who volunteer to control management. This is not the typical situation we observe in the United States, to which the above-mentioned studies refer — the importance of blockholders with private benefits of control notwithstanding.

Building on these assumptions, our model yields several simple and interesting insights. In particular, the analysis shows that a firm is more likely to choose a dispersed ownership structure, other things being equal, if there is more active trading in its secondary market and if regulation facilitates takeovers as a means to acquire control. Complementing this, we find that greater liquidity trading in the secondary market by itself facilitates takeovers by reducing free riding. These observations shed some new light on the issue of why the United States and the United Kingdom have such different capital

6. For publicly traded firms in the United States, see, for example, Wruck (1989) or Hertzel and Smith (1993). For evidence on French and German listed companies, see Franks, Mayer, and Renneboog (1995).

7. Barclay and Holderness (1989), in view of the sizeable number of discounts in their sample, "suggest that block ownership involves private costs as well as private benefits".

and governance structures in large firms from those observed in Germany, France, or Japan. In particular, in the United States and the United Kingdom the takeover mechanism is much less restricted, there are stricter legal restrictions on institutional equity holdings, and secondary market participation by institutional investors is greater and more frequent.[8] All of these features favor ownership dispersion in our model.

More generally, our analysis shows that both types of ownership structure — concentrated or dispersed — can be optimal, depending on the characteristics of the firm and the environment in which it operates. Our comparative statics results show that higher average liquidity demand by investors, lower costs of controlling management, higher potential benefits from correcting managerial failures, and higher transactions costs for secondary market trading all favor a dispersed ownership structure, and vice versa for concentration. Our model is set up to apply in principle to both listed and unlisted firms. Concerning unlisted firms, it is therefore interesting to note that the above characteristics hold — at least to a first approximation — for law and accounting partnerships, which are well-known examples of private firms with dispersed ownership structures (see, *e.g.*, Hansmann (1995)).

For publicly listed companies, where empirical data are best, our model provides a new explanation for why equity block purchase agreements usually are priced at sizeable discounts, but trades of existing blocks are not.[9] Our explanation is that single shares and blocks, when traded, must reflect the anticipated costs of corporate control equally, because by arbitrage, one type of seller cannot be treated differently from another. Anticipating that he will not be fully compensated for holding the block in future trading, however, a block purchaser will demand a discount at the issue stage.

There is a large literature related to several aspects of our model. This literature almost exclusively is concerned with large listed companies, whereas the argument of the present paper applies to privately held firms as well. A closely related paper, by Pagano and Röell (1998), considers a privately held firm with a large shareholder which needs to increase its capital base by bringing in new shareholders. The firm has the option of remaining private and introducing another set of large shareholders, or going public and getting a new set of small shareholders. The benefit of the former option is that the firm does not have to pay listing costs. The downside is that there may be excessive monitoring by large shareholders (as in Burkart, Gromb, and Panunzi (1997)) and the stock is less liquid.

Merton (1987) introduces asymmetric information in the standard CAPM to obtain a model in which investors only trade in the

8. In the United States, actively managed pension funds hold shares for an average of only 1.9 years (Kojima (1995)), and on the NYSE, for example, institutions account for 72 percent of trading volume.

9. See Barclay and Holderness (1989) and Hertzel and Smith (1993) for descriptions of the empirical puzzle.

limited number of shares about which they have information. His model gives rise to the type of limited market participation we consider in the present paper. In fact, our model of secondary market trading can be interpreted as a reduced form of Merton's model for one single stock with an additional emphasis on corporate control issues.

Admati *et al.* (1994) take a similar view to ours on the benefits of large shareholder intervention, and ask to what extent these benefits can be realized by risk-averse investors who optimize their portfolio choice. Kahn and Winton (1998) argue that market liquidity can undermine effective control by a large shareholder by giving him excessive incentives to speculate rather than monitor. In contrast, Holmström and Tirole (1993) argue that insider trading by a large shareholder provides incentives to monitor management but results in a higher cost of capital for the firm.

Recent papers that are related to our analysis of the free-rider problem are Zingales (1995) and Gromb (1993), who show how free riding by small shareholders can be used to increase the *ex ante* value of the firm. Also, Bebchuk (1994) considers the problem of the trading mechanism of controlling blocks when large shareholders obtain both monetary and private benefits of control; he contrasts the equal opportunity rule (according to which minority shareholders can participate in the sale of a block on the same terms as large ones) and the market rule (where no distinction is drawn between shareholders according to the size of their holdings).

In interesting historical studies, Coffee (1991), Bhide (1993), and, more comprehensively, Roe (1994) argue that political considerations have helped shape the development of U.S. capital markets toward higher liquidity and lower investor activism, thus providing evidence for one manifestation of the trade-off studied in our paper. We come back to Bhide's study in Section 4 below.

Finally, it is worth mentioning a recent study by La Porta *et al.* (1996), who take quite a different perspective on the observed international differences in ownership concentration. They regress ownership concentration on several measures of law and law enforcement in different countries and argue that the lack of adequate minority shareholder protection in Germany, France, and Japan relative to the United States (and the United Kingdom) may be a cause for the differences in financial systems. We shall discuss more of the relevant empirical literature in the main body of the paper.

The organization of the rest of this paper is as follows: Section 2 describes our model. Section 3 analyzes the two polar forms of ownership structure relevant in the present model, and Section 4 evaluates the trade-off between the two. Section 5 concludes with some remarks about the scope of the analysis.

2 The Model

Consider a firm that operates for two time-periods, $t = 1, 2$. At time $t = 0$, the original owners want to sell the firm and issue shares, which give rights to the firm's future returns. We assume that because of fixed trading costs these claims will not be traded in arbitrarily fine units, so that the effective number of shares, M, is finite. M is a constant to the model, determined by the costs of trading.

There are a large number of potential investors in the firm's shares. To simplify our analysis, we assume that investors are sufficiently wealthy to buy up the whole firm if they wish.[10] Each investor i can invest in a safe, liquid asset whose net rate of return is normalized to zero, or in shares of the firm. If there are n investors each buying h_0^i shares at $t = 0$, the initial ownership structure is $(h_0^1, \ldots, h_0^n)$, with $\sum_{i=1}^{n} h_0^i = M$. We denote the price of the firm at the issue date $t = 0$ by V_0.

Even if investors can afford to buy the whole firm they may not want to, for liquidity reasons. Following Gorton and Pennacchi (1990) and others, we model investors' demand for liquidity as follows. Each investor has liquidity needs in the future, which arise in either period 1 or 2. At time $t = 0$, the timing of these needs is unknown to everybody, and all investors have the following identical expected utility from consumption in periods $t = 1$ and $t = 2$:

$$u(c_1, c_2) = qc_1 + (1-q)c_2 . \qquad (1)$$

When investors buy shares, they do not know exactly when they will want to consume. If they want to consume early (which happens with probability q), then they have to sell their shares; if they want to consume later, they may buy more shares. The consumption shocks of investors are assumed to be independent. Thus, even though investors are identical *ex ante*, they generally have different liquidity needs *ex post*, and qV_0 can be interpreted as average liquidity demand by existing shareholders. We shall refer to investors who want to consume early as "impatient" and to those who want to wait until period $t = 2$ as "patient". The preferences specified in (1) provide the simplest possible specification of liquidity preferences.[11]

The trading of shares following the liquidity shocks in $t = 1$ typically depends on the institutional framework in which the firm operates. The specific structure of trading is largely irrelevant for our analysis, and we choose the simplest: We assume that after preference shocks have been realized, aggregate liquidity demand

10. Introducing wealth constraints is conceptually not difficult, but technically somewhat complicated, and does not change our main results. We discuss wealth constraints as we go along in the analysis and in the conclusion.

11. In particular, these preferences exhibit risk neutrality with respect to intraperiod consumption. We could have used a more general specification without, however, gaining much further insight. See Jacklin (1987) and von Thadden (1994) for a discussion of more general approaches to modeling liquidity preferences.

becomes publicly known and the following three-stage bidding game is played:

1. Patient investors simultaneously make unrestricted offers for shares.
2. If there are two or more identical offers, one is selected at random.
3. All owners can tender their shares to the selected buyer at the offered price.

This mechanism implies maximum competition between potential buyers and resolves the coordination problem between identical bids which can cause existence problems.[12] Furthermore, outside investors and existing owners bid for shares on equal terms.

Having defined liquidity needs and trading, we now turn to the firm's return structure and, consequently, to the problem of corporate control. We assume that the firm has stochastic returns in $t = 1$ and $t = 2$ which are both determined and publicly observed in $t = 1$ and, for simplicity, assumed to be identical (all we use in the analysis is that first-period returns are informative about second-period returns). With probability π the firm earns high returns, $y = R$ in both periods, and with probability $1 - \pi$ returns are low, normalized to $y = 0$. However, in the bad return state the firm can be reorganized, which generates an added value L, $R > L > 0$, in period $t = 2$.

The problem of corporate control arises from the fact that after the sale of the firm in $t = 0$, the firm is run by managers who always prefer continuation to reorganization.[13] Therefore, reorganization can only be brought about by outside intervention, which typically costs time and resources. We model this by assuming that an owner who intervenes in the bad state improves firm value from 0 to L in $t = 2$, but incurs net private costs of $C < L$. With efficient intervention, the firm's value is, therefore, given by

$$V^* = \pi 2R + (1 - \pi)(L - C) . \qquad (2)$$

We denote per-share values by lowercase letters, *e.g.*, $r = R/M$, $v^* = V^*/M$, etc. Because it is typically difficult to get a group of owners to act collectively in the common interest (Diamond (1984)), we assume that intervention costs cannot be shared among owners, but must be borne individually. This implies that only a single owner with a large enough stake in the firm will intervene in the bad state. In other words, intervention will occur only if its private gain exceeds its cost.

A final and key assumption, which makes the model nontrivial, concerns the secondary market for shares. As discussed in the

12. Because we assume below that an owner can invest a fixed cost in order to control management, the number of shares bought either in Walrasian trading or under standard Bertrand competition determines profits. Therefore, without a coordination stage such as 2, the payoff functions of market participants are not upper-hemi-continuous. The assumption that liquidity demand becomes known before trading simplifies the analysis without qualitative consequences.

13. These managers may well be among the owners of the firm. The important point is that their private interest in running the firm is stronger than the value of cash flow improvements achievable by reorganization.

FIGURE 1

The figure shows the order of events for the model with three time periods, $t = 0, 1, 2$.

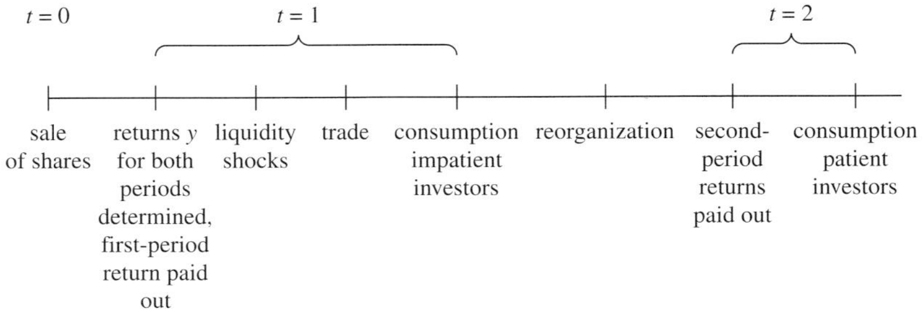

introduction, market participation for any given stock is typically limited by information costs. In the present context this means that there are only a limited number of investors who are able to value and willing to buy shares from existing shareholders when trading at $t = 1$. We model this by assuming that outside investors (those who have not bought shares at $t = 0$) are less willing to intervene in the bad state and, therefore, are only ready to bid 0 in that state. Hence, in the bad state, they provide liquidity only at a discount. This assumption is stronger than necessary for our analysis, but it allows us to capture in a simple way the notion that selling out and "active investing" can be conflicting policies, with potentially different impacts on firm value.[14]

We close the description of the model by recapitulating the timing of activities in the time line shown in Figure 1.

3 Concentration versus Dispersion

As noted previously, only an owner who internalizes the costs of control will intervene and force management to take the efficient continuation/reorganization decision in the bad return state. This is the case if and only if his shareholding h^i after trading in $t = 1$ satisfies

$$h^i l \geq C.$$

Let T denote the smallest solution to this inequality, which we take for simplicity to be integer. It is worth pointing out that the fraction T/M necessary to internalize the cost of controlling management may be well below the threshold of 50 percent, or other majorities required formally for full corporate control. In the United States, for example, blocks of 10-20 percent, if established in a publicly traded company, already can be associated with significant share price increases due to improved corporate control.[15] In fact, if applied to publicly listed U.S. companies, our model should be restricted to blocks of this size or smaller. As Barclay and Holderness (1989) document for large

14. The notion of limited market participation can be modeled by different assumptions of different sophistication. We have chosen the simplest one. One alternative, as in Merton (1987), which gives slightly more complex formulas and the same results, would be to assume that only a limited number of investors can distinguish the good and the bad return states.

15. See, for example, Wruck (1989) and Barclay and Holderness (1991). As these studies show, usually the share price response depends on the nature of the large blockholder.

block trades of NYSE and AMEX firms, block premia in such trades can be substantial for blocks of more than 25 percent, suggesting the existence of private benefits, but are smaller for blocks below 25 percent. Because our model focuses on the private costs of corporate control rather than on the benefits, the model should be restricted to smaller block sizes when applied to the group of firms studied by Barclay and Holderness (1989).

The key determinant of the trade-off between liquidity and control in our model is that achieving a certain level of concentration reduces the number of owners. Because outsiders only buy up shares at a discount in the bad state, this, in turn, reduces the number of trading partners in the secondary market who are ready to provide liquidity in all states. Hence, concentration of ownership, although it improves the incentives for the control of management, reduces valuable trading possibilities for all shareholders.

On the other hand, maximum dispersion of shares among initial owners increases trading opportunities among those who potentially will pay the full price for shares in the bad state, but may lead to a value-reducing lack of control because of ownership dispersion. Notice that dispersion in $t = 0$ does not necessarily imply that there is dispersion in $t = 1$, after liquidity trading. Indeed, one of the patient owners may buy enough shares in the bad state to assemble a stake that makes it profitable for her to intervene. Thus, the old owners, when selling out at $t = 0$, have two principal options: They create a controlling block of shares, hoping that it persists, or they disperse the initial ownership, which creates more trading opportunities in secondary trading, with the hope that a controlling block emerges when necessary in the secondary market.

In this section we consider these two alternatives in turn and provide pricing formulas for each of them. In the next, we determine under what circumstances either of these ownership structures dominates.

3.1 Concentrated Ownership

Maximum dispersion of shares is obtained when there are as many owners as shares, M. With a controlling block the maximum number of owners is $M - T + 1$, because at least one investor holds a block of at least T shares. Yet, when the firm creates a controlling block at date $t = 0$, *a priori* it is not clear that the initial controlling owner will actually control the manager at date $t = 2$ and enforce the efficient continuation/reorganization decision.

The reason is that an initial large owner may himself be impatient, in which case he is only concerned about selling his shares at the highest price. In this case it is possible in principle that he disperses his block in such a way that no large owner emerges *ex post*. However, under the trading structure considered here and under the assumption of no wealth constraints, concentration will necessarily persist in the secondary market. More generally, the reason for this result is the assumption of nonanonymous trading. This assumption reflects the existence of stringent disclosure rules for publicly traded firms in most stock markets and the importance of private communication between owners in privately held firms.

As long as trading is nonanonymous, any attempt by the large owner to unload his block of shares with several buyers would immediately be reflected in the price, which in turn would remove the incentive to disperse the block. Hence, if there is at least one patient shareholder, the large owner either sells his shares as a block or keeps them. In both cases the large block persists, and the efficient continuation/reorganization decision is taken. If none of the initial shareholders is patient, the block and all other shares must be sold to outsiders, in which case the problem of *ex post* concentration is irrelevant.

If the initial ownership structure consists of one large block and a fringe of small owners, *ex post* trading in shares has the following structure.

Lemma 1. *Suppose the firm in* $t = 0$ *has* $M - T + 1$ *owners, one holding* T *shares and the others holding one share each. If in* $t = 1$ *there are at least two patient owners, then shares trade at the price*

$$b(I, r) = r \tag{3}$$

in the good return state, and

$$b(I, 0) = l - \frac{C}{T + I} \tag{4}$$

in the bad state, where I *is the number of impatient small owners. In the bad state, the block is preserved, and the blockholder's* ex post *position is worth* $Tb(I, 0)$, *regardless of whether he is patient or impatient.*

Proof. In the good state, corporate control is not an issue and (3) holds trivially. Suppose that $y = 0$, the large owner is patient, and at least one small shareholder is patient, as well. Then bids by outsiders are irrelevant, because bidding among insiders alone will drive the price up beyond what outsiders are ready to pay (that is, 0).[16] If a small patient shareholder wins the bidding with a bid of b, the maximum number of shares he will attract is $T + I$ (the block and all impatient shares), which will be worth to him $(T + I)(l - b) + l - C$. Hence, the optimal bid by the large share-

16. We assume throughout that bidders do not use weakly dominated strategies, a standard assumption in auction theory.

holder, $b(I, 0)$, keeps the small patient owners indifferent between bidding or not and satisfies:

$$(T+I)(l-b(I,0)) = C, \tag{5}$$

which implies (4). By (5), the large owner's profit from making this bid and attracting the impatient shares is the same as the profit from selling his stake at this price, namely $Tb(I, 0)$.

If the large owner is impatient and $I \leq M - T - 2$, the optimal bid by a small owner satisfies (5) by the same argument. ■

As simple as it is, the lemma contains several interesting insights. First, the large block is not broken up in liquidity trading, except possibly for the extreme case of every owner being impatient. This is consistent with the empirical evidence. Barclay and Holderness (1989), for example, note that "the limited evidence available suggests that large blocks are seldom broken up". Second, expected future intervention costs are partially borne by the small impatient shareholders. Single shares in the bad state trade at less than their *ex post* value, and patient shares are not traded at all.

Third, if in the bad state the large block is sold, it trades at the same price as single shares. This is due to the simple trading structure assumed in this model, which excludes the emergence of several blocks and essentially imposes a nonarbitrage condition on share trades of different size. In reality, things are more complex, as shown by the empirical evidence on premia on large block trades for publicly listed companies in the United States (most importantly, see Barclay and Holderness (1989)). These studies find large variations of premia and discounts and positive median block premia.[17] Furthermore, block size plays a role. When regressing block premia on block size with a sample split at 25 percent, Barclay and Holderness (1989) find a large and significant point estimate for block sizes above 25 percent, and a negative, though insignificant coefficient below 25 percent.[18] As noted previously, for this group of firms our focus on private costs, rather than benefits of control, is therefore only justified when blocks are not too large.

In addition to the focus on private costs, the block trades considered in our model are seller-, and not buyer-, initiated. The available evidence (see, *e.g.*, Holthausen, Leftwich, and Mayers (1987)) suggests that seller-initiated trades are accompanied by significantly lower, sometimes even negative, block premia. Note, however, that Holthausen *et al.* only consider blocks that are large in dollar terms, and typically not in percentage terms. We know of no study distinguishing between seller- and buyer-initiated trades of large percentage blocks. Yet, such differences seem to be plausible also for those

17. For their sample of block trades of NYSE and AMEX firms between 1978 and 1982, Barclay and Holderness (1989) find a median premium for large blocks of shares of 15.7 percent, and block discounts in 20 percent of the transactions.

18. These estimates refer to block premia per share (their Table V, regression 4), which is the measure considered in Lemma 1.

blocks, given the wide variations of block discounts/premia documented by Barclay and Holderness (1989) and, in a related context, by Wruck (1989).

Hence, our model does not incorporate all elements of block pricing. It would be quite possible to include bargaining over block sales and buyer-initiated trades into the model (*e.g.*, by introducing outsiders with random private benefits in $t = 1$, as in Grossman and Hart (1988)), which would generate positive average block premia.[19] Yet, we have preferred to focus on the simpler model with only liquidity trading.

Proposition 1. *The* ex ante *value of the firm with at least one large owner is maximized when there is exactly one large owner with a stake equal to T and all other owners hold only one share. The block is priced at a discount, and the firm's* ex ante *value is*

$$V_0^c = 2\pi R + (1-\pi)(1-q^{M-T+1})(L-C). \tag{6}$$

Proof. To have more than one large owner reduces liquidity and does not provide any improvement in the *ex post* reorganization/continuation decision. To have a single large owner with a stake strictly greater than T reduces liquidity and again does not improve *ex post* efficiency. This establishes that firm value is maximized by having exactly one large owner with a stake T. By Lemma 1, the expected value of the large owner's block, conditional on the bad state occurring, is

$$\begin{aligned} v_B = {} & (1-q)q^{M-T}(L-C) + [1-q^{M-T}(M-T+1) \\ & + q^{M-T+1}(M-T)]Tl - \sum_{i=0}^{M-T}\binom{M-T}{i}q^i(1-q)^{M-T-i}\frac{TC}{T+i} \\ & + (M-T)q^{M-T}(1-q)\frac{TC}{M-1} + q^{M-T}\frac{TC}{M}, \end{aligned} \tag{7}$$

and that of a single share

$$\begin{aligned} v_S = {} & (1-q)q^{M-T}(L-C) - (M-T-1)q^{M-T-1}(1-q)^2\frac{C}{M-1} \\ & - \sum_{i=0}^{M-T-3}\binom{M-T-1}{i}q^{i+1}(1-q)^{M-T-i-1}\frac{C}{T+i+1} \\ & + [1-(M-T-1)q^{M-T-1}(1-q) \\ & + (M-T)q^{M-T-1}(1-q)^2 - q^{M-T-1}]l. \end{aligned} \tag{8}$$

Because $V_0^c = v_B + (M-T)v_S$, (6) follows from (7) and (8) by direct computation. A further straightforward computation shows that

19. An extension of our model in this direction would introduce a separate market for blocks and assume the possibility of pure (costless) diversion from minority shareholders to blockholders in the good state. Under appropriate parameter assumptions, in such a model the median block would trade at a premium and still command a discount at the issue stage.

$$Tv_s - v_B = (T-1)(1-q)q^{M-T}(L-C)$$
$$+ \sum_{i=0}^{M-T}\left(1-\frac{i}{M-T}\right)\binom{M-T}{i}q^i(1-q)^{M-T-i}\frac{TC}{T+i}$$
$$+ q^{M-T}(1-q)\frac{TC}{M-1}, \tag{9}$$

which is positive. ■

Thus, the liquidity cost of having a large owner at date $t = 0$ is measured entirely in terms of the implied reduction in the number of owners from M to $M - T + 1$. The simplicity of the expression for V_0^c comes from the assumption of no wealth constraints. With such constraints, an additional cost of creating a large block is that this block may have to be split up for some realizations of liquidity shocks, thus eliminating the efficiency gains relating to corporate control.

The fact that the block is priced at a discount at the issue date may seem surprising because, by (3) and (4), the shares will trade at their *ex post* value in the good state and in the bad state impatient owners will subsidize the blockholder for the future monitoring costs. Because everyone has the same liquidity preferences *ex ante*, one might expect the costs to be borne equitably at the issue date, and therefore to observe no block discount. This is not the case, however, for two reasons — both of which are reflected in equation (9). First, as shown in Lemma 1, small impatient shareholders only bear part of the expected monitoring costs *ex post*. For the remaining part of these costs, the large blockholder must be compensated *ex ante*. This corresponds to the second term on the right-hand side of (9).

The second component of the block discount is due to an inherent public goods problem in the design of ownership structure. From the point of view of the individual investor, a minimum ownership stake in $t = 0$ is desirable, because this maximizes his liquidity benefits without impairing corporate control *ex post*. This feature of free riding on liquidity provision is quite general[20]; it manifests itself in the present model through the fact that every owner, regardless of his stake, has the same chance of benefiting from liquidity trading *ex post*. In order to persuade an investor to take on more than the one share necessary to obtain this benefit, such shares must receive an additional discount, which is given by the first term on the right-hand side of (9). It is in this sense that the blockholder must be compensated for reduced liquidity in the present model.

Empirically, the discounting of blocks at the issue date is well documented. Wruck (1989) finds small but significant discounts for block equity placements of NYSE and AMEX firms.[21] Consistent with

20. See, for example, Bhattacharya and Gale (1987) for an analysis of the public goods problem in liquidity provision in interbank lending.

21. For reasons we do not know, Wruck (1989) measures the discount with respect to the market price one day before the announcement date. Given that average abnormal returns from day -1 to day 0 alone in her sample are 1.9 percent, her numbers underestimate the block discount as more naively defined.

the prediction of Proposition 1, she suggests that the pricing reflects compensation for reduced liquidity and for "factors other than reduced liquidity".

In a similar vein, for a sample of private equity placements also covering OTC firms, Hertzel and Smith (1993) report mean discounts of 20.1 percent. They, too, "think it unlikely that a pure illiquidity effect can explain the magnitude of the discounts we find," and suggest as an additional explanation, in the spirit of Myers and Majluf (1984) and slightly different from our explanation, costly monitoring by the blockholder at the issue date. In a quite different institutional context, Molin (1996) reports a mean discount of 15.9 percent on private equity placements on the Stockholm Stock Exchange. As another possible application of the above argument, it has been pointed out to us that holding companies in Belgium and Germany generally trade at a discount to the value of their portfolios. We do not have the data to verify this systematically. If this is true, however, it provides another manifestation of the discount established in Proposition 1.[22]

3.2 Dispersed Ownership

When there is no concentration at date $t = 0$, the main question is whether an owner who is large enough to control management emerges after trading in the secondary market in the bad return state. The main factor preventing the emergence of a controlling block at date $t = 1$ is free riding by small patient owners. Small patient owners are willing to sell their shares to a large owner only at the *ex post* value of these shares. Hence, if in the bad state a controlling block were to emerge with probability 1, then small patient owners would only be willing to sell their shares at a price l. But no bidder would offer to buy shares at that price in order to build a controlling block because he needs to be compensated for the intervention cost C. For this reason, the emergence of a controlling block in secondary trading is not guaranteed. There is, however, an important factor favoring the emergence of a controlling block: liquidity selling by the impatient owners. To determine when and how a controlling block emerges, we need to study in detail the response of individual owners to buy offers in secondary trading.

The key observation here is that a small owner considering a selling decision is aware that the decision will have an effect on the overall probability of success of a tender offer. Owners in our model are not atomistic; thus, even if there are many owners, each owner is aware that he may be pivotal with some probability. As is well known from the theory of takeovers (see Kovenock (1984), Bagnoli and Lipman (1988), and Holmström and Nalebuff (1992)), when

22. Because holding companies typically provide real control services, their case is different from the more controversial case of closed-end mutual funds (see, *e.g.*, Lee, Shleifer, and Thaler (1991)).

owners are pivotal there are many Nash equilibria in such tender games. However, one important feature distinguishes our model from this literature: Owners differ according to their impatience to consume. As in the case of concentrated shareholding discussed above, impatient owners will tender their shares with probability 1. But the best response of patient owners is not necessarily unique.

Our problem differs in another way from the existing literature in that we have competition between identical potential bidders as soon as there are at least two patient owners. Thus, in our model the equilibrium tender offer at date $t = 1$ must be such that the owner making the offer is indifferent between remaining a small patient owner and attempting to build a controlling interest. As will be shown below, in the bad state this adds a binding restriction on trading.

In the good state, regardless of liquidity demand, shares trade at their *ex post* value, r, and their allocation is irrelevant for the value of the firm. In the bad state, however, because of the need for intervention, we have to distinguish two cases of liquidity trading: one where the number of impatient owners is at least $T-1$, and the other where it is strictly less than $T-1$.

In the first case equilibrium is easy to characterize. If all owners are impatient, they sell out to an arbitrary outsider at the competitive price 0. If there is exactly one patient owner, he also bids 0 (or slightly more) and acquires the firm at a discount reflecting his insider position. More interestingly, if the number of impatient owners, I, satisfies $T-1 \leq I \leq M-2$, a controlling block can still be built solely with impatient shares, and therefore emerges with probability 1. Each patient owner, by remaining small, gets l in the bad state. Because the successful bidder makes a bid strictly below the *ex post* value of the share, all patient owners hold on to their shares. On the other hand, all impatient owners sell. Thus, if the outstanding bid is b, the new controlling owner gets $l(I+1) - C - bI$. The equilibrium bid is then given by $l(I+1) - C - bI = l$, which implies

$$b(I, 0) = l - \frac{C}{I}. \tag{10}$$

The equilibrium bid $b(I, 0)$ has exactly the same structure as the one in the case of concentrated shareholding, equation (4). Whereas with concentrated shareholding the controlling stake exists *ex ante* and is known to persist, here such a stake does not exist, but is known to emerge with certainty in the bad state. Notice that the controlling interest emerges despite free riding by all the patient owners. Ironically, the intervention cost is entirely borne by the impatient owners. In effect, impatient owners subsidize one patient owner to exercise control in the firm in the future, so that they can sell out in the present. This yields an interesting twist to the famous thesis of "exit, voice, and loyalty" (Hirschman (1970)) as possible responses to organizational failures. Here, owners wishing to sell out can indeed choose the "exit" option. However, although the firm's future does not interest them anymore, they have to pay the price of future corporate control; "exit" is costly.

In the case where the number of impatient owners is smaller, $I < T - 1$, things are more complicated. In this case there are several Nash equilibria in the tender game between patient owners in the bad state; therefore, we shall follow the literature and focus on the unique symmetric mixed strategy equilibrium. Note that, because we suppose that there is maximum dispersion *ex ante*, each owner has only one share to sell at date $t = 1$. Thus, all patient owners are identical. Therefore, it is quite reasonable to suppose symmetric equilibrium behavior by patient owners.

We begin by introducing some notation. Suppose one patient owner makes an offer to buy shares in the bad state. Let $P = M - I - 1$ denote the number of the remaining patient owners. As indicated above, let m be the (symmetric) equilibrium probability of selling for each of these P owners. Let S denote the number of patient shares sold in equilibrium. S is a random variable on $\{0, \ldots, P\}$ with density

$$\sigma^P(S; m) = \binom{P}{S} m^S (1 - m)^{P-S}.$$

Let $K = T - I - 1$ (≥ 1) denote the minimum number of patient shares the offer has to attract in order to generate a controlling stake. Finally, let

$$Q_K^P(m) = \sum_{s=K}^{P} \sigma^P(s; m)$$

denote the equilibrium probability that the tender offer attracts at least K patient shares out of P.

In equilibrium, each of the P potential sellers of shares must be indifferent between selling and not selling. This implies the following relationship between the outstanding bid, b, and the selling probability $m \in (0, 1)$:

$$b = Q_K^{P-1}(m)l, \tag{11}$$

where the left-hand side is the (sure) gain from selling and the right-hand side is the expected gain from holding on to the share. Given b and m, the bidder's expected profits are

$$\Pi = \sum_{s=K}^{P} \sigma^P(s; m)((I + 1 + s)l - C) - \sum_{s=0}^{P} \sigma^P(s; m)(I + s)b. \tag{12}$$

The crucial observation now is the following:

Lemma 2. *For every bid satisfying* (11) *one has* $\Pi < 0$.

The proof of Lemma 2 is in the Appendix. Lemma 2 implies that, whenever there are not sufficient impatient shares to guarantee the success of the tender offer, free riding makes the concentration of shares in the bad state impossible. Any bid that is high enough for patient owners to consider selling — as given by (11) — is too high to pay off for the bidder. Conversely, a bid that is sufficiently low to allow the bidder to recoup future intervention costs does not attract any patient shares. Hence, if $I < T - 1$, dispersion persists with probability 1 in the bad state, and the free-rider paradox, established by Grossman and Hart (1980) for the case of atomistic owners, prevails.

The intuition as to why there is such a stark contrast between the case of high and low liquidity trading is the following. If liquidity demand is high in the bad state, bidders can extract enough value from impatient owners to recoup the intervention costs (as shown in (10)). On the other hand, as soon as a bid needs patient shares to succeed, it has to pay these shares a premium to keep them from free riding. However, because the bidder cannot discriminate between patient and impatient owners, he has to pay this premium to the impatient owners, too, which makes the bid too expensive.[23]

Lemma 2 now immediately implies:

Proposition 2. *If the firm starts out with dispersed ownership in* $t = 0$, *concentration in the bad state obtains with probability*

$$\lambda = \lambda(q, T, M) = \sum_{i = T-1}^{M-1} \binom{M}{i} q^i (1-q)^{M-i}. \qquad (13)$$

The *ex ante* value of the firm is given by

$$V_0^d = 2\pi R + \lambda(1-\pi)(L-C). \qquad (14)$$

Thus the control cost of having no large initial owner is measured entirely in terms of the probability that ownership fails to become concentrated when necessary *ex post*. As in the case of Proposition 1, all *ex post* distortions in liquidity trading wash out *ex ante*. If *all* owners or if *too few* owners are impatient, efficient corporate control fails in the bad return state, but for two different reasons. In the first case, no shareholder *wants* to take on the responsibility (and the costs) of controlling management, in the second case no one *is able* to do it because of excessive free riding by other shareholders.

In practice, of course, a controlling interest is not always built through a simple tender offer. If an owner decides to raise his

23. As in most models of free riding, allowing for bids that are conditional on obtaining 100 percent of the shares would resolve the problem formally. However, empirically this is not appealing.

ownership stake in response to perceived managerial failures, he may be able to buy out some other owners at lower prices, reflecting the imperfections of management control. However, through rising share prices and disclosure requirements the information will get into the market. The preceding analysis suggests that if information disseminates too quickly or if takeovers are very costly, owners will prefer to give up building a controlling interest altogether.[24]

4 • Evaluating the Trade-off

The previous section has analyzed liquidity trading and firm value under two polar ownership structures. It is easy to see that ownership structures with a single block greater than T or with more than one block of size T are suboptimal in our model. Yet, it is less clear whether ownership structures with a block smaller than T (which necessarily involve fewer owners than the fully dispersed structure) may be optimal. Relative to full dispersion such an ownership structure has the advantage of making every shareholder more pivotal in the tender game, thus reducing the free-rider problem of ownership concentration. On the other hand, it has the drawback of providing fewer trading opportunities and, therefore, fewer opportunities to concentrate ownership. *A priori*, it is unclear whether such a structure can give rise to concentration more often when it is needed (that is whether the resulting lambda is higher than in equation (13)).

We do not attempt to determine whether optimal ownership structures in our model can feature small blocks. Based on preliminary calculations and simulations we suspect, however, that ownership structures with a block of size less than T are dominated either by full dispersion or by a structure with a block of size T. The point is that when control is the overriding concern, then even a small reduction in block size below T involves a discrete upwards jump in costs of control loss, compared to only a marginal benefit of higher liquidity. Vice-versa, when liquidity is the primary concern (which means that large blocks cannot be optimal), the marginal benefit of a decrease in control loss is outweighed by the marginal cost of reduced liquidity.

In this section, we discuss how the choice between the two structures analyzed in the last section is influenced by the characteristics of the firm and its environment. Comparison of the expression for V_0^c and V_0^d in equations (6) and (14), respectively, shows immediately that $V_0^c > V_0^d$ if and only if

$$1 - q^{M-T+1} - \lambda > 0 \,. \tag{15}$$

24. Note that Lemma 2 and Proposition 2 do not depend on our assumption that outsiders are less willing to control management than existing owners. This is because the problem is caused by free riding of existing owners. If there are more than $M - T + 1$ patient owners, a tender offer must fail regardless of the number of potential bidders.

This simple condition is a concise description of the trade-off between the costs and benefits of the two ownership structures. If ownership is dispersed, there is a larger group of investors to trade with, but only a reduced chance, measured by λ, of efficient corporate control, due to free riding. Under concentration, corporate control is provided by the large owner, but because of reduced trading opportunities the owners benefit from it only with a reduced probability, $1 - q^{M-T+1}$. As (15) shows, the trade-off depends only on three variables: average liquidity demand q, the total number of shares M, and the efficient controlling stake, $T = (C/L)M$. Other variables, in particular π and R, determinants of the firm's cash flow, do not enter. This is a consequence of our assumption that the costs and benefits of ownership concentration only accrue in bad cash flow states. If ownership structure matters in all states, the comparison becomes more complicated.

We first turn to the question of how ownership structure is affected by the investors' average demand for liquidity, q.

Proposition 3. *There is a critical value* $\bar{q} = \bar{q}(T, M) \in (0, 1)$ *such that concentrated ownership in* $t = 0$ *is optimal for* $q < \bar{q}$, *and dispersed ownership is optimal for* $q > \bar{q}$.

Proof. Ignoring the dependence of λ on M for the moment and writing $\lambda = \lambda(q, T)$, we have $\lambda(0, T) = \lambda(1, T) = 0$. By straightforward calculation the derivative of λ with respect to q is

$$\lambda_q(q, T) = M\binom{M-1}{T-2}q^{T-2}(1-q)^{M-T+1} - Mq^{M-1}.$$

Denote the left-hand side of (15) by $g(q, T)$. We have $g(0, T) = 1$, $g(1, T) = 0$, and

$$g_q(q, T) = -(M-T+1)q^{M-T} - \lambda_q(q, T), \tag{16}$$

hence, $g_q(1, T) > 0$. A further straightforward calculation shows that $g_q(q, T) = 0$ implies $g_{qq}(q, T) > 0$. Hence, g as a function of q can have only local minima. By the above, it therefore has exactly one zero, $\bar{q}$, in $(0, 1)$. ■

At one level, Proposition 3 is intuitive and straightforward: When q is large there is a high value of liquidity (which favors dispersion), and when q is low there is a low value of liquidity (which favors concentration). However, this only concerns the demand for liquidity. The less obvious part of Proposition 3, which our analysis brings out, is that this is also a supply phenomenon. By the assumption of no wealth constraints and maximum *ex post* competition for shares, the supply of liquidity is a constraint only when all shareholders want to sell out simultaneously in the bad state. This happens with probability $(1-\pi)q^n$ where n is the number of initial shareholders. With the remaining probability of $1-(1-\pi)q^n$, shareholders get the full *ex post* value of their shares in both return states — their shares are fully liquid. If q is large, this probability is relatively small, so that increasing it by increasing n is relatively valuable. On the other hand, if q is small, lacking liquidity is relatively less likely and, therefore, reducing n to achieve better corporate control is relatively more valuable.

Proposition 3 shows, in particular, that the existence of a large block in a firm's capital structure can increase as well as reduce firm value. This is because, at the optimum, establishing a block reconciles as well as possible the liquidity needs of investors with the need for corporate control. Away from the optimum, the costs of having a large blockholder may, of course, exceed the gains. This provides a different explanation for the observed variability of stock price reactions to block transactions than the one given by Barclay and Holderness (1989, 1991) and others. There, different stock price reactions are explained by differences in the ability and willingness of blockholders to control management on behalf of the other shareholders. In our model, control by blockholders always has a positive externality on other shareholders, but establishing a block has an opportunity cost that may outweigh the benefit. Of course, these two explanations are mutually compatible.

Proposition 3 implies that if investors are patient, ownership concentration is more likely. This implication is consistent with the empirical observation that shareholdings in Germany and France are more long term than those in the United Kingdom and the United States (*e.g.*, Kojima (1995)). Comparing the ownership structures of French or German publicly listed firms with those in the United States or the United Kingdom, ownership concentration is indeed one of the most striking differences: In the United Kingdom, 16 percent of the largest quoted firms have an owner with a stake of at least 25 percent, against 85 percent in Germany and 79 percent in France (Franks and Mayer (1994)).

We now turn to the relative cost of shareholder intervention. This cost, measured by the size of the efficient intervention stake T, is influenced by two parameters of the model, the actual cost of intervening, C, and the benefit brought about by intervention, L.

Proposition 4. *When T increases, the threshold level of average liquidity demand, $\bar{q}(T, M)$, increases; hence, concentration is more likely to be efficient.*

Proof. We have, for $T \leq (M+1)/2$,

$$g(q, T+1) - g(q, T) = (1-q)q^{T-1}\left(\binom{M}{T-1}(1-q)^{M-T} - q^{M-2T+1}\right). \quad (17)$$

It is not difficult, but lengthy, to verify that this expression is positive if $g(q, T) = 0$. Furthermore, from the proof of Proposition 3, $g_q(\bar{q}(T, M), T) < 0$. This implies the desired result. The case $T > (M+1)/2$ is similar. ■

Proposition 4 states that if intervention becomes relatively more costly (T increases), concentration becomes more valuable at the margin. In other words, when average liquidity demand q is such that investors are indifferent between concentration or dispersion, an increase in the relative cost of intervention makes concentration more attractive than dispersion. Cross-sectionally, one should therefore observe more concentration of ownership if the relative costs of intervention are higher.

This prediction corresponds well to the findings of Demsetz and Lehn (1985) about ownership concentration in large U.S. firms, and also casts some new light on their theoretical arguments. They, too, argue that the costs of monitoring are an important explanatory variable for ownership concentration. They proxy these costs, which are directly unobservable, by the volatility of the exogenous factors influencing corporate performance. The reason for this choice of proxy is that "disentangling the effects of managerial behavior on firm performance from the corresponding effects of these other, largely exogenous factors is costly" (Demsetz and Lehn (1985)). Empirically, they indeed find that firms with higher earnings and stock price volatility tend to have a more concentrated ownership structure. At the same time, however, they predict that ownership concentration should also depend positively on the "control potential", that is, the potential gain from controlling management. Because they measure this variable again by earnings and stock price volatility, they find support for this hypothesis. Our analysis suggests that this might be too quick a conclusion, driven by the fact that Demsetz and Lehn (1985) do not model all the costs of concentration. Indeed, in our model, L can be considered to be a good proxy for the "control potential": the higher L, the larger the gain from intervention in the low return state. Proposition 4 now implies that, with C held constant, increasing L should, on average, decrease concentration. Why this discrepancy? The reason is that an increased benefit from control does not only render *ex ante* concentration more attractive, but also makes it easier to achieve *ex post*, by lowering the stake necessary for efficient intervention. Because *ex ante* concentration has costs in terms of liquidity, it follows that ownership dispersion, with its reliance on *ex post* trading to achieve intervention, becomes more attractive.

Finally, we look at how ownership structure varies with the number of shares, M, which we have argued reflects the transactions costs of trading. Because the comparative statics become more difficult, we only do them asymptotically.

Proposition 5. *For small values of M, both ownership structures, dispersion or concentration, can be optimal, depending on the other parameters. If M tends to infinity, concentration always dominates.*

Proof. Because $C < L$, $q^{M-T+1} \to 0$ and λ is bounded away from 1 for $M \to \infty$. Hence, (15) holds for M large enough. For $M = 2$ (which necessitates $T = 2$) the left-hand side of (15) becomes $(1-q)(1-2q)$, whose sign depends on q. ■

Proposition 5 states that if shares can be arbitrarily finely divided, concentration of ownership is always preferable to dispersion. This is intuitive, because in this case even under ownership concentration the total number of owners $(1 - C/L)M + 1$, can be made large, thus achieving good liquidity without costs in terms of corporate control. This result confirms a conjecture offered by Bhide (1993) in a study of corporate governance issues of publicly traded U.S. companies. Bhide suggests that combining a thick secondary market for shares with the presence of a large controlling block can potentially solve the corporate governance problem. Our analysis shows that, in the framework of our model, this is correct, if shares are arbitrarily divisible. On the other hand, if the transactions costs of trading are taken into account, the denomination of shares is typically bounded below by the costs of transacting and thick secondary markets can no longer be taken for granted. In fact, secondary market liquidity then is one element in the design of corporate ownership structure, and more generally of capital market structure, which is subject to the trade-off analyzed in this paper.

5 • Conclusion

The present paper has developed a simple framework in which to analyze costs and benefits of ownership concentration, if the efficiency of corporate control and secondary market liquidity are both taken into account. An important assumption has been that, in some circumstances, the number of investors holding the firm's stock can be important for secondary market trading. This assumption, which relies on the idea that firms are not monitored perfectly by the market, is a convenient simplification of the general insight that market participation is limited by transaction costs.

A second simplifying assumption of the analysis has been to ignore wealth constraints. This assumption allows us to obtain simple expressions for the pricing of shares in *ex post* trading, because in each contingency owners have enough wealth to pay the *ex post* value of all impatient shares. If this is not the case, *ex post* competition becomes more complicated. However, under reasonable pricing mechanisms the two important qualitative features of *ex post* ownership remain unchanged: With *ex ante* concentration the controlling block, and hence efficient corporate control, persists in bad states of nature, whereas with *ex ante* dispersion a controlling block fails to emerge if liquidity trading is low. For our analysis to hold, this is all that counts (cf. Propositions 1 and 2), because *ex post* distortions and redistributions wash out *ex ante* by symmetry.

The model has one unrealistic implication if one takes the usual interpretation of $t = 2$ as the "long run" seriously. This is that in the long run there is a tendency for ownership to be concentrated. This implication results from the assumption that the firm is put up for sale once and trade afterwards can only result in more concentration, not less. This assumption ignores the fact that if ownership has been concentrated for some time in response to bad firm performance, its owners may well agree to disperse ownership again, thus restarting the cycle of the present paper. Incorporating this feature into a dynamic model of ownership change yields an alternating structure of dispersion and concentration, which is more appealing empirically. We consider such a structure in Bolton and von Thadden (1998) in the context of a model of overlapping generations of investors.

To conclude the paper, it is worth noting that the general problem raised in this paper does not only apply to equity financing. Conceptually, the liquidity-control trade-off is also relevant to debt financing. Thus, one of the benefits of bank financing is that, with a sufficiently large stake, a bank may be willing to monitor the firm and guide managerial decisions. Of course, because the bank itself is not a major shareholder it may not take the *ex post* efficient continuation decision. Nevertheless, even if the bank does not necessarily act in the interest of stockholders, it is likely that its interests are more in line with those of other debt holders. However, for other debt holders, the cost of having a large bank is some lack of liquidity. This is why bond financing may sometimes be preferred to bank financing. An interesting question concerning bond financing then is why there does not seem to be a parallel for bonds to the notion of a controlling interest for stocks. Is this due to regulatory restrictions? Is it due to the fact that with most bonds bondholders are unlikely to ever be in a position where they can exercise control? These are questions for further research.

Appendix: Proof of Lemma 2

Denote by

$$E_K^P(m) = Q_K^P(m)E[S \mid S \geq K] = \sum_{s=K}^{P} s\sigma^P(s; m)$$

the expected number of patient shares including and above the threshold level that are sold in equilibrium. Using the fact that $C = lT$, expected profits from bidding b, given by (11) in the main text, then are

$$\Pi = lE_K^P(m) - lKQ_K^P(m) - (I + mP)b. \tag{A1}$$

Notice that

$$(1-m)Q_K^{P-1}(m) = \sum_{s=K}^{P} \left(1 - \frac{s}{P}\right)\binom{P}{s} m^s (1-m)^{P-s}$$
$$= Q_K^P(m) - \frac{1}{P} E_K^P(m). \tag{A2}$$

Inserting (A2) into (11) and all into (A1) yields

$$\Pi = \frac{l}{1-m}\left[\frac{M-1}{P} E_K^P(m) - (m(M-T) + T - 1)Q_K^P(m)\right]. \tag{A3}$$

Denote the term in brackets in (A3) by $F(m)$. We have

$$Q_{K-1}^{P-1}(m) = Q_K^{P-1}(m) + \binom{P-1}{K-1} m^{K-1}(1-m)^{P-K}.$$

Therefore,

$$F'(m) = ((M-1)K - P(T-1) - mP(M-T))$$
$$\times \binom{P-1}{K-1} m^{K-1}(1-m)^{P-K} - \frac{F(m)}{1-m}. \tag{A4}$$

Remembering that $P = M - I - 1$ and $K = T - I - 1$, we have for $m > 0$,

$$(M-1)K - P(T-1) - mP(M-T) < 0. \tag{A5}$$

Equations (A4), (A5), and the fact that $F(0) = 0$ imply that $F(m) < 0$ for $m \in (0, 1)$. ■

Acknowledgements. We are grateful to the Studienzentrum Gerzensee (ESSET 1995) for its hospitality, and to the Schweizerischer Nationalfonds, the Center for Economic Policy Research (London), and the Ente Luigi Einaudi for financial support. We have received helpful comments from Philippe Aghion, Gabriella Chiesa, Jürgen Dennert, Mathias Dewatripont, Mathias Erlei, Denis Gromb, Oliver Hart, Jürgen Siebel, Jean Tirole, and Josef Zechner. We also thank the participants of the Nobel Symposium on Law and Finance for their comments on an earlier version of this material. An anonymous referee and René Stulz, the editor, have made suggestions that greatly improved the original version.

REFERENCES

[1] Admati, Anat, Paul Pfleiderer, and Josef Zechner, 1994, Large shareholder activism, risk sharing, and financial market equilibrium, *Journal of Political Economy* 102, 1097-1130.

[2] Allen, Franklin, and Douglas Gale, 1994, Limited market participation and volatility of asset prices, *American Economic Review* 84, 933-955.

[3] Bagnoli, Mark, and Bart Lipman, 1988, Successful takeovers without exclusion, *Review of Financial Studies* 1, 89-110.

[4] Barclay, Michael, and Clifford Holderness, 1989, Private benefits from control of public corporations, *Journal of Financial Economics* 25, 371-395.

[5] Barclay, Michael, and Clifford Holderness, 1991, Negotiated block trades and corporate control, *Journal of Finance* 46, 861-878.

[6] Bebchuk, Lucian, 1994, Efficient and inefficient sales of corporate control, *Quarterly Journal of Economics* 103, 957-993.

[7] Bhattacharya, Sudipto, and Douglas Gale, 1987, Preference shocks, liquidity, and central bank policy, in William Barnett and Ken Singleton, eds.: *New Approaches in Monetary Economics* (Cambridge University Press, Cambridge).

[8] Bhide, Amar, 1993, The hidden costs of stock market liquidity, *Journal of Financial Economics* 34, 31-51.

[9] Bolton, Patrick, and Ernst-Ludwig von Thadden, 1998, Liquidity and control: A dynamic theory of corporate ownership structure, *Journal of Institutional and Theoretical Economics*, forthcoming.

[10] Burkart, Mike, Denis Gromb, and Fausto Panunzi, 1997, Large shareholders, monitoring and the value of the firm, *Quarterly Journal of Economics* 112, 693-728.

[11] Coffee, John, 1991, Liquidity versus control: The institutional investor as corporate monitor, *Columbia Law Review* 91, 1277-1368.

[12] Demsetz, Harold, 1968, The cost of transactions, *Quarterly Journal of Economics* 82, 33-53.

[13] Demsetz, Harold, and Kenneth Lehn, 1985, The structure of corporate ownership: Causes and consequences, *Journal of Political Economy* 93, 1155-1177.

[14] Diamond, Douglas, 1984, Financial intermediation and delegated monitoring, *Review of Economic Studies* 51, 393-414.

[15] *The Economist*, 1994, A Survey of Corporate Governance, January 29, 1994.

[16] Franks, Julian, and Colin Mayer, 1994, Ownership and control, Working paper, Oxford University.

[17] Franks, Julian, Colin Mayer, and Luc Renneboog, 1995, The role of large share stakes in poorly performing companies, Working paper, LBS.

[18] Gorton, Gary, and George Pennacchi, 1990, Financial intermediation and liquidity creation, *Journal of Finance* 45, 49-71.

[19] Gromb, Denis, 1993, Is one-share-one-vote optimal?, Working paper, LSE.

[20] Grossman, Sanford, and Oliver Hart, 1980, Takeover bids, the free-rider problem, and the theory of the corporation, *Bell Journal of Economics* 11, 42-64.

[21] Grossman, Sanford, and Oliver Hart, 1988, One share-one vote and the market for corporate control, *Journal of Financial Economics* 20, 175-202.

[22] Hansmann, Henry, 1995, *The Ownership of Enterprise* (Yale University Press, New Haven).

[23] Hart, Oliver, 1995, *Firms, Contracts and Financial Structure* (Oxford University Press, Oxford).

[24] Hertzel, Michael, and Richard Smith, 1993, Market discounts and shareholder gains for placing equity privately, *Journal of Finance* 48, 459-485.

[25] Hirschman, Albert, 1970, *Exit, Voice and Loyalty* (Harvard University Press, Boston).

[26] Holmström, Bengt, and Barry Nalebuff, 1992, To the raider goes the surplus? A reexamination of the free rider problem, *Journal of Economics and Management Strategy* 1, 37-62.

[27] Holmström, Bengt, and Jean Tirole, 1993, Market liquidity and performance monitoring, *Journal of Political Economy* 101, 678-709.

[28] Holthausen, Robert, Richard Leftwich, and David Mayers, 1987, The effect of large block transactions on security prices: A cross-sectional analysis, *Journal of Financial Economics* 19, 237-267.

[29] Jacklin, Charles, 1987, Demand deposits, trading restrictions, and risk sharing, in Edward C. Prescott and Neil Wallace, eds.: *Contractual Arrangements for Intertemporal Trade* (University of Minnesota Press, Minneapolis), 26-47.

[30] Johnson, W. Bruce, Robert P. Magee, Nandu J. Nagarajan, and Harry A. Newman, 1985, An analysis of the stock price reaction to sudden executive deaths: Implications for the managerial labor market, *Journal of Accounting and Economics* 7, 151-174.

[31] Kahn, Charles, and Andrew Winton, 1998, Ownership structure, speculation, and shareholder intervention, *Journal of Finance* 53, 99-129.

[32] Kojima, Kenji, 1995, Corporate governance: An international comparison, Working paper, Kobe University.

[33] Kovenock, Dan, 1984, A note on takeover bids, Note, Purdue University.

[34] La Porta, Rafael, Florencio Lopez-de-Silanes, Andrei Shleifer, and Robert Vishny, 1996, Law and finance, Working paper, Harvard University.

[35] Lee, Charles, Andrei Shleifer, and Richard Thaler, 1991, Investor sentiment and the closed-end fund puzzle, *Journal of Finance* 46, 75-109.

[36] Merton, Robert C., 1987, A simple model of capital market equilibrium with incomplete information, *Journal of Finance* 42, 483-510.

[37] Molin, Johan, 1996, Shareholder gains from equity private placements: Evidence from the Stockholm Stock Exchange, Working paper, Stockholm School of Economics.

[38] Myers, Stewart, and Nicholas Majluf, 1984, Corporate financing and investment decisions when firms have information that investors do not have, *Journal of Financial Economics* 13, 187-221.

[39] Pagano, Marco, 1989, Endogenous market thinness and stock rise volatility, *Review of Economic Studies* 56, 269-288.

[40] Pagano, Marco, and Ailsa Röell, 1998, The choice of stock ownership structure: Agency costs, monitoring and the decision to go public, *Quarterly Journal of Economics*, forthcoming.

[41] Roe, Mark, 1994, *Strong Managers, Weak Owners* (Princeton University Press, Princeton).

[42] Shleifer, Andrei, and Robert Vishny, 1986, Large shareholders and corporate control, *Journal of Political Economy* 94, 461-488.

[43] Shleifer, Andrei, and Robert Vishny, 1997, A survey of corporate governance, *Journal of Finance*, 52, 737-783.

[44] Slovin, Myron, and Marie Sushka, 1993, Ownership concentration, corporate control activity, and firm value: Evidence from the death of inside blockholders, *Journal of Finance* 48, 1293-1321.

[45] von Thadden, Ernst-Ludwig, 1994, Intermediated versus direct investment: Optimal liquidity provision and dynamic incentive compatibility, Working paper, Université de Lausanne.

[46] Wruck, Karen, 1989, Equity ownership concentration and firm value: Evidence from private equity financings, *Journal of Financial Economics* 23, 3-28.

[47] Zingales, Luigi, 1995, Insider ownership and the decision to go public, *Review of Economic Studies* 62, 425-448.

19

Nonlinear Pricing with Random Participation

Jean-Charles Rochet
Lars A. Stole

Abstract

The canonical selection contracting programme takes the agent's participation decision as deterministic and finds the optimal contract, typically satisfying this constraint for the worst type. Upon weakening this assumption of known reservation values by introducing independent randomness into the agents' outside options, we find that some of the received wisdom from mechanism design and nonlinear pricing is not robust and the richer model which allows for stochastic participation affords a more general empirical specification. We develop a multidimensional methodology for addressing this class of problems, providing two important applications to nonlinear pricing. First, with nonlinear pricing by a monopolist the familiar "no-distortion-at-the-top" result persists, but in tandem with the surprising conclusion that there is either no distortion at the bottom or bunching. Second, in a simple model of product differentiated duopolists competing with nonlinear pricing we show that, generally, the duopoly outcome is qualitatively similar to the monopoly outcome. However, when marginal costs are symmetric and competition is sufficiently intense, distortions disappear and the equilibrium outcome takes a remarkably simple form: efficient quality allocations with cost-plus-fee pricing.

1 Introduction

The canonical model of optimal contracting by a principal facing an agent possessing private information[1] makes several simplifying assumptions. First, the private information of the agent is assumed to be one-dimensional, satisfying a single-crossing property with respect to a contractual variable under the control of the principal. Second, the agent's participation decision is modelled as a minimal type-independent level of utility that the agent can obtain if he rejects the offer made by the principal. The effect of

1. This model was introduced by Mirrlees (1971) and later extended and applied to various contexts, notably by Mussa and Rosen (1978), Baron and Myerson (1982) and Maskin and Riley (1984) among others.

these two assumptions is remarkable. The incentive compatibility constraints of the agent can be described by a simple differential equation, with an initial condition given by the participation constraint. From this it follows that the optimal contract exhibits no-distortion for the "best" type agent and downward distortions for all other types. If the agent's type distribution satisfies a common monotone hazard rate property one can also establish the optimality of full separation of types.

Various contributions to the screening literature have explored weakening these two assumptions either by incorporating multi-dimensional types with a corresponding notion of generalized single-crossing[2] or by introducing type-dependent participation constraints.[3] In both variations, the simple results of the standard model disappear except that typically there is no distortion on at least one boundary of the type space. This suggests that we should exercise care in choosing our modelling assumptions if we wish to make more specific claims regarding pricing or allocative efficiency. Unfortunately, even if such a judicious choice of assumptions can be made, the literature on multi-dimensional screening models has demonstrated that in all but the most symmetric and special situations, it is very difficult to obtain closed-form solutions or even a set of loose predictions. The problem arises because, absent a one-dimensional model with a participation constraint which binds for only the lowest type agent, the optimal contract cannot be determined by solving a recursive programme, as for example in the canonical model of Mussa and Rosen (1978). Typically then, we need to rely on numerical simulations with (hopefully) well-chosen parameter values in order to obtain insights. We find this particularly troubling because in a common setting of screening contracts — that of nonlinear pricing — an empirically reasonable model of consumer preferences arguably requires at least two dimensions of type uncertainty and a more general modelling of the participation decision.

The fundamental contribution of this paper is to present and solve a rich class of two-dimensional type preferences in which participation is less than perfectly elastic.[4] Because of a simple (and we think very reasonable) restriction on the contract space, we are able to make a specific set of predictions regarding the nature of optimal contracts for this class. We also find that the methodology which we develop for dealing with the monopoly pricing problem is easily extended to the problem of nonlinear pricing by duopolists, allowing us to make rather strong predictions regarding the nature of duopoly pricing when markets are covered.

Recall the well-known model of Mussa and Rosen (1978), hereafter referred to as simply MR. In their setting, the monopolist

2. McAfee and McMillan (1988) present the conditions of generalized single-crossing. Other contributions on multidimensional screening contracts include Rochet (1984), Laffont, Maskin and Rochet (1987), Lewis and Sappington (1988), Wilson (1993), Armstrong (1996), and Rochet and Choné (1998).

3. See, for example, Lewis and Sappington (1989), Maggi and Rodriguez-Clare (1995) and Jullien (2000).

4. As will be demonstrated, the fraction of participating consumers lies between 0 and 1 under the profit-maximizing price schedule. This is the sense in which we use the term "random participation" in the title.

offers to sell a single good at various levels of quality and price; these offers can be represented as a nonlinear pricing function, $P(q)$, which gives the price schedule for the various offered qualities, q. While precisely speaking it is inaccurate to label this variable-quality setting as "nonlinear pricing" *per se*, it is mathematically equivalent to models in which q is interpreted as quantity and the phrase is appropriate; we will use the phrase "nonlinear pricing" throughout this paper in the broader sense of variable pricing over the characteristics of the final consumption bundle. The consumer's preference (specifically, the consumer's marginal rate of substitution) of quality for money is assumed one-dimensional and denoted by t, with associated gross utility $tq - P(q)$; the consumer's reservation utility is assumed to be independent of type. Under these conditions, Mussa and Rosen show that the optimal contract induces all but the highest consumer type to choose inefficiently low qualities.[5] This simple model has since been used extensively by applied theorists studying regulation, auctions, and labour contracts, to name a few prominent areas of research.

One primary motivation for developing a broader nonlinear pricing methodology is empirical: the need to extend the canonical model to a richer set of two-dimensional preferences is an empirical necessity in the context of nonlinear pricing. As an illustration, consider what an econometrician would find when estimating the price elasticities of demand for the consumers depicted in Mussa and Rosen's model. Most strange, she would observe that if the firm increases its pricing schedule by a small amount (*i.e.* $P(q)$ is shifted upward by a small constant), then the units sold at every quality level except the lowest would remain unchanged. This is because a shift in $P(q)$ has no effect on any of the incentive compatibility conditions since the shift occurs on both sides of the constraints. Moreover, the participation constraint is active only for the lowest type of consumer who is purchasing, and it is irrelevant for all higher types.

As we will see, introducing uncertainty over the participation constraint restores the possibility of smooth demand effects for all consumers. To this end, we extend the MR setting by modelling the participation constraint as a random variable, x, which is also private information to the consumer. Hence, a consumer of type (x, t), has preferences over q and money given by $tq - P(q)$ as before, but importantly this consumer purchases if and only if $\max_q \{tq - P(q)\} \geqq x$. Now, following a general price increase of δ, each consumer's indirect utility of purchasing from the firm falls by δ, which reduces the market share at the low-quality end of the market more greatly than at the high-quality end of the market.[6] This is illustrated in Figure 1. All points of demand, however, are affected.

5. In Maskin and Riley (1984), the contractible variable is quantity rather than quality, but this has no effect on the reported results. We could equally well model q in this paper as quantity rather than quality if we introduced a diminishing marginal utility of q into the consumer's preferences and required (in our oligopoly context) that a consumer purchase from at most one firm in equilibrium. Indeed, instead of letting $u = tq - P(q)$ and costs be given by $C(q) = \frac{1}{2}q^2$, we could alternatively choose $u = tq - \frac{1}{2}q^2 - P(q)$ and $C(q) = cq$. After shifting the support of t by c, the mathematics are precisely the same.

6. To be more precise, the high end market share is affected less than the low end following a uniform increase in prices whenever the distribution of x is log-concave.

FIGURE 1

Changes in market share from a uniform price increase. The shaded region represents the set of parameter values (x, t) for which purchasing occurs. As shown, a uniform increase in $P(q)$ changes the proportions of each t-type purchasing

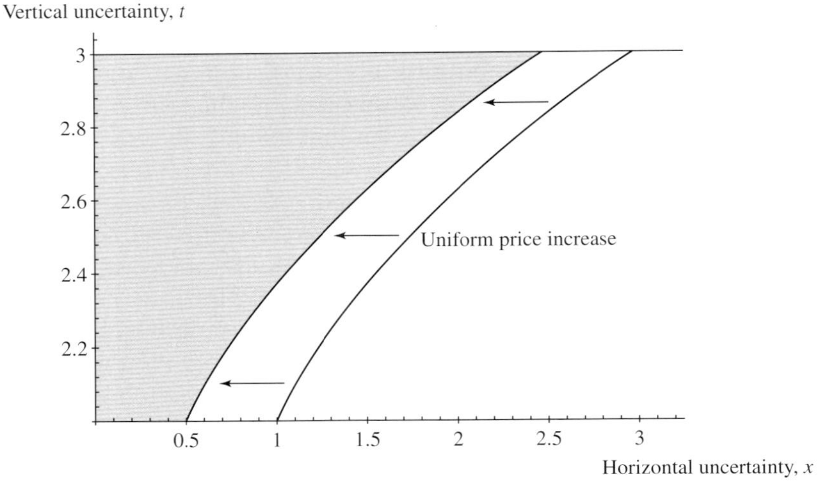

So far, we have motivated our approach by focusing on monopoly models of nonlinear pricing without addressing the issues of imperfect competition. As the previous discussion suggests, however, this is easily incorporated into this framework by taking the distribution of the outside options to be brand specific, x_j, letting j index the different firms. Indirect utilities can be associated with a particular firm's product offerings, $u_j(t) = \max_{q_j} tq_j - P_j(q_j)$, so we can model a consumer of type $(t, x_1, \ldots, x_N)$ consuming brand j if $u_j(t) - x_j \geqq \max\{0, \max_k u_k(t) - x_k\}$ which is endogenously determined by rival firms' price-quality offerings. As we will suggest below, this framework for modelling oligopoly markets is quite general; we only need posit some distribution of horizontal preferences.[7] What is fundamental is that our proposed model affords both a vertical preference parameter along the lines of Mussa and Rosen (1978) while also incorporating a measure of imperfect competition by allowing for distinct horizontal preferences.[8] In this regard, the analysis builds upon the nonlinear pricing work of Stole (1995) which considered oligopoly models of vertical and horizontal preference uncertainty *in isolation*.

We are struck by the fact that, in this instance, econometric practice is ahead of the theoretical literature. It has long been an accepted practice when estimating consumer demands in discrete-choice, multiproduct environments to include an additive disturbance to capture consumer heterogeneity in choice. A common formulation for denoting the utility of consumer i from consuming a product of quality q_k of firm/brand k is

$$U_{ik} = \alpha q_k - \beta p_k + \xi_i + \varepsilon_{ik},$$

7. Such a framework, for example, has been usefully employed recently by Laffont *et al.* (1998*a*, 1998*b*) and Dessein (2000) for studying competition between telecommunications networks. In Dessein (2000), which is closest to the present analysis, both horizontal differentiation between firms and vertical variation over consumer valuation for quality are combined much as in the present analysis. Ivaldi and Martimort (1994) model competition between two firms with heterogenous products using a two-dimensional type model, but their setting ultimately aggregates to a one-dimensional model. Finally, in a recent theoretical and empirical paper by Verboven (1999), a similar setting as the present paper with horizontal and vertical heterogeneity is explored, but the vertical types are limited to two, and the corresponding quality levels are fixed *a priori* and not endogenous.

8. This modelling of competition is in the spirit of some recent empirical work on price discrimination. Leslie (1999), for example, in his study of Broadway theatre ticket pricing finds it useful to incorporate heterogenous valuations of outside alternatives to capture the presence of competing firms while

where ξ_i captures a fixed effect specific to consumer i and ε_{ik} has a zero mean. The consumer optimizes by choosing the k with the highest associated utility, leading to easily computable derived demands. As is now well known, such a specification can generate rather strange empirical implications. Berry, Levinsohn and Pakes (1995), for example, note that the cross-price elasticities are identified by observed market shares, resulting in such absurd results as Yugos and Mercedes automobiles having a similar cross-price elasticity as that of BMWs and Mercedes because BMWs and Yugos have similar market shares. To address this problem, random coefficients are typically introduced, modifying the previous formulation by introducing a cross term, $v_i q_k$:

$$U_{ik} = \alpha q_k - \beta p_k + \xi_i + v_i q_k + \varepsilon_{ik}.$$

This resulting preference characterization allows the data an additional degree of freedom, disconnecting cross-price elasticities from a fixed relationship with relative market shares. What is noteworthy about this formulation is that by redefining $t = (\alpha + v_i)/\beta$ as consumer i's preference for quality and redefining $x_k = (\xi_i + \varepsilon_{ik})/\beta$ as consumer i's outside reservation utility relative to brand k, we have precisely our proposed two-dimensional representation of preferences: *i.e.* up to a multiplicative rescaling, $U_{(t, x_k)} = tq_k - p_k - x_k$. Our approach, therefore, has the advantage of allowing substantially greater freedom in the consumer's preferences so as to fit empirical distributions of prices and consumption better than the benchmark model. The fact that some rather strong conclusions can still be made about the optimal contract in this more general environment is therefore quite significant. Moreover, because we are optimizing over both prices and qualities, we have generated additional implications about the nature of profit-maximizing product designs and allocations.

In Section 2, we present the general class of two-dimensional preferences with which we are interested and the basic programme of a profit-maximizing firm. In Section 3, we begin an analysis of this programme with the simpler case in which t can take on only two values: $t \in \{t_1, t_2\}$. Although some aspects of the two-type case lack robustness, a considerable amount of economic intuition can be learned about monopoly and duopoly nonlinear pricing in this setting. We then proceed in Section 4 to the case in which t is continuously distributed on $[t_1, t_2]$ which may be a better approximation to the real world. Here, some of our results for the two-type case reappear in full generality. In the case of monopoly, we demonstrate that the optimal quality allocation is downward-distorted and bounded below by the Mussa-Rosen allocation. In the case of duopoly, we show that under an economically interesting set of assumptions — providing that the market is covered and that firms are symmetric in

maintaining a distinct form of vertical heterogeneity (in this case, income) to capture variation in preferences over quality. Because Leslie (1999) takes the quality of theatre seats as fixed, he does not solve for the optimal quality-price schedule. Similarly, Ginsburgh and Weber (1996) use a Hotelling-type model to study price discrimination in the European car market, Ivaldi and Martimort (1994) study the market for electricity, and Verboven (1999) studies the automobile engines market.

terms of costs and quality valuations — equilibrium nonlinear price schedules are cost-plus-fixed-fee, and hence all allocations are efficient. When these assumptions are not satisfied, we alternatively find that the resulting nonlinear price schedules nonetheless lie between the case of perfect competition and monopoly.

In Section 5, we take the opportunity to suggest the applicability of our analysis to more general problems in economics, beyond the stylized framework of nonlinear pricing.

2 Incorporating Random Participation

The model we examine is one of standard nonlinear pricing but with random participation decisions. In part for tractability and in part to facilitate comparison, we adopt the linear framework of Mussa and Rosen (1978) and append to the consumer preferences an additive, random component. Like in Mussa and Rosen, a customer with privately known type $t \in T$ obtains *gross* utility $tq - p$ from consuming a unit of output with quality q at a price p. Net utility v (or gain from trade) is obtained by subtracting an outside opportunity cost x. It is therefore equal to

$$v = tq - p - x .$$

Importantly for our purposes, the outside opportunity cost is separable from quality in this preference formulation.[9] The consumer's type t is one-dimensional, but the type space T may be either discrete or continuous. The cost to the firm of producing quality q is $C(q) = \frac{1}{2} q^2$, and the principal's profit margin (per-unit profit conditional on the agent purchasing) is given by

$$\pi = p - C(q) .$$

Joint surplus from trade is given by

$$S(q, t) \equiv tq - \frac{1}{2} q^2 - x .$$

Note that the full-information first-best allocation that maximizes $S(q, t)$ is simply[10] $q^{fb}(t) = t$.

Our main departure from the standard nonlinear pricing environment is our assumption regarding the distribution of x. Typically, it is assumed that $x = \underline{U}$ is a fixed, exogenous parameter representing the agent's outside option.[11] In this case, the probability that an agent of type $t \in T$ purchases from the firm is simply the density[12] of type t, say $f(t)$, providing that $u(t) \geqq \underline{U}$. In the present setting, we consider a more general distribution of x which includes the

9. We have thus assumed that only q can directly screen on the vertical preference component: $\partial^2 v/\partial q \partial t > 0$, while $\partial^2 v/\partial q \partial x = 0$. This is restrictive. One can easily imagine (as in Spulber (1989) and Stole (1995)) that the less brand-sensitive a consumer, the lower the consumer's marginal valuation of quality. Here, we are only allowing brand preferences to affect consumers by shifting utility by a fixed constant, independent of q. Thus, the relative value that a consumer obtains from purchasing a Peugeot instead of a Chevrolet is independent of whether the automobiles are basic models or laden with extra features. While we find this somewhat restrictive and less than ideal, in many consumer markets the amount that brand sensitivity affects preferences for quality seems to be of a second order compared to the effect of q on the marginal willingness to pay for the product.

10. The quadratic cost specification is not very restrictive. Indeed, if C is any strictly convex cost function, q^{fb} is characterized by $C'(q^{fb}) = t$. Since the measurement units of consumers' types and products qualities are not intrinsic, they can be redefined in such a way that costs are quadratic and the first-best allocation is the identity.

11. Che and Gale (2000) consider an auction environment in which potential consumers have random income as well as marginal valuations. In their framework, the consumer can only purchase at a price that does not exceed his wealth level. Although similar in spirit with the present paper, all consumer types participate in the random income setting, so participation is not endogenous.

standard setting as a special case. Specifically, we denote the probability that a consumer of type t with associated indirect utility, $u = \max_q tq - P(q)$, purchases from the firm is given by a smooth market-share function $M(u, t)$.

$$M(u, t) = \text{Prob}\ [(x, t) \mid x \leqq u].$$

Note that this formulation includes the possibility that x and t are correlated, although many of our results will assume independence. In what follows, it will be useful to define the inverse hazard rate of M (over u):

$$H(u, t) \equiv \frac{M(u, t)}{M_u(u, t)}.$$

Throughout the analysis we will require that $H(u, t)$ is nondecreasing in u.

We restrict attention to non-random nonlinear pricing schedules in the general form of $P(q)$. Because a consumer of type t has preferences over the available price-quality allocations which are independent of x conditional on purchasing from the firm, it is without loss of generality to consider direct revelation mechanisms of the form $\{p(t), q(t)\}_{t \in T}$ in the analysis which follows. More precisely, we consider direct revelation mechanisms, taking the consumer's decision to purchase from the firm as given. For any given mechanism offered by a firm, we define the indirect utility of an agent who truthfully reports his type as $u(t)$ and use this to determine the consumer's choice of whether to purchase anything from the firm at all.[13] As such, we model the consumer's choice of purchasing from the firm as an indirect mechanism; no report of $\hat{x}$ is actually made. This is all without loss of generality given our restriction to non-random price schedules.

The restriction to non-random price schedules comes possibly at a slight cost: in general, a firm may benefit by asking its potential customers to announce their private information (x, t), followed by a lottery which determines whether or not the customer consumes the product, and if so, the quality of the product. By randomizing over the probability of consumption, the firm may be able to sort over x as well as t. Unfortunately, when utilizing these two instruments in tandem, a closed-form solution is not generally available and the analysis is considerably more complex.[14] More importantly, random contracts are seldom used in practice. In fact, there are at least two theoretical rationalizations for deterministic contracts which are persuasive and worth noting. First, if we assume that any consumer has the option to anonymously return to a firm to make another purchase (presumably, because the first supply realization was unfavourable),

The impact of the random financial constraint is to append a corner condition to the consumer's standard first-order purchasing condition rather than to affect participation as in the current setting.

12. Strictly speaking, the term density is only appropriate when t is continuously distributed. In the discrete model of this section, $f(t)$ is just the (unconditional) probability of t.

13. This is of course in the spirit of the large literature of discrete choice theory; see Anderson, *et al.* (1992) for thorough survey. More directly related is Bliss (1988), who considers the use of an indirect utility function to model consumer choice among retail stores offering a variety of products and prices. Armstrong and Vickers (2001) follow up this analysis applying the methodology to competitive models of second- and third-degree price discrimination, which we discuss in more detail in Section 4.

14. See Rochet's (1984) extension of Baron and Myerson (1982) to the case of regulating a monopolist with private information over fixed and marginal costs for an early work on this problem.

then there is no value to utilizing random contracts because the consumer's purchasing decision is stationary.[15] Second, if one literally interprets the horizontal uncertainty component as a transportation cost which must be sunk before making a selection from a firm's offerings, there is again no value to randomization. For our purposes, we will content ourselves with the view that random contracts are not feasible and leave the precise reason open.

Because all types of agent with outside options less than $u(t)$ will participate in this mechanism, the unconditional probability of a participating agent of type t is $M(u(t), t)$. The firm's programme is to maximize

$$\int_T M(u(t), t)[S(q(t), t) - u(t)]dt,$$

subject to the incentive compatibility of $\{u(t), q(t)\}_{t \in T}$. The solution of this programme depends upon the underlying structure of T and the underlying joint distribution of (x, t) (which in turn may depend upon the equilibrium market structure under oligopoly). We provide a detailed analysis of this programme for two settings: the discrete case of $T = \{t_1, t_2\}$ (Section 3) and the continuous case of $T = [t_1, t_2]$ (Section 4). In each setting, we consider the possibilities of monopoly and duopoly.

3 A Simple Model with Two Vertical Types

In this section, we assume that $t \in \{t_1, t_2\}$, $t_2 > t_1$, using subscripts $i = 1, 2$ to identify these types. In the two-type setting, we will represent a price-quality schedule as a menu, $\{(p_2, q_2), (p_1, q_1)\}$; such a menu is incentive compatible if and only if for the qualities, q_i, and associated gross utilities, $u_i \equiv t_i q_i - p_i$, $i = 1, 2$,

$$q_2 \Delta t \geqq u_2 - u_1 \geqq q_1 \Delta t, \tag{1}$$

where $\Delta t \equiv t_2 - t_1$. The first inequality is the upward incentive compatibility (UIC) constraint, which requires that the low-type consumer does not prefer to choose the high-type's allocation; the second inequality is the downward incentive compatibility (DIC) constraint and requires that the high-type does not choose the low-type's allocation.

It will be convenient to refer to the profit margins, π_i, on each product. By definition:

$$\pi_i \equiv p_i - C(q_i) \equiv S(q_i, t_i) - u_i. \tag{2}$$

15. To see this, consider the general class of nonlinear price schedules, $P(\phi)$, defined over lotteries of quality, $\phi(q)$. Fix the consumer of type profile (x, t) and some lottery choice ϕ. Then the consumer's indirect utility is given by $u(x, t) = \int_Q \phi(q) \max\{tq - x, u(x, t)\} dq - P(\phi)$, where the second argument of the maximum in the integrand represents the consumer optimally exercising the option to return to the store for another purchase following an unfavourable realization of ϕ. Note that we have assumed the "cost" of x is born only upon consumption of the good and not at each time a lottery is purchased. Denote $\bar{Q}_\phi$ as the subset of qualities in which the consumer is content and chooses not to return to the firm. Then we have $u(x, t) = \dfrac{\int_{\bar{Q}_\phi} tq\phi(q)dq - P(\phi)}{\int_{\bar{Q}_\phi} \phi(q)dq} - x$. Hence, there is no ability to sort over x using a lottery over q. Given that the consumer's preferences are linear in quality and costs are convex, any lottery is suboptimal from the firm's viewpoint.

The incentive compatibility constraints (1) are equivalent to the following conditions on these margins:

$$\Delta S - q_2 \Delta t \leqq \pi_2 - \pi_1 \leqq \Delta S - q_1 \Delta t, \qquad (3)$$

where $\Delta S \equiv S(q_2, t_2) - S(q_1, t_1)$.

In the deterministic participation model (*i.e.* $x = 0$), the market structure determines, in a somewhat extreme fashion, which of these constraints bind. More specifically, in the Mussa-Rosen monopoly case (MR), the downward incentive constraint is always the unique binding constraint, whereas in the oligopoly case (*i.e.* Bertrand competition), profit margins are zero, quality is efficiently provided, and therefore neither IC constraint ever binds. We are now going to see that the random participation model lies between these extremes. We start by examining the monopoly situation.

3.1 Monopoly Nonlinear Pricing

If types t_1 and t_2 were observable, the monopolist would independently choose $\{q_1, u_1\}$ and $\{q_2, u_2\}$ to maximize its profit on each market: *i.e.* to maximize

$$B_i(q_i, u_i) \equiv M(u_i, t_i)(S(q_i, t_i) - u_i).$$

Clearly, chosen qualities would be efficient, $q_i = \arg\max_q S(q, t_i) = t_i$, total surpluses would be $S(q_i, t_i) = \frac{1}{2} t_i^2$, and optimal profit margins would be given (implicitly) by the classical monopoly pricing formula:[16]

$$\pi_i = \frac{1}{2} t_i^2 - u_i = \frac{M(u_i, t_i)}{M_u(u_i, t_i)} = H(u_i, t_i).$$

Since types are not observable, however, the monopoly has to take into account the IC constraints in (1) when maximizing its expected profit: $B = B_1(q_1, u_1) + B_2(q_2, u_2)$.

Which incentive constraints (if any) are binding is determined by whether one type prefers to consume the other's allocation when vertical information is known and horizontal information is private information. As a consequence, the nature of incentive compatibility will depend upon the shape of the horizontal distribution of locations. If the distribution generates sufficiently greater rents for the lower (higher) types, t_1 (t_2), then DIC (UIC) is more likely to bind. To be precise, the incentive-constrained programme gives rise to four possibilities, corresponding to the various possible sets of binding

16. If we let $M(t_i q_i - p_i, t_i)$ represent the demand by type t_i for quality q_i at price p_i with the notation $D_i(p_i)$, then the classical monopoly formula (*i.e.* $MR = MC$) is $p_i + D_i(p_i)/D_i'(p_i) = C(q_i)$. In our notation, marginal revenue is equivalently represented by $p_i - H(u_i, t_i)$ and our formula follows after substitution for π_i.

incentive constraints: both DIC and UIC bind (*i.e.* pooling), only DIC binds, only UIC binds, and neither constraint binds. The first case of pooling can be eliminated by noting that both constraints binding imply $q_2 \geqq q_2^{fb} > q_1^{fb} \geqq q_1$; hence, it cannot be that $q_2 = q_1$.[17] The case in which only the upward incentive constraint is binding can also be eliminated given our assumption about the monotonicity of $H(u, t)$ over u, providing that we make an additional assumption that H is also nondecreasing in t.

Lemma 1. *If classical monopoly margins increase with type t_i (for which it is sufficient that H be nondecreasing in t) then the upward constraint is always slack.*

Proof. Because prices are optimal given qualities, q_1 and q_2, *monopoly margins* are implicitly defined by:

$$\pi_i = H(u_i, t_i) = H\left(\frac{1}{2} t_i^2 - (\pi_i, t_i)\right).$$

Suppose that the UIC constraint binds. That is

$$\Delta\pi = \Delta S - q_2 \Delta t,$$

where $\Delta\pi \equiv \pi_2 - \pi_1$. Necessary conditions for such a constrained optimum require $q_1 = t_1$ and $q_2 \geqq t_2$. Over the set of all $q_2 \geqq t_2$, the right-hand side of the binding UIC constraint is maximized at $q_2 = t_2$ with a value of $-\frac{1}{2}(\Delta t)^2$, hence

$$\Delta\pi = \Delta S - q_2 \Delta t \leqq -\frac{1}{2}(\Delta t)^2 < 0.$$

If $H(u, t)$ is nondecreasing in u and t (and by (1), $u_2 \geqq u_1$), then $\Delta\pi \geqq 0$, a contradiction. The lemma is proved. ■

The assumption that profit margins increase with quality seems reasonable in several contexts (*e.g.* cars, computers, etc.), but one could imagine situations where the reverse is true. In such a case, it is possible that the upward incentive constraint is binding, and hence excessive provision of quality will emerge in equilibrium. For example, if there is perfect correlation between x and t, then we are in a principal-agent setting with one-dimensional type-dependent participation constraints; as has been shown by Lewis and Sappington (1989), Maggi and Rodriguez-Clare (1995) and Jullien (2000), upward distortions can arise.

Coming back to our context, we have thus established that, because only the downward incentive constraint is relevant, the optimal allocation always satisfies $q_2 = q_2^{fb}$ and $q_1 \leqq q_1^{fb}$. To say more about the equilibrium quality allocations, additional assumptions are useful. In particular, we assume for the remainder of this paper that t and x are independently distributed with t having the probability

17. This result also identifies a severe limitation of the two-type model.

distribution $f(t)$ and x having a log-concave cumulative distribution of $G(x)$ on $[0, +\infty)$, with density $g(x)$ satisfying $\lim_{x \to +\infty} xg(x) = 0$. In the context of monopoly,[18] this implies that

$$M(u, t) = G(u)f(t),$$

which further implies that H is independent of t:

$$H(u) = \frac{G(u)}{g(u)}.$$

Let us introduce an auxiliary function for the profit margin at S:

$$\pi(S) \equiv \arg\max_{\pi} \pi M(S - \pi, t). \tag{4}$$

$\pi(S)$ represents the unit profit extracted by the monopolist when the total surplus from trade is S (ignoring incentive compatibility issues). Notice that log concavity of G (and hence M) implies that $\pi(S)$ is uniquely defined by the first-order condition of (4):

$$\pi(S) = H(S - \pi(S)). \tag{5}$$

Because $H(u)$ is monotonic, so is $\pi(S)$, which implies that the upper incentive constraint never binds; this is a particular case of Lemma 1.

In order to characterize further the cases in which the downward constraint binds, we find it convenient to assume that H is convex in u. This additional assumption is equivalent to the property that the (relative) share of surplus extracted by the monopolist, namely $\pi(S)/S$, does not decrease with S.[19] Under this assumption, the monopoly solution can be completely characterized. Indeed, the following proposition establishes that the DIC binds and q_2 is distorted downward when the total gains from trade are large relative to the consumers' heterogeneity. On the contrary, if the surplus is small (or the consumers' heterogeneity over T is large) we obtain the surprising result that the monopoly solution involves *no quality distortion* (*i.e.* the allocation is identical to the complete information solution). In order to see this, let us introduce some new notation:

- $\gamma \equiv t_2/t_1$, which is a (relative) measure of consumers' vertical type heterogeneity;
- $S_1 \equiv \frac{1}{2} t_1^2$, which measures the gains from trade for t_1 at the (first-best) efficient level; note that for a given γ, an increase in S_1 proportionally increases $S_2 = \frac{1}{2} t_2^2 = \gamma^2 S_1$, so S_1 also measures the gains from trade for t_2.

18. As we will see, this is not the case for duopoly in general as the outside option depends upon the indirect utility generated by the other firm's price schedule.

19. To see this, note that $\pi(S) = H(S - \pi(S))$ is equivalent to $S = \pi(S) + H^{-1}(\pi(S))$. Since the left-hand side is linear in S, π is convex iff H is convex. This is also equivalent to the property that the mark-up (defined as unit profit divided by price) increases with quality (ignoring incentive compatibility issues). Again, this property seems plausible for the type of markets we have in mind (*e.g.* cars, computers, etc.) but its validity is ultimately an empirical question.

Proposition 1. *If H is convex, the monopoly solution has two regimes:*

- *For* $\gamma > 1 + 2H'(0)$ *and* S_1 *small enough (specifically,* $S_1 \leqq S^*(\gamma)$*), qualities are not distorted.*
- *In all other cases, the low quality is distorted downward.*

Proof. For the parameters of (γ, S_1) in which DIC is slack, necessary conditions for optimality require $q_i = t_i$ and hence $S(q_1, t_1) = S_1$ and $S(q_2, t_2) = \gamma^2 S_1$. Thus, DIC slackness is equivalent to

$$\frac{\pi(\gamma^2 S_1) - \pi(S_1)}{S_1} \leqq (\gamma - 1)^2 . \tag{6}$$

When H is strictly convex, so is π (see footnote 19) and the left-hand side of (6) is an increasing function of S_1. Hence, there exists a function $S^*(\gamma)$ such that DIC binds for all $S_1 > S^*(\gamma)$. When S_1 tends to zero, the left-hand side of (6) converges to $\pi'(0)(\gamma^2 - 1)$. Differentiating (5) at $S = 0$ we obtain

$$\pi'(0) = H'(0)(1 - \pi'(0)),$$

or

$$\pi'(0) = \frac{H'(0)}{1 + H'(0)} .$$

Therefore the DIC constraint is satisfied for S_1 close to 0 if and only if

$$\frac{H'(0)}{1 + H'(0)} (\gamma^2 - 1) < (\gamma - 1)^2 ,$$

which is equivalent to $\gamma > 1 + 2H'(0)$. Hence, $S^*(\gamma) > 0$ for $\gamma > 1 + 2H'(0)$. ■

Let us now add another dimension to our comparative statics analysis by introducing a scale parameter for the horizontal consumer heterogeneity: $\sigma > 0$. We assume from now on that the reservation utility of the consumer is σx, where x is, as before, a random variable drawn from the c.d.f. G. The introduction of σ allows us to encompass both the previous case $(\sigma = 1)$ and the Mussa-Rosen framework $(\sigma = 0)$, among others. The profit function now becomes

$$B(q, u, t, \sigma) = \left(tq - \frac{1}{2} q^2 - u\right) G\left(\frac{u}{\sigma}\right) .$$

By the envelope theorem, we know that profit will always be decreasing in σ.[20] Because of our linear-quadratic preferences, this function satisfies the following homogeneity property:

$$B(q, u, t, \sigma) = \sigma B\left(\frac{q}{\sqrt{\sigma}}, \frac{u}{\sigma}, \frac{t}{\sqrt{\sigma}}, 1\right) .$$

20. The result that profits are decreasing in σ must be interpreted carefully, as σ has both a mean effect as well as a dispersion effect.

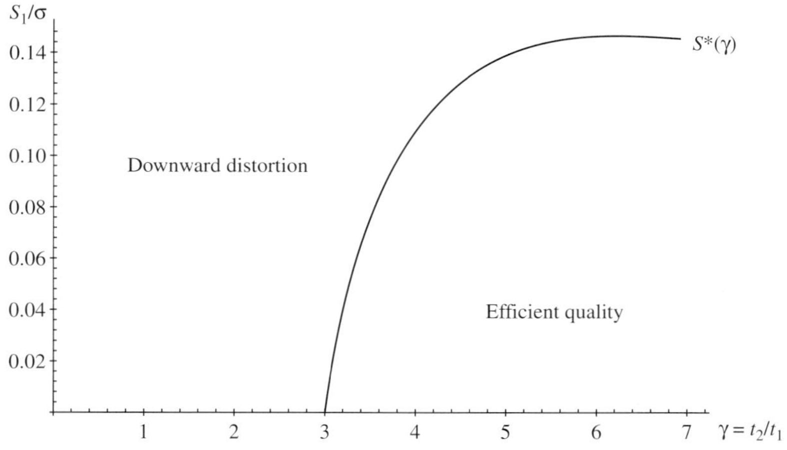

FIGURE 2

The monopoly solution with a discrete 2-type distribution of t and an exponential distribution of x: $G(u) = 1 - e^{-u}$

Therefore, a simple adaptation of Proposition 1 allows us to study the influence of σ in the monopoly setting.

Proposition 1′. *If H is convex and $\gamma > 1 + 2H'(0)$, then the monopoly solution involves no quality distortion if $\sigma \geqq S_1/S^*(\gamma)$.*

Proof. By the homogeneity property, the condition for no distortion from Proposition 1 becomes

$$\frac{1}{2}\left(\frac{t_1}{\sqrt{\sigma}}\right)^2 \leqq S^*((t_2/\sqrt{\sigma})/(t_1/\sqrt{\sigma})).$$

After simplification we obtain

$$\sigma \geqq \frac{S_1}{S^*(\gamma)}. \quad \blacksquare$$

As an illustration of Propositions 1 and 1′, consider the case in which G is an exponential distribution as depicted in Figure 2. In this case, $1 + 2H'(0) = 3$. For greater (vertical) heterogeneity than $\gamma = 3$, large σ and/or low gains from trade, efficient quality allocation emerges.[21]

Compared to the MR setting, we have already one clear distinction: there exists a range of parameters for which qualities are not distorted. Intuitively, when the heterogeneity over x is sufficiently high, the monopolist finds it is more effective to set quality efficiently, thereby increasing market penetration, than to distort quality and extract higher rents from high type customers, thereby lowering the high type's market participation.

A natural second line of inquiry is to compare the magnitude of the classic MR distortion with the distortion (when it occurs) in the

21. Readers familiar with the two-type version of Mussa-Rosen's model may wonder about the optimality of offering two different qualities when γ is sufficiently large. In the MR setting where t is uniformly distributed, for example, the monopolist will not serve the $t = t_1$ customer whenever $\gamma \geq 2$. When x is stochastic and unbounded above, however, it can be shown that the firm will always offer a full product line in the efficiency region.

random-participation model. Whenever the downward-local incentive condition is binding (*i.e.* there is a distortion), the firm's first-order conditions can be simplified to

$$S_q(q_1, t_1) = \Delta t\left(\frac{f(t_2)G(u_2)}{f(t_1)G(u_1)}\right)\left(1 - \frac{g(u_2)}{G(u_2)}[S(q_2, t_2) - u_2]\right).$$

Comparing this to the MR model of fixed market share in which $G(u) = 1$ for all u,

$$S_q(q_1, t_1) = \Delta t\left(\frac{f(t_2)}{f(t_1)}\right),$$

we can see that the distortion is reduced in the presence of horizontal heterogeneity for the intuitive reason that leaving rents to the high type now has a benefit which is absent under the standard MR setting. If more rents are left to the high type, the benefit of distorting quality is reduced, as we see by the fact that the additional term $1 - (g(u_2)/G(u_2))(S(q_2, t_2) - u_2)$ is less than 1. This term can be interpreted as the marginal cost of leaving rents to the high types; it is less than unity because there is an added benefit of increased market share which is not present in the standard MR setting.

It is also the case that the presence of horizontal uncertainty tilts the distribution of types toward weighting the high-type; this effect is present in the $G(u_2)/G(u_1) > 1$ term and, other things equal, increases the value of extracting rents from the high types. It is possible, therefore, that the absolute level of the distortion increases in the presence of horizontal uncertainty, but this is an artifact of our particular two-type framework and will be absent in the uniform, continuous-type setting analysed in Section 4.[22]

3.2 Duopoly Nonlinear Pricing with Two Types

Consider now the case of duopolists (two firms denoted "left" and "right", $j = L, R$) competing on a horizontal market segment with unit length as in Hotelling's (1929) model of spatial product differentiation, and suppose each firm competes by offering a nonlinear price schedule, $P_j(q_j)$, from which the consumer chooses a quality if the consumer decides to purchase a product. Denote the gross utility which the consumer obtains from firm j as $u_j(t) \equiv \max_q tq - P_j(q)$. By analogy to the monopoly case, we will denote by σ the transportation cost per unit distance. The net utility of a consumer who

[22] We thank Meg Meyer for pointing out this second effect. As a numerical example, consider first $t_1 = 2$, $t_2 = 3$, $G(u) = u$ and an uniform distribution on t: $f(t_1) = f(t_2) = \frac{1}{2}$. Simple calculations reveal that $q^{fb} = 2 > q_1 = 1.6 > q_1^{mr} = 1$. On the other hand, if $f(t_1) = 0.9$ and $f(t_2) = 0.1$, the second inequality is reversed: $q_1 = 1.87 < q_1^{mr} = 1.89$.

purchases from firm j is thus $u_j(t) - \sigma x_j$ where $x_L = x$ and $x_R = (1-x)$. Hence, the marginal customer (indifferent between purchasing from firm L or R) is defined by the location

$$\hat{x}(t) = \frac{1}{2} + \frac{u_L(t) - u_R(t)}{2\sigma}.$$

When the marginal consumer prefers purchasing to not purchasing, firm L's market share is simply the measure of consumers lying to the left of $\hat{x}$. When the marginal-L consumer prefers to buy from no one rather than from firm R, we are in a case of local monopolies and firm L's market share is the measure of consumers to the left of $u_L(t)/\sigma$. Combining these notions, we characterize firm L's market share as a function of u_L and t,

$$M_L(u_L, t) = G\left(\min\left\{\frac{u_L}{\sigma}, \frac{u_L - u_R(t) + \sigma}{2\sigma}\right\}\right) f(t),$$

and define the associated inverse hazard rate as

$$H_L(u_L, t) = \frac{M_L(u_L, t)}{\partial M_L(u_L, t)/\partial u_L}.$$

Notice that although x is distributed independently of t, t enters G through $u_R(t)$. We also extend our assumption of the log concavity of G to require that $1 - G$ is similarly log concave.

The complete solution of the competitive two-type case is tedious because of the presence of a kinked demand curve similar to that in the original Hotelling framework. At prices (and associated utilities) which make the marginal customer indifferent among all three alternatives (firm L, firm R, and no consumption), each firm's demand curve exhibits a kink: higher prices generate a monopoly response while lower prices result in a competitive response. Of course, when more types are introduced, the measure of consumers which are present at a kink goes to zero, so this is not a concern in the continuous-type model of Section 4. For our present purposes, we ignore the kinked region and instead focus on the other more economically relevant regimes.

For σ sufficiently large (*e.g.* transportation costs are sufficiently high) in equilibrium both types of consumers will consider only options of either purchasing from the nearest firm or not purchasing at all. This is a case of *local monopolies*: $u_L(t) + u_R(t) < \sigma$ for $t \in \{t_1, t_2\}$. The analysis is as before: qualities are either efficient (for sufficient heterogeneity among the types) or distorted downward.

For σ sufficiently low, on the other hand, both types of customers will view their second-best as consuming from the more distant firm in equilibrium; the option of not consuming at all is dominated. This is a case of *full competition*: $u_L(t) + u_R(t) > \sigma$ for $t \in \{t_1, t_2\}$. Remarkably, quality allocations are set at their efficient levels under full competition.[23]

Proposition 2. *Under full competition, there exists a unique equilibrium outcome in which firms allocate the same qualities. In such an equilibrium, qualities are not distorted and can be implemented using cost-plus-fixed-fee prices:* $P_j(q) = C(q) + F_j$.

The proof is provided in the Appendix. Briefly, uniqueness within the class of symmetric quality outcomes follows from applying the argument used in Lemma 1: neither DIC nor UIC can bind for the firms, hence if there is an equilibrium, it must arise with slack incentive constraints. The existence of such a symmetric equilibrium is easily demonstrated by construction: providing that the rival offers cost-plus-fixed-fee prices, a firm will find it optimal to sell efficient quality levels using cost-plus-fixed-fee pricing. The only asymmetry which arises within this class is potentially on the size of the fixed fees. For any given distribution of location, $G(x)$, there is a unique pair of fixed fees which may differ in magnitude when the distribution G is not symmetric on $[0, 1]$.

Under full competition, each firm offers price schedules which are cost-plus-fixed-fee: $P_j(q) = C(q) + F_j$. The fixed fees are set as by a monopolist, trading off the marginal rent of an additional customer against the inframarginal loss from lower fees. Fundamentally, the cost-plus-fixed-fee result requires that (i) the market is covered, and (ii) neither firm has a comparative advantage in providing utility through quality (*i.e.* costs and preferences for quality are symmetric). A similar finding has been noted by Armstrong and Vickers (2001).[24] The result is intuitive if one views the firms as competing in utility space which is the approach emphasized in the methodology of Armstrong and Vickers (2001). In this sense, because each firm's competitive advantage is derived from location and not quality provision, there is no reason to introduce a distortion in quality. Note that symmetry in G is not relevant for the result as the location advantage does not interact with quality provision when the market is covered. As we will see in Section 4, however, any departure from full coverage or cost symmetry alters this result. Additionally, if we were to introduce correlation between location and t (or equivalently if transportation costs were correlated with vertical preferences, as explored in the network competition model of Dessein (2000)), the conclusion of this proposition would not be valid.

23. The existence of asymmetric equilibria remains an open question.

24. Also related in spirit, Schmidt-Mohr and Villas-Boas (1999) consider a competitive model with two-types in the vertical dimension and a standard Hotelling framework in the horizontal dimension. Due to their economic setting of adverse selection in credit markets (*i.e.* the competing firms are directly affected by the consumer's vertical type), they do not find full efficiency in equilibrium.

The intuition behind Proposition 2 deserves some comment. Suppose that the R firm offers cost-plus-fee pricing. For the moment, suppose that firm L actually observes t_i and can contract directly on it. In this case, qualities would be chosen at their efficient levels, $q_{L,i} = t_i$, and prices would be chosen to maximize profits given R's offers. This requires (when the market is covered) that

$$\pi_{L,i} = 2H_L\left(\frac{\frac{1}{2}t_i^2 - \pi_{L,i} - u_{R,i} + \sigma}{2\sigma}\right).$$

Using the fact that R is offering cost-plus-fixed-fee pricing (*i.e.* $\pi_{R,i} = \frac{1}{2}t_i^2 - u_{R,i} = F_R$), this expression simplifies to

$$\pi_{L,i} = 2H_L\left(\frac{F_R - \pi_{L,i} + \sigma}{2\sigma}\right).$$

The solution to this equation has the optimal profit margin for firm L independent of i because the right-hand side of the equation is constant across t_i. Hence, we can write $\pi_{L,i} = F_L$. As a consequence, L's optimal pricing schedule is to offer $q_i = t_i$ at a price of $F_L + \frac{1}{2}t_i^2$ to each type i. But even without the ability to price discriminate *directly* on t_i, firm L can implement this allocation by offering a cost-plus-fixed-fee price schedule without observation of t_i. Hence, cost-plus-fixed-fee pricing is an equilibrium and the equilibrium profits are precisely the same as those in the Hotelling model in which qualities are *exogenously* fixed to their efficient levels and self-selection is not an issue.[25] The crucial ingredient in this argument is that when the market is covered, the market share function is independent of t at the efficient qualities. In short, each firm's demand becomes independent of t when the market is covered and quality is efficiently provided by competitors, so distortions to segment the market over t are not desirable.

A remaining case to consider is the mixed regime in which transportation costs are such that in equilibrium the high-type quality market is competitive while the low-quality market contains two local monopolies: $u_{L,2} + u_{R,2} \geqq \sigma \geqq u_{L,1} + u_{R,1}$. In this mixed setting, the high-type consumer still obtains efficient quality, while the low-type customer may be served inefficiently low quality to reduce the rents going to the high-end of the market. Whether or not a downward distortion emerges on the low end of the market depends (as in the monopoly case) on the ratio of the two type parameters and the size of transportation costs. Rather than explore this mixed regime in the context of two-types, we defer such an analysis until the general

25. Verboven (1999) considers such a setting with exogenous qualities and shows that cost-plus-fixed-fee pricing emerges in a Hotelling market.

FIGURE 3

The duopoly solution with a uniform distribution over $\{t_1, t_2\}$ and a uniform distribution over x: $G(x) = x$. Note that $S^*(\gamma)$ (represented by the dotted line) is vertical at $\gamma = 3$ because $G(u)$ is uniform and hence H is linear (and only weakly convex)

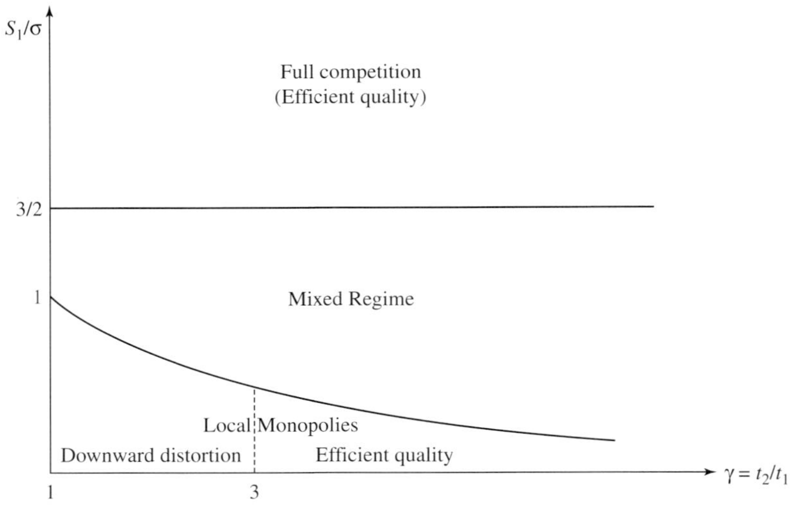

model in Section 4. Figure 3 illustrates our main findings for the two-type duopoly, in the case of a uniform distribution of customers.

4 • A General Model with Continuous Types

Although useful for building simple intuitions, the two-type specification may be misleading, since it generates some non-robust results (for example pooling is impossible in a two-type model). In order to go further, we could have studied the general discrete specification with N types. For the sake of transparency, we study instead the continuous types model, which is in fact very close to the specifications used in econometric studies of differentiated products markets (see for example Berry *et al.* (1995) and the references therein). We start by developing a general methodology (Subsection 4.1). Then we apply it to the monopoly case (Subsection 4.2) and to the duopoly case (Subsection 4.3).

4.1 Characterization of a Firm's Optimal Strategy

We keep the same notation as before: $q(t)$, $p(t)$ and $u(t)$ are respectively the quality, price and utility for a consumer of type t. The only change with respect to Section 3 is that the type space T is now the interval $[t_1, t_2]$.

As is standard in the literature, the following lemma characterizes the set of implementable allocations.

Lemma 2. *A piecewise-smooth quality function, $q(t)$ is implementable by some price function $p(t)$ if and only if $q(t)$ is nondecreasing, $u(\cdot)$ is absolutely continuous, and $\dot{u}(t) = q(t)$ at all continuity points of $q(\cdot)$.*

Consider now the probability $M(u(t), t)$ of a purchase by a consumer of type *t*. If the firm is a monopoly, a purchase will be made by type (x, t) iff $u(t) \geqq \sigma x$, *i.e.* with conditional probability $G(u(t)/\sigma)$. The unconditional measure of consumers of type *t* who participate is thus:

$$M(u(t), t) = G\left(\frac{u(t)}{\sigma}\right)f(t).$$

If instead the firm is the "left" duopolist in a Hotelling model, we have a more complicated formula:

$$M(u(t), t) = G\left(\min\left\{\frac{u(t)}{\sigma}, \frac{1}{2} + \frac{u(t) - u_R(t)}{2\sigma}\right\}\right)f(t),$$

where $u_R(t)$ represents the utility provided by the "right" duopolist to a consumer of type *t* (see Section 4.2).

In spite of the different forms of these probabilities $M(u(t), t)$, the methodology we are going to develop will apply to both cases. Let us now turn to this methodology.

Given that the unconditional probability of an agent of type *t* who also purchases is $M(u(t), t)$, the firm's programme is to maximize

$$\int_{t_1}^{t_2} M(u(t), t)[S(q(t), t) - u(t)]dt,$$

subject to $\dot{u}(t) = q(t)$ and $\dot{q}(t) \geqq 0$ for all *t*.[26]

This programme seems simple enough, but unlike the standard paradigm with certain participation constraints, it is not easily solved. First, it is nonlinear in $u(t)$, which prevents us from integrating the objective function by parts and incorporating the agent's incentive compatibility condition into the programme directly; and because *u* and *q* are nonseparable in the objective function, unlike the problem of Mussa and Rosen, this programme is inherently nonrecursive. Second, as we will demonstrate below, even with strong restrictions on *G*, pooling will typically emerge in optimal pricing schedules whenever the ratio t_2/t_1 is sufficiently large. Thus, we find it useful to proceed using more powerful control-theoretic techniques.

26. Strictly speaking, this inequality has to be taken in a generalized sense: $\dot{q}(t)$ is a positive measure (since *q* is not necessarily differentiable). However, we check *ex post* that the solution is such that $\dot{q}(t)$ is in fact a piecewise continuous function.

As we show in the Appendix, when full separation is optimal, then the following second-order differential (Euler) equation characterizes the optimal utility profile:

$$M_u(u,t)\left(u - \frac{1}{2}\dot{u}^2\right) + M(u,t)(2-\ddot{u}) + M_t(u,t)(t-\dot{u}) = 0, \quad (7)$$

with the boundary conditions that $q(t) = q^{fb}(t)$ for $t = t_1$ and $t = t_2$, and the incentive compatibility requirement that $q(t)$ is given by $\dot{u}(t) = q(t)$.[27]

One curious change already is evident: there is efficiency for both the high *and the low* types when there is full separation. Because full separation can occur (as shown below), we have substantial departure from the traditional results of screening contracts. Indeed, the efficiency on the boundary result is a common occurrence in many multi-dimensional settings (*e.g.* Rochet and Choné (1998)), as well as in the optimal taxation literature (*e.g.* Seade (1977) and Ebert (1992)). In the present setting, the economic intuition at the top is distinct from that at the bottom. Efficiency at the top arises for a familiar and robust economic reason: the only purpose for distorting quality for type t is to extract rents from higher types, which do not exist at $t = t_2$. Efficiency at the bottom, however, is based on more subtle reasoning. In short, the first-order condition with respect to $u(t_1)$ is very close to the marginal social product of quality at $t = t_1$, where "very close" is related to the distance between adjacent types; we explore this intuition more formally in the first part of the Appendix. Hence, in the discrete setting, efficiency at the bottom does not arise when incentive constraints bind, but the distortion decreases to zero as the type space T becomes finer. In the limit as t is distributed continuously, efficiency emerges at the bottom.[28]

Another notable feature of this programme is that after substitutions are performed, the solution is found by solving a second-order boundary-value problem rather than a first-order ordinary differential equation as in the standard setting. This increasing complexity illustrates the non-recursive nature of our multi-dimensional problem. In the standard one-dimensional setting, $q(t)$ and $u(t_1)$ are chosen optimally, then $u(t)$ is constructed by straightforward integration of $q(t)$, and then $p(t)$ is constructed to conform with utility, $p(t) = tq(t) - u(t)$. In the present setting, the functions of $q(t)$ and $u(t)$ are jointly determined as evident by the fixed-point nature of a boundary-value problem.

Unfortunately, the quality levels associated with the solution to (7) will sometimes fail to be monotonic. In such a setting, the optimal screening contract will necessarily have regions of bunching in which an interval of customers consumes the same allocation. It is

27. In the general case, (7) will hold over any fully separating region of t, but the endpoints will not necessarily be efficient.

28. Note as Proposition 1 indicates, efficiency at the bottom also arises when the incentive constraints do not bind.

straightforward to show that in such a case, a similar boundary-value problem arises for each region of separation, but now the boundary values for the region are determined endogenously. Again, the non-recursive nature of the problem rears its head.

We now turn to a more complete analysis of the monopoly solution.

4.2 Monopoly Nonlinear Pricing with Continuous Types

To illustrate in greater detail how random participation constraints can be incorporated into nonlinear pricing problems, we take the distribution of types to be distributed uniformly on $[t_1, t_2]$ (and independently of x) with $2t_1 \geqq t_2$ for the remainder of this paper. As Mussa and Rosen (1978) have shown, the optimal quality allocation in such a setting with a *fixed* participation constraint is simply

$$q^{mr}(t) \equiv q^{fb(t)} - (t_2 - t) \equiv t - (t_2 - t) = 2t - t_2 .$$

That is, the Mussa-Rosen allocation is the first-best full-information allocation, $q^{fb}(t) = t$, less an informational rent term $(t_2 - t)$. Our assumption that $2t_1 \geqq t_2$ ensures that $q^{mr}(t) \geqq 0$ for all t in $[t_1, t_2]$.

Coming back to our random-participation model and applying the Euler equation (which must hold over all regions of separation) to this simplified setting yields:

$$g\left(\frac{u(t)}{\sigma}\right)\left(u(t) - \frac{1}{2}\,\dot{u}(t)^2\right) = \sigma G\left(\frac{u(t)}{\sigma}\right)(\ddot{u}(t) - 2) . \qquad (8)$$

Notice that the Mussa-Rosen allocation $\dot{u}(t) = 2t - t_2$ satisfies (8) when $g(u) = 0$ and $G(u) = 1$; more generally, it will not. Notice also that the homogeneity property with respect to σ still holds in the continuous framework: if u_1 solves (8) when $\sigma = 1$, then $u_\sigma(t) = \sigma u_1(t/\sqrt{\sigma})$ solves it for arbitrary σ. The following characterization result is proven in the Appendix.

Proposition 3. *When G is log-concave, pooling can only occur at the bottom. To be precise, the monopolist's optimal nonlinear pricing contract satisfies the following conditions:*

- *there exists a lower interval $[t_1, t_0]$ of the type space (perhaps degenerate, $t_1 = t_0$) over which consumers buy the same product q_0 at price $p_0 = t_0 q_0 - u_0$, where u_0 is the indirect utility of types t_0;*
- *in the upper interval of the type space, $[t_0, t_2]$, u satisfies the differential equation*

$$g\left(\frac{u(t)}{\sigma}\right)\left(u(t)-\frac{1}{2}\dot{u}(t)^2\right) = \sigma G\left(\frac{u(t)}{\sigma}\right)(\ddot{u}(t)-2) \qquad (9)$$

and the boundary conditions that $\dot{u}(t_0) = q_0$, $u(t_0) = u_0$, *and* $\dot{u}(t_2) = t_2$.

Proposition 3 provides an informative characterization. As is standard in the nonlinear pricing literature with certain-participation constraints, the monopolist's optimal quality allocation exhibits no distortion for $t = t_2$. At $t = t_1$, however, either no distortion occurs or there is bunching. Either of these results is a departure from the standard results in the literature.[29]

There is a third distinction between the characterization in Proposition 3 and the standard Mussa-Rosen setting that is more general than our present model: full coverage of the market by a monopolist is never optimal. When the support of x is unbounded, it is clearly never profitable to sell to some measure of the low-t and high-x population. However, even if we considered bounded distributions of $x \in [0, \bar{x}]$, full coverage remains suboptimal. The generality of this result in multi-dimensional environments was first noted by Armstrong (1996). In the present context, suppose that the market was just covered so that no consumer surplus accrued to type $(t_1, \bar{x})$. The firm could uniformly increase the price schedule by ε while suffering a loss of consumers of order ε^2. This form of optimal non-coverage is not present in one-dimensional models of the Mussa-Rosen variety.

There is one very strong sense under which the Mussa-Rosen results remain robust: it provides a lower bound for the quality which can arise in the more general two-dimensional setting. Making use of the monotonicity of $G(u)/g(u)$, we obtain the following conclusion regardless of the degree of pooling.

Proposition 4. *The monopolist's allocation satisfies* $q(t) \in (q^{mr}(t), q^{fb}(t)]$ *for all* $t \in (t_1, t_2)$.

Thus far, a few clear distinctions emerge from the standard fixed-participation-constraint models. First, even with probability distributions which satisfy the standard monotone hazard rate condition and preferences which are quadratic, pooling can emerge for the lower types of consumers. Second, when such pooling does not emerge, lower types will receive first-best quality allocations, and the resulting range of equilibrium allocations correspond with that of the first best. Finally, the introduction of uncertainty over participation reduces the firm's incentive to distort quality and enlarge the product spectrum.

In the Appendix, we develop an algorithm for numerically calculating the optimal contract. Here, we provide a few numerical examples as a means of illustrating the various possibilities.

29. It is noteworthy that optimal screening contracts with risk-averse agents exhibit a similar pattern, but for different reasons; see Salanié (1990) and Laffont and Rochet (1998) for details. The optimal taxation literature provides a mathematically closely-related result: for the lowest type there is either efficiency or pooling (see Ebert (1992)). This result is a local one, however; to our knowledge global solutions to the setting with bunching and separation have not been characterized.

FIGURE 4

The monopoly solution with a uniform distribution of t on $[1, 2]$ and an exponential distribution of x: $G(u) = 1 - e^{-u}$

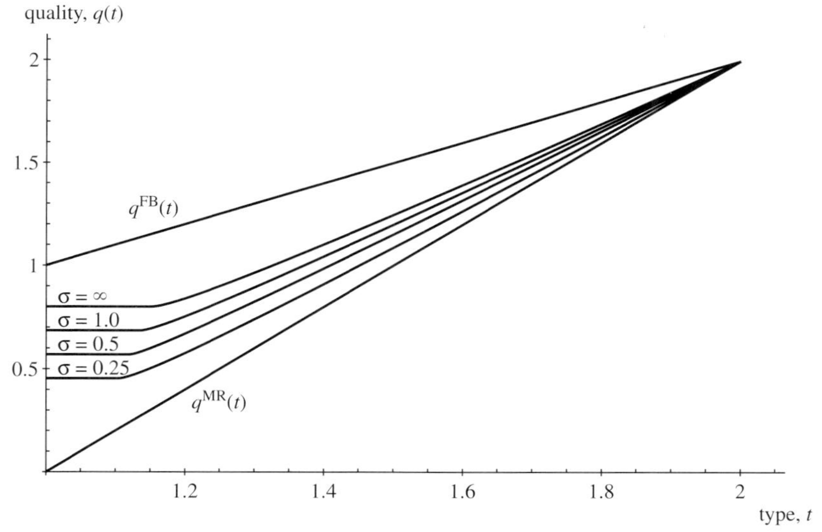

Numerical Example: Exponential distribution. Consider the following numerical example. Let $G(u/\sigma) = 1 - \exp\{-u/\sigma\}$, the exponential distribution defined over $[0, \infty)$. Note that when σ increases, u is more dispersedly distributed. In the limit when $\sigma \to \infty$, $G(u/\sigma)$ behaves like a uniform distribution over any finite support. Initially, we choose t to be uniformly distributed on $[1, 2]$ and we record the solutions for $\sigma = \frac{1}{4}, \frac{1}{2}, 1$ and $\sigma \approx \infty$. The results are presented in Figure 4.

Several relationships appear to emerge from this example. First, Proposition 4 is illustrated as the monopolist's quality allocation is bounded above by the efficient allocation and below by the Mussa-Rosen allocation. Second, for low values of σ (*i.e.* a tight distribution around 0), the monopolist's quality allocation appears to approach that of Mussa-Rosen. We formalize this result, and generalize it beyond our example.

Proposition 5. *Let $u_\sigma(t)$ be the solution of the monopolist problem, and $q_\sigma(t)$ denote its derivative, that is the optimal quality allocation for the monopolist. Then*

$$\lim_{\sigma \to 0} q_\sigma(t) = q^{mr}(t), \qquad \forall t.$$

Hence, there is no discontinuity in the Mussa-Rosen solution as we introduce a small amount of noise into the participation constraint.

A third apparent result is that no matter how disperse the distribution, in our example pooling always *seems* to occur. This result, however, does not generalize, as another numerical example will illustrate. Consider similar simulations ($\sigma = \frac{1}{4}, 1, 4$ and 5.07) but with t uniformly distributed on $[4, 5]$.

FIGURE 5

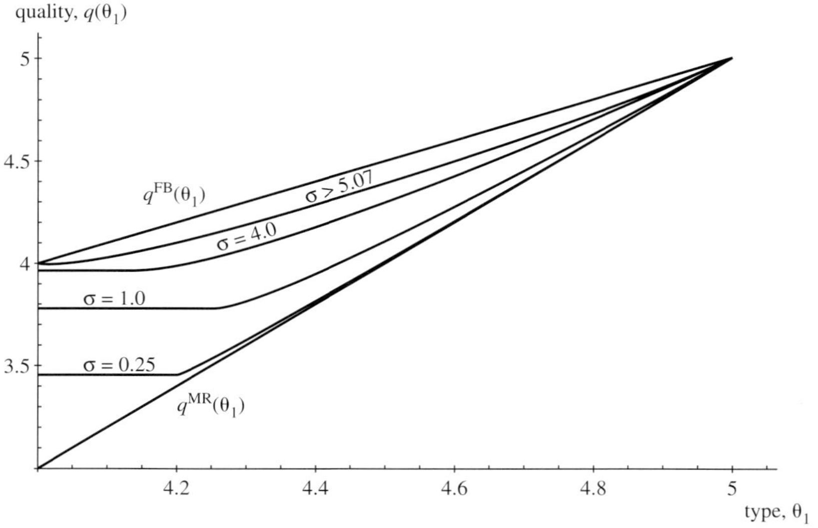

As Figure 5 indicates, once again a reduction in dispersion yields a quality schedule closer to the Mussa-Rosen allocation, with pooling for an interval of low types. When σ becomes large, however, the pooling region vanishes and the optimal allocation is monotonic without constraint.[30] This suggests that full separation may occur whenever type uncertainty is relatively small in a proportional sense (*i.e.* $\gamma = t_2/t_1$ sufficiently small), providing that $G(u)$ is disperse.[31]

Finally, using the same notation as in Section 3, we can study when the monopoly solution involves full separation as a function of three parameters. Recalling that σ measures the heterogeneity on x, $\gamma = t_2/t_1$ measures the heterogeneity on t, and $S_1 = \frac{1}{2}t_1^2$ measures the total gains from trade, we can make the following precise statement. Providing that t is uniformly distributed, for all S_1 and σ, full separation always occurs when γ is sufficiently small. Moreover, there exists a constant, $\gamma^* \approx 1.319$, such that if $\gamma < \gamma^*$, then full separation occurs when S_1/σ is sufficiently small.[32]

4.3 Duopoly Nonlinear Pricing with Continuous Types

We return to the application of two firms competing on either ends of a market with unit length and transportation cost σ. Specifically, in the spirit of Hotelling's linear market model, consider some distribution $G(\cdot, t)$ of customers on the interval $[0, 1]$ with one firm positioned at each end. Each firm simultaneously posts a publicly observable price schedule, $P_i(q_i)$, after which each consumer decides which firm (if any) to visit and which price-quality pair to select.

30. In this numerical example, the pooling region disappears for all $\sigma > 5.07$. We thank an anonymous referee for pointing out that the extent of the pooling region is not monotonic in σ: it is zero both for $\sigma = 0$ and $\sigma = 5.07$.

31. It is tempting to conclude from this proposition that empirically one should expect to find a large measure of consumers bunched on the lowest quality offering in some settings. Unfortunately, given that firms offer only a finite number of qualities, it is empirically difficult to distinguish pooling from separation without knowing the underlying distribution of consumer heterogeneity.

32. The proof of this result appears in an earlier version of this paper and is available upon request.

Let $G_j(x_j, t)$ be firm j's distribution function similar to before, where x_j is the consumer's distance to firm j. We will use j and k subscripts to generically represent the two distinct firms. The market share of firm j among consumers of type t can be computed easily:

$$M_j(u_j, u_k(t)) = G_j\left(\min\left\{\frac{u_j}{\sigma}, \frac{1}{2} + \frac{u_j - u_k(t)}{2\sigma}\right\}\right). \qquad (10)$$

This comes from the fact that the marginal consumer of firm j is located at a distance that is the minimum of $u_j(t)/\sigma$ (which occurs when the total market shares are less than one — the *local monopoly* regime) and $\frac{1}{2} + (u_j - u_k)/2\sigma$ (which occurs when all the market is served — the *competitive* regime). Using again the dual approach, we can write the total expected profit of firm i as a functional involving the consumers' rents $u_i(\cdot)$ and $u_j(\cdot)$ taken as the strategic variables of the two firms:

$$u_j(t) \equiv \max_q \; tq - P_j(q),$$

where P_j is the price schedule chosen by firm j. We obtain:

$$B_j(u_j, u_k) = \int_{\underline{t}}^{\bar{t}} \{S(t, q_j(t)) - u_j(t)\} M_j(u_j(t), u_k(t)) dt \qquad (11)$$

where q_i is again related to u_i by the first-order differential equation $\dot{u}_j(t) = q_j(t)$.

We now look for a Nash equilibrium of the normal form game defined by (10) and (11), where the strategy spaces of the firms have been restricted to u_i consistent with nondecreasing quality allocations. The corresponding price schedules will be called *duopoly nonlinear prices*. This turns out to be a difficult task in general, because of the monotonicity conditions (remember that $q_L(\cdot)$ and $q_R(\cdot)$ have to be non-decreasing). However, if we neglect these monotonicity conditions (which can be checked *ex post*, as usual) competitive nonlinear prices can be characterized by a set of Hamiltonian equations which are presented in the Appendix (in Proposition 8).

A numerical example is illustrative. Consider, for example, the case when t is uniformly distributed on $[4, 5]$, which is shown in Figure 6. For σ sufficiently large (*i.e.* $\sigma > 14.8$) the market shares of the two firms do not adjoin: each firm is in a (local) monopoly situation and the quality allocation is exactly the same as in our previously analysed monopoly setting.[33] Interestingly, when the market shares are adjoining for some t (*i.e.* $u_1(t) + u_2(t) \geqq \Delta$, which occurs at the top of the distribution of types) but not all t (which means that $u_1(t_1) + u_2(t_1) < \Delta$) the qualitative pattern of the solution remains

33. This local monopoly solution involves full separation.

identical (*cf.* Figure 6 below for $\sigma = 10$). However, when $u_1(t_1) + u_2(t_1) \geqq \Delta$ (the fully competitive regime), it turns out that quality distortions disappear completely (*cf.*, Figure 6 below, $\sigma < 16/3$). In this particular case, the equilibrium pricing schedules are cost-plus-fee schedules.

The next proposition characterizes duopoly pricing in the region of full market coverage.

Proposition 6. *If σ is sufficiently small so as to guarantee that every consumer in $[0, 1] \times [t_1, t_2]$ purchases, then in the symmetric equilibrium each firm offers a cost-plus-fee pricing schedule, $P_j(q) = C(q) + F_j$, and each customer consumes the efficient allocation $q^{fb}(t)$ from one of the two firms. The fixed pricing components, F_L and F_R, and the marginal consumer, $\hat{x}$, are jointly determined by*

$$F_L + \sigma\hat{x} = F_R + \sigma(1 - \hat{x}),$$

$$\frac{G_L(\hat{x})}{g_L(\hat{x})} = \frac{F_L}{2},$$

$$\frac{G_R(1 - \hat{x})}{g_R(1 - \hat{x})} = \frac{F_R}{2}.$$

Example. Consider a uniform distribution of t and a quadratic distribution of x on $[0, 1]$: $G_L(x) = x^2$. Such a distribution — which has a median of $\sqrt{1/2} > \frac{1}{2}$ — clearly favours firm R. Assume that S_1/σ is sufficiently large such that the market is competitive for all t ($S_1/\sigma > 1.29$ is sufficient). Then the equilibrium outcome

FIGURE 6

Quality choices in the oligopoly equilibrium for three regimes: fully competitive ($\sigma < 16/3$), mixed ($\sigma = 10$), and local monopoly ($\sigma > 14.8$). We assume that u is uniform on $[0, 1]$; t is uniform on $[4, 5]$

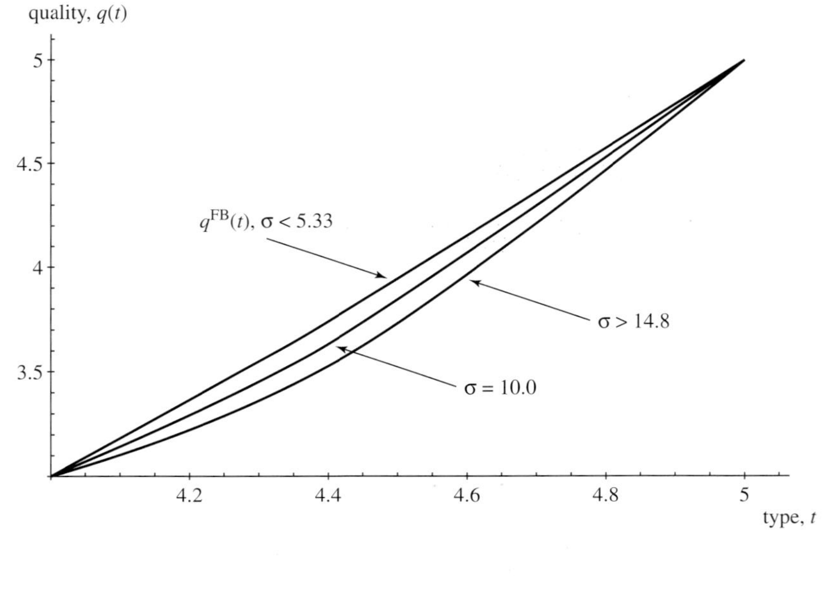

is $F_L = 0.64$, $F_R = 0.92$, and the marginal consumer is located at 0.64, to the left of the median consumer. In equilibrium, firm R captures more than half of the market and uses a higher fixed fee to take advantage of the relatively greater number of nearby (*i.e.* inelastic) consumers.

The result in Proposition 6 is quite general. As in the two-type setting, fundamentally the result relies upon the inverse hazard rate being constant over t in equilibrium for each firm, which in turn relies upon market coverage and symmetry in production. More generally, we could think about an N-firm oligopoly with a joint distribution of $(x_1, \ldots, x_N)$. Formally, let $G_i(u_1, \ldots, u_N) \equiv \text{Prob}\ [u_i - \tilde{x}_i \geqq \max_j u_j - \tilde{x}_j]$ and let the inverse hazard rate be given by

$$H_i(u_1, \ldots, u_N) = \frac{G_i(u_1, \ldots, u_N)}{(\partial/\partial u_i)G_i(u_1, \ldots, u_N)}.$$

We can state a straightforward extension of our previous no-distortion result.

Proposition 7. *Let $S_i^*(t)$ represent the surplus generated from efficient consumption of quality by consumer of type t from firm i. Let $\hat{u}(t) = \{\hat{u}_j(t)\}_j$ represent the vector of utilities which arise as an equilibrium outcome of the pricing game in which firms are restricted to cost-plus-fixed-fee pricing and can only set their fixed fee. Then cost-plus-fixed-fee pricing is an equilibrium in the unrestricted game if for all i and t*

$$\sum_{j=1}^{n} \frac{\partial H_i(\hat{u})}{\partial u_j} \frac{d}{dt} S_j^*(t) = 0. \tag{12}$$

Economically, this condition means that the equilibrium profit margins are constant over qualities. An immediate application of the proposition is that when $(d/du)H_i(u, \ldots, u) = 0$ for all i and u and firms have the same marginal costs (*i.e.* $(d/dt)S_j^*(t) = (d/dt)S^*(t)$ for all j), then efficient quality provision supported by cost-plus-fixed-fee pricing is an equilibrium outcome. For example, if the x_i are distributed independently according to the extreme-value distribution and there is no outside option of non-purchasing (*i.e.* the market is covered), then

$$G_i(u_1, \ldots, u_N) = \frac{\alpha_i \exp(u_i/\sigma)}{\Sigma_j \alpha_j \exp(u_j/\sigma)},$$

and the inverse hazard rate has the desired property. Hence, cost-plus-fixed-fee pricing is an equilibrium if firms have identical marginal costs. In a simpler setting, if $\alpha_j = \alpha$ for all j, then in equilibrium the hazard rate reduces to $H_i(u, \ldots, u) = \sigma(N/N-1)$. The efficiency result of the theorem, however, does not apply to the extreme-distribution setting when there is an outside option of fixed value; in such a case full market participation never arises and the required equilibrium condition over the hazard rate does not arise.[34] Armstrong and Vickers (2001) have independently found an efficiency result similar to Proposition 6, but in a slightly different context: They assume a uniform distribution of x (which is not needed here), but allow for multiple goods and more general (higher-dimensional) preferences.[35,36]

This surprising cost-plus-fixed-fee result (which gives an interesting motivation for restricting attention to simple price schedules when examining competition between multiproduct firms) is not valid in the mixed regime where the market is covered for high t but not for low t. As can be seen in Figure 6, the quality choice in the mixed regime involves downward distortions everywhere, except at the extremes ($t = t_1$ or t_2).

In Rochet and Stole (1997) we give a complete solution to the duopoly equilibrium in the particular case of Mussa-Rosen preferences and a uniform distribution of t and x when the conditions of Proposition 6 does not hold. There, we show that (in general) the properties of this solution are qualitatively similar to those of the monopoly solution: downward distortion of qualities everywhere, except at the top and the bottom.

5 Extensions and Concluding Remarks

We take this opportunity to suggest the applicability of our analysis to more general problems in economics, beyond the stylized framework of nonlinear pricing. Although the methodology we present was initially motivated by a perceived need to further our understanding of nonlinear pricing in more general environments, it is easy to see that the class of preferences we examine naturally includes other screening environments.

For example, with a simple change in notation, one can immediately derive results for the optimal regulation of a public utility with unknown marginal *and* fixed costs along the lines of Baron and Myerson (1982). Suppose the public utility's variable profits are given by $\pi = P(q) - tq$ and total profits are $\pi - x$; here $P(q)$ is the rate schedule allowed by the public utility commission and $C(q) = tq + x$ is the cost of producing q. Now, t is the marginal cost of production and x is the fixed cost. The regulator desires to maximize consumer surplus, but takes into account the possibility that the

34. As an aside, note that the theorem does not explicitly require coverage, although coverage is typically an ingredient in satisfying the required hazard rate condition. To take an example which differs from the setting in this paper, suppose that x is exponentially distributed on $(-\infty, 0]$ with parameter λ and $S^*(t) \leqq \lambda$; then a monopoly would not introduce a quality distortion for its served customers, although it would not serve the entire market.

35. Biglaiser and Mezzetti (1999), in a different context, consider the case of auctions for incentive contracts of a restricted form. Because sellers have heterogeneity over their ability to provide quality, each seller's objective function takes a similar form as the present paper and that of Armstrong and Vickers (2001). Nonetheless, because of the structure of preferences and contracts, efficient cost-based pricing only emerges in the limit as preferences become homogeneous, but interestingly, the standard DIC constraints do not bind, just as in our discrete-type model with market competition.

36. It is worth remarking that there are also some similarities between the efficiency result and the recent work of Inderst (2000) in the setting of matching models of buyer-seller exchange. Here, Inderst demonstrates that when the costs of delay enter payoffs additively, in equilibrium the buyer's outside option is equally attractive for all types, and an efficient allocation of quality arises even when such delay costs are not small. When delay costs are instead modelled as positive discount rates, the relative attractiveness of a buyer's outside option depends upon type, and efficiency only arises in the limit as traders become more patient.

firm will refuse to serve an area. That is, the public utility commission maximizes

$$G(\pi)(S(q, t) - \pi),$$

where $\pi(t) \equiv \max_q P(q) - tq$. Formally, this setting is identical to our nonlinear pricing model, and as a consequence, all of the results regarding the reductions in distortion, the presence of bunching or efficiency at the bottom, among others readily apply.

Broader questions of how to regulate an industry in which entry is endogenous (due to a distribution of entry costs) present more complicated extensions on our analysis, but extensions for which our results can be productively utilized. Likewise, more general models of optimal auctions with private valuations and private bid-preparation costs are also in this same vein. We leave these and related questions to future research.

Appendix

Intuition for "Efficiency at the Bottom"

The intuition is best illustrated in the context of a finite-type setting. Assume that the type space is discrete with N components, each of length $\Delta t = 1/N$. In addition, assume without argument that all downward-local incentive compatibility constraints are binding: $u_{i+1} = u_i + q_i \Delta t$ and hence $u_i = u_1 + \Delta t \sum_{j=1}^{i-1} q_i$. We can rewrite the firm's expected profit function as simply

$$\frac{1}{N} \sum_{i=1}^{N} G\left(u_1 + \Delta t \sum_{j=1}^{i-1} q_i\right)\left(S(q_i, t_i) - u_1 + \Delta t \sum_{j=1}^{i-1} q_i\right).$$

Differentiating with respect to q_N yields the familiar result that q_N is first-best efficient for the well-known reason that there is no gain from distorting q_N downward in order to extract rents from higher types. The first-order condition for u_1 (a first-order condition which is notably absent from the standard approach) requires that

$$\frac{1}{N} \sum_{i=1}^{N} [g(u_i)(S(q_i, t_i) - u_i) - G(u_i)] = 0.$$

This condition is familiar to standard monopoly pricing: the optimal base level of consumer surplus, u_1, is found by trading off the average gain from increased market share for all types against the average loss of profit from reduced rents to inframarginal consumers. Now, consider the first-order condition for q_1 (multiplied by N).

$$\Delta t \sum_{i=2}^{N} [g(u_i)(S(q_i, t_i) - u_i) - G(u_i)] + G(u_1) S_q(q_1, t_1) = 0.$$

Using the first-order condition for u_1, the first term is $-\Delta t[g(u_1)(S(q_1, t_1) - u_1) - G(u_1)]$, which is of the order $1/N$. As N gets large, the second term must converge to 0, and hence efficiency at $t = t_1$ emerges in the limit. Now we can begin to understand the source of the efficiency result. Suppose to the contrary that q_1 is far from efficient. By choosing the base price, $P(q_1)$, the firm will still wish to balance market share against profit/customer by satisfying the first-order condition for u_1. But if q_1 is sufficiently different from the first-best level, a cheaper way to achieve this end is to raise u_1 by raising q_1. Of course, this begs the question, why not set q_1 exactly at the first-best level when N is finite? To answer, suppose to the contrary that q_1 was at this first-best level. Then a small change will have only second-order consequences on profits, but such a variation will enable the firm to move u_2 from its previous level; the gain from this is that the ideal value of u_2 from the firm's point of view satisfies $\Delta t \sum_{i=2}^{N} [g(u_i)(S(q_i, t_i) - u_i) - G(u_i)] = 0$, rather than $\Delta t \sum_{i=1}^{N} [g(u_i)(S(q_i, t_i) - u_i) - G(u_i)] = 0$, which is the condition for u_1. Hence, the marginal return to u_2 is negative, and the ideal u_2 is lower than that which emerges from the first-order condition for u_1, and hence the difference between these two conditions determines the optimal size of the distortion for q_1 in the finite case.

Proof of Proposition 2. In the class of equilibria in which firms implement symmetric quality allocations over types, t, note that each firm will face identically binding IC constraints. Thus we need only consider the programme of one firm (the left, for sake of the argument). Define $x_i^L \equiv (u_i^L - u_i^R)/2\sigma + \frac{1}{2}$. Firm L maximizes

$$B_L = \sum_{i=1,2} G(x_i^L) f(t_i)(s(g_i^L, t_i) - u_i^L),$$

subject to

$$q_1^L \Delta t \leqq u_2^L - u_1^L \leqq q_2^L \Delta t.$$

Let $\lambda_D(\lambda_U)$ be the multiplier on the downward (upward) IC constraint. The Lagrangian for this programme is

$$\mathcal{L} = B_L + \lambda_D(u_2^L - u_1^L - q_1^L \Delta t) + \lambda_U(q_2^L \Delta t - u_2^L + u_1^L).$$

First-order necessary conditions include:

$$\frac{\partial \mathcal{L}}{\partial u_1^L} = -G(x_1^L) f(t_1) + \frac{1}{2\sigma} g(x_1^L) f(t_1) \pi_1^L - \lambda_D + \lambda_U = 0.$$

$$\frac{\partial \mathcal{L}}{\partial u_2^L} = -G(x_2^L)f(t_2) + \frac{1}{2\sigma} g(x_2^L)f(t_2)\pi_2^L + \lambda_D - \lambda_U = 0 .$$

Suppose $\lambda_U > 0$ and $\lambda_D = 0$. Then in a symmetric-quality equilibrium,

$$\pi_1^L < 2\sigma \frac{G(x_1^L)}{g(x_1^L)} < \pi_2^L .$$

But following the same argument as in Lemma 1, it must be that when UIC binds, we have $\pi_2^L - \pi_1^L < 0$, generating a contradiction.

Suppose that $\lambda_U = 0$ and $\lambda_D > 0$. Then in a symmetric-quality equilibrium,

$$\pi_1^L > 2\sigma \frac{G(x_2^L)}{g(x_2^L)} > \pi_2^L .$$

But when DIC binds, it must be that $q_2 = t_2$ and $q_1 < t_1$. Hence,

$$\pi_2^L - \pi_1^L = \Delta S - q_1 \Delta t = \frac{1}{2} t_2^2 - q_1 t_2 - t_1^2 \geqq \frac{1}{2}(t_2 - t_1)^2 > 0 ,$$

again generating a contradiction.

To see that an equilibrium exists in which IC constraints are slack, we show that such cost-plus-fixed-fee pricing satisfies each firm's relaxed optimization programme. Firm j's first-order condition for the unconstrained programme is simply $u_j(t) = \frac{1}{2} t^2 - H_j(\frac{1}{2} + (F_k - F_j)/2\sigma)$, when at the candidate equilibrium. The difference in indirect utilities is $u_{j,2} - u_{j,1} = \frac{1}{2}(t_2 + t_1)\Delta t$ which lies between $t_2 \Delta t$ and $t_1 \Delta t$ as required for DIC and UIC. ■

Preliminary results for proving Propositions 3-5

The Monopoly control problem. The following Hamiltonian-Lagrangian is defined for the principal's problem:

$$\mathcal{L}(u, q, z, t, \lambda_1, \lambda_2, \mu) \equiv M(u, t)(S(q, t) - u) + \lambda_1 q + \lambda_2 z + \mu z ,$$

where u and q are state variables, λ_1 and λ_2 are the associated co-state variables, z is a control variable (equal to $\dot{q}$) and μ is the Lagrange multiplier associated with the monotonicity constraint. Throughout we restrict attention to piecewise continuous controls, z, and so therefore to piecewise smooth quality schedules. Following Seierstad and Sydsæter (1987), we construct necessary conditions for an optimal nonlinear pricing contract in order to characterize the optimal pricing schedule.

The first step is to maximize $\mathcal{L}$ with respect to the only control variable, z. We obtain

$$\mathcal{L}^* = M(u,t)(S(q,t)-u) + \lambda_1 q,$$

with the auxiliary requirements that $\mu = -\lambda_2 \geqq 0$, $\dot{q} = z \geqq 0$, and $\mu z = 0$. The second step is to solve the system of Hamiltonian equations:

$$\dot{\lambda}_1 = -\frac{\partial \mathcal{L}^*}{\partial u} = -\frac{\partial}{\partial u}([M(u,t)(S(q,t)-u)]), \tag{13}$$

$$\dot{\lambda}_2 = -\frac{\partial \mathcal{L}^*}{\partial q} = -[M(u,t)S_q(q,t) + \lambda_1], \tag{14}$$

together with the boundary conditions: $\lambda_1 = \lambda_2 = 0$ for $t = t_1, t_2$.

For any open subinterval of $[t_1, t_2]$, there are two possibilities: full separation or pooling. To provide some intuition for the mechanics of the result, we briefly consider the scenario of full separation over the type space before turning to the case of pooling. When pooling of types is absent, formally we have $z > 0$ for all $t \in [t_1, t_2]$. Thus, $\mu = \lambda_2 = 0$ for all t. In such a setting, (14) implies that

$$\lambda_1(t) = -M(u(t),t)S_q(q(t),t). \tag{15}$$

Using this relationship in (13), we obtain the Euler equation for the firm's programme. Specifically, the solution solves (15) above and the following boundary-value problem

$$\frac{d}{dt}[M(u(t),t)S_q(q(t),t)] = \frac{\partial}{\partial u}[M(u(t),t)(S(q(t),t)-u(t))] \tag{16}$$

with $q(t) = q^{fb}(t)$ for $t = t_1$ and $t = t_2$, and $q(t)$ given by $\dot{u}(t) = q(t)$. Following substitution, (16) simplifies to a second-order differential equation:

$$M_u(u,t)\left(u - \frac{1}{2}\dot{u}^2\right) + M(u,t)(2-\ddot{u}) + M_t(u,t)(t-\dot{u}) = 0.$$

In the particular case where $M(u,t) = G(u/\sigma)$, we obtain

$$g\left(\frac{u}{\sigma}\right)\left(u - \frac{1}{2}\dot{u}^2\right) + \sigma G\left(\frac{u}{\sigma}\right)(2-\ddot{u}) = 0,$$

which establishes (8).

A useful order-reduction technique:[37]

First, by the homogeneity property, we can restrict ourselves to the case $\sigma = 1$. Second, we make use of the following

37. We are indebted to Serge Resnick for suggesting this technique for reducing the order of our differential equation.

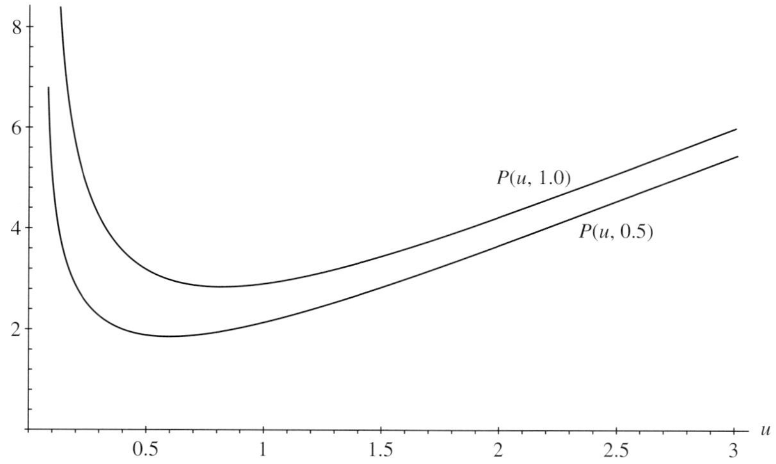

FIGURE 7

Graphs of $P(u, K)$ for $G(x) = 1 - e^{-x}$ and $K = 0.5, 1.0$

order-reduction technique in order to characterize the optimal contract more fully. Define the auxiliary function

$$P(u, K) \equiv u + \frac{K + \int_0^u G(s)ds}{G(u)}, \tag{17}$$

where K is a given constant. An illustration may prove useful, so we graph the function for the exponential distribution with K taking on values of $K = 0.5$ and $K = 1.0$ in Figure 7. Define

$$K(t) \equiv G(u(t))\left[\frac{1}{2}\,\dot{u}(t)^2 - u(t)\right] - \int_0^{u(t)} G(s)ds\,.$$

Then

$$\frac{dK}{dt} = \dot{u}(t)G(u(t))\left(\ddot{u}(t) - 2 - \frac{g(u(t))}{G(u(t))}\left(u(t) - \frac{1}{2}\,\dot{u}(t)^2\right)\right).$$

Because $\dot{u}(t) = q(t) > 0$, $K(t)$ is constant over t if and only if (8) is satisfied. Hence, we can restate the Euler condition as simply

$$\dot{u}(t)^2 = 2P(u(t), K)\,. \tag{18}$$

As shown below in Lemma 3, $P(u, K)$ is quasi-convex in u because G is log-concave. This implies several useful results. First, for any K we have at most two solutions of (18) to consider. Second, because any solution must have $q(t) = \dot{u}(t)$ increasing in t, we know we must restrict attention to the solutions on the upward-sloping portion of $P(u, K)$ as (18) also implies $\ddot{u} = P_u(u, K)$. Thus, if a convex solution to the Euler equation exists for a given set of boundary conditions, it is unique. Third, $P(u, K)$ has a single trough; once $u(t)$ becomes convex (*i.e.* $P_u(u(t), K) \geqq 0$), it remains convex for all higher t. These results place sufficient structure on the optimal contract and we can characterize the monopolist's nonlinear pricing schedule.

Lemma 3. *The function $P(u, K)$ is quasi-convex in u on* $[0, +\infty[$.

Proof of Lemma 3. More precisely we prove that $P(u, K)$ (as given by equation (17)) is single-peaked in u over $[0, \infty)$ for any $K \geqq 0$, and $P(u, K)$ is increasing in u over $[0, \infty[$ for any $K < 0$. To substantiate this claim, consider an arbitrary extremum (providing one exists), $\hat{u}$, of $P(u, K)$. Note that

$$G(\hat{u})^3 P_{uu}(\hat{u}, K) = -G(\hat{u})^2 g(\hat{u}) + [-G(\hat{u})g'(\hat{u}) + 2g(\hat{u})^2]\left(K + \int_0^u G(s)ds\right).$$

The defining condition for an extremum that $P_u(\hat{u}, K) = 2 - (g(\hat{u})/G(\hat{u})^2)\left(K + \int_0^u G(s)ds\right) = 0$ can be used to simplify the above expression: $G(\hat{u})^3 P_{uu}(\hat{u}, K) = -G(\hat{u})^2 g(\hat{u}) + 2(G(\hat{u})/g(\hat{u}))(2g(\hat{u})^2 - G(\hat{u})g'(\hat{u}))$. Simplifying again,

$$P_{uu}(\hat{u}, K) = \frac{g(\hat{u})}{G(\hat{u})^2}(g(\hat{u})^2 + 2(g(\hat{u})^2 - G(\hat{u})g'(\hat{u}))) > 0,$$

where the inequality follows from the monotonicity condition on $G(u)/g(u)$. Therefore any extremum of $P(u, K)$ must be a minimum. Now consider whether or not an extremum exists. Suppose first that $K > 0$. At $u = 0$, $\lim_{u \to 0} P_u(u, K) = -\infty$; moreover, $\lim_{u \to \infty} P_u(u, K) = 2$ because $\lim_{u \to \infty} g(u) \int_0^u G(s)ds \leqq \lim_{u \to \infty} g(u)u = 0$. Thus, if $K \geqq 0$, an extremum must exist, and according to the above argument, it must represent the unique minimum. If, however, $K < 0$, then $P_u(0, K) = +\infty$, $P_u(\infty, K) = 2$ and so no extremum can exist; therefore $P_u > 0$ for all $u \geqq 0$. ■

Lemma 4. *The monopolist's optimal allocation of q will exhibit pooling at most on an interval at the bottom of the type space,* $[t_1, t_0]$.

Proof of Lemma 4. Suppose that there is an interval $(t', t'') \subset (t_1, t_2)$ over which there is full separation. It is straightforward to demonstrate that in such an interval, the same Euler equation as above must be satisfied: $\dot{u}(t)^2 = 2P(u(t), K)$. But if the resulting $u(t)$ over this interval is convex (*i.e.* $P_u(u(t), K) \geqq 0$ for all $t \in (t', t'')$), then no pooling can occur above this interval because P is quasiconvex; *i.e.* once $P_u(u(t), K) \geqq 0$, it remains so for all higher values of $u(t)$. Hence, pooling can only occur for the lower interval of the type space, $t \in [t_1, t_0]$, for some $t_0 \leqq t_2$. ■

Proof of Proposition 3. Using Lemma 4, there can be at most one interval of pooling and such an interval must take the form of $[t_1, t_0]$. Using this result, we demonstrate that the Pontryagin necessary conditions for the Hamiltonian-Lagrangian associated with the monopolist's problem imply the conditions of the proposition.

Because $q(t)$ is piecewise smooth, it follows that $z(t) = \dot{q}(t)$ is piecewise continuous, and as such, the necessary conditions for an optimum are (see Seierstad and Sydsæter (1987), pp. 276-77):

(a) $\lambda_1(t)$ and $\lambda_2(t)$ are continuous and piecewise smooth and $\mu(t)$ is piecewise continuous;

(b) $\lambda_2(t) = -\mu(t)$ for all *t*;

(c) $\mu(t) \geqq 0$, $\dot{q}(t) \geqq 0$ and $\mu(t)\dot{q}(t) = 0$ for all *t*;

(d) $\dot{\lambda}_1(t) = G(u(t)) - g(u(t))\left(tq(t) - \frac{1}{2}q(t)^2 - u(t)\right)$ virtually everywhere;[38]

(e) $\dot{\lambda}_2(t) = -G(u(t))(t - q(t)) - \lambda_1(t)$ virtually everywhere;

(f) $\lambda_1(t_1) = \lambda_1(t_2) = \lambda_2(t_1) = \lambda_2(t_2) = 0$.

Evaluating using the lemma that a pooling region exists for an interval of types $[t_1, t_0]$, and applying the requirements of incentive compatibility (namely $\dot{u}(t) = q(t)$), implies that $q(t) = q_0$ and $u(t) = tq_0 - p_0 = u_0 - (t - t_0)q_0$ for $t \in [t_1, t_0]$.

Consider the non-bunching region $[t_0, t_2]$. Over this region $\dot{q}(t) > 0$, so $\mu(t) = 0$. Conditions (a) and (b) imply that $\mu(t)$ is piecewise smooth and that we can replace $-\lambda_2(t)$ throughout with $\mu(t)$. Hence, $\lambda_2(t_0) = 0$ and integrating condition (e) over $[t_1, t_0]$ implies (19).

$$\lambda_2(t_0) = \int_{t_1}^{t_0} \{G(u(s))(s - q_0) + \lambda_1(s)\}ds = 0. \tag{19}$$

In addition, $\dot{\mu}(t) = -\dot{\lambda}_2(t) = 0$, and as such condition (e) implies that

$$G(u(t))(t - q(t)) = -\lambda_1(t), \qquad \forall t \in [t_0, t_2]. \tag{20}$$

Because $\lambda_1(t_0)$ is given by integrating condition (d) over $[t_1, t_0]$ and using $\lambda_1(t_1) = 0$ (condition (f)), the continuity of $q(t)$ implies equation (21).

$$\lambda_1(t_0) = \int_{t_1}^{t_0} \{G(u(s)) - g(u(s))(S(q_0, t_0) - u_0)\}ds$$
$$= -G(u_0)(t_0 - q_0). \tag{21}$$

38. Following Seierstad and Sydsæter's (1977), a property holds virtually everywhere iff it is true at all but a countable number of points.

Because $u(t)$ and $q(t)$ are continuous over t, $\dot{q}(t)$ is also continuous, and so this differential equation is defined for all $t \in (t_0, t_2]$. The boundary conditions of $q(t_0) = q_0$ and $u(t_0) = u_0$ are required by continuity of the state variables. Lastly, the condition in (f) that $\lambda_1(t_2) = 0$ implies that $q(t_2) = q^{fb}(t_2) = t_2$. Hence, the fourth condition of the proposition must be satisfied. ■

The following lemma is useful for many of the results in the monopoly setting.

Lemma 5. $\lambda_1(t) \leqq 0$ *for all* $t \in [t_1, t_2]$ *with equality on the end points. Furthermore, if the optimal allocation is fully separating, then* $\frac{1}{2} q(t_1)^2 = \frac{1}{2} t_1^2 > u(t_1)$*; if the optimal allocation has pooling over* $[t_1, t_0]$*, then* $\frac{1}{2} q_0^2 > u_0$.

Proof of Lemma 5. Proving $\lambda_1(t) \leqq 0$ is equivalent to proving $q(t) \leqq q^{fb}(t)$. Over any pooling region $[t_1, t_0]$, it is sufficient to show that $q_0 \leqq q^{fb}(t_1) = t_1$. Consider the Pontryagin conditions in the proof of Proposition 3. $-\lambda_2(t) = \mu(t) \geqq 0$, so $\lambda_2(t) \leqq 0$ for all t. Additionally, $\lambda_2(t_1) = 0$ implies that $\dot{\lambda}_2(t_1) \leqq 0$ (to ensure that $\lambda_2(t) \leqq 0$ in the neighbourhood around $t = t_1$). Using condition (e) of the proof, together with $\lambda_1(t_1) = 0$, implies that $G(u(t_1))(t_1 - q_0) \geqq 0$. Hence, $q_0 \leqq q^{fb}(t_1)$.

Over the region $(t_0, t_2]$, $q(t) > q^{fb}(t)$ iff $\lambda_1(t) > 0$ (the multiplier associated with the state variable $u(t)$) for some $t > t_0$. Suppose that there exists such a $t > t_0$ with $\lambda_1(t) > 0$. Because $\dot{\lambda}_1$ is piecewise smooth, $\lambda_1(t_0) < 0$ and $\lambda_1(t_2) = 0$, if such a point exists, λ must have a local maximum for some $t^* > t_0$ such that $\dot{\lambda}_1(t^*) = 0$ and $\ddot{\lambda}(t^*) \leqq 0$. Differentiating $\lambda_1(t)$ twice,

$$\ddot{\lambda}_1(t) = g(u(t))q(t) - g'(u(t))q(t)\left(tq(t) - \frac{1}{2}q(t)^2 - u(t)\right) - g(u(t))(t - q(t))\dot{q}(t).$$

$\ddot{\lambda}_1$ at t^* (*i.e.* using $\dot{\lambda}_1(t^*) = 0$),

$$\ddot{\lambda}_1(t^*) = q(t^*)\left(g(u(t^*)) - g'(u(t^*))\frac{G(u(t^*))}{g(u(t^*))}\right) - g(u(t^*))\dot{q}(t^*)(t^* - q(t^*)) > 0,$$

where the inequality follows from the monotonicity of $G(u)/g(u)$ and the supposition that $q(t^*) > q^{fb}(t^*) = t^*$, thereby yielding a contradiction. Hence, for all of $t \in [t_1, t_2]$, $q(t) \leqq q^{fb}(t)$ and $\lambda_1(t) \leqq 0$. Suppose that the optimal allocation is fully separating. Because $\lambda_1(t_1) = 0$, our result implies that $\dot{\lambda}_1(t_1) \leqq 0$. Then from (d) in the proof of Proposition 3,

$$\dot{\lambda}_1(t_1) = G(u(t_1)) - g(u(t_1))\left(t_1 q(t_1) - \frac{1}{2}q(t_1)^2 - u(t_1)\right) \leqq 0,$$

which in turn implies

$$0 < \frac{G(u(t_1))}{g(u(t_1))} \leqq \frac{1}{2}\, t_1^2 - u(t_1)\,,$$

thereby proving $\frac{1}{2}\, t_1^2 > u(t_1)$ in an optimal separating allocation. Suppose instead that the optimal allocation exhibits pooling over the region $[t_1, t_0]$. Over this region, the firm's profit per customer served is constant, $\pi_0 = t_0 q_0 - \frac{1}{2}\, q_0^2 - u_0$, and utility is given by $u(t) = u_0 - (t_0 - t)q_0$. Using (21) from the proof of Proposition 3, we have after simplification,

$$G(u_0)\left(\frac{1}{2}\, q_0^2 - u_0\right) = \left(\int_{u(t_1)}^{u_0} G(z)dz + G(u(t_1))\right)\pi_0 > 0\,,$$

thus proving $\frac{1}{2}\, q_0^2 > u_0$ in an optimal pooling allocation. ■

Proof of Proposition 4. The upper bound of $q(t)$ is immediate from Lemma 5.

Consider the lower bound, $q^{mr}(t)$. Suppose by contradiction that $q(t) < q^{mr}(t)$ for some interval of t, $(t', t'') \subset [t_1, t_2]$, where $q(t'') = q^{mr}(t'')$. Two possibilities exist. Over a portion of this interval there is pooling or there is not. If there is pooling, it must be the case that $q_0 < q^{mr}(t_0)$. Let $\dot{q}(t_0)$ be the right-defined derivative whenever the derivative does not exist. At that point, we have $\dot{q}(t_0) < 2$ because of (8) and $u_0 < \frac{1}{2}\, q_0^2$ (Lemma 5). Now define $\Delta q(t) \equiv q^{mr}(t) - q(t)$. By our above argument, we know that $\Delta\dot{q}(t_0) > 0$; by construction, $\Delta\dot{q}(t'') < 0$, because $t'' < t_2$. By continuity, we have an interior extremum, t^*, which maximizes the value of $\Delta q(t)$ and therefore satisfies $\Delta\dot{q}(t^*) = 0$ and $\Delta\ddot{q}(t^*) \leqq 0$. We demonstrate a contradiction by showing at such, $\Delta\ddot{q}(t^*) > 0$. Indeed, (8) can be written as

$$H(u(t))\Delta\dot{q}(t) + u(t) - \frac{1}{2}\, q^2(t) = 0\,.$$

Now $\Delta\dot{q}(t^*) = 0$ implies $u(t^*) = \frac{1}{2}\, q^2(t^*)$. Moreover, differentiating the above equation gives

$$H_u(u(t))q(t)\Delta\dot{q}(t) + H(u(t))\Delta\ddot{q}(t) + q(t) - q(t)\dot{q}(t) = 0\,.$$

For $t = t^*$, $\Delta\dot{q}(t^*) = 0$ and $\dot{q}(t^*) = 2$, thus

$$H(u(t^*))\Delta\ddot{q}(t^*) = q(t^*) > 0\,,$$

a contradiction.

The second possibility is that there is full separation over the subinterval $(t', t'') \subset [t_1, t_2]$, in which $q(t) < q^{mr}(t)$. Using a similar argument as in the pooling case, $\Delta q(t') = \Delta q(t'') = 0$ and $\Delta \dot{q}(t') \geqq 0 \geqq \Delta \dot{q}(t'')$, hence there exists an interior maximum over the interval, t^*, such that $\Delta \dot{q}(t^*) = 0$ and $\Delta \ddot{q}(t^*) \leqq 0$. But $\Delta \ddot{q}(t^*) > 0$, as shown above, yielding a contradiction. Hence $q(t) \geqq q^{mr}(t)$ for all $t \in [t_1, t_2]$. ■

Proof of Proposition 5. We begin by demonstrating that a well-defined limit point exists for q_σ. First, note that the class of optimal allocations belongs to a uniformly bounded set, $\mathcal{Q}$. We first establish that this set is equicontinuous. Because an optimal allocation is continuous and bounded (*e.g.* $q(t) \in [q^{mr}(t), q^{fb}(t)]$), it is sufficient for equicontinuity to establish that $\dot{q}_\sigma(t) \leqq M$ for all σ and t. To this end, note there are two relevant cases: (i) it contains a lower interval of pooling, or (ii) the allocation is strictly increasing.

Case (i). If a lower interval of pooling arises, Lemma 5 holds that $\frac{1}{2} q_\sigma(t_0)^2 > u(t_0)$. If $\dot{q}_\sigma(t) \geqq 1$, this inequality remains true, and according to (8), $\dot{q}_\sigma(t) \leqq 2$; if $\dot{q}_\beta(t)$ falls below unity, then trivially $\dot{q}_\sigma(t) \leqq 2$.

Case (ii). If full separation occurs, Lemma 5 holds that $\frac{1}{2} t_1^2 = \frac{1}{2} q_\sigma t_1^2 > u(t_1)$, and a similar argument applies, establishing that $\mathcal{Q}$ is equicontinuous for $M = 2$.

By the theorem of Arzela-Ascoli the set $\mathcal{Q}$ is compact, and therefore any infinite sequence $q_\sigma(t)$ as σ tends to zero has at least one limit point. We arbitrarily select a limit point, $\bar{q}(t)$ (and associated $\bar{u}(t) = \int_0^t \bar{q}(s)ds + \bar{u}(0)$), for analysis and demonstrate that it must be identical to the Mussa-Rosen allocation.

In the region in which $\bar{q}(t)$ is increasing we have

$$K = \lim_{\sigma \to 0} G(\bar{u}(t)/\sigma)\left(\frac{1}{2}\,\bar{q}(t)^2 - \bar{u}(t)\right) - \int_0^{u(t)} G(s/\sigma)ds,$$

or $K = \frac{1}{2}\,\bar{q}(t)^2 - 2\bar{u}(t)$. Differentiating with respect to t and imposing $\bar{q}(t_2) = t_2$ establishes that $\bar{q}(t) = 2t - t_2 = q^{mr}(t)$.

What remains to be shown is that t_0 from Proposition 3 converges to t_1 as σ approaches 0 (*i.e.* the pooling region vanishes in the limit). Integrating (and simplifying) equation (21), using the fact that $G(u/\sigma) \to 1$ for any $u > 0$, yields the relationship

$$\bar{t}_0 - t_1 + \bar{t}_0 - \bar{q}_0 = \lim_{\sigma \to 0} \int_{t_1}^{t_0} g(\bar{u}(s)/\sigma)\pi_0 ds.$$

Given that $\lim_{x \to \infty} g(x) = 0$, the right-hand side must equal 0, and hence $\bar{t}_0 - t_1 + \bar{t}_0 - \bar{q}_0 = 0$. Because $\bar{t}_0 \geqq t_1 \geqq \bar{q}_1$, it must be that $t_1 = \bar{t}_0$. ■

An Algorithm for Numerically Calculating Optimal Nonlinear Pricing Schedules

Given (t_0, q_0), the Euler equation (8) from Proposition 3 on $[t_0, t_2]$ and the boundary conditions of $\dot{u}(t_0) = q_0$ and $\dot{u}(t_2) = t_2$ provide a well-posed boundary-value problem. Using our previous results, we can recast this problem more simply: For a given (t_0, q_0), we have to find $(u_0, u(t_2), K)$ such that

$$q_0^2 = 2\bar{P}(u_0, K), \tag{22}$$

$$t_2^2 = 2\bar{P}(u(t_2), K), \tag{23}$$

$$t_2 - t_0 = \int_{u_0}^{u(t_2)} \frac{du}{\sqrt{2\bar{P}(u, K)}}, \tag{24}$$

where $\bar{P}(u, K)$ is the upward-sloping portion of P. The third equation is obtained by noting that $\dot{u}(t)^2 = 2\bar{P}(u(t), K)$ implies $du = \sqrt{2\bar{P}(u, K)}dt$; separating the variables and integrating yields the equation. The result of this programme is a mapping from (t_0, q_0) to a value $u_0 = u(t_0)$. This relationship, combined with equations (19) and (21) from the proof to Proposition 3 which provide two additional equations to determine (t_0, q_0), yields a system of three equations and three unknowns. Upon finding a solution to this system, we can uniquely construct the functions $u(t)$ and $q(t)$ (as well as the pricing equation). To check the sufficiency of our necessary conditions (equations (19), (21)–(24)), we can then construct $\lambda_1(t)$ and $\lambda_2(t)$ from $q(t)$ and $u(t)$ and numerically check whether the modified Lagrangian of Seierstad and Sydsæter (1977) is maximized by $(q(t), u(t))$ for all $t \in [t_1, t_2]$.[39] In the fully separating case, $t_0 = q_0 = t_1$ and the problem reduces to a system of three equations (22)–(24) in three unknowns: $u_1 = u_0$, $u(t_2)$ and K.

The following result is discussed in the text and is used in the proof of Proposition 6, below.

Proposition 8. *In the absence of bunching, duopoly nonlinear prices can be characterized by the following conditions:* For all t and j, $q_j(t)$ maximizes

$$\mathcal{L}_j(t, u_j, u_k, q_j) = (S(q_j, t) - u_j)M_j(u_j, u_k) + \mu_j qj,$$

39. The modified Lagrangian is given by $\mathcal{L}(q, u, t) = G(u)(S(t, q) - u) + \{\lambda_1(t) + \lambda_2(t)\}q\dot{\lambda}_1(t)u$. Seierstad and Sydsæter (1977) demonstrate that this condition is sufficient.

$\mu_j(\cdot)$ solves the Hamiltonian equation:

$$\dot{\mu}_j = -\frac{\partial \mathcal{L}_j}{\partial u_j} = M_j(u_j, u_k) - (S(q_j, t) - u_j)\frac{\partial M_j}{\partial u_j}(u_j, u_k) \quad \forall t \in (t_1, t_2), \tag{25}$$

$$\mu_j(t) = 0, \quad \text{for } t = t_1, t_2 \tag{26}$$

and $q_j(\cdot)$ is given by

$$\dot{u}_j(t) = q_j(t). \tag{27}$$

Proof of Proposition 8. Follows from application of standard necessary conditions for control-theoretic programmes. See Seierstad and Sydsæter (1977) for details. ■

Proof of Proposition 6. We suppose that the market is covered, proving the conditions of the proposition comprise an equilibrium. We then demonstrate that for σ sufficiently small, the market is indeed covered.

Ignore monotonicity concerns and consider the Hamiltonian for the duopolist i's problem, taking $u_j(t)$ as given:

$$\mathcal{H}(q, u_i, t, \lambda) \equiv G_i(x_i(u_i, u_j(t)))(S(q, t) - u) + \lambda_q,$$

where $x_i = (u_i - u_j + \sigma)/2\sigma$. The necessary conditions are $\lambda(t_1) = \lambda(t_2) = 0$,

$$\dot{\lambda}(t) = G_i(x_i(u_i(t), u_j(t))) - g_i(x_i(u_i(t), u_j(t)))\left(\frac{\partial x_i}{\partial u_i}\right)[S(q(t), t) - u_i(t)],$$

$$G_i(x_i(u_i(t), u_j(t)))S_q(q(t), t) = -\lambda(t).$$

Because the pricing functions $P_i(q) = C(q) + F_i$ implement efficient allocations of quality, $q(t) = q^{fb}(t)$, it must be that $\lambda(t) = 0$ and $S(q(t), t) - u_i(t) = F_i$ for all t. This in turn requires that $\dot{\lambda}(t) = 0$ for all t, and thus

$$\frac{G_i(x_i(u_i(t), u_j(t)))}{g_i(x_i(u_i(t), u_j(t)))} = \frac{1}{2}F_i.$$

Because x and t are independently distributed, the left-hand side of this expression only depends upon t only if $x_i(u_i(t), u_j(t))$ depends upon t at the equilibrium allocations. Because preferences are symmetric and qualities are efficient, $u_i(t) - u_j(t)$ is constant, and therefore x_i is constant. Hence, a solution to the three equations and three unknowns satisfies the necessary conditions for an optimal allocation.

These conditions are also sufficient if, following the argument along the lines of Seierstad and Sydsæter (1977), we further have

$$u_i(t) = \underset{u \in [0, \infty)}{\arg\max}\ G_i(x_i(u_i, u_j(t)))(\max_q S(q, t) - u_i).$$

But this will be true because G_i is log-concave.

Finally, we need to demonstrate that for σ sufficiently small that indeed the market is covered. To see this, note that $u_L(t_1) = u_R(t_1) > \sigma \max\{x, 1 - x\}$, so for σ sufficiently small, the market will be covered. ■

Proof of Proposition 7. Consider a Nash equilibrium to the restricted cost-plus-fixed-fee game in which each firm is forced to supply first-best qualities and can only choose the fixed fee. In this setting, each firm i can be thought of as choosing its optimal gross consumer utility pointwise in t:

$$\max_{u_i(t)}\ G_i(u_i(t), u_{-i}(t))(S_i^*(t) - u_i(t)).$$

In vector notation, the first-order conditions which characterize the Nash equilibrium are given by

$$u(t) = S^*(t) - H(u(t)),$$

where each argument is an n-length vector. Because this relationship is true for all t, we can differentiate to obtain,

$$\dot{u}(t) = \dot{S}^*(t) - DH(u(t))\dot{u}(t),$$

where DH is the matrix of derivatives of H, evaluated at $u(t)$.

Now consider the unrestricted pricing game. A necessary and sufficient condition for efficient qualities to arise in an equilibrium is that $S_i^*(t) - u_i(t)$ is constant. Hence, an efficient-quality equilibrium arises iff at the equilibrium utilities of the restricted game, we have

$$DH(\hat{u}(t))\dot{u}(t) = 0.$$

Using our characterization of the Nash equilibrium, the condition is

$$DH(\hat{u}(t))[I + DH(\hat{u}(t))]^{-1}\dot{S}^*(t) = 0.$$

The condition of the proposition can be restated in vector notation as $DH(\hat{u}(t))\dot{S}^*(t) = 0$ for all t, which implies the above equation holds. ■

Acknowledgements. We are grateful to Patrick Bolton, Bernard Caillaud, Kent Daniel, Mathias Dewatripont, Rob Gertner, Igal Hendel, Bruno Jullien, Steve Matthews, Meg Meyer, Amil Petrin, Canice Prendergast, Serge Resnick, Sherwin Rosen, Hyun Shin, Jean Tirole, Bob Wilson, two anonymous referees, numerous seminar participants, and especially Mark Armstrong and Yossi Spiegel. The first author thanks the CNRS for financial support. The second author thanks the National Science Foundation PFF Programme for support. An earlier version of this paper appeared under the title of "Selection Contracts with Uncertain Participation: Re-examining Monopoly and Competitive Nonlinear Pricing." Any errors are our own.

REFERENCES

[1] Anderson, S., De Palma, A. and Thisse, J.-F. (1992) *Discrete Choice Theory of Product Differentiation* (Cambridge: MIT Press).

[2] Armstrong, M. (1996), "Multiproduct Nonlinear Pricing", *Econometrica*, **64**, 1-76.

[3] Armstrong, M. and Vickers, J. (2001), "Competitive Price Discrimination", RAND *Journal of Economics* (forthcoming).

[4] Baron, D. and Myerson, R. (1982), "Regulating a Monopolist with Unknown Costs", *Econometrica*, **50**, 911-930.

[5] Berry, S., Levinsohn, J. and Pakes, A. (1995), "Automobile Prices in Market Equilibrium", *Econometrica*, **63**, 841-890.

[6] Biglaiser, G. and Mezzetti, C. (2000), "Incentive Auctions and Information Revelation", *RAND Journal of Economics*, **31**, 145-164.

[7] Bliss, C. (1988), "A Theory of Retail Pricing", *Journal of Industrial Economics*, **36**, 375-391.

[8] Che, Y.-K., and Gale, I. (2000), "The Optimal Mechanism for Selling to a Budget-constrained Buyer", *Journal of Economic Theory*, **92**, 198-233.

[9] Dessein, W. (2000), "Network Competition in Nonlinear Pricing" (Mimeo, ECARE, Brussels, August 2000).

[10] Ebert, U. (1992), "A Reexamination of the Optimal Nonlinear Income Tax", *Journal of Public Economics*, **49**, 47-73.

[11] Ginsburgh, V. and Weber, S. (1996), "Product Lines and Price Discrimination in the European Car Market", (Mimeo, March 1996).

[12] Hotelling, H. (1929), "Stability in Competition", *Economic Journal*, **39**, 41-57.

[13] Inderst, R. (2000), "Price Discrimination in a Market with Frictions" (Mimeo, University College London).

[14] Ivaldi, M. and Martimort, D. (1994), "Competition under Nonlinear Pricing", *Annales d'Economie et de Statistique*, **34**, 71-114.

[15] Jullien, B. (2000), "Participation Constraints in Adverse Selection Models", *Journal of Economic Theory*, **93**, 1-47.

[16] Laffont, J.-J., Maskin, E. and Rochet, J.-C. (1987), "Optimal Nonlinear Pricing with Two-Dimensional Characteristics", in T. Groves, R. Radner and S. Reiter, (eds.), *Information, Incentives and Economic Mechanisms* (Minneapolis: University of Minnesota Press, 1987).

[17] Laffont, J.-J., Rey, P. and Tirole, J. (1998*a*), "Network Competition: Overview and Non-discriminatory Pricing", *RAND Journal of Economics*, **29**, 1-37.

[18] Laffont, J.-J., Rey, P. and Tirole, J. (1998*b*), "Network Competition: Price Discrimination", *RAND Journal of Economics*, **29**, 38-56.

[19] Laffont, J.-J. and Rochet, J.-C. (1998), "Regulation of a Risk-averse Firm", *Games and Economic Behavior*, **25**, 149-173.

[20] Leslie, P. (1999), "Price Discrimination in Broadway Theatre" (Mimeo, UCLA, November).

[21] Lewis, T. and Sappington, D. (1988), "Regulating a Monopolist with Unknown Demand and Cost Functions", *Rand Journal of Economics*, **19**, 438-457.

[22] Lewis, T. and Sappington, D. (1989), "Countervailing Incentives in Agency Problems", *Journal of Economic Theory*, **49**, 294-313.

[23] Maggi, G. and Rodriguez-Clare, A. (1995), "On Countervailing Incentives", *Journal of Economic Theory*, **66**, 238-263.

[24] Maskin, E., and Riley, J. (1984), "Monopoly with Incomplete Information", *RAND Journal of Economics*, **15**, 171-196.

[25] McAfee, P. and McMillan, J. (1988), "Multidimensional Incentive Compatibility and Mechanism Design", *Journal of Economic Theory*, **46**, 335-354.

[26] Mirrlees, J. (1971), "An Exploration in the Theory of Optimum Income Taxation", *Review of Economic Studies*, **38**, 175-208.

[27] Mussa, M. and Rosen, M. (1978), "Monopoly and Product Quality", *Journal of Economic Theory*, **18**, 301-317.

[28] Rochet, J.-C. (1984), "Monopoly Regulation with Two Dimensional Uncertainty" (Mimeo, Université Paris 9).

[29] Rochet, J.-C., and Stole, L. (1997), "Competitive Nonlinear Pricing" (Mimeo, August 1997).

[30] Rochet, J.-C. and Choné, P. (1998), "Ironing, Sweeping, and Multidimensional Screening", *Econometrica*, **66**, 783-826.

[31] Salanié, B. (1990), "Sélection Adverse et Aversion pour le Risque", *Annales d'Economie et de Statistique*, **18**, 131-149.

[32] Schmidt-Mohr, U. and Villas-Boas, M. (1999), "Oligopoly with Asymmetric Information: Differentiation in Credit Markets", *RAND Journal of Economics*, **30**, 375-396.

[33] Seade, J. (1977), "On the Shape of Optimal Tax Schedules", *Journal of Public Economics*, **7**, 203-236.

[34] Seierstad, A. and Sydsæter, K. (1977), "Sufficient Conditions in Optimal Control Theory", *International Economic Review*, **18**, 367-391.

[35] Seierstad, A. and Sydsæter, K. (1987) *Optimal Control Theory with Economic Applications* (Amsterdam: North-Holland).

[36] Spulber, D. (1989), "Product Variety and Competitive Discounts", *Journal of Economic Theory*, **48**, 510-525.

[37] Stole, L. (1995), "Nonlinear Pricing and Oligopoly", *Journal of Economics and Management Strategy*, **4**, 529-562.

[38] Verboven, F. (1999), "Product Line Rivalry and Market Segmentation — with an Application to Automobile Optional Engine Pricing", *Journal of Industrial Economics*, **47**, 399-426.

[39] Wilson, R. (1993), *Nonlinear Pricing*, (Oxford: Oxford University Press).

[40] Wilson, R. (1996), "Nonlinear Pricing and Mechanism Design", in H. Amman, D. Kendricks and J. Rust (eds.), *Handbook of Computational Economics*, Chap. 5, (Amsterdam: North-Holland).